Technology and Oligopoly Capitalism

Technology and Oligopoly Capitalism is a major contribution to our understanding of how technology oligopolies are shaping America's social, economic, and political reality.

Technology oligopolies are the most powerful socioeconomic entities in America. From cradle to grave, the decisions they make affect the most intimate aspects of our lives, how we work, what we eat, our health, how we communicate, what we know and believe, whom we elect, and how we relate to one another and to nature. Their power over markets, trade, regulation, and most every aspect of our governance is more intrusive and farther-reaching than ever. They benefit from tax breaks, government guarantees, and bailouts that we must pay for and have no control over. Their accumulation of capital creates immense wealth for a minuscule elite, deepening disparities while politics and governance become ever more subservient to their power. They determine our skills and transform employment through the tools and services they create, as no other organizations can. They produce a vast array of goods and services with labor, marketing, and research that are more intrusively controlled than ever, as workplace rights and job security are curtailed or disappear. Our consumption of their products—and their capacity to promote wants—is deep and far reaching, while the waste they generate raises concerns about the survival of life on our planet. And their links to geopolitics and the martial domain are stronger than ever, as they influence how warfare is waged and who will be vanquished.

Technology and Oligopoly Capitalism's critical, multidisciplinary perspective provides a systemic vision of how oligopolistic power shapes these forces and phenomena. An inclusive approach spans the spectrum of technology oligopolies and the ways in which they deploy their power. Numerous, previously unpublished ideas expand the repertory of established work on the topics covered, advancing explanatory quality—to elucidate how and why technology oligopolies operate as they do, the dysfunctions that accompany their power, and their effects on society and nature. This book has no peers in the literature, in its scope, the unprecedented amount and diversity of documentation, the breadth of concepts, and the vast number of examples it provides. Its premises deserve to be taken into account by every student, researcher, policymaker, and author interested in the socioeconomic and political dimensions of technology in America.

Luis Suarez-Villa is Professor Emeritus of Social Ecology and of Planning, Policy, and Design at the University of California, Irvine. Among his previous books are *Corporate Power, Oligopolies, and the Crisis of the State*; *Globalization and Technocapitalism*; and *Technocapitalism.*

Technology and Oligopoly Capitalism

Luis Suarez-Villa

Routledge
Taylor & Francis Group
NEW YORK AND LONDON

Designed cover image: © Shutterstock

First published 2023
by Routledge
4 Park Square, Milton Park, Abingdon, Oxon OX14 4RN

and by Routledge
605 Third Avenue, New York, NY 10158

Routledge is an imprint of the Taylor & Francis Group, an informa business

Library of Congress Cataloging-in-Publication Data
Names: Suarez-Villa, Luis, author.
Title: Technology and oligopoly capitalism/Luis Suarez-Villa.
Description: Abingdon, Oxon; New York, NY: Routledge, 2023. |
Includes bibliographical references and index.
Identifiers: LCCN 2022050527 (print) | LCCN 2022050528 (ebook) |
ISBN 9781032386188 (hardback) | ISBN 9781032386157 (paperback) |
ISBN 9781003345893 (ebook)
Subjects: LCSH: High technology industries–United States. |
Oligopolies–United States. | Capitalism–United States. |
Corporate power–United States. | Technology and state–United States.
Classification: LCC HC110.H53 S83 2023 (print) | LCC HC110.H53
(ebook) |
DDC 338.4/760973–dc23/eng/20230106
LC record available at https://lccn.loc.gov/2022050527
LC ebook record available at https://lccn.loc.gov/2022050528

ISBN: 978-1-032-38618-8 (hbk)
ISBN: 978-1-032-38615-7 (pbk)
ISBN: 978-1-003-34589-3 (ebk)

DOI: 10.4324/9781003345893

Typeset in Bembo
by Deanta Global Publishing Services, Chennai, India

Contents

Chapter 1

Introduction

Technology captivates our attention today like no other subject. Our work and social life depend on myriad technologies that help us stay in touch, save effort and expense, and cut down time. Our health depends on technologies that test, diagnose, modify our genes and organs, or prescribe for any affliction. Our movements depend on technologies that chart our trajectories and determine how we go, where and when we rest, and what we see. And we entrust our intimate lives to technologies that program our routines, whom we meet, and what we learn, know, or believe.

This seemingly wondrous domain is owned by entities that are like no other in history. They are the richest and most powerful businesses that have ever existed, with revenues that dwarf the economies of most nations on the planet. They can cause politicians to win or fail, and they can bring down governments without firing a shot or hiring an army. Guided by their propaganda and affectation for our wellbeing, we purchase and use their products boundlessly, paying most any price they set. The news they feed us we accept at face value, without doubt or question. And, awed by their capabilities, we allow them to appropriate our data identities without much thinking or regret. Can anyone be faulted for believing technology companies to be the proverbial *deus ex machina* of our time?

But, regardless of whether we agree, is it not disturbing that so little is known about the deeper structures that sustain these most powerful entities? What sort of phenomena have helped create these organizations that so influence and intrude into most everything we do? Do these companies—in addition to generating the wondrous effects mentioned earlier—not also exploit us, expropriate our resources, damage nature, shortchange our governance, and otherwise compromise our future and that of all life on the planet? Can we be justified in thinking that their negative effects may make the entire panorama of their existence—and ours—unsustainable? And, if we can so suspect, is that fateful panorama worth the ephemeral benefits that we have or might yet receive?

Having a broad, critical look at the seemingly magical, inscrutable domain of large technology corporations will be the main objective of this book. To

DOI: 10.4324/9781003345893-1

do so will require an unapologetic grasp of our current reality—the one that many of us may not notice or know about. Concepts and historical perspective—indispensable for a book with this scope—will be considered critically. The deeper structures and phenomena that sustain technology oligopolies will be the focus of discussions. Much attention will be devoted to numerous examples that can help us understand the reality we face. And a vast amount of bibliography will provide documentation and place discussions in perspective.

A few definitions seem necessary at this point. The term *technology corporation* (or corporation and company) will refer to organizations that create products using technologies that emerged after the middle of the twentieth century. In some cases, these organizations originated the technologies they use. More frequently, they acquired or merged with companies that use them. Or, they adopted the technologies to expand their markets. Some corporations may be dedicated to patenting and licensing—essentially serving as commercial repositories of knowledge.

The term *oligopoly* will refer to a high degree of control by a few corporations over a market segment—be it for products and services or for labor and inputs. This term will encompass *monopoly*, in cases where a company has sole control over a market. The term *duopoly* will apply to cases where such control is shared with another company. In some markets a company may have a monopoly, while in others the same company may share oligopolistic control. In such scenarios, the term *oligo-monopolistic* may be used.

Some labor or input markets may be controlled by one, two, or a few companies. In such cases the terms *monoposony*, *duopsony*, and *oligopsony* may be used. The circumstances of control may vary. In some cases, for example, a company may have control over labor or inputs through a new technology. In others, control may involve areas or markets that have few or no competitors. In this book, the term oligopoly will encompass all of these meanings, although differentiation may be noted when addressing specific situations.

All technology oligopolies have a national base, and it would be remiss to ignore this reality. Although many companies portray themselves as being "international"—and a look at their reach may confirm that they operate in numerous nations—they nonetheless have a home base. Analyses of their most important decisions typically reveal that these are in accord with the interests of their home nation. This applies to important operational areas—such as research, intellectual property, and investment. It also applies to their involvement with geopolitics and military contracting. Due to space limitations, this work will focus on oligopolistic companies headquartered in the United States.

The question of when a company can be considered oligopolistic also needs to be addressed. On this matter there is, unfortunately, no clear or easy guide. If we apply the criteria used by the U.S. Department of Justice to challenge mergers in the late 1960s—a time when antitrust enforcement was more active (and more credible)—then practically all technology corporations comprised by both the S&P 500 and the Fortune 500 indexes today can be considered oligopolistic.

Market share—a limited indicator—has long been an important benchmark for antitrust enforcement. A proposed merger or acquisition involving a company with more than a three percent market share—by another company with a share greater than 15 percent of the same market segment—would have been challenged by federal regulators in the late 1960s.[1] This criterion might be taken as a reference, but we should be aware that it will exclude many oligopolistic companies.

A company with less than three percent market share that is the sole seller of a product—due to patent protection—can impose pricing. Limited demand for the product, due to technical complexity or high price, can ensure that market share remains low. As we will see later in this book, this scenario can be found in some product niches in nanotechnology, genomics, and biotechnology.

There are technology companies with low market share that may also be considered oligopolistic. One or a few other companies may rule their markets and set prices. If the company with low share engages in follow-the-leader pricing, may it not be considered oligopolistic? This can occur out of self-interest—or to avoid retaliation and unwanted takeover attempts, should it not follow the larger companies' guidance. Small, specialized companies in software, bio-pharmacology, and nanoelectronics can be found in this situation.

How a market segment is defined can also affect share calibration—potentially introducing distortions or making comparisons difficult. Generally, statistical criteria tend to avoid too narrow a definition for a product segment. Thus, fairly inclusive definitions for certain product ranges can make the previously noted scenarios possible. Complex or expensive technology products may then be subject to an oligopolistic price setting, despite their producers' low market share.

And, product differentiation—common in technology—can add further complexity. Some differentiated products may be placed in narrow market categories, thus ensuring that they will have a high market share despite low sales. Should companies marketing these products be considered oligopolistic? Also, some differentiated products—protected by patents, but nonetheless similar to others in usage—can make calibration and comparisons difficult.

Control over intellectual property—important for advanced technologies—could be a complementary (or alternative) benchmark. However, the complexities of this metric can pose challenges. Companies that own a significant number of patents related to one or several technologies may have a minute market share in any product segment. Such companies could be exclusively

1 See U.S. Department of Justice Archives, *1968 Merger Guidelines*, www.justice.gov/ (accessed July 16, 2022); Gregory J. Werden, "The 1968 Merger Guidelines," *Review of Industrial Organization* 53 (2018), 445–52; *The Economist*, "Silicon Valley, We Have a Problem," January 20, 2018, 21.

focused on licensing patents they own—a not uncommon situation for some advanced technologies. They may therefore evade categorization as oligopolies—even though they hold a monopolistic right conferred by every patent they own and impose license pricing. The latter may, in turn, induce price setting by licensees in their market niches.

Also, the licensees may have low shares of their respective market segments. Thus, they may not be considered oligopolistic either—even though their licenses confer an exclusive right to produce and market a product. And, similar products may not be available for purchase in any market. Thus, they would be the only sellers of the product, able to impose pricing at will. May the licensee be considered oligopolistic—or, more specifically, monopolistic? And, should license pricing by the owner of the patents be considered a form of monopolistic control?

Market share and segment composition are thus also subject to complexity when combined with the intellectual property dimension. As intellectual property is accompanied by a monopoly right, should the market share of products sold under licensing—or directly by the owner of a patent—be considered equal to those of products that are not privileged by licensing, or by any patent right? If not, how should either product be evaluated to determine market share? Many technology products and market segments can be found in this situation—as patents expire but the previously protected products continue to be sold.

Market share is further complicated by the value dimension. Most technology products are created through global chains that involve multiple sourcing of inputs and processing in various locations. Value is thus added to or captured by a product (or its raw materials) at every stage of the chain. And, most technology companies today are not in charge of the entire chain—and some may not be directly involved in any part of it, if they subcontract all stages. Estimation of market share based on the net value of products may thus be more meaningful than the conventional metric based on final sale pricing or the number of product units sold. Especially when—in an oligopolistic market—pricing or unit sales may not reflect value due to price, output, or demand manipulation.

Yet another complication is that technology oligopolies sell their products in multiple market segments and niches. Thus, a company may sell some products in a competitive segment, while other products are sold in oligopolistic niches, and yet others in monopolistic ones. This is fairly common among technology conglomerates, or in companies that sell many different products. The latter can be in the thousands in some cases, placed in hundreds of market niches. A further complication of this scenario is that some or many of the products may be sold by fully or partially owned subsidiaries—an increasingly common reality as spin-offs, specialized units, or modular segmentation proliferate.

These considerations make it unwise to set a rigid metric for examining oligopolistic power. Most any benchmark that may seem appropriate for one group of companies is bound to be invalid or spurious for others. The challenge will be to find common elements that can provide a meaningful understanding of technology oligopolies and the phenomena that sustain them.

Another aspect that needs to be addressed involves the choice of technology sectors. Technologies that emerged or came into use since the mid-twentieth century will be considered—whenever it is appropriate to do so and information is available. Examples will draw from microelectronics, computing, software, the internet and telecommunications (including tech-service platforms and social media), biotechnology (including agro-biotech), genomics, nanotechnology, robotics, aerospace, and biopharmaceuticals. In many cases, these technologies have been embedded in older products—a matter that will be taken into account as information and space allow. The importance of intellectual property for oligopolistic power will also be considered, along with the nexus of technology oligopolies with geopolitics and the martial domain.

Understanding the labyrinthine character of the oligopolistic technology domain poses many challenges. Possibly the most difficult one is the need to grasp the general panorama—the "big picture," in a manner of speaking—without losing sight of the distinctive features and phenomena involved. As the technologies considered in this book are most likely to be symbolic of the twenty-first century, we must also try to grasp their long-term significance. This is not an easy undertaking as many of these technologies are nascent, and their full parameters and consequences are unknown. A certain sense of introspection is therefore called for as one explores the contents of this book.

Numerous examples will be anchored by references—current and from recent decades. Many related concepts and theories will be discussed critically. Providing credit to their proponents—and references to their work—has been carefully looked after. I felt it was my duty to do so—in gratitude and recognition, regardless of whether I concur with their views. As most chapters contain hundreds of references, readers may find many of these useful for further reading or research. With this in mind, I labored to provide as much documentation as possible on most every argument.

Our journey will start with a look at the sources of power that sustain technology oligopolies. Doing so at this early stage will provide a platform of reference for subsequent chapters. A systemic, critical approach in the coming chapter—*Power*—will deal with the panorama of influences that perpetuate technology oligopolies. Major institutional, regulatory, political, juridical, and organizational constructs—that have been used to justify the *modus operandi*—will be considered. Contradictions between reality and reason—on social justice, the collective interest, and public governance—will be addressed. Historical perspectives will help reflect on the systemic continuity of the power structures that rule our reality.

The subsequent chapter—*Accumulation*—will consider the accumulative dynamic of oligopolistic capital, its contradictions, and the embedded relations of power. Commodity value, exchange, and use value—and the systemic creation of value through technology—will be at the core of the phenomena examined. The market domains of oligopolistic capital accumulation will be explored critically. A schematic dimensional model of accumulative flows will provide perspective on each domain. Combinations of oligopolistic market power scenarios, and major aspects of capital accumulation and labor, will be considered. Differences between investment and speculative capital in the accumulative dynamic will be examined. Conceptual ideas that can help our understanding of oligopolistic accumulative phenomena will be part of the repertory.

The chapter *Transformation* will explore the productive dynamic of technology oligopolies. Transformation of commodities through production and labor will take center stage—along with R&D and the way research regimes structure innovation and product development. Prior discussions on the accumulative dynamic will be extended to consider the domain of production—for tangible and intangible technology products. The role of finance capital in production will be considered and differentiated from speculative capital. The twin pillars of commodification and reproduction will be examined critically, relating them to the transformative dynamic. Typologies of transformation will help place the division of functions involving technology oligopolies, and the embedded relations of power, in context.

The chapter *Dysfunction* will consider the panorama of distress generated by technology oligopolistic power. Micro- and macro-level dysfunctions grounded in employment, consumer exploitation, wants promotion, data exploitation, the generation of waste, and oligopolistic expropriation of the commons will be discussed. Abuse at various levels and in multi-faceted ways will be a core concern. The systemic generation of waste by technology oligopolies will be explored through its effects on nature and life on the planet—taking into account proposed techno-fixes and their feasibility. This chapter's contents will add to the topics considered in prior chapters, to provide additional perspective.

The symbiotic relationship between technology oligopolies, geopolitical power, and the martial domain will be explored in the chapter *Domination*. Commodity chains are a major component of this panorama, as they link input extraction, processing, labor, and value arbitrage. The multi-faceted global hierarchy of control upon which commercial and military technology oligopolies depend—involving biotechnology, intellectual property, cybernetics, financial transaction technologies, and socio-political media technologies—will be explored. Ways of enforcement of domination involving the martial domain, military spending, and taxpayer exploitation will be considered—to provide as inclusive a treatment as possible of this difficult part of our reality.

The final chapter—*Techno-Oligarchy*—will consider the supra-structure that sustains technology oligopolistic power. Vacating functions of the state, the supra-structure becomes its substitute—a sort of fragmented, totalistic *alter* state ruled by a privileged elite. The phenomenon of social alienation—a deep-seated component of our reality—will be related to the modes of control that sustain the techno-oligarchy. Trajectories that might achieve systemic change will be considered. As it brings this book to a close, this chapter will invite reflection on our possibilities for bringing about meaningful, constructive change.

This book is dedicated to all readers and scholars with an interest in the social dimensions of technology. Many scholars provided insights over the years on the topics covered in this work. Out of respect for their privacy, I will refrain from disclosing their identities, but they know that their efforts are deeply appreciated.

It took seven years of patient toil to research and complete this book. To my spouse I owe much gratitude for her encouragement. Her philosophical insights, deep aesthetic sense, and wide-ranging creativity nurtured my dedication to this project.

To Routledge editor Michael Gibson, I must express my gratitude for his outstanding work overseeing the review and publication of this book. To the anonymous reviewers who examined the manuscript, their painstaking efforts and excellent critiques are deeply appreciated. Their detailed reviews guided all revisions and helped improve the contents of this book considerably. To the publication committee, and to the production and marketing staff at Routledge, I express my gratitude for their efforts. Their professional commitment to see that this work reaches readers deserves much praise.

Chapter 2

Power

Technology is dominated by some of the most powerful corporations in history. Their power allows them to affect our lives, the economy, our governance, and nature in ways that would have elicited disbelief not long ago. Their reach now encompasses most every activity and life form, creating risks that we do not yet understand. Their appropriation of creativity restricts its benefit to society, unleashing effects over which we have no control. Yet, we seem inured to the deleterious effects of their power, tolerating and compromising with the reality they have imposed on us.

The power of technology oligopolies is built on an ensemble of interrelated functions that have far-reaching consequences. This ensemble—fragmented and multi-faceted but internally coherent—is the source of their influence. Its labyrinthine character often defies and confuses our attempts to decipher its workings. And it can create misperceptions that shield its deeper structure.

This chapter will provide an overview of that ensemble, to examine the structures and strategies that sustain oligopolistic power. Concepts and constructs that have been used to legitimize such power will be approached critically. Numerous references and examples—with documentation on developments in recent decades—will be provided to help place discussions in perspective.

Pricing

A most important source of power involves control over pricing. Once technology oligopolies establish control over a market, sustaining pricing power is a fundamental priority. This typically guarantees greater revenue to nurture their influence. Greater revenue usually offsets short-term fluctuations in market share. Thus, even when an oligopolist experiences some loss of share, greater cash flow over the short or medium term will likely more than compensate for it.

The inverse scenario occurs when labor comes under oligopolistic control. Thus, what in product markets is an upward pricing tendency, in the case of labor the objective is to depress compensation to the lowest possible level. The

DOI: 10.4324/9781003345893-2

same can be said for pricing in input markets. In the case of labor and inputs, oligopolistic power therefore depends on reducing costs and prices.

Co-respectiveness

Following a higher price lead sustains pricing power. Price wars tend to be self-defeating. Usually, they result in losses for all. Among technology oligopolists, price wars are not only counterproductive but also unnecessary. Output adjustments or product differentiation can ensure sustenance of higher prices, even when some loss of market share occurs. Also, the novelty and status appeal of many technology products can help sustain pricing.

Price wars undermine *co-respectiveness*—a necessary element of trust needed to safeguard oligopolistic power in times of stress.[1] Shortchanging the collective interest can have negative consequences for everyone. Outcries from the public—and inquiries by regulators—are often overcome by presenting a common front.

If there is any competition, it will likely occur for leadership in setting higher prices. The inverse is typically the case for labor and inputs. Reducing labor and input costs is an important—but often overlooked—aspect of co-respectiveness. Offshoring is a common way to lower such outlays. Certain tactics—such as pitting contractors, suppliers, or locales against each other—are customary and can be handled by consultants. Co-respective action to lower labor costs and input prices may thus be kept out of the public eye.

Price rises and follow-the-leader behavior are often pursued cautiously. Temporal delays—from several weeks to a few months—may be adopted to avoid attracting unwelcome attention. And higher pricing may be accompanied by engineered-in limitations that require customers to make additional purchases. Requiring purchase of accessories and apps—or additional services—will increase nominal pricing of a core product. This tends to attract follow-the-leader action, especially in niche markets.

Co-respective action in reducing labor costs may be aided by automation—if offshoring or outsourcing are not feasible. This often attracts imitation, as labor usually accounts for the largest outlays in production. For processes that resist automation, offshoring or outsourcing, externalizing work tasks can reduce costs. Execution usually involves furloughs, and in some cases the hiring of former employees as "contractors" or "vendors"—paying lower compensation and no benefits. This approach became an important way to reduce costs

1 The term is often associated with Joseph Schumpeter—see his *Capitalism, Socialism, and Democracy* (New York: Harper, 1942), 87–106. Critical insights on the history and meaning of the term are in Paul M. Sweezy's *Modern Capitalism and Other Essays* (New York: Monthly Review Press, 1972), Chapter 3.

during the last decade—accounting for the rise of contingency labor among technology oligopolies.[2]

Shareholder Returns

The panorama of oligopolistic pricing power found theoretical support in one of the most widely practiced concepts in corporate management—agency theory. Articulated in the late 1970s by two prominent business school economists, this construct became the strategic norm for managerial decisions.[3] A perceived need *to align the interests of shareholders and of corporate management* was its core premise—executives being viewed as "agents" of shareholders in all aspects of corporate stewardship. Eliminating divergence between shareholders and management was thus turned into a precept—all other aspects of the corporate domain relegated to lesser importance.

Agency theory posited "maximization of shareholder value" to be the prime strategic and operational objective of corporate organizations. Although not explicitly advocating oligopolistic pricing power, practice of the theory tacitly became a vital support. As the most effective way to optimize "shareholder value" is through pricing power, the construct can be seen as a major justification for consolidation. And, being routinely taught in business schools, its widespread use was guaranteed.[4]

Agency theory is consonant with the ideological perspective of Nobel laureate Milton Friedman—one of the twentieth century's most influential economists. Friedman's longtime advocacy of profit maximization to be the sole concern of corporate management was very much in line with the concept's core objective.[5] The association of optimal shareholder value with maximal profitability thus seems inescapable—along with the similarly close relation-

2 See Mark Bergen and Josh Eidelson, "Inside Google's Shadow Workforce: About Half of Google's Workers are Contractors Who Don't Receive the Same Benefits as Direct Employees," *Bloomberg*, July 25, 2018, www.bloomberg.com/; Ellen Sheng, "Silicon Valley's Dirty Secret: Using a Shadow Workforce of Contract Employees to Drive Profits," *CNBC*, October 22, 2018, www.cnbc.com/; Lauren Weber, "The End of Employees: U.S. Companies Shift Work Once Considered Core to Contractors, Pruning Costs and Job Security," *Wall Street Journal*, February 3, 2017, A1.

3 Michael C. Jensen and William H. Meckling, "The Theory of the Firm: Managerial Behavior, Agency Costs, and Ownership Structure," *Journal of Financial Economics* 3 (1976), 305–60. An early exploration—related to accounting—that may be considered a precursor is William W. Cooper's "A Proposal for Extending the Theory of the Firm," *Quarterly Journal of Economics* 65 (1951), 87–109.

4 See Fabrizio Ferraro, Jeffrey Pfeffer and Robert I. Sutton, "Economic Language and Assumptions: How Theories can Become Self-Fulfilling," *Academy of Management Review* 30 (2005), 8–24; Lex Donaldson, *American Anti-Management Theories of Organization: A Critique of Paradigm Proliferation* (Cambridge: Cambridge University Press, 1995), chapters 1, 6.

5 Milton Friedman's *Capitalism and Freedom* (Chicago: University of Chicago Press, 1962) sets the tone early on for his subsequent works on aspects related to profit and what he saw as the need to rid corporate governance of concerns unrelated to profit maximization—among them the important question of social responsibility.

ship of shareholder value and profit *with* market pricing power. The implicit contradiction between such power—which can only be achieved by an oligopolist—and Friedman's belief in competitive markets was largely ignored by his followers—and by advocates of agency theory. Thus, many economists and management specialists who favored competitive markets would end up finding that the construct's usage generated the opposite of what they had theoretically cherished.

This dissonance between optimization of shareholder returns—and its outcomes—can be taken as a symptom of what Herbert Simon—the 1978 Nobel laureate—characterized as "bounded" rationality in decision-making.[6] The straitjacket into which agency theory fits corporate decisions—and the resulting undesirable outcomes and societal effects—were often brushed off as happenstance or bad luck.[7] Such interpretations could be taken as symptoms of the limited rationality that Simon attached to optimization—due to the usually narrow decision parameters. Often, corporate management—no matter how competent—could thus not anticipate how decisions based on agency theory might play out.[8] But, despite its flaws, the construct would become very influential.

For publicly traded technology oligopolies, agency theory became especially important, as it provided a simple heuristic to judge strategic decisions. Such decisions all too often revolve around boosting pricing power—the fundamental support of "shareholder value" optimization. Most any aspect of the usually complex operation of technology oligopolies could thus be tied to that simple criterion. And it was one that would appeal greatly to financial oligopolies and speculators—whose favor was needed to boost share prices, especially over the short term.[9] Decisions on research, labor, inputs, marketing, and other aspects could thus be justified on the basis of a simple heuristic.

6 Herbert A. Simon, *Models of Bounded Rationality: Behavioral Economics and Business Organization* (Vol. 2) (Cambridge, MA: MIT Press, 1982); James G. March and Herbert A. Simon, *Organizations* (New York: Wiley, 1958), 157–92.

7 Such justifications were made easier as there are practically no external checks (or regulation) on managerial application of agency theory. And, shareholders are seldom informed about a company's internal decision processes. See Ferraro, Pfeffer and Sutton, "Economic Language and Assumptions"; Donaldson, *American Anti-Management Theories of Organization*.

8 See the critiques in Lynn Stout, *The Shareholder Value Myth: How Putting Shareholders First Harms Investors, Corporations, and the Public* (San Francisco: Berrett-Koehler, 2012); Luis Suarez-Villa, *Corporate Power, Oligopolies, and the Crisis of the State* (Albany: State University of New York Press, 2016), 204–05, 232–33, 310; and his *Technocapitalism: A Critical Perspective on Technological Innovation and Corporatism* (Philadelphia: Temple University Press, 2009), 114–15; *The Economist*, "Out with the Old: Management Theory is Becoming a Compendium of Dead Ideas," December 17, 2016, 61.

9 An endemic feature, inasmuch as large companies typically have multiple layers of "agents"—who need favorable short-term results to ascend the corporate ladder or increase their compensation. See *The Economist*, "Executives, Not Investors, May Be to Blame for Short-Termism," February 6, 2021, 54; Lucian A. Bebchuk, "Don't Let the Short-Termism Bogeyman Scare You," *Harvard Business Review*, January 2021, https://hbr.org/.

The association of pricing power with "shareholder value optimization" may thus be seen as a significant motive for oligopolistic consolidation during the past five decades. The logic behind this association became a very important rationale for the elimination of restraints to oligopolistic consolidation and pricing power. As financial betting became a cultural phenomenon and pension systems became involved with stock, bond, and options markets, shareholder activism would enthrone agency theory as a fundamental precept. Any deviance from the core tenet of this construct came to be seen as justification to sack corporate management, restructure a company, or call for others to acquire it.

Mergers and Acquisitions

A very important way to deepen and extend oligopolistic control over pricing is to pursue mergers and acquisitions. Tens of thousands of M&A deals—amounting to over three percent of U.S. Gross Domestic Product (GDP)—were reported in the last decade.[10] This is thought to be partly responsible for the de-listing from stock markets of large numbers of companies—a long-term trend that has reduced investment possibilities.[11]

M&A deals have been the single most important force driving technology oligopolistic consolidation during the past six decades.[12] The five largest technology and tech-service "platform" oligopolists—Microsoft, Apple, Amazon, Alphabet-Google, Meta-Facebook—reportedly acquired 519 companies over a 10-year period during the last decade.[13] Mostly because of M&A deals, one-half of the largest 30 American corporations in the S&P 500 index are technology and tech-service corporations—all of them oligopolistic—including the five largest (by market capitalization).[14]

10 See Yelena Larkin and Roni Michaely, *Are U.S. Industries Becoming More Concentrated?* SSRN, October 27, 2018, https://papers.ssrn.com/; Richard Henderson, "The Incredible Shrinking Stock Market," *Financial Times*, June 27, 2019, www.ft.com/; John C. Bogle, "The Father of the Index Fund Sees a Reckoning Ahead: John Bogle Says It's Likely Just a Matter of Time Before a Handful of Firms Own Half of All U.S. Stocks," *Wall Street Journal*, December 1, 2018, B1; PitchBook, *Mergers and Acquisitions*, www.get.pitchbook.com/ (accessed June 17, 2021); Barry C. Lynn, *Cornered: The New Monopoly Capitalism and the Economics of Destruction* (Hoboken: Wiley, 2010), chapters 1, 4.

11 See Bogle, "Father of the Index Fund"; Henderson, "Incredible Shrinking."

12 See Larkin and Michaely, *Are U.S. Industries Becoming*; Robert W. McChesney, *Digital Disconnect: How Capitalism is Turning the Internet against Democracy* (New York: New Press, 2013), 120–29, 130–58; PitchBook, *Mergers and Acquisitions*.

13 Growth Marketing Agencies, *The Big Five Tech Companies and Their Big Five Acquisitions*, April 18, 2018, www.growthmarketingagencies.com/. See also *The Economist*, "Crony Capitalism," April 15, 2017, 59; McChesney, *Digital Disconnect*, 120–29, 130–58.

14 See Federal Reserve Bank of St. Louis, *Economic Research, S&P 500*, https://fred.stlouisfed.org/ (accessed June 26, 2022); Growth Marketing Agencies, *Big Five Tech Companies*; PitchBook, *Mergers and Acquisitions*.

By historical standards, technology corporations are today among the largest companies that have ever existed—largely due to M&A-driven consolidation. The ranks of the largest companies in history—East India Company (1813), Standard Oil, and U.S. Steel (early 1910s)—were joined by IBM in the late 1960s, AT&T in the mid-1970s (a regulated tech-service monopolist), and Microsoft in the 1990s. In this century, Apple, Alphabet-Google, Monsanto, and Dow (after their respective mergers with Bayer and DuPont)—along with tech-service oligo-monopolists Meta-Facebook and Amazon—joined this select group.[15]

Merger deals often involve companies in activities that are complementary to those of suitors, although companies in control of some of the same market segments can be pursued. The latter can practically guarantee an oligo-monopoly on product pricing. Acquisitions in technology often involve small companies that have the potential to enter new product segments—or that can help the suitor control pricing. The M&A strategy has thereby contributed to make many technology oligopolists "too big to fail"—thus engineering the possibility that taxpayers will end up paying for their bailouts when a crisis or insolvency occurs. This strategy also contributes to reduce labor costs for the companies that merge by cutting employment—often by the thousands—a trend observed during the last decade.[16]

In most every case, oligopolistic finance has been heavily involved in technology M&A deals—through funding, debt creation, and speculation. Much of the overwhelming oligopolistic power that American finance has attained during the past three decades is due to its link with technology M&A activity.

15 *The Economist*, "History's Biggest Companies: What 19th Century Opium Dealers and 1970s Telecoms Monopolies can Teach Silicon Valley," July 7, 2018, 56; Stephen Menendian, *The Era of Corporate Consolidation and the End of Competition: Bayer-Monsanto, Dow-DuPont, and ChemChina-Syngenta* (Berkeley: Haas Institute, 2018). See also Charles R. Geisst, *Monopolies in America: Empire Builders and their Enemies from Jay Gould to Bill Gates* (New York: Oxford University Press, 2000); Thom Hartmann, *The Hidden History of Monopolies* (San Francisco: Berrett-Koehler, 2020); Myron Gordon, "Monopoly Power in the United States Manufacturing Sector, 1899 to 1994," *Journal of Post-Keynesian Economics* 20 (1998), 323–35.

16 During a five-year period, for example, more than 156,000 were estimated to have been laid off in the biopharmaceuticals sector—substantial M&A activity in subsequent years also generating large employment losses. See Andrew Dunn, "NewLink's two-decade run ends in Reverse Merger, Layoffs," *Biopharma Dive*, October 20, 2019, www.biopharmadive.com/; Sy Mukherjee, "Three Major Trends Driving Layoffs in Biotech and Pharma," *Biopharma Dive*, May 27, 2015, www.biopharmadive.com/; Peter Loftus, Marta Falconi and Hester Plumridge, "In Drug Mergers, there's One Sure Bet: The Layoffs," *Wall Street Journal*, April 29, 2014, www.wsj.com/. Companies in every technology sector have also experienced layoffs after M&A deals—see, for example, Sridhar Natarajan, "Goldman Warns of More Job Losses with Jumbo Mergers on the Rise," *Bloomberg*, October 17, 2020, www.bloomberg.com/; Rich Laden, "Microchip Technology Cutting 200 to 275 Jobs at Colorado Springs Plant," *The Gazette*, December 29, 2019, https://gazette.com/; Alan B. Krueger, *Where Have All the Workers Gone? An Inquiry into the Decline of the U.S. Labor Participation Rate*, Brookings Papers on Economic Activity, September 7, 2017, www.brookings.edu/.

Myriad ways to "package" debt have been engineered—such as derivatives, collateralized loan obligations, hedge funds, and shadow (unregulated) financial vehicles. And it is very doubtful that finance would have had so much interest in facilitating M&A deals without the strong market pricing power that technology oligopolies command.

Oligopolistic technology corporations also often purchase other oligopolists' shares and long-term debt, as a way to secure backdoors to potential acquisitions or mergers.[17] And they can engage in speculation outside the technology domain—to raise cash. Real estate can provide such opportunity—an activity that does not require much in the way of hiring labor, setting up marketing operations, investing in machinery or plants, or looking for offshore contractors.[18] Becoming a quasi-financier is another. Some of the largest technology corporations became shadow hedge funds during the last two decades—speculating in myriad activities.[19] These can help deepen pricing power, as speculative cash is redeployed to execute M&A deals and fence- in markets.

An important incentive to pursue technology M&A deals involves executive compensation. M&A deals—undertaken by chief executives—may be considered a very important factor in the substantial rise in compensation in recent times. Compensation for chief executives in technology oligopolies is typically the highest in the American economy, with "packages" that can amount to hundreds of millions of dollars annually per CEO. This can be as much as 20 times the average compensation of top executives in the largest non-technology sector corporations.[20]

Analysts in recent times have thus found a substantial disconnection between chief executive compensation and company performance—especially in very large corporations.[21] This raises the possibility that M&A deals may have a strong positive effect on executive compensation—that escapes the usually

17 A practice frequently observed during the last decade. See, for example, Claire Boston, "Apple Buys More Company Debt than World's Biggest Bond Funds," *Bloomberg*, May 4, 2017, www.bloomberg.com/.

18 A trend that attracted concern during the last decade. See, for example, Brittany Shoot, "Google's $1 Billion Bay Area Buy is the Second Biggest U.S. Real Estate Deal of 2018—Who's Number One? Also Google," *Fortune*, November 27, 2018, www.fortune.com/.

19 See Thomas Gilbert and Christopher Hrdlicka, "Apple is a Hedge Fund that Makes Phones: Big Companies Need to Disclose More about their Investments," *Wall Street Journal*, August 23, 2018, www.wsj.com/; Brad Cook, "Apple Creates Braeburn Capital to Manage $8.7 Billion Stash," *Mac Observer*, April 5, 2006, www.macobserver.com/.

20 Alphabet-Google's chief executive, for example, received $281 million in compensation for 2019, compared to an average of $14 million annually for the 50 largest S&P 500 corporations—*The Economist*, "Executive Compensation: Pay Guaranteed, Performance Optional," July 11, 2020, 50. See also Federal Reserve Bank of St. Louis, *Economic Research*.

21 See Lawrence Mishel and Julia Wolfe, *CEO Compensation has Grown 940% since 1978: Typical Worker Compensation has Risen only 12% Since that Time*, August 14, 2019, Economic Policy Institute, www.epi.org/; Rick Marshall, *Out of Whack: U.S. CEO Pay and Long-Term Investment Returns*, MSCI, October 2017, www.msci.com/.

short-term metrics of company performance. In any case, the vast disparity in compensation in technology oligopolies—compared to that in other sectors—seems unjustified, considering the dysfunctions and abuses that will be addressed later in this book. Also, the high levels of executive compensation provide a deep contrast with employee compensation.[22] A substantial proportion—one-half or even greater—of the workforce in some of the largest and wealthiest technology oligopolies is of the contingency (*precariat*) or TVC (temporary–vendor–contractor) mode.[23]

The spread of M&A deals and rising oligopolistic power found theoretical and regulatory support in one of the most important formulations of the second half of the twentieth century—transaction cost theory. At the core of this construct, posited in the 1930s in embryonic form by Ronald Coase—the 1991 Nobel laureate—was the notion that corporate organizations were better suited than markets to enforce contracts.[24] Diminishing "opportunistic behavior" would lead to lower transaction (or exchange) costs. Such behavior was assumed to be common in non-standardized transactions—typically those subject to negotiation. Although not explicitly addressed, oligopolistic M&A deals fit very well the scenario envisioned by the theory.

A second component, posited in 1960—also by Coase—assumed that corporate disputes involving social costs would arrive at better outcomes when parties negotiate—as opposed to having a court or regulatory agency impose solutions.[25] In the oligopolistic context, however, negotiation and resolution would end up in the hands of the most powerful entity. Negotiations involving M&A transactions illustrate this asymmetry on a regular basis, as the more powerful entities usually set conditions. Also, the scenario where regulatory agencies, legislators, and even the judicial system favor the most powerful corporations was left out of the construct. This is common in a political system where revolving-door appointments of corporate executives to head regulatory agencies are frequent—along with the influence of corporate-funded political organizations, lobbying, and campaign donations. The need for socially just, equitable outcomes was thus largely left out of consideration—when negotiations involve oligopolies.

The implicit notion that markets would be competitive was another problem. This assumption was quite unrealistic, given the advance of oligopolies in Coase's time—and the fact that their power over important market segments

22 See Dean Baker, Josh Bivens and Jessica Schieder, *Reining in CEO Compensation and Curbing the Rise of Inequality*, June 4, 2019, Economic Policy Institute, www.epi.org/.

23 See Julia C. Wong, "Revealed: Google's 'Two-Tier' Workforce Training Document—Exclusive Internal Document Shows How Google Employees are Trained to Treat Temps, Vendors and Contractors," *The Guardian*, December 12, 2018, www.theguardian.com/; Bergen and Eidelson, "Inside Google's Shadow Workforce"; Sheng, "Silicon Valley's Dirty Secret."

24 Ronald H. Coase, "The Nature of the Firm," *Economica* 4 (1937), 386–405.

25 Ronald H. Coase, "The Problem of Social Cost," *Journal of Law and Economics* 3 (1960), 1–44.

had long been pointed out by various scholars.[26] Transaction cost theory would thus come to ignore the case of oligopolistic power over both non-standardized and conventional market transactions.

And it also ignored the fact that oligopolies impose their pricing power on consumers—who have no way of negotiating the terms of their submission, and usually have no competitive market to turn to. Much the same applies to labor markets controlled by oligopolistic companies—as all too often occurs whenever labor organizations are weak or non-existent. Negotiation is also usually irrelevant for input suppliers that serve oligopolistic customers, as the latter all too often impose the terms of exchange.

Following Coase's work, in the 1970s and 1990s, Oliver Williamson—the 2009 Nobel laureate—and Oliver Hart and Bengt Holmström—2016 Nobel laureates, jointly—looked into additional aspects of transactions and contracts. Important in their work—relevant to M&A transactions and oligopolistic power—were the impossibility of specifying all obligations, the problem of incomplete contracts, differences between short- and long-term contracting, and the character of non-contractible rights in transactions.[27] All of these aspects embed important motivations for engaging in M&A transactions—as a way to reduce opportunistic behavior and uncertainty—and to expand oligopolistic pricing power. Acquiring or merging with a contractual partner, in particular, becomes desirable when non-contractible rights are involved, as it is usually too expensive or impossible to specify all transactional needs. All the more so if the contractual relation is foreseen as being longer term, requiring adaptation, is expensive to end, and litigation is likely to occur at some point. Unfortunately, their contributions left out the social dilemmas and

26 Rudolf Hilferding's seminal analysis of the transformation of capitalism into monopoly—as it became integrated with finance—had been published over a quarter century before Coase's work. See Hilferding, *Das Finanzkapital: eine Studie über die jüngste Entwicklung des Kapitalismus* (Vienna: Brand, 1910) [translated as *Finance Capital: A Study of the Latest Phase of Capitalist Development* (London: Routledge and Kegan Paul, 1981)]. Almost half a decade before the first publication of Coase's work, Joan Robinson's *The Economics of Imperfect Competition* (London: Macmillan, 1933)—a pioneering analysis of the economics of monopolies and oligopolies—was published, following her earlier work and public lectures on the topic. Edward Chamberlin's work on monopolies and duopolies had also appeared in print well before Coase's formulation—see Chamberlin's *The Theory of Monopolistic Competition: A Re-Orientation of the Theory of Value* (Cambridge, MA: Harvard University Press, 1933); and his "Duopoly: Value Where Sellers are Few," *Quarterly Journal of Economics* 44 (1929), 63–100.

27 Williamson is credited for first academic usage of the term "institutional economics." See Oliver E. Williamson, "Transaction Cost Economics: The Governance of Contractual Relations," *Journal of Law and Economics* 22 (1979), 233–61; and his "The Economics of Organization: The Transaction Cost Approach," *American Journal of Sociology* 87 (1981), 548–77. See also Oliver Hart, *Firms, Contracts and Financial Structure* (New York: Oxford University Press, 1995), 73–94; Bengt Holmström and John Roberts, "The Boundaries of the Firm Revisited," *Journal of Economic Perspectives* 12 (1998), 73–94. A broad critique of aspects of their (and Coase's) work can be found in *The Economist*, "The Theory of the Firm: Coase Call," July 29, 2017, 59–60.

the relations of power posed by oligopolies—and the differences between the idealized corporate organizational contexts they portrayed and the reality of the oligopolistic domain.

The Coase construct also left unanswered the question of whether oligopolistic corporate behavior may not actually be very opportunistic, compared to that of companies engaged in competitive market transactions. After all, is opportunistic behavior not often deployed by the more powerful on those with less power—as all too often occurs with both non-standardized and conventional transactions in oligopolistic markets? The proliferation of lawsuits alleging not only deception in M&A transactions but also engineered-in obsolescence, harmful product performance due to insufficient testing or poor design, theft of IP, reverse engineering, and outrageous pricing of many products and services would seem to indicate so. Thus, perhaps the greatest opportunism on transactions—unconventional or not—can be found in oligopolistic organizations. Technology oligopolies are no exception to this panorama, as opportunistic behavior involving most any aspect of their operations—of which many examples will be provided in this book—becomes ever more poignant.

Overlooked by the construct, therefore, was the reality that costs may actually be higher when transactions—unconventional or not—are under the control of oligopolistic corporate organizations. Possibly the highest transaction costs that can be found today involve oligopolistic market pricing. This is acute for technology products because of their usually high demand due to novelty, wants contrivance schemes, psychological manipulation, and branding effects. And we must add the costs of flawed performance, engineered-in obsolescence, abusive maintenance contracts, and other aspects that affect many tech products and services—all of which fit the rubric of transaction costs.

Opportunistic behavior on M&A deals also generates high transaction costs for many people, as it leads to greater concentration and rising prices for those who depend on the affected market. And, in stock and bond markets, the reduced number of listed companies that results from M&A transactions generates higher transaction costs. This occurs through heightened risk for those who bet on their shares and debt. The fact that many such transactions now involve oligopolistic shadow hedge funds and banks increases the risk—not only for those who bet. When crises occur, the cost of government bailouts of too-big-to-fail oligopolists is borne by taxpayers—a form of transaction cost that is usually ignored. When all of these costs and the oligopolistic pricing markups on the range of products and services in existence are added up, the amounts may surpass the gross economic product of most nations around the world.

The notion that corporate organizations are more effective than markets in reducing non-routine transaction costs also found theoretical and regulatory justification in the work of the seventeenth century's best-known socio-political philosopher. The fact that decisions on transactions in the corporate domain are made by fiat—a fundamental, explicit aspect in Coase's construct—was thought to be consonant with Thomas Hobbes's belief in the need for an "autocratic" authority to rule society.[28] Hobbes surmised that such authority was necessary to avoid society's descent into a "primitive" condition—or what he referred to as "a state of nature"—that would lead to widespread chaos, strife, and behaviors associated with opportunism and lawlessness.

About a century and a half later, classical economists such as Adam Smith and David Ricardo would adopt contrarian positions to Hobbes's, based on the belief that markets—not authoritarian political power—were best suited to rule over society. Thus, they thought, the preponderance of markets and their self-organizing discipline—not only on transactions but on decisions related to supply and demand—would allow Hobbes's formulation to be dispensed with.[29] Many neoclassical economists would later also subscribe to the need for a predominance of markets over society, as would most every neoliberal policy-maker in the late twentieth century—without recognizing that the markets in question were meant to be competitive.

The reality of powerful corporate entities that were already the "visible hand" controlling market transactions—through such vital aspects as pricing, mergers, output, labor, and production, if not also regulation—was thus lost on those who advocated both the predominance of markets and the transaction cost theory approach. Both camps ignored that neither oligopolistic corporate organizations nor oligopolistic markets may be capable of either reducing non-routine transaction costs *or* of being a self-organizing social force. The reduction of such costs even for (or within) oligopolistic corporate organizations is in doubt, and such reduction—if it should occur—must be balanced against the social costs they generate. Realistically, however, Hobbes's vision of autocratic authority is what actually prevailed as oligopolies gained control over society, the economy, and governance. Only not monolithically, as Hobbes envisioned, but in fragmented and sometimes contradictory ways—features applicable to oligopolistic power in our time, which will be explored later in this book.

Entry Barrier Engineering

Oligopolistic control over market pricing is also supported by an ensemble of strategies that can be referred to as entry barrier engineering. The objective is twofold.

28 See Thomas Hobbes, *Leviathan or the Matter, Form and Power of a Commonwealth Ecclesiastical and Civil* (London: Andrew Crooke, 1651); and his *The Elements of Law, Natural and Politic* (London: Routledge, 1969; orig. publ. 1650).

29 A view that would—in a general way—be echoed by sociologist Max Weber long after but focusing more on the market discipline and (spontaneous) transactional self-organization generated by shared religious and community values. See his *The Protestant Ethic and the Spirit of Capitalism*, trans. Talcott Parsons (London: Unwin Hyman, 1930; orig. publ. 1905 as *Die protestantische Ethik und der Geist des Kapitalismus*).

Preventing companies from entering a market segment (or niche) under oligopolistic control is most important. This preempts the possibility that pricing may be undercut—as an entrant tries to capture market share. Co-respective behavior among oligopolists in control of the market can be expected, as any price reduction would damage their common interest.

Entry barrier engineering also seeks to prevent customers from switching out of an oligopolist's control. Making it difficult or expensive for existing customers to become clients of an entrant, or to terminate a purchasing relationship, are examples.[30] The former can also be achieved by making it costly for an entrant to operate—such that customers that switch face higher pricing or limited performance. Enforcing little-noticed contractual stipulations or changing rules of purchase—such as those that involve equipment changes or penalties—can make it difficult and expensive for customers to switch.[31] A fenced or locked-in market segment is the outcome.

A very important mode of entry barrier engineering is posed by networks and network-based platforms. Oligopolistic control over *network extent*—an array of quantitative and qualitative aspects that help magnify pricing power—is crucial. In a previous book, I discussed three dimensions of network extent, all relevant to technology oligopolistic pricing power.[32] Range (the scale and heterogeneity of participants), accessibility, and composition are vital. Although scale and accessibility are the most frequently considered features, heterogeneity and composition are very important, as they can reveal the diversity of a network's customer base.[33]

Oligopolistic pricing power tends to be strongest when network extent is very large in scale—with easy access, a diverse customer base, and a vast range of interests.[34] Expanding network extent can allow a technology oligopolist

30 The trouble of switching databases can be very discouraging—a matter that reportedly allowed Oracle to "extract huge profits." Among the tactics was pursuing adversarial measures to intimidate clients—such as carrying out "audits to verify their use of software by workers" and imposing "hefty charges"—if they should "exceed license limits." Quoted from *The Economist*, "Oracle: Larry's Last Stand," September 26, 2020, 59.

31 One way is to break up data clouds into "sub-clouds," such that switching becomes costly and complicated, compromising security and privacy—*The Economist*, "Oracle," 60.

32 Suarez-Villa, *Technocapitalism*, 57–67.

33 Effects of pricing power built up through network extent can be seen in the capitalization of four important technology oligopolists—Apple, Alphabet-Google, Meta-Facebook, and Amazon. Their aggregate value rose by about $1.3 trillion in four years during the last decade (2013–17). Microsoft—the third most valuable American corporation—was excluded from this estimate. See Scott Galloway, *The Four: The Hidden DNA of Amazon, Apple, Facebook, and Google* (New York: Portfolio, 2017), chapters 2–5, 8.

34 Evidence on the effects of network extent expansion can be found in unusual practices. Tech-service oligopolist Netflix, for example, set up "no-rules-rules" management that allowed the sealing of multimillion dollar contracts by lower-echelon executives—without approval from higher-level executives. This practice has been referred to as "management on the edge of chaos" by the company's chief executive—see *The Economist*, "The Hastings Doctrine," September 12, 2020, 52–53.

to set up stronger entry barriers while capturing multiple market segments.[35] Thus, an array of product markets can come under the pricing power of a single oligopolist.[36] Pricing power that cuts across market segments can then become a major source of revenue. And a network-based platform that makes this scenario possible can be the most valuable entry barrier that a technology oligopolist might hope for.

This occurs because platforms—in contradiction with a fundamental principle of economics—increase in value with abundance of network extent, as opposed to its scarcity. Abundance, *not* scarcity, becomes the key to greater pricing power and value—and to the engineering of entry barriers. A principle that for over three centuries has been the cornerstone of economic rationality, and of pricing theory, is thereby invalidated. Abundance of network extent thus begets greater pricing power and stronger entry barriers—a dynamic that can build upon itself rapidly.[37]

And how can network extent expand, to generate greater pricing power for the oligopolist in control? The answer is to provide easy access—nominally "free" or without apparent monetary cost—to anyone who wishes to join. It should not surprise, then, that oligopolists in network-based platforms that "give away" access have become some of the wealthiest corporations in history. This is reflected by their market capitalization—now greater than the gross product of many nations.

The common notion that access to such networks is "given away"—or that it is "free"—is a fallacy. Users do pay for access—but not monetarily—by having to acquiesce to the appropriation of their intimate data—one of the most valuable resources of our time. Pervasive surveillance has thus become the norm in network-based platforms. The data compiled can include contacts, purchases, finances, location, health, gender preferences, legal problems,

35 The growing power of many tech oligopolies in recent times can be attributed to the rapid expansion of platform-based network extent. See Jonathan Taplin, *Move Fast and Break Things: How Facebook, Google and Amazon Cornered Culture and Undermined Democracy* (New York: Little, Brown, 2017), chapters 6–9; Franklin Foer, *World Without Mind: The Existential Threat of Big Tech* (New York: Penguin, 2017), chapters 2–5; McChesney, *Digital Disconnect*, chapters 4, 5; Tim Wu, *The Master Switch: The Rise and Fall of Information Empires* (New York: Random House, 2010), chapters 12, 18–21.

36 During the last decade, Facebook, for example, acquired Instagram, WhatsApp, Oculus VR, and TBH—all in niches that could be linked to its core activity—to expand its power over social media. See Greg Ip, "The Antitrust Case against America's Technology Behemoths: Amazon, Google and Facebook are as Dominant as Ma Bell Once Was," *Wall Street Journal*, January 17, 2018, A1, A10.

37 Limits to this condition tend to result from hardware technicalities or regulatory restrictions. Robert Metcalfe's hypothesis about Ethernet network connections assumed that the square of the number of devices in a system is proportionately related to their effect. This formulation has been researched by various authors in different settings and has been related to the cost of exclusion. See Carl Shapiro and Hal Varian, *Information Rules: A Strategic Guide to the Network Economy* (Cambridge, MA: Harvard Business School Press, 1999), chapters 5–7.

ethnicity, race, property, finance, travel, family history, daily timing, news, and other aspects. A monetary estimate is difficult to place on such data, but amounts would likely be substantial—given the vast revenue generated. These databases also become a formidable entry barrier as they accumulate—one that can be impossible to overcome.

But, if there is no price on access to a network platform, how can the oligopolist impose pricing control and obtain such immense revenue? The answer is advertising—especially the targeted kind.[38] And, in many cases, setting up related businesses that can feed on network extent. Oligopolistic pricing power is thus exercised on advertisers and on any merchant that wants to be placed on the platform.[39] Listing order of search entries can be considered a form of advertisement, as viewers are most likely to select the first entry or the next. This is a cognitive subtlety commonly exploited by search engine and merchandise oligopolists.[40]

As will be discussed in the next and subsequent chapters, usage—even if it is not monetarily charged for—can be considered equivalent to *labor.* The expropriation of personal data and the intrusive surveillance of online behavior, after all, generate immense revenue for the oligopolists in control. This phenomenon is not yet well understood, and it is part of the reason why platform oligopolists have been allowed to set up formidable entry barriers, and to become so intrusive and wealthy—while disregarding norms that other businesses have to observe. Such platforms are the backbone of "Big Data"—the cloud-based accumulation of intimate information based on network extent.

The cloud data platforms of Apple, Alphabet-Google, Microsoft, Meta-Facebook, and Amazon are so vast that they are larger than the combined databases of all governments on the planet—including those of their intelligence

38 Google—one of the best examples—was estimated to receive almost 90 percent of every dollar paid for new online advertisements during the last decade—and controlled over 85 percent of global search engine advertising revenue. See *The Economist*, "Silicon Valley, We Have a Problem," January 20, 2018, 19–20; Douglas MacMillan, "Google Blasts through Hurdles," *Wall Street Journal*, July 24, 2018, A1; Eric Rosenberg, *How Google Makes Money*, Investopedia, June 23, 2020, www.investopedia.com/.

39 During the last decade, Google's vast network extent made it possible for it to control the system of algorithms that reports when any advertisement is viewed—including the technical definition of what such "viewing" means. Merchants also paid Google to list their products by rank order—an important factor in attracting sales. See Denyse O'Leary, "Google Engineer Reveals Search Engine Bias," *Mind Matters*, July 27, 2019, https://mindmatters.ai/; Alistair Barr, "'Search Bias' is at Heart of Case," *Wall Street Journal*, April 16, 2015, A10.

40 Advertisers are usually required to bid to place their ads in search listings. Each bid can be attached to a keyword that the advertiser believes can be related to a search for its product. Then, advertisers must pay every time anyone clicks on an ad. Advertisements can be targeted to specific searches based on location, time of day, purchasing history, and a vast array of intimate details appropriated from each user. See Rosenberg, *How Google Makes*; *Economist*, "Silicon Valley"; Anna C. Redding, *Google It: A History of Google* (New York: Macmillan, 2018), chapter 8; Rolfe Winkler, "Key Word for Google? Advertising," *Wall Street Journal*, October 14, 2013, B2.

agencies.[41] And the market capitalization of these oligo-monopolies is much greater than the gross economic product of almost every nation on earth.[42] The data platforms owned by Monsanto and Bayer, along with Dow and DuPont (after their respective mergers), contain more information on crops, food chains, farms, farmers, chemical and agribusiness companies than that of all combined agricultural agencies in history.[43] The vast amount of intimate individual and business data that the clouds of these seven oligopolists encompass is thus one of the most important corporate assets in existence—*and* it is also a formidable entry barrier.

The intimate data appropriated by oligopolists in control of clouds should be considered a *commodity*. All the more so as it is analogous to a raw material used to manufacture a product. The product—advertising—can be considered the real output of search and social media oligopolists. Production then involves mining the appropriated data and devising algorithms that target users for ads. Research and development (R&D) activities usually revolve around the design of the algorithms—and behavioral analyses of mined data and ad propaganda.

Data are an inexhaustible resource—the more an oligopolist has, the more it can usually accumulate. This creates a dynamic circuit that builds upon itself, aided by the growing network extent.[44] It also allows the oligopolist in control to detect any incipient rivals or potential entrants—based on users' activities, payments, and the like—so that they can be targeted for entry barriers or acquisition.[45] Data also tend to be non-rivalrous—they can be used by the oligopolist in control and by any companies that purchase placement in its platform. Therefore, data appropriated by the oligopolist does not preclude its use by a client—so long as the latter subjects itself to the imposed pricing. In many platforms, pricing power is thus about advertisement.

In agro-biotech, vast network extent and data clouds provide formidable pricing power and customer lock-in—a most important entry barrier.

41 Mainly because of the vast network extent and its data platform, Google was estimated to control close to 90 percent of all online searches worldwide during the last decade. Facebook was found to control over two-thirds of all social media—and Apple and Amazon were found to control about one-half of all smartphone web traffic and online retail activity, respectively. See Statcounter, *Global Stats*, https://gs.statcounter.com/ (accessed June 20, 2022); *The Economist*, "Special Report: Fixing the Internet, Regulation," June 30, 2018, 11.

42 See Hartmann, *Hidden History*; *Economist*, "History's Biggest Companies."

43 See Menendian, *Era of Corporate Consolidation*; *Economist*, "History's Biggest Companies."

44 The immediate effect of this dynamic is noticeable in personal text communications that are restricted to be brief (140 characters in Tweeter's case, initially). An early example was France's Minitel (officially Teletel) in the 1980s—that allowed telephone users to send and receive brief text messages. See Nick Bilton, *Hatching Twitter: A True Story of Money, Power, Friendship, and Betrayal* (New York: Portfolio, 2013), chapters II-IV; Mark Stoner, "French Connections with Minitel: The Future has Arrived in France," *Online*, March 1988, www.questia.com/.

45 See Billy Gallagher, "Copycat: How Facebook tried to Squash Snapchat," *Wired*, February 16, 2018, www.wired.com/.

Genetically engineered cropping can be tailored to suit the priorities of an agro-biotech oligopolist—placing them above the needs of farmers, the preservation of ecologies, and public health. Planting programs can thus be devised that seek to maximize sales of genetically engineered seeds—instructing farmers on how to demarcate and use land, and the crops that may be chosen.[46] Each program can then be individually tailored for every farm and farmer—based on intimate data mining.

Network extent and the clouds can include terabytes of systematically archived information on yields for hundreds of thousands of genetically engineered seeds—along with detailed information on who uses them, and who might do so based on soil characteristics, land area, climate, and other factors. Then, the use of each seed type by any given farmer—along with yields obtained over time, financial situation, and personal details—can be placed in the cloud. Such data can be made available, under contract, to agribusiness oligopolies such that they can target a specific farmer for purchase of her land—based on underperformance, financial difficulties, age, and other intimate information. Similarly, crop insurance oligopolists can be sold access to such data to find new customers or adjust premiums.

In the case of a platform oriented toward shoppers, network extent can make it easier to use the data to recruit merchants—and to require them to bid for placement order in a search listing. And, to charge commissions on every sale they execute. Vast network extent can also make it easier for the oligopolistic owner of the platform to integrate other functions. Thus, a merchandise platform with substantial network extent can be extended to include logistics—down to the point of delivery to each customer.[47] If network extent is substantial, this scenario poses an entry barrier that is very difficult to overcome, even with much capital on hand and years of patience.

And the merchandise platform can include finance and banking, as almost all purchases are performed using credit, debit, or bank transfer instruments. Telecommunications can also be part of this panorama, as a vast network extent that services shoppers, merchants, logistics, and finance depends on it. Home management services might also be added to the platform, to execute automatic purchases before products are depleted. This panorama can result in

46 Monsanto's "prescriptive planting"—to instruct farmers on where, what, and how to plant—is considered to be one of the most important programs devised since the creation of genetically engineered seeds. See Peggy Connolly, Ruth A. Althaus and Robert B. Skipper, *Big Farma: Prescriptive Planting*, Markkula Center for Applied Ethics, ww.scu.edu/ (accessed June 17, 2022); *The Economist*, "Digital Disruption on the Farm," May 24, 2014, 64.

47 The numerous merchants on its platform allowed Amazon to become a merchandise search engine, a retailer, and a logistics operator. Amazon's low (or in some years inexistent) profitability—that allowed it to pay very low taxes—also became a form of entry barrier. See Galloway, *The Four*, chapter 2; *The Economist*, "How Far can Amazon Go?" June 21, 2014, 11.

an oligo-monopoly of sorts, with price control over many market niches and segments. And a formidable entry barrier.

The power of vast network extent can also be seen in the filtering of news. Vast oligo-monopolistic platforms that control our searches essentially operate as shadow news agencies, with tacit censorship and omission powers—that surpass those of all the largest government propaganda machines in history. Those platforms, moreover, have practically taken control of news distribution—targeting users based on online behavior and appropriated data.[48] And, the oligo-monopolists in charge have tended to co-opt conventional news outlets—partly to gain legitimacy for their tacit censorship and omissions—taking advantage of those companies' difficult finances.[49]

News carried in platforms with much network extent can thus become an important entry barrier. The vast majority of Americans receive their "news" through multi-use platforms—that convey selected details on recent events along with much trivia—and can capture attention as no news agency or government propaganda ever could. Conveniently, algorithms designed to perform filtering and tacit censorship tend to be blamed when complaints arise—obscuring the fact that they are programmed by the oligo-monopolist in control.[50]

Neo-Conglomerates

Adding company acquisitions to mega-platforms with a vast network extent not only helps set up stronger entry barriers but also extends pricing power. In recent times, this has led to the creation of technology *neo-conglomerates* sustained by numerous acquisitions—that build up a sort of "ecology" of related products.[51] The companies might seem independent, but they are owned by

48 During the last decade, conventional news outlets—newspapers and news agencies—largely lost control of news distribution to oligo-monopolistic platforms—such as Google's and Facebook's. See *The Economist*, "Bad News," October 17, 2020, 58.

49 This remark by a conservative magazine—owned by one of the largest conventional publishers in the world—is revealing: "The gratitude for big tech's largesse shows how desperate newspapers are for payment of any kind"—*The Economist*, "Bad News," 58.

50 In Google's case, its oligo-monopoly over about 85 percent of all news searches allows it immense discretion in filtering news—to suit its interests and those of its advertisers (the main source of revenue of its search engine). See Paul Chesser, *Yet Another Study Reveals Bias in Google's News Search*, National Legal and Policy Center, May 16, 2019, https://nlpc.org/; Nicholas Diakoupoulos, *Automating the News: How Algorithms are Rewriting the Media* (Cambridge, MA: Harvard University Press, 2019); Olivia Solon and Sam Levin, "How Google's Search Algorithm Spreads False Information with a Rightwing Bias," *The Guardian*, December 16, 2016, www.theguardian.com/.

51 During the last decade, Alphabet—the umbrella corporation created to further Google's oligo-monopolistic power through acquisitions—extended its already formidable entry barriers. This enabled Google to subsidize acquired companies (if needed) through the revenues of its core operations—which are mainly drawn from advertising. The fact that Google's two co-founders controlled well over one-half of all shareholder voting guaranteed that any unwelcome initiatives

the oligopolist in control and contribute all appropriated data to its cloud.[52] Embedding the acquired companies in the mega-platform expands possibilities for data mining, as all purchases of a product can be communicated to all the other companies. These mega-platform clouds are a very important asset and can help target acquisitions—such that entire market segments can be captured and stronger entry barriers erected.

The mega-platforms of a neo-conglomerate involve both horizontal and vertical integration. Thus, unlike in the old tech and heavy industrial conglomerates, acquired companies have technical, production, usage, marketing, or research connections that deepen and extend the range of functions.[53] Acquired companies are thereby related to those embedded in the mega-platform. The interrelationships can be complex and in some cases unidirectional, but technology mega-platforms tend to have many links—more so as their network extent expands.

Several elements bind a neo-conglomerate's acquired and embedded companies in a mega-platform. All of them contribute to set up entry barriers, extend pricing power, and expand network extent. One binding element is the appropriated data placed in the cloud, to be mined intensively and continuously. Another linking element is pervasive surveillance of all users or customers, to promote sales and appropriate more data. Advertising to users or customers is a binding element that can generate immense revenue. Using proprietary technical tools and standards—such as operating and payment systems, apps, and accessories—to make purchases of ancillary products unavoidable is yet another element.[54] Then there is finance—an element that has grown in

---

would be ignored. See Alistair Barr and Rolfe Winkler, "Google Creates Parent in Shake-Up," *Wall Street Journal*, August 11, 2015, A1; Nicolás Rivero, "The Acquisitions that Made Google a Search Monopoly," *Quartz*, October 20, 2020, https://qz.com/.

52 Among Alphabet-Google's many acquisitions—in a relatively short period of time—were YouTube (entertainment, online video), Calico (life sciences), Nest (smartphone devices, thermostats), Fiber (internet service), Sidewalk (urban technologies), and DeepMind (artificial intelligence). Acquired companies can allow Google to enter new sectors and market segments—such as urban development, transportation, entertainment, household management, and finance. Some existing units in its mega-platform were spun off as subsidiaries or began to be managed in quasi-independent ways—such as Waymo (formerly Google X, self-driving vehicles), Google Home, Google Maps, Google Capital, and Google Ventures. See Rivero, "The Acquisitions"; Rosenberg, *How Google Makes*; *The Economist*, "Google's Hippocampus," December 17, 2016, 55–56.

53 General Electric (founded in 1878) is possibly the most important example of an old tech conglomerate. Its M&A activity started in the 1890s, setting up some of the most formidable entry barriers of its time. It amassed a vast array of companies—many of which were functionally unrelated, or weakly related, to the other subsidiaries. See Thomas Gryta and Ted Mann, *Lights Out: Pride, Delusion, and the Fall of General Electric* (New York: Houghton Mifflin, 2020), chapters 15–19.

54 Alphabet-Google's Android operating system, for example, reportedly controls over four-fifths of the world's smartphones—that are inevitably linked in various ways to products in its mega-platform. See Rivero, "The Acquisitions"; Rosenberg, *How Google Makes*; *Economist*, "Silicon

importance among tech neo-conglomerates in recent times, to the point that some are considered to operate, in part, as shadow hedge funds.[55]

Neo-conglomerates can also be found among hardware-focused oligopolists. Network extent is very important, and their mega-platforms tend to embed acquired companies with products that complement existing ones.[56] The mega-platforms may be less extensive than those of their cyberspace counterparts, but they can be as formidable an entry barrier. And the revenues obtained through maintenance, updates, and repair are usually much greater than those derived from hardware sales. Service contracts are thus important for customer lock-ins—and they typically strengthen entry barriers.

In hardware-focused mega-platforms, pricing control is extended and deepened as more companies are acquired. These often involve interrelated technologies that share workers, hardware, marketing, distribution, and warranties—all of which generate much data and create a strong entry barrier. The data appropriated from clients through sale of products and services can thus be as important an asset as those provided by cyberspace mega-platforms, although the clientele is usually smaller. Mining the data and acquiring related companies—to expand network extent—are important for pricing power.

The neo-conglomerate phenomenon reverses what in the last part of the twentieth and the initial years of the twenty-first centuries was a tendency toward decomposition of companies in new technology sectors.[57] That scenario involved modular decentralization, the spinning off of some units as autono-

Valley"; Liz Hoffman, "The Conglomerate is Embraced by Google," *Wall Street Journal*, August 12, 2015, C4.

55 See Tyler Durden, "The World's Biggest 'Hedge Fund', $30 Billion Bigger than Bridgewater, Remains Mysterious as Ever," *ZeroHedge*, July 23, 2015, www.zerohedge.com/; Gilbert and Hrdlicka, "Apple is a Hedge Fund that Makes Phones"; Cook, "Apple Creates Braeburn Capital"; Shoot, "Google's $1 Billion Bay Area Buy". At the onset of financialization in the 1980s, General Electric became a sort of shadow hedge fund—extending its prior consumer finance operation to become a speculator. As the 2007–9 financial crisis set in, GE was bailed out by the federal government—through debt guarantees of $84 billion—while simultaneously being allowed to borrow vast amounts at 0.25 percent annual interest (a negative real rate at the time). After the bailout, GE reportedly closed 40 plants in the United States over a five-year period, laying off tens of thousands of workers—while its chief executive was reportedly compensated $20.6 million (in 2012 alone). See *UPI*, "GE is Quiet Bailout Recipient," June 29, 2009, www.upi.com/; Gryta and Mann, *Lights Out*.

56 Honeywell acquired 84 companies over a 13-year period, in seemingly diverse areas that nonetheless fit into its expanded mega-platform—grounded in navigation and communication systems. It benefited greatly from its military technology contracting to expand over the years—while also engaging commercial clients. Other hardware technology oligopolists that serve both commercial and military clients—United Technologies and Danaher, for example—have set up mega-platforms. Danaher was estimated to have acquired more than 400 companies since the 1980s (up to the last decade). See Ted Mann, "A Conglomerate Finds Love among the Breakups," *Wall Street Journal*, September 2, 2015, A1; Sriram Nadathur and L. Jay Bourgeois, *Danaher: The Making of a Conglomerate*, Darden School, University of Virginia, 2013, https://store.darden.virginia.edu/.

57 See Suarez-Villa, *Technocapitalism*, 86–122.

mous entities, or the setting up of a quasi-subsidiary to target specialized niches. Research was a binding element and the main entry barrier—through the intellectual property it generated and the chance to seize new markets. Missing was a platform upon which all the units were embedded—to systematically conduct surveillance, appropriate data, and build up pricing power. Financial speculation was missing, as it was considered extraneous to a technology company.

Beyond the effects of network extent and data appropriation, another point that can help explain why platform oligopolists have become so powerful is that they are not government sanctioned (as, say, AT&T was for decades). Regulation would restrict their pricing power—along with other aspects, such as their exploitation of data they appropriate and surveillance of users. Government inaction, however, has led to a massive buildup of oligopolistic power among data platform corporations and neo-conglomerates that would have been considered unthinkable in previous times. Also, the fact that they are not government sanctioned has itself been used to justify why they should be allowed to accumulate power, in what amounts to an inversion of regulatory logic. This panorama results from neglect by antitrust regulators to act, due to the nature of the political and regulatory system—aspects that will be dealt with later in this chapter and book.

An outcome of this panorama is a winners-take-all situation that allows oligopolistic pricing power to grow rapidly. Unregulated, rapidly expanding network extent—especially in platform oligopolies and neo-conglomerates—is part of the problem. One symptom of this dynamic during the last decade was the appearance of so-called "blockbusters" that captured market niches—using pricing power and visibility to prevent others from entering.[58] This can occur in subtle ways by, for example, ensuring that search listings favor the company in control. Other companies in the market niche thus end up being placed lower in listings and are noticed less—executing fewer sales.

Creating barriers for customers to switch out of a neo-conglomerate's control can be supportive of pricing power and the winners-take-all scenario. Making it difficult to switch out to another product or service can involve expense and inconvenience. The barriers can involve not only customers but also entrants into a market segment, as the latter would find it more difficult to gain sales and market share. Platforms with significant network extent pose a formidable obstacle to switching, as relationships and links can be lost or require restructuring. Such difficulties can be compounded by aggressive tactics. Schemes may be concocted to surreptitiously undermine business, appropriate innovations, and shortchange sales of departing customers as a warning to others.[59]

58 As in entertainment platforms—see Anita Elberse, *Blockbusters: Hit-Making, Risk-Taking, and the Big Business of Entertainment* (New York: Holt, 2013), chapters 2, 3.

59 Aggressive strategies are often recommended by consultants. Their use against customers can lead to bankruptcies, theft of intellectual property, or substantial loss of revenue. See George Stalk Jr.

Standards Setting

Setting technical standards can build pricing power and become an entry barrier. Locking a market into a technology standard often involves co-respective consent. Protecting pricing power—by sharing ownership of a standard—is an existential priority for those in control. Even when ownership is not shared, the benefit of protecting pricing power is simply too important to be ignored.

Setting a standard can be done tacitly, by a company that pioneers a technology. One of the best examples involved Microsoft's PC operating system in the 1980s.[60] Acquiring a new technology through M&A can have much the same effect. Then, after a significant number of products are in use, any entrant may find it unavoidable to adopt the standard. Especially when alternatives are too expensive to develop—or are incompatible with accessories and services.

Setting technical standards thus helps sustain pricing power, by preventing entry of companies with products that do not comply. Devising protocols that favor a proprietary technology is important, as they usually set the stage for long-lasting revenue streams. The protocols can be "designed" to seem logical, through technicalities that exclude the larger panorama of alternatives. And only those with deep knowledge of the technology may be able to decipher what the alternatives might be. The protocols can—in addition to preventing entry—turn owner-oligopolists into rentiers.

Setting a standard can occur in numerous ways. Imposing diagnostic criteria for biotechnology or biopharmaceutical products can generate entry barriers and pricing power—even when the technology deployed is not proprietary. This can be achieved by setting higher test thresholds for certain conditions—previously considered not to pose significant risk—such that they can lead to treatment or medication.[61] If the targeted conditions can generate surgeries, revenues can be further increased. This may explain in part why American health care is controlled by layers of oligopolistic corporations, and why so

---

and Robert Lachenauer, "Hardball: Five Killer Strategies for Trouncing the Competition," *Harvard Business Review*, April 2004, 62–71; George Stalk Jr., Robert Lachenauer and John Butman, *Are You Playing to Play or Are You Playing to Win?* (Boston: Harvard Business School Press, 2004).

60 IBM—pioneer in mass PC production—commissioned Microsoft to provide the OS software. IBM, however, did not appropriate Microsoft's software nor did it retain rights to the PC. Massive cloning of IBM's PCs then allowed Microsoft to become a standard setter, as it retained rights to the OS. See Hal R. Varian, Joseph Farrell and Carl Shapiro, *The Economics of Information Technology* (Cambridge: Cambridge University Press, 2004), 37–38, 49–50, 70–72; IBM, *The Birth of the IBM PC*, www.ibm.com/ (accessed June 28, 2022); Randall Stross, *The Microsoft Way* (New York: Basic, 1996), chapters 3, 8–10.

61 See H. Gilbert Welch, Benjamin L. Mazer and Adewole S. Adamson, "The Rapid Rise in Cutaneous Melanoma Diagnoses," *New England Journal of Medicine* 384 (2021), www.nejm.org/; H. Gilbert Welch, Lisa Schwartz and Steven Woloshin, *Overdiagnosed: Making People Sick in the Pursuit of Health* (Boston: Beacon, 2011); H. Gilbert Welch, "Diagnosis as Disease," *Wall Street Journal*, May 6, 2011, A29.

much more is spent by consumers while obtaining worse outcomes than in other advanced nations.[62]

The multiplier effects of this standard-setting mode can be wide ranging. Not only can sales and pricing power for biotechnology and biopharmaceutical oligopolists increase but also those of—usually oligopolistic—hospital corporations, clinics, testing companies, and insurers.[63] Side effects of treatments and medications can then generate additional revenue streams—more so if they are irreversible and require attention for the rest of a lifetime. And, numerous conditions for which treatments, medications, or surgeries make little or no difference can compound pricing power and entry barriers.

Imposing standards in new areas of biotechnology, such as genetic editing, can influence future treatments and medications.[64] Even though the technologies involved have a limited proprietary life, the methods may themselves become an entry barrier. High complexity can help generate this situation, as only relatively few specialists may be able to perform procedures. All the more so if the latter cannot be automated. As genetic editing expands to most life forms, including humans, entry barriers may be extended not by proprietary restrictions but by complexity and pre-established procedures or protocols.

Setting standards based on software operating systems and large network extent can also create formidable entry barriers. These systems determine a host of other functions down the line.[65] Thus, the multiplicative effects of operating system (OS)-based entry barriers must be taken into account. Setting up an OS as a standard, tacitly or by collusion, will pave the way for sales generated by dependent systems—as now occurs with the vast array of apps that are needed to make smartphones and other gadgets work.[66] And the revenue

62 See Jake Novak, "Hospital Monopolies are Making Us Poorer and Sicker," *CNBC*, January 21, 2020, www.cnbc.com/; *The Economist*, "Health-Care Profits: Which Firms Make the Biggest Killing from America's Health Care System?" March 17, 2018, 66.

63 See Susie Cagle, "How Hospital Monopolies Broke the Health Care System," *The Nation*, December 2, 2020, www.thenation.com/; *The Economist*, "Health-Care Profits"; Jerome P. Kassirer, *On the Take: How America's Complicity with Big Business Can Endanger Your Health* (New York: Oxford University Press, 2005).

64 See Rasmus O. Bak, Natalia Gomez-Ospina and Matthew H. Porteus, "Gene Editing on Center Stage," *Trends in Genetics* 34 (2018), 600–11; Patrick D. Hsu, Eric S. Lander and Feng Zhang, "Development and Applications of CRISPR-Cas9 for Genome Engineering," *Cell* 157 (2014), 1262–78.

65 Microsoft's oligo-monopoly over PC operating systems in the 1980s made it possible for it to bundle its Internet Explorer browser with its Windows OS in the 1990s—eventually vanquishing Netscape and its Navigator browser. See Cal Jeffrey and Julio Franco, "What Ever Happened to Netscape Navigator?" *Techspot*, August 25, 2020, www.techspot.com/.

66 Alphabet-Google's Android OS has been estimated to operate over four-fifths of all smartphones worldwide—a result of entry barriers supported by vast network extent. Google reportedly "effectively forces" smartphone manufacturers to have its OS as the default on their devices. Then, through its Android OS Google requires smartphone manufacturers and users to install its own apps—sold by the millions monthly by its store. This inevitably leads smartphone manufacturers

obtained through them can be important for an oligopolist's market capitalization. Increases in the latter often pave the way for acquisitions of potential entrants that help erect stronger entry barriers.

The longevity of set technical standards can be substantial—decades in many cases. And this form of lock-in can be practically impossible to overturn, once a large number of products are in use. All the more so when regulators are co-opted into acquiescing, because of the absence of an alternative standard or due to corruption. The result will be to lock in customers, to prevent entrants that can offer alternatives, and—most of all—to sustain the pricing power of those in control.

Setting up any of the previously discussed entry barriers is often accompanied by disinformation campaigns, to justify abuses. One such justification is to argue that customer lock-in increases "choices." The very opposite is often the case, however, as the range of choices that would occur without an entry barrier may be greater. Also, the choices would be provided not by one or a set of colluding oligopolists but by independent, competing providers.

And, the choices may involve rights and benefits for customers that are absent when lock-in occurs. Compensation for appropriation of intimate data that each user or customer is made to give up would be an important right. Similarly, the right to refuse that intimate data be appropriated and still receive the product—along with the right to switch at any time without incurring charges, or the possibility of choosing to remove one's data. And, the right to refuse to be targeted for advertisements without incurring charges. On the interphase between platforms, services, and hardware, among the choices could be voiding the need to purchase accessories to make a product work and compensation for flawed or insufficiently tested products. The choices available would on balance be greater, as competing platforms would likely generate different possibilities down the line.

Another false justification involves the argument that entry barriers and lock-in "lower prices." This not only seems irrational but also deceptive, as it has been shown repeatedly during most of the last and current centuries that competitive market pricing scenarios provide lower prices. Price markups would evaporate quickly when an oligopolistic market segment becomes competitive. This is a reality that has unfortunately become a rarity in our time, as oligopolies have taken over most every sector in the American economy.[67]

---

to install its Play Store, its Maps, and dozens of other programs as standard equipment. See Ryan Browne, "Google's Smaller Rivals Say It's Not Playing Fair After Record EU Antitrust Fine," *CNBC*, September 29, 2020, www.cnbc.com/; Rolfe Winkler, "Scrutiny Turns to Android Software," *Wall Street Journal*, April 16, 2015, A10.

67 See Federico J. Diez, Daniel Leigh and Suchanan Tambunlertchai, *Global Market Power and Macroeconomic Implications*, IMF Working Paper WP/18/137 (Washington: International Monetary Fund, 2018), www.imf.org/; Jan De Loecker and Jan Eeckhout, *Global Market Power*, NBER Working Paper 24768 (Cambridge: National Bureau of Economic Research, 2018), and their *The*

Thus, it can be argued that the combination of lower pricing and greater choice would only occur when entry barriers, lock-ins, and oligopolistic pricing power are dissolved.

Deregulation

The spread of oligopolistic standards setting, entry barriers, and greater pricing power found tacit theoretical and policy justification in an important and influential construct—contestable markets theory. Articulated by one of the best-known economists of the late twentieth and early twenty-first centuries—William Baumol—the construct's ideological perspective was largely aligned with 1976 Nobel laureate Milton Friedman's longstanding advocacy of a minimalist role for government.[68] At the core was the assumption that markets would provide better outcomes than regulatory intervention and—left unimpeded—would generate faster growth. Thus, *undertaking deregulation to place "free" market processes above all other considerations was the prime objective.* This occurred at a time—the late 1970s and early 1980s—when fears spread about capitalism's capacity to survive crises that conflated stagnation with high inflation.

Behind the construct's theoretical façade was the advocacy for market processes to rule over society—an aspect that may recall the neo-Hobbesian perspective of classical economists, discussed earlier. Contestable markets theory was thus used to push for deregulation to disengage markets from oversight and to place the interests of businesses above those of the public. Favored by many mainstream economists and neoliberal policy-makers, the construct also essentially minimized the effects of entry barriers and M&A deals. And, although it

---

Rise of Market Power and the Macroeconomic Implications, NBER Working Paper 23687 (Cambridge: National Bureau of Economic Research, 2017), www.nber.org/; Geisst, *Monopolies in America*; Hartmann, *Hidden History*; Larkin and Michaely, *Are U.S. Industries Becoming*. The Herfindahl-Hirschman index has long indicated a sustained rise in oligopolistic concentration in the American economy—see Investopedia, *Herfindahl-Hirschman Index-HHI*, www.investopedia.com/ (accessed July 24, 2019); William Galston, "The Perils of Corporate Concentration," *Wall Street Journal*, June 20, 2018, A15.

68 See William J. Baumol, "Contestable Markets: An Uprising in the Theory of Industry Structure," *American Economic Review* 72 (1982), 1–15; William J. Baumol, John C. Panzar and Robert D. Willig, *Contestable Markets and the Theory of Industry Structure* (New York: Harcourt, Brace, Jovanovich, 1982). Friedman's *Capitalism and Freedom* (first published in 1962)—where he articulated his ideological and politico-economic perspective—is possibly most closely related to the tenets of contestable markets theory. In Chapter 8—in what may be considered the eventual core idea of contestable markets theory—Friedman advocated for an end to government-regulated monopolies. In his view, corporations' prime concern should be solely with profit, and not at all with what he referred to as "social responsibility"—a matter that he regarded as a serious "subversion" of the ethos of capitalism. Friedman's ideas would eventually be translated into policies—first implemented by the Pinochet regime in Chile in the 1970s and subsequently by the governments of Margaret Thatcher and Ronald Reagan.

provided no blanket endorsement of oligopolistic consolidation, its application nonetheless proved to be a major support.[69]

A major flaw with the construct was its failure to understand the dynamics of deregulation with government-sanctioned monopolies and oligopolies, where the lifting of restrictions initially creates a competitive scenario for a relatively short period, followed by rapid oligopolistic concentration—as occurred in the United States with telecommunications, public utilities, finance, the airlines, and other sectors.[70] Thus, it can be argued that the construct legitimized the asset stripping of previously regulated monopolies and the societal resources they had managed.[71] And the brief spell of competition that ensued set the stage to bring assets that belong to the public under freewheeling oligopolistic control. Paradoxically, many neoliberal ideologues viewed the newly created oligopolistic concentration as "competition"—a blatant contradiction that sought to legitimize the new reality, arguing that such concentration was a direct result of "competitive forces" and should be left unregulated.[72]

Another problem with the construct was the assumption that a deregulated market provides free entry, even when oligopolies become engaged in building up considerable market power. Related to this view was the notion

69 Particularly among conservative jurists, who would lead the drive for deregulation in most every area of the American economy—see Robert H. Bork's *The Antitrust Paradox: A Policy at War with Itself* (New York: Basic Books, 1978).

70 See the discussion in Suarez-Villa, *Corporate Power, Oligopolies*, 39–44. The equivocal notion that oligopolies that emerged after deregulation were acceptable—and should be considered "competitive"—was adopted by many who followed the precepts of contestable markets theory.

71 See Philip Mirowski, *Science-Mart: Privatizing American Science* (Cambridge, MA: Harvard University Press, 2011), chapters 1, 6, 7; John Bellamy Foster, Robert W. McChesney and R. Jamil Jonna, "Monopoly and Competition in Twenty-First Century Capitalism," *Monthly Review*, April 2011, https://monthlyreview.org/.

72 A view that has been propagated through business school curricula and academics and by the management literature. An article in the conservative magazine The Economist, for example, called attention to the mistaken interpretation of oligopolistic consolidation as "competitive" by stating: "The first idea is that business is more competitive than ever. Skim popular titles … and you will be left with the impression of a hyper-competitive world in which established giants are constantly being felled by the forces of disruption. A glance at the numbers … should be enough to expose this as fiction. The most striking business trend today is not competition but consolidation. The years since 2008 have seen one of the biggest-ever bull markets in mergers and acquisitions, with an average of 30,000 deals a year worth 3% of GDP. … Technology is high on the list of industries that are concentrating. In the 1990s Silicon Valley was a playground for startups. It is now the fief of a handful of behemoths"—*The Economist*, "Out with the Old," 61. Among the publications denounced in this article were Ram Charan's *The Attacker's Advantage: Turning Uncertainty into Breakthrough Opportunities* (New York: PublicAffairs, 2015) and Rita G. McGrath's *The End of Competitive Advantage: How to Keep your Strategy Moving as Fast as your Business* (Cambridge, MA: Harvard Business Review Press, 2013). Among others in the news media who have called attention to the downfall of competition—and the rapid rise of oligopolistic consolidation—is Paul Krugman's "Barons of Broadband," *New York Times*, February 16, 2014, www.nytimes.com/. See also Foster, McChesney and Jonna, "Monopoly and Competition."

that scale cannot provide appreciable advantages to larger companies—to block others from entry or from competing in the same market.[73] Markets ruled by government-sanctioned monopolies or oligopolies were thus assumed to be "contestable" by the theory—as any company that sought to enter them was supposed to be able to do so once they were deregulated.

The contestable markets construct also posited that *only* government regulation—antitrust legislation included—and labor unions blocked the path to greater economic growth and efficiency. Thus, prescriptions to do away with regulations that restrict corporate power over markets, most of all on entry and pricing—along with legislation that preempted or blocked labor unions—became established in the American policy panorama. And, the notion that oligopolies and monopolies should not be restricted unless it could be shown that they directly harm consumers—in a very narrow way—became a standard prescription for regulatory endeavors.

Policies that followed the precepts of contestable markets theory benefitted technology oligopolies greatly and allowed them to build up formidable entry barriers, greater pricing power, and larger scale. And it allowed tech oligopolists to escape antitrust regulatory attention if they provided new services that involved little or no monetary cost to consumers—while building up diverse entry barriers to lock in market segments and niches. Thus, for tech oligopolists, forgoing significant product price increases could be more than made up through strategic ploys—such as expanding network extent, expropriating more data, setting up mega-platforms, imposing technical standards, building up vast intellectual property monopolies, structuring neo-conglomerates, tacitly enlisting platform users as unpaid workers, and capturing entire market segments through M&A deals and entry barriers. And, betting that their eventual imposition of higher product pricing on consumers would be ignored or protected by their economic clout, political influence, and regulatory co-optation.

Innovation

The orientation of research and development (R&D) toward wants creation is another important source of technology oligopolistic power. Modifying existing products such that they can be presented as "necessary"—and novel—has become the main objective of R&D operations.[74] The overarching hope is that a differentiated

73 Despite evidence showing that numerous entry barriers could be found in just about every industrial sector. One analysis published at the time when contestable markets theory was most fervently advocated, for example, found 22 entry barriers to be very common in American industry—see William G. Shepherd, *The Economics of Industrial Organization* (Englewood Cliffs: Prentice-Hall, 1979), chapters 9, 10.

74 Thorstein Veblen noticed long ago the early symptoms of this tendency, in *The Instinct of Workmanship and the State of the Industrial Arts* (New York: Macmillan, 1914), 314–15.

product will generate greater demand. Product development (the D in R&D) is thus turned into a marketing machine, whose primordial objective is to sell.[75]

Development versus Research

Research is largely subordinated to product development in the ever pressing drive to sell more, sustain pricing power, expand network extent, and strengthen entry barriers. Boosting revenue, executive compensation, and market capitalization become the most desirable results—to be attained immediately and continuously. Cutting-edge research is thus relegated to a lower plane in the oligopolistic scale of priorities, if it is retained at all. Such research is simply too costly and uncertain, and the payoff—notable as it might be—may only be obtained at a distant time. Out of range, in other words, for the near-term perspectives of executives, shareholders, and speculators.

The preponderance of product development over research is very noticeable in technology platforms. Most everything that platform-based oligopolists do on R&D involves finding a product marketing opportunity. Data in clouds are mined intensively and continuously, and the prime objective is to concoct ways to convince customers or users to buy more. If there are "innovations" in this scenario they might occur in the form of algorithms that streamline ad targeting and data mining, so that more sales can occur. Or, in behavioral analyses that may make it easier to identify those susceptible to believe certain propaganda.[76]

Acquiring companies with significant intellectual property—or with research that can be commercialized right away—is a way to offset the downgrading

75 Greater emphasis on product development and marketing—and its contribution to economic waste—can be traced to the early days of oligopolistic concentration in the American economy. Among the prominent critics was Vance Packard, and his *The Waste Makers* (New York: McKay, 1960), chapters 2–4, 6, 14. See also David Hamberg, "Invention in the Industrial Research Laboratory," *Journal of Political Economy* 71 (1963), 95–115. The rise of advertising as an important economic activity—and of advertising oligopolies soon after—was one of the outcomes. An early analysis of advertising and its tactics to reach consumers can be found in Louis Cheskin's *Why People Buy: Motivation Research and its Successful Application* (New York: Liveright, 1959). Prior to this era, economist Alfred Marshall—in his *Industry and Trade* (London: Macmillan, 1919), 305–06—had categorized advertising as either "constructive" (one that brings up possibilities) or "combative" (mainly persuasive or manipulative in scope). The rise of the American advertising juggernaut in the 1950s took up the second, to the near complete exclusion of the first. Advertising thus began to concentrate on psychological influence—to induce each and every individual to purchase, regardless of need.

76 Analyses for this purpose gained attention during the last decade, as social media, online gaming, and sales in merchandise platforms expanded rapidly. See *The Economist*, "Getting Hooked: How Digital Firms Create Products that Get Inside People's Heads," January 3, 2015, 53; Nir M. Eyal and Ryan Hoover, *Hooked: How to Build Habit-Forming Products* (London: Portfolio Penguin, 2014), chapters 1, 6–8.

of in-house research.[77] Merging with another company that possesses substantial IP is another. These two possibilities may help understand why the drive toward oligopolistic consolidation in technology sectors has been so intense in recent times.

Nonetheless, the road to research through acquisitions may not involve an easy ride. An acquired company's IP may not be as promising as assumed—due to changing external conditions or a rival's early marketing of similar products. Risk is uncertainty that can be measured, but uncertainty—on its own—is a gamble, a bet whose probability escapes calibration. And research, even when it has generated IP in acquired companies, is all too often an uncertain endeavor.

The vast majority of patents are never put to any use, and most of those that are utilized never yield much in the way of financial rewards. Also, all patents expire.[78] Products based on patents become generic when they expire—the underlying invention being available for any company to use.[79] This means that even if an acquired company has seemingly valuable patents, their eventual expiration can render the acquisition less valuable—or even worthless.[80]

Also, acquisitions can be problematic when they involve startups. About nine-tenths of all startups fail. Among those that manage to survive, it can be difficult to tell whether any of their IP or ongoing research might be turned into profitable products. If a tech startup does not possess IP, its chances of being acquired are practically none. And patent application reviews can take years for a decision to be made—thus, by the time a patent is granted, a startup may no longer exist.

77 Some biotechnology oligopolists devised a "distributed model" of research during the last decade—to help decide on financing research projects for smaller companies that may eventually be acquired. See Alessandro Delfanti, *Distributed Biotechnology*, University of Toronto, 2016, https://tspace.library.utoronto.ca/; *The Economist*, "Biotechnology: Fever Rising," February 15, 2014, 56–57. In some cases, however, acquisition of established companies is the preferred way to increase an IP portfolio and strengthen market pricing power. A company that reportedly pursued this strategy—to substitute for in-house research—was biopharmaceutical oligopolist Valeant—see William Alden, "Valeant's History of Deal-Making," *New York Times*, April 21, 2014, https://dealbook.nytimes.com/; Jonathan D. Rockoff and Dana Mattioli, "Build it or Buy it? Drug Bid Puts R&D in Focus," *Wall Street Journal*, June 11, 2014, A1.

78 See U.S. Patent and Trademark Office, *2701 Patent Term [R-10.2019], 35 U.S.C. 154 Contents and Term of Patent; Provisional Rights*, www.uspto.gov/ (accessed June 28, 2022). The possibility that a patent might be extended—or a substitute granted for much the same invention, through clever tweaking—is always uncertain. Even if a patent is granted in such cases, the award may be contested.

79 Revenue losses from patent expiration can be substantial—see Eric Sagonowsky, "The Decade's Top 10 Patent Losses, Worth a Whopping $915 Billion in Lifetime Sales," *Fierce Pharma*, August 17, 2017, www.fiercepharma.com/.

80 A related problem is the frequent use of the PTAB (Patent Trial and Appeal Board, created in 2012) to challenge patents' validity retroactively—each case potentially costing as much as one million dollars, if not more, to those challenged—in addition to revenue losses if a case is lost. See *The Economist*, "The Trouble with Troll-Hunting: Rules to Curb Frivolous Patent Claims May Encourage Infringement," December 14, 2019, 60.

Another problem with startups is fraud and the prevalence of exaggerated claims.[81] In the rush to be acquired, the prospects for any potential products or IP can be highly inflated—all the more so if similar products do not already exist. The spread of so-called "accelerators" that train would-be startup owners—playing on the dreams of those who believe they will become rich quickly—might be considered partly responsible for this scenario.[82] Acquiring a startup to substitute for in-house research can thus be a costly and wasteful bet.

Cost reduction efforts in technology oligopolies have long targeted in-house research. The importance of cost reduction for technology oligopolies should not be underestimated, as it is an operational aspect that they actively compete on. After labor cost reduction (discussed earlier), lowering the cost of research is often a major priority. In labor's case, however, cost reduction through pricing power over a labor market can be relatively straightforward. With research, reducing costs often turns out to be more complicated.

Seizing innovations from open-source platforms can help reduce costs. This can eliminate the need to hire qualified personnel, purchase equipment, build facilities, and manage a research regime. Modifying or reverse-engineering open-source innovations—to embed them in products or claim them as proprietary—can and does occur. This is a matter that an oligopolistic corporation can get away with, given the relations of power involved.[83] The cost of

81 Exaggerated claims seems to be a perennial problem with biotech startups and may explain why less than 16 percent have any profit—see Nasdaq Global Indexes, *NASDAQ Biotechnology (NBI)*, https://indexes.nasdaqomx.com/ (accessed June 22, 2022); *The Economist*, "Biotechnology: Just What the Doctor Ordered," August 14, 2021, 51. Exaggerated claims are also often connected to fraud—see, for example, Graham Winfrey, "New HBO Documentary Seeks to Explain How Theranos Founder Elizabeth Holmes Created a $9 Billion Scam," *Inc.*, March 18, 2019, www.inc.com/; David Folkenflik, "'The Inventor': Elizabeth Holmes' Theranos Scam that Rocked Silicon Valley," *WBUR*, March 22, 2019, www.wbur.com/; Telis Demos, Shira Ovide and Susan Pulliam, "Tech Startups Play Numbers Game," *Wall Street Journal*, June 10, 2015, A1. The reality of startups' problems may evade attention, however, if we believe the promotional literature—see Peter Thiel and Blake Masters, *Zero to One: Notes on Startups, or How to Build the Future* (New York: Crown Business, 2014), chapters 1, 3, 7–10.

82 Accelerators—known as "incubators" in the 1990s—increased rapidly in the twenty-first century, partly because of the growing insecurity of conventional employment and the high cost of management education. But the training tuition charged by accelerators can be quite expensive, given startups' very high failure rates. Generally, training involves recipes that boil down what an entrepreneur supposedly does to a template of tasks—and can include some basic notions of accounting, financial solicitation, legal aspects, and IP application routines. See Steve Blank and Bob Dorf, *Startup Owner's Manual: The Step-by-Step Guide for Building a Great Company* (Hoboken: Wiley, 2020); Steve Blank, *The Four Steps to the Epiphany: Successful Strategies for Products that Win* (Hoboken: Wiley, 2020). See also *The Economist*, "Venture Capital: The Next Stage," November 27, 2021, 69–70; and its Special Report on Startups, "A Cambrian Moment," January 18, 2014, 3–4, 6.

83 See Synopsys, *Open Source Vulnerabilities, 2020 Open Source Security and Risk Analysis (OSSRA) Report*, www.synopsys.com/; Brian Proffitt, "How Scary are GPL Violations?" *Computerworld*, November 21, 2011, www.computerworld.com/.

litigation against a tech oligopolist for open-source pilfering can be immense and the outcome uncertain. Nonetheless, seizing innovations from open-source research has major drawbacks—repertories are limited and quality can disappoint, dependent as they are on the interests, capabilities, and number of participants.

Schemes involving cost reduction in research gained greater urgency through the practice of agency theory in technology oligopolies during the past four decades.[84] The theory's placement of "shareholder value" optimization above all other concerns—and its prescribed role for executives to exclusively become "agents" of shareholders—can be held responsible for the downgrading of research and the reorientation of R&D for wants creation. And, its premise that shareholders "own" the company to which they provide capital is fallacious, inasmuch as they are only entitled to a portion of the profit (and the right to vote on certain decisions).[85] All the more so as the American legal system considers corporations to be "legal persons" that own themselves.[86] Shareholders, not being owners, are thus shielded from liability if bankruptcy occurs—their wealth being exempt from seizure. Many shareholders also only hold their stock for short periods, especially if the purchase is speculative.

It can be argued that the widespread practice of agency theory has also been prejudicial for those who provide the single most important resource for innovation—creativity. Skilled labor is the source of this most valuable quality, yet their interests are typically placed far below those of shareholders in the corporate scale of priorities.[87] The fact that such labor—employee-inventors—are typically expropriated of the patents they are awarded adds injustice to this reality. Patents are only granted to individuals, but corporations require ownership to be reassigned to them as a condition for employment. This usually applies even when the employee comes up with an invention outside work-time and with her own resources. And any reward provided—usually in the form of bonuses or stock options—seldom ever reflects the future cumulative revenue streams that the invention will provide.

Behind the panorama of cost cutting and deployment of R&D for wants creation lies an important reality. This is the declining significance of innovations

84 See Jensen and Meckling, "Theory of the Firm."

85 A matter long pointed out by management and business law specialists. See Sumantra Ghoshal, "Bad Management Theories are Destroying Good Management Practices," *Academy of Management Learning and Education* 4 (2005), 75–91; Stout, *Shareholder Value Myth*; Donaldson, *American Anti-Management Theories of Organization*, Chapter 6; Paddy Ireland, "Company Law and the Myth of Shareholder Ownership," *Modern Law Review* 62 (1999), 32–57.

86 A principle reaffirmed by a landmark 2010 U.S. Supreme Court decision—see Wikipedia, *Citizens United v. FEC*, and its *Corporate Personhood*, https://en.wikipedia.org/ (both accessed June 15, 2022); Ciara Torres Spelliscy, *The History of Corporate Personhood*, Brennan Center for Justice, April 8, 2014, www.brennancenter.org/.

87 See the critique on this point in Suarez-Villa, *Technocapitalism*, 114–15. See also Ghoshal, "Bad Management Theories."

in the United States. Innovations classified as "important" reportedly dropped by over four-fifths since the decade of the 1970s.[88] And the sharp decrease in the number of such innovations in recent decades may—in part—be considered a result of cutbacks in cutting-edge research.

The decline of basic research in technology contrasts with the rising importance of financial speculation with patents. Substantial efforts to trade with patent rights in financial markets—much as occurs with any stock, bond, or derivative—by betting on the revenue they might generate have been undertaken in recent times. This might help explain the frequent calls for greater patent protection. Yet, strengthening patent protection has not been found to lead to a significant rise in innovation—even in technology sectors that depend greatly on them.[89]

Technological Barriers

Another, larger problem—one often not taken into account—also contributes to the declining importance of innovation and research. *These are the technological barriers on performance that affect innovative quality*. These barriers—conflated with pressures to reduce cost—may also be posing a serious obstacle to technological advancement. And oligopolistic technology power, despite the vast resources at its disposal, seems ill suited to overcome them.

In microelectronics, the current slowdown and likely end of Moore's law may limit the expansion of performance in most every product that uses microprocessors.[90] A doubling of capacity about every 18 months—the essence of

88 Analyses of innovations classified as "award winners," originating in Fortune 500 corporations—all technology oligopolies included—by *R&D World* magazine reportedly declined from an annual average of 44 in the 1970s to 9 in the 2000s—declining further in the 2010s decade—see R&D World, *R&D World Archive*, www.rdworldonline.com/ (accessed November 10, 2021). And, many award winners in recent decades may be considered differentiations of prior innovations and thus not really "new"—see Michael S. Malone, "An Innovation Slowdown at the Tech Giants," *Wall Street Journal*, July 2, 2014, A13; Fred Block and Matthew R. Keller, *Where Do Innovations Come From? Transformations in the U.S. National Innovation System, 1970–2006*, Information Technology and Innovation Foundation, July 2008, www.itif.org/; and the articles in their edited volume, *State of Innovation: The U.S. Government's Role in Technology Development* (New York: Routledge, 2011), 1–26, 154–72; William Galston, "Government is a Good Venture Capitalist," *Wall Street Journal*, August 28, 2013, A13.

89 See Michele Boldrin and David K. Levine, *Against Intellectual Monopoly* (New York: Cambridge University Press, 2008), chapters 8–9; their "Market Size and Intellectual Property Protection," *International Economic Review* 50 (2009), 855–81; and their *Growth and Intellectual Property*, NBER Working Paper 12769, December 2006, www.nber.org/. See also *The Economist*, "Protection Racket: How to Think about Vaccines and Intellectual Property in a Pandemic," April 24, 2021, 66.

90 See Semiconductor Industry Association, *2015 International Technology Roadmap for Semiconductors 2.0 (ITRS), Executive Report*, www.semiconductors.org/ (accessed June 28, 2022); Rachel Courtland, "Transistors Could Stop Shrinking in 2021: A Key Industry Report Forecasts an End

Moore's law—has been so predictable that it has long been taken for granted. This has been at the core of advancements in electronics during the past half-century. A consequence for technology-dependent activities may be stagnation in performance—leading to diminished productivity and revenue.[91] Innovations, such as compartmentalization of uses or the application of high-powered lasers, may be unlikely to overcome it.[92]

In biotechnology and biopharmaceuticals, the complex nature of R&D, its multidisciplinary character, high cost, need for extensive testing, and uncertainties regarding results are another barrier.[93] Research programs in many fields can only be profitable over the long term—if at all. Their high cost and long-term horizons cause them to have lower priority, yet they are important for our future wellbeing. Genomics, genetic engineering, and bio-nanotechnology are among the affected fields. Biopharma and biotech research on viruses for epidemic and pandemic preparedness are another case. Many research programs in these and other areas may need more funding or direct involvement by government-backed laboratories.[94] But funding reductions and dismantlement of much government bio-research in past decades—largely due

to Traditional Scaling of Transistors," *IEEE Spectrum*, July 22, 2016, spectrum.ieee.org/; Tom Simonite, "Moore's Law is Dead: Now What? Shrinking Transistors Have Powered 50 Years of Advances in Computing—But Now Other Ways Must Be Found to Make Computers More Capable," *Technology Review*, May 13, 2016, www.technologyreview.com/; Kevin Krewell, "The Slowing of Moore's Law and its Impact," *Forbes*, July 30, 2015, www.forbes.com/.

91 See Asa Fitch, "Intel's Success Came with Making its Own Chips—Until Now," *Wall Street Journal*, November 6, 2020, www.wsj.com/; *The Economist*, "The Semiconductor Industry: Silicon Crumble," February 25, 2017, 53–54; Betsy Morris, "Smartphones Turn to Software Advances: Services, Instead of Hardware, Are Expected to Drive Industry as It Enters Second Decade," *Wall Street Journal*, January 12, 2017, B4; Don Clark, "Turning 50, Tech Axiom Moore's Law Shows Age," *Wall Street Journal*, April 18, 2015, A1.

92 High-powered semiconductor lasers, in particular, suffer substantial degradation from high temperature and voltage, as well as static electrical discharges (that can be unpredictable and very difficult to control). See the collection of articles and research reports in Science Direct, *Semiconductor Lasers*, www.sciencedireect.com/; and Nature Portfolio, *Semiconductor Lasers: Latest Research and Reviews*, www.nature.com/ (both accessed May 11, 2022).

93 See Andrew Nusca, "Here's the Problem with Today's Human Clinical Trials," *Fortune*, March 20, 2018, https://fortune.com/; Luis Suarez-Villa, *Globalization and Technocapitalism: The Political Economy of Corporate Power and Technological Domination* (Burlington: Ashgate, 2012), 56, 149–53. Breaking up trial processes for biopharmaceuticals—into small groups of test subjects—has been a way to try to accelerate testing, reduce costs, gain faster approval, or speed up marketing. Such groups are often made up of individuals with specific traits assumed to be relevant to the product being tested. However, this can increase future risk due to negative side effects—when the genetic makeup of a patient does not match the one used for testing. See Garth Sundem, "With Smaller Clinical Trials, It May be Up to Doctors to Notice Rare Drug Side Effects," *Medical Xpress*, April 22, 2020, htpps://medicalxpress.com/.

94 Private philanthropy may not be able to garner the funding and patience needed to sustain the extensive cost and lengthy time horizons involved—as it all too often operates in ways similar to those of the oligopolistic corporate domain. See Henry A. J. Ramos, *Shortcomings of Modern Philanthropy*, National Committee for Responsive Philanthropy, 2015, www.ncrp.org/.

to pressures from oligopolistic interests—has made performance barriers difficult to overcome.[95]

Intangibles

In addition to technological barriers, innovative research quality is often affected by another structural problem. *This is the inability of the corporate domain to reproduce internally the sophisticated intangibles needed to undertake cutting-edge research.*[96] Creativity, tacit knowledge, curiosity, cross-disciplinary learning, scientific aptitude, and deep experience are most important.[97] Their complex, qualitative (and sometimes esoteric) character poses difficulties that the corporate domain seems ill suited to resolve.

The difficulties of overcoming this obstacle are underlain by several features. First, high uncertainty and risk permeate their deployment—more so than for any other resource in the corporate domain.[98] This is a vexing and costly problem that corporate management usually tries to evade or cannot adequately address. Second, intangibles—unlike tangible resources—are not depleted with use. Usage actually improves their quality and impacts.[99] This makes it more difficult to appropriate and control them. Their usually specialized character can also make their understanding elusive—as only those who possess the necessary knowledge may figure out how they can be used.

A third characteristic of intangibles is their transferability—they can be learned and can be embodied in products other than those they were intended for.[100] This makes it difficult for them to be manipulated and appropriated—as any company that has experienced an exodus of researchers knows.

95 An example is the federal agency charged with research on pandemics—see Deb Riechmann, "Trump Disbanded NSC Pandemic Unit that Experts Had Praised," *ABC News*, March 14, 2020, https://abcnews.go.com/.

96 See Suarez-Villa, *Corporate Power, Oligopolies*, 175–222; and his *Globalization and Technocapitalism*, 67–95; *Technocapitalism*, 31–55, for extensive treatments of this topic.

97 Research creativity has long been a target for corporate appropriation (much like personal data in cyberspace platforms)—see Michael Perelman, *Steal this Idea: Intellectual Property Rights and the Corporate Confiscation of Creativity* (New York: Palgrave Macmillan, 2002), 1–12, 45–74.

98 Much more so than capital. In some cases, however, intangibles have been considered equivalent to (or a substitute for) capital—see Jonathan Haskel and Stian Westlake, *Capitalism Without Capital: The Rise of the Intangible Economy* (Princeton: Princeton University Press, 2018), Chapter 2.

99 An aspect that may account for their value when embedded in both tangible and intangible products. Intangibles have been estimated to account for as much as four-fifths of the price of most products and services—see Ahmed Bonfour, *The Management of Intangibles: The Organisation's Most Valuable Assets* (London: Routledge, 2003), 45–79.

100 An example is the knowledge embedded in the magnetron tube—a device used during the Second World War to generate radio waves for short-range radars. Its owner, Raytheon—a military technology oligopolist—found that it could be used to heat food, leading to the creation of the microwave oven. Decades later, a more powerful version would be used to shoot down drones. See Ed Adamczyk, "Raytheon Shoots down Drone with Lasers, Microwaves in Air Force Test," *UPI*,

Transferability also makes products and services that incorporate them easier to copy or pilfer—something that someone with the necessary skills can figure out how to do. This characteristic is one of the reasons why reverse engineering has gained much favor in the corporate domain. It avoids the uncertainty, expense, and time of having to undertake the necessary research—along with the intangibles to do so—and it facilitates immediate marketing.

A fourth and most important characteristic is their dependence on external societal influences—over which oligopolistic power usually has little or no control. The influences are myriad, difficult to quantify, and practically impossible to program.[101] Mostly, they are qualitative in character and depend on resources that only society at large can provide. Considerable tacit knowledge accumulation, creativity, experience, social or professional interactions, patience, and time are needed to impart or learn them.

Problems with reproducing intangibles, technological barriers, and the decline of important innovations raise doubts about Joseph Schumpeter's conceptualization of a process that has attracted much attention during the past nine decades. This is the notion that a "perennial gale of creative destruction" will invariably occur.[102] Its central assumption—that established technologies and related economic activities will be swept away, opening possibilities for new ones to emerge—has been at the core of much work on technology and economic change up to our time.

Schumpeter also assumed that waves of innovations—largely created by oligopolists—would transform economies endogenously. He therefore saw large companies as the most important vehicles for such transformation. His approach, however, ignored that executive power and shareholder expectations can subordinate research to product development, as short-term considerations—such as cost reduction and profitability—take over managerial decisions. The widespread influence of agency theory—previously discussed—on technology management during the past four decades needs to be taken into account in this regard.

May 1, 2019, www.upi.com/; Evan Ackerman, "A Brief History of the Microwave Oven," *IEEE Spectrum*, September 30, 2016, https://spectrum.ieee.org/.

101 See Suarez-Villa, *Corporate Power, Oligopolies*, 175–222; his *Globalization and Technocapitalism*, 67–95; and his *Technocapitalism*, 31–55.

102 Schumpeter, *Capitalism, Socialism*, 83–85, 87–106. Critical insights on Schumpeter's thoughts on this matter can be found in Paul A. Baran and Paul M. Sweezy, *Monopoly Capital: An Essay on the American Economic and Social Order* (New York: Monthly Review Press, 1966), 73–74; John Bellamy Foster, "Theories of Capitalist Transformation: Critical Notes on the Comparison of Marx and Schumpeter," *Quarterly Journal of Economics* 98 (1983), 327–31. Although the term "creative destruction" is commonly associated with Schumpeter, its origin was traced to Werner Sombart—see Hugo Reinert and Erik S. Reinert, "Creative Destruction in Economics: Nietzche, Sombart, Schumpeter," in Jürgen G. Backhaus and Wolfgang Drechsler, eds., *Friedrich Nietzche (1844–1900): Economy and Society* (New York: Springer Verlag, 2006), 55–85.

Schumpeter's assumptions on both "creative destruction" and endogenous economic change also ignored that insufficient reproduction of intangibles and technical barriers can bar both scenarios indefinitely. Such difficulties have long posed a serious obstacle to certain technologies and their related economic activities. Among them, for example, the development of commercial supersonic air travel and definitive cures for such diseases as cancer. The end of the effect known as Moore's law (discussed earlier) may pose a similar obstacle to advancements in electronics and microprocessor technology—and related economic activities—in decades to come.

Doubts are also raised—by difficulties in reproducing intangibles, the decline of innovation and research, and technological barriers—on the notion that marketing of new technologies causes efficiency gains to be underestimated—and inflation to be overestimated.[103] The rationale was that purchasing a new technology product results in greater efficiency—due to its better performance over the model it replaces. This implicitly assumed that non-oligopolistic pricing of both the new and the replaced product would be the same—or, if not, that adjusting for the efficiency improvement would show a lower real price.

Overlooked, however, was the fact that many new technology products usually require additional purchase of accessories (apps included) to make them work. The additional expense may more than offset any efficiency gains. Another problem is the sale of insufficiently tested products, with flaws that lead to replacement—providing little or no gain in efficiency for the additional expense. Such products can also compromise efficiency, as their usage may not lead to any increase in productivity. And repair costs—to try to avoid replacement—can add substantially to the initial purchase price, with no added efficiency gain. Even in such cases, replacement may be unavoidable, requiring repeat purchase of the same or a similar product, without any real efficiency gain.

The engineering-in of programmed obsolescence to boost sales is another aspect that needs to be taken into account. In this case, the expense of replacement may not justify any efficiency gain, and the expense itself may be regarded as both unnecessary and involuntary. The expense of replacement must be added to the price of the original product, or it must be adjusted for the loss of use of that product. The result may be an actual loss of efficiency, in addition to the additional cost. Then, there is the fact that oligopolistic pricing power will impose a higher price above what competitive pricing would—in all of these cases, and indeed for all product purchases. This may likely, by itself, more than offset any efficiency gain.

103 See Graham Tanaka, *Digital Deflation: The Productivity Revolution and How it will Ignite the Economy* (New York: McGraw-Hill, 2004), chapters 2, 3, 5; and his statements in "Letters to the Editor," *Wall Street Journal*, July 25, 2015, A10. Optimism generated by the so-called "new economy" in the 1990s and early 2000s—fueled by advances in informatics, computing, microelectronics, the internet, and the web—likely contributed to the assumptions posited in this work.

Yet another overlooked aspect is the waste that many new technology products can involve and that detract from any efficiency gain. This can occur through unforeseen behavior and complications related to use, the characteristics of a product, or its effect on people other than the individual who purchased it. Incessant or addictive videogaming or smartphone use that waste much time and cause expense, distractions while driving that lead to accidents, disability or death, online gambling that depletes income and savings, theft of personal identity that damages finances and consumes time, demotion or dismissal from work due to distractions and addictions—all lead to expense and to declining personal and collective productivity.[104]

Thus, the expected additional efficiency provided by a new technology product—assumed to trigger higher productivity in the economy—may only be a mirage. In an extrapolation to the larger economy, it was posited that ignoring the additional efficiency provided by new technology products—and discounting prices accordingly—results in an overestimation of inflation. This, in turn, was assumed to cause interest rates to be set higher than necessary—thus shortchanging economic growth, if not also the supposed greater benefits of "creative destruction." These effects are also doubtful, due to the previously discussed aspects, and because of a larger problem—the disregard of oligopolies.

The work in question overlooked technology oligopolistic power and its control over pricing. It thus implicitly assumed that competitive market conditions are the norm for technology products. But with oligopolistic pricing, the posited price deflation—to adjust for any efficiency gain of a new technology product—largely evaporates. Even if there would be an efficiency gain, it would likely come at a higher price, thus wasting consumers' budgets—and offsetting the benefit of a gain. Thus—in the oligopolistic scenario—the effect may *not* be lower real inflation or higher macroeconomic productivity but more waste, expense, and lesser (or stagnant) productivity. As for interest rates, their setting

104 See Kyle Stock, Lance Lambert and David Ingold, "Smartphones are Killing Americans, But Nobody's Counting: Amid a Historic Spike in U.S. Traffic Fatalities, Federal Data on the Danger of Distracted Driving are Getting Worse," *Bloomberg*, October 17, 2017, www.bloomberg.com/; Leslie Scism and Nicole Friedman, "Smartphone Use Lifts Car-Insurance Rates," *Wall Street Journal*, February 21, 2017, A1; Chaelin K. Ra, Junhan Cho, Matthew D. Stone, *et al.*, "Association of Digital Media Use with Subsequent Symptoms of Attention-Deficit/Hyperactivity Disorder Among Adolescents," *Journal of the American Medical Association* 320 (2018), 255–63; Kate Richards, Kai Wong and Mansoor Khan, "Augmented Reality Game Related Injuries," *New Horizons in Clinical Case Reports* 2 (2017), 27; Susan Scutti, "WHO Classifies 'Gaming Disorder' as Mental Health Condition," *CNN*, June 18, 2018, www.cnn.com/; Mara Faccio and John J. McConnell, *Death by Pokémon GO: The Economic and Human Cost of Using Apps While Driving*, NBER Working Paper 24308, June 4, 2018, https://papers.ssrn.com/; Julie Jargon, "You Spent $1,500 on a Virtual What? Kids are Splurging on Digital Goods such as Outfits for their Videogame Avatars, as 'Money Turns Magical' with Virtual Spending," *Wall Street Journal*, July 17, 2019, A15.

may not be higher than necessary unless other—non-technological—factors are at work.

Long-term productivity in the American economy, moreover, has for many decades been found to be largely stagnant.[105] The posited efficiency effect of new technology products on the economy has thus likely not occurred. The long-term stagnation (very slow growth) in GDP since the 1960s—sustained despite reductions in corporate and personal income taxes over the years and significant deregulation of numerous sectors—is consonant with this scenario.[106]

And this occurred even though many new technologies were coming into use in the economy—computing, microelectronics, informatics, biotechnology, digital communications, genetic engineering, nanotechnology, robotics, new energy technologies, advances in land, sea and air transportation, along with their myriad effects. Thus, it may seem reasonable to conclude that oligopolistic pricing power, the decline of important innovations, difficulties in reproducing intangibles, and performance barriers may have tended to neutralize the impact of new technologies.[107]

International Projection

An important source of oligopolistic power is its international projection. This involves trade, the dollar, and investment. Although these strongly support the power of American technology oligopolies, as we shall see they also entail problems for the international economy.

105 Increases in total U.S. factor productivity peaked in the 1950s and have mostly remained stagnant (growing very slowly) since. See U.S. Bureau of Labor Statistics, *Multifactor Productivity*, www.bls.gov/; Federal Reserve Bank of St. Louis, Economic Research, *Total Factor Productivity at Constant National Prices for the United States*, https://fred.stlouisfed.org/ (both accessed March 15, 2022). The alleged underestimation of total factor productivity has been found to have declined over the years, and for some time it has remained at historically low levels—see Brent R. Moulton, *The Measurement of Output, Prices, and Productivity: What's Changed since the Boskin Commission?* Hutchins Center on Fiscal and Monetary Policy, Brookings Institution, July 2018, www.brookings.edu/.

106 See Federal Reserve Bank of St. Louis, Economic Research Division, *Industrial Production Index* (St. Louis: Federal Reserve Board, various years), http://research.stlouisfed.org/; U.S. Bureau of Economic Analysis, *National Income and Product Accounts* (Washington: B.E.A., various years), www.bea.gov/.

107 The stagnation in total factor productivity has occurred despite continuous—and historically high—increases in R&D spending (as a share of GDP)—see American Association for the Advancement of Science, *Historical R&D Data*, www.aaas.org/; OECD, *Gross Domestic Spending on R&D*, https://data.oecd.org/ (both accessed March 15, 2022). The previously discussed, long-standing subordination of research to product development in R&D may have contributed greatly to this scenario.

Trade and the Dollar

About four-fifths of international trade involves oligopolistic corporations—including all technology oligopolies.[108] American influence in setting trade rules has conditioned this reality. It has also made the dollar the predominant currency in trade. This is an important advantage for technology oligopolies, as it simplifies offshoring deals, product pricing, and investment.

The dollar accounts for over four-fifths of all global currency transactions, over one-half of all debt issuance, and makes up almost two-thirds of all central bank reserves.[109] And, most trade occurs in dollars—even when U.S. companies are not involved.[110] Thus, the volume of global trade that uses the dollar far surpasses the amount of foreign trade carried out by the United States.[111] The dollar is also the usual metric for pricing technology products and offshore contracting. And it is the world's preferred vehicle for investment, the main currency for payments, and the prime reference for exchanges.

The dollar's predominance also supports oligopolistic pricing power. Direct exports from offshore locales to third nations are mostly in dollars.[112] And

108 Partly because of the vast amount of trade they are involved in, the profitability of American companies abroad increased from an average of about 6 percent during the 1960s to well over a quarter during the last decade. At the same time, the annual revenue of the 500 largest corporations (all engaged in business abroad) has in recent times accounted for more than one-half of world income. See U.S. Bureau of Economic Analysis, *Corporate Profits*, www.bea.gov/ (accessed July 2, 2022); Reade Pickert, "U.S. Companies' Repatriated Cash Hits $1 Trillion Under Tax Law," *Bloomberg*, December 19, 2019, www.bloomberg.com/; Niall McCarthy and Statista, *The U.S. Companies with the Highest Overseas Earnings*, October 26, 2017, www.statista.com/; Andrew W. Hodges, *Comparing NIPA Profits with S&P 500 Profits*, March 2011, https://apps.bea.gov/.

109 Gustavo Adler, Camila Casas, Luis Cubeddu, Gita Gopinath, *et al.*, *Dominant Currencies and External Adjustment*, International Monetary Fund, Research Department, July 2020, 8–21, www.imf.org/; *The Economist*, "Greenback Dominates: Buck Up," August 29, 2020, 54–55. Central bank reserves include dollar-denominated instruments such as U.S. Treasury bonds.

110 Emine Boz, Camila Casas, Georgios Georgiadis, Gita Gopinath, *et al.*, *Patterns in Invoicing Currency in Global Trade*, International Monetary Fund, July 2020, www.imf.org/; *The Economist*, "Greenback Dominates," 55.

111 *The Economist*, "Greenback Dominates," 55. Adler, Casas, Cubeddu, Gopinath, *et al.*, *Dominant Currencies*. The dollar's global share of trade has been estimated to be about five times the amount of U.S. imports and three times the amount of exports.

112 China—the most important tech exporter in the world—has in the past settled over four-fifths of its trade in U.S. dollars. South Korea, a major tech exporter—that usually receives less than one-fifth of its imports from the U.S.—usually invoices more than four-fifths of its imports in dollars. These trends—and those of other significant technology exporters—have remained stable over the years. See Adler, Casas, Cubeddu, Gopinath, *et al.*, *Dominant Currencies*; Boz, Casas, Georgiadis, Gopinath, *et al.*, *Patterns in Invoicing Currency*; *The Economist*, "Greenback Dominates," 54; Linda S. Goldberg and Cedric Tille, *Vehicle Currency Use in International Trade*, NBER Working Paper 11127, February 2005, www.ssrn.com/; and their *Macroeconomic Interdependence and the International Role of the Dollar*, November 2007, www.imf.org/.

offshore processing costs—including labor—are also mostly priced in dollars.[113] If the dollar appreciates, consumers are unlikely to see lower prices for technology products made offshore, as an oligopolist's pricing power will likely prevent it. And, should demand decrease, output can be reduced to avoid discounting. Dollar pricing for offshore production facilitates this dynamic, especially for products that require multiple inputs from different nations (as most technology products do).

For offshore processing nations, an important consequence is that they may not be able to benefit much by devaluing their currencies.[114] Devaluation has been a common policy in the past to reduce exports' prices abroad, increase their demand, and generate growth at home. A major policy tool long invoked by economic development and international trade specialists to promote exports and domestic growth is thus largely neutralized.

This panorama also invalidates the longstanding notion that trading parties will adopt the exporter nation's currency for their transactions. This assumption was at the core of one of the most important theoretical contributions on the economics of trade and currencies—the Mundell–Fleming model—for which Robert Mundell was awarded the Nobel Prize in 1999.[115] The model assumed that no currency would dominate trade—as the dollar overwhelmingly does today.[116] At its core was the notion that perfect capital mobility is the

113 Despite the fact that arm's length contracting characterizes most technology offshore operations. See World Bank, *Special Focus 2, Arm's Length Trade: A Source of Post-Crisis Trade Weakness*, Global Economic Prospects, June 2017, 61–69.

114 This occurred when South Korea, Malaysia, and Thailand, among other nations, devalued their respective currencies by as much as two-thirds during the financial crisis of the late 1990s. Despite the sharp devaluations, their export volumes either fell or remained largely stagnant, as almost all of their exports were priced in dollars. Also, their trade was mostly carried out through oligopolistic corporations—an aspect that at the time went unnoticed. See Boz, Casas, Georgiadis, Gopinath, *et al.*, *Patterns in Invoicing Currency*; Adler, Casas, Cubeddu, Gopinath, *et al.*, *Dominant Currencies*; *The Economist*, "Greenback Dominates," 55.

115 See Robert A. Mundell, "Capital Mobility and Stabilization Policy under Fixed and Flexible Exchange Rates," *Canadian Journal of Economics and Political Science* 29 (1963), 475–85; J. Marcus Fleming, "Domestic Financial Policies under Fixed and Floating Exchange Rates," *IMF Staff Papers* 9 (1962), 369–79. See also Sven Grassman, "A Fundamental Symmetry in International Payment Patterns," *Journal of International Economics* 3 (1973), 105–16; and his "Currency Distribution and Forward Cover in Foreign Trade: Sweden Revisited, 1973," *Journal of International Economics* 6 (1976), 215–21. Grassman's findings supported the Mundell–Fleming assumption of symmetry on the use of the exporter's currency, using Swedish data (except for exports to the United States, which always used the dollar). In Sweden's case, however, few oligopolies existed at the time. As the global reach of oligopolies intensified after the 1970s, Grassman's—along with Mundell and Fleming's—assumptions began to be contradicted by new data. See Goldberg and Tille, *Vehicle Currency Use*, and their *Macroeconomic Interdependence*.

116 This assumption was taken up despite doubts expressed in the late 1940s about the symmetrical use of currencies in trade—see Joan Robinson, *Essays in the Theory of Employment* (Oxford: Blackwell, 1947), Chapter "Beggar-My-Neighbor Remedies for Unemployment." Earlier, Robinson had written extensively on the effects of monopolies and oligopolies—see, for

norm—any differences in domestic asset returns or interest rates across nations being equalized by the interplay of supply and demand. The model's premises were considered very important for economic development policies, as taking advantage of national currency depreciation was assumed crucial for promoting exports and raising national income.

Another important assumption of the model was that currency use and value would reflect trade balances. Nations with an export surplus were thus assumed to experience gains in the value of their currencies, whereas those that had deficits would see devaluation. The use of the dollar as the world's predominant trading currency has mostly invalidated this assumption, however—at least insofar as technology trade and offshore processing are concerned.

The dominance of the dollar has also undermined assumptions about the supposed advantages of flexible currency exchange rates. For the United States, changes in officially set interest rates all too often affect the dollar's global value—an often overlooked effect of Federal Reserve decisions. Thus, fluctuations in the value of the dollar can be more a function of domestic U.S. policy and can overshadow such factors as trade balances and risk.

A Federal Reserve policy that, say, sets lower interest rates may devalue the dollar. This makes technology products cheaper abroad and can increase their demand. Conversely, when U.S. interest rates are raised, the dollar may strengthen—making technology products more expensive abroad, reducing their demand, and lowering trade volume.[117] The impact of the latter on other nations seldom seems to be taken into account by the Federal Reserve, although the resulting capital flight, recessions, and unemployment can plunge millions into poverty and cause fiscal crises. These impacts can be advantageous for technology oligopolies, as they strengthen their negotiating position on, say, labor, processing cost, and raw materials.

Most important, the Mundell–Fleming model overlooked the role of oligopolistic power in the trade and currency panorama. Oligopolistic consolidation in the United States during the past seven decades can be considered an important reason for the model's invalidation. Without the sort of concentration that the world has witnessed, the global predominance of the U.S. dollar would most likely not have occurred. Or, the negative impacts noted before would have likely been milder. The international projection of oligopolies also

---

example, her *Economics of Imperfect Competition*. She apparently surmised that a symmetrical use of currencies would be unrealistic as oligopolistic concentration increased and extended its global reach.

117 Dollar appreciation tends to reduce credit by banks abroad (when used to finance trade)—leading to decline in exports. See Valentina Bruno and Hyun Song Shin, *Dollar and Exports*, Bank for International Settlements, Working Paper 819, 2020; their *Cross-Border Banking and Global Liquidity*, Working Paper 458, 2014; and their *Global Dollar Credit and Carry Trades: A Firm-Level Analysis*, Working Paper 510, 2015 (all at www.bis.org/); Boz, Casas, Georgiadis, Gopinath, *et al.*, *Patterns in Invoicing Currency*.

derailed the expectation that currency fluctuations can or should reflect the terms of trade—as oligopolies twisted those to their advantage.

The national interest on trade and currencies was therefore subordinated to the interests of oligopolistic power. Neutralizing a nation's sovereign prerogative to promote the depreciation of its currency—or the opposite—mattered little or nothing to oligopolies, as the convenience of using a single currency overruled sovereignty. Thus, nations that are important offshore processing sites for technology products may not be able to depreciate their currencies much—to promote growth at home or to diversify their economies.

Those nations have thus been bound to a trade currency—the dollar—over which they have no control. And their promotion of domestic growth may then be left up to the question of labor costs. Thus, the only policy measure left to a government may be to promote stagnant or reduced labor compensation—such that it can be more globally "competitive." Most of all in labor-intensive activities, as are those that involve processing of technology products.

The international projection of American technology oligopolies brings up another aspect that may be taken into account. This is the likelihood that greater oligopolistic concentration raises risks for the international economy. Despite its potentially catastrophic consequences, such risk has not been considered or assessed much.

Cross-Shareholding

Cross-shareholding is common in international finance, among technology oligopolies, and between the latter and companies in other sectors. Corporate cross-shareholding has long been assumed to be a way of diversifying investment risk. That cross-shareholding often leads to consolidation through acquisitions, entry barriers, mergers, greater pricing power—and more concentrated risk—seems to have been overlooked.[118] Neglect of oligopolies and the risks they pose for the international economy are the apparent root cause.

The rationale for large-scale cross-shareholding to try to avert crises is that when a company's shares weaken, other companies will either step in to purchase due to the lower price or take a long-term view and avoid selling. Much the same was assumed to apply to corporate bonds when underlying assets lose value or yields and prices decline. Technology oligopolies in the United States have long engaged in cross-shareholding—as have oligopolies in other sectors—partly for speculative reasons or to gain insights that can be used for an acquisition. Reducing or diversifying systemic risk seem to have had very little weight among the motivations for this strategy.

118 See Chris Brooks, Zhong Chen and Yeqin Zeng, "Institutional Cross-Ownership and Corporate Strategy: The Case of Mergers and Acquisitions," *Journal of Corporate Finance* 48 (2018), 187–216.

In this regard, the influence on chief executives and governing boards of a small group of consulting firms (typically oligopolistic in their specialties) may be taken into account. These firms tend to use much the same models to advice their global oligopolistic clients, yet their counsel seems guided by heuristics that are questionable.[119] Also, they often have longstanding relationships with their clients—becoming co-dependent—and base their advice on "best practices" guidelines formulated by themselves. Deviating from those guidelines can be perilous, as it would likely lead to blame, loss of a client, and even lawsuits when a desired level of performance does not materialize. Greater oligopolistic consolidation is a result, as the objective of maximizing profit and power takes precedence over other aspects. And, in the absence of global restrictions, the larger panorama of risk tends to be ignored.[120]

A higher concentration of cross-shareholdings among fewer oligopolies—as acquisitions reduce the number of listed companies—can add substantial risk to the global economic panorama. A global network analysis using data from over 40,000 large corporations—including those of most every technology oligopoly in existence—provided some insights in recent decades. The study comprised over half a million nodes embedding more than a million cross-shareholding and ownership ties—based on sample data obtained from 30 million economic organizations.[121] The network extent was the largest and most comprehensive ever used to research this topic—a very difficult aspect given the complexity of the data and the relationships involved. A most important insight gained from the analyses was that *less than one percent of the corporations were found to be in control of almost half of the wealth of all the organizations engaged in cross-shareholdings.*

This is an astounding level of concentration that should generate concern among those who have heretofore dismissed oligopolies and the risks they pose. And it seems reasonable to assume that the pace of consolidation during the last decade and in recent years has raised global concentration to a much higher level. Especially so in technology, where consolidation has increased substantially within and across sectors—as noted earlier.

The risks of extensive oligopolistic cross-shareholding at the global level have been much neglected in investment finance, and the effects of this

119 See *The Economist*, "The Smuggest Guys in the Room: McKinsey's Partners Suffer from Collective Self-Delusion," March 6, 2021, 65.

120 The influence of certain global organizations—such as the Mount Pelerin Society and the World Economic Forum—should also be considered. These entities organize venues that feed social networking among technology executives and directors that promote the interests of oligopolistic corporations. Considerations of global risk, oligopolistic concentration, and the impacts of crises all too often tend to be overlooked. See the discussion in Suarez-Villa, *Corporate Power, Oligopolies*, 82–83.

121 See Stefania Vitali, James B. Glattfelder and Stefano Battiston, *The Network of Global Corporate Control*, September 2011, https://arxiv.org/. Their analysis used the Orbis 2007 database. See also the related discussion in Suarez-Villa, *Corporate Power, Oligopolies*, 80–83.

phenomenon are practically unknown. Complex derivatives, obscure options, shadow trading vehicles, and esoteric debt instruments are routinely bundled with oligopolistic cross-shareholdings, with effects that even the most seasoned specialists cannot anticipate or do not fully understand. And extensive financial engineering and deregulation during the past four decades created innumerable shadow banks and hedge funds—with more money at their command than that of the gross domestic product of most nations.

The most important model for evaluating risk in finance—the Black–Scholes–Merton model—ignored the effects of oligopolistic power.[122] Unfortunately, how oligopolies distort assessments of uncertainty and risk neutrality—in a highly concentrated cross-shareholding scenario—was neglected by this construct. It also ignored how and whether the oligopolistic shareholders of other (also oligopolistic) shareholders—including mutual ones—evaluate risk and uncertainty. The volatility dimension in such cases was also ignored. The dynamic adjustments that all such scenarios would require—to render decisions risk neutral—were also left out of consideration. And the model ignored the question of whether its own evaluation of these and other scenarios—relevant to oligopolies—could capture reality, *and* the catastrophic outcomes that could occur—if the model's assumptions happen to be wrong.

It provides little comfort that in 1998 one of the largest hedge funds in existence—Long-Term Capital Management, in which Myron Scholes and Robert Merton, authors of the model and 1997 Nobel laureates, were the main shareholders—had to be bailed out to save the U.S. banking system from collapse.[123] Cross-shareholding—one of its most important trading strategies—had followed the principles outlined in the model. Prior to that event, some analysts had blamed the widespread use of their model for the 1987 crisis—the so-called Black Monday crash—that brought the U.S. financial markets, if not also the economy, close to a near-complete collapse.[124]

One potential peril of cross-shareholding concentration for the international economy is a major meltdown, through waves of corporate insolvencies. Rising, unsustainable levels of corporate debt can be a trigger for such a crisis—a situation that would affect technology oligopolies greatly, as well as many other companies across the United States and abroad. Another potential cause can be the high concentration of investment and speculation in

122 See Fischer Black and Myron Scholes, "The Pricing of Options and Corporate Liabilities," *Journal of Political Economy* 81 (1973), 637–54; Robert Merton, "Theory of Rational Option Pricing," *Bell Journal of Economics and Management Science* 4 (1973), 141–83.

123 See Kimberly Amadeo, "Long-Term Capital Management Hedge Fund Crisis," *The Balance*, January 8, 2020, www.thebalance.com/; Tim Harford, "Black-Scholes: The Maths Formula Linked to the Financial Crash," *BBC*, April 27, 2012, www.bbc.com/.

124 See Pablo Triana, *Lecturing Birds on Flying: Can Mathematical Theories Destroy the Financial Markets?* (Hoboken: Wiley, 2009), 177–244; Harford, "Black-Scholes"; Amadeo, "Long-Term Capital Management."

fewer companies—and the oligopolistic banks and shadow financial operators involved—that could initiate the crisis or compound it. These potential causes are now present in the international investment panorama.

Adding to the peril of this scenario is the high indebtedness of many governments, and the possibility that they may not be able to provide liquidity or rescue companies as they have in the past. Or, that so many oligopolies may become insolvent that it would be impossible to rescue most, thus triggering a deep and long depression. The amounts that might be required for rescuing a dozen technology oligopolies alone seem staggering and might reach into the hundreds of trillions of dollars.

Net U.S. government debt has been projected to reach 117 percent of GDP in 2030—the highest level in peacetime.[125] This estimate excludes government obligations—pensions, medical care, veterans' support, unemployment and disability compensation, and other contracted expenses (that are not accounted for as debt). These obligations—added to the (official) net debt—were estimated by a Wall Street investment firm to amount to as much as 1,832 percent of GDP (2019 dollars)—a proportion that is certain to grow in coming years and decades.[126] Estimates of how much additional (official) net indebtedness the U.S. government could incur do not typically include (or consider) such obligations.[127]

Public Governance

Influence on public governance is a fundamental source of power for technology oligopolies. Several vehicles of influence condition their relationship with government and the institutions established to serve the public interest. All of these vehicles are vital for oligopolistic power, as they affect regulation, politics, and the judiciary.

Anti-regulatory Praxis

Anti-regulatory praxis is a multi-faceted vehicle that may at times seem contradictory. But its effects can be far-reaching. Among these are the norms of jurisprudence and the legality of oligopolistic power. The fragmented character of anti-regulatory efforts may explain why it may be difficult to place them in the spectrum of corporate influence.

125 *The Economist*, "Pace Your Debts: New Research Explores the Limits to Government Borrowing," June 5, 2021, 66.

126 AllianceBernstein Holding, www.alliancebernstein.com/. See Jeff Cox, "Real U.S. Debt Levels Could Be 2,000% of Economy, A Wall Street Report Suggests," *CNBC*, September 9, 2019, www.cnbc.com/.

127 See Atif R. Mian, Ludwig Straub and Amir Sufi, *Indebted Demand*, National Bureau of Economic Research, Working Paper 26940, April 2020, www.nber.org/; *The Economist*, "Pace Your Debts."

The overarching objective of anti-regulatory praxis is to co-opt—or eliminate—rules and initiatives that diminish oligopolistic power. Sustaining and deepening pricing power is one consequence. Allowing the proliferation of entry barriers is another. Getting regulators to ignore M&A deals and their contribution to oligopolistic consolidation, price manipulation, systemic consumer abuse, and the reduction of investment possibilities are also important. Sustaining anti-regulatory praxis requires a diffuse apparatus that must influence public opinion, concoct propaganda to prevent or end regulation, render antitrust lawsuits ineffective, and deploy corporate structures that can evade regulatory action.

A core argument of anti-regulatory agendas has involved the notion that oligopolistic corporations should not be "punished" for being "successful."[128] Corporate success is thus equated with attaining oligopolistic power. Tacitly, this argues for certain corporations—those that can most successfully engineer, manipulate, or otherwise set the relations of power in their favor—to be allowed to impose themselves on society. A sort of neo-Darwinian socioeconomic perspective pervades this argument, although this is seldom articulated clearly.

Herbert Spencer—one of the nineteenth century's most influential philosophers—is credited with using the term "survival of the fittest" to describe a human society that operates on the basis of the principles of natural selection and reproductive success.[129] This perspective would be extrapolated to the case of oligopolistic power later, as consolidation in industry advanced. By and large, the application of natural selection to socioeconomic life evades awareness of the most important qualities that have allowed human society to advance beyond primitive conditions—among them social justice, fairness, solidarity, and equity. The importance of these qualities would be largely dis-

128 An accompanying argument is that antitrust regulation should be solely concerned with "consumer welfare"—narrowly. Robert Bork—one of the late twentieth century's most influential jurists—expressed this sentiment in a study commissioned by Google to oppose its own investigation for antitrust violations. Bork wrote that regulatory action would be: "punishing Google for being a successful competitor" (p. 686)—Robert H. Bork and J. Gregory Sidak, "What does the Chicago School Teach about Internet Search and the Antitrust Treatment of Google?" *Journal of Competition Law and Economics* 8 (2012), 663–700. See also *CNBC*, "Bork and Sidak Joint Statement on Google Antitrust Claims," November 11, 2012, www.cnbc.com/. Arguments by Bork on the role of regulation can be found in his *The Antitrust Paradox: A Policy at War with Itself* (New York: Basic Books, 1978), chapters 6, 7, 21, 22. An important critique of this perspective can be found in Lina M. Khan, "The Ideological Roots of American's Market Power Problem," *Yale Law Journal* 127 (2018), www.yalelawjournal.org/. See also her "Amazon's Antitrust Paradox," *Yale Law Journal* 126 (2017), 564–907.

129 See Herbert Spencer, *Principles of Sociology* (London: Williams and Norgate, 1876), Vol. I (parts I, II), Vol. II (parts IV, V); and his *The Principles of Ethics* (New York: Appleton, 1897), Vol. II (parts IV, V, VI). These works are part of Spencer's ten-volume *A System of Synthetic Philosophy* (originally published in 1862–92). Richard Hofstadter, in his *Social Darwinism in American Thought* (Boston: Beacon, 1944), (chapters 2, 3), argued that Spencer's work influenced Andrew Carnegie's and William Graham Sumner's views on oligo-monopolistic capitalism.

missed in favor of letting the proverbial "animal spirits" run rampant—a term used frequently by those who advocate, tacitly or not—for the rule of a neo-Darwinian corporate order.

This worldview is often conflated with the notion that "merit"—most of all in the case of technology—attaches to oligopolistic supremacy. Accumulating and wielding oligopolistic power is thus equated with "fitness" to survive, attaching to it a meritocratic aura—one that regulation should not interfere with. The immense wealth and growing power of oligopolistic corporations is thereby justified as socioeconomic virtuosity—as opposed to its being a product of machinations, exploitation, systemic abuse, and the accumulation of privilege. To restrict such power through regulation would therefore be tantamount to rewarding the "less fit"—a condition that is assumed to lead to greater inefficiency, the negation of merit, and an irrational socioeconomic order.

In mainstream economics, there is a long history of assumptions and arguments—often tacitly articulated—that view business success in markets as a symptom of greater "fitness." Markets are thus assumed to operate as selection processes—analogous to those of natural selection—that reward rational optimizers with survival. And corporations are implicitly assumed to be living organisms. Lost to this argument is that both markets and corporate organizations are human inventions and do not exist in nature.

Companies that fail to optimize in the market domain are assumed to become acquisition targets—that can make the acquirer more "fit." Or, they are expected to experience bankruptcy and liquidation—the price to be paid for being suboptimal (or less fit). Selection processes that operate through markets are thus posited to generate efficient outcomes, and the "ecology" of surviving companies is supposed to encompass the most "fit" to exist.[130]

Anti-regulatory action in this area has been closely associated with the work of Milton Friedman, one of the twentieth century's most influential economists.[131] Although Friedman did not explicitly relate his work to socioeconomic Darwinism, his precepts and prescriptions nonetheless fit well with it. What is usually overlooked, however, is that Friedman assumed that the markets in

130 In the 1980s, the emerging specialty of organizational ecology distanced itself from socioeconomic Darwinism. Its approach to research on organizations—utilizing sociological empirical methods and concepts to explore their workings—thus avoided links to notions of natural selection. See Michael T. Hannan and John Freeman, *Organizational Ecology* (Cambridge, MA: Harvard University Press, 1989), 35–37. In economics, Richard R. Nelson and Sidney G. Winter [in their *An Evolutionary Theory of Economic Change* (Cambridge, MA: Harvard University Press, 1982), chapters 9–11] took the position that natural selection does not necessarily lead to efficient organizations.

131 See Milton Friedman, *Essays in Positive Economics* (Chicago: University of Chicago Press, 1953), 3–46, 100–16; Milton Friedman and Rose D. Friedman, *Free to Choose: A Personal Statement* (New York: Harcourt, 1980), chapters 1–3, 7.

which rational optimizers would succeed were all competitive. Market competition was the most important common denominator in his views on rational choice, optimization, and enterprise success. Thus, what happens in markets under oligopolistic control was left out of consideration—presumably because, in his approach, such markets cannot lead to efficient outcomes—or improve business "fitness" in ways that are optimal.

Some arguments and calls for action in the anti-regulatory repertory revolve around the notion that any regulation that diminishes oligopolistic power would stifle innovation.[132] The long-term decline in the importance of innovations—an apparent outcome of greater oligopolistic concentration, discussed previously—is thus conveniently ignored. Much the same applies to the widespread submission of research to wants contrivance in the technology oligopolistic domain. The fact that much oligopolistic technology "research" actually involves neither invention nor innovation—cutting-edge, least of all—but finding ways to increase sales is also overlooked.

Another component of the anti-regulatory repertory involves the notion that oligopolies "compete" on pricing.[133] This assertion ignores mounting evidence on the deleterious effects of pricing power and market manipulation, and the myriad ways in which oligopolies subvert market competition. Among these are the numerous entry barriers concocted, frequent M&A deals to extend or deepen pricing power, the mega-platforms that turn network extent into a formidable anti-competitive weapon, the numerous lock-in schemes imposed, the widespread data expropriation that users and consumers are subjected to, the confiscation of IP from employee-inventors, and the imposition of proprietary standards over entire sectors and product lines.

The notion that oligopolies "compete" on market pricing has been partially propagated through business school curricula and concepts, much as decades earlier occurred in the case of agency theory.[134] Business-oriented media have

132 Bork and Sidak in "Chicago School," for example, wrote that antitrust regulation of Google would have "chilling effects on innovation" (p. 673) and that "punishing Google … would stifle innovation" (p. 687). Similar statements (or versions thereof) can be found in most every defense of oligopolistic corporations investigated for antitrust violations.

133 In Google's antitrust defense, for example, Bork and Sidak ("Chicago School," 687) wrote that "punishing Google would stifle … dynamic competition." Arguments by defense attorneys proclaiming oligopolies to be "competitive" on market pricing (generally and specifically) can be found in most every antitrust trial conducted during the past four decades.

134 See *The Economist*, "Management Theory is becoming a Compendium of Dead Ideas," December 16, 2016, 61. This article—in an ideologically conservative, pro-business global publication—notes that "management theories are organized around four basic ideas, repeated *ad nauseum* in every business book you read or business conference you attend, that bear almost no relation to reality. The first idea is that business is more competitive than ever. Skim popular titles such as … and you will be left with the impression of a hyper-competitive world in which established giants are constantly being felled by the forces of disruption. … The most striking business trend today is not competition but consolidation."

also contributed to disseminate this fallacy, magnifying what business curricula preach. Inappropriate analogies, formulation of heuristics that have little or nothing to do with the reality of oligopolistic power, and the generation of biases and fallacies that persist are among the tools used to mold mindsets and behavior.[135]

A related effort involves propagating the notion that lasting price competition will occur if monopolies somehow find themselves having to share a market segment or niche with other companies—thus becoming duopolies or oligopolists.[136] This argument ignores the importance of co-respectiveness among oligopolists—most of all on market pricing—a condition addressed earlier.[137] Accumulated evidence on co-respective behavior is substantial and can be regarded as one of the more noticeable effects of oligopolistic power. And, the reality that entry barriers, M&As, network effects, lock-ins, and other means typically foreclose the possibility of price competition—soon after a monopolist has to share a market—is also overlooked.

Anti-regulatory advocates have argued that the embedding of businesses in oligopolistic tech-owned platforms renders the latter competitive.[138] This argument has been aided by the deployment of corporate modes that neutralize regulations involving profit, taxes, liability, and investment. Master Limited Partnership (MLP)—also known as "pass-through"—corporate structures, and BDC (Business Development), RIC (Regulated Investment), and REIT (Real

135 Research on how individual and collective biases (and heuristics) are constructed can help understand how opinion, attitudes, and collective behavior are influenced. See the articles in Daniel Kahneman, Paul Slovic and Amos Tversky, eds., *Judgment under Uncertainty: Heuristics and Biases* (New York: Cambridge University Press, 1982), parts II–IV.

136 Experience with deregulation of government-sanctioned monopolies has shown that price competition—if any occurs—tends to be very short-lived. When AT&T was deregulated in the 1980s and the telecommunication sector became oligopolistic, charges for basic services went up substantially in a very short time—increasing by 614 percent for having an unlisted telephone number and by 226 percent for those who sought direct assistance with calls, among others. See *California Senate Office of Oversight and Outcomes, Gaps Emerge in Consumer Protections after Phone Deregulation* (Sacramento: California Senate, 2012); and the discussions in Suarez-Villa, *Corporate Power, Oligopolies*, 39–41.

137 An editorial on American technology companies in a globally circulated publication, for example, stated that "an oligopoly of rivals is much better than a monopoly," wishfully noting later that "oligopolistic competition could benefit consumers." The benefits claimed would be "boosting choice," "raise standards as platforms differentiate themselves by trust," and "spur innovation." See *The Economist*, "The Dust-Up: A New Phase in the Global Tech Contest is Under Way," February 27, 2021, 9.

138 Various versions of this argument have been at the core of support for technology oligopolies in antitrust lawsuits since the 1990s. See, for example, *NPR*, "Antitrust Lawsuits: Google 2020 vs. Microsoft 1998," October 20, 2020, www.npr.org/; U.S. Department of Justice, *U.S. v. Microsoft: Court's Findings of Fact*, 1998, www.justice.gov/atr/. It may be argued that embedding businesses in oligopolistic platforms actually increases the power of its owner—see *The Economist*, "Raining on the Parade: The Risks of Writing Blank Cheques to a Cloud-Computing Oligopoly," July 3, 2021, 68.

Estate Investment Trust) companies are found in such platforms. Companies operated under MLP and similar structures—some of which can be oligopolistic in their market niches—avoid taxes and regulations applied to conventional corporations by distributing profits annually while limiting the liability of their owners under LLC or LLP arrangements.[139] Their owners (or "members")—analogous in some ways to shareholders, but with nominally greater direct oversight—declare the amounts as "income" to avoid the higher tax rates that would otherwise apply. And they may even end up paying no taxes if a trust is arranged to receive the amounts.

Adolf Berle and Gardiner Means—in one of the most influential contributions to corporate governance and law of the twentieth century—set the conceptual stage for these corporate structures to emerge.[140] Their work argued that the separation of ownership from management in large corporations had undermined the institutional notion of property. Shareholding—which they interpreted to be equivalent to ownership—had become divorced from key decision-making and day-to-day management. This condition, they posited, could only be overcome by providing shareholders with the means to be more active—voting rights and direct scrutiny of managerial decisions being important recommendations. As time went by and oligopolistic consolidation increased—along with the expansion of shareholding and its fragmentation into different categories—their recommendations would become difficult to fulfill. Thus, many would come to believe, alternative structures had to be created.

Companies that operate under the MLP and similar structures were eventually set up to bring individuals who provide capital closer to managerial decisions. In practice, this aspect seems illusory, as the owners of capital do not usually participate in decisions—although they might be informed *a priori*. The main incentive to invest in these structures is the lower or null taxes that can be paid, compared to shareholding in conventional companies. And, MLPs and similar structures can be publicly traded, allowing owners to sell their stake.[141]

139 See Internal Revenue Service, *Characteristics of a Limited Liability Company (LLC)*, 5.1.21.3 (and subsequent sections), and its *Partnerships* [Publication 541 (03/2021)], www.irs.gov/, (both accessed June 27, 2022). LLCs are governed by laws enacted by states—Wyoming being the first to do so in 1977. LLPs emerged widely, also at the state level, in the early 1990s, and tend to follow guidelines provided by the Uniform Partnership Act. See Wikipedia, *Limited Liability Company*; its *Limited Liability Partnership*; and its *Uniform Partnership Act*, https://en.wikipedia.org/ (all accessed June 26, 2022).

140 Adolf A. Berle and Gardiner C. Means, *The Modern Corporation and Private Property* (New York: Harcourt, Brace and World, 1932), 47–118, 141–254. Berle was a member of President Franklin D. Roosevelt's "Brain Trust" group of advisers.

141 See Legal Information Institute, Cornell University, *Publicly Traded Partnerships*, www.law.cornell.edu/ (accessed June 15, 2022); David A. Sussman, *Publicly Traded Partnerships*, December 2014, www.duanemorris.com/.

Much as oligopolies do, companies established under these structures can exercise pricing power over customers while evading the sort of regulatory scrutiny that their conventional counterparts might attract. Acquisitions or mergers between MLPs and similar businesses can be executed and may also evade scrutiny, as laws in the states where they are registered tend to facilitate them. The low level of scrutiny they enjoy is sometimes cited by anti-regulatory advocates as a model for what the entire corporate domain should be in the United States. And the structures can include technology activities, such as systems consulting or design, research, clinical trials, product development, testing, marketing, and business processes.

MLPs and similar structures have received over one-third of all equity raised in U.S. financial markets in recent times, accounting for over two-thirds of all new companies formed.[142] Their numbers—now well over twice those of conventional companies (also known as "C" corporations)—may indicate why the rapid reduction of stock investment possibilities due to oligopolistic concentration has not attracted greater concern. Much capital that would have been invested in conventional companies has thus been placed in MLPs and similar structures. Their proliferation may also partly account for lower relative levels of federal and state tax revenue—amounts that could have supported public needs, such as education, health care, or infrastructure construction.

Sheltered by "limited liability" clauses and registered under the names of individual owners, MLPs and similar structures can appear to be independent from a tech oligopolist that funded or created them. In some cases, certain executives of an oligopolistic technology corporation (of the "C" type) may appear as nominal owners, if state regulations allow it. Technology oligopolies can thus embed their lesser-known subsidiaries or spin-offs in the platforms they control—structuring operations such as real estate or stock market speculation, purchasing targeted companies' bonds and stocks, setting up stealthy operations to acquire companies or prepare the ground for mergers, and establishing mechanisms to externalize workers as "franchisees."

The fact that embedded MLPs and similar structures are subject to the power of the oligopolists that own the platforms invalidates the notion that the latter—and in many cases the embedded companies themselves, if they happen to be oligopolistic—are competitive. In these platforms, the embedded businesses not controlled by the oligopolistic platform owner face a scenario not unlike that of consumers in a market subject to oligopolistic pricing power. But the MLPs and similar structures provide anti-regulatory advocates with a model for the future elimination of corporate taxes, such that government financing can

142 See MLP Data, *Top 10 MLPs*, https://mlp.com/ (accessed June 15, 2022); Rohan Reddy, *MLP Monthly Report: June 2021*, globalxetfs.com/; *The Economist*, "Rise of the Distorporation," October 26, 2013, 29; Rodney D. Chrisman, "LLCs are the New King of the Hill," *Fordham Journal of Corporate and Financial Law* 15 (2010), 459–89.

be shifted entirely to individual taxpayers—who will likely not benefit from any MLP or similar structure, or be significant shareholders in conventional corporations. By and large, the pursuit of this model may thus lead to a social panorama where the rich get much richer, and the poor and middle-level income earners remain as they are or become poorer.

Rendering antitrust lawsuits ineffective is another component in the repertory of anti-regulatory praxis. One approach is to narrow the scope of lawsuits such that settlements have minimal effect on oligopolistic power.[143] Thus, only a small part of an oligopolist's operation will be scrutinized, making it more likely that a lawsuit will fail or may not be pursued in the first place.[144]

Raising the burden of proof on regulators is a related tactic—often deployed when favorable judicial interpretations are likely or legal maneuvers can be mounted to challenge evidence. This is a tactic that can lead to compromises that would not otherwise occur and that tend to favor a powerful corporation under investigation.[145] Coping with this tactic can be time-consuming for regulators and may require internal data that can be difficult to obtain. Insufficient data can also lead to a narrow scope for lawsuits, limited evidence, and the likelihood that it will be inconsequential even if it succeeds.[146]

Antitrust lawsuits are hampered in part because they are *ex-post*.[147] Accumulated power and influence are difficult to challenge, particularly with technology oligopolies. Settlements are likely to specify minimal restrictions while imposing penalties that are pittances compared to annual revenues. Restrictions may have little or no consequence if violated—especially when there is no continuous oversight. Change of executives in regulatory agencies and external political influence may also render judgments ineffective—especially when there is political capital in doing so. And legislators can neutralize sanctions by passing new laws that loosen restrictions.

143 See Gerrit De Vynck, "How an Antitrust Suit Could Save Google Money," *Bloomberg*, September 30, 2020, www.bloomberg.com/; *The Economist*, "Technology and Competition: Search Query—American Trustbusters take on Google," October 24, 2020, 58.

144 As occurred in the case against Google in the mid-2010s. See L. Gordon Crovitz, "Why Google was Spared," *Wall Street Journal*, March 30, 2015, A11—as noted by its author, some details provided in this article became known because of carelessness on regulators' part, when a 160-page internal analysis was inadvertently released. See also Edward Wyatt, "Critics of Google Antitrust Ruling Fault the Focus," *New York Times*, January 6, 2013, www.nytimes.com/.

145 See Brandon L. Garrett, *Too Big to Jail: How Prosecutors Compromise with Corporations* (Cambridge: Belknap, 2014), chapters 3, 8–10.

146 An aspect overlooked by arguments that consider antitrust lawsuits to be a substitute for regulation (assuming they are successful and lead to new rules). See Andrew P. Morriss, Bruce Yandle and Andrew Dorchak, *Regulation by Litigation* (New Haven: Yale University Press, 2009), chapters 3, 4, 7.

147 See *The Economist*, "Regulating Big Tech: Ex-antics—Antitrust Lawsuits May Not be the Most Potent Tool to Rein in Technology Giants," October 10, 2020, 57–59.

More effective for anti-regulatory action is to pursue *ex-ante* efforts. Prevention of regulation can require extensive use of the media to influence politicians, regulators, and the public. Spreading the notion that technology oligopolies "compete" on market pricing, discussed earlier, can be part of the agenda. A related tactic is to foster the impression that oligopolistic power is on balance harmless or even positive, using oligopolies' global projection or philanthropic works as examples. And, whenever more restrictive rules are proposed, targeting legislators' reports can be part of the repertory—to focus on details that distract and limit the scope of regulators' attention.[148]

Associated with this approach is the argument that an oligopoly cannot be such if it does not sell anything. This is used to forestall regulation of oligopolists in social media networks, clouds, search, messaging, and related activities. This argument misses the point that even if access is nominally "free"—users not being made to monetarily pay—they are nonetheless paying by having to give up one of the most valuable resources of our time: personal data.

But users not only pay for access with their data. They are also made to pay by having to give up what is essentially labor—the provision of online behaviors and preferences that will be mined for profit, along with their personal time and effort. And—should the data be stolen—additional effort will be expended by users to rectify the problem, along with money and time. As will be discussed later in this book, the form of free labor that users are made to give up is a prime source of the vast wealth and power amassed by some technology oligopolists.[149]

Online behaviors and preferences—and the related time and effort expended—may thus be considered analogous to inputs that are processed to generate targeted advertisements—advertisements that lead to sales of products and services and that are commissioned and paid for by oligopolistic ad-placement companies and their—usually also oligopolistic—clients. Advertisers and clients pay for users' viewings even when a sale does not occur. Viewings are based on insights provided by the mining of intimate details—insights that users are not informed about. The entire apparatus of "free" usage is thus sustained by a vast net of data expropriation, mining, advertising, unrecognized labor, surreptitious analysis, and oligopolistic control that empower some of the wealthiest corporations in history.

148 As occurred with the 450-page report prepared by the U.S. House of Representatives' Committee on the Judiciary, *Digital Markets Investigation: Antitrust Investigation on the Rise and Use of Market Power Online and the Adequacy of Existing Antitrust Laws and Current Enforcement Levels*, 2019, https://judiciary.house.gov/; *Economist*, "Regulating Big Tech," 57.

149 "Facebook ... has built a $92 billion-per-year advertising business by selling space alongside posts by its 2.8 billion ... unpaid user-suppliers. Twitter makes $3.4 billion a year flogging ads among the free editorial typed by its 350 million contributors"—*The Economist*, "Serfing the Web," May 8, 2021, 24.

Discriminatory strategies that can be considered prejudicial to the interests of users—who are made to provide what is essentially free labor—are overlooked. Searches can be "directed" to entities (often also oligopolistic) that have paid more (or bid highest) for a listing spot—regardless of whether this suits the interests of users. Thus, users may end up not knowing about certain products or services that may be better suited to their needs. Large network extent can magnify this problem, as users who are disadvantaged in this way can be in the tens of millions for a single search listing.[150]

Network extent may also be used in differentiated ways by "giving away" some services—such as email, maps, searches—while charging for others. Or, all services may be given away over a period of time. Apps, streaming, video, gaming, or films may thus be provided at no charge until a network reaches significant extent. Thereafter, monetary payment may be required. Or, some services may continue to be given away while others are charged for, in what amounts to a cross subsidy by some users.[151]

Bait-and-switch tactics may thus be part of this scenario, if certain items—such as apps, software, game consoles—are given away initially to build up user dependence. As network extent expands, monetary charges may be introduced for some items. Even when switching costs are minimal, inertia, habits, addiction, or routines may nonetheless keep users dependent and paying—providing a vast revenue flow to the oligopolist in control. And targeted advertising—achieved through the appropriation and mining of users' data, preferences, online behaviors, effort, and time—may generate a parallel and substantial revenue flow that cements oligopolistic power.[152]

Large network extent combined with this panorama of data appropriation, mining, free labor, and oligopolistic control poses a formidable entry barrier. All the more so when it is based in platforms and data clouds that serve a multiplicity of purposes and that are global in scope and reach. And when they

150 This also applies to those who pay to the so-called "influencers"—content providers who sell subscriptions to view their material or participate in games. Very few providers—a very minute proportion of any given segment or category—can attract revenue that will cover their costs, much less make profit. Very long "tails" are the most common graphic evidence whenever, say, percent of paying subscribers by category (such as gaming, online videos) is taken as a share of the total in each segment—see *The Economist*, "Serfing the Web," 25.

151 A related matter is the question of "net neutrality," to guarantee—through regulation—that pricing for bandwidth usage (if not also internet access itself) does not discriminate in favor of businesses. At the core of this concern is that differentiated pricing for bandwidth would shortchange individuals and households. See Shira Ovide, "The Long, Painful Path of Net Neutrality," *New York Times*, February 25, 2021, www.nytimes.com/; American Civil Liberties Union, *What is Net Neutrality?* December 2017, www.aclu.org/; Tim Wu, "Network Neutrality, Broadband Discrimination," *Journal of Telecommunications and High Technology Law* 2 (2003), 141–80.

152 This challenges the argument that if there is another company that also targets advertisements (in the same market segment), then neither one should be considered oligopolistic. See Bork and Sidak, "Chicago School," 679–83.

are under the control of some of the most powerful corporations in history. Google's control over more than three-quarters of all web searches in the United States—and Amazon's control over more than three-quarters of all e-book sales—are testimony to the power that can be amassed in a relatively short time.[153] Troubling as it is, this panorama is nonetheless ignored by anti-regulatory advocates who argue that such power should be neither regulated nor considered harmful.[154]

These considerations are also overlooked by those who advocate against regulation of the internet as a public resource. If so treated, access to the internet would be regulated in much the same way as utilities are—electricity or potable water being relevant analogies. Doing so would recognize that the internet has become a necessity of life. Challenges posed by this regulatory mode would not be difficult to resolve, as a vast amount of experience has been accumulated over many decades with utility provision.

Fundamentally, regulation of the internet as a public utility would aim to provide corporate operators a revenue (or profit) rate comparable to that of a competitive market. Thus, the estimated rate would be based on the cost—to a potential entrant—of duplicating the assets of an existing oligopolist, such that the revenue (or profit) rate is about equal to the cost of capital.[155] This would reduce the high markups that internet oligopolists obtain, such that users can be compensated for the appropriation of their data, for revealing preferences and behaviors, expending time, and providing free labor through usage.

With regulation, users might have to pay for access, but the compensation they would receive would more than offset access charges. Such compensation could be as much as 300 percent or more than what they would pay for access—as part of the advertising revenue captured by oligopolists is distributed among users.[156] Rates would be adjusted periodically, to ensure that the internet remains accessible—as occurs with electricity or water. Users would need

153 See U.S. House of Representatives' Committee on the Judiciary, *Digital Markets Investigation*; *NPR*, "Antitrust Lawsuits: Google 2020"; *The Economist*, "Technology and Competition"; and its "Everybody Wants to Rule the World: Online Businesses can Grow Very Large Very Fast," November 29, 2014, 19–22.

154 See the arguments against regulating Google during its early 2010s investigation in Bork and Sidak, "Chicago School," 680–83; and a more general treatment of entry barrier issues in Bork, *Antitrust Paradox*, Chapter 16. Thiel and Masters, in their *Zero to One* (Chapter 4), in particular, argue that the power of monopolies represents success, while competition should be understood to be synonymous with failure.

155 Customarily assumed when competitive market operations are compared with their competitive counterparts. See *The Economist*, "What if Large Tech Firms were regulated like Sewage Companies?" September 23, 2017, 63; Robert E. Litan, *Regulating Internet Access as a Public Utility: A Boomerang on Tech if It Happens*, Brookings Institution, June 2014, www.brookings.edu/.

156 Assuming the cost of capital and returns for corporate operators to be approximately 12 percent each—an amount that would allow for reinvestment and operational risk. See *The Economist*, "What if Large Tech Firms."

to be informed about how their data is used and would have the choice of opting out of any provision. Procedures for compensation would address any unauthorized use of their data or its theft.[157]

Partly to prevent this scenario, internet oligopolists have bundled their operations by acquiring companies that provide diverse services in multiple market segments. Thus, companies that are seemingly unrelated to the acquiring oligopolist's core business end up becoming the means to set up entry barriers and pricing power—even when they retain their names and legal identities. This has allowed acquirers to establish vast clouds based on acquired companies' databases and to appropriate content from suppliers—to build up network extent and set up internet-based mega-platforms.[158] Bundling has also allowed oligopolists to appropriate users' details across services and markets, thus becoming the largest repositories of intimate data on the planet.

Bundling has been facilitated by mobile communication devices that allow oligopolists to decide which services the users of their gadgets (or software) will see or have access to. Sizes of screens and human visual scale limitations are often used as alibis for limiting listings and choices, while technologies that would overcome such limitations are neglected. This contradicts the argument that regulation of the internet would stifle innovation. Internet and tech (hardware and software) oligopolists thus seem to have avoided moving toward holographic or projected amplification of displays. These technologies would allow larger (virtual) screen sizes and the possibility of seeing diverse choices. A result of this neglect is that users face app-enabled walled patios and search listings—all "sponsored" by the oligopolist in control.

As internet oligopolists seize AI and faster communication technologies with greater connectivity, their control over services related to most everything we do—such as self-driving vehicles, shopping, personal finance, work routines,

157 Calibrating the value of a user's personal data could start from a general baseline (applicable to all users) that would include consideration of the risk of theft and malfeasance by third parties (but also possibly through neglect by internet operators). The baseline estimate could then be adjusted upward, with increments calculated as a function of the total amount of a user's purchases from advertisers over a period of time. This approach might compensate for the risks users take on when they shop online, related to data security, scams, and other considerations.

158 Microsoft—although not considered to be an internet access provider—engaged in bundling through acquisitions in diverse sectors that essentially turned it into one. Companies unrelated to its core software business—such as LinkedIn, GitHub, Nokia, and Skype—allowed it to be in control of a vast data cloud that is very important for internet services and access. See *The Economist*, "Video Gaming: High Score, Microsoft places a $69bn Bet on the Future of Entertainment," January 22, 2022, 57; and its "Method in the Madness: Why the World's Biggest Software Firm Looks Increasingly Acquisitive," April 17, 2021, 57–58. Much the same occurred with tech-service oligopolist Amazon—see Christopher Mims, "Amazon is Leading Tech's Takeover of America: The Tentacles of a Handful of Tech Giants are Reaching into Industries No One Ever Expected Them To, Reshaping Our World in their Image," *Wall Street Journal*, June 16, 2017, www.wsj.com/.

movement, household activities, travel, and intimate contacts—is bound to increase. Bundling and AI may thus facilitate oligo-monopolistic control over all layers of internet-based services, from smartphone apps to social networking and web searches, to the protocols that govern modes of usage. What has been emerging from this panorama of bundled power are platforms that operate as walled fiefs, to which users can be bound indefinitely—bundling insuring that they always end up with "sponsored" services and purchases. This situation contrasts with the early days of the internet and the web, when usage occurred through desktop computers, with browsers and search engines that allowed the possibility of free-flowing searches and discoveries.[159]

Lax antitrust regulation—supported by anti-regulatory action and advocacy—has made this scenario of bundled control possible. Regulation of the internet as a public utility may thus face difficulties unbundling services. A common platform that would allow single access to the internet—and all related services—such that users do not have to switch providers, or pay for access to each service separately, would have to be devised. This is not as daunting as it may sound, as such arrangements have long been used to provide essential services that require integration—health care among them.

Those who oppose regulation of the internet as a public utility also argue that innovation would be shortchanged. This argument, however, ignores that "innovation" by internet oligopolists is mostly about concocting ways to more effectively appropriate and mine data, exploit the free labor that users provide, and contrive wants such that sales through advertising can increase. Few of these activities involve technological innovation as such. And the technological innovations that are put to use by internet oligopolists usually originate externally. Moreover, innovations that can limit oligopolistic control—such as the previously mentioned virtual augmentation possibilities for screens and viewings—tend to be disregarded. Even if the argument on innovation is taken seriously, the benefit of internet regulation as a public utility is bound to be greater for users than any potential innovative shortfall.

Lobbying and Patronage

A second set of vehicles of influence that sustains technology oligopolistic power involves lobbying and the politics of patronage. So ingrained have these vehicles become in American public governance that it is impossible to address the power of technology oligopolies without them. Because of the relations of influence

159 A profound evolution that has been critiqued by scholars such as McChesney in his *Digital Disconnect*, 98–145; and Niall Ferguson in *The Square and the Tower: Networks and Power, from the Freemasons to Facebook* (New York: Penguin, 2019), Part VIII. See also *The Economist*, Special Report (Fixing the Internet), "More Knock-On than Network: How the Internet Lost its Decentralised Innocence," June 30, 2018, 5–6.

involving money, favors, co-optation, and payoffs they embed, the workings of this vehicle amount to a legalization of corruption. That is, corruption made legal simply by *not* considering them illegal—or by formally making them legal and deploying rules that stipulate some restrictions. The latter often result from compromises, and they tend to have a cosmetic function, so as to make the embedded practices seem necessary.

The justification for the system of *legalized corruption* closely associated with lobbying and political patronage is relatively simple. Politicians and regulators, it is argued, must "hear" from corporate constituents—and "intercede" on their behalf—such that legislation can be proposed or rules modified. After all, it is posited, this is what "representative" government is about.

The overarching objective—it is claimed—is to make the economy, regulation, and laws more efficient and to address perceived needs. A common argument posits that oligopolies must be allowed to have such influence because they give us jobs and make products we consume. This is often framed by the belief that oligopolies operate in "competitive" markets and that their pricing schemes obey the rules of competition—consumers being depicted as the ultimate decision-makers on prices and whatever is sold, producers being seen as mere "price takers."[160]

Technology oligopolies are of particular importance in this scenario, because of their association with novelty and the public interest they attract. Support for their lobbying and political patronage often rests on the assignment of anthropomorphic qualities to their corporate identities. This seeks to induce the public to relate to technology oligopolies *as if they were people*. A targeted effect is to promote feelings of loyalty, admiration, or pride toward them—and to view their power as we do that of any human being. The ultimate objective is to promote the belief that corporations have "rights"—in much the same way as people do. Therein lies the notion of "corporate personhood" as an American political, regulatory, and legal concept.[161]

Thus, implicitly, the lobbying and campaign contributions that oligopolistic corporations deploy are not to be conceived as being any different from the political activism and contacts that individual humans undertake. Much the same perspective is applied to the taxes and regulations that apply to technology oligopolies. This allows those taxes and regulations to be seen as heavy and

160 See Tyler Cowen, *Big Business* (New York: St. Martin's, 2019), chapters 1, 5, 6, 8.

161 A belief at the core of a major decision by the U.S. Supreme Court in 2010, with important ramifications for future cases involving oligopolistic power. See Supreme Court of the United States, *Citizens United v. Federal Election Commission: Appeal from the United States District Court for the District of Columbia* (Washington: U.S. Government Printing Office, 2010); Federal Election Commission, *Citizens United v. FEC*, www.fec.gov/ (accessed April 29, 2022). See also Jeffrey Toobin, "Money Unlimited: How Chief Justice John Roberts Orchestrated the Citizens United Decision," *New Yorker*, May 14, 2012, www.newyorker.com/; *New York Times* (editorial), "The Rights of Corporations," September 21, 2009, www.nytimes.com/.

onerous when compared with the ones that individual citizens or households must pay. Sympathy, or at least empathy, for the oligopolies is the targeted effect—to keep out of mind the fundamentally different realities involved.

The contemporary spread of this mindset can be traced to the economic crisis of the 1970s—until then the most profound one since the Great Depression—and to efforts by large corporations to eliminate limitations on their influence.[162] A key enabling figure in this scenario was a prominent twentieth-century jurist—Lewis Powell, appointed in 1971 to the U.S. Supreme Court—and his pro-corporate views.[163] Powell's advocacy became a most important ideological support for corporate political influence during the following decades.[164] And although he did not explicitly favor oligopolies, his ideological position and decisions helped them immensely.

The amounts spent on lobbying are staggering—large corporations accounting for over four-fifths of the handful of billions spent annually at the federal level.[165] Lobbying state and local governments added up to a billion dollars or

162 Grounded on the notion that lifting them would help eliminate "stagflation" (stagnation with high inflation)—the most difficult macroeconomic problem at the time. For critical perspectives on this troubled period, see Harry Magdoff and Paul M. Sweezy, *The End of Prosperity: The American Economy in the 1970s* (New York: Monthly Review Press, 1977), and the discussions in Suarez-Villa, *Corporate Power, Oligopolies*, 277–93.

163 Possibly the most important document encapsulating the precepts behind pro-corporate and pro-oligopolistic Supreme Court rulings to come was a confidential memorandum commissioned by the U.S. Chamber of Commerce—Lewis F. Powell, Jr., *Attack on the American Free Enterprise System—Reframed*, August 23, 1971, www.nowforourturn.org/. This document was thought to be a reaction to efforts seeking to hold corporate power accountable—exemplified at the time by Ralph Nader's leadership and his denunciation of an iconic General Motors product (the Chevrolet Corvair) and its technical shortcomings, in his *Unsafe at Any Speed: The Designed-In Dangers of the American Automobile* (New York: Grossman, 1965). David Harvey—in his *A Brief History of Neoliberalism* (New York: Oxford University Press, 2005), 42–45—credits Powell's influence for the post-1970s rise of neoliberal ideology in the United States. See also Jane Mayer, *Dark Money: The Hidden History of the Billionaires Behind the Rise of the Radical Right* (New York: Anchor, 2016), chapters 8–10—for details on the interests that led to landmark Supreme Court rulings favoring corporate political engagement (largely following Powell's precepts).

164 The organization that commissioned Powell's confidential 1971 memorandum—and lobbied strongly for his appointment to the Supreme Court—would become a very important advocate for corporate interests. See Alyssa Katz, *The Influence Machine: The U.S. Chamber of Commerce and the Corporate Capture of American Life* (New York: Spiegel and Grau, 2015), chapters 4, 6, 7, 10; Mayer, *Dark Money*, chapters 8, 9.

165 See Center for Responsive Politics, *Influence Watch*, www.influencewatch.org/, its *Interest Groups*, its *Top Spenders*, and its *Lobbying Data Summary*, www.opensecrets.org/ (all accessed April 25, 2022); U.S. Senate, *Lobbying Disclosure Act (LDA) Reports: Contributions Reports*, https://lda.senate.gov/ (accessed April 29, 2022); Statista, *Total Lobbying Spending in the United States from 1998 to 2020*, www.statista.com/ (accessed May 29, 2022). Lobbying labor union-linked politicians reportedly made it easier for large corporations to negotiate collective-bargaining agreements—see Michael Kazin, *What It Took to Win* (New York: Farrar, Strauss and Giroux, 2022), chapters 6–9.

more annually during the last decade.[166] Also, the figures compiled are incomplete and pertain to a narrow definition—based on what registered lobbyists declare. This excludes various other forms of corporate lobbying that take place—shrouded in diverse terminology, such as "government relations," "public affairs," "legislative communications," and the like.[167]

The largest technology and tech-service oligopolists can hire hundreds of lobbyists each from dozens of highly experienced lobbying firms. A corporation's annual expense for this endeavor can be in the tens of millions—and budgets have grown several-fold in recent times.[168] Beyond such budgets, a focused lobbying effort to defeat—politically—an antitrust investigation can involve considerable amounts—as in Google's estimated $25 million expense in the early 2010s and its very costly recent campaigns.[169] The repertory of lobbying themes can be broad, diverse, or specialized. In recent times, they have included such interests as promoting tax breaks, securing government contracts, influencing policy formulation, protecting profitability, preventing adoption of generic treatments and medications, or preempting scrutiny of M&A deals that extend pricing power and entry barriers.[170]

166 Linda King, *50-State Assessment of the Costs and Availability of Lobbying Expenditure Data*, National Institute on Money and State Politics and Sunlight Foundation, 2011, www.followthemoney.org/; Jason Clemens, Julie Kaszton, Karrie Rufer and Laura Sucheski, *State-Level Lobbying and Taxpayers: How Much Do We Really Know?* (San Francisco: Pacific Research Institute, 2010), Part III. Regretfully, recent aggregate data on state-level lobbying could not be found.

167 Lee Drutman, *The Business of America is Lobbying: How Corporations Became Politicized and Politics Became More Corporate* (New York: Oxford University Press, 2015), chapters 1, 3–5, 7, 9, 10. Details on lobbying networks and influence are difficult to find due to secrecy—an exception being John A. Farrell, *Koch's Web of Influence: Koch Industries is Spending Tens of Millions to Influence Every Facet of Government that Could Affect its Global Empire*, Center for Public Integrity, May 19, 2014, https://publicintegrity.org/. See also Frank Yu and Xiaoyun Yu, "Corporate Lobbying and Fraud Detection," *Journal of Financial and Quantitative Analysis* 46 (2011), 1865–91.

168 Center for Responsive Politics, *Top Spenders*, www.opensecrets.org/ (accessed May 5, 2022); Megan R. Wilson, "Lobbying's Top 50: Who's Spending Big," *The Hill*, February 7, 2017, https://thehill.com/.

169 L. Gordon Crovitz, "Google's $25 Million Bargain," *Wall Street Journal*, January 13, 2013, www.wsj.com/; Edward Wyatt, "A Victory for Google as FTC Takes No Formal Steps," *New York Times*, January 3, 2013, www.nytimes.com/. See also Ben Gilbert, "Amazon and Google Spent $7.5 Million Lobbying Politicians in the First 3 Months of 2021," *Business Insider*, April 23, 2021, www.businessinsider.com/.

170 See Lee Fang, "Pharmaceutical Industry Dispatches Army of Lobbyists to Block Generic Covid-19 Vaccines," *The Intercept*, April 23. 2021, www.theintercept.com/; Alfred Ng and Maddy Varner, "The Little-Known Data Broker Industry is Spending Big Bucks Lobbying Congress," *The Markup*, April 1, 2021, https://themarkup.org/; *The Economist*, "Health-Care Profits"; Brody Mullins, Laura Stevens and John D. McKinnon, "Amazon Rises as One of D.C.'s Most Powerful Players," *Wall Street Journal*, June 21, 2018, A1; Farrell, *Koch's Web of Influence*; Occupy Monsanto, *Monsanto's Lobbying Expenses 2002–12*, May 16, 2012, and its *Why Senator Bernie Sanders' GMO Labeling Amendment to the Farm Bill Failed: Monsanto's GMO Money*, June 27, 2012, www.occupy-monsanto.com/.

The benefit of lobbying for a technology oligopolist can be substantial. A single data cloud contract for the U.S. government can amount to several billion dollars annually—making up as much as one-fifth or more of total yearly revenue.[171] Tens of millions of dollars spent on lobbying annually can thus pay for themselves many times over through a single contract. This is a matter that every technology oligopolist is aware of. And even when a major contract is not involved, the return to a single dollar spent lobbying has been estimated to be as much as 22,000 percent—a level far higher than that of most any corporate investment.[172]

This matter is usually ignored by the workforce, as the data are not made public—at least not when efforts to form a union are underway or agreements have to be renegotiated. A large proportion of workers in technology corporations that spend greatly on lobbying may rely on welfare, food stamps, Medicaid, or public housing to sustain themselves or their families because of insufficient pay.[173] Many such workers can be considered *precariat* labor, toiling from day to day without stable employment or with contracts that are issued only for specific tasks under TVC (temporary–vendor–contractor) arrangements. These aspects—to be addressed later in this book—are among the more blatant yet lesser known labor problems of technology oligopolistic power.

Also largely ignored by the workforce are the tax breaks and loopholes that their oligopolistic employers secure through lobbying. Among the lesser known are tax breaks for R&D and the apparent inflation of costs to reduce taxes or secure additional breaks. An investigation on the biotech and pharmaceutical sector during the last decade, for example, found that the actual average cost of research to bring a new medication or treatment to market was as much as 94 percent below the advertised amounts.[174] And about one-fifth of

171 See Jon Swartz, "Microsoft Wins Pentagon's $10 Billion JEDI Cloud Contract, Beating Amazon," *MarketWatch*, October 28, 2019, www.marketwatch.com/; Mullins, Stevens and McKinnon, "Amazon Rises," A10.

172 For tax breaks on repatriated earnings, an aspect of crucial importance to many technology oligopolies—Raquel M. Alexander, Stephen W. Mazza, and Susan Scholz, "Measuring Rates of Return for Lobbying Expenditures: An Empirical Case Study of Tax Breaks for Multinational Corporations," *Journal of Law and Politics* 25 (2009), www.lawandpolitics.org/. The returns to lobbying have likely increased since the publication of this research, given the loosening of restrictions—particularly after 2017. Unfortunately, a dearth of specific data and of empirical studies prevents comparisons up to our time. See also Bruce A. Kibler and Kathleen V. Kibler, "Corporate Lobbying: The Tradeoff Between Payback, Accountability/Responsibility, and Democracy," *Journal of Leadership, Accountability and Ethics* 13 (2016), 103–15; Cliff Scott, "Lobbying: A Critical Dimension of Business Strategy," *Journal of Law and Management* 57 (2015), 17–27; Suarez-Villa, *Corporate Power, Oligopolies*, 69–75; *The Economist*, "Investment and Lobbying: Money and Politics," October 1, 2011, 82.

173 See Mullins, Stevens and McKinnon, "Amazon Rises," A10.

174 Donald W. Light and Rebecca Warburton, "Demythologizing the High Costs of Pharmaceutical Research," *BioSocieties* 6 (2011), 34–50. See also Sammy Almashat, "Pharmaceutical Research Costs: The Myth of the $2.6 Billion Pill," *Public Citizen*, September 2017, www.citizen.org/;

corporations listed in the Fortune 500 Index—many of them technology corporations—typically pay no federal taxes at all, and the vast majority of those that do contribute at rates far below those that apply.[175] This situation is compounded by the self-reported, highly inflated estimates of taxes paid, which are said to have reached $100 billion for the six largest technology oligopolists during the last decade.[176]

One of the largest technology oligopolists—conglomerate General Electric—reportedly enjoyed substantial net *negative* federal tax treatment for many years, thus being effectively subsidized by taxpayers.[177] Such fiscal welfare does not usually benefit workers—whose toil and creativity are so vitally important. In addition to having inventions and other IP they create appropriated as a condition for employment—a matter noted earlier that will be addressed later in this book—the taxpaying workforce therefore subsidizes their employers through their tax contributions. Such subsidies aside, if oligopolistic corporate tax breaks and loopholes during the last two decades were added up, the total would likely be in the trillions of dollars. This panorama of fiscal welfare at taxpayers' (and the workforce's) expense is a longstanding reality—and it reflects the power of oligopolistic corporate lobbying over tax legislation.[178]

Lobbying for tax breaks and loopholes has been accompanied by the preemption of legislation limiting executive compensation—a matter of vital interest to the technology managerial elites. CEO compensation was estimated to have risen nearly one-hundred-fold during the past four decades, while that of the corporate workforce increased by barely one-tenth.[179] The CEO-to-workforce compensation ratio for the largest 350 corporations—all

---

Alison Kodjak, "Prescription Drug Costs Driven by Manufacturer Price Hikes, Not Innovation," *NPR*, January 7, 2019, www.npr.org/. Much biotech and pharmaceutical data on R&D are difficult to verify independently as companies are the sole sources.

175 Institute for Taxation and Economic Policy, *Corporate Tax Avoidance in the First Year of the Trump Tax Law*, December 16, 2019, www.itep.org/; Jesse Pound, "These 91 Companies Paid No Federal Taxes in 2018," *CNBC*, December 16, 2019, www.cnbc.com/.

176 Rupert Neate, "'Silicon Six' Tech Giants Accused of Inflating Tax Payments by Almost $100 Billion: Study Claims Firms Paid $96 Billion Less in Tax Between 2011 and 2020 than the Notional Figures Cited in their Annual Reports," *The Guardian*, May 31, 2021, www.theguardian.com/.

177 Matthew Gardner, Robert S. McIntyre and Richard Phillips, *The 35 Percent Corporate Tax Myth: Corporate Tax Avoidance by Fortune 500 Companies, 2008 to 2015*, Institute on Taxation and Economic Policy, 2017, https://itep.org/; Americans for Tax Fairness, *General Electric's Special Tax Loophole Lets Company Dodge Billions in Taxes*, https://americansfortaxfairness.org/ (accessed May 9, 2022); Andy Kroll, "GE, Exxon, 10 Other Major Corporations Paid Negative Tax Rate," *Mother Jones*, June 2, 2011, www.motherjones.com/.

178 See Robert S. McIntyre, Matthew Gardner, Rebecca J. Wilkins and Richard Phillips, *Corporate Taxpayers and Corporate Tax Dodgers 2008–10* (Washington, DC: Citizens for Tax Justice and Institute on Taxation and Economic Policy, 2011), www.ctj.org/; Kroll, "GE, Exxon, 10 Other."

179 Lawrence Mishel and Julia Wolfe, *CEO Compensation has Grown 940% since 1978: Typical Worker Compensation has Risen only 12% During that Time*, Economic Policy Institute, 2019, www.epi.org/.

oligopolistic, including technology—was found to be 278-to-1 in recent years compared to 20-to-1 in 1965.[180] This dynamic is at the core of the vast wealth accumulated by the top one percent of the population—that includes all the technology managerial and owner elites.[181]

Lobbying also helps technology oligopolists consolidate walled patios that provide substantial pricing power—through labyrinths of intermediaries. In health care, biotechnology and pharmaceutical oligopolists have been found to operate through several layers of "facilitators"—five insurers, three pharmacy chains, three wholesale commercial chains, and three benefit management companies (all of them oligopolistic).[182] This multi-level division of functions—partly a result of lobbying and political campaign contributions—introduces much waste in American health care. It is considered to be an important reason why U.S. health spending is so much more than in any other advanced nation—yet results are worse.[183] Tens of millions of Americans—including many technology sector workers—have no health insurance coverage, while thousands of dollars more per person are spent on health care than in any other advanced nation.[184] Meanwhile, corporate profits in health care, biopharmaceuticals, and tech-based health services surpass those of most other sectors.[185]

Intelligence on legislative agendas—and issues to target—is often obtained by lobbying politicians whose campaigns an oligopolist contributes to.[186] The lobbyists themselves can be former legislators. In recent times, almost two-thirds of retiring or defeated members of the U.S. Congress have taken up lobbying as their business.[187] "Insider" intelligence on political agendas—provided by current and former politicians-turned lobbyists—is of special importance to technology oligopolies, to preempt or counter actions such as antitrust investigations, limits on executive compensation, and unfavorable changes in IP rules. Such intelligence is also vital for oligopolistic military technology contractors

180 Mishel and Wolfe, *CEO Compensation*.

181 It is also at the core of the vast amounts of money channeled by those elites into politics. See, for example, Ryan T. Beckwith, "Billionaires' Political Spending Grew 37-Fold in 10 Years," *Bloomberg*, July 1, 2020, www.bloomberg.com/.

182 *The Economist*, "Health-Care Profits."

183 *The Economist*, "Health-Care Profits"; Kodjak, "Prescription Drug Costs"; Almashat, "Pharmaceutical Research Costs."

184 *The Economist*, "Health-Care Profits"; Light and Warburton, "Demythologizing the High Costs."

185 *The Economist*, "Health-Care Profits"; Almashat, "Pharmaceutical Research Costs."

186 See Center for Responsive Politics, *Top Recipients of Contributions from Lobbyists, 2020 Cycle*, 2021 (and previous years), www.opensecrets.org/; Lawrence Lessig, *Republic, Lost: How Money Corrupts Congress—and a Plan to Stop It* (New York: Twelve, 2011), chapters 1, 9, 14.

187 Alan Zibel, *Revolving Congress: The Revolving Door Class of 2019 Flocks to K Street—Nearly Two-Thirds of Former Members of 115th Congress Working Outside Politics and Government Have Lobbying or Strategic Consulting Jobs*, Public Citizen Organization, 2019, www.citizen.org/; Center for Responsive Politics, *Top Recipients of Contributions*; Lessig, *Republic, Lost*, 99, 123.

to gain or renew contracts, increase the amounts awarded, or have budget overruns approved.

Money in Politics

Influence through political contributions tends to work in tandem with lobbying, as politicians who are lobbied are often those whose campaigns are financially supported. And those whose campaigns have not been monetarily supported know that in the future they may be—if they provide results. Thus, catering to the interests of contributors and lobbyists is built into the system—money being so much of what American political campaigning is about.

The amounts spent on political contributions are quite substantial. Technology oligopolies are the most important corporate contributors.[188] A small fraction—say, two or three percent—of a technology oligopolist's annual profit can be greater than the total spent on presidential campaigns. And the total spent on a presidential campaign by a single candidate now tends to be greater than two billion dollars for each electoral cycle.[189] The two-billion-dollar-or-more threshold has even been taken by some political analysts as an indicator of whether a candidate is "electable" for the presidency of the United States.

Technology oligopolies are an important factor in these campaigns, not only because of their substantial contributions. The strategic apparatus of a presidential candidate today rests on a very important asset controlled by oligopolistic technology power. This is the vast data clouds with intimate personal information that can encompass most of the voting population. Such clouds—typically used for and derived from online commerce, social media, personal communications, and most any activity dependent on connectivity—are thus a very important political asset.[190]

188 See Center for Responsive Politics, *Donor Lookup*, and *Who Are the Biggest Donors?* www.opensecrets.org/; HowMuch, *The Thirty Biggest Political Donors on the Fortune 500: Political Donations Between the Years 2007 and 2017*, https://howmuch.net/ (based on data analyses by Zippia, https://research.zippia.com/); Campaign Finance Institute, *Historical Statistics*, www.cfinst.org/; Adam Bonica, *Database on Ideology, Money in Politics, and Elections: Public Version 2.0*, Social Science Data Collection, Stanford University Libraries, https://data.stanford.edu/ (all accessed May 18, 2022).

189 The total spent by both candidates in the 2020 presidential election campaign was estimated to be almost four billion dollars. Spending on other political campaigns can add substantially to this amount. See Center for Responsive Politics, *2020 Election to Cost $14 Billion, Blowing Away Election Records*, October 28, 2020; and its *2020 Presidential Race*, www.opensecrets.org/ (accessed May 18, 2022).

190 A matter reflected by the extensive use and misuse of such data during the last decade. See, for example, Nicholas Confessore, "Cambridge Analytica and Facebook: The Scandal and the Fallout So Far," *New York Times*, April 4, 2018, www.nytimes.com/; Carole Cadwalladr and Emma Graham-Harrison, "Revealed: 50 Million Facebook Profiles Harvested for Cambridge Analytica in Major Data Breach," *The Guardian*, March 17, 2018, www.theguardian.com/.

Lest we forget, the data in these clouds are routinely appropriated from users by the oligopolists in control, as a condition for access. Such clouds are now recognized as one of the most important corporate assets that a technology company can possess. But their significance as a political asset has not been widely understood. A political "donation" to a candidate in the form of access to such clouds can be more important than any monetary contribution. And such "donations" can be arranged through third parties—consultants, foundations, political action committees (and super-PACs), think-tanks, and lobbying firms—to avoid a direct link. Analyses of data in the clouds can be crucial for strategy, such as identifying which states and local areas are worth spending money in—based on whether they can provide enough Electoral College votes for victory.

Political contributions by technology oligopolists can occur in other ways that are practically impossible to trace—and can evade electoral regulations. These contributions-by-other-means can involve speaker fees for which large payments are disbursed—a single lecture or appearance at an event garnering, say, half a million dollars in addition to travel expenses. Funding for such payments may be provided by an oligopolist as a philanthropic "donation" to a non-profit organization set up to organize the event. Hiring of a politician's relatives and close associates, as consultants or employees, is another way. Such employment can involve assignments that are actually performed by others—salary being a form of payoff for political favors.

Arranging to purchase goods and services supplied by a business run by a politician's relatives or associates is yet another way. And the supply contract may specify a time limit that happens to coincide with the end of the favored politician's term in office—the contract being tacitly subject to renewal if reelection occurs. Facilitating financing for a project conceived by a politician's associates or family can also be part of the repertory. This can be arranged through an oligopolist's subsidiaries, such as those set up to speculate in real estate or the bond market. The web of payoffs and favors can be rather complex, and minimal disclosure regulations can ensure that the motives will not be found out.

Revolving Doors

Another vehicle of influence involves revolving-door appointments of high-level corporate executives to important government positions. This vehicle also operates in reverse, as top government officials and ex-politicians are often recruited for corporate executive positions. Or it can operate in a roundtrip fashion, as executives return to high-level corporate positions with their former (or similar) employers after government appointments. In all or any of its modes, revolving-door influence is typically entwined with lobbying, patronage, political contributions, and anti-regulatory schemes.

This vehicle of influence can be traced to the mid-twentieth century and General Electric—long a symbol of American technological prowess and one of the largest and wealthiest conglomerates in history. Its top executive joined the Roosevelt and Truman administrations to manage national industrial production and wages during and after the Second World War—returning to GE between appointments.[191] His time in government was characterized as anti-union and pro-corporate—and he was often referred to as the "co-president" of the United States due to his vast influence. This instance was followed by the appointment of General Motors' top executive to a powerful federal position in the early 1950s—Secretary of Defense—overseeing the military-industrial complex and its ties with some of the most powerful oligopolies of that time.[192]

The rising power of oligopolies—fueled by consolidation throughout the American economy in the 1950s and thereafter—sent a strong message to the political establishment that the interests of powerful corporations should have the highest priority in government. As pre-War restrictions on corporate interface with the public sector were relaxed and—later on—largely diluted, the revolving-door vehicle gained increasing importance. Cabinet appointments, regulatory agency directorships, and departments that could restrict or benefit the corporate domain became targets of interest for oligopolistic power. Actual and potential conflicts of interest were quietly swept aside, shielded by the argument that the public interest would be better served if those with experience—in corporations subject to regulation—took command of agencies charged with their oversight.[193]

Technology oligopolies in various sectors—health, communications, agro-biotech, aerospace, military—would benefit from this panorama of influence that the revolving-door vehicle provided.[194] However, one key regulation—largely intended to keep appearances and ensconce the conflicts of interest that often arise—forbade executives from receiving monetary benefit from their

191 See Wikipedia, *Charles Edward Wilson (businessman)*, https://en.wikipedia.org/ (accessed May 19, 2022); Alden Whitman, "Charles E. Wilson of G.E. Dies; Mobilized Industry in Two Wars," *New York Times*, January 4, 1972, www.nytimes.com/.

192 Wikipedia, *Charles Erwin Wilson*, https://en.wikipedia.org/ (accessed May 19, 2022).

193 Exposure of conflicts of interest is typically muted, if they are reported at all, in the mainstream news media—possibly because of dependence on corporate advertisers. Pentagon-related conflicts can attract some exposure, as advertising for companies in this area tends to be less than for those that sell to the public—but mainstream media coverage nonetheless tends to be sparse. See Jason Paladino, *The Chairman of the Revolving Door: Dunford Gave Lockheed a Crucial F-35B Approval; Six Years Later, It Gave Him a Job*, Project on Government Oversight, March 6, 2020, www.pogo.org/; Peter Castagno, "New Defense Secretary Poised for Confirmation Despite Vast Conflicts of Interest," *Citizen Truth*, July 29, 2019, https://citizentruth.org/. See also Sam Bright, "Government Departments Breaking Guidance on Board Members' Conflict of Interest," *Byline Times*, April 19, 2021, https://bylinetimes.com/.

194 Related discussions can be found in Suarez-Villa, *Corporate Power, Oligopolies*, 42–43, 75–78. The financial sector attracted much attention in recent decades, mainly because of the repeal of the Glass-Steagall Act in the late 1990s and the 2007–9 economic crisis.

corporate employers when they joined the government. This restriction posed a major obstacle as the use of "golden parachutes" spread—becoming a customary executive compensation scheme.

The problem revolved around the vesting of stock—often amounting to tens of millions of dollars, if not more—granted by corporate employers to executives as partial compensation. To keep executives from cashing in and departing, vesting is granted over a period of years of employment or after a pre-specified term—shareholders usually bearing the cost. A remedy—adopted by most oligopolistic corporations—was to accelerate vesting to occur just before executives sign up for government appointments, regardless of the pre-specified contractual time parameters. In this manner, corporations granted departing executives sizable early payouts—that actually violated the contractual terms of their employment.[195] Much the same can be said for an alternative scheme—to keep vesting on schedule but without disbursement, as if the departing executive continued with the corporate employer.[196]

The contractual violations involved were, of course, conveniently swept under the carpet. In the corporate domain, any other breach of contract that involved the large amounts granted by "golden parachutes" would have been pursued fiercely. No effort would be spared to claw back every dollar paid out to, say, a supplier that violates contractual clauses involving the amounts in question. And, most any individual in the TVC labor category would be terminated—and likely blacklisted as well—if a contractual violation involves only a minute fraction of the amounts typically vested through this scheme.[197]

Shareholders—who usually end up paying for the "golden parachutes"—are typically not consulted beforehand about such costly contractual violations.[198]

195 A prominent former federal official (with much experience in the corporate domain) commented on a proposed government appointee who would receive a substantial accelerated "golden parachute" vesting from his employer (a large financial corporation): "Only in the Wonderland of Wall Street logic could one argue that this looks like anything other than a bribe. We want people entering public service because they want to serve the public. Frankly, if they need a $20 million incentive, I'd rather they stay away." Quoted in Jennifer Bendery, "Obama Nominee Antonio Weiss Takes More Hits over Qualifications for Treasury Post," *Huffpost,* December 9, 2014, www.huffpost.com/. See also Richard Trumka, "The Paratroopers of Crony Capitalism," *Wall Street Journal*, February 11, 2015, A11.

196 The justification that these schemes are necessary—because departing executives experience a substantial reduction in compensation while in government—seems to ignore the problem of executive overcompensation and its rapid rise in recent decades. See Mishel and Wolfe, *CEO Compensation*.

197 See Daisuke Wakabayashi, "Google's Shadow Workforce: Temps Who Outnumber Full-Time Employees," *New York Times*, May 28, 2019, www.nytimes.com/; Bergen and Eidelson, "Inside Google's Shadow Workforce"; Sheng, "Silicon Valley's Dirty Secret."

198 The costs of accelerated vesting of "golden parachutes" tend to be spread over many shareholders, thus diluting the magnitude of the payout per share (or per shareholder). Shareholders may not be informed clearly about the payouts or may not notice them in the accounting summaries that might be provided. Doubts and objections on these schemes were voiced early on by some

For them, the presumed calculus is that the cost of the "golden parachute" payout will be more than made up by the benefits that the corporation will gain from the departing executive's doings in government. And, what might those benefits be? The myriad specific forms would be too long to list and discuss here, but among the more important are the preemption of antitrust investigations, the award of rich government contracts, and the approval of (or turning a blind eye to) sizable M&A deals that create formidable entry barriers and increase pricing power.

A systemic consequence of the revolving-door vehicle has been a substantial *shift of risk* from the corporate domain to the public sector—taxpayers bearing the cost, without vote or consent. This phenomenon becomes more noticeable in the generous bailouts that occur during crises. General Electric was provided with an estimated $182.5 billion rescue in 2008, during the financial crisis.[199] In addition, GE Capital—a subsidiary that was practically run as a hedge fund—had to be provided with federal guarantees for $139 billion of its accumulated debt.[200] During that year, GE reportedly spent almost $19 million on lobbying, while executives and employees contributed $1.35 million in direct political donations—in addition to the nearly $3 million provided by GE's Political Action Committee.[201]

The taxpayer-supported welfare granted to oligopolies to cover insolvencies may not only not be fully repaid (if any occurs) when a corporation refloats its finances—but its top executives are unlikely to see any reduction in their compensation. And, usually, certainly not an abrogation (or reduction) of the sizable "golden parachutes" they feel entitled to cash in when vesting occurs. Also, in many cases, the same executives who are left to cash in their "parachutes"—often shortly after bailouts—were responsible for decisions that led to a company's insolvency.

---

legal scholars and corporate policy specialists—see Susan L. Martin, "Platinum Parachutes: Who's Protecting the Shareholder?" *Hofstra Law Review* 14 (1986), http://scholarlycommons.law.hofstra.edu/; National Legal and Policy Center, *Boeing Shareholder Proposal Targets 'Golden Parachutes'*, April 24, 2009, https://nlpc.org/.

199 Phil Kerpen, "General Electric: The Worst Bailout in the World," *Fox News*, March 26, 2009, www.foxnews.com/; Robert Lenzner, "GE, AmEx, GM—Bailout USA," *Forbes*, November 15, 2008, www.forbes.com/. See also Wikipedia, *The Emergency Economic Stabilization Act of 2008*, https://en.wikipedia.org/.

200 *New York Times*, *DealBook*, "F.D.I.C. to Back $139 Billion in GE Capital Debt," November 12, 2008, https://dealbook.nytimes.com/. See also Geoffrey Colvin and Katie Benner, "GE Under Siege: For Years GE Capital's Profits Powered its Parent's Earnings and Helped Finance its Vast Array of Businesses; Now GE's Biggest Asset has Turned into a Liability that Puts the Future of the Entire Company at Risk," *CNN Money*, October 15, 2008, https://money.cnn.com/.

201 Timothy P. Carney, "Obama's Hidden Bailout of General Electric," *Washington Examiner*, March 4, 2009, www.washingtonexaminer.com/. Compensation packages for GE executives continued to be paid at high levels, even during periods of depressed revenue. In 2020, GE's CEO reportedly received $73 million, a 300 percent increase from 2019—*The Economist*, "For Some American CEOs it was as if Covid-19 did Not Happen," May 15, 2021, 61.

For taxpayers, the revolving-door vehicle can involve a dystopian practice of *agency-theory-in-reverse*—as revolving-door executives in government end up *not* safeguarding the public interest but actually damaging it—to benefit oligopolistic power. In multiple ways—as corporations and shareholders that pay "golden parachutes" and excessive executive compensation often also happen to contribute little in the way of taxes. And, what they contribute tends to be well below the rates that apply. Loopholes, deductions, and breaks make this reality possible—an astounding corporate welfare benefit that revolving-door executives and lobbyists assiduously guard and promote.

Judiciary System

The judiciary system is a very important vehicle of influence for technology oligopolistic power, as it defines legality and imposes rulings and penalties on society. Influence here tends to be indirect compared to the other vehicles. An appearance of independence and impartiality is sought for rulings—to maintain credibility and a semblance of legitimacy. Without influence over the judiciary apparatus, it would be impossible for technology oligopolistic power to sustain the other vehicles—lobbying politicians and regulators, providing monetary contributions to try to engineer election outcomes, deploying the revolving-door scheme, and obtaining favorable results in myriad anti-regulatory efforts. Influence over the judiciary system therefore sets the legal platform upon which the other vehicles operate.

The assignment of anthropomorphic qualities to corporate power, noted earlier, is a most important conceptual premise guiding the judiciary vehicle of influence. Decisions that set corporations—most of all oligopolies—on an equal plane with personhood and its political rights have cemented their power considerably. This is a matter that percolates from the cusp of judiciary power down to the lower levels of adjudication. Thus, for technology oligopolistic power to have its political backers pack the Court with a majority who are ideologically favorable—and subscribe to the notion of corporate personhood—is of paramount importance.

As precedent is important in American jurisprudence, the anthropomorphic outlook that guides rulings on corporate influence sets the parameters for future decisions. Any request to the Supreme Court will thus be affected by prior rulings. And in lower courts, decisions that contradict precedent may likely be scrutinized, if not avoided. Deviant rulings may then be appealed to the Supreme Court—cost posing no obstacle to oligopolistic power and its wealthy elites.[202]

202 The Supreme Court has the option of declining to take up an appeal—thus letting a lower court's decision stand. Cases brought against the Federal Elections Commission are often important, however, and draw attention—all the more so if they can set or cement precedent. U.S. District Courts

Thus, the expense that might be a barrier to an individual or public interest organization will be easily covered when it comes to appeals against unfavorable lower court rulings. All the more so if a precedent is likely to be set—to further strengthen the political hand of oligopolistic power. Only an enlargement of Supreme Court membership that results in a majority less ideologically favorable to corporate power might change this panorama—a very unlikely possibility given the political establishment's subservience to corporate oligopolies and their bountiful monetary contributions.[203] Supreme Court nominees must, after all, be approved by a majority of politicians in the Senate.

And those politicians' campaigns will have most likely received significant donations from oligopolistic corporations—and their political organizations. The records, ideas, and philosophical bent of Supreme Court nominees are always scrutinized, especially with regard to how they view the corporate domain and its relationship with politics and governance. Potential candidates whose thinking might deviate from the expected parameters can thus be disqualified before nominations are made.[204] This does not mean that a monolithic thought mode rules this process, but nominees who win appointment will most likely fit general expectations.

The spread of favored political action committees (PACs) since the late 1940s is testimony of how entwined oligopolistic power became with the judiciary system and politics.[205] Many PACs virtually operate as political front organizations for technology oligopolies—advocating ideas and agendas, engaging in pervasive advertising, launching attacks against candidates perceived to be threats, and supporting the favored ones through donations and events.[206] Their scope may be narrow or broad (or both), but the overarching objec-

are usually the locus of suits when the F.E.C. cannot satisfactorily resolve compliance problems—appeals to the Supreme Court can be the next step. See Federal Election Commission, *Court Cases*, and its *Mission and History*, www.fec.gov/ (both accessed June 1, 2022).

203 During the Great Depression—one of the worst economic downturns in U.S. history—an attempt to enlarge the Supreme Court failed. This effort was pursued after the Court ruled against important New Deal programs, arguing that they were unconstitutional—largely on ideological grounds. The Court had been packed during the 1920s with a majority of pro-corporate judges—terms lasting until voluntary retirement or death. See William E. Leuchtenburg, "When Franklin Roosevelt Clashed with the Supreme Court—and Lost," *Smithsonian*, May 2005, www.smithsonianmag.com/.

204 Historically, an emphasis on putting forth nominees who are generally "safe" for the system may explain why rejection rates have been low—see U.S. Senate, *Supreme Court Nominations (1789-present)*, www.senate.gov/ (accessed June 1, 2022).

205 See Center for Responsive Politics, *Political Action Committees (PACs)*, www.opensecrets.org/; Federal Election Commission, *Political Action Committees (PACs)*, www.fec.gov/ (both accessed May 30, 2022); Joanna Banthin and Leigh Stelzer, "Political Action Committees: Fact, Fancy and Morality," *Journal of Business Ethics* 5 (1986), 13–19. PACs were created after the U.S. Congress banned direct contributions from labor unions to political parties and candidates.

206 See Karl Evers-Hillstrom, *Why Corporate PACs have an Advantage*, Center for Responsive Politics, February 14, 2020, www.opensecrets.org/.

tive is to support those whose views and agendas can be favorably associated with corporate interests. Informal contacts, clues, and information—including those provided through advertisements and the media—make it reasonable to assume that some coordination will occur between PACs and campaign organizations, despite regulations.[207] And even if coordination between PACs and candidates or their campaigns does not take place, the vast disbursements of money, advertisements, and programmed activities often set the stage for election victories.

Technology oligopolies have created PACs and devoted special attention to them because of their capacity to influence voters, channel campaigns, and elections and because the very tools that technology provides are indispensable to their operation.[208] Thus, technology oligopolies tend to benefit on all counts—through the PAC-dispensed financial support that backs their favored candidates, through the judicial appointments and laws those politicians will make when they are in office, and through the products and services they sell and which PACs and campaigns deploy in their activities. The latter can, in many cases, also provide demonstration effects to attract customers—as political gatherings often serve to show off tech gadgets and services.

Employees of technology oligopolies are encouraged or induced to contribute to a favored PAC—and also directly to candidates' campaign organizations.[209] Even when individual contributions are modest, the totals from the workforce of a single company can be substantial. Employees who contribute to a favored PAC and its chosen politicians may be tacitly rewarded through career advancement or continued employment. And contractors or temporary workers may be advised to contribute to a PAC as a demonstration of loyalty—and in the hope that contracts may be renewed. Such practices reflect the

207 Violations of campaign rules often go unnoticed and are not penalized—see Campaign Legal Center, *CLC Complaints Allege Illegal Coordination between Super PACs and Two Senate Campaigns*, December 17, 2020, https://campaignlegal.org/; Kenneth P. Doyle, "Lax Campaign Law Enforcement May Empower Big Money in 2020," *Bloomberg Government*, June 5, 2019, https://about.bgov.com/; Adam Wollner and National Journal, "10 Ways Super PACs and Campaigns Coordinate, Even Though They are Not Allowed To: Campaigns and Super PACs Have Become Adept at Working Around Rules Barring Them from Directly Working Together," *The Atlantic*, September 27, 2015, www.theatlantic.com/; Patrick O'Connor, "Campaigns Drop Clues to PACs: Barred from Direct Planning with Groups, Candidates Send Signals to Keep Them on Message," *Wall Street Journal*, July 7, 2012, A4.

208 See Center for Responsive Politics, *Microsoft Corp PAC Profile, its US Apple Assn PAC Profile, its Google Inc PAC Profile, and its Amazon.com PAC Profile*, www.opensecrets.org/; Ballotpedia, *Google NetPAC*, https://ballotpedia.org/ (all accessed May 30, 2022).

209 Firings of employees who refused to follow corporate instructions on this matter became possible during the last decade. See Alexander Hertel-Fernandez, "Employer Political Coercion: A Growing Threat—Since Citizens United, Companies can Legally Require Workers to Participate in Politics, and Fire Them If They Refuse," *American Prospect*, November 23, 2015, https://prospect.org/.

relations of power that the judiciary system—through many decades of rulings and precedent—has endorsed.

For technology oligopolistic power and its judicial influence, a 2010 Supreme Court ruling—*Citizens United v. Federal Election Commission*—stood out in the landscape of favorable decisions.[210] By allowing unlimited corporate monetary contributions and loosening campaign finance rules, this decision sets a very important precedent.[211] It also sets the stage for further future deregulation to favor corporate influence not only over politics but—indirectly—over the judiciary system itself. First and Fourteenth Amendment rights—free speech and equality under the law—were invoked by the ruling, applying to corporations what the U.S. Constitution stipulates for citizens.

Conceptually, the ruling affirmed and extended the anthropomorphic notion of political and constitutional rights for corporate organizations—oligopolies, most of all—as it judged explicitly that corporations' First Amendment rights would be violated if they were to continue being restricted from contributing to politics.[212] Thus, a corporate organization—an inanimate and artificial construct invented by humans—was assumed to have much the same constitutional right to freedom of speech—and the capacity to generate speech itself—as a human does. Also, the ruling affirmed that the corporate act of spending money on politics had to be considered a form of "free speech"—thereby equating money with human speech. Or, allowing the substitution of money for the exercise of human speech.

The fact that humans exist through and from nature, whereas a corporate organization does not, was thus cast aside—along with the reality that the character, scale, and powers of corporate organizations are completely different from those of a human being. Also, the reality that the existence of either revolves around very dissimilar purposes and functions, with different consequences. Corporations, at the bottom of it all, have no speech of their own—only what certain powerful humans in charge express using their brand, legal name, or label. Attributing such a precious human quality as speech to corporate organizations seemed to obey *not* a rational premise, but one imposed by the power of interests to which the judiciary system is subservient.

210 See Supreme Court of the United States, *Citizens United v. Federal Election Commission*; Federal Election Commission, *Citizens United v. FEC*.

211 See Tim Lau, *Citizens United Explained: The 2010 Supreme Court Decision Further Tilted Political Influence Toward Wealthy Donors and Corporations*, Brennan Center for Justice, New York University Law School, 2019, www.brennancenter.org/; Deborah Tedford, "Supreme Court Rips Up Campaign Finance Laws," *NPR*, January 21, 2010, www.npr.org/; Toobin, "Money Unlimited."

212 See Adam Winkler, *We the Corporations: How American Businesses Won their Civil Rights* (New York: Liveright, 2018), chapters 2, 4, 5, 8, 10; Thom Hartmann, *Unequal Protection: How Corporations Became "People"—And How You Can Fight Back* (San Francisco: Berrett-Koehler, 2010), chapters 2, 10–22, 24.

The Fourteenth Amendment of the U.S. Constitution—invoked in the *Citizens United* ruling—was enacted after the Civil War to grant former slaves equal treatment under the law, at least nominally. In 1886, the Supreme Court ruled that equal protection to that granted citizens was to be applied to corporate businesses (initially the railroads—among the earliest oligo-monopolistic sectors in the United States).[213] As a consequence, of the 307 Fourteenth Amendment cases decided by the Supreme Court before 1910, 93 percent were brought up by corporations—*not* citizens or former slaves. And the contrast between rulings on the rights of former slaves and those of corporations was remarkable—as in the 1896 case *Ferguson v. Plessy*, when the Court ruled against the constitutional right of a citizen who, having been classified as (or considered to be) Afro-American, was forced to sit in the "colored" (segregated) compartment of railroad cars.[214]

A long trail of Supreme Court and lower court decisions would follow the 1886 ruling, granting corporate businesses equal treatment to that afforded citizens. Such rulings would gain greater importance as oligopolistic consolidation advanced. By and large, the rising economic, political, and legislative influence of very large corporations could consider itself safe from adverse decisions, even during times of deep economic distress for the American people.[215] For the new technology oligopolies that emerged in the second half of the twentieth century, the trajectory of rulings would provide a formidable legal platform upon which to build up their power—and influence the judiciary, the regulatory, and the political apparatus.

The *Citizens United* ruling also practically disabled a 36-year ban on political contributions by federal contractors—a less noticed aspect with important implications for technology oligopolies.[216] Almost all tech oligopolies are engaged in federal contracting in multiple forms and benefit greatly from what

213 See Adam Winkler, "'Corporations are People' is Built on an Incredible 19th Century Lie: How a Farcical Series of Events in the 1880s Produced an Enduring and Controversial Legal Precedent," *The Atlantic*, March 5, 2018, www.theatlantic.com/; Alex Park, "10 Supreme Court Rulings—Before Hobby Lobby—that Turned Corporations into People," *Mother Jones*, July 10, 2014, www.motherjones.com/.

214 See Wikipedia, *Plessy v. Ferguson*, https://en.wikipedia.org/ (accessed June 6, 2022); Keith W. Medley, *We as Freemen: Plessy v. Ferguson* (Gretna: Pelican, 2003), chapters 1–3, 5, 7.

215 See Leuchtenburg, "When Franklin Roosevelt Clashed"; Federal Election Commission, *Court Cases*.

216 See Sophia Gonsalves-Brown, *Federal Contractors Continue to Ignore Contribution Ban and Donate to Super PACs*, Campaign Legal Center, October 28, 2020, https://campaignlegal.org/; Donald Shaw, "Government Contractors are Making Political Contributions, Despite Longstanding Ban: Federal Election Law Prohibits these Kinds of Donations Because of Concerns Over Pay-to-Play Contracting, but Contractors are Still Making Them—and the FEC is Not Actively Working to Stop Them," *Sludge*, March 20, 2019, https://readsludge.com/; Ian Duncan and Matea Gold, "Federal Contractors Donate to 'Super PAC' Backing Romney," *Los Angeles Times*, August 16, 2012, and their "Romney Backers Test a Ban on Donors: Federal Contractors Give to a 'Super PAC' Despite a Law Barring Such Activity," *Los Angeles Times*, March 19, 2012, www.latimes

are often the largest and most profitable awards. Revenues from such contracts can amount to billions over a short period of time and can affect awardees' stock market valuations significantly. Concerns about conflicts of interest, their corrosive influence, waste, corruption, and myriad other problems were thus largely cast aside—preparing the ground for future rulings that could further eliminate restrictions.

Along the trajectory of favorable judicial rulings, a federal appeals court case—the 2010 *SpeechNow.org v. Federal Election Commission*—eliminated spending limits for individuals set by the Federal Election Campaign Act.[217] Individuals donating to political advocacy organizations—independently from campaigns and political parties—were thus allowed to spend any amount to support or oppose any candidate. This complemented the influence of corporate political donations allowed by the Supreme Court's *Citizens United* ruling. Oligopolistic elites—the wealthiest one-half of one percent in American society—were thus freed to spend and compound the political influence of the corporations from which they derive their vast wealth.[218] As a result, the combined effect of these rulings substantially neutralized both the Election Campaign Act and F.E.C. oversight over elections spending.

The *SpeechNow.org* ruling added to an earlier Supreme Court decision—2007 *F.E.C. v. Wisconsin Right to Life Inc.*—in which the McCain–Feingold Act, passed by Congress in 2002 (also known as the Bipartisan Campaign Reform Act), was partially disabled.[219] In addition to restrictions on "soft" campaign money, the Act had prohibited 501(c)(4), 501(c)(5), and 501(c)(6) entities—non-profit organizations as coded by the Internal Revenue Service—from broadcasting any communication that contained a candidate's name within 60 days before a primary and 30 days prior to a general election.[220] Created to further "social welfare" and community affairs, these entities became involved in political activities, partly because of the Supreme Court's deregulation of

.com/; Wikipedia, *Federal Election Campaign Act*, https://en.wikipedia.org/ (accessed June 6, 2022).

217 See Federal Election Commission, *SpeechNow.org v. FEC* (accessed June 8, 2022), and its *Federal Election Campaign Laws*, 2019, www.fec.gov/. SpeechNow.org subsequently appealed to have the donor disclosure-and-identification requirement—left in place by the District Court decision—eliminated, but the Supreme Court declined to consider the request. See also Britannica, *SpeechNow.org v. Federal Election Commission*, www.britannica.com/ (accessed June 8, 2022).

218 See Beckwith, "Billionaires' Political Spending."

219 Federal Election Commission, *FEC v. Wisconsin Right to Life Inc.*, www.fec.gov/; Legal Information Institute, Cornell University, *Federal Election Commission v. Wisconsin Right to Life; McCain v. Wisconsin Right to Life*, www.law.cornell.edu/ (all accessed June 12, 2022).

220 Legal Information Institute, Cornell University, *Bipartisan Campaign Reform Act of 2002*, www.law.cornell.edu/; Wikipedia, *Bipartisan Campaign Reform Act*, https://en.wikipedia.org/ (both accessed June 13, 2022).

contributions and electoral oversight.[221] The combined effect of the Court's *Citizens United* and *SpeechNow.org* rulings—and the partial elimination of the McCain–Feingold Act—made it possible for corporate—most of all oligopolistic—power to deepen and extend their influence over politics.

Coordinating with PACs, many 501(c)-type organizations thus became more deeply involved in elections.[222] Technology oligopolies and their associated elites could donate substantial amounts to a 501(c) non-profit, with the benefit of tax deductibility—and then all or part of the donation could be given by the 501(c) entity to a PAC, to be spent to support chosen candidates or attack those considered unfavorable. This process can help conceal the identities of donors, as PACs may disclose only the 501(c) non-profits as sources of donations. The phrase "dark money in politics" is largely derived from the deployment of this scheme—an operation that the judiciary system enabled and preserves.[223] A sort of political donation identity laundering was thus set up—voters largely remaining ignorant about donors.

The 501(c)-type organizations and PACs are also active in judicial elections at the state and local levels. In over three-quarters of all U.S. states, trial and appellate court judges are elected—to occupy a judgeship or decide if appointees are retained.[224] Spending on these campaigns increased substantially during the past three decades, as money gained greater importance for the judiciary

221 Tax Exempt World, *501C Classifications*, www.taxexemptworld.com/; Internal Revenue Service, *Types of Tax Exempt Organizations, and its Types of Organizations Exempt Under 501(c)(4)*, www.irs.gov/ (all accessed June 13, 2022).

222 See Citizens for Truth, *PACs, Super PACs, and 501(c)4s*, https://citizensfortruth.wordpress.org/ (accessed June 13, 2022); Lee Fang, "Five 501(c)(4) Groups that Might Have Broken the Law: While the IRS was Scrutinizing Tea Party Groups, Other Organizations were Clearly Using the Majority of their Funds for Political Activity," *The Nation*, May 21, 2013, www.thenation.com/. See also Suarez-Villa, *Corporate Power, Oligopolies*, 68–69, 71–72, for a discussion of 501(c)-type organizations in lobbying.

223 See Brennan Center for Justice, New York University Law School, *Dark Money: Citizens United Unleashed Unlimited Spending in Our Elections, and Groups Can Now Spend Hundreds of Millions Without Disclosing their Sources of Funding*, www.brennancenter.org/ (accessed June 13, 2022); Mayer, *Dark Money*; Maya Miller, *How the IRS Gave Up Fighting Political Dark Money Groups*, ProPublica, 2019, www.propublica.org/; ProPublica, *Contributions to Top Dark Money Spenders*, 2017, htpps://projects.propublica.org/; Kurt Eichenwald, "The *Real* IRS Scandal that No One is Talking About," *Vanity Fair*, May 17, 2013, www.vanityfair.com/; Susan Pulliam and Brody Mullins, "Companies Discover Campaign-Finance Loophole: Some Funnel Money through Groups that Back Gubernatorial Candidates," *Wall Street Journal*, December 30, 2017, A1.

224 See Ballotpedia, *Judicial Election Methods by State*, https://ballotpedia.org/ (accessed June 13, 2022); Jeri Zeder, "Elected vs. Appointed? Shugerman Explores the History of Judicial Selection in the U.S.," *Harvard Law Today*, July 1, 2012, https://today.law.harvard.edu/; Joe Palazzolo, "More Judges Forced to Hit Campaign Trail: GOP Group Pours Money into Judicial Elections, Eroding Traditions under Which Jurists Could Avoid Electioneering," *Wall Street Journal*, October 13, 2014, A4.

system.[225] Tens of millions of dollars have been spent annually in a single judicial election cycle at the state and local levels—amounts that keep increasing with each cycle. This dynamic seems symptomatic of the fusion of interests of the judiciary system, the political apparatus, and oligopolistic corporate power. A fusion of interests, it seems appropriate to say, that is driven by money and the anthropomorphic attribution of constitutional rights to corporate entities—most of all oligopolies.

Further voidance of restrictions on corporate spending in elections came in a 2014 Supreme Court ruling—*McCutcheon, et al. v. Federal Election Commission*.[226] For technology oligopolistic power, this decision was highly favorable, as it eliminated limits on what the elites linked to tech oligopolies can contribute to all federal candidates and PACs. In so doing, the ruling helped set the stage for the so-called "super-PACs"—many of which are political fronts for corporate oligopolies and the wealthy elites connected to them.[227] Such organizations, with their vast amounts of money, donor anonymity, and unlimited contributions, can determine election outcomes.[228] And the amounts they have expended in recent times are much greater than the total spent by presidential candidates of both major parties.

The 2014 ruling also established the notion and precedent that the U.S. Congress cannot reduce the amount of money that goes into politics and that giving unlimited amounts to candidates cannot be considered to lead to corruption. "Ingratiation and access"—the Supreme Court ruling stated—that result from political contributions "are not corruption."[229] This decision complemented an earlier ruling—*Skilling v. United States* (2010)—that narrowed the definition of corruption and fraud in so-called "pay-to-play" cases, through which politicians receive contributions in tacit exchange for favors, legislation,

225 Brennan Center for Justice, New York University Law School, *Money in Judicial Elections*, www.brennancenter.org/; Scott Greytak, Alicia Bannon, Allyse Falce and Linda Casey, *Bankrolling the Bench: The New Politics of Judicial Elections, 2013–14*, Brennan Center for Justice, www.brennancenter.org/ (both accessed June 14, 2022).

226 Federal Election Commission, *McCutcheon, et al. v. FEC*, www.fec.gov/ (accessed June 7, 2022). See also Jess Bravin and Colleen M. Nelson, "Court Lifts Caps on Political Giving," *Wall Street Journal*, April 3, 2014, A1.

227 See Campaign Legal Center, *CLC Complaints Allege*; Wollner and National Journal, "10 Ways Super PACs and Campaigns Coordinate."

228 During the last decade, the Supreme Court prevented disclosure of donors' identities—staying a lower court's order that required the F.E.C. to come up with regulations to pursue this matter. See Andrew Duehren, "Campaign Spending: Roberts Stays Ruling on Disclosing Donors," *Wall Street Journal*, September 17, 2018, A4.

229 Federal Election Commission, *McCutcheon, et al. v. FEC*; Robert E. Mutch, *Campaign Finance: What Everyone Needs to Know* (New York: Oxford University Press, 2016), chapters 6–8; Bravin and Nelson, "Court Lifts Caps," A4. See also *Wall Street Journal* (editorial), "The Menendez Indictment," April 16, 2015, A14.

contracts, or appointments.[230] As a result, the Federal Election Commission was further disabled on its oversight of aspects that deal with electoral fairness and justice, while a heavier burden of proof was placed on the U.S. Department of Justice in political corruption cases.[231] The potential for vast inequality and imbalances that the rulings created were disregarded, along with the possibility that dozens of very wealthy donors—and the corporate oligopolies from which they derive their wealth—may practically decide who is elected to federal office (including the presidency of the United States).[232]

The 2010 *Skilling v. United States* ruling also favored technology oligopolistic power, as the narrower definition of malfeasance made it very difficult to win prosecutions in cases in which creative forms of corruption occur. Thus, attempting to prosecute an executive's provision of, say, a mansion or an aircraft to a politician for vacations that involves no payment of money—but which occurs in response to a favor, such as an intervention to prevent a regulatory inquiry—would likely fail.[233] More so if, in addition, the individuals involved have a longstanding acquaintance or friendship and there are no recorded transfers of money. As technology oligopolies are recipients of some of the largest contracts awarded by government, and are subject to antitrust inquiries—among other important actions—providing creative forms of payoffs will be more difficult to prosecute.

These important cases were accompanied by other judicial decisions that supported and extended oligopolistic power. Thus, Supreme Court rulings guided by the notion of corporate personhood that lifted limits on donations were complemented by lower court decisions against antitrust suits. One such decision involved tech-service oligopolist AT&T—at the time the largest combined telecommunication–entertainment corporation—and its acquisition of the (also-oligopolistic) media and entertainment company Time Warner for $80 billion (2017 dollars).[234]

The decision of the federal judge who ruled in favor of AT&T was based on very narrow perceptions of consumer welfare and vertical consolidation. Conceptually, the ruling followed jurist Robert Bork's 1970s ideas on

230 U.S. Department of Justice, *Skilling v. United States-Brief (Merits)*, www.justice.gov/; Legal Information Institute, Cornell University, *Skilling v. United States*, www.law.cornell.edu/ (both accessed June 8, 2022).

231 See Shaw, "Government Contractors"; Mutch, *Campaign Finance*, chapters 6–7; Legal Information Institute, *Skilling v. United States*; *Wall Street Journal*, "Menendez Indictment."

232 A point made shortly before the 2014 Supreme Court ruling by Kenneth P. Vogel in his *Big Money* (New York: Public Affairs, 2014), chapters 6, 7, 9. See also Mutch, *Campaign Finance*, Chapter 6.

233 See *Wall Street Journal*, "Menendez Indictment."

234 See Brent Kendall and Drew FitzGerald, "AT&T Beats U.S. in Antitrust Fight: Judge Backs $80 Billion Time Warner Deal as Media Companies Eye Wave of Consolidation," *Wall Street Journal*, June 13, 2018, A1; *Wall Street Journal* (editorial), "Justice's Antitrust Humiliation," June 13, 2018, A14. Symptomatic of lax antitrust enforcement—and the difficulties of pursuing cases in court—40 years had passed since the Justice Department attempted to stop a vertical merger.

consumer welfare as the sole and exclusive concern of antitrust action.[235] In line with Bork's thinking, a merger that results in greater vertical integration was assumed to be harmless to consumer welfare.[236] The ruling's static, narrow orientation ignored the dynamic interplay of vertical and horizontal integration after mergers and the fact that the fusion of new technologies in media and telecommunication render differences between one and the other practically meaningless—insofar as consumer welfare is concerned. Thus, the reality that what seems to be a vertical merger will actually turn out to be horizontal one (or both)—when such aspects as bundling, entry barriers, network extent, market segment domination, emphasis on wants contrivance and sales in place of research, and data appropriation are taken into account—was ignored.

In AT&T's vast oligopolistic domain, as the boundary between its services increasingly blurs, what might seem beneficial to consumers in one market niche can be prejudicial in another. Greater bundling of services—a result of the merger—would contribute to this panorama and would most likely diminish consumer welfare as pricing power increases. Thus, to use the static view of vertical integration and the straitjacket of consumer welfare—both improperly and inadequately cast to begin with—to guide the decision seemed erroneous. The ruling gave approval to one of the largest mergers ever, with the consequent effect that future antitrust actions that might be pursued may likely be crippled or abandoned—as judiciary power marches in lockstep with precedent and the interests of oligopolistic power.

Perhaps then, it should not surprise that three years after the merger's approval, AT&T spun out Time Warner to gain even greater power—by acquiring one of the largest content providers, Discovery (also oligopolistic). This allowed AT&T to further bundle multiple services and enlarge the vast oligopolistic power it acquired through the ruling.[237] This acquisition could thus count on the inaction of antitrust regulators, given their prior defeat. And, as for consumer welfare, it would most likely be further damaged as bundling incorporates new services under AT&T's vast data cloud, its far-reaching platform, and its more powerful control over pricing.

235 Bork, *Antitrust Paradox*, chapters 5, 6; Bork and Sidak, "Chicago School." For a critique of the focus on consumer welfare for antitrust actions see Tim Wu's *The Curse of Bigness: Antitrust in the New Gilded Age* (New York: Columbia Global Reports, 2018), chapters 4–6.

236 Bork, *Antitrust Paradox*, chapters 10, 11; Steven Pearlstein, "How Judge Leon Blew It with U.S. v. AT&T," *Washington Post*, June 15, 2018, www.washingtonpost.com/; Brent Kendall, "DOJ's Behind-the-Scenes Struggles with Judge in AT&T Case," *Wall Street Journal*, August 8, 2018, www.wsj.com/.

237 See Lauren Feiner, "AT&T Battled the DoJ to Buy Time Warner, Only to Spin It Out Again Three Years Later," *CNBC*, May 17, 2021, www.cnbc.com/; Grace Dean and Claire Atkinson, "AT&T is Combining Warner Media with Discovery to Create a New Streaming Giant," *Business Insider*, May 17, 2021, www.businessinsider.com/

The apparatus of power of technology oligopoly capitalism is complex and fragmented. It draws legitimacy from a desire for novelty and efficiency that we believe will improve our condition. In a sort of Faustian bargain, we seem to have acquiesced to its deployment of practices that exploit most everything we do and trounce some of our most cherished values. And so we tolerate deleterious conduct, such as its co-respective pricing power, its compulsion for consolidation, the penchant to concoct entry barriers and walled patios, its diminishment of research by wants contrivance schemes, and its appropriation of our data identities and creative endeavors.

The systemic power of technology oligopoly capitalism co-opts the most important organs of governance, diminishing their legitimacy. And such co-optation now seems deep-seated and expansive. A judiciary system that confers anthropomorphic qualities and the rights of citizens to corporate organizations, a political system ever more dependent on money, legislation tailored to favor oligopolies, a legalization of corrupt practices, revolving-door appointments that skew regulation and build subservience, and the institutionalization of lobbying to preserve its privileges—all of these seem to be part of the Faustian bargain that sustains its power.

These features call on us to comprehend the larger processes and phenomena that make it possible for this reality to exist and to be imposed on us. The following chapters will provide a panoramic vision of those processes and their place in the sustenance of technology oligopoly capitalism. The accumulation of capital—the topic of the next chapter—is of vital importance, as it generates the means for its power to be deployed and reproduced. It also generates fateful contradictions, raising questions about how long the Faustian bargain can be sustained.

Chapter 3

Accumulation

Technology oligopolies are sustained by a dynamic accumulation of capital grounded in social notions of value and power. Understanding the market domains where power is deployed and value is appropriated is vital for our journey through the labyrinths of technology oligopoly capitalism. Consideration of these domains will be part of the agenda for this chapter—supported by systemic insights and numerous examples on contemporary trends and events from recent decades.

Control over multiple market domains has made technology oligopolies the most powerful corporate entities of our time. Their accumulation of capital and their market reach are unprecedented, with implications that are still largely unknown. Understanding the accumulative dynamic of technology oligopolies—and the relations of power it encompasses—is necessary, if we are to grasp the myriad effects of this most important phenomenon of our time.

Value

Capital accumulation fundamentally depends on the generation of value. A most characteristic form of value in capitalism is *commodity value*—that which accrues to any product, tangible or not, whenever it is created to be sold or exchanged. A commodity acquires *exchange value* through the social dimension—the human labor expended, the interaction of buyers and sellers, the social relations embedded in transactions, and the asymmetries of power involved. Exchange values are thus variable and depend on the terms of exchange at any given place and time.[1]

The *use value* of a commodity depends on its socially necessary utility. Use value can be considered a depository of exchange value, in the sense that it

1 The variable character of exchange value was noted by Marx as "a quantitative relation, as the proportion in which values in use of one sort are exchanged for those of another sort, a relation constantly changing with time and place." Karl Marx, *Capital: A Critique of Political Economy*, F. Engels, ed. (New York: International Publishers, 1974; orig. publ. Hamburg: Verlag von Otto Meissner, 1867), Vol. I, 36.

DOI: 10.4324/9781003345893-3

embeds the terms of exchange through which the use or utility of a commodity is acquired. Use values are the real source of wealth, inasmuch as they are based on need.[2] Thus, whereas exchange value is subject to the vagaries of market supply and demand—or the manipulation of pricing—use value represents an objective need that must be fulfilled. Use value and exchange value are both fundamentally rooted in human labor—a crucial aspect that is often lost sight of in analyses of technology.[3]

An important feature of oligopoly capitalism is that it distorts exchange value—and, implicitly, the accumulative dynamic—through the manipulation of markets. This involves setting the terms of exchange to benefit the corporate entities in control. Perceptions of use value are also distorted under oligopolistic power, as unnecessary wants are contrived to induce unnecessary purchases. The spread of consumerism during the past 80 years—a consequence of oligopoly capitalism—provides ample evidence of this distortion. The rift between use value and exchange value that results from these distortions is harmful not only to human society but also to nature. One of the consequences is waste. Waste on an unprecedented scale, that now threatens nature and all forms of life on Earth.

Commodity Value

Distortions of valorization under oligopoly capitalism extend to our understanding of the relationship between commodity value and technology. Non-human forms of life, inanimate substances, and elements—many of which are very important for technology—become commodities by acquiring value in the capitalist accumulation dynamic. Usage, necessity, and market exchange are instrumental for determining such value. But commodity value ultimately depends on human

2 "Use values become a reality by use or consumption: they constitute the substance of all wealth, whatever may be the social form of that wealth.... They are, in addition, the material depositories of exchange value." Marx, *Capital*, Vol. I, 36.

3 "As use values, commodities are, above all, of different qualities, but as exchange values they are merely different quantities.... If then we leave out of consideration the use value of commodities, they have only one common property left, that of being products of labor." Marx, *Capital*, Vol. I, 37–38. With technology, as in other aspects of the economy, labor can be seen to represent use value for the capitalist that employs it, whereas for the worker her toil becomes mere exchange value—in the sense that she sells it for money or a wage (itself a result of exchange value from the commodity she produced). This is a fine point discussed by Marx that explores the juxtaposition of use value and exchange value, when the interests of labor and capitalist employers are taken into account—see his *Grundrisse: Foundations of the Critique of Political Economy* (New York: Penguin, 1973; based on writings in seven notebooks drafted in 1857–58), 306. The fundamentally important *qualitative* dimension of value and its roots in labor is an aspect that must be kept in mind throughout this discussion. For incisive discussions on this aspect, and its relationship with capital accumulation and technical change, see David Laibman, *Value, Technical Change and Crisis: Explorations in Marxist Economic Theory* (New York: Sharpe, 1992), chapters 1, 2.

labor—a fundamental factor needed to transform commodities into products. This applies to products created through automated processes, as human intervention is required for the latter to be created in the first place.

In many cases, inanimate substances, non-human life, and natural elements also become commodities as inputs to research activities. Many components of nature, however, never become commodities—and thus have no economic value—but are nonetheless thought to be valuable for other reasons. This involves *intrinsic value*—the perceived significance of any form of life, substance, or element, in and of itself.

Intrinsic value may thus be considered independent of commodity value. A perception of intrinsic value for any form of life, inanimate substance, or natural element may occur, for example, because of its contribution to nature, its association with human history, or for esthetic reasons. Such perceptions can be disengaged from any assessment of exchange value. Intrinsic value may thus be perceived in the absence of capitalist accumulation (or of capitalism itself). Technology, however, has long been assumed to result from human labor, with use value and exchange value mediating its role in the accumulative dynamic.

Technology may thus be considered anthropocentric—as human labor and social relations are always posited to be at the core of motives for its existence. Technology—even when it affects nature very negatively—thus ends up being perceived through the filter of humanity. This has been characteristic of views on most everything technological since the first written accounts. And oligopoly capitalism has magnified this perception greatly, through consumerism. These considerations may explain why some authors consider the value of nature—as provider of resources to human labor and capital accumulation—to have been sorely neglected.[4]

Such neglect may also be explained by the fact that non-human forms of life lack three fundamental attributes needed to create and deploy technology. Consideration of these attributes is typically missing from discussions on the value of nature.[5] The capacity to use creativity in a way that transcends the

4 See Jason W. Moore, *Capitalism in the Web of Life: Ecology and the Accumulation of Capital* (New York: Verso, 2015); Raj Patel and Jason W. Moore, *A History of the World in Seven Cheap Things: A Guide to Capitalism, Nature, and the Future of the Planet* (Oakland: University of California Press, 2018); Paul Hawken, Amory B. Lovins and L. Hunter Lovins, *Natural Capitalism: Creating the Next Industrial Revolution* (New York: Earthscan, 2010); Robert Costanza, Ralph D'Arge, Rudolf de Groot, Stephen Farber, *et al.*, "The Value of the World's Ecosystem Services and Natural Capital," *Nature*, 387 (1997), 253–60.

5 This includes approaches that downplay the importance of human labor and that in some ways attempt to deconstruct the Marxian labor theory of value. Perceptions of "work" by non-human life forms, inanimate substances, or elements (energy, gases, water, biochemicals) have been posited to be of equal (or greater) importance than human labor. This has led to components of nature being considered "nature capital" because of their contribution to capitalist accumulation—much as some neoclassical economists and neoliberal advocates decades ago started to think of humans as a form

subject's immediate existential need is the first attribute. A vital aspect of technology is to consciously and deliberately generate effects that extend beyond the immediate needs of the creator, such that other species and populations may benefit. This allows others to improve techniques, in ways that can add to their utility. And new discoveries based on a known technique can further cumulate effects, as they are applied through the social milieu.

A second missing attribute involves the capacity to engage in transactions using monetary means. This is essential for generating exchange value. It is also vital for technology, as exchange value is crucial for determining economic importance. Exchange thus reflects human relations and the social division of labor. And markets are, after all, a human invention. Neither markets nor the use of money have been found to be part of non-human ecologies.

The third missing attribute is the capacity to entertain notions of fairness—beyond the subject's own specific need to benefit or survive. This involves conscious decisions that take into account the wellbeing of other species or populations. Questions of fairness and justice, broadly conceived, are very important in the diffusion of technology. They condition exclusion and privilege and are at the core of programs devised to remedy unjust effects.

The expenditure of energy in nature—by any non-human life form—cannot substitute for these attributes. Nor can it bring them into existence. Neither can any commodity-based pricing of such life forms. Nor, for that matter, can conceiving them to be a form of capital. Despite millions of years of adaptation, evolution seems to have been incapable of generating the three previously mentioned attributes in non-human organisms.

The distortion of value under oligopoly capitalism—and especially the rift between use value and exchange value, and its effect on nature—has thus led to a misunderstanding of the difference between commodity value *and* intrinsic value.[6] The latter does not preclude the former, as many commodities are perceived to have intrinsic value before or after they are transformed—even

---

of capital, regarding innovation and technology. Thus, the term "human capital" was concocted—a contradiction in terms that has become common in some circles. John Bellamy Foster's incisive critique of the "nature capital" approach in his *Ecology against Capitalism* (New York: Monthly Review Press, 2002), and his "Value Isn't Everything," *Monthly Review*, November 2018, 1–17, provides many important insights in this regard. See also Paul Burkett, *Marxism and Ecological Economics: Toward a Red and Green Political Economy* (Leiden: Brill, 2006). In some respects, positing nature as the source of *all* value—leading to the notion of nature capital—is reminiscent of the physiocrats and their view of land as the source of all economic value. Karl Marx's nineteenth-century critique of that approach seems quite relevant in this regard—see his *Theories of Surplus Value* (New York: Prometheus, 2000), chapter II, "The Physiocrats," 44–68.

6 A confusion of intrinsic value with commodity value in the environmental literature—related to current notions about "nature capital"—has been traced to the early 1970s and the emergence of the environmental movement in the United States. See Foster's *Ecology against Capitalism* and his "Value Isn't Everything," 2. In some respects, the "nature capital" approach—like the "human capital" conception of earlier decades—seems oriented (consciously or not) to validate (or even motivate) the

as they forsake their natural condition. But the value of a commodity under capitalism depends on necessity, human labor, and the social relations through which work, technology, and exchange occur. Economic necessity, use value, and exchange value are, unfortunately, all too often extraneous to intrinsic value—as perceptions of the latter tend to transcend the actual or potential worth of the former.

Product Markets

Product markets have been the most important historical locus of capital accumulation. They have also provided the setting where goods are priced and where pricing power is imposed. The interplay of supply and demand is, after all, largely a result of product market pricing. And, the question of whether competitive or oligopolistic conditions exist is all too often decided in the context of product markets.

Competition

An overview of oligopolistic accumulation must necessarily start with a competitive product market scenario. Competitive conditions are the standard presumption of mainstream (neoclassical) economic theory, and they provide the platform upon which its concepts are built. Mainstream economic analyses typically assume that competitive conditions are highly desirable—regardless of the context or economic activity. And, practically every major policy measure taken by the mainstream economic technocracy during the past one hundred years has been founded on the need for competitive market conditions to exist. Such assumptions also apply to technology, as competitive markets are typically thought to provide the impetus for its creation and use.

The assumption of "perfect" competition—unrealistic as it is—has for so long been built into economic models that it is impossible to disassociate it from their workings. This wide-ranging belief in competitive market conditions as the "normal" state of affairs is a legacy of the early era of industrial capitalism—the late eighteenth and the first half of the nineteenth centuries—when classical economics emerged and competition in the nascent industries was apparent. That stage of capitalism—grounded in the new technologies created during the Industrial Revolution—was marked by limited enterprise size and market power.[7]

---

conquest of a new frontier—the larger panorama of nature in this case—for finance and oligopoly capitalism.

7 See Eric J. Hobsbawm, *The Age of Capital: 1848–75* (London: Weidenfeld and Nicolson, 1975), chapters 2, 3, 12; Joan Robinson, *The Economics of Imperfect Competition* (London: Macmillan, 1934), Chapter 27; Michel Beaud, *A History of Capitalism, 1500–2000* (New York: Monthly Review Press, 1983).

One keen observer of the economic and social changes taking place at that time was Karl Marx. The changes were, by and large, grounded in the role of capital as a new—and very important—element of economic and social transformation. Marx's understanding of those changes placed the process of capital accumulation—and the social, economic and political power it generated—at the center of the new era.[8] His conceptualization of capital as a prime social, economic and political resource was both novel and revolutionary, and it would stand the test of time as capitalism evolved and new economic activities emerged.

In Marx's presentation of the accumulative dynamic of capitalism, three phases were considered, involving (i) the use of money-capital to acquire commodities, (ii) the transformation—through production—of the acquired commodities into new commodities, and (iii) the exchange of the new commodities into new money-capital.[9] These phases, working together systemically, were at the core of the new era that Marx sought to decipher, and they provided a platform for his critical insights. In his view, production took center stage in the accumulative dynamic, becoming the prime and indispensable enabler of capital formation. Without the continuous re-initiation and completion of the three linked phases—the *productive cycle*—the accumulative dynamic of capitalism could not be sustained.

Each iteration of the accumulative dynamic would have to generate sufficient new money-capital, such that the productive cycle can be completed. This scenario can be represented as:

$$M \rightarrow C \rightarrow C' \rightarrow M' \text{ where } M' = M + \Delta m$$

—with M as initial money-capital, C the initial commodity (purchased with M), C′ the new commodity (a product or service) created through transformation of the initial commodity C (involving production), and M′ the new

8 See Marx, *Grundrisse*, 140–53.

9 Marx, *Capital*, Vol. I, Part II, Chapter IV: "The General Formula for Capital," 146–55; Vol. I, Part VII, "The Accumulation of Capital," chapters XXIII–XXV, 566–647; and Vol. II, Part I, Chapter I, "The Circuit of Money-Capital," 23–62. Marx mainly used the term *transformation* to refer to the *conversion* of labor effort (or labor power) embodied in a commodity—produced through the relations of production in phase (ii)—*into* new money-capital through market exchange—encompassed in phase (iii). It is noteworthy that Marx used the term in the context of competitive market conditions, as oligopolies had *not* yet arisen as a significant factor in his time. *In this book, the term transformation will be used to refer to the second phase*—a topic that will be addressed in the following chapter. This modification seems justified, given the expanded scope of the relations of production in oligopolistic technology corporations—that can encompass *not only manufacturing but also research, product development, intangibles such as intellectual property, and myriad service activities.* The fact that market exchange under oligopolistic conditions acquires a very different character from that of a competitive scenario adds another level of complication. And, the relatively recent emergence of finance, and of financial market speculation, as a major endeavor of many technology oligopolies further complicates this panorama.

money-capital (or total exchange value) acquired through sales of C′. *Surplus value*, Δm, denotes the monetary equivalent of *surplus labor* obtained by the capitalist—above and beyond what is required to allow workers to regenerate their capacity for labor.

Surplus value remains with the capitalist after new money-capital (M′) is obtained and all costs [embedded in initial money-capital (M)]—labor, input supplies, production, distribution, market exchange—are covered.[10] Surplus value is thus often considered equivalent to profit, although conceptually it involves a range of aspects that are typically excluded by mechanistic notions of profitability. For our purposes, *surplus labor*—the basis of surplus value (Δm)—will be considered *uncompensated labor*. This is of fundamental importance, for without it capitalists can neither enrich themselves nor expand the productive cycle in the competitive market scenario.

For the productive cycle to expand, surplus value must increase with each iteration, and part (or all) of the increase must be reinvested to raise the quantum of initial money-capital in the productive cycle.[11] This is crucial for an expansion of output that can, in turn, lead to a larger quantum of new money-capital. This schematic presentation, simple as it is, encapsulates the basic components of the accumulative dynamic and provides a starting point for our journey into the realm of accumulation. It will be brought up again later—to consider oligopolistic power in various market domains.

It seems easy to assume that surplus value is solely derived from new money-capital, since the capitalist obtains it through the exchange value of the new commodity (C′) produced. However, the root of surplus value is to be found in the use of labor in production (embedded in C→C′). This is an important point that can be traced to the work of some of the best-known late eighteenth- and early nineteenth-century thinkers.[12] Classical economists before Marx's time—most prominently Adam Smith and David Ricardo—considered

10 The cost of external financing to support or expand production may also be placed among the costs included in initial money-capital (M). Future debt repayment obligations will thus likely reduce the level of new money-capital (M′) available to restart a productive cycle.

11 Although it is possible that external financing—in the form of debt, sale of stock, or investment from other parties—might make up for any shortfalls in surplus value over the short term. The frequent repetition of this recourse would be unsustainable over the medium or long term, however, as mounting debt or the inability to provide returns to shareholders and investors—coupled with surplus value shortfalls—would render the enterprise insolvent. The latter (or its likelihood) often leads to acquisitions or mergers among technology companies (a topic addressed in the previous chapter).

12 The work of political economists dating from the late seventeenth century—in Britain—along with Pierre L. P. de Boisguillebert and Jean C. L. de Sismondi in France must be noted. A critical discussion of contributions from that period can be found in Ronald L. Meek's *Studies in the Labour Theory of Value* (London: Lawrence and Wishart, 1973)—specifically the chapters "Value Theory Before Adam Smith," "Adam Smith and the Development of the Labour Theory," and "David Ricardo and the Development of the Labour Theory."

labor to be not only the main element of production but, fundamentally, the source of value in capitalism.[13]

Writing on this matter, Smith stated that "labour, not money, is the true measure of value"—adding that the "labour of every nation is the fund which originally supplies it with all the necessaries and conveniences of life which it ... consumes."[14] On market value, Smith added: "labour ... is the real measure of the exchangeable value of all commodities."[15] These thoughts on labor's fundamental importance were affirmed by prominent philosophers of the time, among them John Locke, who stated that labor "puts the difference of value on everything," adding that "of the products of the earth useful to the life of man, nine-tenths are the effects of labour."[16]

Capital and Labor

These views were grounded on the premise that capital cannot be accumulated without labor, whereas labor can exist and produce without capital—as any examination of human history doubtlessly revealed. Labor had, since the earliest times, been engaged in production and the fulfillment of needs without capital—crafting goods and using skills to exchange for other necessary goods and skills. Moreover, labor costs—since the beginnings of industrial capitalism—were the most important cost component of production for most economic activities—a condition that has largely prevailed up to our time and that applies to technology production.

13 The work of Adam Smith is particularly important, regarding his understanding of labor's contribution—see his *An Inquiry into the Nature and Causes of the Wealth of Nations* (Glasgow: Strahan and Caddell, 1776), Part I, chapters "Of the Component Parts of the Price of Commodities," "Of the Natural and Market Price of Commodities," "Of the Wages of Labour," and "Of Wages and Profit in the Different Employments of Labour and Stock." See also David Ricardo's *On the Principles of Political Economy and Taxation* (London: Murray, 1817), chapters "On Value," "On Natural and Market Price," "On Wages," and "Value and Riches, their Distinctive Properties." Karl Marx, in particular, defined classical economics with reference to political economists who had analyzed labor and the relations of production—see his *Capital*, Vol. I, Parts III through V (on surplus value), his *Grundrisse*, "Theories of Surplus Value," 549–602, and Section 3, on the transformation of surplus value into profit, 745–78. Important shortcomings of their work were—in Marx's view—their failure to consider the difference between exchange value *and* use value, the systemic character of labor exploitation, and the relations of power between workers and capitalists.

14 The first quotation is from Adam Smith, *Lectures on Justice, Police, Revenue, and Arms: Delivered in the University of Glasgow*, Edwin Canaan, ed. (Oxford: Clarendon Press, 1896)—the contents of this work are often referred to as the "Glasgow Lectures" and were published on the basis of notes taken in 1763, during a course given by Smith. The second quotation is from his *Wealth of Nations*, Part I, 1.

15 Smith, *Wealth of Nations*, Part I, 32.

16 John Locke, *An Essay Concerning the True Original Extent and End of Civil Government* (Boston: Edes and Gill, 1773), 137.

The fundamentally important role of labor in classical economics would later be ignored—and in various ways repudiated—by the early neoclassical economists in the second half of the nineteenth century, when they re-conceptualized economics by adopting assumptions based on individual mental calculation—with an exclusive focus on self-interest.[17] This emphasis on individual calculation eventually paved the way for neoclassical economics' tacit validation of oligopolistic power—and the misguided interpretations of "competition" that have persisted to this day.[18] The neoclassical approach thus largely involved a disregard of the larger social panorama, the relations of production, and labor's role in them—placing pure personal self-interest, and to a great extent mathematical esthetics, at the center of their economic vision.

Neoclassical economists' disregard of labor's fundamental importance in capitalism seems to have been largely driven by fear of the rising social awareness of labor injustice and by growing interest in Karl Marx's work during the second half of the nineteenth century and thereafter. Their efforts to legitimize the belief that economics should be solely concerned with individual self-interest—disregarding considerations of social justice and exploitation—went so far as to engineer the creation and award of Nobel prizes in economics.[19] Marx's

17 The work of Jevons, Menger, and Walras must be taken into account in this regard—see William S. Jevons, *A General Mathematical Theory of Political Economy* (London: Royal Statistical Society, 1862); Carl Menger, *Principles of Economics* (Auburn: Von Mises Institute, 1976; orig. publ. 1871); Léon Walras, *Elements d'Économie Politique Pure* (Lausanne: Rouge, 1896; orig. publ. 1874). See also Eugen Böhm-Bawerk and William Smart, *The Positive Theory of Capital* (London: Macmillan, 1891), and Vilfredo Pareto's *Cours d'Economie Politique* (Geneva: Droz, 1896), for elaborations of this approach. A contemporary critical analysis of this panorama can be found in Jonathan Aldred, *Licence to be Bad: How Economics Corrupted Us* (London: Allen Lane, 2019). A broad, comparative perspective on the neoclassical approach may be found in Richard D. Wolff and Stephen A. Resnick, *Contending Economic Theories: Neoclassical, Keynesian, and Marxian* (Cambridge, MA: MIT Press, 2012), chapters 1, 2, 5, 7.

18 Despite occasional assertions on the importance of competitive pricing by some of the best-known advocates of neoclassical precepts. Friedrich Hayek, for example, asserted that "the price system will fulfill its function only if competition prevails, that is, if the individual producer has to adapt himself to price changes and cannot control them," in his *The Road to Serfdom* (Chicago: University of Chicago Press, 1944), 49.

19 The creation of the Riksbank (Swedish Central Bank) Nobel Prize in 1969—unconnected as it was to the Nobel endowment, but nonetheless using its name—was particularly important in this regard. Awards over the years have overwhelmingly favored neoclassical economic ideology—in particular those who find ways to extend its ideo-theoretical apparatus. The contributions of scholars (such as Joan Robinson, John Kenneth Galbraith, and Paul Sweezy) who questioned (or were at least skeptical of) the new order that oligopolistic consolidation was imposing were thus ignored. The approach taken by the Riksbank Nobel selection committees was allegedly orchestrated by a conservative economist—Assar Lindbeck—who apparently sought to legitimize economists who had ideological perspectives close to his. His *The Political Economy of the New Left: An Outsider's View* (New York: Harper and Row, 1971) reflected that agenda. The Riksbank Nobel thus came to be seen by many as an award that—with few exceptions—would reward those who contributed to legitimize neoclassical economic ideology and, indirectly, oligopolistic power. Perhaps then, it

ideas, in contrast, drew on the work of classical economists such as Smith and Ricardo, but in a critical way, while (in consonance with their work) placing labor at the center of the emerging era that he sought to analyze.[20] In his analyses, Marx understood surplus value to be the rightful claim of labor in the context of capitalist accumulation. Surplus value was, in his view, appropriated by the capitalist—a *systemic* feature of the new era and a root cause of the panorama of social injustice.

Marx therefore saw the surplus appropriated by the capitalist as a direct result of uncompensated labor obtained from workers—*above and beyond what was necessary to sustain their capacity for labor.*[21] Regenerating labor's capacity for work was considered essential to sustain accumulation—a matter that capitalists had to undertake to preserve their power and wealth. Without such sustenance—in the form of wages that could provide sufficient nutrition, health care, housing, and the like—the productive cycle could not be adequately sustained. Nonetheless, in Marx's time, insufficient compensation to support basic, day-to-day needs was the norm—accompanied by high labor turnover and large numbers of unemployed.[22]

Surplus value has often been regarded as synonymous with profit in the competitive capitalist enterprise. Marx, however, drew an important conceptual distinction between the two—based on the relations of production between capitalists and labor.[23] Estimating surplus value without taking into account its root cause—the uncompensated surplus labor obtained from workers—seemed incomplete and unjust, a point that has been taken up by progressive and radical thinkers since the late eighteenth century.

Unfortunately, in our time, this aspect has been largely ignored by neoclassical economic theory, as it is assumed (more or less automatically) that profit is the sole outcome of product sales. Thus, the relations of production involving

should not surprise that among the early winners of the prize were the most important economic advisors and supporters of the Pinochet military regime in Chile—one of the bloodiest dictatorships in Latin American history.

20 Historical perspectives were lost as the neoclassical paradigm took over the field of economics in the mid-twentieth century—most notably after the 1970s, when economics departments in American universities practically expelled economic historians and those who critically challenged the neoclassical dogma. For a critique of multiple aspects of this panorama, see Michael Perelman, *Railroading Economics: The Creation of the Free Market Mythology* (New York: Monthly Review Press, 2006), "Introduction" and chapters 1, 2, 8.

21 Marx, *Capital*, Vol. I, Part III, "The Production of Absolute Surplus Value," Chapters IX, X, 212–302.

22 See Friedrich Engels, *The Condition of the Working Class in England in 1844*, F. Kelley, trans. (New York: Lovell, 1887).

23 Marx, *Capital*, Vol. III, Chapter III, "The Relation of the Rate of Profit to the Rate of Surplus-Value," 49–69. Meek, in his *Labour Theory*, quotes Marx on this aspect: "profit is ... that disguise of surplus-value which must be removed before the real nature of surplus-value can be discovered. In the surplus-value, the relation between capital and labour is laid bare," 187.

labor—as the source of value—and surplus value are missed. This state of affairs seems to have been the dream (if not the objective) of the early neoclassical economists, who wanted profit to be seen as purely an outcome of market demand and supply.[24]

Another consideration is the likelihood that surplus value may be null at some point in time—a possible outcome in competitive scenarios. In such cases, the uncompensated surplus labor would have nonetheless been obtained by the capitalist. This aspect can be missed whenever surplus labor is considered exclusively as an outcome of market exchange rather than as a function of the relations of production.[25] A non-monetary outlook has thus been adopted by some authors, to try to overcome this problem. Thinking of surplus labor in terms of worktime and skills deployment can provide an alternative to the monetary valorization of surplus value, conceptually and empirically—a matter that will be discussed in the following chapter.

In the competitive accumulative dynamic, surplus value is crucial in deciding whether an increase in the magnitude of production (relative to the prior cycle) might occur. Declining levels of surplus value can thus constrain—and eventually jeopardize—the accumulative dynamic, leading to a reduction in the initial money-capital available to restart the productive cycle.[26] Economic crises and recessions can result from—and also trigger—such declines, because of the lack of pricing power for the capitalist in the competitive market scenario. The relationship between surplus value and market pricing power is therefore of great importance in deciding the sustainability of the accumulative dynamic.

Thus, surplus value can be considered a critical component of capitalist accumulation under competitive market conditions—an aspect that changes remarkably under oligopoly, as will be discussed shortly. It must also be noted that—in the competitive scenario—the lack of pricing power makes it impossible to cut production in order to sustain market prices in the face of lower demand—as doing so would only depress further the level of surplus value obtained. The

24 See Meek, *Labour Theory*, 204–11.

25 See Michael Heinrich, *Die Wissenschaft vom Wert* (Münster: Westfälisches Dampfboot, 1999), 232, and the critique in Christian Fuchs, *Digital Labour and Karl Marx* (New York: Routledge, 2014), 45.

26 Three possibilities can be considered regarding the reproduction of capital in the accumulative dynamic. The first one is the case of *simple reproduction*, in which initial money-capital (M) remains constant—compared to the prior iteration. In this case, the magnitude of new-money capital (M′) obtained would remain the same as before. Simple reproduction, if repeated, would translate into stagnant accumulative cycles. The second possibility is *expanded reproduction*, involving an increment in initial money-capital compared to the prior iteration. In this case, all or part of the surplus value obtained would be reinvested—thus increasing M—leading to an expansion of the accumulative cycle. See Marx, *Capital*, Vol. I, Part VII, "The Accumulation of Capital," 564–712. The third possibility—*contracted reproduction*—implies a declining level of M relative to the prior cycle. This situation is most commonly associated with crises, as occurs when economies enter a period of cyclical decline—see, for example, Ernest Mandel, *Long Waves of Capitalist Development* (Cambridge: Cambridge University Press, 1980), chapters 3, 4.

result is a tendency for surplus value to experience a long-term decline toward nullity in the competitive market scenario, a point elaborated by Marx in his declining rate of profit concept.[27] Eliminating this fundamental feature of a competitive market economy—the lack of pricing power of capitalist producers—may therefore be considered a very important motive for oligopoly formation.

Early in the second half of the nineteenth century, tendencies toward larger enterprise scale and consolidation in some industrial sectors began to emerge—a trend that did not escape Marx's attention.[28] Marx posited that further consolidation would eventually gain ground, as pricing power through larger size and greater market control would be used to increase capital accumulation. His prescient observation—unique among economic and social theorists of that time—would become all too realistic toward the end of the nineteenth century, when natural resource-based monopolies emerged.

Accumulation and Pricing

Capitalist accumulation would thus become associated with pricing power over markets—as eliminating competition led to larger surpluses, wealthier corporate elites, and

27 Marx, *Capital*, Vol. III, Part III, "The Law of the Tendency of the Rate of Profit to Fall," 211–66. The assumption of the long-term tendency of profits to decline rests—in the competitive scenario—on all other aspects remaining equal (the *ceteris paribus* assumption commonly used in economic theory).

28 Marx's discussion on the "centralization" of capital—in *Capital*, Vol. I, Part VII, Chapter XXV, Section 2, 621–27—noting its tendency to be "stronger than ever before"—is revealing in this regard. Elaborating on this point, he argued that "capital can grow into powerful masses in a single hand because there it has been withdrawn from many individual hands. In any given branch of industry centralisation would reach its extreme limit if all the individual capitals invested in it were fused into a single capital. In a given society the limit would be reached only when the entire social capital was united in the hands of either a single capitalist or a single capitalist company" (Marx, *Capital*, Vol. I, Part IV, Chapter XV, Section 6, 441). Noting the relationship between "centralization" and accumulation, and the tendency toward acquisitions and mergers, Marx added: "centralisation completes the work of accumulation by enabling industrial capitalists to extend the scale of their operations. Whether this latter result is the consequence of accumulation or centralisation, whether centralisation is accomplished by the violent method of annexation—when certain capitals become such preponderant centres of attraction for others that they shatter the individual cohesion of the latter and then draw the separate fragments to themselves—whether the fusion of a number of capitals already formed or in process of formation takes place by the smoother process of organising joint-stock companies, the economic effect remains the same" (Marx, *Capital*, Vol. I, Part IV, Chapter XV, Section 6, 441). Marx's statements were prescient, given that industrial capitalism during his time was still in what may be referred to as its early stage, with individual (or family) ownership of enterprises as the norm. Formation of private joint-stock companies issuing shares and debt—the genesis of what would become large corporate entities—mostly started in Britain during the late 1860s. Before that time, the large joint-stock companies in existence were mostly those established to build transportation infrastructure (such as railroads and canals) or undertake mining projects (mostly for coal)—undertakings made possible by the introduction of new, general-purpose technologies (steam propulsion and steel manufacture, for example).

more money-capital to expand output. The early twentieth century would provide further confirmation of this trend, as some companies grew to a large size in various industrial sectors. Oligopolies would consequently emerge as larger enterprise scale promoted greater market pricing power. Thus, small numbers of very large companies started to dominate entire market segments.[29]

Oligopolies also emerged after some monopolies were broken up by regulators. Technological considerations were given high priority in such cases, mostly because of a need for large scale to maintain efficiency and reduce costs. In the United States, possibly the best-known case was that of Standard Oil and its breakup into several regional oligopolies.[30]

Antitrust regulations—one of the most important legislative achievements of the early twentieth century—thus provided ground for oligopolies to arise, even as they led to breakups of monopolistic companies. Economic crises—most of all the Great Depression—then led to more antitrust action, a trend that was tempered by the Second World War and the need to expand scale economies in production. After the War and for the next three decades, antitrust action was subdued—large corporations taking over numerous market segments as consumerism gained ground. With the start of the neoliberal era in the 1980s, however, regulations on monopolies in telephony and public utilities were lifted, leading to mergers and the expansion of pricing power.

The emergence of new technology corporations in the 1980s reinforced this dynamic, as they grew to a very large size in a few years and imposed their power over new markets. Personal computing software was one such sector, with Microsoft becoming an important example.[31] By and large, antitrust regulations were diminished or not enforced as the neoliberal era advanced, resulting in unprecedented consolidation across the American economy—most of all in technology sectors. This trend was empirically confirmed by the Herfindahl–Hirschman index—a measure of consolidation that, using market share data, estimated increases in concentration of over 50 percent, from the late 1990s up to the start of the last decade.[32]

Belief in the infallibility of markets for efficiently allocating resources was important in this changing panorama. The prime justification given was that

29 A trend that would become all too obvious by the middle of the twentieth century, as noted by Paul A. Baran and Paul M. Sweezy in their *Monopoly Capital: An Essay on the American Economic and Social Order* (New York: Monthly Review Press, 1966), chapters 2, 3, 8.

30 See Bruce Bringhurst, *Antitrust and the Oil Monopoly: The Standard Oil Cases, 1890–1911* (Westport: Greenwood, 1979), and the articles in Eleanor M. Fox and Daniel A. Crane, eds., *Antitrust Stories* (New York: Foundation Press, 2007).

31 See James Wallace and Jim Erickson, *Hard Drive: The Making of the Microsoft Empire* (New York: Wiley, 1992); Jennifer Edstrom and Martin Eller, *Barbarians Led by Bill Gates: Microsoft from the Inside, How the World's Richest Corporation Wields Its Power* (New York: Holt, 1998).

32 See Investopedia, *Herfindahl-Hirschman Index-HHI*, www.investopedia.com/ (accessed July 24, 2022); William Galston, "The Perils of Corporate Concentration," *Wall Street Journal*, June 20, 2018, A15.

deregulation would promote greater competition—and that such competition would lead to greater efficiency in the economy. Competition thus became the prime ideological justification for neoliberal policies that, paradoxically, ended up creating oligopolistic conditions in many sectors—thereby eliminating or reducing competition. This contradiction between neoliberal ideology and the outcome of neoliberal policies would become very poignant as the twenty-first century started, when corporate oligopolies in the American economy—and in most other advanced capitalist nations—gained unprecedented power.[33]

Oligopolistic Accumulation

Product markets are a major scenario for technology oligopolies, and they are also the source of much of their power. A new element needs to be considered: *the surplus obtained through oligopolistic pricing power over a product market—or, the quantum above and beyond what competitive conditions would provide.* This quantum will be specified as ΔN—the oligopolistic surplus obtained through the exercise of pricing power over a market.[34] Taking this scenario into account requires a re-specification of the accumulative dynamic, such that:

$$M \rightarrow C \rightarrow C' \rightarrow M^N \text{ where } M^N = M + \Delta m + \Delta N$$

—with M^N as new money-capital obtained from the exchange of the new commodity (C′) in a market under oligopolistic control.

Surplus value (Δm) has historically been assumed to correspond to uncompensated surplus labor, and it continues to exist under oligopolistic conditions. It occurs through the transformation of commodities (embedded in C → C′) and the relations of production that this vital component of accumulation encompasses. Under competitive conditions, surplus value (Δm) was assumed to be the only surplus appropriated by the capitalist.[35] Taking Δm into account

33 See Luis Suarez-Villa, *Corporate Power, Oligopolies, and the Crisis of the State* (Albany: State University of New York Press, 2016), Chapter "Oligopolies," 9–86.

34 This definition refers to the enterprise (or establishment). Aggregation of these surpluses for a technology sector, or across all sectors, may be considered an indicator of oligopolistic power. Note, however, that this approach is different from that taken by Baran and Sweezy in their estimate of aggregate economic surplus—as explained and demonstrated in their *Monopoly Capital*, "Appendix," 369–91. Their aggregate estimate included surplus value, whereas the definition of oligopolistic surplus (ΔN) provided in this book does not.

35 Marx's definition of surplus value—conceptually represented in this book by Δm—was closely related to the labor theory of value, and it is often identified with the sum of profit, rent, and interest. It is unclear, however, whether Marx meant to include rent and interest in his definition. Marx's derivation of profit from surplus value—in his *Capital*, Vol. III, Part I, "The Conversion of Surplus-Value into Profit and the Rate of Surplus-Value into the Rate of Profit," 25–141—deserves further study in this regard. Piero Sraffa's discussion in his *Production of Commodities by Means of Commodities: Prelude to a Critique of Economic Theory* (Cambridge: Cambridge University Press, 1960), Part I, Section II, "Production with a Surplus," 6–11, also needs to be taken into account. Baran and

and comparing it to ΔN can thus reveal the difference between the oligopolistic and the competitive scenarios. *The differential between* Δm *and* ΔN *may thus help us understand the importance of oligopolistic power to corporate interests*, and the attention that its preservation receives in the technology corporate domain.

One aspect in the oligopolistic product market scenario must not be lost sight of. This is that the root source of the oligopolistic surplus (ΔN, encompassed in M^N) is the labor expended in production. Thus, although the surplus (ΔN) represents the product market advantage obtained by the oligopolist, this fundamentally owes its existence to *labor*. The importance of this advantage for corporate power cannot be overemphasized. *For oligopolistic technology corporations, sustaining or increasing the quantum of the oligopolistic surplus* (ΔN) *over time is an objective of the highest order.*

An oligopolistic corporation's stock market value can be severely affected by significant changes in this surplus—with an unwanted takeover or even insolvency becoming likely when it declines (or fails to rise) over time. The magnitude and increase of this surplus are also fundamental for sustaining the entry barriers that support a corporation's market power. Some (or all) of the funds needed to acquire rivals—or to merge with other oligopolistic companies—depend on it. Without its sustenance and increase, the oligopolistic corporation—and its privileged elite—will find their power diminished over time not only materially but also politically.

It is also important to keep in mind the difference between the oligopolistic surplus (ΔN) and surplus value (Δm) in this scenario. The oligopolistic surplus, as specified in this book, does *not* encompass—conceptually or empirically—the meaning (or magnitude) of surplus value. Both, however, make up the *overall surplus* that the product market oligopolist appropriates. Thus, the overall surplus—made up exclusively by surplus value under competitive conditions—must, under oligopoly, include the oligopolistic surplus as well.

The overall surplus for the oligopolist may thus be specified as (Δm + ΔN), taking into account that M encompasses all costs involving input purchases and the transformation of commodity inputs (C) into new commodities (C′). And, that M^N includes all revenue obtained through oligopolistic control over the product market where the new commodity (C′) is sold.[36] The separate treatment of surplus value in this book respects the fact that uncompensated surplus labor has been obtained—as discussed before—and that this represents a material benefit to the oligopolist, *beyond what it obtains from consumers (or customers) in the product market*. At the same time, surplus value can serve as reference to

Sweezy's estimate of aggregate surplus (in *Monopoly Capital*, "Appendix," 369–91) included profit, rent, and interest payment data.

36 Thus, the overall surplus for a given oligopolist may be specified as: (M^N – M), or [(M + Δm + ΔN) – M] = (Δm + ΔN).

compare oligopolistic advantage—a matter that should be of interest for antitrust action.[37]

In this market scenario, the magnitude of the oligopolistic surplus (ΔN) is derived from product prices set by the corporations in control. Empirical research on markups—a plausible measure of the difference between oligopolistic and competitive pricing—with very large databases, has shown substantial increases over extended periods.[38] For biotechnology, the estimated average markup was 419 percent over nearly four decades.[39] Measured as pricing percentage above marginal cost, aggregate markups in the American economy were found to have been close to 50 percent over six decades.[40] A larger study—using selling prices relative to production costs—of 70,000 corporations in 134 nations found the average markup increase to have been almost 60 percent over nearly four decades.[41]

The oligopolist has the power to set or manipulate pricing and output, such that its supply of the product is less than the market demand generated by consumers. This is often achieved by adjusting productive capacity, such that output is reduced when market demand declines. Or, whenever the oligopolist deems it convenient to set a higher price—and thereby obtain larger surpluses. Sustaining idle productive capacity is not crippling to the oligopolist—as it would be for the capitalist in a competitive scenario—because of the surpluses accumulated over time, part of which can be kept as a ready reserve to cover the cost.

Also, it is important to consider that price setting in technology product markets often occurs through follow-the-leader behavior. Price wars between oligopolists are uncommon—and tend to be short-lived if they occur—because they all too often lead to losses for all, compared to the collusive alternative. Tacit collusion—an outcome of co-respectiveness, discussed in the previous chapter—typically leads to advantages for the group of oligopolists as a whole.[42]

37 Periodic measurements of the level of profit, above and beyond what a competitive scenario would provide, could prove useful. Although such estimates may involve some complexity, they are nonetheless feasible given the vast amount of corporate data accumulated. One approach could, for example, involve tracking changes in the composition of profit attributed to capital or labor—see Simcha Barkai, *Declining Labor and Capital Shares*, LBS Research Paper (London: London Business School, 2017).

38 Markups increased by an average of 42 percent for all U.S. corporations in the database (1980–2016). See Federico J. Diez, Daniel Leigh and Suchanan Tambunlertchai, *Global Market Power and Macroeconomic Implications*, IMF Working Paper WP/18/137 (Washington: International Monetary Fund, 2018), www.imf.org/.

39 Diez, Leigh and Tambunlertchai, *Global Market Power and Macroeconomic Implications.*

40 Jan De Loecker and Jan Eeckhout, *The Rise of Market Power and the Macroeconomic Implications*, NBER Working Paper 23687 (Cambridge: National Bureau of Economic Research, 2017), www.nber.org/.

41 Jan De Loecker and Jan Eeckhout, *Global Market Power*, NBER Working Paper 24768 (Cambridge: National Bureau of Economic Research, 2018), www.nber.org/.

42 An aspect addressed by Joseph Schumpeter in his *Capitalism, Socialism, and Democracy* (New York: Harper and Brothers, 1942), 87–106. Schumpeter's understanding of co-respectiveness

Differences between oligopolistic and competitive pricing can be substantial—especially for new technology products and services. One hundred percent or even higher price markups for technology products under oligopolistic control are not uncommon. Moreover, as a product segment or niche comes under oligopolistic control, the opportunity to compare with pricing under competitive conditions can evaporate.

Another aspect that deserves consideration is automation. Differences in performance due to automation may diminish over the long term in the oligopolistic technology context. However, old and new productive technologies (including automated ones) can coexist within the same oligopolistic corporate domain for long periods of time. This seemingly contradictory aspect can occur because greater productive efficiency is sometimes pursued only if the resulting output can be sold at a higher price—such that the oligopolistic surplus can be increased. Thus, whereas in the competitive scenario, lower unit costs—and greater productive efficiency—might be sought as a matter of survival, in the oligopolistic case other considerations may rule over the adoption of new techniques. Oligopolistic technology corporations typically have much leeway in this regard, given their vast resources and the importance they attach to strategy.

An additional issue is that the effort to raise oligopolistic surpluses all too often leads to a contrivance of wants (or demand) in product markets. This is important and feasible for technology oligopolists, because of the novelty factor in many of their products. The prime means for this phenomenon are the corporate "product development" departments (the D in R&D)—typically embedded in the transformative (C→C′) component of the accumulative dynamic.

Advertising—and all the psychological factors associated with it—plays a very important role. The establishment of advertising as an important economic activity was largely a result of growing oligopolistic power over product markets in the American economy, starting in the late 1940s. Augmenting such power through marketing of many superfluous products also became a prime objective for the advertising companies that would themselves become oligopolies in the 1950s and 1960s.

One example was the wasteful (and unnecessary) designs concocted by the American automotive oligopolies during the 1950s.[43] Automobile styling changed substantially from one year to another, for no other purpose than to entice consumers to purchase and boost the manufacturers'

unfortunately missed the asymmetrical relations of power that occur between purchasers (or consumers) and the oligopolists in control.

43 Design schemes typically appealed to socio-behavioral factors, related to the decision to purchase. See, for example, David Gartman, *Auto Opium: A Social History of American Automobile Design* (New York: Routledge, 1994).

surpluses. Not purchasing a new model every year even came to be regarded by many as a symptom of diminished social or economic status. Advertising campaigns that appealed to personal vanity, desire for peer approval, fantasies of flight, and feelings related to mastery of motion were a major factor in this regard.

The designs in question did not enhance safety, economize on personal resources, allow shorter travel time, help the environment, or even provide a more reliable product. One study estimated the cost of such design changes in American automobiles throughout the 1950s to amount to about 25 percent of purchase prices—a cost paid by consumers, given the oligopolistic character of the industry dominated by General Motors, Ford, and Chrysler.[44] In our time, consumer-targeted technology products—for which self-esteem and peer show-off are important in the purchasing decision—also depend greatly on extensive advertising. Appearance—along with packaging—are used to promote purchases of what are often superfluous improvements, while utility is limited through programmed obsolescence.

Differentiating products can thus help extend their market life cycle, even when improvements have limited or no utility for the purchaser. Brand loyalty and social status inference can help this matter. Thus, consumers may end up finding practically no difference in utility between products in a market niche. Smartphones, a sector where three oligopolists—Apple, Samsung, and Huawei—controlled a substantial proportion of the market during the last decade provide an example.[45] Other smartphone manufacturers can find themselves having little or nothing to offer technically—beyond what the dominant oligopolists provide—and experience stagnant or declining sales. Lowering prices often does not help them, as it can lead to reduced revenue and fewer resources to put into product development and advertising. In such cases, a weaker manufacturer will underperform or become insolvent, possibly becoming an acquisition target.

Beyond these considerations, it should be evident that a major consequence of—and also a motive to impose or sustain—oligopolistic power over a product market is that the new money-capital (M^N) obtained is typically much greater than its counterpart under competitive conditions (M'). In this sense, therefore, $M^N > M'$—a simple consequence of the relations of power imposed through oligopolistic control. Such power is derived from—and it is also a cause of—the oligopolistic surplus (ΔN) obtained, for without it the material benefit and other advantages embodied in M^N evaporate.

44 Franklin M. Fisher, Zvi Griliches and Karl Kaysen, "The Costs of Automobile Model Changes Since 1949," *Journal of Political Economy* 70 (1962), 433–51. At the time, the proportion of imported automobiles sold in the United States was relatively insignificant.

45 See Geoffrey A. Fowler, "An Edgy Bid to Win over Phone Buyers," *Wall Street Journal*, March 30, 2017, B1.

The difference between M^N and M'—and the larger magnitude of M^N—may be partly attributed to entry barriers set up by the oligopolist in its product market.[46] Such barriers can be quite diverse and depend on the characteristics of a sector and the technologies involved. Also, acquiring actual or potential rivals—or merging with other oligopolists—can be very important in this regard. Consolidation can fence in a market overnight—and is often accompanied by expanded capital resources.

Consolidation

The weakening of antitrust enforcement in the United States during the past four decades made consolidation quite feasible and strengthened oligopolistic power over technology product markets. It should not surprise, therefore, that historical records have been set on technology merger and acquisition activity in the United States in recent times.[47] An outcome of consolidation is the stock market de-listing of one of the corporations involved, thus reducing the spectrum of investment possibilities.

Examples of consolidation among technology companies in recent times abound, and they surpass those of all other sectors.[48] Microsoft's acquisition of professional networking niche oligopolist LinkedIn in the last decade—one of the most expensive in the history of information technology—expanded the acquirer's product market power while taking a promising company out of the public investment panorama.[49] Verizon's acquisition of Yahoo—which included the latter's substantial stakes in Alibaba Group Holding and Yahoo Japan—guaranteed expanded power for the acquirer and a global market

46 Twenty-two categories of entry barriers were identified by William G. Shepherd in *The Economics of Industrial Organization* (Englewood Cliffs: Prentice-Hall, 1979)—all of them applicable to contemporary technology sectors.

47 See *PC*, "The Biggest Tech Mergers and Acquisitions of All Time," April 12, 2021, www.pcmag.com/; *Techfunnel*, "Biggest IT Mergers and Acquisitions of 2021," May 25, 2021, www.techfunnel.com/; Scott Carey, "Biggest Technology Acquisitions of 2020," *Computer World*, December 15, 2020, www.computerworld.com/; Dana Mattioli and Dana Cimilluca, "Hot M&A Market is on Pace for Record: Tech Disruption and Court Decision on AT&T Make Conditions Ripe for More Deals," *Wall Street Journal*, July 2, 2018, R1; *The Economist*, "Mergers and Antitrust in America: Pushing the Limits," December 12, 2015, 63–64.

48 See *Mirror Review*, "16 Biggest Mergers and Acquisitions of the Decade (2010–20)," August 2021, www.mirrorreview.com/; Carey, "Biggest Technology Acquisitions"; *PC*, "Biggest Tech Mergers."

49 *The Economist*, "Technology Deals: Linked Up; Microsoft's Purchase of LinkedIn is One of the Most Expensive Tech Deals in History," June 18, 2016, 65–66. Microsoft's acquisition of new app-making companies in various communications niches also added to its power—see Jay Greene, "Microsoft Gets a Reboot: After Missteps, Software Giant is the Rare 1990s Tech Titan Figuring Out the Post-Desktop World," *Wall Street Journal*, December 17, 2016, A1.

reach.[50] United Technologies' acquisition of Rockwell in the last decade was the most important in aerospace history up to that time.[51] A more narrow and shallow range of investment possibilities for investors was a largely unnoticed consequence.

During the last decade, consolidation in biotechnology and biopharmaceuticals was the key to the larger surpluses generated by new medications—numerous companies being taken out of the stock market (or losing the possibility of a listing). Many of Astra Zeneca's most promising and profitable medications in recent times were acquired through acquisitions or mergers, for example.[52] And, biotechnology acquisitions by biopharmaceutical oligopolists in the last decade showed the importance of product market control—as in Sanofi's acquisition of Bioverativ and Celgene's purchase Juno Therapeutics.[53] Prior acquisitions can also increase interest in a company, as in AbbVie's purchase of Allergan at the end of the last decade—one of the largest ever in the biotech–biopharmaceuticals sector.[54] In medical technology, Abbott Laboratories' purchase of Alere allowed expanded oligopolistic control over diverse areas of health care, such as diagnostics and implant devices—promising fields for investment that were significantly narrowed as a result.[55]

Despite accumulating evidence, mainstream media during the last decade tended to ignore oligopolistic consolidation as a cause of the rising shortage of investment opportunities, blaming regulation instead.[56] In the late 1990s, the United States had more than 7,000 companies listed in its stock markets—two decades later, listings had declined by almost half.[57] This astounding reduction of listed companies occurred despite the vast and rapidly growing amounts of

50 *The Economist*, "Verizon Buys Yahoo: Does It Add Up? The Telecoms Giant Has Made a Bold Bet on the Future of Advertising," July 30, 2016, 49–50.

51 David Benoit, Dana Mattioli and Thomas Gryta, "United Technologies Sets Rockwell Deal," *Wall Street Journal*, September 5, 2017, A1.

52 *The Economist*, "Decentralising Drug Research: Pharmed Out," May 24, 2014, 63.

53 Jonathan D. Rockoff, "Drug Firms Bet Billions on Biotech," *Wall Street Journal*, January 23, 2018, A1.

54 Cara Lombardo, Jonathan D. Rockoff and Dana Cimilluca, "Drugmakers Strike $63 Billion Deal: AbbVie Agrees to Buy Allergan, Maker of Botox, in One of 2019's Largest Mergers," *Wall Street Journal*, June 26, 2019, A1.

55 Imani Moise, "Abbott, Alere Reach Pact," *Wall Street Journal*, April 15, 2017, B3.

56 Jon Sindreu, "A Shortage of Safe Assets Looms," *Wall Street Journal*, February 17, 2017, B11. Conservative neoclassical economists largely ignored oligopolistic consolidation—attributing many of its effects to cultural factors. See Tyler Cowen, *The Complacent Class: The Self-Defeating Quest for the American Dream* (New York: St. Martin's, 2017).

57 See Jason Zweig, "Disturbing New Facts About Winner Take-All Capitalism in U.S.," *Wall Street Journal*, March 4, 2017, B1; and his "Stock Pickers Struggle as Public Shares Shrink," *Wall Street Journal*, June 24, 2017, A1; *The Economist*, "Death and Transfiguration: The Golden Age of the Western Corporation May Be Coming to an End," September 19, 2015, 66; Gustavo Grullon, Yelena Larkin and Roni Michaely, "Are US Industries Becoming More Concentrated?" *SSRN*, May 31, 2015, htpps://papers.ssrn.com/.

investment capital available in the American economy—due largely to low interest rates and the growth of finance. The relatively short period of time involved is also significant, reflecting lax antitrust enforcement. Two important consequences of this trend were a reduction of stock market diversity and the increase in oligopolistic product market pricing power.

New or small companies are frequent acquisition targets—a tactic that can increase the acquirer's product market control. The objective can be preemption—to keep the acquired company from growing or gaining market share. And it often allows the acquiring oligopolist to expand its product market—or to capture new niches and capabilities. Acquisition of small companies engaged in 3-D printing during the last decade, for example, enabled oligopolistic conglomerate General Electric to extend its control to a new technology relevant to its turbine products.[58] Large accumulated surpluses facilitated this and many other acquisitions.

Microsoft's acquisition of 36 small and medium-size companies (such as SwiftKey, Accompli, Minecraft, and Xamarin) over a two-year period, allowed it to secure capabilities in mobile computing, telephony, and videogaming—areas vital to expand its market power over software.[59] Social media, search engine, and telecom oligopolists—such as Facebook, Google, and Apple—aggressively acquired numerous niche companies during the last decade, to expand their control over most every aspect of mobile telephony, messaging, searches, images, gaming, and related activities.[60] Acquisition strategies in these cases largely revolved around the quantity of users' data owned by the targeted company—given their importance for advertising and sales. The compulsory requirement for users to provide intimate personal data to gain access was a major factor.

Acquisition of small and medium-size companies is also pursued by technology oligopolists to appropriate valuable intellectual property and to establish control over new product market niches. IP can help generate future revenue streams for the acquiring oligopolist, due to the monopoly rights involved and the possibility of fencing in new niches. Biotech and pharmaceutical

58 Ted Mann and Eyk Henning, "GE Expands 3-D Printing," *Wall Street Journal*, September 7, 2016, B3.

59 Dan Gallagher, "Microsoft Mines More Out of 'Minecraft'," *Wall Street Journal*, April 12, 2017, B1; Jay Greene, "Microsoft Gets a Reboot," *Wall Street Journal*, December 17, 2016, A1.

60 See Dana Mattioli, Jack Nicas and Dan Strumpf, "Google Set to Acquire Design Unit of HTC," *Wall Street Journal*, September 21, 2017, B1; Jack Nicas, "YouTube Notches Global Video Milestone: Google Unit's Viewers Watch More than 1 Billion Hours a Day, On Pace to Eclipse TV," *Wall Street Journal*, February 28, 2017, B1; *The Economist*, "Imperial Ambitions," April 9, 2016, 11; and its "The New Face of Facebook: How to Win Friends and Influence People," April 9, 2016, 22. In some cases, launching a new service that mimics what a new or startup company has developed can be used to lay the groundwork for an acquisition—see Betsy Morris and Deepa Seetharaman, "For Tech Innovators, Facebook Looms Large: Startup Houseparty Created a Hot Video-Chat App—Then a Big Rival Noticed," *Wall Street Journal*, August 10, 2017, A1.

oligopolists have frequently engaged in this strategy in recent times. In the last decade, biopharmaceutical oligopolist Johnson and Johnson, for example, made the most important (and costly) acquisition in its history—for a biotech research company—while Pfizer negotiated a substantial all-cash purchase of another biotech company—both of which owned promising IP.[61]

Research collaboration with new or small companies can pave the ground for acquisitions, by providing detailed knowledge of operations and capabilities. Such collaboration is often narrowly targeted for specific projects or products, at least initially.[62] In biotechnology and pharmaceuticals, collaboration for specific projects has been fairly common—such as Bayer's research joint venture with Crispr Therapeutics during the last decade, to develop treatments using genetic-editing techniques.[63] Even when acquisition does not occur, research collaboration can help increase product market control—as in the case of AstraZeneca and Sanofi, when they agreed to share thousands of their proprietary compounds.[64]

In addition to facilitating acquisitions, collaboration can make it easier to set standards that lead to greater product market control. In mobile telephony, companies have often collaborated to "contribute" designs that establish network protocols. Such designs can be in the thousands over a few years' time. The protocols then help determine access and service provision guidelines to be imposed on consumers. For fourth-generation (4G) mobile telephony networks, for example, Ericsson provided over 7,000 designs over a seven-year period.[65] Huawei, its closest rival, provided 6,500—while Nokia and Alcatel-Lucent contributed close to 3,000 each during the same period.[66] The designs helped increase contributors' market power considerably.

Acquiring small or medium-size companies can also be attractive if the target already has products that secure a significant revenue stream. This is an

61 Denise Roland and Jonathan D. Rockoff, "J&J to Pay $30 Billion for Biotech," *Wall Street Journal*, January 27, 2017, B1; Jonathan Rockoff, "Pfizer Near $14 Billion Deal for Biotech," *Wall Street Journal*, August 22, 2016, B1; and his "Deal for Medivation is the Latest in a Line of Similar Acquisitions," both in *Wall Street Journal*, August 23, 2016, B3.

62 See Denise Roland, "Drugmakers Mine DNA Troves for Research," *Wall Street Journal*, July 24, 2019, B1; Josh Beckerman, "Novartis: Drug Maker, Amgen Team on Alzheimer's," *Wall Street Journal*, September 2, 2015, B3.

63 Amy D. Marcus and Joe Palazzolo, "Gene Tool Draws Investors, Discord," *Wall Street Journal*, September 23, 2016, B1.

64 Denise Roland, "Drug Giants Seek Edge by Sharing Secrets," *Wall Street Journal*, November 20, 2015, B1.

65 *The Economist*, "Culture Clash: As 'Third Generation' (3G) Networks Proliferate, the Focus Shifts to 4G," July 19, 2008, 76; and its "Wireless: The Next Generation; A New Wave of Mobile Technology is on its Way, and Will Bring Drastic Change," February 20, 2016, 53–54.

66 *The Economist*, "Wireless," 54. Collaborative standards setting in the telecom sector will likely gain greater importance, as data flows increase. The introduction of 5G, for example, was expected to increase data volumes 1,000-fold during the first half of the 2020s. See Data Center Dynamics, *How 5G Will Affect the Structure of Data Centers*, February 6, 2020, www.datacenterdynamics.com/.

aspect that some Wall Street hedge funds understood long ago, when they funded existing biotech or biopharmaceutical companies that—using the patron fund's capital—purchased established products and then raised their prices substantially. In that way, the hedge fund-backed companies became attractive acquisition targets, due to the product markets they controlled. And, even when products become generic, their necessity—if there is a lack of effective alternatives—guarantees a captive market and substantial surpluses.

With finance placing the highest priority on short-term returns, such opportunities are prized—compared to the uncertainty and risk of marketing new products. This was the case with Daraprim—used to treat life-threatening parasitic infections in newborns, compromised immune systems across age groups, and malaria—during the last decade. The price of this biomedication was raised by 5,456 percent overnight after its marketing rights were purchased.[67] In another case, a dystrophy biotreatment underwent a 5,462 percent price increase.[68] In such cases, the acquiring oligopolist often re-brands the product after purchase and—using its market power—raises the price significantly.

Speculative Finance

In recent decades, the advance of speculative finance attracted technology oligopolies. *Some of the larger corporations thus became speculators or even shadow hedge funds to support their technology product markets.*[69] Financial "product markets" were set up—the controlling tech oligopolist being either the only "client" or among only a handful. And the latter are all too often its subsidiaries or those in which it possesses cross-holdings. Myriad speculative schemes have been pursued through these operations, with vast amounts of money that can surpass those of banks and hedge funds.

In contemporary finance, most any activity with a probabilistic dimension can become a betting possibility. Speculative operations are typically disconnected from such core functions as manufacturing, R&D, or the marketing of

67 Andrew Pollack, "Drug Goes from $13.50 a Tablet to $750, Overnight," *New York Times*, September 20, 2015, http://nytimes.com/; *The Economist*, "Drug Pricing in America: Painful Pills," September 26, 2015, 66.

68 After an uproar over this medication's pricing, its owner sold the medication to another niche oligopolist, who initially discounted its price but then proceeded to increase it in small increments—see Joseph Walker, "Drug's Price Rises to $65,250 a Year," *Wall Street Journal*, January 19, 2018, B6.

69 See Thomas Gilbert and Christopher Hrdlicka, "Apple is a Hedge Fund that Makes Phones: Big Companies Need to Disclose More about their Investments," *Wall Street Journal*, August 23, 2018, www.wsj.com/; Tyler Durden, "The World's Biggest 'Hedge Fund', $30 Billion Bigger than Bridgewater, Remains Mysterious as Ever," *ZeroHedge*, July 23, 2015, www.zerohedge.com/; Josh Arnold, "GE: A Hedge Fund in Disguise," *Seeking Alpha*, December 31, 2012, https//:seekingalpha .com/; Brad Cook, "Apple Creates Braeburn Capital to Manage $8.7 Billion Stash," *Mac Observer*, April 5, 2006, www.macobserver.com/.

products and services—the prime objective being *to obtain money as quickly as possible, and amass cash.*[70] Most important is that financial speculation does not require managing the productive cycle and complexities.

The self-serving priorities of executives, particularly on compensation, are also very important in such operations—despite the substantial losses that can occur when bets go wrong. Nonetheless, relatively little effort is needed to keep the cash flowing in, compared to what managing a technology product market requires. And the cash flow can augment surpluses from product markets.[71] Amassed cash can also be used to fence in new market niches or acquire other companies. Deregulation in the United States made this phenomenon possible, when barriers to financial speculation were taken down to try to promote growth.[72]

It is possible to confound speculative activities with components of the accumulative dynamic—or to place them in the productive cycle as if they were "normal" components of accumulation. Financial speculation is, however, an artificial endeavor in the context of capitalist accumulation—in the sense that it primarily involves *making money out of money.*[73] The productive

70 In some cases, large-scale financial speculation developed out of consumer product financing—see Andy Kessler, "General Electric's Long Unwinding: The Company Turned Out to be a Hedge Fund Masquerading as an Industrial Giant," *Wall Street Journal*, June 24, 2018, www.wsj.com/; General Electric Company, *The G.E.C.: Its History, Structure and the Future* (London: General Electric, 1953).

71 Thus, the cash obtained through financial speculation may be co-mingled with new money-capital (M^N) obtained from sales in the oligopolist's product market. And, conversely, money used for speculation may originate from the pool of new money-capital obtained from a product market. In such cases, the difference between the money amassed through speculation—and the money-capital obtained from an oligopolistic product market—must be kept in mind. Conceptually, this is important, since only money-capital deployed in productive transformation can be considered *capital* in the full functional sense of the term.

72 The emergence of financial speculation as a widespread phenomenon—and the immense weight of finance in advanced capitalism, in general—has been referred to as the "financial explosion" and as "financialization." The cause lies in what has been conceptualized as the "stagnation-financialization trap"—and the effort to evade long-term stagnation through speculation, particularly after the 1970s. See Harry Magdoff and Paul M. Sweezy, *Stagnation and the Financial Explosion* (New York: Monthly Review Press, 1987); Greta R. Krippner, *Capitalizing on Crisis: The Political Origins of the Rise of Finance* (Cambridge, MA: Harvard University Press, 2012).

73 The speculative dynamic may thus be specified as: $F \rightarrow F^F$, where $F^F = F+\Delta f+\Delta F$, with F as initial speculative money, F^F as new money—obtained through speculative activities—and ΔF as the oligopolistic speculative surplus. The component that should rightfully belong to personnel who execute transactions, analyze data, provide advice, and the like is represented by Δf. The representation of Δf thus implicitly recognizes employee exploitation. The competitive scenario may be specified as $F \rightarrow F'$, where $F'=F+\Delta f$, with F' as new speculative money. Employee exploitation in this scenario must be understood to be distinctive from labor exploitation, in the sense that *labor* is assumed to occur as such *solely in the context of the capitalist accumulative dynamic.* This distinction reflects the fact that speculative finance—disengaged as it is from the productive cycle of capitalist accumulation—vacates capital accumulation, *essentially becoming betting and the amassment of money to obtain more money.*

transformation of commodities—and the accumulative dynamic in which it is embedded—are thus banished from this scenario. And, money cannot be considered a commodity in and of itself but merely a medium for exchange.

Money-capital (M, M^N) can thus only be considered such—*capital*—when it is involved with the productive cycle ($M \rightarrow C \rightarrow C' \rightarrow M^N$). This is far from a mere classificatory issue. It is, rather, an aspect of philosophical substance that is rooted in the nature and definition of capitalism and that can be traced to the earliest classical economists.[74] The confusion in our time in this regard results in part from the overwhelming emphasis placed by mainstream economics on individual mental calculation—and on the end results of such calculation—as the sole basis of economic phenomena.

Financial speculation cannot be considered a "new stage" (or a new form) of capitalism but, rather, a *distortion* of the accumulative dynamic—and of the essence of capitalism. A distortion that leads to crises grounded in the instruments of speculation—such as debt, the pricing of stocks, bonds and derivatives, and perceptions of betting risk. Understanding this distortion is particularly important in the case of technology oligopolies, as *without their transformative component* ($C \rightarrow C'$) *such enterprises lose their raison d'être as productive entities*. Greatly so, since new technologies can only emerge from the productive cycle embedded in the accumulative dynamic.

New Technologies

Corporations that pioneer a new technology often gain oligopolistic control over their product market. The early phases are crucial, as they are most propitious for building market power. Control over related IP tends to be very important. The monopoly rights provided by patents are a crucial support, but secrecy may be preferred when a new technology is difficult to reverse engineer.[75]

74 Marx, for example, considered money obtained through financial speculation to be "fictitious capital," because of its disengagement from production—see Marx, *Capital*, Vol. III, Part V, Chapter XXV, "Credit and Fictitious Capital," 400–13. The disengagement of finance from production, due to speculation, was noticed and elaborated upon in the early twentieth century by Rudolf Hilferding, in his pioneering work *Das Finanzkapital: eine Studie über die jüngste Entwicklung des Kapitalismus* (Vienna: Brand, 1910), translated as *Finance Capital: A Study of the Latest Phase of Capitalist Development* (London: Routledge and Kegan Paul, 1981). Hilferding alluded to the incipient emergence of a financial "establishment" in his time—separate from the productive or industrial base but not wholly unrelated to it. That establishment, he presciently noted, would eventually gain substantial power in advanced capitalist economies.

75 Two decades of a patent-protected monopoly can be a short time for an oligopolist with a longer-term perspective. Also, the fact that details in patent applications become public information can be a deterrent when long product life is anticipated. The case of Coca-Cola's chemical formula provides an example. Its pioneering role in the industrialization of soft beverages allowed this company to fence in a market that had been artisanal and local. See, for example, Frederick Allen, *Secret Formula* (New York: HarperBusiness, 1994).

Strategic considerations regarding product life can make all the difference. When new products are expected to have a very short market life, forgoing patenting may be preferred. In such cases, ensuring that they will only work with an oligopolist's proprietary system (or platform) can help retain control. Thus, although the larger platform might itself be patented, doing so for an accessory or an app may be avoided—as they would likely be obsolete before a patent can be awarded.

Understanding this panorama can lead a company to establish wide-ranging product market control in the early phases.[76] This is important when a new technology can collapse cost, time, or effort significantly—over the one it seeks to replace. In such cases, the accumulation of oligopolistic surpluses can become exponential.

Creating derivative products based on the new technology is advantageous. It is often accomplished by acquiring companies that have related products. The vast "apps" platform developed by Apple—considered to be a "digital ecosystem" by some authors—is an example.[77] In Microsoft's case, creating a Windows-based software platform upon which many small companies could develop their businesses—non-competitive to its power—helped expand its product market considerably.[78]

The trajectory of capitalism provides many examples of new technologies that were deployed in unintended ways. In most cases, product market power and the surpluses obtained provided the resources needed to establish derivative products. This has been the case in biotechnology and biopharmaceuticals, with numerous medications and treatments.[79] Software, initially introduced to perform simple computational tasks, became indispensable in aviation—allowing avionics technology oligopolists to set up new market niches.[80]

A novel form of oligopolistic market control can be found in corporations that are solely specialized in research. In this case, the new commodity (C′) in the accumulation dynamic is a patent that grants monopolistic power for a limited time. Production of patents through research is their only productive

76 Its early start with PC operating system software, for example, provided Microsoft with a formidable advantage. See Wallace and Erickson, *Hard Drive*.

77 Numerous acquisitions early in the last decade helped Apple extend its control over its app market. See Daisuke Wakabayashi and Douglas Macmillan, "Apple Buys Twitter Data Tool," *Wall Street Journal*, December 3, 2013, B1; *The Economist*, "Another Digital Gold Rush," May 14, 2011, 85–87.

78 This feature of Microsoft's platform was used to help it evade antitrust sanctions in the late 1990s. The fact that Microsoft's platform is very important for this corporation's immense oligopolistic surplus was largely lost in the arguments. See U.S. Department of Justice, *United States v. Microsoft* (Washington: U.S. Government Printing Office, 1999); Paul Andrews, *How the Web was Won: Microsoft from Windows to the Web* (New York: Broadway, 1999).

79 See Denise Roland, "Some Rejected Drugs Get a New Life," *Wall Street Journal*, March 14, 2017, B1; Emma Jay, "Viagra and Other Drugs Discovered by Accident," *BBC News*, January 20, 2010, www.news.bbc.co.uk/.

80 See "Honeywell," *Wikipedia*, http://wikipedia.org/ (accessed June 6, 2022).

endeavor (embedded in C→C′). Researchers and research materials are the main commodities (C) along with laboratory equipment and facilities.

The exclusive ownership rights created by researchers is the most important factor in these companies' market control. Only by licensing such rights to others can a surplus be obtained. One such corporation, for example, imposed its market power by inducing other companies—that manufactured products which could be related to any of the patents it owned—to purchase its licenses.[81] Companies that declined were then sued for patent infringement. Litigation—or the fear of it—thus became the means to exert power over its market. The high cost of litigation, the long timelines involved, the uncertainty of court outcomes, and the extensive effort required to document how an invention was used contributed to that power.

Companies that provided a service—linked in any way to technologies related to its patents—were also targeted. Such services could include, for example, technical assistance, installation, maintenance, or repair. Thus, a derivative approach that targeted both producers and service providers was enlisted to build market power. In this scenario, companies that refuse to accept licensing "invitations" can be driven into insolvency through serial litigation—and be made ripe for takeover by a hedge fund. And the latter may have previously invested in the litigating patent owner. In such cases, the patent-owning corporation becomes a medium for takeovers—if or when the potential licensee refuses to comply.

Litigation on IP can thus be part of a company's business model to "create" market power. If done serially, this strategy can intimidate or prevent others from entering a market. Perhaps, it should not surprise that, in the United States, this form of litigation has become the best compensated and most sought-after specialty in the legal profession. The very large budgets allocated to it by some of the most powerful technology corporations attests to its growing importance. Intel's litigation budget, for example, was said to have exceeded one billion dollars by the middle of the twenty-first century's first decade.[82]

By the end of the twenty-first century's first decade, the total cost of IP litigation in the United States was estimated to be well above the profit that corporations obtain from licensing their patents to others.[83] The deployment of

81 Don Clark, "Rambus Expands with Own Chip Brand: Move is Part of Firm's Effort to Leave Behind Business Model Linked to Patent Litigation," *Wall Street Journal*, August 17, 2015, B4; Abhirup Roy, "Tech Licensor Rambus to Start Selling Chips Under Own Brand," *Reuters*, August 17, 2015, http://reuters.com/.

82 See Dennis Crouch, "Intel Successfully Defends its Patent Case but Owes its Own Attorneys $9 Million for the Defense," *Patentlyo*, August 13, 2014, www.patentlyo.com/; Intel, *Intellectual Property Policy*, www.intel.com/ (accessed July 8, 2022).

83 James Bessen and Michael J. Meurer, *The Direct Costs from NPE Disputes*, Boston University School of Law Working Paper 12–34 (Boston: Boston University School of Law, 2012); L. Gordon Crovitz, "Why Technologists Want Fewer Patents," *Wall Street Journal*, June 15, 2009, A13.

IP as an oligo-monopolistic product market weapon can thus be part of a larger strategy aimed at expanding a corporation's market control. The accumulation of surpluses (ΔN) and the resulting aggregate new money-capital (M^N) make it possible to implement such strategies.

Input Markets

Technology corporations may exercise oligopsonistic control over their input markets. This can occur when a company has a large number of suppliers to choose from, and the suppliers have a very small set of purchasers. In some cases, suppliers can be highly specialized and may not have the means to diversify. This can happen across input chains and can involve raw materials, parts, or services. The oligopsonistic surplus obtained through input chain control can be substantial compared to a competitive situation. Small supplier companies tend to be vulnerable in this regard.

Imposing Terms

The oligopsonist thus imposes its terms on a supplier—on price, most of all, but also possibly on technical features, timing, and quantity. In some cases, tacit collusion among oligopsonists—to set terms for suppliers through a follow-the-leader tactic—may occur. This situation can, for example, be found in the aerospace sector, where a global duopoly—Boeing and Airbus—impose their power.

Boeing's input chain strategy, in particular, helped it gain greater control by expanding the number of potential suppliers. Its United States-focused input supply chain thus acquired a global scope in the 1990s.[84] Control over its input chains then led to larger surpluses—due to the price reductions imposed on suppliers.

Apple provides another example of how a corporation imposes its terms. It contracts with different suppliers for most every part in its iPhones.[85] Various suppliers may thus provide one part type. Apple then demands discounts as a condition to renew contracts. Because it uses several suppliers for the same part, it can switch companies, change quantities, or cancel contracts—if a supplier does not bend to its terms.

Because of its power, Apple can also engage in a tactic known as a "double cut"—the imposition of price discounts *and* the reduction of supplies.[86] This

84 See Edward S. Greenberg, Leon Grunberg, Sarah Moore and Patricia B. Sikora, *Turbulence: Boeing and the State of American Workers and Managers* (New Haven: Yale University Press, 2010).

85 A matter that led to disputes during the last decade. See Stu Woo, "Apple Supplier Talks Fight Over Patent," *Wall Street Journal*, April 4, 2017, B4; Daisuke Wakabayashi and Peg Brickley, "Apple Supplier Cries Foul," *Wall Street Journal*, November 8, 2014, B3.

86 Eva Dou, "Apple Squeezes Suppliers on Prices," *Wall Street Journal*, September 2, 2016, B1. See also Brian Merchant's *The One Device: The Secret History of the iPhone* (New York: Little, Brown,

tactic was resorted to when an iPhone model's demand declines or when it has been in the market for some time and its replacement is not ready to be marketed. The typically short market life cycle of iPhones—intended to stimulate demand—and the high volumes sold worldwide allow Apple to increase surpluses substantially. Suppliers can thereby find their revenue declining—a situation that may push them closer to insolvency and makes them all the more vulnerable to Apple's conditions. Suppliers' workers also bear the consequences, as reductions in supply volume or prices usually mean furloughs or reduced compensation.

Small, research-oriented biotechnology companies that provide specialized inputs—such as biochemical compounds and organisms requiring regulatory testing or trials—to biopharmaceutical oligopolists provide another example. Experimentation in many small biotech firms usually has long timelines, with failure rates for potential compounds that can be as high as 8,000 to one.[87] These rates are a symptom of these suppliers' fragility—compounded by long delays and high research expenses.[88] To protect their investment, these companies often secure patents for the inputs they provide.[89] Obtaining a patent can take as long as five years, depending on its complexity, and can involve much uncertainty.

For biotech suppliers, the fact that a patent application's details become public information is more than offset by the need to protect their investment in research. A shortage of capital often plagues their operations, because of long timelines, the complexity of research tasks, and the uncertainty involved.[90] These companies' need for capital therefore makes them highly dependent on the biopharmaceutical corporations they supply.[91] Also, to secure capital they

2017), chapters 11–13.

87 Rates that may reflect an experimentalist ethos uncommon in technology businesses of previous times. See Luis Suarez-Villa, *Technocapitalism: A Critical Perspective on Technological Innovation and Corporatism* (Philadelphia: Temple University Press, 2009), chapters "Experimentalism" and "Experimentalist Organizations."

88 Clinical testing of proposed medications is usually done in phases, with about 70 percent passing Phase 1 and about one-third of those passing Phase 2—see U.S. Food and Drug Administration, *Selected FDA GCP/Clinical Trial Guidance Documents*, http://www.fda.gov/ScienceResearch.htm (accessed July 30, 2022).

89 Securing potentially valuable patent awards is also important for undertaking an initial public offering (IPO) in the stock market—see, for example, Corrie Driebusch, "During Covid-19 Pandemic, Biotech IPOs Already Surpass Records," *Wall Street Journal*, August 10, 2020, www.wsj.com/; and her "Big Paydays for Unproven Biotechs," *Wall Street Journal*, July 29, 2015, C1.

90 The urgent need for capital has also driven some biotech firms to seek a listing in stock markets, despite their lack of marketable products. See, for example, Driebusch, "During Covid-19 Pandemic"; *The Economist*, "All about the Base: New Businesses Eye the Opportunities in Managing Genome Data," June 25, 2016, 55–56.

91 Partly because of this dependence, results of clinical trials tend to be selectively published—potentially shortchanging patients. One report from the last decade noted, for example, that only 17 percent of trials paid for by corporations had their results published—the majority of trial failures thus

often must commit to supply only their oligopsonistic patron. Small biotech suppliers thus find themselves at the mercy of their customer—who will dictate the terms of their relationship. And, they often have no choice but to agree to be acquired—if or when the possibility arises—thus giving up any chance of independent growth (or of keeping their IP).

Dual Oligopoly: Inputs, Products

To take into account control over *both* product and input supply markets, the accumulative dynamic may be re-specified as:

$$M_S \rightarrow C \rightarrow C' \rightarrow M^N{}_S$$

where $M_S = M - \Delta S$ *and* $M^N{}_S = M^N + \Delta S$ (with $M^N = M + \Delta m + \Delta N$ as before) —with M_S as initial money-capital for the oligopsonistic purchase of inputs. Such inputs are assumed to be *non-labor* commodities—that will undergo transformation (embedded in C→C′). As before, M represents the initial money-capital that—under *competitive* input supply conditions—would be expended to purchase all inputs necessary to undertake the transformation of commodities (C) into new commodities (C′). Through its control over the input market, the oligopsonist is able to obtain a surplus (ΔS) in the form of a lower payment. This surplus renders $M_S < M$—thus making the initial money-capital needed (M_S) lower than its counterpart under competition (M).[92]

Thus, the oligopsonistic surplus obtained from the input market (ΔS) *effectively discounts the initial money-capital needed to purchase inputs.* In this scenario, ΔS is derived from both M^N *and* M_S—in the sense that the market exchange of the product (C′) is the conduit through which the oligopsonist's benefit is obtained. Product market exchange ($M^N{}_S$)—and the transformative component (C→C′)—are thus linked to obtainment of the oligopsonistic surplus.

When oligopolistic control is exercised over both product and input markets, $M^N{}_S$ represents the quantum of aggregate new money-capital obtained through the combination of new money-capital (M^N) derived from a product market *and* the oligopsonistic surplus obtained from the input market (ΔS). The latter thus augments the monetary benefit obtained by the oligopolist—a

remaining undisclosed. See *The Economist*, "Clinical Trials: Spilling the Beans; Failure to Publish the Results of All Clinical Trials is Skewing Medical Science," July 25, 2015, 62–63.

92 The possibility that oligopolistic control may only be exercised over the input market can be taken into account. In this case, the accumulative dynamic may be specified as $M_S \rightarrow C \rightarrow C' \rightarrow M'_S$ where $M'_S = M' + \Delta S$ *and* $M' = M + \Delta m$—with M'_S and M' both denoting a competitive product market and $M_S = M - \Delta S$ (as before). Here, ΔS would be derived through market exchange—revenues embedded in M_S and M'_S—since the input market oligopolist would only be able to obtain its monetary benefit when M'_S is appropriated.

matter of crucial importance to any technology corporation. A company that only controls its input market would nonetheless be in an advantageous position—due to ΔS—compared to one facing competition in both input and product markets.

Insofar as the accumulative dynamic is concerned, the surplus (ΔS) obtained through oligopsonistic control over the input supply market cannot benefit the oligopsonist-*cum*-oligopolist *unless* the transformation (C→C′) of commodity inputs takes place, *and* product market exchange of the new commodity occurs. This is a fundamental aspect of accumulation that cannot be ignored, as control over the input market alone cannot complete the accumulative dynamic. Only through productive transformation can the sale of the new commodity be undertaken, such that M^N_S—aggregate new money-capital that includes *both* input and product market surpluses—can be obtained and the productive cycle completed.

Without the completion of the productive cycle, the oligopsonist-*cum*-oligopolist would be unable to restart the accumulative dynamic—even when it retains control over its input market. The history of technology provides many cases of companies that managed to establish control over input suppliers but failed to market their products. Or, lacking oligopolistic control over their product market failed to obtain sufficient new money-capital (M'_S) to cover initial outlays (M_S). New, complex technologies whose utility was difficult to establish, were very expensive, or did not have a ready market often accompanied or triggered such failures.

Control over both input and product markets makes a corporation more powerful—and more capable of exercising influence over society. Although not as common as product market oligopoly, the rapid expansion of technology oligopolies during the past four decades makes this scenario more likely to occur. More so for new technologies that are complex, require rare inputs that undergo intensive research and testing, and have products with high market value.

We may refer to a corporation's control over its input and product markets as *dual oligopolistic power*. And, the aggregate surplus in this scenario can be specified as:

$$(M^N_S - M) \text{ or } [(M + \Delta m + \Delta N + \Delta S) - M] = (\Delta m + \Delta N + \Delta S)$$

Dual oligopolistic power thus magnifies the surpluses and allows the company in control to expand its influence. Also, the aggregate new money-capital (M^N_S) accumulated—supported by the product market (ΔN) *and* input market (ΔS) surpluses—means that $M^N_S > M^N > M'$, thus making dual oligopolistic power all the more desirable. The fact that such scenario is difficult to achieve makes it all the more likely that a company will try to sustain it, once attained. Acquiring input suppliers and potential rivals, preempting regulatory action, and erecting entry barriers can thus acquire great priority.

Labor Markets

Technology corporations can also establish oligopsonistic control over their labor market. Concentrations of unemployed or underemployed labor—and very few appropriate employers—can provide the setting.[93] M&A activity can make this imbalance worse by eliminating small and medium-size companies.

Oligopsonistic employers tend to provide lower compensation than small or medium-size companies.[94] Oversupply of workers with suitable skills—essentially a reserve army of potential labor—can help sustain control, placing current and potential workers at the mercy of their employers. The oligopsonist can then impose the terms for compensation, benefits, performance, discipline, safety, and other aspects.

Insecurity

Insecure employment—along with loss of workplace rights, limited compensation, and greater exploitation—are outcomes. Undercompensated labor, a systemic feature of capitalism that dates back to its earliest days—and underlies the appropriation of surplus value (Δm) in the accumulative dynamic—is part of the panorama. Underemployment and long-term unemployment tend to make this situation worse. And, high labor turnover can keep employees submissive.[95] Technology startups were no exception to this panorama during the last decade.[96]

In the United States, significant real jobless rates—also referred to as "nonemployment" rates—have been found since this statistic started to be collected. This indicator is more revealing than the official unemployment data, partly because it includes the long-term unemployed and has a broader scope than tabulations based on unemployment compensation. Over the long term, the level of real joblessness has been several times the official unemployment rate—a condition favorable to oligopsonistic power.[97]

93 Promoting labor displacement (involving physical mobility or migration) became a hallmark of neoliberal theory and policy agendas for dealing with oligopsonistic labor markets—in place of antitrust enforcement. Such displacement would contribute to undermine labor unions, whose power to organize workers is often locally rooted.

94 An aspect that attracted attention during the last decade. See Theo Francis, "Bigger Company but Not Big Pay: U.S. Workers Moving from Smaller Firms No Longer Get as Big a Boost in Compensation," *Wall Street Journal*, January 11, 2018, B6; Philip Mattera, *Grand Theft Paycheck: The Large Corporations Shortchanging their Workers' Wages*. Corporate Research Project of Good Jobs First and Jobs with Justice Education Fund, 2018, www.goodjobsfirst.com/; Lydia DePillis, "Big Companies Used to Pay the Best Wages: Not Any More," *CNN Business*, January 18, 2018, https://money.cnn.com/.

95 See Mattera, *Grand Theft Paycheck*; Francis, "Bigger Company"; DePillis, "Big Companies Used."

96 See Stephanie Gleason and Rachel Feintzeig, "At Startups, Pink Slips Come Early and Often," *Wall Street Journal*, December 13, 2013, B1; Rachel Feintzeig and Rachel Silverman, "Haggle Over Salary? It's Not Allowed," *Wall Street Journal*, May 27, 2015, B1.

97 Close to one-fifth of men and one-third of women (both aged 25 to 54), and over 40 percent of men and women aged 18 to 24, were estimated to be in this condition during the first half of the

Even when technology corporations do not have oligopsonistic power over their labor market, rising trends toward outsourcing have provided similar advantages. The main advantage has been to keep labor costs low by depressing compensation, making employment less secure and forgoing provision of health insurance and retirement—while transferring the costs of unemployment, health, retirement, and other benefits to the state or to the workers themselves. At Google, for example, by the end of the last decade, an estimated 70,000 temporary workers, vendors, and individuals contracted independently for specific tasks—a general category of labor known as TVC (temporary–vendor–contracted)—were managing data and marketing projects, reviewing legal documents, testing cars with self-driving software, providing customer and technical assistance, and performing numerous other tasks that would have been done by in-house labor.[98] And, Google's parent—Alphabet—was estimated to have about the same number of TVC workers as full-time, in-house labor—a condition that has become fairly common among some of the largest technology oligopolists.[99]

During the last decade in some sectors—such as biopharmaceuticals and software—TVC workers were estimated to be twice as many as in-house labor.[100] One report calculated TVC workers' income to be about 25 percent less than that of full-time, in-house labor—with more than 26 percent of all TVC workers receiving welfare support, food stamps, health care, and other taxpayer-provided benefits.[101] As many as 20 million people in the American economy were estimated to be in the TVC category—with long-term predictions for most employment growth to occur in this area.[102] And, it has been

last decade. See U.S. Bureau of Labor Statistics, *Population Level* and *Employment Level*, 1952–2013 series, http://data.bls.gov/; Mattera, *Grand Theft Paycheck*; Fred Magdoff and John Bellamy Foster, "The Plight of the U.S. Working Class," *Monthly Review*, January 2014, 1–22. Because of the cyclical character of the economy, this panorama is likely to reoccur.

98 Lauren Weber, "The End of Employees: U.S. Companies Shift Work Once Considered Core to Contractors, Pruning Costs and Job Security," *Wall Street Journal*, February 3, 2017, A1. See also Mattera, *Grand Theft Paycheck*.

99 Weber, "End of Employees," A1.

100 Weber, "End of Employees," A10.

101 *The Economist*, "Temporary Work: How the 2% Lives; Temp is On the Increase, Affecting Temps and Staff Workers Alike," July 16, 2016, 62–63. See also Mattera, *Grand Theft Paycheck*.

102 Lawrence F. Katz and Alan B. Krueger, *The Rise and Nature of Alternative Work Arrangements in the United States, 1995–2015*, March 29, 2016, https://krueger.princeton.edu/. The magnitude of contingency labor in the American economy has proven difficult to estimate, mainly because Bureau of Labor Statistics (BLS) surveys measure only those whose primary job is as a contractor, vendor, or freelancer. Therefore, workers that are included in any payroll but are also employed as temporary or independent contractors, freelancers, or vendors are not included. The disparity between BLS data and the reality of contingency labor has been noted by some sources—see McKinsey Global Institute, *Independent Work: Choice, Necessity and the Gig Economy*, October 2016, www.mckinsey.com/; MBO Partners, *MBO Blog: Worker Misclassification*, www.mbopartners

anticipated that many technology companies might soon have no full-time employees of their own, except executives.[103]

Technology oligopolies also strengthened their control over labor during the last decade by promoting the scrapping of labor safeguards and laws—making it easier to reduce employment security, rights, and compensation.[104] A well-known review of state-level legislative changes, for example, noted that:

> they undermine the wages, working conditions, legal protections, and bargaining power of either organized or unorganized employees.... The consequence of the legislative agenda is to undermine the ability of workers to earn middle-class wages, and to enhance the power of employers in the labor market. These changes did not just happen but were the results of an intentional and persistent campaign by business groups.[105]

The "business groups" in question were all prominently funded, led by, or otherwise obeisant to, the interests of oligopolistic corporations across the American economy. Weak or docile labor unions—and continuous declines in union membership—have been a consequence of those state-level changes. Union membership among private sector employees in the United States has declined to historically low records and will likely decline further in coming years. This trend has been accompanied by increasingly lax safety enforcement by authorities. U.S. Occupational Safety and Health Administration staff, for example, were estimated to be capable of inspecting each workplace only once every 99 years.[106]

Collusion among oligopsonistic corporations has been part of the effort to achieve and sustain greater control over labor markets. Tacit agreements

.com/ (accessed June 16, 2022); Liya Palagashvili, "Don't Be So Sure the Gig is Up," *Wall Street Journal*, June 13, 2018, A21.

103 Accenture PLC—one of the world's largest broker-consultants on this specialty—has forecast this scenario. See Accenture, *Future Workforce Insights*, and its *Workforce Market Place*, www.accenture.com/ (both accessed December 13, 2020); Weber, "End of Employees." Some TVC worker-providing companies—that essentially serve as intermediaries between individual workers and the contracting corporation—may become oligopsonists in their sector.

104 See Don Clark, "HP, HP Enterprise Hit with Claims of Age Discrimination," *Wall Street Journal*, August 29, 2016, B6; Lauren Weber, "Companies Block Staff from Filing Lawsuits," *Wall Street Journal*, April 1, 2015, B1, and her "Some Tech Workers are Underpaid," Wall Street Journal, January 11, 2017, B7; Mattera, *Grand Theft Paycheck*.

105 Gordon Lafer, *The Legislative Attack on American Wages and Labor Standards, 2011-12*, Economic Policy Institute, Briefing Paper 364, October 31, 2013, http://epi.org

106 U.S. Department of Labor, Occupational Safety and Health Administration, *Data and Statistics*, www.osha.gov/ (accessed March 3, 2022). See also Magdoff and Foster, "Plight of the U.S. Working Class"; Kris Maher, "House Bill Would Boost Federal Authority Over Workplace Safety," *Wall Street Journal*, April 18, 2013, www.wsj.com/. The proposed legislation (noted in the last article) was never approved.

to forgo recruiting employees from each other are an example of this practice. One case involved some of the world's largest and wealthiest technology corporations—Apple, Google, Intel, Adobe Systems, Intuit, and the Pixar and Lucasfilm subsidiaries of Walt Disney. These corporations continuously engaged in this practice during a four-year period in the twenty-first century's first decade (2005-09)—an unusually long period of time.[107]

Extensive documentation on meetings between executives and their communications revealed how they agreed to this strategy and executed it. Among the vast number of documents found were regular reports by top executives, detailing how many employees left for companies outside the colluding group—along with the sharing of ideas to aggressively obstruct such departures. The evidence also showed that one of the legendary executives of the tech corporate universe—Steve Jobs—was a key participant in this scheme to curtail employee rights, suppress their compensation, and otherwise shortchange their careers.[108]

The colluding oligopsonists thereby sought to artificially create a situation of imbalance between highly skilled jobs and labor, by impeding the latter from leaving while obstructing higher compensation in the former. Boosting their surpluses—even as they enjoyed historically high revenues—was a key objective. The fact that this strategy was carried out by some of the world's best-known technology corporations—which all too frequently boast about their great workplace culture—is revealing about the strategies deployed to exercise greater control over labor.

Curtailment or elimination of retirement benefits—another feature of oligopsonistic labor markets—has added to the insecurity panorama. In the United States today, the majority of workers do not have any old-age retirement plan. The widespread elimination of conventional—or guaranteed benefit—plans by companies during the past three decades was a major contributor. For the few technology companies that offer guaranteed benefit retirement, a common tactic has been to induce workers to choose "lump sum" payments.[109] If chosen, the employee often purchases an annuity from an (usually oligopolistic) insurer, but the income eventually received is often less than what would be obtained with a guaranteed benefit program. And, during the last decade,

107 Jeff Elder, "Tech Giants Discussed Hiring, Say Documents," *Wall Street Journal*, April 21, 2014, A1; David Streitfeld, "Bigger Settlement Said to be Reached in Silicon Valley Antitrust Case," *New York Times*, January 14, 2015, http://nytimes.com/.

108 Elder, "Tech Giants," A4.

109 See Stephanie AuWerter, *How to Choose Between a Pension and Lump Sum Payout*, AARP September 11, 2020, www.aarp.org/; Lydia DePillis, "It Just Became Easier for Employers to Dump Retirees' Pensions," *CNN Business*, March 20, 2019, www.cnn.com/; Emily Chasan and Kristin Lin, "Pension Buyouts Gain Luster: More Companies Move to Cut Obligations, Costs by Offering Ex-Workers Lump-Sum Payments," *Wall Street Journal*, September 8, 2015, B5.

about one-fifth of all lump sum payees were estimated to deplete their funds in less than six years.[110]

The preferred tactic for technology corporations, however, has been to replace guaranteed benefit retirement plans with "defined benefit"—also known as 401(k)—programs, a trend that started four decades ago. During the last decade, it was found that almost three-quarters of all employees—typically full-time, in-house—in the United States who have *any* workplace plan are covered solely by these programs.[111] And they basically require continuous stock and bond market betting by employees to have any hope of securing enough income to live on, when they reach old age.

The burden placed on employees by these plans is overwhelming, as individuals are forced to guess their longevity and future spending, evaluate the different risks of stocks or bonds, divine what inflation might be like, decide on allocations, anticipate fees, and assess if the employer allows a choice—whether other retirement fund companies can provide better returns. Moreover, it has been a longstanding practice—among the retirement-fund corporations contracted for 401(k) programs—to favor their own funds over those of other companies. Doing so often constrains choices and can shortchange employees' returns.[112]

Risks can also be magnified, especially when a 401(k) program holds a significant proportion of the corporate employer's own stock—while high fees can consume the amounts contributed by employees out of their salaries. During the last decade, Boeing's 190,000 employees and retirees, for example, had to sue to try to stop its longstanding practice of allowing high fees to be levied on them along with risky bets on stocks and bonds—including inducements to purchase large amounts of its own stock—in addition to favoring stock purchases of client companies.[113] Other technology oligopolists—such as Lockheed Martin and IBM—faced similar lawsuits. Boeing's 401(k) plan was the second largest in the United States—after IBM's—and served as a model for those of many other companies. In 2009, it stopped offering any pension benefits to new non-union employees and thereafter gradually stopped providing them for union labor as well. In 2014, Boeing then unilaterally announced

110 MetLife, *Retirement Plan Lump Sums Being Depleted Too Quickly*, April 11, 2017, www.metlife.com/; AuWerter, *How to Choose.*

111 For an overview of the panorama and policies that have supported this situation, see Suarez-Villa, *Corporate Power, Oligopolies*, 119–25.

112 Aspects that attracted attention during the last decade, due to cyclical stock market downturns. See Andrew Blackman, "All in the Fund Family; Investors Beware: A Study Shows How Providers of 401(k)s Favor their Own Funds on the Menu," *Wall Street Journal*, July 5, 2016, R4; John Sullivan, "Plan Providers Biased toward their Own Mutual Funds: Pension Research Council," *401k Specialist*, June 18, 2015, https://401kspecialistmag.com/.

113 Sara Randazzo, "Boeing Fights Suit over its 401(k) Plan," *Wall Street Journal*, August 26, 2015, B1.

it would freeze all pre-existing, guaranteed-benefit pension plans for its more than 68,000 non-union employees, replacing them with 401(k) programs.[114]

Helping these practices is the notion that inducing employees to purchase large amounts of their employer's stock leads to a feeling of "co-ownership," when all too often the "stake" purchased by employees merely becomes a form of consent to their own exploitation.[115] A prominent jurist—the Chief Justice of Delaware's Supreme Court—once referred to workers in these programs as "forced capitalists"—a term intended to denote the compulsory enlistment of labor in the domain of financial speculation.[116] This scenario has contributed to a more insecure and exploitable labor force, as fear takes over minds—particularly for those over 50 years of age who have not been lucky enough or have not managed to accumulate sufficiently to retire. Insecure employment—for that segment of the workforce—usually means that the individual will be unable to retire. And, should the worker become unemployed or disabled, taxpayer-funded welfare programs would have to provide support—shifting the cost to taxpayers and the state.

Contingency Labor

The term contingency labor is often used to refer to those who experience underemployment, TVC-type work, and insecure employment. Such labor is now very much a part of the technology panorama. During the last decade, contingency labor was estimated to be about one-third of the American workforce—and it is now projected to increase to one-half by the second half of the 2020s.[117]

114 Randazzo, "Boeing Fights Suit."

115 See Timothy W. Martin, "401(k) Pioneers Lament What They Started: Retirement-Saving Vehicles Fall Short of Early Backers' Rosy Expectations," *Wall Street Journal*, January 3, 2017, A1; Anne Tergesen, "Plaintiffs Ramp Up 401(k) Lawsuits," *Wall Street Journal*, July 14, 2017, B1. Favorable views on stock purchases by employees ("co-ownership") have long been diffused by the media—see, for example, *The Economist*, "When Workers are Owners," August 22, 2015, 56.

116 See Leo E. Strine, Jr., *A New Deal for this Century: Making Our Economy Work for All*, New York University Law School, October, 2019, www.law.nyu.edu/; *The Economist*, "Reinventing the Deal," October 24, 2015, 21–24.

117 See U.S. Bureau of Labor Statistics, *A Profile of the Working Poor*, various years, http://bls.gov/ (accessed July 10, 2022); Lauren Weber, "The Flip Side of the New U.S. Economy: Millions of Contractors Struggle for Career Advancement, Stability and Respect at Work," *Wall Street Journal*, September 15, 2017, A9; Anna Louie Sussman and Josh Zumbrun, "'Gig' Economy Spreads Broadly," *Wall Street Journal*, March 26, 2016, A1; Ann Lowrey, "Caught in a Revolving Door of Unemployment," *New York Times*, November 16, 2013, http://nytimes.com/; Krueger and Katz, *Rise and Nature*. The U.S. Congress stopped funding data collection on irregular work—the Labor Department's biannual Contingent Workers Survey—in 2005. Thus, the contingency labor population does not seem to show up in—and cannot be differentiated from—other statistical employment categories. See Josh Zumbrun and Louie Sussman, "Proof of 'Gig Economy' Revolution Hard to Find in the Data," *Wall Street Journal*, July 27, 2015, A2. Contributing to this problem is the practice of paying contingent workers in cash (or cash-equivalent means) and treating such

This labor market is particularly important for many technology oligopolists. Today, contingency labor is so common that the term "1099 worker"—indicating the type of tax form to be filed—has become part of the employment vocabulary. Employing labor so designated does not require an employer to contribute payroll taxes; comply with minimum wage and safety regulations; or pay for health insurance, training programs, unemployment, sick leave, overtime, vehicle expenses, retirement benefits, severance, and travel.[118]

A related practice during the last decade—grounded in the online "app" platforms owned by Apple and Microsoft—was for oligopsonic tech-service corporations (many of which are also oligopolists in their product markets) to classify individual employees as "franchisees" or limited liability company (LLC) "owners."[119] The LLC and franchise "ownership" arrangements involve one person—the employee. This allows a corporation to take the employee off its payroll—thereby lowering costs—and it also provides the legal means to charge the employee for "owning" the "franchise" or the "LLC" arrangement required by the employer. And the "franchisee" fee imposed by the employer can be as high as $35,000 or more, depending on the activity.[120]

For a tech-service oligopolist, the additional surpluses provided by these arrangements can be very advantageous. They also allow the employer to transfer risk to employees. Thus, the employee—the new "franchisee" or LLC "owner"—will be forced to secure her own insurance, for work tasks that the employer previously paid for. For the employer, the immediate result will be lower operating costs, larger surpluses, higher executive compensation, and greater control over the workforce.

Many tech-based services—the so-called "on-demand startups"—many of which can be considered oligopolistic, depend greatly on contingency labor. The business models of these mobile app-enabled corporations are based on short timelines for certain services—transportation, food delivery, personal or home tasks. One such corporation—Uber Technologies, considered to be a

compensation as payment for an "external service"—separately paid from hired part- or full-time employees. Those performing contingent work are thus often not counted as employees. The individuals concerned may also tend to avoid reporting their status for various reasons (tax avoidance, maintaining eligibility for welfare, and other benefits, for example). Another aspect is the widespread recognition that official unemployment statistics are incomplete—typically missing or undercounting the underemployed.

118 App-enabled daily or hourly payment of contingent workers (in place of weekly or monthly payouts) that places compensation in debit cards—such that the amounts can be spent immediately—is a common practice. The ready availability of such cash is thought to make it harder to build savings and can lead to longer (poorly compensated) worktime. See Kelsey Gee, "Apps Give Workers Early Access to Pay," *Wall Street Journal*, November 25, 2017, A1.

119 See Lauren Weber, "Some Bosses Reclassify Employees to Cut Costs," *Wall Street Journal*, July 1, 2015, B1.

120 Weber, "Some Bosses Reclassify," B7.

model of this type of business—has tens of thousands of "contract" (or 1099) workers in the United States alone, yet it has claimed to have no employees of its own.[121] During the last decade, this company's employment contracts were found to require workers to waive their right to any legal class-action arbitration involving pay or benefits—such as health and unemployment insurance or work-related expenses such as fuel, road tolls, or car repairs.[122]

Contingency labor now also encompasses R&D activities. Having an advanced degree is therefore less likely to provide stable employment than at any previous time. Simplification of tasks—and automation—have made it easier to externalize R&D work through TVC arrangements. Implementation of AI routines in research—a topic that will be dealt with in the following chapter—has also made many highly skilled workers redundant.

When certain skills are scarce, immigration can be resorted to. U.S. authorities, and the ready availability of consultants abroad that can screen applicants, has made this possibility easier than ever to pursue. The highly skilled immigrant worker may then receive compensation that is lower than that of TVC labor. And, the conditions imposed by visa laws typically favor the employer.[123]

To maintain residency and avoid deportation, an immigrant must remain employed, and the employer that recruited the individual must routinely certify it to authorities. Switching employers for a higher salary or better conditions is therefore out of the question, and—should the worker be furloughed—time limitations may make it necessary to find employment on short notice or face deportation. Recurring to immigration thus contributes to the contingency labor population at home while making skilled work less secure. And it sends a message to those with advanced degrees or high qualifications that they are vulnerable.

121 See Brian Chen and Maya Pinto, *Uber's New Worker Bill is the Same Old Trick: Deregulation and Special Treatment for Exploitive Companies*, National Employment Law Project, June 20, 2021, www.nelp.org/; Ankita Rao, "Uber was Designed to Exploit Drivers," *Vice*, May 8, 2019, www.vice.com/; Greg Bensinger, "Startups Scramble to Define 'Employee'," *Wall Street Journal*, July 30, 2015, B1. See also Steven Hill, *Raw Deal: How the "Uber Economy" and Runaway Capitalism are Screwing American Workers* (New York: St. Martin's Press, 2015); *The Economist*, "From Zero to Seventy (Billion): The Life and Times of the World's Most Valuable Startup," September 3, 2016, 17–19. Self-drive vehicle technology may eventually make it possible for Uber to reduce its "1099" workforce immensely, if not almost completely—see Greg Bensinger and Jack Nicas, "Uber Plans Self-Drive Taxis," *Wall Street Journal*, August 19, 2016, B1.

122 See Chen and Pinto, *Uber's New Worker Bill*; Rao, "Uber was Designed."

123 See U.S. Citizenship and Immigration Services, *Combatting Fraud and Abuse in the H2-B Visa Program*, www.uscis.gov/ (accessed July 10, 2022); Sarah Jaffe, "'You're Fired!' The Abuses of 'Skilled' Worker Visa Programs," *The Progressive*, February 22, 2016, https://progressive.org/; Tekla S. Perry, "Migrant Tech Workers Abused by Contract Labor Firms, Investigation Shows," *IEEE Spectrum*, October 30, 2014, https://spectrum.ieee.org/.

Uselabor

A novel form of labor market control involves social media. In this case, however, the distinction between oligopsony and oligopoly is blurred. *Users can be considered a form of uncompensated labor,* as they are made to freely give away their intimate data—along with their time, effort, and online experiences. *Such data are among the most valuable commodities of our time.* And *users are also customers,* as they view and purchase advertised products. One mode of control feeds the other.

The corporations in control *sell* access to users' data *to* advertisers—the other customers.[124] Ad targeting opportunities—and, potentially, sales—are the products sold in this case. App developers gain access to users' data and may also be considered customers.[125] Legally binding "terms of service" agreements for users—requiring consent for intimate data to be appropriated, mined, and sold to third parties—set this oligopsonistic-*cum*-oligopolistic dynamic in motion. All required for users to gain access to the network and communicate with others—a vital human social necessity. Vast amounts of personal data are thus appropriated by the corporations that own the networks—an extremely profitable undertaking that most users are not aware of.

A similar situation occurs for search engine users, whose preferences and habits are appropriated, mined, and sold—as ad targeting opportunities and potential sales.[126] In addition, search engine oligopolists can sell access to the appropriated-and-mined users' data—to merchants who pay for listings in comparison-shopping programs, for example. Skewing search results on the latter—to prioritize its merchant-clients' listings—can benefit a search engine oligopolist greatly.[127] Merchants may thus be made to bid and pay for listing

124 An aspect that attracted some attention during the last decade—see Abby McCourt, *Social Media Mining: The Effects of Big Data in the Age of Social Media,* Yale Law School, MFIA, April 3, 2018, htpps://law.yale.edu/; Jacob Silverman, "The Facebook Scandal Isn't Really about Social Media; It's About Capitalism," *Washington Post,* December 20, 2018, www.washingtonpost.com/; Bruce Schneier, *Data and Goliath: The Hidden Battles to Collect Your Data and Control Your World* (New York: Norton, 2015), chapters 1–4, 8.

125 See Sam Schechner and Mark Secada, "You Give Apps Sensitive Personal Information, then They Tell Facebook," *Wall Street Journal,* February 22, 2019, www.wsj.com/. See also Gabriel J. X. Dance, Nicholas Confessore and Michael LaForgia, "Facebook Gave Phone Makers Vast Access to Users' Data," *New York Times,* June 4, 2018, www.nytimes.com/.

126 See Bennett Cyphers, *Google Says It Doesn't 'Sell' Your Data; Here's How the Company Shares, Monetizes, and Exploits It,* Electronic Frontier Foundation, March 19, 2020, www.eff.org/; Natalia Drozdiak and Jack Nicas, "Google User-Data Policy Examined," *Wall Street Journal,* January 25, 2017, A1.

127 A matter that raised concerns from European Union regulators during the last decade (but not from their U.S. counterparts)—see Josie Co, "Google Hit with Record Fine Over 'Unfair' Shopping Searches," *Independent,* June 27, 2017, www.independent.co.uk/. See also Sam Schechner, Natalia Drozdiak and Alistair Barr, "Google Digs in for Protracted Antitrust Fight," *Wall Street Journal,* August 28, 2015, B1.

rank order and possibly also give up a percentage of sales. The higher a merchant's product is placed in search result listings, the more likely it is that a sale will occur—and the higher the eventual revenue for the search engine oligopsonist-*cum*-oligopolist.[128]

As intimate contact data cannot usually be appropriated through web searches, free email service may be provided. Search companies can then scan messages for email contacts and contents—subject to much the same "terms of service" agreements as social media network access.[129] And, even when mining of email content is curbed, other data—such as locations, search histories, routines, and website viewing preferences—can be compiled, mined, and sold.[130] App developers also gain access to users' data, as their product is indispensable for smartphone searches and communication. Developers may thus sell users' data they appropriate—independently.

The advertisement corporations that purchase access to the data, in turn, are hired by (usually oligopolistic) clients in most every sector of the economy. Individually targeted advertisements are the objective—a most important source of surpluses. Mobile targeted ads alone accounted for over 80 percent of Facebook's advertisement sales in the last decade, becoming a major source of its surpluses.[131]

Partial advertisement blockage can sometimes become a strategic tool, to achieve greater control over accumulated data—especially when ads to be blocked were placed by a rival.[132] Curtailing data access to non-advertisers can also help bolster control—as in the case of Facebook's exclusion of researchers and some service providers—when it decided to take over their activities during the last decade.[133] Thus, any new technology that can serve as a medium for targeted advertisements is bound to be exploited rapidly—and

128 Beyond shopping, priority of search listings—and favoritism—attracted concern during the last decade. See Kirsten Grind, Sam Schechner, Robert McMillan and John West, "How Google Interferes with Its Search Algorithms and Changes Your Results," *Wall Street Journal*, November 15, 2019, www.wsj.com/.

129 Douglas MacMillan, Sarah Krouse and Keach Hagey, "Yahoo, Bucking Industry, Scans Emails for Data to Sell: Web Giant Pushes Harder to Analyze Inboxes for Advertisers," *Wall Street Journal*, August 29, 2018, A1; *NBC News*, "Google Faces $5 Billion Lawsuit in U.S. for Tracking 'Private' Internet Use," June 2, 2020, www.nbcnews.com/.

130 Jack Nicas, "Google to Curb Mining of User Emails for Ads," *Wall Street Journal*, June 24, 2017, B1; *NBC News*, "Google Faces $5 Billion Lawsuit."

131 See Ad Age, *10 Major Issues Digital Marketing May Face in the Future*, July 15, 2020, https://adage.com/; Deepa Seetharaman, "Facebook Rides Mobile-Ad Surge," *Wall Street Journal*, July 28, 2016, B1.

132 Daisuke Wakabayashi and Jack Marshall, "Apple's Ad Blockers Rile Publishers," *Wall Street Journal*, August 31, 2015, B1. In this case, Apple justified its ad blockage by claiming that the ads in question "compromised performance" in its proprietary gadgets (iPhones, iPads). See also Jack Marshall, "Facebook Fights Back against Ad Blockers," *Wall Street Journal*, August 10, 2016, B4.

133 Deepa Seetharaman and Elizabeth Dwoskin, "Facebook Restricts Access to Its Data Trove," *Wall Street Journal*, September 22, 2015, B1.

any regulatory effort to block ads is bound to be opposed fiercely. It should not surprise, then, that acquisitions by social media network oligopolies are often pursued on the basis of the personal data bases (and clouds) owned by a targeted company.[134]

The kind of personal data mined and sold by the social media network and search engine oligopolists can be very diverse. They can include, for example, shopping, health, politics, family circumstances, race, sexual preferences, fitness, physical appearance, sports, betting, finances, location, legal problems, properties, recreational habits, travel, and educational interests. No activity and preference expressed or performed online—or anything that can be related to one's personal profile—is likely to be spared. Practically everything that an individual can do online may thus end up being mined, archived, updated, and reused—anywhere, anytime—for most any purpose that serves the interests of the company that appropriated the data.

Such information is a treasure trove for contriving demand for any item that a product development outfit (the D in R&D) can conceive. In the case of social media, personal preferences can also be diffused to online contacts—to promote imitation effects that can benefit advertisers. Beyond advertisements, personal information can be sold to numerous parties—among them marketing consultants, financiers who bet on corporations that advertise, political consultants, potential hackers or criminals, and government agencies that use the data for various purposes—including law enforcement, tax compliance, surveillance, espionage, warfare, or network analyses.[135]

Users thus become revenue generators for social media and search corporations—and for other parties upstream. Since most advertisement companies are themselves oligopolists in their sector—and many of their clients are also oligopolistic—the *social media–search–advertisement oligopolistic combine* constitutes a formidable power base—one that most every social media or search engine user may not even know exists. *As a labor market, it is possibly the most peculiar combination of technology with corporate power and labor exploitation that has ever existed.* So well camouflaged is this collusion of oligopolistic corporate interests and power that not even regulators seem to understand it well.

134 An aspect that attracted attention during the last decade. See McCourt, *Social Media Mining*; Schneier, *Data and Goliath*; Deepa Seetharaman and Brian R. Fitzgerald, "WhatsApp Shifts on Sharing Data with Facebook," *Wall Street Journal*, August 26, 2016, B5.

135 See Zak Doffman, "Your Social Media is (Probably) Being Watched Right Now, Says New Surveillance Report," *Forbes*, November 6, 2019, www.forbes.com/; Michael Grothaus, "How Our Data Got Hacked, Scandalized, and Abused in 2018," *Fast Company*, December 13, 2018, www.fastcompany.com/; Matthew Cagle, "Facebook, Instagram, and Twitter Provided Data for a Surveillance Product Marketed to Target Activists of Color," *Free Future-American Civil Liberties Union*, October 11, 2016, www.aclu.org/; Jonah Engel Bromwich, Daniel Victor and Mike Isaac, "Police Use Surveillance Tool to Scan Social Media, A.C.L.U. Says," *New York Times*, October 11, 2016, www.nytimes.com/.

Those exploited through this oligopsonistic-*cum*-oligopolistic work regime may be referred to as *uselabor*—as usage is combined with work to generate data *and* enrich the corporations in control. Work *and* usage are thus entwined, and the boundaries between the two become blurred.[136] All too often, it is impossible to separate one from the other. Much the same can be said about usage that involves play and gaming.[137] Play helps conceal the nature of uselabor, mainly because many consider it "entertainment"—even though uselaborers contribute vast amounts of uncompensated time, effort, experiences, and personal data to enrich the companies in control.

Oligopsonistic-*cum*-oligopolistic control over the uselabor market depends a lot on automation. Appropriating personal data from uselaborers was initially automated through the use of software robots—chatbots—that sped up and refined data collection, "inviting" uselaborers to interact online.[138] Such "interactions" help the companies in control add much detail to the data they appropriate, and they are important for targeting advertisements. Algorithms and chatbots also make it possible for no two uselaborers with similar interests to receive the same social media feeds or search results.[139] One consequence is that the web's original objective of becoming a digital commons has been preempted, as all searches and feeds are personalized.[140]

136 Attempts to provide terms that might represent this phenomenon have included, for example, Alvin Toffler's "prosumption"—combining production and consumption [in his *The Third Wave* (New York: Morrow, 1980)]—and Julian Kücklich's "playbour," denoting the fusion of play with labor, in his "Precarious Playbour: Modders and the Digital Game Industry (FCJ-025)," *Fibreculture Journal*, December 5, 2005, http://fibreculturejournal.org/; and his *Playability: Prolegomena zu einer Computerspielphilologie* (Saarbrücken: Müller, 2008). Earlier, Dallas Smythe provided important critical analyses, by conceptualizing how audiences become commodities—"audience labor"—in his "Critique of the Consciousness Industry," *Journal of Communication* 27(1977), 198–202; and his *Dependency Road: Communication, Capitalism, Consciousness, and Canada* (Norwood: Ablex, 1981).

137 In "e-sports," it was found that uselaborer-players can generate substantial revenue for the corporations in control, whenever advertisements appear alongside videos that highlight play. See Ed Dixon, "Study: Global E-sports Revenue to Hit Almost $1.1 Billion in 2021," *SportsPro*, March 9, 2021, www.sportspromedia.com/; Sarah E. Needleman, "Newest Job in Sports: Videogame Coach," *Wall Street Journal*, July 29, 2015, B1.

138 See Daria Zaboj, "Key Chatbot Statistics You Should Follow in 2021," *ChatBot* May 6, 2020, www.chatbot.com/; Victoria Klochkova, *Four Real Time Uses of Chatbots in Social Media Marketing*, Search Engine People, August 31, 2017, www.searchenginepeople.com/; Robert MacMillan, "Facebook Focuses on Smarter Chatbots," *Wall Street Journal*, April 18, 2016, B5.

139 Josh Loh, "Targeting, Chatbots, and Personalisation—How the AFL Broke Records on Facebook," *Marketing*, September 12, 2018, www.marketingmag.com.au/; Klochkova, *Four Real Time Uses*; *The Economist*, "Growing Up: How the Internet Lost Its Free Spirit," March 26, 2016, 93–94; MacMillan, "Facebook Focuses."

140 See Christian Fuchs, *Communication and Capitalism: A Critical Theory* (London: University of Westminster Press, 2020), chapters 5, 6; Scott Malcolmson, *Splinternet: How Geopolitics and Commerce are Fragmenting the World Wide Web* (New York: OR Books, 2016), chapters 1, 3; Robert W. McChesney, *Digital Disconnect: How Capitalism is Turning the Web against Democracy* (New York: New Press, 2013), chapters 3–5.

Another outcome is that the social media and search oligopolists know more about us than most of us know about ourselves—in a very intimate way.[141] No intelligence agency in history—or all of them combined—ever managed to accumulate as much data on individuals as the social media and search companies have.[142] Thus, over 80 percent of the internet is now fenced in by corporations such as Facebook and Google—whose decisions and algorithms are largely unknown to uselaborers and the public. Online ads—targeted using the intimate data they have appropriated—have therefore become a most important source of wealth for these companies. And, since the middle of the last decade, advertising corporations have spent much more in placing ads online than on television, radio, and print media combined.[143]

In tandem with the vast control exercised by the social media and search companies, concentration in the advertising sector has generated much power for some corporations. One company, for example, has claimed that it issues contracts for one-third of all ads placed in the world.[144] Those corporations—and the social media and search companies—have effectively appropriated the web and bent rules to their advantage—placing ads on an equal footing with other communications.[145] And they also managed to eliminate much mobile ad blockage. Advertising companies targeting billions of uselaborers thus now control the web, and their power is bound to increase as online transactions increase.[146]

141 See Christian Fuchs, *Social Media: A Critical Introduction* (London: Sage, 2021), chapters 5–8, 12; Julia Angwin, Terry Parris, Jr. and Surya Mattu, "Facebook Doesn't Tell Users Everything It Really Knows About Them: The Site Shows Users How It Categorizes Them, It Doesn't Reveal the Data It is Buying About their Offline Lives," *ProPublica*, December 27, 2016, www.propublica.org/; Cagle, "Facebook, Instagram, and Twitter."

142 See Fuchs, *Social Media*, chapters 3, 9; Julia Angwin, "You Know Who Else Collected Metadata? The Stasi," *ProPublica*, February 11, 2014, www.propublica.org/; Nicole Collins Bronzan, "ProPublica: When U.S. Companies Help the NSA," *ProPublica*, October 21, 2014, www.propublica.org/; Cagle, "Facebook, Instagram, and Twitter"; Bromwich, Victor and Isaac, "Police Use Surveillance Tool."

143 BI Intelligence, "Interpublic Shifts $250 Million from TV Ad Budgets to YouTube," *Business Insider*, May 5, 2016, www.businessinsider.com/; PwC Advisory Services LLC and Interactive Advertising Bureau, *IAB Advertising Revenue Report*, April 2016, https://www.iab.com/. The Media Rating Council considered an advertisement to have been viewed if at least one second is spent looking at half of its text, images, or sound—see Media Rating Council, "MRC Viewable Ad Impression Measurement Guidelines (Desktop)," 2015, and its "MRC Mobile Viewable Ad Impression Measurement Guidelines," Public Comment Draft, 2016, mediaratingcouncil.org; *The Economist*, "Digital Advertising: Invisible Ads, Phantom Readers," March 26, 2016, 69–70. See also Fuchs, *Communication and Capitalism*, Chapter 6; and his *Social Media*, Chapter 7.

144 See Group M's website—see https://www.groupm.com (accessed July 17, 2022).

145 *The Economist*, "Growing Up"; Matthew Broughton, "The Fight against Ad Blocking: Why Blocking the Blockers is Not Enough," *Exchange Wire*, June 12, 2019, www.exchangewire.com/; *The Economist*, "Mobile Advertising," March 26, 2016, 70.

146 See Fuchs, *Social Media*, chapters 5–8; Malcolmson, *Splinternet*.

Global annual spending on advertising through social media and search oligopsonists-*cum*-oligopolists is projected to rise to hundreds of billions of dollars in the near future—an amount that will be larger than the economic product of most nations.[147] This is the most important support for capital accumulation in the social media–search–advertising combine. Sustaining this panorama is that advertisement companies charge their clients between three and seven times more for targeted ads than the blindly placed ones.[148]

The effectiveness of targeted ads is at the core of this panorama, as the chances of executing a sale and showing more products are much higher. When shopping is added, the combined amount obtained by the social media–search–advertising combine may reach several trillion dollars annually in a few years' time. The projected future number of uselaborers—at least five billion worldwide, all of whom would be freely giving up their personal data—is also astounding.[149]

Facebook's uselaborer population may soon be several billion—on a monthly basis—a formidable fenced-in market.[150] Ad-based revenue has consistently grown rapidly annually, and its profitability will likely be among the highest of all corporations in the world for many years. During the last decade, Google's estimated annual profit rose to several billion dollars annually, as it imitated some of Facebook's tactics and mined its own uselaborers' data intensively—especially email communications and shopping habits.[151]

147 Statista, *Social Network Advertising Spending in the United States from 2016 to 2022*, www.statista.com/ (accessed July 12, 2022). See also *The Economist*, "Marketing in the Digital Age: A Brand New Game," August 29, 2015, 51–52; Robert W. Gehl, *Reverse Engineering Social Media: Software, Culture, and Political Economy in New Media Capitalism* (Philadelphia: Temple University Press, 2014), chapters 1, 2.

148 Based on a study funded by the Digital Advertisement Alliance, http://www.aboutads.info/ (accessed July 12, 2022). See also *Social Network Advertising Spending*; Elizabeth Dwoskin, "'Do Not Track' Compromise is Pitched," *Wall Street Journal*, August 6, 2015, B6; Katy Bachman, "Advertisers Pay 3 Times More for Cookie-Based Ads: But Will Consumer Privacy Regulation Alter the Landscape?" *Adweek*, February 10, 2014, http://www.adweek.com/news/.

149 StatCounter, *Social Media Stats Worldwide*, https://gs.statcounter.com/ (accessed July 12, 2022). Increasing returns due to larger network extent—a fundamental feature of most digital networks—must be taken into account. For a discussion of network extent, see Suarez-Villa, *Technocapitalism*, 57–67.

150 Statista, *Number of Monthly Active Facebook Users Worldwide as of 4th Quarter 2021*, www.statista.com/ (accessed July 22, 2022). See also Willa Plank and Carlos A. Tovar, "The Short Answer: Who are Facebook's Biggest Friends?" *Wall Street Journal*, April 9, 2015, B5. To expand its global pool of uselaborers during the last decade, Facebook offered free online access in India. The program, Free Basics, was considered to be a "gateway drug" to enlist uselaborers—see *The Economist*, "Facebook in India: Can't Give It Away," January 9, 2016, 55.

151 Rolfe Winkler and Jack Marshall, "Google Imitates Facebook with Email Marketing," *Wall Street Journal*, April 14, 2015, www.wsj.com/. To further raise revenue, during the last decade, Facebook and Google started asking companies that contract advertisers to hand over their customers' information and emails—along with data in loyalty programs.

Facebook's high surpluses—obtained through its vast uselaborer population—have allowed it to mount serial acquisitions. Two such companies—WhatsApp and Instagram—were purchased in the last decade for little more than 10 percent of its own market capitalization.[152] Its acquisitions also allowed Facebook to gain control over diverse communication platforms and to expand into such areas as artificial intelligence, messaging, and virtual reality. As a result, more than one in three of all mobile internet usage in the United States is done through its apps, while its global uselaborer population encompasses more than one-third of all internet-connected people.[153] Its acquisitions thus allowed Facebook to embed itself ever deeper into everyone's daily lives and routines.

This crucial aspect was not lost on other web-based companies, as attracting finance capital came to depend greatly on pervasive uselaborer data mining. In Apple's case, expanding its uselaborer population and mining their data attracted much interest in Wall Street. Apple had long been viewed by financiers as a "hardware" company—with stock prices that were well below those of social media and search engine companies.[154] Companies in the search, software, and mobile telephony sectors—such as Google, Microsoft, and Apple—are thus continuously refining their exploitation of uselaborer data.[155] And it is expected that they will intensively refine their software—which already operate most of the world's smartphones—to more accurately predict uselaborers' behavior and preferences.[156]

Some of the most powerful corporations in the social media–search–advertising combine—Facebook, Google, Apple, Microsoft, and Twitter, in particular—became the most important news providers during the last decade. Thus, the majority of all adults in the United States today receive their first exposure to breaking news—particularly on politics and government—from

152 Gabrielle Canon, "Facebook Faces Antitrust Allegations over Deals for Instagram and Whatsapp," *The Guardian*, December 8, 2020, www.theguardian.com/.

153 Statista, *Number of Monthly Active Facebook Users*.

154 Macrotrends, *Apple—41 Year Stock Price History/AAPL*, www.macrotrends.net/ (accessed July 13, 2022). See also Erik Holm, "For Goldman, Apple's Content is King," *Wall Street Journal*, November 19, 2015, C4. Perception of Apple as a "hardware" company dated from the time when it was focused on designing and manufacturing PCs (starting in the 1970s).

155 See Statista, *Statistics and Facts on Google, Amazon, Facebook, Apple, and Microsoft (GAFAM)*, www.statista.com/ (accessed July 14, 2022); Kaled M. Ahmed, "Effects of Design Elements for Social Media Ads on Consumers' Purchasing Decision," *Global Media Journal*, March 2020, www.globalmediajournal.com/.

156 Ahmed, "Effects of Design Elements"; Dokyun Lee, Kartik Hosanagar and Harikesh Nair, "Advertisement Content and Consumer Engagement on Social Media: Evidence from Facebook," *Management Science*, 64 (2018), https://repository.upenn.edu/; Carolyn A. Lin and Tonghoon Kim, "Predicting User Response to Sponsored Advertising on Social Media via the Technology Acceptance Model," *Computers in Human Behavior* 64 (2016), 710–18; Daisuke Wakabayashi and Alistair Barr, "Apple and Google Race to Predict What You Want," *Wall Street Journal*, August 4, 2015, B1.

social media.[157] This further increased the surpluses obtained through targeted advertising.[158] Providing news keeps uselaborers on platforms longer, allowing more time and opportunities to target ads and mine data.[159] Issues of tacit censorship and selectivity in the news fed to uselaborers thus raise questions about how perceptions are being shaped.[160]

Since personal data mining determines both the advertisements to target to uselaborers *and* the news they will be fed, the two operations—ad targeting and news—are highly correlated. Individually targeting news involves much the same automated procedure as targeting advertisements, thereby providing economies of scale and function. As the dominant providers of news around the world, these oligopsonists-*cum*-oligopolists can therefore influence greatly what people know, learn, and feel. Provision of censored, biased, or fake news has thus become easier than ever.[161]

Also, the personalization of news means that no two uselaborers with similar interests may be fed the same news reports—as the data mining algorithms decide what is "best" for them to know (much as occurs with advertisements).[162] Tacitly targeting, omitting, censoring, or spinning news content thus seems to be built into their systems—even when such practices are not explicitly

157 See Statista, *Share of Adults Who Use Social Media as a Source of News in Selected Countries Worldwide as of February 2022*, www.statista.com/; Mike Vorhaus, "People Increasingly Turn to Social Media for News," *Forbes*, June 24, 2020, www.forbes.com/; Pew Research Center, *News Media Trends*, www.journalism.org/ (accessed July 17, 2022); Jane Wakefield, "Social Media 'Outstrips TV' as News Source for Young People," *BBC*, June 15, 2016, www.bbc.com/.

158 See Vorhaus, "People Increasingly Turn"; Deepa Seetharaman, "Facebook's Ad Shifts Power Its Earnings," *Wall Street Journal*, July 26, 2017, B1.

159 See Vorhaus, "People Increasingly Turn"; Christopher Mims, "How Facebook's Master Algorithm Powers the Social Network: The Algorithm Behind Facebook's News Feed, A 'Modular Layered Cake' Extracts Meaning from Every Post and Photo," *Wall Street Journal*, October 22, 2017, www.wsj.com/articles/.

160 See *Reuters*, "Social Media Firms Put Profit Above Principle: Singapore Minister," January 12, 2021, www.reuters.com/; *The Economist*, "Technology Companies and Censorship—The Deciders: Social-Media Platforms Have Travelled Further Down the Road of Censoring What People Say and See than Users Probably Realise," September 8, 2018, 52–54.

161 See Stephanie Panke, "Social Media and Fake News," *AACE Review*, April 10, 2019, www.ace.org/; Benjamin Mullin and Deepa Seetharaman, "Big Tech Asked How it Fights Fake News: Lawmakers Question Facebook, Twitter and Google, Revealing a Muddled Approach," *Wall Street Journal*, July 18, 2018, B4. Corporate advertisements were considered to have funded some fake news sites and postings during the last decade—see, for example, Jack Nicas, "Big Brands' Ads Give Boost to Sites Touting Fake News," *Wall Street Journal*, December 8, 2016, A1.

162 See *The Economist*, "Technology Companies and Censorship"; Mims, "How Facebook's Master Algorithm"; Jeffrey Herbst, "The Algorithm is an Editor," *Wall Street Journal*, April 14, 2016, A15. During the last decade, Facebook's designation of articles that attracted uselaborers' attention as "clickbait"—guided by whether viewers return to the plaform after viewing them—reflected the importance placed on news content—see, for example, Deepa Seetharaman, "Facebook Demotes 'Clickbait' News Again," *Wall Street Journal*, August 5, 2016, B4.

approved by executives.[163] And, the fact that the companies in the social media–search–advertising combine do not have news reporters of their own makes it easier for these practices to occur. It also makes it possible to deny—and conceal—the vast influence that they have over what uselaborers see and believe.

Expanding and refining control over the uselabor market can include new capabilities. These often involve marginal changes on what is already provided. This has been the case with the corporations that control mobile computing and communication. Among the new capabilities, for example, is signaling a caller's type of business activity to recipients, based on feedback obtained through a social network. Uselaborers are thus tacitly enlisted to provide information on the calls they receive—becoming enablers of the new capability. Once a caller's telephone number or email is associated with a certain activity, this information can be reused indefinitely—and uselaborers can even be surveyed and the data they provide can be sold to callers and advertisers.

Introducing new capabilities can therefore provide substantial advantages. During the last decade, for example, Google's Android platform achieved control over more than three-quarters of the mobile-computing sector in a short time. This was aided by the fact that any new, competing operating system would require app providers to write new programs—an expensive undertaking with uncertain results.[164] Also during the last decade, Apple gained control over almost one-fifth of mobile computing due to its power over hardware, its apps, and its proprietary software.[165] Google and Apple thus gained control over 95 percent of mobile computing, making it very difficult and risky for new (or small) companies to establish themselves. And, also during the last decade, Facebook's introduction of camera-centric capabilities, imitating features already provided by another (smaller) company—along with video content and films—helped expand its formidable uselaborer market.[166]

163 See Siobhan Ryan, "Facebook's Australian News Wipeout Showed It can Delete Our History at Any Time," *The Guardian*, February 28, 2021, www.theguardian.com/. Another case involved Facebook's deletion of a photo from the Vietnam war, that provided evidence of U.S. bombing of civilians—Kjetil Malkenes Hovland and Deepa Seetharaman, "Facebook Rethinks Policy: Protests from Norway Prompt Reversal of Decision to Delete Vietnam War Photo," *Wall Street Journal*, September 10, 2016, B3.

164 See *The Economist*, "Mobile Operating Systems: Alpine Android," August 8, 2015, 54. The fact that apps can have serious flaws—that may only be resolved after substantial usage—also contributes to this effect—see A. J. Dellinger, "Many Popular Android Apps Leak Sensitive Data, Leaving Millions of Consumers at Risk," *Forbes*, June 7, 2019, www.forbes.com/.

165 John Koetsier, "Apple's 'Time to Walk' Reveals Monopoly Power," *Forbes*, January 25, 2021, www.forbes.com/. See also Lucas Nolan, "Apple Exec: iPhone App Store Monopoly is Necessary Because Macs Aren't Safe," *Breitbart*, May 20, 2021, www.breitbart.com/; Andy Chalk, "Epic Games Sues Apple Over 'Monopolistic Practices'," *PC Gamer*, August 13, 2020, www.pcgamer.com/.

166 Deepa Seetharaman, "Facebook's Additions Flatter Snapchat—and Put Pressure on It," *Wall Street Journal*, March 29, 2017, B4, and her "Facebook Embraces 'Video-First' Future," *Wall Street Journal*, September 9, 2017, B1.

Uselaboring through the social media–search–news–advertisement combine has proliferated rapidly, partly because those who provide this form of labor believe they are receiving a "free" service—as there is no monetary payment for access or usage. The fundamental human social need to communicate with others underlies this phenomenon, all the more so as social alienation has become pervasive. Unfettered consumption—all too often fueled by contrived demand and high indebtedness—is another factor, helped by the expansion of online purchases. *Uselabor is a form of uncompensated labor, however, and any personal benefit obtained is greatly overshadowed by the vast amount of revenues and surpluses it generates for the oligopolists in control.*

This observation also applies to most every situation where some learning or problem resolution occurs—as the personal benefits are often very temporary or trivial. Moreover, the cost and risk of giving up personal privacy are seldom taken into account. Similarly, the amount and cost of personal time spent online is almost never analyzed by users or compared to other individual—and potentially more beneficial—endeavors. It is quite possible that, if such costs were analyzed, the individual waste of time involved is quite substantial and expensive—relative to any personal benefit obtained.

Unproductive time can also accumulate greatly and rapidly—compromising finances, health, and psychological wellbeing. And, in some cases personal harm can result, if uselaboring ends up involving illegal acts, sanctions, anti-social behavior, or retribution. Beyond the sphere of the individual uselaborer—and all the pros and cons involved—the fact remains that an immense concentration of power over an immense (and uncompensated) labor market is now controlled by a small group of very powerful corporations.

Dual Oligopoly: Labor, Products

Returning to the general formulation of the accumulative dynamic, it is possible to consider a scenario where control is exercised over a labor market *and* over a product market. The accumulative dynamic may thus be re-specified as:

$$M_L \rightarrow C \rightarrow C' \rightarrow M^N_L$$

where $M_L = M - \Delta L$ *and* $M^N_L = M^N + \Delta L$ (with $M^N = M + \Delta m + \Delta N$ as before); with ΔL representing the surplus obtained by the oligopsonist through its labor market control. It must be noted that this surplus is conceptually independent from the surplus labor obtained in production. The latter involves surplus value (Δm), as noted earlier. In this scenario, ΔL is a consequence of the oligopsonist's control over its labor market *and* of its need to expend labor in productive transformation (embedded in $C \rightarrow C'$). Through this control, the oligopsonistic surplus translates into a lower payment for the purchase of labor, such that $M_L < M$. This makes the initial money-capital needed (M_L) *less* than its counterpart under competitive labor market conditions (M).

As a result, *the surplus obtained discounts the initial money-capital that would be necessary to purchase labor*—under competitive conditions. M^N_L therefore represents the aggregate new money-capital obtained by the oligopsonist-*cum*-oligopolist through its control over *both* labor and product markets—the oligopolistic product market surplus being represented by ΔN (as before). The total surplus extracted in this scenario may thus be specified as:

$$(M^N_L - M) \text{ or } [(M + \Delta m + \Delta N + \Delta L) - M] = (\Delta m + \Delta N + \Delta L)$$

This form of dual oligopolistic power and the magnitude of the surplus obtained have many implications for labor's wellbeing and for work-related social justice. And, as in the case of oligopolistic control over input suppliers, only through product market exchange of the new commodity (C′) can the benefit of labor market control be obtained.[167]

Taking the social media example into account, the accumulative dynamic is set in motion as the oligopolist requires uselaborers to give up their personal data.[168] The production process (embedded in C → C′) thus depends on uselaborers being made to provide their intimate data—adding individual time, effort, experiences, and feedback that can make targeted advertising more effective. The network controlled by the oligopsonist-*cum*-oligopolist—including all hardware and software—is merely the means that allows this peculiar production process to operate. Although some conventional labor is used—programmers and administrative staff—it is the uselaborer population that makes this production process work and generate revenue.

But, what does this unusual production process generate? Its product—the source of new money-capital (M^N_L) for the oligopsonist-*cum*-oligopolist—is targeted advertising. The product market customers are thus the advertisers—all of which have to pay to have their ads presented to uselaborers. *And* the uselaborers themselves who—in addition to being customers—*pay* for access with their data, time, effort, and experiences—all mined by the company in control. The targeted ads must draw the attention of uselaborers such that they

167 If control is *only* exercised over the labor market, the accumulative dynamic can be specified as $M_L \rightarrow C \rightarrow C' \rightarrow M'_L$ where $M'_L = M' + \Delta L$ *and* $M' = M + \Delta m$—with M'_L and M' denoting a competitive product market, and $M_L = M - \Delta L$. In this case, ΔL would represent the discount on the cost of labor obtained through control over the labor market. And, the labor market oligopsonist would not be able to obtain its benefit unless product market exchange—and, previously, productive transformation (embedded in C → C′)—occur.

168 Regarding the accumulative dynamic under oligopsonistic-*cum*-oligolistic labor *and* product market conditions—applied to the social media example—it is assumed that the corporation in control would *not* have such power over: (i) its input chain—the manufacturers (or sellers) of the servers and other hardware it uses, for example—and (ii) its conventional labor market (programmers and administrative staff).

will view the ads (even if no purchase occurs) for a limited time—so that the advertiser can be charged a fee.[169] And, the advertisers have no alternative but to pay the corporations in control, to deploy their targeted ads. Uselaborers—as customers of *both* social media companies *and* the advertisers—have no alternative either, if they are to engage in social contact.

Contribution of uselaborer time, effort, online preferences, and experiences should be added to intimate data—as they are uncompensated labor *and* payment for access. Social media and search companies keenly target these aspects for intensive mining and for sales to third parties. Among the latter are app developers, marketing companies, retailers, political consultants, financiers, law enforcement agencies, and intelligence contractors. Identity thieves and hackers—although unauthorized—also often receive such information.

The surplus obtained through control over the uselabor market (ΔL) can be considered equivalent to the compensation that the oligopsonist-*cum*-oligopolist would have to pay its uselaborers for their personal data—*if* each uselaborer could forgo providing such data *and* still be able to use the network. The latter situation would most likely dissolve oligopsonistic control over social media—as far as uselabor is concerned—thus leading to a competitive market scenario. In either case, uncompensated surplus labor must be taken into account. The latter, as noted earlier, underlies surplus value (Δm) and would apply to conventional labor *and* to compensated uselabor—no matter how partial or incomplete the latter may be. Thus, Δm and ΔL must be considered independently.

In the accumulative dynamic, ΔL indicates the discount obtained by the oligopsonist through its control over the uselabor market. And this discount can be considered complete, since uselaborers' provision of personal data (including time, effort, online preferences, and experiences) is not compensated. *Even when uselaborers derive some personal benefit, this is typically non-monetary—while, on the other hand, the oligopsonist's benefit is completely monetary*. This asymmetry is usually lost on analyses of social media usage.

In the accumulative dynamic of social media, M^{N}_{L} thus represents aggregate new money-capital obtained by the oligopsonist-*cum*-oligopolist through its control over *both* uselaborers and targeted advertising (its main product market). The surplus generated by the latter is represented by ΔN—derived from pricing imposed on advertisers. This product market surplus is obtained whenever uselaborers view ads presented to them. And, the eventual purchase of a product is important to the corporation in control *and* the advertisers. The

169 Drawing attention is therefore very important for targeted ads—see, for example, Ahmed, "Effects of Design Elements"; Lee, Hosanagar and Nair, "Advertisement Content and Consumer Engagement"; Lin and Kim, "Predicting User Response"; Tim Wu, *The Attention Merchants: The Epic Scramble to Get Inside Our Heads* (New York: Knopf, 2016), 276–88.

expectation that such purchases will occur is what keeps advertisers coming back (and paying).

The uselabor time giveaway is very important for targeted advertising. The more time a uselaborer spends on the network, the more likely it is that she will purchase (or at least share comments on) an advertised product. And, the monetary value of the time giveaway by uselaborers is a matter that deserves evaluation. Even if accounted for at the level of the legal minimum hourly wage—in their respective nations or places—the amounts involved would likely be very substantial.[170] Facebook alone has billions of uselaborers spending considerable amounts of time on its network every month, and even the more specialized social media companies have hundreds of millions of users giving away their time.

How can the personal data that uselaborers give up be valued? Estimating it as, say, a fraction of each uselaborer's weekly income would no doubt generate a very large aggregate figure. If it is valued at the level of what it would cost an individual to repair a case of identity theft, the collective amount involved could also be quite substantial—even if non-recurrence is assumed. Alternatively, assuming its value to be a fraction of each uselaborer's financial net worth would also likely yield a vast sum. Such valuations of personal data would be no more subjective than the values that Wall Street all too often places on many types of derivatives. Although it is not the purpose of this discussion to estimate the fair value of uselabor, it seems reasonable to assume that the surpluses obtained through the social media–search–advertisement combine very likely amount to several times the annual economic product of most nations.

Compound Oligopoly

Technology corporations can establish control over their labor, input supply, and product markets. This is the most complete scenario of oligopolistic control. Corporations that pioneer or take over a new technology are most likely to be

170 Using minimum legal wages as reference would tacitly involve the application of labor laws to uselabor. Using the median wage level—a common metric for monetary estimates of worktime—as an indicator would likely yield vast sums. An estimate of idle worktime, for individuals employed full-time outside their homes in the United States—using the median wage level as reference—estimated its annual value at about $100 billion. See Andrew Brodsky and Teresa Amabile, "The Downside of Downtime: The Prevalence and Work Pacing Consequences of Idle Time at Work," *Journal of Applied Psychology*, 103 (2018), https://nrs.dash.harvard.edu/. Adding reported aggregate profit *per* the total number of uselaborers in a network could also be taken into account. Treating appropriated personal data as a form of labor has been advanced by some authors, arguing that compensation can be allocated by markets—see Eric A. Posner and E. Glen Weyl, *Radical Markets: Uprooting Capitalism and Democracy for a Just Society* (Princeton: Princeton University Press, 2018); *The Economist* (*World If* supplement), "If People Were Paid for their Data: Data Workers of the World, Unite," July 7, 2018, 11–12.

found in this situation.[171] The new technology typically requires knowledge that is unknown or uncodified. Controlling the new product market may not be difficult, and much the same may occur with inputs if they are rare. In the case of labor, control can be established through in-house training.

Few or no other companies may possess similar knowledge, and employment possibilities may be very limited. Compound oligopoly is thus most likely to depend on a new technology that is so unfamiliar and complex that very few will have worked with it. This scenario can be difficult to sustain once knowledge becomes codified enough. As this occurs, the compound oligopolist may become a partial one, possibly retaining control over its product, labor, or input markets—but not over all three.

Returning to the general formulation of the accumulative dynamic, the case of compound oligopoly may be represented as follows:

$$M_{SL} \rightarrow C \rightarrow C' \rightarrow M^{N}{}_{SL}$$

$$\text{where } M_{SL} = M - \Delta S - \Delta L \textit{ and } M^{N}{}_{SL} = M^{N} + \Delta S + \Delta L$$

$$(\text{with } M^{N} = M + \Delta m + \Delta N \text{ as before})$$

where M_{SL} stands for initial money-capital—based on the oligopolistic surpluses obtained from the input (ΔS) and labor (ΔL) markets. The initial money-capital that would be expended under competitive conditions (M) is thereby discounted by these two types of surpluses. In aggregate new money-capital ($M^{N}{}_{SL}$), the surplus obtained through the product market (ΔN) is thus augmented by the labor and input surpluses.

The aggregate surplus in the compound oligopolistic scenario must therefore include these surpluses, such that:

$$(M^{N}{}_{SL} - M) \text{ or } [(M + \Delta m + \Delta N + \Delta S + \Delta L) - M] = (\Delta m + \Delta N + \Delta S + \Delta L)$$

The compound oligopolist cannot obtain its benefit without product market exchange—and, previously, production and the expenditure of labor (embedded in C→C′). It may not be difficult to see why, for any oligopolistic corporation, compound oligopoly is the most desirable scenario, as $M^{N}{}_{SL} > M^{N}{}_{S}$ (or

171 Vertically integrated companies that pioneered or used new technologies in the late nineteenth and early twentieth centuries—in oil extraction and refining, steel, and mass production—are examples. Standard Oil, Ford, and Carnegie established control over raw material deposits, labor markets, and their product distribution. Antitrust laws, labor struggles, and diffusion of knowledge eventually splintered their control, leading to regulated oligopolies. See Bringhurst, *Antitrust and the Oil Monopoly*; Charles R. Geisst, *Monopolies in America: Empire Builders and their Enemies from Jay Gould to Bill Gates* (New York: Oxford University Press, 2000).

$M^N{}_L) > M^N > M'$. Sustaining a compound oligopolistic situation for as long as possible may thus become a crucial priority.

A range of vitally important aspects—from executive compensation to profits, share pricing, lobbying, political and regulatory influence—depend on the possibility of sustaining this scenario. Failing to maintain compound oligopolistic power nonetheless often leads to dual or sole market oligopolistic control—over products, inputs, or labor. Or, to acquisitions that might offset the loss of compound surpluses.

Complexity and Lock-In

Examples of compound oligopoly can be found in complex new technologies. In biotechnology, discoveries in genetics and molecular biology made it possible to combine new knowledge.[172] The multiple fields involved—among them genomics, biochemistry, proteomics, immunology, and bio-pharmacology—contributed much complexity to the new technology. This meant that no established discipline could provide—on its own—the necessary knowledge or skills. Also, the small scale of organisms and processes, and the high failure rates, made it difficult to establish skill standards and diffuse knowledge. And, the expensive—and often customized—hardware required substantial investment.

In agro-biotech, Monsanto established early control over genetically engineered seeds. As it developed skills in-house, it appropriated the technology by obtaining patents. Thus, in a relatively short time, about 80 percent of all soybeans and cotton harvested in the United States had at least one of Monsanto's patented seeds.[173] And, also in a short time, this corporation ended up supplying almost 75 percent of all genetically engineered seeds for field corn.[174] A designed lifetime window of one crop (or harvest) for each seed, moreover, meant that new seeds had to be purchased for every crop—guaranteeing a continuous stream of surpluses. And, once farmers started using the seeds, it was often impossible to return to the natural ones.

172 See Center for Drug Evaluation and Research, Food and Drug Administration, *Biological Products—Larger, Complex and Diverse*, www.accessdata.fda.gov/ (accessed July 14, 2022); James C. Mullen, "Gene Therapy," *Wall Street Journal*, April 27, 2007, A17. In clinical biotechnology, trials may take as long as five years, and failure rates can be as high as 8,000:1 for a single compound—see Luis Suarez-Villa, *Globalization and Technocapitalism* (London: Ashgate, 2012), 56, 103.

173 Reset, *The Privatisation of Seeds*, https://en.reset.org/ (accessed July 15, 2022); Marie-Monique Robin, *The World According to Monsanto* (New York: New Press, 2010), chapters 1–2; Roger Parloff, "Seeds of Discord," *Fortune*, May 24, 2010, 94–106.

174 Reset, *Privatisation of Seeds*; Robin, *World According*; Helena Paul and Ricarda Steinbrecher, *Hungry Corporations: How Transnational Biotech Companies Colonise the Food Chain* (London: Zed, 2003); Daniel Charles, *Lords of the Harvest: Biotech, Big Money, and the Future of Food* (Cambridge, MA: Perseus, 2002). A critical historical perspective on the links between commercialization, seeds, and biotechnology can be found in Jack R. Kloppenburg, Jr., *First the Seed: The Political Economy of Plant Biotechnology, 1492–2000* (Madison: University of Wisconsin Press, 2004), chapters 7–9.

Monsanto's compound oligopolistic power was strengthened by its merger with Bayer during the last decade.[175] This allowed the combined companies to impose their pricing power over most agro-biotech and biochemical market segments. And also downstream—on most any crop grown and marketed by agribusiness companies, farmers, and their clients (food processors, distributors, grocery companies, and eventually consumers).[176] The merger's approval reflected the failure of antitrust regulation in the United States, due to its negative implications for health, ecosystems, and food pricing.

Earlier, Monsanto's power over the engineered seed market had allowed it to establish control over pesticides—a necessary companion to its seeds. Its pesticides thus came to be used in about 90 percent of all soybean and corn crops in the United States—a large market that further raised surpluses.[177] As the required pesticides destroyed existing ecologies—and weeds evolved, became resistant, and returned—the pesticides had to be strengthened and made more toxic, thus guaranteeing more surpluses for Monsanto.[178] Strengthening the toxicity of the pesticides, however, eventually led to substantial crop damage, to warnings about their negative health effects, and to lawsuits and court decisions over their link to cancer.[179]

175 After almost two years of intense lobbying pressure, the U.S. Department of Justice's antitrust division approved the merger, requiring only some minor asset sales—in place of changes in either company's operations. See Jacob Bunge and Christopher Alessi, "Monsanto Deal Creates Farm Giant," *Wall Street Journal*, September 15, 2016, A1; Christopher Alessi, "Bayer Seeks to Offset Rules: Europe Bans Many GMOs, but Monsanto Acquisition Offers Foothold in U.S. Market," *Wall Street Journal*, September 19, 2016, B3; Brent Kendall and Jacob Bunge, "U.S. to Allow Bayer's Monsanto Takeover," *Wall Street Journal*, April 10, 2018, A1.

176 See Marc Steiner, "Bayer-Monsanto Merger: Endangering Our Health, Food, Farms and Planet," *Real News Network*, February 1, 2019, https://therealnews.com/; Ben Popken, "Monsanto to Drop Name After Sale to Bayer: The New Owner of Monsanto, Synonymous with Deadly Chemical Warfare and Genetically Modified Plants, is Ditching the Name," *NBC News*, June 4, 2018, www.nbc.news.com/; Erin Brodwin, "After a $66 Billion Merger, Monsanto is Disappearing—Sort Of," *Business Insider*, June 7, 2018, www.businessinsider.com/.

177 See Christopher Walljasper and Ramiro Ferrando, "Glyphosate Use Increases Dramatically across the Midwest," *The Counter*, October 28, 2019, htpps://thecounter.org/; Paul and Steinbrecher, *Hungry Corporations*; Charles, *Lords of the Harvest*.

178 See Pesticide Action Network, *Monsanto's Superweeds and Superbugs*, www.panna.org/ (accessed July 14, 2022); Walljasper and Ferrando, "Glyphosate Use Increases"; Ian Berry, "Pesticides Make a Comeback: Many Corn Farmers Go Back to Using Chemicals as Mother Nature Outwits Genetically Modified Seeds," *Wall Street Journal*, May 22, 2013, B1; Scott Kilman, "Superweeds Hit Farm Belt, Triggering New Arms Race," *Wall Street Journal*, June 4, 2010, A1. The negative ramifications of higher toxicity for human health are not fully known, but might likely be serious—see, for example, Rob Wallace, *Big Farms Make Big Flu: Dispatches on Infectious Disease, Agribusiness, and the Nature of Science* (New York: Monthly Review Press, 2016); Daniel Cressey, "Widely Used Herbicide Linked to Cancer: The World Health Organization's Research Arm Declares Glyphosate a Problem Carcinogen. What's the Evidence?" *Scientific American*, March 25, 2015, www.scientificamerican.com/.

179 Glyphosate usage is more than four times that of atrazine (the second most heavily used pesticide) and is regularly found in food, water, and the air. See Walljasper and Ferrando, "Glyphosate Use Increases"; World Health Organization, International Agency for Research on Cancer, *IARC*

In many cases, farmers that used Monsanto's engineered seeds—and pesticides—could not revert to their prior methods and seeds, as the supporting ecology was destroyed by the pesticides. They thus remained locked into this oligopolist's power.[180] Agribusiness oligopolies then benefited from this scenario, as many small farmers were forced into bankruptcy and had to sell their land—when they could not pay the prices Monsanto imposed. The agribusiness oligopolies, in turn, deployed factory-farming regimes by consolidating acquired land—and became Monsanto's best customers.

The vast surpluses Monsanto obtained allowed it to acquire numerous companies in related activities—among them input suppliers, marketers, and research providers. In the first decade of the twenty-first century, for example, Monsanto acquired more than 20 companies—a trend that has continued since.[181] Its additional resources also allowed Monsanto to influence regulators and their reviews of its products—including those with effects on human health.[182] And Monsanto's merger with Bayer may be seen as a way to offset the erosion of compound oligopolistic power, as agro-biotech technologies become better known.[183]

Corporations in other sectors have also exercised compound oligopolistic power using complex new technologies. Fairchild Semiconductor had control over research, manufacturing, marketing, and labor as it engineered microprocessors six decades ago.[184] And it was able to control its input suppliers by

Monograph on Glyphosate (Lyon: IARC, 2015), www.iarc.fr/; Center for Food Safety, *Glyphosate and Cancer Risk* (Washington: CFS, 2015), www.centerforfoodsafety.org/. The first lawsuit against Monsanto's highly profitable Roundup pesticide resulted in a substantial award—see Sam Levin, "Monsanto Ordered to Pay $289 Million as Jury Rules Weed Killer Caused Man's Cancer: Court Rules in Favor of DeWayne Johnson, Ill Man Who Was First to Take Roundup Maker to Trial Over Allegations," *The Guardian*, August 10, 2018, www.theguardian.com/; *The Economist*, "Glyphosate and Cancer: Bayer Beware; A Big Lawsuit Against Monsanto Could Have Big Consequences," August 18, 2018, 54–55.

180 See Center for Biological Diversity, *Farmers, Conservationists Challenge Approval of Monsanto's Crop-Damaging Dicamba Pesticide*, August 14, 2019, www.commondreams.org/; Walljasper and Ferrando, "Glyphosate Use Increases"; Berry, "Pesticides Make a Comeback"; Jacob Bunge, "Farmers Reconsider GMO Revolution," *Wall Street Journal*, September 15, 2016, A1; Robin, *World According*; Dominic Clover, *Monsanto and Small Holder Farmers: A Case Study on Corporate Accountability*, IDS Working Paper (Brighton: Institute for Development Studies, University of Sussex, 2007); Suarez-Villa, *Corporate Power, Oligopolies*, 59–61.

181 *The Economist*, "The Parable of the Sower," November 21, 2009, 71–73. One of the acquired companies, Climate Corp., allowed Monsanto to expand its power over data-driven farming services—see, for example, Jacob Bunge, "Monsanto's Data Unit Gets New CEO," *Wall Street Journal*, March 24, 2016, B2.

182 See Center for Biological Diversity, *Farmers, Conservationists*; Steiner, "Bayer-Monsanto Merger". A senior scientist employed by the company declared that Monsanto scientists had "ghostwritten" sections of regulatory reviews of the company's agricultural chemicals—Jacob Bunge, "Questions Dog Monsanto Product," *Wall Street Journal*, March 16, 2017, B6

183 See Bunge and Alessi, "Monsanto Deal Creates"; Alessi, "Bayer Seeks to Offset"; Steiner, "Bayer-Monsanto Merger."

184 See Gordon E. Moore, "The Role of Fairchild in Silicon Technology in the Early Days of 'Silicon Valley'," *Proceedings of the IEEE* 86 (1998), 53–62; Christophe Lécuyer and David C. Brock,

setting standards. The latter allowed it to select which companies would supply it and the prices it would pay. Its initial funding by the Pentagon—and subsequent contracts— helped its standards setting and compound oligopolistic power greatly.[185]

Later, Intel—Fairchild's successor—was able to prolong its predecessor's power through rapid miniaturization. The new personal computer market thus came to depend on its microprocessors.[186] After a rival emerged (AMD), Intel was able to sustain its compound power by focusing on the most advanced chips.[187] As the technology became better known, however, companies abroad began to manufacture at lower cost. Intel's compound power thus narrowed to the most advanced microprocessors. It then used its accumulated surpluses to acquire small, technologically advanced companies with promising products.[188]

One of the acquisitions involved the $15 billion purchase of Mobileye, a vehicle-camera company—one of the most expensive in Intel's history—with the aim of extending its power to computer-assisted driving.[189] The acquisitions made it possible for Intel to sustain its power over a narrow band of its product market, even though its control over its labor and input markets diminished. Control thus metamorphosed from a compound scenario to a more limited—but nonetheless very powerful—position.

IBM had achieved oligopolistic power during the decades when it partially controlled the typewriter and office machine markets.[190] Industrializing gadgets for activities and skills that were primarily artisanal had long been part of its power-building capabilities. With mainframe computers, its power was compounded through this technology's complexity, its product market, and by setting standards in multiple areas.[191] Its global projection then allowed IBM to impose terms for its main inputs—among them electronic circuitry, switches,

---

Makers of the Microchip: A Documentary History of Fairchild Semiconductor (Cambridge, MA: MIT Press, 2010), Chapter 2, Appendix.

185 See Alex Press, "Big Tech's Unholy Alliance with the Pentagon," *New Republic*, February 7, 2019, https://newrepublic.com/; Lécuyer and Brock, *Makers of the Microchip*.

186 Tim Jackson, *Inside Intel* (London: Harper Collins, 1997), parts 2, 3; Intel, *Defining Intel: 25 Years/25 Events*, 1993, www.intel.com/.

187 See Hector Ruiz and Lauren Villagran, *Slingshot: AMD's Fight to Free an Industry from the Ruthless Grip of Intel* (Austin: Greenleaf, 2013), chapters 2–4, 8; Jackson, *Inside Intel*.

188 See Asa Fitch, "Intel to Buy Networking Startup," *Wall Street Journal*, June 11, 2019, B4; Don Clark, "Intel Deal Shows Pull of Artificial Intelligence," *Wall Street Journal*, August 10, 2016, B4; *The Economist*, "The Semiconductor Industry: Silicon Crumble," February 25, 2017, 53–54.

189 Ted Greenwald, "Intel Joins Race for 'Servers on Wheels'," *Wall Street Journal*, March 14, 2017, A1.

190 See IBM, *IBM Archives: Chronological History of IBM*, www.ibm.com/ (accessed July 15, 2022); James W. Cortada, *Before the Computer: IBM, NCR, Burroughs, and Remington Rand and the Industry They Created, 1865–1956* (Princeton: Princeton University Press, 1993), parts 1, 2.

191 Emerson W. Pugh, *Building IBM: Shaping an Industry and Its Technology* (Cambridge, MA: MIT Press, 1995), chapters 7, 12, 14–16, 20; IBM, *IBM Archives*.

magnetic metallurgy, and the celluloid film technology needed to store data.[192] IBM's power also allowed it to impose control over the labor market needed to manufacture and develop this product.

The nascent field (and profession) of computer programming thus practically became an extension of IBM's operations. This required knowledge from multiple fields—electrical engineering, mathematics, physics, mechanical engineering. Its mainframe computers became indispensable for many activities, such as corporate and government payroll processing, transportation, higher education, statistical analyses, ballistic missile control, and space exploration.[193] Its compound oligopolistic power then allowed IBM to acquire new or smaller companies that had the potential to grow—or to become competitors.

IBM would set hardware standards when microprocessors made it possible for PCs to emerge. But when desktop PCs superseded mainframes for many uses—and portable PCs became ubiquitous—IBM saw its compound power erode. To try to refocus its power, it sold its PC business to Lenovo and concentrated on providing computing services to corporations.[194] One such service—that strengthened IBM's oligopolistic power (though not in a compound way)—was cloud computing.[195] Its largest acquisition ever (at the time it occurred) was for open-source cloud computing company Red Hat.[196]

In software, Microsoft exercised compound oligopolistic power through its control over PC operating systems. When PC software was practically unknown—and very few individuals had the skills to create it—Microsoft established control over its labor market. Keeping its software proprietary allowed Microsoft to build up compound power—as manufacturers of IBM-based PCs had to purchase it.[197] Later, it sustained its power by creating platforms upon which non-competing businesses could operate.[198]

Microsoft's products were intangible—allowing it to forgo establishing control over raw materials. Its most important input—coding knowledge—was labor embodied and also intangible. And, it undertook much skills training in-house. In its early phase, Microsoft was thus able to set the terms for

192 See IBM, *IBM Archives*; Emerson W. Pugh, *Memories that Shaped an Industry: Decisions Leading to IBM System/360* (Cambridge, MA: MIT Press, 1984); and his *Building IBM*, chapters 17–19.

193 Pugh, *Building IBM*, chapters 18, 19; IBM, *IBM Archives*.

194 *EE Times*, "IBM Sells PC Business to Lenovo," August 12, 2004, www.eetimes.com/.

195 See Micah Maidenberg, "IBM Turns Corner with Newer Businesses: More than Half of Sales in Latest Quarter Came from Initiatives like Cloud Computing," *Wall Street Journal*, July 19, 2018, B4.

196 Asa Fitch, "IBM Closes its Biggest Deal Ever," *Wall Street Journal*, July 10, 2019, B1.

197 See Wallace and Erickson, *Hard Drive*; Cheryl D. Tsang, *Microsoft First Generation* (New York: Wiley, 2000).

198 See Microsoft, *Power Platform*, https://powerplatform.microsoft.com/. (accessed July 15, 2022); Wallace and Erickson, *Hard Drive*.

compensation, hiring, and workplace rules.[199] Microsoft's product also benefited from exclusivity, as its software was necessary to make PCs operate.

This symbiosis made it possible for Microsoft to control almost all of the PC operating software market. And, Microsoft's clout emerged even though IBM itself had not established proprietary control over its PC hardware. Later, when IBM's PC was cloned by multiple manufacturers, Microsoft would expand its power by licensing its software to them.

Creating rapid obsolescence for its software—aided by advances in PCs—boosted Microsoft's oligopolistic surpluses, even as software skills and knowledge spread.[200] Then, as the company saw its compound power diminishing, it sought to diversify by targeting specialized niches—such as gaming, video entertainment, mobile telephony, data clouds, and artificial intelligence.[201] Producing an intangible product—while depending on others to manufacture the hardware—helped Microsoft capture selected niches.

At this point, it seems relevant to note that the surpluses discussed in this chapter——for product (ΔN), input (ΔS), and labor (ΔL) markets—are vitally important for oligopolistic capital accumulation. Obtaining these surpluses depends on the transformation of commodities (embedded in $C \rightarrow C'$). Unless this occurs, no labor can be employed, no commodities can be produced or exchanged, and no technology can be made use of. The sustenance of the productive cycle of technology oligopoly capitalism therefore depends on the relentless pursuit of these surpluses.

The use of commodities to produce other commodities—a fundamental characteristic of technology oligopoly capitalism—is thus inextricably tied to capital accumulation. In the scenarios considered in this chapter, technology should be regarded as a tool used in—and that also results from—the accumulative dynamic. A most troublesome aspect of the panorama of control is that so much of it is in the hands of such few and very powerful entities.

199 Microsoft's approach to workplace control was characterized as a "casual, confrontational, male-dominated, youth-oriented" activity manipulated by a small group of individuals (the owners) to give the impression that it was consensual and participatory—see Richard Sharpe, "'Globalization': The Next Tactic in the Fifty-Year Struggle of Labor and Capital in Software Production," in Rick Baldoz, Charles Koeber and Philip Kraft, eds., *The Critical Study of Work: Labor, Technology, and Global Production* (Philadelphia: Temple University Press, 2001), 218.

200 See Wallace and Erickson, *Hard Drive*; G. Pascal Zachary, *Show-stopper! The Breakneck Race to Create Windows NT and the Next Generation at Microsoft* (New York: Free Press, 1994).

201 See *The Economist*, "Video Gaming: High Score, Microsoft Places a $69bn Bet on the Future of Entertainment," January 22, 2022, 57; its "Method in the Madness: Why the World's Biggest Software Firm Looks Increasingly Acquisitive," April 17, 2021, 57–58; and its "Microsoft: Head in the Cloud," March 18, 2017, 64–65. Serial acquisition of small innovative companies—and capture of new market niches—by an established oligopolist can neutralize the notion that new companies possessing "disruptive innovations" will end (or diminish) oligopolistic power, as assumed by Tim Wu in his *The Master Switch: The Rise and Fall of Information Empires* (New York: Knopf, 2010), parts III, V.

Chapter 4

Transformation

Technology oligopolies are creators *and* users of new technologies—an aspect that sets them apart in the panorama of capitalism. Their involvement with productive transformation is grounded in both of these functions, while their existential identity tends to be rooted in the former. In the oligopolistic domain, they often contradict each other, yet both are indispensable for understanding the deeper structure of technology oligopoly capitalism.

Exploring the multidimensional character of transformation will be the main objective of this chapter. The relations of power at the core of how commodities are transformed into new commodities—denoted by (C→C′) in the accumulative dynamic—will be addressed critically. Use of the term *transformation* in this chapter thus encompasses the full panorama of productive endeavors in the oligopolistic technology domain.[1]

Elements and phenomena of productive transformation will be addressed first. The embedded relations of power will be of particular interest and will be related to the exercise of control. Numerous examples, and reference to contemporary trends and events of recent decades, will place discussions in perspective.

1 The spectrum of productive activities—raw material input extraction and processing, production and its labor processes (including factory assembly of parts and components), research and product development—is thus subsumed by the term. Transformation should not be confused with the process of selling a new commodity (C′) in a product market to obtain new money-capital (M′ or M^N). As noted in the previous chapter, that process is referred to as *market exchange* (or exchange) in this work. This is meant to avoid any misinterpretation related to the first translation of Marx's manuscript—the one that would become the first volume of *Capital: A Critique of Political Economy*, F. Engels, ed. (New York: International Publishers, 1974; orig. publ. Hamburg: Verlag von Otto Meissner, 1867); Vol. I, Part II, "The Transformation of Money into Capital," 146–76. Written in German (and translated years later), the sense of the term "transformation" provided by Marx has been interpreted to be synonymous with "umwandlung," "verwandlung," or "veränderung"—used to denote monetary conversions (or transactions).

DOI: 10.4324/9781003345893-4

Elements

The elements of productive transformation are interrelated. Considering the ensemble at the core of transformation—labor, capital, production, research, and product development—is essential for understanding how technology oligopolies operate. This section will set the stage to explore the phenomena at the core of commodity transformation and their influence on the panorama of production.

Labor

In all its forms and diversity of skills, labor is the most important element of transformation. It is also a fundamental commodity in the context of oligopoly capitalism. No achievement in technology, no capital accumulation or surplus, no innovative activity, and no output in production or research is possible without it.[2] *Labor, as the source of economic value and of new ideas, must therefore be regarded as the single most important element of the transformative apparatus.*

Labor has been an indispensable component of economic activity since humanity's beginnings—before capital and capitalism.[3] It might escape attention that classical economists placed much emphasis on labor as the source of *all* value. Adam Smith, for example, stated: "Labour … is alone the ultimate and real standard by which the value of all commodities can at all times and places be estimated and compared. It is their real price; money is their nominal price only."[4]

Smith thus considered labor to provide *the standard of value*, in reference to which all commodities should be evaluated. This consideration would be supported by other classical economists and would be at the core of Marx's work.[5] In another passage, Smith noted:

2 A brief (and perhaps unexpected) passage from Lincoln's 1861 State of the Union address seems appropriate: "Labor is prior to and independent of capital. Capital is only the fruit of labor, and could never have existed if labor had not first existed. Labor is the superior of capital, and deserves much the higher consideration." Abraham Lincoln, *Message of the President of the United States to the Two Houses of Congress at the Commencement of the Second Session of the Thirty-Seventh Congress*, Vol. 1 (Washington: Government Printing Office, 1861), 78th paragraph. See also Gerhard Peters and John T. Woolley, "Abraham Lincoln: First Annual Message, December 3, 1861," *The American Presidency Project*, http://www.presidency.ucsb.edu/ (accessed July 18, 2022). Earlier, Benjamin Franklin had noted that "trade in general being nothing but the exchange of labor for labor, the value of all things is … most justly measured by labor"—in Henry Stueber, ed., *The Works of Dr. Benjamin Franklin* (Baltimore: Hickman, 1835), 264.

3 The importance of labor in human evolution has long been a topic of interest in the social literature. Friedrich Engels, in particular, envisioned a dialectical relationship between the use of tools, the development of language, social culture, and the emergence of major differences between human and animal life—see his *The Part Played by Labour in the Transition from Ape to Man* (Moscow: Foreign Languages Publishing, 1963); Friedrich Engels, Clemens Palme Dutt and John B. S. Haldane, *Dialectics of Nature* (New York: International Publishers, 1940).

4 Adam Smith, *An Inquiry into the Nature and Causes of the Wealth of Nations* (Glasgow: Strahan and Caddell, 1776), Part I, 35.

5 See Ronald L. Meek, *Studies in the Labour Theory of Value* (London: Lawrence and Wishart, 1973), 121, 177.

> What is bought with money or with goods is purchased by labour, as much as what we acquire by the toil of our own body … Labour was the first price, the original purchase-money that was paid for all things. It was not by gold or by silver, but by labour, that all the wealth of the world was originally purchased; and its value, to those who possess it, and who want to exchange it for some new productions, is precisely equal to the quantity of labour which it can enable them to purchase or command.[6]

David Ricardo—a very important figure in the emergence of the field of economics—also dealt with the question of labor's value, stating: "I know no other criterion of a thing being dear or cheap but by the sacrifices of labour made to obtain it. Every thing is originally purchased by labour—nothing that has value can be produced without it."[7] Marx took these considerations further by assuming labor—and the associated relations of production—to be the prime factor influencing value in market exchange, noting: "In principle, there is no exchange of products—but there is the exchange of labour which co-operated in production. The mode of exchange of products depends upon the mode of exchange of the productive forces."[8] To Marx, the value of labor—embedded in every commodity—represented value *independently* of money or market prices, thus concurring with Smith's and Ricardo's earlier observations. Referring to the "exchange of the productive forces," he placed the relation between worker and capitalist—most of all, the exchange of labor for a wage—at the center of the relations of production.

Wages aside, the notion of labor's claim to the value of what it produced—central to Marx's perspective—was by no means new. Seventeenth-century social and political philosophers, such as John Locke, believed that expenditure of labor provided an *inalienable right of property* to the worker, on the product of his toil.[9] This observation, by one of the best known philosophers of the Enlightenment, who came to be regarded as the father of Liberalism, would set the tone for subsequent work on the subject. In the nineteenth century, social philosophers would embrace Locke's notion to

6 Smith, *Wealth of Nations*, Part I, 32–33. Critical perspectives on this aspect—valuing labor on the basis of product exchange—may be found in Laibman, *Value, Technical Change and Crisis*, chapters 1–4.

7 David Ricardo, *The Works and Correspondence of David Ricardo*, Piero Sraffa, ed. (Cambridge: Cambridge University Press, 1952), Part IV, 397.

8 Karl Marx, *The Poverty of Philosophy*, H. Quelch, trans. (Chicago: Kerr, 1913), 65–66.

9 "The 'labour' of his body and the 'work' of his hands … are properly his. Whatsoever, then, he removes out of the state that Nature hath provided and left it in, he hath mixed his labour with it, and joined to it something that is his own, and thereby makes it his property. It being by him removed from the common state Nature placed it in, it hath by this labour something annexed to it that excludes the common right of other men. For this 'labour' being the unquestionable property of the labourer, no man but he can have a right to what that is."—John Locke, *Two Treatises of Government* (Glasgow: Griffin, 1823), Chapter V: "Of Property," 116. See also his *Of Civil Government* (London: Dent, 1943), 136–37; Meek, *Studies in the Labour Theory*, 125.

advocate for the rights of labor—a view that converged with Marx's vision of labor justice.

In appropriating the results of work, Marx observed that the capitalist compensates the worker for *less than* the full exchange value obtained from the sale of the product.[10] This difference is what classical economists—Adam Smith and David Ricardo, in particular—referred to (under *competitive* market conditions) as the gain or "level of profit," which they considered to be a "reward" to the capitalist for undertaking production and sales.[11] This aspect caught Karl Marx's attention, as it made capitalism distinctive from previous eras—in particular, from craftwork and the conditions of individual or family-run workshops.[12] In these pre-capitalist scenarios, production had been largely artisanal, small in scale and scope, and based on relations that were personal or community oriented.[13]

Industrial capitalism—in Marx's view—had broken with the past, as the worker was prevented from receiving the *full* value of what he produced. Part of that value was paid to the worker in the form of a wage, while the rest was kept by the capitalist as *surplus value* (or Δm, noted in the previous chapter).[14] In Marx's view, the relations of production between worker and

10 Use of the term *worker* (or laborer) in this chapter will refer to any individual who sells her labor to obtain compensation (in any form). The term *work* will refer to the personal effort and time that a worker sells to a capitalist. In neoclassical economics, "work" has often been treated as a form of disutility—a necessary evil (involving coercion, pain, or fatigue), necessary to generate income so as to consume. In classical materialist philosophy, however, work was seen as a creative human necessity—vital not only for practical reasons but also for understanding the purpose of human existence. Broad perspectives on the meaning of work for human and social wellbeing can be found in Herbert Applebaum, *The Concept of Work: Ancient, Medieval, and Modern* (Albany: State University of New York Press, 1992); André Gorz, *Paths to Paradise: On the Liberation from Work* (London: Pluto, 1985).

11 See Meek, *Labour Theory*, 12–18, 45–59, 86–96.

12 Karl Marx, *Theories of Surplus Value: Books I, II and III* (Amherst: Prometheus, 2000), Chapter IV, "Theories of Productive and Unproductive Labour," 152–304; Meek, *Labour Theory*, Chapter 4, "Karl Marx's Theory of Value," 121–56. Paul M. Sweezy's *The Transition from Feudalism to Capitalism* (New York: Verso, 1992) provides important insights on the emerging industrial capitalist order that drew Marx's attention.

13 Craftwork generated value—through utility—and a sense of worth to its producer. The latter typically obtained some gain—beyond operating cost—an aspect that was considered fair and necessary. The question of what should be the fair level of that gain became a topic of much interest among Canonist authors (before the emergence of classical economics)—see Ronald L. Meek, *Studies in the Labour Theory of Value* (London: Lawrence and Wishart, 1973), Chapter 1, "Value Theory Before Adam Smith," 12–14; Rudolf Kaulla and Robert D. Hogg, *Theory of the Just Price* (London: Allen and Unwin, 1940).

14 Marx, *Capital*, Vol. I, Part III, "The Production of Absolute Surplus-Value," 177–311, and Part IV, "Production of Relative Surplus-Value," 312–507. In the literature, surplus value (under competitive market conditions) has often been assumed to be equivalent to profit. This simplification is unwarranted, however, as the calculus of profit typically includes outlays for inputs and other assets needed to undertake production.

capitalist became impersonal, often oppressive in the imposition of rules, tasks, or the pace of work, and paying a wage that was usually inadequate.

Automation then increased alienation and the appropriation of surplus value, by deskilling work and reducing labor's possibilities of controlling its tasks and routines.[15] As industrial capitalism advanced, this would become a key feature of programs advocating workplace rights and labor justice. The spread of oligopolies deepened alienation and deskilling—management becoming more intrusive, labor more insecure, benefits being cut or disappearing altogether. Thus, the "reward" to capitalists that classical economists had envisioned—under competitive conditions—lost its meaning.[16]

Automation also reduced worktime and effort—an aspect that has accelerated with the spread of artificial intelligence (AI) in our time. This has led to the question of how to measure the exploitation of labor. For—as software algorithms and machines replace humans—how can exploitation be defined and measured, and what metric of value might be used? This questioning is by no means new, as Marx himself raised it in the mid-nineteenth century—machinery then coming into greater use in factories—without fully answering it.[17]

Measuring labor exploitation therefore remains an open question. *Surplus labor*—labor expended that is equivalent to *surplus value* (Δm) under *competitive* market conditions—was conceptually posited by Marx to represent exploitation.[18] Measuring labor exploitation this way may seem simple enough—

15 A matter that would become more noticeable in the twentieth century, as factory scale increased. See Harry Braverman, *Labor and Monopoly Capital: The Degradation of Work in the Twentieth Century* (New York: Monthly Review Press, 1974), chapters 7–10. Increased stratification in factory production regimes was part of the deskilling panorama—see Katherine Stone, "The Origins of Job Structures in the Steel Industry," *Review of Radical Political Economics*, 6 (1974), 113–73.

16 Under oligopoly capitalism, the "reward"—seen by some classical economists, such as Adam Smith, as just compensation to the capitalist for his efforts and risk—evolved into appropriating as much uncompensated work as possible from labor. See Paul A. Baran and Paul M. Sweezy, *Monopoly Capital: An Essay on the American Economic and Social Order* (New York: Monthly Review Press, 1966), chapters 2, 3, 8; Eric J. Hobsbawm, *Age of Extremes: The Short Twentieth Century, 1914–91* (New York: Vintage Books, 1994), chapters 3–7.

17 The following statement is at the core of debates on the value of labor, its measurement, and its contribution to use value: "As soon as labour in the direct form has ceased to be the great well-spring of wealth, labour time ceases and must cease to be its measure, and hence exchange value [must cease to be the measure] of use value," (p. 705) in Karl Marx, *Grundrisse: Foundations of the Critique of Political Economy* (London: Penguin, 1973), based on notes compiled in seven (rough draft) notebooks in 1857–58. These notes were not fully published until 1953, in German [*Grundrisse* (Berlin: Dietz Verlag)]. See also the discussion in Michael Heinrich, "Crisis Theory, the Law of the Tendency of the Profit Rate to Fall, and Marx's Studies in the 1870s," *Monthly Review*, April 2013, 16–17. The need to understand value generation in (and through) labor as a *qualitative* matter—beyond any (quantitative) consideration of labor time—was stressed by David Laibman in his *Value, Technical Change and Crisis: Explorations in Marxist Economic Theory* (New York, Sharpe, 1992), Chapter 1.

18 This equivalence brings into question whether exchange (or market) value—the reference monetary calibration of surplus value—may diverge from the socially necessary value (*use value*) of a

inasmuch as the monetary calibration of surplus value would be equivalent to surplus labor—*and* to exploitation.

However, the scenario where labor is expended and exploited, yet *no* surplus value is obtained by the capitalist—not uncommon under competitive market conditions—makes it impossible to calculate exploitation ratios.[19] This matter is complicated by labor's rightful claim to the oligopolistic surpluses (ΔN, ΔS, ΔL) obtained from product, input, and labor markets (discussed in the previous chapter)—a panorama missing in Marx's time due to the inexistence of oligopolies. These surpluses would necessarily have to be added to surplus value, if labor exploitation is to be calibrated.[20]

The problem noted above—and the addition of labor's claim to the oligopolistic surpluses—indicates the need to find a non-monetary valuation of exploitation.[21] Among the possibilities that might be considered could be worktime and a composite metric that can represent effort and skill. These indicators, however, come up against the fact that AI and production hardware have *reduced* worktime, effort, and skills. Thus, this approach would show the value of exploitation (and of labor expended) to have declined over time—simply

---

commodity—a point raised by Marx in *Capital*, Vol. I, Part I, Chapter III, 94–145. Marx's objective seems to have been to point out that pricing *might* provide a *semblance* of value, even *if* a commodity's exchange value (or market price) happens to be greater than its use value. This aspect was addressed by Moishe Postone in his *Time, Labor, and Social Domination: A Reinterpretation of Marx's Critical Theory* (New York: Cambridge University Press, 1993), 134–35. The potential divergence between the utility *and* the market price of a commodity was also apparent to Smith, when he stated: "The word value … has two different meanings, and sometimes expresses the utility of some particular object, and sometimes the power of purchasing other goods which the possession of that object conveys. The one may be called 'value in use'; the other, 'value in exchange'. The things which have the greatest value in use have frequently little or no value in exchange; and … those which have the greatest value in exchange have frequently little or no value in use"—Smith, *Wealth of Nations*, Part I, 30.

19 A matter apparently overlooked in estimates of labor exploitation ratios that have used operating profit as proxy for surplus value—as numerator—with initial money-capital (M), total employment, *or* total wage disbursements as denominators. It is unclear if the operating profit data utilized in the estimates included outlays for non-labor inputs. If so included, the ratios would provide a combined measure of labor exploitation *and* consumption of inputs in production. The case of negative or null profit (profit loss) for any year (or time period) would, however, lead to a missed estimate. See the discussions in Joan Robinson, *An Essay on Marxian Economics* (London: Macmillan, 1942), 16; Meek, *Studies in the Labour Theory*, 237; Christian Fuchs, *Digital Labour and Karl Marx* (London: Routledge, 2014), 358.

20 Labor's claim on the oligopolistic surplus is partial, however, as consumer exploitation—a matter that will be considered in the following chapter—needs to be taken into account.

21 Conceptually, the disengagement of labor expended in production from monetary measures is by no means novel. In the early nineteenth century, for example, David Ricardo endorsed this approach, stating: "The value of a commodity … depends on the relative quantity of labour which is necessary for its production, and not on the greater or less compensation which is paid for that labour." See his *Works and Correspondence*, Part I, 11. See also the discussion in Meek, *Studies in the Labour Theory*, 97.

because labor was replaced by hardware. Yet, exploitation of labor continued and possibly increased, and its expended value would no doubt exist—but both aspects would be missed.

The measurement of labor exploitation, and labor value, has therefore remained elusive. This should not detract from recognizing that labor exploitation is a very serious problem in the context of technology oligopolies. Devising a metric that can account for the labor expended in inventing, developing, and maintaining the AI and hardware—that replaces employment in production—might be one possibility. The value of such labor might then be adjusted according to the serial usage of AI and the hardware that replace workers—taking the exchange value of output as a guide. This approach would likely not be more complex than the methods commonly used in finance to estimate, say, the value of derivatives or of collateralized debt obligations (among other instruments).

Despite the widespread use of AI and hardware, all indications are that the importance of labor—and its exploitation—has increased over time.[22] Labor is today the most important operational cost factor in technology production and a major concern of global arbitrage (a topic that will be dealt with later in this work). Labor is also at the core of automated processes and AI—as it is essential for their invention, development, and maintenance. And labor intangibles—creativity, knowledge, and experience—are fundamentally important in technology research and product development.

Novel forms of labor associated with new technologies—and with technology oligopolies—need to be taken into account. *Uselabor*, an uncompensated form of labor—defined and discussed in the previous chapter—defies longstanding notions of work. Social media oligopolies have turned this form of labor into an immense source of surpluses and power, enlisting billions of human beings around the world.[23] Personal data appropriated from uselaborers are mined to sell access to advertisers and other parties.[24] The fact that the financial value of these companies depends on their uselaborer population—and the intimate data appropriated—is all too often ignored. If the value of

22 Nonetheless, returns to labor in the American economy declined during the last four decades—a matter that reflects the rapidly increasing contingency labor workforce (and its exploitation), the erosion of incomes for working people, the spread of AI and automation, and rapid oligopolistic consolidation. See David Autor, David Dorn, Lawrence F. Katz, Christina Patterson and John Van Reenen, *Concentrating on the Fall of the Labor Share*, NBER Working Paper 23108, 2017, www.nber.org/; and their *The Fall of the Labor Share and the Rise of Superstar Firms*, MIT Economics Working Paper, 2017, https://economics.mit.edu/.

23 See Christian Fuchs, *Culture and Economy in the Age of Social Media* (New York: Routledge, 2015), chapters 4–6; and his *Digital Labour and Karl Marx* (New York: Routledge, 2014), chapters 11, 12.

24 Through data cloud platforms that are considered "lean," in the sense that they largely eliminate labor outlays through AI—see, for example, Nick Srnicek, *Platform Capitalism* (Malden: Polity, 2017), Chapter 2.

uselaborers and their exploitation were to be calibrated, it would most likely be higher than the economic product of many nations.

Diverse modes of uselabor arose during the last decade—as differences between work, games, entertainment, and consumption became blurred.[25] Also, enlistment of uselaborers cut across age groups—to involve even children, with unknown long-term consequences for mental health and social wellbeing.[26] Rather than helping foster democracy—a frequent claim by network oligopolists—social media seems to have fostered much waste of time and effort, addictions, censorship, false perceptions, and a shallow understanding of many topics.[27] Calibrating the value of wasted time alone could amount to a substantial portion of lifetime income for many uselaborers. And, despite the confusion surrounding uselabor, this ubiquitous form of work fits quite well in the transformative dynamic of technology oligopoly capitalism.

A related development was the proliferation of open-source networks during the last two decades. Initially intended to be collaborative vehicles for software development, open-source networking became a *quasi*-uselabor operation for many oligopolistic technology corporations.[28] Open-source activities have long moved beyond software, to include contributions in robotics, biopharmaceuticals, AI, genomics, microelectronics, biomedicine, and nanotechnology, among other fields. Although open-source contributions are not proprietary, they can nonetheless be seized and used to increase oligopolistic market power—with little or no risk of attracting lawsuits. In many cases, modifying an open-source contribution significantly can practically render it proprietary—as it becomes impossible to separate what contributors provided from what a corporation added.

25 Use of the terms *play* or *hobby* in this book will refer to activities performed for self-development or amusement—results *not* being appropriated by a capitalist or business (social media oligopolists included). If appropriation occurs, then the hobby or play become *work*, the toil involved becomes *labor*, and the individual becomes a worker. If hobby or play generates products or services that are sold—to gain individual or household income—then they can be considered artisanal self-employment. In the case of social media oligopolists, play or gaming activities, and hobbies, become *uselabor* (as defined and discussed in the previous chapter).

26 See Tobbi Dyer, "The Effects of Social Media on Children," *Dalhousie Journal of Interdisciplinary Management* 14 (2018), https://ojs.library.dal.ca/; Jean M. Twenge, *iGen: Why Today's Super-Connected Kids are Growing Up Less Rebellious, More Tolerant, Less Happy—and Completely Unprepared for Adulthood (and What this Means for the Rest of Us)* (New York: Atria, 2017). One concern often cited is the 31 percent suicide rate increase for 15- to 19-year-olds (2007–15) in the United States—see *The Economist*, "Mental Health: Me, Myself and iPhone; Teenagers are Anxious and Depressed. Could the Culprit Be in their Pocket?" November 25, 2017, 26–28.

27 See Siva Vaidhyanathan, *Antisocial Media: How Facebook Disconnects Us and Undermines Democracy* (New York: Oxford University Press, 2018); Nicholas G. Carr, *The Shallows: How the Internet is Changing the Way We Think, Read and Remember* (London: Atlantic, 2011).

28 For an overview of the promise initially attributed to open-source networking, see Johan Söderberg, *Hacking Capitalism: The Free and Open Source Software Movement* (New York: Routledge, 2007), chapters 1–3, 5.

A major difference between uselaborers and open-source contributors is that the latter may not be required to provide personal data to participate, and their collaborative behaviors (or data) may not be mined and sold to advertisers. Data developers who purchase access to information on uselaborers—to mine or advertise to—are thus largely missing from the open-source spectrum. Also, the open-source network is not typically owned or controlled by the corporate oligopolist that seizes contributions.

But one important aspect that uselaborers and open-source contributors share is that the labor appropriated by the oligopolist is uncompensated. Much the same can be said for corporate schemes that target customer feedback or "user engagement"—to obtain ideas for product improvement, through which corporate resources are saved.[29] The now ubiquitous customer or user surveys provide opportunities to enlist this form of uselabor, and the personal data given up is often mined for advertising or sold to other companies.

Capital

The transformative apparatus requires *capital*. Here, the term will refer to active monetary support for all aspects of productive transformation in technology oligopolies. This will render it equivalent to money-capital in the accumulative dynamic—and will help differentiate it from passive uses, such as speculation, rentier activities, and lending.[30]

Capital—in its active form—takes up several functions. *All of them reflect the relations of power in productive transformation and the predominance of the owners of capital.* One of the functions involves fixed capital—the use, purchase (or lease) of facilities, and equipment to undertake transformation. Some oligopolistic technology corporations—such as social media and search providers—have partially dissipated this function, by shifting the expense of facilities and equipment to uselaborers. In other cases—such as on-demand tech services—the cost of equipment and facilities has been shifted to labor through external arrangements. Reduced outlays for real estate, rent, utilities, insurance, workspace, or upkeep have thus helped boost surpluses, stock valuations, and executive compensation.

It should not surprise, therefore, that so many technology oligopolists are externalizing their workforce. "Temporary-vendor-contractor" (TVC),

29 Some of these schemes were euphemistically labeled "democratic" by some authors—see, for example, Eric von Hippel, *Democratizing Innovation* (Cambridge, MA: MIT Press, 2005). Few customers seem to be aware that their freely provided work can save considerable management effort and expense—see, for example, *The Economist*, "Barely Managing: User-Rating Systems are Cut-Rate Substitutes for a Skillful Manager," June 30, 2018, 65.

30 Differentiation between active and passive uses of money can be traced to classical economists—and the long-running debate on the rewards of either form. See Smith, *Wealth of Nations*, Part I, 338–39; Marx, *Capital*, Vol. I, Part II, "The Transformation of Money into Capital," 146–76.

"franchisee," and "1099" arrangements—app developers included—are thus likely to become the norm for most tech oligopolies in the near future.[31] Many companies may therefore retain only a nucleus of executives as in-house staff (along with the necessary production facilities—server farms included). Further reductions in fixed capital outlays may therefore be expected—possibly up to a point where corporate headquarter facilities become "command-and-coordination centers" that operate with minimal use of space (and in-house staff). Research, which often requires significant fixed capital outlays—in such sectors as biotechnology and biopharmaceuticals—may follow this pattern, as research units are spun off and treated as external entities. Researcher activities in which physical space outlays, along with hardware or equipment, can be loaded unto workers—through externalization—also seem bound to become the norm.

Another function involves circulating capital—necessary to cover outlays for non-labor inputs.[32] Raw and processed materials, shipping, waste disposal, taxes, and intangible inputs—such as externally based accounting, marketing, advertising, and technical assistance—are supported by this function. Circulating capital outlays are often high, due to the market reach of oligopolistic technology production. Also, some inputs—such as rare-earth minerals—may be found in few locations, requiring much expense to extract, refine, or transport. A peculiar advantage of some technology oligopolies—as in the case of social media and search engines—is that their circulating capital outlays tend to be low, due to the intangibility of their products.

Intangibility of products—such as software, social media interactions, and web searches—is thus a distinctive aspect. This can explain, in part, why circulating capital outlays are usually so low and surpluses so high for oligopolists Facebook, Alphabet-Google, Microsoft, and others—compared to companies that depend on hardware. In cases where hardware and software are core functions, as with Apple, high surpluses can be attributed to low circulating capital due to software production (in Apple's case the Android operating system). Low circulating capital outlays can definitely boost share valuations and

31 An aspect noticed during the last decade. See Lawrence F. Katz and Alan B. Krueger, *The Rise and Nature of Alternative Work Arrangements in the United States, 1995–2015*, March 29, 2016, https://krueger.princeton.edu/; Lauren Weber, "The End of Employees: U.S. Companies Shift Work Once Considered Core to Contractors, Pruning Costs and Job Security," *Wall Street Journal*, February 3, 2017, A1.

32 Use of the term *constant* to refer to both fixed and circulating capital will be omitted—see Marx, *Capital*, Vol. II, Part II, 213–14, 218–19. Although relevant to competitive conditions (in Marx's time), the meaning of this term seems unsuited to productive transformation in technology oligopolies. This is due to the distinctive character of fixed capital in technology, noted previously, and the (no less distinctive) function of circulating capital. Each of these forms of capital became significantly differentiated from each other, as oligopolistic consolidation advanced in the American economy during the past eight decades.

executive compensation—and release funds that can be used for acquisitions, entry barriers, and lobbying.

Variable capital involves direct support for production and includes such outlays as wages and benefits. As labor outlays tend to be a most important factor in productive transformation, variable capital receives considerable attention in the oligopolistic technology domain. Offshoring and outsourcing—through labor arbitrage (to be discussed later in this book)—are important for reducing such outlays. At home, externalizing the workforce (noted earlier) seems set to become the norm.

For social media and web search oligopolists, variable capital outlays are unnecessary regarding uselabor. Thus, expenses incurred for conventional labor tend to be very low in relation to the uselaborer workforce—and to surpluses.[33] And, much of the work performed by conventional labor—to manage data mining algorithms, arrange apps development, ad targeting, and the like—tends to be offshored.[34] This aspect—in concert with their uncompensated uselabor population—may explain why and how social media oligopolies have accumulated their vast wealth in a short period of time.

The finance capital function supports productive transformation by providing (or increasing) money-capital (M) in the accumulative dynamic. This mode of capital usually involves external sources, such as loans or the issuance of bonds and shares. It has been an important support for production since the early stages of capitalism.[35] Under oligopolistic conditions, however, the accumulation of surpluses—in the form of ΔN, or possibly ΔS and ΔL (or all of these, as discussed in the previous chapter)—provide a reservoir that can supplant loans and debt.[36]

Finance capital can nonetheless play a part in technology oligopolies through speculative schemes. Share buybacks—a way to increase share prices (or stop their decline) artificially—is a common practice. Issuing bonds when real interest rates are negative (or null) is a favored strategy among many technology

33 Keeping conventional employment low is a major priority for many social media oligopolists. See, for example, Finances Online, *Number of Facebook Employees 2020/2021: Compensation, Tenure and Perks*, https://financesonline.com/ (accessed July 20, 2022); Lauren Weber, "For Videogame Makers, Hiring is a Last Resort," *Wall Street Journal*, April 11, 2017, A1.

34 See Alex Melnichuk, "The Current State of IT Offshoring: Review by nCube," *nCube*, May 1, 2021, https://ncube.com/; Statista, *IT-Outsourcing Services Market Revenue in the World from 2016 to 2021*, www.statista.com/; Tech World Times, *Offshore Software Development Trends in 2020*, https://techworldtimes.com/ (both accessed July 22, 2022).

35 See Eric J. Hobsbawm, *The Age of Capital: 1848–75* (London: Weidenfeld and Nicolson, 1975), chapters 1–3, 7, 13; Pierre Vilar and Judith White, *A History of Gold and Money, 1450 to 1920* (London: Verso, 2011).

36 Research on 74 nations over a 36-year period concluded that capital investment from external sources tended to decline in large corporations—see Federico J. Diez, Daniel Leigh and Suchanan Tambunlertchai, *Global Market Power and Macroeconomic Implications*, IMF Working Paper WP/18/137 (Washington: International Monetary Fund, 2018), www.imf.org/.

oligopolists.[37] This can provide funds to acquire other companies, set up entry barriers, and lobby regulators and politicians. Such bonds can then be repurchased—using part of the vast surpluses obtained through market control, or the idle cash accumulated—if interest rates rise or trading in bond futures turns negative.

Production

Production is a vital element of productive transformation. It is at the core of the transformative dynamic (C→C′)—making it possible for a new commodity (C′, in the form of a product or service) to exist. And it is fundamentally important for the accumulative dynamic, as noted in the previous chapter. Without it, capital accumulation and market exchange are unsustainable.[38]

Production regimes establish managerial control over labor and all aspects of production, including the technologies deployed. But these technologies are not neutral—as the ways of their usage are part of their design. *Technology thus often becomes a tool to impose managerial power over production.* The fact that AI-enabled technologies may not use any (or few) workers can be considered a result of their design—even though the latter was itself a result of labor. Highly skilled labor, that is, but labor nonetheless.

Labor processes—a vital component of production regimes—are the vehicle to structure work tasks and the specific uses of technology, such that uncompensated surplus labor (equivalent to surplus value, Δm) can be obtained by the oligopolist. Exploitation in the form of uncompensated surplus labor is thus an

37 Negative real interest rates for an extended period—unprecedented in its duration—became important for oligopolistic technology finance during the last decade. See Edward N. Gamber, *The Historical Decline in Real Interest Rates and its Implications for CBO's Projections*, Congressional Budget Office, Working Paper 2020-09, December 2020, www.cbo.gov/.

38 The accumulative dynamic would be vacated without production, becoming simple amassment of money through money. Or, $F \rightarrow F^F$, where $F^F = F + \Delta f + \Delta F$, with F as initial speculative money, F^F as new money, Δf as the speculative surplus obtained under competitive conditions, and ΔF as the oligopolistic speculative surplus obtained through control over a betting scenario (above and beyond the quantum of Δf). Productive transformation is thus eliminated—replaced by speculative routines, heuristics, or schemes (automated—as in the case of e-trading—or not). Some authors have wrongly considered this scenario to be a "new" (or another) mode of capitalism, referring to it as "financial capitalism" or in some cases financialization. In my book *Corporate Power, Oligopolies, and the Crisis of the State* (Albany: State University of New York Press, 2016), 87–174, I referred to this panorama as *financialism*—a mode of money amassment that is outside the capitalist accumulative dynamic, and that has acquired mass cultural features. I believe this interpretation to be consistent with the notion of "fictitious capital" elaborated by Rudolf Hilferding in his *Das Finanzkapital: eine Studie über die jüngste Entwicklung des Kapitalismus* (Vienna: Brand, 1910) [translated as *Finance Capital: A Study of the Latest Phase of Capitalist Development* (London: Routledge and Kegan Paul, 1981), Part III, Chapter 15, 237–38]—based in part on Marx's discussion of fictitious capital in his *Capital*, Vol. III, Part V, Chapter XXV, 400–13.

outcome of labor processes. Transformed commodities (C′)—embedding the uncompensated labor (along with the compensated one)—are the result.

The organization of labor processes—and of the production regimes in which they operate—thus determines the technologies that will be deployed, what kind of work will be done, where and when, the skills that will be used, and how much creativity workers will be allowed. And, how exploitive the execution of tasks may turn out to be. Through the labor processes, oligopolists require workers to surrender their effort, time, and creativity—along with any claim to what they produce—in exchange for salaries (and possibly some benefits).

Structuring labor processes to increase productivity is a customary way to obtain more surplus labor—the key to increments in surplus value (Δm).[39] Keeping productivity on an upward path is thus an important goal of technology oligopolistic management, as it tends to increase surpluses. But because increased labor productivity is seldom accompanied by commensurate increases in wages or benefits, uncompensated surplus labor—and surplus value—tend to rise relative to surpluses. Reducing skills through automation and AI thus tends to perpetuate this scenario and increase labor turnover—along with share valuations.[40]

A consequence of this practice is greater control over production and more labor insecurity, allowing oligopolists to unilaterally set performance rules.[41] Another consequence has been a long-term reduction of employment in production across technology sectors.[42] Offshoring has contributed to this dynamic, allowing oligopolists to evade regulations on safety, benefits, and compensation.[43] Reductions in employment offer the advantage of cut-

39 Historically, higher labor productivity has been related to increases in surplus value—under *competitive* conditions—in two distinctive ways (both drawn from Marx's original propositions in his *Capital*, Vol. I, parts III, IV, V). The first one—relevant to automation—involves a *relative* increase in surplus value through gains in productivity from greater output produced during the same amount of time *or* the same output in less time. The second one involves an *absolute* increase in surplus value through additional productivity provided by an increment in worktime. Under oligopolistic conditions, however, these relationships tend to be distorted—as labor's claim to the surpluses (ΔN, ΔL, and ΔS) obtained through market price manipulation must be added to the surplus value appropriated from labor.

40 High turnover has often helped increase surplus labor—a longstanding problem since the early days of industrial capitalism. See Sumner H. Slichter, *The Turnover of Factory Labor* (New York: Appleton, 1919), chapters I-IV, VI, VII, IX, XI; Eric J. Hobsbawm, *Labouring Men: Studies in the History of Labour* (London: Weidenfeld and Nicolson, 1979), chapters 2, 8, 16, 17.

41 A scenario compounded by the externalization of in-house labor during the past three decades. See Katz and Krueger, *Rise and Nature of Alternative Work*; Weber, "The End of Employees."

42 A significant trend since the 1960s, interrupted by cyclical upturns. See John Bellamy Foster and Robert W. McChesney, *The Endless Crisis* (New York: Monthly Review Press, 2012); Katherine S. Newman, *Laid Off, Laid Low* (New York: Columbia University Press, 2008).

43 Empirical research with data for a 36-year period and 74 nations found that offshoring and outsourcing contributed to increases in oligopolistic markups, by reducing labor cost—see Diez, Leigh

ting labor costs—thereby increasing surpluses. Offshoring and outsourcing (at home) can thus be important means of obtaining more uncompensated labor or raising productivity—through longer work shifts, lower wages, or reduced benefits. Offshoring can thereby translate into greater control over production and labor, as the bargaining power of workers is diminished, and fear of insecure employment takes over minds.

Greater automation in production can increase output. The latter might be welcomed by a company in a competitive scenario. However, *under oligopolistic conditions, an increase in output through automation would likely occur only if the resulting output of a product can be lower than its market demand.* On this calculus rides the possibility of retaining control over pricing.[44]

Thus, any output increase that automation brings may likely be less than the demand for the product. A mistake in this calculus can have negative consequences for capital accumulation, share pricing, and executive compensation. At the core of any decision to automate is therefore the expectation that the product market surplus (ΔN) obtained *after* automation will be greater than that obtained before. More so, because the cost of automating will likely be amortized through the additional surpluses. And, increments in the surplus—above and beyond the level of amortization—would need to be greater than the amounts obtained from alternatives.

This calculus may explain why usage of new technology in production tends to be secondary to sustaining pricing power. Thus, the oligopolist's *usage* of new productive technologies and its *creation* of new technologies through research—to be embedded in products and services—are two different matters. This asymmetry has sometimes baffled those who analyze the oligopolistic domain.[45] It may help explain why offshoring—where older production technologies are often used—might be preferred to automating at home. And, this often occurs even when the oligopolist pioneers new technologies and embeds them in its products. *The coexistence of old production techniques with the creation of new technologies—or of both new and old production technology within the same plant and organization—may thus seem contradictory but it is actually quite rational, when the calculus of oligopolistic power is taken into account.*

---

and Tambunlertchai, *Global Market Power.*

44 In the case of input or labor markets, the objective would be to sustain demand below the prior level of inputs or labor—provided product market demand remains the same. On labor, such action may contribute to sustain (or increase) a reserve pool of unemployed or underemployed workers and consequently stabilize (or reduce) wages. On inputs, it may lead to lower input prices from suppliers. These actions may maintain or increase the surpluses obtained through input (ΔS) or labor (ΔL) market control, as discussed in the previous chapter.

45 The coexistence of old and new production technologies—within the same plants and companies—was noticed long ago by Baran and Sweezy, *Monopoly Capital*, 95–97. A survey of production plants in the 1950s can provide additional insights—see Dexter M. Keezer, *New Forces in American Business* (New York: McGraw Hill, 1959), chapters 1–3, 8, 10.

A novel form of production involves the social media oligopolies. Production in this scenario depends on uselaborers being made to give up their personal data, time, effort, and experiences. The network is the means—or platform—that makes it possible. The production regime involves data mining—a largely automated process—while the oligopolist dictates the technology—the general software and hardware—that must be used.

Uselaborers—along with their data, time, effort, and experiences—may be considered *both* labor and raw material providers in this production regime. The latter structure the online protocols to be followed—including the rules for access, contact, and usage. The general parameters in which uselaborers can communicate are thus imposed—much as factory production regimes set rules for performing tasks or utilizing machinery. Some flexibility is necessary—more so than a factory regime would allow—as online behavior can occur in diverse ways—time, speed, content, contacts, and usage varying substantially between uselaborers.

One result of this unusual production regime is that the uncompensated surplus labor—underlying surplus value (Δm)—is practically the totality of labor provided by uselaborers. In other words, uselabor is *not* monetarily compensated—a phenomenon not seen in human history since the times of slavery (although slaves did receive nutrition, housing, clothing, and possibly medical care from their masters). Thus, if monetary value is estimated for uselabor, its quantum could likely be many times the value of the annual surpluses obtained by the oligopolies in control.

Uselabor tasks in this production regime also involve viewing advertisements (and possibly purchasing). Placements of such ads are, in effect, the product market that the social media oligopolist controls—frequency of viewings by uselaborers being a most important aspect.[46] Advertisement is thus the source of surpluses (ΔN, ΔL) and new money-capital (M^N). And, the number of uselaborers in the network, and their viewings—along with the data, time, effort, and experiences they are made to give up—are paramount for pricing the advertisements.

Research and Product Development

Another vital element of the transformative apparatus involves research and product development (R&D). This element reflects the dual nature of

46 An aspect that drew attention during the last decade—see Jack Marshall, "Facebook Says It Sells Only Viewable Ads," *Wall Street Journal*, February 23, 2015, B6. The overwhelming importance of having as many viewings as possible has in many cases neglected objectionable aspects—see, for example, *BBC*, "Fake Ads on Facebook Spoil Real Life Fairy Story," June 18, 2021, www.bbc.co.uk/; Leslie Chiou and Catherine Tucker, *Fake News and Advertising on Social Media: A Study of the Anti-Vaccination Movement*, National Bureau for Economic Research, Working Paper 25223 (Cambridge: NBER, 2018); Jack Nicas, "Big Brands' Ads Give Boost to Sites Touting Fake News," *Wall Street Journal*, December 8, 2016, A1.

technology oligopolies as users and providers of new technologies. Of prime importance for oligopolies is *the capacity of R&D operations to differentiate products or services to increase sales*. Tweaking existing products so that they can be advertised as novel—or at least more effective—is a major preoccupation. Research may be enlisted to differentiate products, especially when technical complexities are significant.[47] Identifying ways to promote sales, however, tends to be a most important objective.[48]

Research operations may also be tasked with internal projects, such as adapting technologies that can lower production cost.[49] Seeking licensing revenue may motivate companies to patent ideas—especially when cost and uncertainty are limited.[50] Technology oligopolists also engage in "second-mover" R&D—reverse engineering other companies' products to differentiate and market them.[51] Reverse engineering has become easier than ever and can be done (confidentially) by contracting "tear-down" consultants.[52]

Patent infringement can be made undetectable or very difficult to prove, particularly when evidence is not readily available. And, the notion that pilferage and imitation tend to be more profitable than investing in research has long been understood in the corporate domain.[53] In the case of new processes or formulas, knowledge that can be used in second-mover projects can be

47 The drive to find uses for AI in the home is one example. See Ommid Saberi and Rebecca Menes, *Artificial Intelligence and the Future for Smart Homes*, International Finance Corporation, February 2020, www.ifc.org/; Andrew Weinreich, "The Future of the Smart Home: How Homes Powered by Artificial Intelligence will Know and Care for You," *Forbes*, February 8, 2018, www.forbes.com/; Laura Stevens and Tripp Mickle, "Alexa, Siri and Rivals Battle for the Home," *Wall Street Journal*, September 2, 2017, A1.

48 An aspect noticed long ago by Baran and Sweezy in their *Monopoly Capital*, 104–07. Their insights would be confirmed four decades later—see *The Economist*, "Out of the Dusty Labs: Technology Firms Have Left the Big Corporate R&D Laboratory Behind, Shifting the Emphasis from Research to Development," March 3, 2007, 74–76.

49 Through greater use of AI for example—see Jack Warner, "How AI and Machine Learning are Reshaping the Manufacturing Sector," *Manufacturing Automation*, January 12, 2018, www.automationmag.com/; Ian Wright, "Bringing Artificial Intelligence to Manufacturing," *Engineering.com*, September 19, 2017, www.engineering.com/.

50 See Asa Fitch, "Oracle Gets Boost from Licensing Software," *Wall Street Journal*, June 20, 2019, B1.

51 Martin S. Bressler and C. W. Von Bergen, "When Running Second Wins the Race: Examining the Benefits of Second-Mover Advantage," *Journal of Management and Marketing Research*, 20 (2017), https://aabri.com/; Luis Suarez-Villa, *Globalization and Technocapitalism: The Political Economy of Corporate Power and Technological Domination* (Farnham: Ashgate, 2012), 128–30.

52 EMS, *Steps Involved in Reverse Engineering a Part*, www.engineeredmechanicalsystems.com/; Boston Consulting Group, *Product Teardown*, www.bcg.com/ (both accessed July 22, 2022); Carl Hoffman, "The Teardown Artists," *Wired*, February 2016, 136–39; *The Economist*, "The Business of Dissecting Electronics: The Lowdown on Teardowns," January 23, 2010, 62–63.

53 A matter established long ago by William L. Baldwin and Gerald L. Childs, "The Fast Second and Rivalry in Research and Development," *Southern Economic Journal* 36 (1969), 18–24.

obtained by hiring away R&D staff—a tactic that gained attention during the last decade.[54]

Corporate espionage also gained importance in the technology oligopolistic domain in recent decades, as product development gained priority. As much as $600 billion in intellectual property (IP) were estimated to be stolen annually during the last decade, mainly through espionage.[55] The latter can involve diverse R&D endeavors, such as strategic plans for new products and technologies, their design, test results, performance features, and marketing programs. It can also encompass tech-based services that seek to expand into new niches.[56] Consultants specialized in espionage can play an important role in deploying this strategy.[57] Much the same techniques used by government-run intelligence agencies tend to be applied by such consultants, and the individuals in charge can be former intelligence analysts or agents.

In some of the more complex technology sectors—nanotechnology, genetic engineering, bio-pharmacology, for example—companies may place significant emphasis on research. Operations may be grounded in what I have referred to as a *systematized research regime*—the research equivalent of the factory production regime.[58] A prime objective is to *continuously* generate novel processes, formulas, gadgets, or ideas—and IP.

Systematized research regimes may account for the rising tide of litigation over IP in recent decades—and of numerous avoidance schemes. Among the more unusual ones was Allergan's nominal transfer of patent rights for its

54 See Mark S. Reisch, "U.S. Charges DuPont Employee with Trade Secrets Theft," *Chemical and Engineering News*, April 17, 2017, www.cen.acs.org/; Ed Silverman, "Glaxo Scientists Indicted for Stealing Trade Secrets," *Statnews*, January 20, 2016, www.stanews.com/pharmalot/; Justin Scheck and Lauren Pollock, "Former H-P Executive Pleads Guilty: Malhotra Could Get Jail Time for Stealing IBM Trade Secrets," *Wall Street Journal*, July 14, 2008, B8. Confidential settlements have made it more difficult to find reports on research or trade secrets theft.

55 Commission on the Theft of American Intellectual Property, *Update to the IP Commission Report 2017*, www.ipcomission.org/report/, and other years (accessed August 2, 2022). See also Peter Loftus, "Industrial Espionage Cases Soar in U.S.," *Wall Street Journal*, September 20, 2017, A1. Corporate espionage and IP theft have been a longstanding concern among corporate specialists—see Adam L. Penenberg and Marc Barry, *Spooked: Espionage in Corporate America* (Reading: Basic Books, 2008); Pat Choate, *Hot Property: The Stealing of Ideas in an Age of Globalization* (New York: Knopf, 2005); Hedieh Nasheri, *Economic Espionage and Industrial Spying* (Cambridge: Cambridge University Press, 2005).

56 See Greg Bensinger, "Uber Formed Covert Unit to Steal Trade Secrets, Ex-Employee Says," *Wall Street Journal*, November 29, 2017, A1.

57 See ORC International, Expert Advisory Services, *Corporate Espionage Experts*, http://www.orcexperts.com/ (accessed May 11, 2022); Loftus, "Industrial Espionage"; George Chidi, "Confessions of a Corporate Spy," *Inc.*, February 2, 2013, www.inc.com/; Rhymer Rigby, "Spotting Corporate Espionage," *Financial Times*, December 21, 2010, www.ft.com/.

58 See Luis Suarez-Villa, *Technocapitalism: A Critical Perspective on Technological Innovation and Corporatism* (Philadelphia: Temple University Press, 2009), 124–35.

best-selling eye medication (Restasis) to the St. Regis Mohawk nation.[59] The latter's sovereign status placed disputes out of reach of U.S. federal courts, thus preempting lawsuits. Efforts to stem IP litigation by involving the U.S. government created other problems—as patent agency ("*Inter Partes*") reviews supplanted judicial due process.[60]

Among the more significant examples of IP litigation tied to systematized research regimes have been those involving genomics.[61] Appropriation of IP related to this field has gained vital importance for oligopolistic power, as it holds the key to create and modify life. Innumerable commercial products, therapies, and services stand to be marketed in the near future as this field matures. Thus, most any aspect of IP connected to genomic R&D is attracting intense attention from the corporate domain—and Wall Street.

The research regime's drive to generate IP is often accompanied by measures intended to achieve rapid results, particularly through tasking—much as workers' routines are controlled in a production regime.[62] The drive for fast results has even involved setting strict time limits in some regimes. Google's imposition of two-year time frames for some research projects, for example, drew attention during the last decade.[63] In biotechnology, deadline setting has often been linked to pressures to obtain patents quickly, partly because of high research outlays.[64]

Automation of some tasks—through expert systems or AI—is often employed in the research regime, much as might occur in factories. Thus, efforts to speed up research have resorted to the use of virtual reality, to simulate outcomes[65] In some cases, resorting to artisanal-type techniques—such as

59 Jonathan D. Rockoff, "Mylan Hits Patent Sale to Tribe," *Wall Street Journal*, October 16, 2017, B3.

60 See Brent Kendall, "Supreme Court Hears Patent Case: Justices Appear Divided Over Process that Pits Biotech Firms Against Tech Titans," *Wall Street Journal*, November 28, 2017, B4.

61 See Arindam Purkayastha, "After Intense Patent Litigation Bio-Rad and 10x Genomics Settle through Cross Licensing," *Mondaq*, August 2021, www.mondaq.com/; Rebecca Tapscott, "Complete Genomics Sues Illumina for Antitrust and Unfair Competition Violations," *IP Watchdog*, January 15, 2021, www.ipwatchdog.com/; Joe Palazzolo and Amy D. Marcus, "Patent Case Heads to Court: Rival Research Teams Battle Over Commercial Rights to Crispr-Cas9, a Gene-editing Tool," *Wall Street Journal*, December 6, 2016, B3; and their "Gene Tool Draws Investors, Discord," *Wall Street Journal*, September 23, 2016, B1.

62 See Suarez-Villa, *Technocapitalism*, 127–29.

63 Alistair Barr, "Google Lab Puts a Time Limit on Innovations: Mobile-Focused Projects Get Two Years to Prove Themselves; Hiring Mostly outside Experts," *Wall Street Journal*, April 1, 2015, B6.

64 Shen Lin, "Invasion of Patent Trolls into the Biotech Sector," *Medium*, October 14, 2018, https://medium.com/; National Human Genome Research Institute, *The Human Genome Project Turns the Big 3-0!* September 30, 2020, www.genome.gov/.

65 Carla Brown, *Virtual Reality in Clinical Research: Potential Implementation and Challenges*, Anju Life Sciences Software, December 17, 2019, www.anjusoftware.com/; Poonam Verma, Suyash Arora, Karan Chauhan and Krishan Gupta, "Digital Simulations and Virtual Reality," *International Journal of Engineering, Pure and Applied Sciences* 2 (2017), 7–11; *The Economist*, "Virtual Reality: Get Real," July 8, 2017, 55–56.

three-dimensional (3-D) prototype fabrication—has helped speed up results, by avoiding the need to order and wait for manufactured parts.[66] And, the combination of artisanal techniques and mass production has often reduced the time to fabricate, especially when diverse product ranges are involved. *A permanent state of urgency is thus an important characteristic of the systematized research regime—anticipation of the unexpected and fast response being considered essential.*[67]

Systematized research regimes may thus help speed up IP appropriation. An unsavory aspect is that they typically dispossess research workers of any claim to what they create. Researchers must therefore renounce ownership of IP awards, such as patents—all of which are issued to individuals—and agree to transfer the rights to employers.[68] When additional compensation is provided—in the form of stock options, for example—the tendency is to bind researchers to corporate risk and to provide an impression of co-ownership.

This seems to be a clever way of concealing that researchers will not benefit from future revenue streams generated by the IP they create. Especially since share pricing does not usually reflect those revenue streams—due to the vagaries of speculation or circumstantial factors that have little or nothing to do with the IP involved. The practice also allows corporate executives to present IP as the impersonal result of a research department—or of the corporation—rather than of individual creators. And this situation has been easier to implement if contracting of researchers—as external employees or TVC-type workers—is arranged.[69]

The modularization of research regimes—by spinning off research units as subsidiaries or autonomous entities—can provide greater control over researchers and their IP productivity.[70] It may also allow the oligopolistic parent to evade blame for layoffs. Externalization of research regimes—by incorporating them as nominally independent units, along with their workers—stands to

66 Zach Winn, "3D Printing Tiny Parts for Big Impact," *MIT News*, June 2, 2021, https://news.mit.edu/; Stephanie Yang, "3-D Printing Fuels Demand for Powdered Metals," *Wall Street Journal*, December 29, 2016, B10; Christopher Gregory, "Will 3-D Printers Change the World?" *New York Times*, August 11, 2014, www.nytimes.com/.

67 See Suarez-Villa, *Technocapitalism*, 132–35.

68 See Suarez-Villa, *Globalization and Technocapitalism*, 182–85; and his *Technocapitalism*, 52–53. See also Haseltine Lake LLP, *Employee Inventor Compensation—Are Some Companies "Too Big to Pay"?* November 7, 2017, www.haseltinelake.com/.

69 As increasingly occurred during the last decade. See, for example, Lauren Weber, "The Flip Side of the New U.S. Economy: Millions of Contractors Struggle for Career Advancement, Stability and Respect at Work," *Wall Street Journal*, September 15, 2017, A9; and her "The End of Employees: U.S. Companies Shift Work Once Considered Core to Contractors, Pruning Costs and Job Security," *Wall Street Journal*, February 3, 2017, A1.

70 During the last two decades, compartmentalizing units in this manner helped attract interest from Wall Street. See Allison Prang, "Honeywell Spinoffs on Track," *Wall Street Journal*, August 24, 2018, B4; and the articles in Raghu Garud, Arun Kumaraswamy and Richard Langlois, eds., *Managing in the Modular Age: Architectures, Networks, and Organizations* (Oxford: Blackwell, 2003).

become the norm. This approach can reduce fixed and variable capital outlays while shielding the oligopolistic parent from IP-related lawsuits.

When a corporation has a market monopoly, modularization may allow engineering of obsolescence into products. This can reduce a product's market life cycle by limiting its capabilities. Engineering obsolescence can also occur through modularization of the research regime, when rapid performance improvements can be generated. This was partly the case with microprocessors. Systematized research regimes were important for generating rapid increases in processing capacity—practically doubling it every 18 months since the 1970s.[71] Generating rapid increases in processing capacity, in turn, shortened product life and allowed oligopolistic chip makers to capture new markets.

In the automotive sector, for example, microprocessors were introduced for most every vehicle control function.[72] The introduction of medical diagnostic equipment and surgical tools changed many procedures. Smartphones were made possible by continuous miniaturization. Graphics processing unit (GPU) microprocessors made it possible to provide online gaming and AI applications.[73] And, in such mundane activities as shipping packages or reading utility meters, faster and more precise data transmission became a reality.

Commodification

The previously discussed elements are entwined with an important phenomenon of the transformative apparatus—commodification. Labor—along with inputs, products, and IP—are subject to commodification in technology oligopolies. Any of these resources become a commodity whenever they are appropriated and used in productive transformation.

Until capitalism's emergence, labor, materials, and resources had not been systematically calibrated in monetary terms. The conversion of most everything into a monetary quantity then started to become ubiquitous as capitalism and oligopolies spread. An important result was that value—a qualitative notion based on social relations and perception since the earliest times—became monetized.

71 A trend predicted by semiconductor engineer Gordon Moore that became known as Moore's Law. See Gordon E. Moore, "Cramming More Components onto Integrated Circuits," *Electronics*, April 19, 1965, 114–17; Arnold Thackray, David C. Brock and Rachel Jones, *Moore's Law: The Life of Gordon Moore, Silicon Valley's Quiet Revolutionary* (New York: Basic Books, 2015), chapters 6, 9, 10. The expected end of the effect predicted by Moore's law poses major challenges, as many products' performance may stagnate—see David Rotman, "We're Not Prepared for the End of Moore's Law," *MIT Technology Review*, February 24, 2020, www.technologyreview.com/.

72 See Eric Tingwall, "Electronics Account for 40 percent of the Cost of a New Car," *Car and Driver*, May 2, 2020, www.caranddriver.com/.

73 See Stephen McBride, "Nvidia's Chips have Powered Nearly Every Major AI Breakthrough," *Forbes*, December 15, 2020, www.forbes.com/.

As capitalism deepened and oligopolies emerged, everything that a human could do or possess came to be viewed in monetary terms. And, through the use of money-capital in production and market exchange—any form of labor, any material, or resource perceived to have value could be turned into a commodity. *The use of commodities to produce other commodities would thus become a distinctive feature of the transformative apparatus in technology oligopoly capitalism.*

Commodity Fetishism

The commodification of most every endeavor as capitalism advanced generated some peculiar cultural notions and misperceptions. One of the most important was *commodity fetishism*—a term provided by Marx to criticize *the subjective belief that a commodity is inherently good—by its mere existence, or because of its desired possession and the results that may generate.*[74] Commodity fetishism, in his view, ignored the relations of production through which a commodity—any commodity—is made to exist. The expenditure of labor, the conditions of work, exploitation, the dominant social role of the capitalist, and the social injustices that result were thus ignored as commodity fetishism became a cultural phenomenon.

The social relations of production involving those who produced and those who consumed were then turned into mere relations between commodities. This narrow focus on the terms of exchange was accompanied—and legitimized—by mainstream economics' espousal of individual mental calculation as the sole basis of economic action. This panorama deepened as labor became more impersonal and as capitalists' control over production and society erased public awareness of how and why commodities were produced. Marketing propaganda aided this phenomenon, by focusing on psychological factors—to promote consumption through enhancement of self-esteem, individual gratification, and peer show-off behavior.

Branding and the emergence of advertising—along with the oligopolization of the American economy—were important forces for commodifiction.[75] The arrival of mass media technologies in the first half of the twentieth century—radio, films, television—provided many possibilities to reach individual consumers with commercial propaganda. And, the fact that the new media outlets depended greatly on corporate sponsorship was a major factor.[76] Advertising

74 Marx, *Capital*, Vol. I, Part I, Chapter I, "Commodities," 35–83.

75 Aspects noted early in the postwar period, as oligopolistic consolidation advanced. See Paul A. Baran and Paul M. Sweezy, "Theses on Advertising," *Science and Society* 28 (1964), 20–30; Rosser Reeves, *Reality in Advertising* (New York: Knopf, 1961).

76 See Robert W. McChesney, *Telecommunications, Mass Media, and Democracy: The Battle for Control of U.S. Broadcasting, 1928–35* (New York: Oxford University Press, 1993), chapters 2, 5, 9.

and branding thus turned commodity fetishism into an existential feature of life under oligopoly capitalism.[77]

The effects of this cultural phenomenon could be found everywhere, as psychologically targeted propaganda campaigns reached into most every aspect of life.[78] In the minds of millions of individuals around the world, for example, the jingle music—or key phrases—associated with a brand's advertisement could take hold for long periods of time, leading to favorable attitudes toward the brand (or its corporate owner). And, the concoction of brand images to reflect the illusion of higher social status or greater personal gratification became part of the apparatus of commodity fetishism everywhere. Lost in this panorama was the dimension of production and transformation and the oligopolistic takeover of technology.

Oligopolistic corporate ownership of news media—and of most every form of mass entertainment technology—helped this dynamic greatly. The public could thus be indoctrinated on the importance of brand-based consumption for self-esteem and peer approval—ads being shown incessantly alongside news and entertainment. And the branded advertisements—and the news and entertainment—could target age groups, interests, and occupations. The arrival of the web and social media then opened a universe of possibilities, by allowing the fine-tuning of advertisement.[79]

During the past two decades, commodification cut across age groups—as teenagers and children became important targets for advertisement and brand-based commodity fetishism. Many started to spend increasing amounts of time on networking and gaming platforms, with potentially negative effects on their health and education.[80] Children, from a very young age, were also made conscious of the importance of associating one's personality with a certain brand and its image.[81] And, advertising that targeted pre-teens became an important generator of revenue for entertainment and social media oligopolists—such as

77 See Sut Jhally, *The Codes of Advertising: Fetishism and the Political Economy of Meaning in the Consumer Society* (New York: Routledge, 2009), chapters 2, 3, 5.

78 See Emily Gould and Rumaan Alam, "The Way We Shop Now: You'll Wear What They Tell You to Wear," *New York Times*, October 24, 2017, www.nytimes.com/; Jhally, *Codes of Advertising*.

79 See the articles in Robert W. McChesney, Ellen Meiksins Wood and John Bellamy Foster, eds., *Capitalism and the Information Age: The Political Economy of the Global Information Revolution* (New York: Monthly Review Press, 1998), chapters 6, 7, 12; and in Robert W. McChesney, Russell Newman and Ben Scott, eds., *The Future of Media: Resistance and Reform in the 21st Century* (New York: Seven Stories Press, 2005), parts 1, 4.

80 Research tracking 2,500 teenagers over a two-year period—monitoring use of social media and videogaming—found they were at higher risk of developing attention-deficit hyperactivity disorder (ADHD) with prolonged usage—see Chaelin K. Ra, Junhan Cho, Matthew D. Stone, *et al.*, "Association of Digital Media Use with Subsequent Symptoms of Attention-Deficit/Hyperactivity Disorder among Adolescents," *Journal of the American Medical Association* 320 (2018), 255–63.

81 See Joel Bakan, *Childhood under Siege: How Big Business Targets Children* (New York: Free Press, 2014), chapters 3, 4, 9, 10.

YouTube and Facebook—that captured not only the attention of many millions of children but also their predators.[82]

Despite videogaming's addictive potential, this form of play—that all too often becomes uselabor—attracted much attention from tech and tech-service oligopolists.[83] The fusion of videogaming with uselabor then became an important way to feed clouds that contain the most extensive collection of intimate data ever assembled. Storing and mining such information are important for targeting advertising at any individual throughout a lifetime—thus tracking their existential trajectory. Multi-billion dollar acquisitions of videogame companies with products intended for pre-teens—with no income of their own—as in the case of Microsoft's purchase of Minecraft, pointed to the importance of commodifying gaming uselabor.[84]

Technological Fetishism

The emergence of a related feature, *technological fetishism*, can be considered a byproduct of this panorama. *Commodification thus promoted the notion that technology—the tool that helps create commodities—is good in and of itself.* That belief opened the gates for commodification of most everything technological, setting the stage for oligopolistic control. Personal and collective resignation to the effects of technology aided this phenomenon. After all, in a world where the positive effects of technology are massively divulged—and the negative ones all too often omitted—consent seems guaranteed.

The harmful effects of technology—that detract from the interests of oligopolistic corporate power—can thus be easily covered up. If, after all, technology facilitates the production of all those "desirable"—now fetishistic—commodities that are constantly advertised, how can it be otherwise? Negative impacts that the public might notice every now and then—as in the case of technologically induced disasters, ecological damage, and individual harm—can conveniently be blamed on "mistakes" or on rotten individuals who have strayed from the path of progress.

82 See Matt Binder, "YouTube's Pedophilia Problem: More than 400 Channels Deleted as Advertisers Flee Over Child Predators," *Mashable*, February 21, 2019, https://mashable.com/; Stu Woo and Sam Schechner, "YouTube Deals With Another Advertiser Backlash," *Wall Street Journal*, November 25, 2017, B1; Betsy Morris and Deepa Seetharaman, "Facebook Offers App for 6-Year-Olds," *Wall Street Journal*, December 5, 2017, B1. Children's predators include identity thieves—one credit-reporting company estimating that about 25 percent of all minors in the U.S. will be affected; see Yuka Hayashi, "Now Even Children Face ID Theft," *Wall Street Journal*, August 29, 2018, A2.

83 Sarah E. Needleman, "Game Developers are Making It Hard for Players to Stop," *Wall Street Journal*, August 21, 2018, B4; Mike Brooks, "'Gaming Disorder' Identified by World Health Organization," *Psychology Today*, June 29, 2018, www.psychologytoday.com/.

84 Dan Gallagher, "Microsoft Mines Out of 'Minecraft'," *Wall Street Journal*, April 12, 2017, B1.

Product development units (the D in R&D)—and their close links to marketing—helped this misperception, by blotting out the critical understanding of not only how commodities are produced but also the role of technology in their existence. And, the cultivation of fetishism—in terms of commodities *and* of technology—advanced greatly as oligopolies gained greater power. Thus, the links between commodity and technological fetishism—and oligopolistic power—deepened and reinforced one another. In recent decades, the emergence of social media oligopolies—and the vast uselaborer population they enlisted—took technological fetishism to new heights. Most everything that anyone can do is now accompanied by an unprecedented level of tech-enabled commodification—and it is one that goes largely unquestioned.[85]

It follows, therefore, that *the commodification of everything in human existence—and of nature—intensified greatly as oligopolies and their productive apparatus captured new markets.* Commodification started to penetrate new fields and dimensions. Oligopolistic technology corporations have begun to commodify nature in unexpected ways as, for example, they search the oceans to seize little-known animal and plant species—to decode and adjust their DNA, RNA, or proteins; apply for patents; or create repositories to sell to corporate labs. Or, to extract minerals that can be used in diverse products—from biotech treatments to electronic circuitry. Newly discovered deep-ocean species and minerals have thus become a target for appropriation—much as any other commodity.[86]

Life—in the form of commodified genetic codes—is thus appropriated and sold. Transformation here involves genetic decoding, experimentation, and creating a product that can be marketed—or obtaining a patent that can be licensed. Surplus labor—and surplus value—are obtained much as would occur in a factory, except that the workers tend to be individuals with advanced degrees and complex knowledge. The future revenue streams that their work generates—from patents or sales—are appropriated by the corporate employer, much as any product would be in a factory setting. One difference with the latter may involve patents, however. So-called patent trolls may intimidate—with costly infringement litigation—other companies selling products and services that might (in any way) be linked to the patented knowledge.[87]

85 Such intrusion influences not only our social attitudes but also the most intimate aspects of personal and household life—an aspect explored in Christian Fuchs's *Digital Labour*; and his *Social Media: A Critical Introduction* (Los Angeles: Sage, 2017), chapters 10–12.

86 See Kate Lyons, "Mining's New Frontier: Pacific Nations Caught in the Rush for Deep-Sea Riches," *The Guardian*, June 23, 2021, www.theguardian.com/; Greenpeace International, *Deep Trouble: The Murky World of the Deep Sea Mining Industry*, December 9, 2020, www.greenpeace.org/. Deep-ocean explorations undertaken with public funds have been an important resource for some technology corporations—see, for example, Gautam Naik, "Census Uncovers Oceans' Deep Secrets: Survey Names More than a Thousand New Species, But Scientists Are Most Surprised by Huge Variety of Microbial Level," *Wall Street Journal*, October 5, 2010, A8.

87 This tactic became fairly common during the last decade and has increased since. See, for example, Stefan Lederer, "The Growing Problem of U.S. Patent Trolls, and What Should Happen

Like life itself, health, medicine, and even human evolution are targets for commodification. Techniques involving Clustered Regularly Interspaced Short Palindromic Repeats (CRISPR) and their corporate appropriation provide an example. This technology allows editing of genetic codes in every living organism. Editing human germline cells will allow passing genetic changes to offspring that—when legally and ethically approved—will likely become a major source of oligopolistic power and profit.[88]

Human genetic editing using body cells (to make changes that cannot be passed on) is already a reality.[89] During the last decade, gene editing was commercially undertaken for certain healthcare purposes.[90] Thus, the genetic engineering of humans becomes subject to commodification—along with the future prospect of engineering human evolution itself. This new technology is likely to become a thriving oligopolistic market—as the notion that unhappiness or personal failure can be genetically corrected is likely to be advertised, and possibly believed.[91] A vast, oligopolistic neo-eugenics market could thus become a reality.

Effects of the commodification of gene editing for medicine will likely be far-reaching, particularly in the treatment of disease. Yet, as a commodity, it will all be subject to oligopolistic appropriation. The replacement and transplant of human organs would then be subject to commodification and appropriation as well. And, as multiple genetic editing is introduced, its commodification seems inevitable—as it would expand the spectrum of interventions that can be placed under oligopolistic control. It should not surprise, therefore, that during the last decade research-dedicated corporations—such as Crispr Therapeutics, Editas, Intellia, and Caribou Biosciences, all pioneers in the use of CRISPR techniques—started to fence in market niches.[92]

Next," *Forbes*, July 22, 2021, www.forbes.com/; John D. McKinnon, "Case Challenges 'Patent Trolls'," *Wall Street Journal*, March 24, 2017, A1; Don Clark, "New Venture Enters Patent Fray: San Francisco Startup Plans to Recruit Companies to Deter Legal Threats Against its Members," *Wall Street Journal*, April 8, 2013, B3; Charles Duhigg and Steve Lohr, "The Patent, Used as a Sword," *New York Times*, October 7, 2012, www.nytimes.com/; Ashby Jones, "Patent 'Troll' Tactics Spread," *Wall Street Journal*, July 9, 2012, B1.

88 Henry T. Greely's *CRISPR People: The Science and Ethics of Editing People* (Cambridge, MA: MIT Press, 2021) provides an analysis of the first (illegal) editing of human germline cells and its ethical implications (parts I–III), along with a discussion of the issues (Part IV) that need to be considered.

89 The history and work of one of the Nobel-winning scientists behind this technique—in Walter Isaacson's *The Code Breaker: Jennifer Doudna, Gene Editing, and the Future of the Human Race* (New York: Simon and Schuster, 2021)—provides insights on the vast commercial prospects of this technology (parts 4, 9).

90 Peter Loftus, "FDA Approves First 'Gene Silencing' Drug," *Wall Street Journal*, August 11, 2018, B3; Amy D. Marcus, "In U.S. First, Scientists Edit Out Gene Defect," *Wall Street Journal*, August 3, 2017, A1; and her "Gene-Editing Hits New Milestone," *Wall Street Journal*, August 11, 2017, A3.

91 For a critical analysis of gene-centric ideologies and social tendencies by a medical academic and practitioner, see Stuart A. Newman, "The Divisive Gene," *Monthly Review*, November 2017, 38–44.

92 Intrado Globe News Wire, *CRISPR Therapies Pipeline Insights 2021: Analysis of Key Companies, Emerging Therapies, Recent Happenings and Futuristic Trends*, April 12, 2021, www.globenewswire

In agro-biotech, the commodification of genetic editing long ago opened the gates for powerful oligopolies to control how crops are produced—with substantial implications for farming, ecosystems, the food chain, and human health.[93] Much the same applies to animal life, as commodification will encompass engineering the evolution of entire species—and their ecologies. Obtaining or appropriating patents for CRISPR techniques has thus become very important for commodification and oligopolistic power. More than ever, patents have become commodities—subject to be licensed, traded, and sold or to have their knowledge embedded in most any other commodity.

Data Commodification

The commodification of data is a distinctive feature of productive transformation in technology oligopolies. Facilitated by new technologies during the past four decades, it is now part of the elements and phenomena discussed in this chapter. The emergence of data clouds and AI as major corporate assets—and the rising profile of data analytics, bioinformatics, and data science—attest to its importance for technology oligopolies.

Data commodification gained greater visibility during the last decade through uselabor. Social media oligopolies turned intimate data into a commodity—much as a raw material would be in factory production.[94] Uselabor itself became a commodity—as all effort, time, and online experiences were appropriated, to be mined and sold—raising many concerns about privacy.[95] And this trend also applied to search and email oligopolists—as search histories, messages, preferences, and site visits were compiled.[96] Much the same occurred

.com/; Ben Adams, "CRISPR Therapeutics Raises a $56M IPO, but Patent Battles, Potential Stock Drops Loom," *FierceBiotech*, October 19, 2016, www.fiercebiotech.com/.

93 See Economic Research Service, U.S. Department of Agriculture, *Recent Trends in GE Adoption*, www.ers.usda.gov/ (accessed July 25, 2022); Alliance for Science and Boyce Thompson Institute, Cornell University, *The GMO Debate*, August 18, 2018, allianceforscience.cornell.edu/; Dennis Berman, "Data Science Will Transform Farming: Hugh Grant of Monsanto and James C. Collins Jr. of DuPont on the Impact of New Gene-Editing Technologies and Big Data," *Wall Street Journal*, October 16, 2017, R7.

94 An aspect that attracted concern during the last decade—see Ursula Huws, *Labor in the Global Digital Economy: The Cybertariat Comes of Age* (New York: Monthly Review Press, 2014); Fuchs, *Social Media*; and his *Digital Labour*.

95 See Shosahana Zuboff, *The Age of Surveillance Capitalism* (New York: Public Affairs, 2019), chapters 2, 5, 6; Rosalie Chan, "The Cambridge Analytica Whistleblower Explains How the Firm Used Facebook Data to Sway Elections," *Business Insider*, October 5, 2019, www.businessinsider.com/; Alyssa Newcomb, "Facebook Data Scandal Widens to 87 Million People," *NBC News*, April 4, 2018, www.nbcnews.com/; Georgia Wells, "Facebook Details Data Sharing: Company Discloses More Firms than Previously Known Got Special Access," *Wall Street Journal*, July 2, 2018, A1.

96 See Reuters, "Google Faces $5 Billion Lawsuit in U.S. for Tracking 'Private' Internet Use: Google 'Cannot Continue to Engage in the Covert and Unauthorized Data Collection from Virtually Every American with a Computer or Phone', the Complaint Said," *NBC News*, June 2, 2020, www

with data on choices and viewing histories by the oligopolies that control gaming and entertainment.[97]

Data on purchases and preferences became a commodity to be sold. And the value of the data depends on the scale of databases. The larger the scale, the more valuable—and the more likely that ads will be placed. Placement of ads is sold to advertising companies that—by paying for viewings—provide social media oligopolists with revenue. And, data obtained from uselaborers is largely costless—outlays for server farms, utilities, conventional labor, and the like being incurred, but these tend to be minute relative to the value of the data obtained.

The cost of sustaining a data network is sensitive to scale. Thus, the larger the network, the lower the operational cost—per uselaborer—and the more exploitive commodification becomes.[98] Operational items—conventional labor, server farms, facilities—are also commodities, in the sense that they are purchased to carry out production—a very peculiar form of production, no doubt. This chain of commodification—focused on uselaborers, their data, time, effort, online experiences, and the targeted advertisements—is possibly the most profitable one ever to arise. Taking into account the very recent emergence of the social media sector—and the vast wealth accumulated—the prospects for this novel form of commodification seem promising.

So profitable is the commodification of data for targeted advertising that internet service provider (ISP) oligopolists began to imitate some of the practices of social media. Thus, during the last decade, regulators and politicians were lobbied and induced to scrap most personal privacy restrictions—to allow the commodification and sale of ISP customer data.[99] Auctions to sell everyone's data to the highest bidder were also made legal, whenever the oligopolistic owners decide to do so.

.nbcnews.com/; Davey Winder, "Microsoft Security Shocker as 250 Million Customer Records Exposed Online," *Forbes*, January 22, 2020, www.forbes.com/; Douglas MacMillan and Robert McMillan, "Google Exposed User Data, Feared Repercussions of Disclosing to Public," *Wall Street Journal*, October 8, 2018, www.wsj.com/.

97 A sector associated with some scandals during the last decade. See Stacey Grant and Yerin Kim, "15 of YouTube's Most Horrifying Scandals and Controversies: From Fake Murders to Allegations of Abuse, These Events Shocked the Internet," *Seventeen*, January 28, 2020, www.seventeen.com/; Binder, "YouTube's Pedophilia Problem"; Jack Nicas, "YouTube Notches Global Video Milestone," *Wall Street Journal*, February 28, 2017, B1; Michael D. Smith and Rahul Telang, *Streaming, Sharing, Stealing: Big Data and the Future of Entertainment* (Cambridge, MA: MIT Press, 2016).

98 Greater extent makes a network more valuable by increasing its exploitive potential—see Suarez-Villa, *Technocapitalism*, Chapter "Networks as Mediators," 56–85.

99 Tom Wheeler, "How the Republicans Sold Your Privacy to Internet Providers," *New York Times*, March 29, 2017, www.nytimes.com/; Jack Marshall, "Internet Privacy for Sale," *Wall Street Journal*, March 31, 2017, B1. See also Chan, "Cambridge Analytica Whistleblower"; Wells, "Facebook Details Data Sharing."

The amount and quality of data collected by ISPs can be greater and more intimate than those appropriated by social media and search oligopolists. ISP customers pay for access, and their credit histories, bank accounts, debit or credit card data, and other financial information have to be disclosed to obtain service. In addition, ISP oligopolists compile identity details, social security numbers, family members' information, home configurations, routines, residential features, and travel information, among other aspects. Telecommunication services are often provided by ISP oligopolists, and contact details, places called, duration of calls, frequency, and related information are also compiled. Data leaks, hacks, and identity theft—frequent during the last decade—may thus pose problems for customers, but it would be naïve to think that such malfeasance will curb data collection.[100]

Interconnectivity, AI, and cloud computing also make it possible for a provider to appropriate data on home remote control features—lighting, utilities usage, daily routines, timing, and security. Data on movements may also be compiled—including vehicle usage, routings, timing, maintenance, and locations. The largest and most valuable databases tend to be compiled when customers are induced to "bundle" services, such that they are all purchased from a single provider. The intimate data appropriated may then become an important source of uselabor—as data on usage, connectivity, ad viewings, purchases, and other details are appropriated and sold. Paying customers can thus become uncompensated uselaborers.

Another instance of data commodification involves oligopolistic control over corporate databases—involving most everything a business can do. Most every aspect—customers, financing, employment, shareholders, compensation, production, marketing, sales, profit, investments, security, facilities, taxes, and lobbying, for example, can be part of this sort of commodification. Since the middle of the last decade, three global oligopolists—Amazon, Microsoft, Alphabet-Google—gained control over vast amounts of such vital corporate information in their clouds.[101] Combined, they have expended tens of billions of dollars annually to appropriate, commodify, and store such data using the most sophisticated technologies.

Already, each one of them—separately—controls more sensitive corporate data than any government, or any global statistical or regulatory agency. Each of these three global oligopolists possibly holds more corporate information than all the government data agencies in the world combined. Never before have such few corporations been able to amass so much information from so

100 See PYMNTS, *Comcast Faces Fallout from Bug that Leaked Customer Data*, May 22, 2018, https://pymnts.com/; Ryan Knutson, "Verizon Makes It Personal," *Wall Street Journal*, September 6, 2017, B1.

101 Google, *Data Centers*, www.google.com/ (accessed July 26, 2022); Mark Haranas, "Microsoft will Build Up to 100 New Data Centers Each Year," *CRN*, April 28, 2021, www.crn.com/; Jay Greene, "A New Arms Race for Tech: Sector's Heavy Hitters Spend Heavily on Data Centers to Power On-Demand Services," *Wall Street Journal*, April 10, 2017, B4.

many companies. And, due to their global scope, the concentration of control may lead to major security problems—not only for client companies but also for entire nations and economies.

The payoff to the oligopolists in charge involves providing most any processing operation that a corporate client will ever need. The vast data troves also make it possible to provide consulting services—on most any endeavor, from strategy formulation to labor deployment, production, R&D, marketing, financing, offshoring, and acquisitions, among others. Such a diverse repertory of possibilities will likely provide oligo-monopolistic power in certain market niches—and turn some clients into acquisition targets.

Data commodification oligopolists can also control blockchain-type transaction technologies. Cryptography and clouds are enablers of this new mode of commodification—as trust itself is turned into a commodity. Records of transactions—in such diverse areas as research, shipping, crypto-currencies, real estate, food safety, precious stones, health care, finance, or government records—can be kept encrypted and accessible to speed up verification, negotiations, contracting, testing, approvals, and sales. Encrypted blocks with sensitive data—uniform in content—are kept in each participating computer system or cloud, records being blocked from changes unless all participants agree and record them.

Blockchain-enabled data commodification is being felt across the economy in multiple ways.[102] For technology oligopolies, this form of commodification provides many advantages. Systematized research regimes engaged in collaborative research—or that require regulatory approvals—can store and access data on tasks, clinical trials, prototypes, and testing methodology, without having to request approval from each of the participants—or from a central repository. In production, a technology oligopolist and its subsidiaries or contractors can keep track of shipments, capacity utilization, and product mix—aspects that help calibrate output and sustain pricing power. Adjustments to avoid excessive output can thus enhance control and be made more dynamic.

Standardizing and Systematizing

Important for commodification in production and research regimes are standardization and systematization—control modes that support (and are supported by) large-scale computing. *This involves control by the oligopolist over the*

102 See Maggie Potter, "What are the Environmental Effects of Blockchain Technology?" *Environmental Magazine*, April 2, 2020, https://emagazine.com/; Knowledge-at-Wharton and Swift Institute, University of Pennsylvania, *How the Blockchain will Impact the Financial Sector*, November 16, 2018, https://knowledge.wharton.upenn.edu/; Rob Marvin, "Blockchain: The Invisible Technology that's Changing the World," *PCMag*, August 29, 2017, www.pcmag.com/; Don Tapscott and Alex Tapscott, "The Impact of the Blockchain Goes beyond Financial Services," *Harvard Business Review*, May 10, 2016, https://hbr.org/.

relations of production—on work routines, automation, and compensation. Detailed data on employee performance facilitate such control, especially for multi-establishment oligopolists. The latter tend to depend greatly on systematic record-keeping and the standardization of labor management procedures across branches or subsidiaries.

Technology corporations often achieve standardization and systematization through protocols that, even though narrow in scope, can nonetheless allow flexibility in terms of execution. The case of uselabor in social media illustrates this seemingly contradictory aspect. Billions of uselaborers (on a monthly basis) are subjected to standardized protocols for access and to systematic rules of online conduct. The kind of intimate data they are required to give up is standardized—and the coding and mining of online experiences are systematically organized so that profitable usage (targeted advertising and sales) can occur.

This allowed Facebook, for example, to have little paid employment, while achieving the highest uselaborer-to-conventional labor ratio of any social media oligopolist during the last decade. By the end of the last decade, Facebook's ratio was about 100,000 uselaborers per conventional full-time employee—on a *monthly* basis.[103] Although its conventional (full-time) employment rose from barely a handful in the early 2000s to nearly 45,000 by the end of the last decade, its uselaborer force increased much faster—and prospects are for the ratio to grow larger as AI takes over more data mining and advertising.[104]

Standardization supports (and is supported by) the use of AI to analyze uselaborer-related functions, while systematization reduces operating costs. Nonetheless, Facebook's high level of both standardization and systematization allow much flexibility in online behaviors. Thus, uselaborers can change their preferences for contact and content anytime, anywhere, and for any purpose—or for no purpose at all. Such flexibility helps keep uselaborers in the network and helps attract new ones.

Systematization is important for research-oriented technology oligopolists, particularly in biotechnology and biopharmaceuticals.[105] Systematized research regimes can be made flexible—in terms of approaches to experimentation—despite the standardized experimental procedures and safety protocols that usually need to be followed. High failure rates—customary in biotech

103 Statista, *Number of Full-Time Facebook Employees from 2004 to 2020*, www.statista.com/ (accessed July 22, 2022).

104 Statista, *Number of Full-Time*. An inverse relation therefore seems to have set in, as Facebook's conventional labor is projected to level off, due to AI and the vast scale of its operations—see Nancy Scola, "Facebook Employees Fear 'Golden' Years are Over," *Politico*, March 22, 2018, www.politico.com/; Mya Frazier, "Facebook Won't Hire You for Its Data Center," *Bloomberg Businessweek*, September 25, 2017, www.bloomberg.com/.

105 See Suarez-Villa, *Technocapitalism*, 124–35.

clinical testing—make such flexibility necessary, as a form of risk reduction.[106] Nonetheless, the payoff for companies that have a successful medication or treatment can be very substantial. An analysis of companies that obtained first-ever U.S. Food and Drug Administration approval for a single cancer therapy medication during the last decade, for example, estimated that median research expenses of $648 million generated median revenues of $1.66 billion.[107]

Flexibility to restructure is important in this commodification scenario, as research projects often require major adjustments on short notice. The need for collaboration and feedback—in the lab or with peers outside—also makes it necessary to allow flexibility as a way of reducing mistakes and uncertainty and to increase productivity. Such flexibility helps obscure the apparatus of control—giving the impression that researchers have the "freedom" to use their own initiative, when the real purpose is to increase their productivity and expand surpluses. In this way, flexibility becomes a convenient artifice to conceal that the value of what research workers create is far above what they will be compensated for.

One effect of standardization in research regimes—that contributes to an impression of flexibility—is a tendency to modularize activities. Modules can make it easier to reconfigure routines and systematize new standards to meet a project's changing needs—or start a new experimental stage.[108] This can facilitate shedding unnecessary labor, by compartmentalizing furloughs and firings—thereby helping streamline commodification. Thus, the specific module—rather than the top executives—may end up being blamed for such actions. Flexibility through modularity can also lead to higher researcher productivity—as desirable an outcome for the oligopolist in control as it is in factory production.

Commodification in factory production regimes in technology sectors has involved greater standardization and less flexibility than in the previous cases. With the emergence of factory oligopolies in the early twentieth century, serial tasking, systematic programming, and standardized measurability took center stage in the commodification of labor. As factory workers became more of a commodity—and more expendable—raising efficiency gained paramount importance.

The standard to accomplish this objective was provided by Frederick Taylor's vision of factory performance—often referred to as Taylorism, or

106 See Biotechnology Innovation Organization, *New Clinical Development Success Rates 2011–20 Report*; its *Clinical Development Success Rates 2006–15*; and its *BIO Releases Largest Study Ever on Clinical Development Success Rates*—all at www.bio.org/ (accessed July 27, 2022).

107 Vinay Prasad and Sham Mailankody, "Research and Development Spending to Bring a Single Cancer Drug to Market, and Revenues After Approval," *JAMA Internal Medicine*, September 11, 2017, https://jamanetwork.com/.

108 See Suarez-Villa, *Technocapitalism*, 105, 134–35.

(generically) as "scientific management."[109] The systematization of his ideas placed task execution speed as a major benchmark for evaluating performance. Raising efficiency through speed thus became the overarching objective of any and all labor processes—and of the commodification of factory work. Taylor's principles are still applied, mostly in production where much labor is used—as in the case of offshore assembly factories. Assembly processes for smartphones, computers, and numerous electronic products follow Taylor's ideas. Some tech-service oligopolists, such as Amazon, also follow this model despite the fact that logistics and distribution are their core operations, rather than production.

Systematically simplifying labor tasks became essential for implementing Taylor's ideas, leading to deskilling—an aspect that deepened as oligopoly capitalism advanced.[110] Alienation of the worker and the depersonalization of work thereby became permanent features of factory labor processes—along with command-and-control management. Taylor's ideas thus became *the* guide for managing labor processes in factory production, and the greatest beneficiaries were industrial oligopolies—most of all those that would implement mass production technologies.

Henry Ford's assembly plants were among the beneficiaries—and an early example of the compound oligopolistic scenario, discussed in the previous chapter. Ford's main plant, for example, employed close to 100,000 workers, had 100 miles of railroad track within the factory grounds, and used 16 million square feet of factory space—where all the necessary raw materials were processed (assembly operations included).[111] His vertically integrated oligopoly exercised control over every aspect of labor and production—from raw material mining to dealerships.[112] Ford's industrial labor practices—also known as Fordism—thus provided a practical guide for the commodification and exploitation of labor in mass production—a model that would be imitated innumerable times throughout most of the twentieth century. Offshore subcontracting

109 Frederick W. Taylor and Frank B. Copley, *Two Papers on Scientific Management: A Piece-Rate System and Notes on Belting* (London: Routledge, 1919). Optimality ruled Taylor's approach—see Robert Kanigel, *The One Best Way: Frederick Winslow Taylor and the Enigma of Efficiency* (New York: Viking, 1997).

110 See Braverman, *Labor and Monopoly Capital*; Paul Cockshott, *How the World Works: The Story of Human Labor from Prehistory to the Modern Day* (New York: Monthly Review Press, 2019); Frederic L. Pryor and David L. Schaffer, *Who's Not Working and Why: Employment, Cognitive Skills, Wages, and the Changing U.S. Labor Market* (Cambridge: Cambridge University Press, 1999).

111 Ford Motor Company, *The Ford Industries: Facts About the Ford Motor Company and Its Subsidiaries* (Detroit: Ford Motor Company, 1925).

112 See Stephen Meyer, *The Five Dollar Day: Labor Management and Social Control in the Ford Motor Company, 1908–81* (Albany: State University of New York Press, 1981); David Gartman, *Auto Slavery: The Labor Process in the American Automobile Industry, 1897–1950* (New Brunswick: Rutgers University Press, 1986).

for mass production has used the Fordist model extensively, especially for consumer technology products.

Standardization in factory production regimes deepened with automation, making it possible to establish greater control over the commodification of labor.[113] Commodification thus became easier and more profitable, as automation allowed greater precision in forecasting input volumes and timing. For multi-plant oligopolists, the standardization that automation provided also helped reduce labor greatly. This scenario has been replicated many times in the case of technology oligopolists that tried to avoid offshoring.

Systematized flexibility in factory production regimes—a feature of the late twentieth century still found in many factories—has depended greatly on automation. "Flexible production" systems became common in many factories that assembled consumer technology products. Its standardization then facilitated the systematic implementation of "just-in-time" routines, taking commodification to a new plane. A very important outcome was closer coordination between output, labor processes and shipping—to eliminate warehousing and speed up deliveries. For workers, the combination of systematization and standardization that this panorama created led to very intrusive monitoring of tasks and more oppressive workplaces—a feature that has persisted and increased up to our time.[114]

Reproduction

Reproduction is a fundamental phenomenon of the transformative apparatus. In the context of technology oligopolies, reproduction refers to the *systemic regeneration* of vital processes and resources. *Capitalism's capacity to evolve—despite its crises and dysfunctions—has depended on this phenomenon.* Three modes of reproduction are at the core of technology oligopoly capitalism's evolution and of its capacity to reconstitute itself—capital, the capacity for work, and labor intangibles. All of them are essential for commodification and the previously discussed elements to function.

113 See David F. Noble, *Forces of Production: A Social History of Industrial Automation* (New York: Knopf, 1984); Braverman, *Labor and Monopoly Capital.*

114 See Ellen Sheng, "Employee Privacy in the U.S. at Stake as Corporate Surveillance Technology Monitors Workers' Every Move," *CNBC*, April 15, 2019, www.cnbc.com/; Ellen R. Shell, "The Employer-Surveillance State," *The Atlantic*, October 15, 2018, www.theatlantic.com/; *The Guardian*, "Amazon's Diaries: 'They Treat Us as Disposable'," November 21, 2018, www.theguardian.com/; Patience Haggin, "As Wearables in the Workplace Spread, So Do Legal Concerns: Companies Can Now More Easily Monitor their Employees' Health and Habits; But How Are they Allowed to Use that Information?" *Wall Street Journal*, March 14, 2016, R7; *The Economist*, "Digital Taylorism: A Modern Version of 'Scientific Management' Threatens to Dehumanise the Workplace," September 12, 2015, 63.

Capital Resources

The reproduction of capital is vital for sustaining productive transformation. Recalling the oligopolistic accumulative dynamic, capital's reproduction involves continuous recurrence of: (a) purchase of commodity inputs (M→C, labor included), (b) production (embedded in C→C′), (c) exchange (or sale) of transformed commodities ($C' \rightarrow M^N$), and (d) consumption or usage, through consumers' (or customers') purchase of the transformed commodity (C′). The latter generates new money-capital (M^N) through market pricing.

The oligopolistic surpluses (ΔN, ΔL, ΔS) *and* surplus value (Δm) can be considered the fuel and lubricants of this dynamic. Without the initial money-capital (M) they provide, it would be impossible to sustain the productive cycle. As such, they are fundamentally important for the recurrence of the four components of the productive cycle *and* for the reproduction of capital.

The realization of profit—subsumed in the oligopolistic surpluses *and* surplus value—thus depends on the reproduction of capital in productive transformation. In the context of technology oligopolies, profit is a form of income appropriated by the owners of capital—the oligopolists—through their use of labor and technology in productive transformation. For the oligopolists in control, this is different from other forms (or sources) of income—such as interest on money and rent on land or property.[115]

The four components of the accumulative dynamic noted above—operating continuously—allow oligopolies to sustain and restart the productive cycle. The previously discussed capital modes—fixed, circulating, variable, finance—are part of this panorama. Their relationship in technology oligopolies is symbiotic, in the sense that none can function (and be reproduced) on its own.

Fixed capital is indispensable for production, but its relevance for the other components must not be lost sight of. Variable capital is fundamental for purchasing labor—the vital commodity in productive transformation. Circulating capital is essential for input purchases, while finance capital is vital for all components. The fusion of all these modes in money-capital (M and M^N in the accumulative dynamic) sustains productive transformation.

The reproduction of capital tends to be more dynamic—paradoxically perhaps—in the case of production regimes where variable, fixed and circulating capital outlays are lowest—relative to new money-capital (M^N). This is the case with social media oligopolies, where capital's reproduction takes on the

115 On his part, Adam Smith regarded profit as "altogether different" from other sources of income and believed it to be "regulated by quite different principles." See Smith, *Wealth of Nations*, Part I, 50–51; Meek, *Studies in the Labour Theory*, 24. Marx regarded profit as a social class-based form of income derived by the capitalist (the owner of capital) through his use and exploitation of labor in production. See Marx, *Capital*, Vol. III, 35–48. Although profit has sometimes been assumed to have equivalence to surplus value in the literature, it must be noted that the former usually includes outlays for inputs and various assets that are not part of Marx's conception of surplus value.

appearance of an automatic, self-perpetuating process. Facebook provides possibly the best example of this condition. Its variable capital outlays are extremely low, given that its main workforce—uselaborers—are uncompensated and that the conventional labor it employs is a minute fraction of that workforce.

Facebook's dynamic reproduction of capital has allowed it to acquire most any company that can add to its power.[116] Expanding into new market niches is thus a matter of its own choice. And Facebook's dynamic reproduction of capital has allowed it to undertake projects under the semblance of public service or even philanthropy—to increase its visibility and enhance its image.

Reproduction of capital can be more difficult for oligopolists specialized in research, in such fields as biotechnology and nanotechnology. Fixed capital outlays tend to be high, because of the custom-made laboratory equipment, specialized facilities, or expensive computing hardware. In many cases, the laboratory equipment either becomes obsolete quickly or has to be discarded upon completion of a project. Circulating capital outlays may also be high, especially when rare or difficult-to-find inputs are utilized—as in the case of deep-ocean organisms or of microorganisms and raw materials found in few places. Variable capital may also be high, compared to other technology sectors, due to the specialized personnel.

Capacity for Work

Replenishing labor's capacity for work is a vital support for productive transformation. This mode is rooted in the imperative of regenerating the possibility of performing work tasks—as a systemic economic necessity. Labor's importance in the creation of technology goods and services makes it unavoidable.

As the oligopolist purchases labor, it tacitly commits itself to provide sufficient compensation to support workers' nutritional, housing, health care, rest, and related needs—such that the capacity for work can be restored.[117] Compensation must also take into account household work performed by partners or relatives.[118] All these aspects are indispensable for the recurrent performance of work.

116 See Infographics, *Facebook Acquisitions—The Complete List*, www.techwyse.com/; Wikipedia, *List of Mergers and Acquisitions by Facebook*, https://en.wikipedia.org/ (both accessed July 28, 2022).

117 Fulfilling these needs became a concern for some early industrial capitalists, who built housing and sanitary facilities around their factories. Such projects—categorized as utopian by some historians—allowed control over most aspects of workers' lives. See Charles Fourier's *L'Harmonie Universelle et le Phalanstère* (Paris: Librairie Phalanstérienne, 1849); Robert Owen, *A New View of Society* (London: Longman, 1817) and his *Narrative of the Thirty Years' Experiments at New Lanark* (publisher unknown, 1849, avail. at Princeton University Library, https://catalog.princeton.edu/).

118 Households must, in this regard, be seen as productive units of a kind that generate not money-capital or commodities but a form of *use value* that helps regenerate labor's capacity for work.

One of the great injustices of capitalism since its earliest days has been the undercompensation of labor. This has persisted in different forms up to our time—shifting responsibility to taxpayers and the state to provide subsistence support. It affects many technology and tech-service workers—particularly those engaged in TVC-type arrangements, and the so-called "franchisee" and "1099" categories.[119] The precarious (or contingency) workforce in technology oligopolies has increased substantially in recent times—in some large companies reaching one-half of total employment.[120]

During the last decade, it was estimated that at least $150 billion of taxpayer-provided funds were expended annually—to sustain underpaid workers with Medicaid and food assistance.[121] Estimates indicate that the contingency worker population will become the most important segment of the American labor force in the near future.[122] Contributing to this panorama are such

Such *quasi*-use value does not (directly) result in exchange value but—unlike uselabor—household work should not be considered free labor. Neglect of household work in political economy over the years has led to debates on its importance—see Tithi Bhattacharya, "Liberating Women from 'Political Economy'," *Monthly Review*, January 2020, 1–13; Susan Ferguson, *Women and Work: Feminism, Labour, and Social Reproduction* (London: Pluto, 2020); Kevin Floyd, "Automatic Subjects: Gendered Labor and Abstract Life," *Historical Materialism* 24 (2016), 79–80.

119 See U.S. Bureau of Labor Statistics, *A Profile of the Working Poor*, various years, http://bls.gov/ (accessed July 10, 2022); Lauren Weber, "The End of Employees: U.S. Companies Shift Work Once Considered Core to Contractors, Pruning Costs and Job Security," *Wall Street Journal*, February 3, 2017, A1; Anna Louie Sussman and Josh Zumbrun, "'Gig' Economy Spreads Broadly," *Wall Street Journal*, March 26, 2016, A1; Fred Magdoff and John Bellamy Foster, "The Plight of the U.S. Working Class," *Monthly Review*, January 2014, 1–22; Ann Lowrey, "Caught in a Revolving Door of Unemployment," *New York Times*, November 16, 2013, http://nytimes.com/.

120 William R. Kerr and Carl Kreitzberg, *Google: To TVC or Not to TVC?* Harvard Business School, Faculty and Research, December 2019, www.hbs.edu/; Mark Bergen and Josh Eidelson, "Inside Google's Shadow Workforce: About Half of Google's Workers are Contractors Who Don't Receive the Same Benefits as Direct Employees," *Bloomberg*, July 25, 2018, www.bloomberg.com/; Julia C. Wong, "Revealed: Google's 'Two-Tier' Workforce Training Document," *The Guardian*, December 12, 2018, www.theguardian.com/; Lauren Weber, "The Flip Side of the New U.S. Economy: Millions of Contractors Struggle for Career Advancement, Stability and Respect at Work," *Wall Street Journal*, September 15, 2017, A9.

121 U.S. Bureau of Labor Statistics, *Profile of the Working Poor*; Ricardo Antunes, "The New Service Proletariat," *Monthly Review*, April 2018, 23–29; Patricia Cohen, "Working, but Needing Public Assistance Anyway," *New York Times*, April 12, 2015, www.nytimes.com/; Clare O'Connor, "Report: Walmart Workers Cost Taxpayers $6.2 Billion in Public Assistance," *Forbes*, April 15, 2014, www.forbes.com/.

122 U.S. Bureau of Labor Statistics, *Profile of the Working Poor*; Robert Reich, "Almost 80% of US Workers Live from Paycheck to Paycheck: Here's Why—America Doesn't Have a Jobs Crisis, It has a 'Good Jobs' Crisis, Where Too Much Employment is Insecure, and Poorly Paid," *The Guardian*, July 29, 2018, www.theguardian.com/. See also Antunes, "New Service Proletariat"; and his *The Meanings of Work: Essay on the Affirmation and Negation of Work* (Boston: Brill, 2013), chapters 3, 7; Guy Standing, *The Precariat: The New Dangerous Class* (London: Bloomsbury Academic, 2011), chapters 1–3, 5; Ursula Huws, *Labour in the Circuits of Global Markets: Theories and Realities* (London: Analytica, 2014).

arrangements as "zero-hour" employment—whereby workers remain indefinitely at their employer's disposal, waiting to be called, and being compensated only for worktime (if that should occur).[123] Also, voucher-paid work in place of monetary compensation—that is often below the overtime or minimum wage equivalent.[124]

Oligopolistic consolidation worsened this panorama during the last three decades—M&A activity often leading to employment reductions, stagnant labor compensation, and the loss of inter-corporate competition for workers.[125] At the same time, executive compensation increased rapidly. The latter reached historical records—rising by an average of 725 percent over three decades.[126] Disparities between executives' and workers' compensation in technology oligopolies have been the highest ever. By the end of the last decade, for example, compensation for Apple's chief executive was found to be about 300 times that of the company's average employee.[127] Oligopolistic technology CEO compensation is now the highest ever and may continue to set new records.[128]

At the same time, the ranks of the permanently unemployed and the underemployed increased relative to the total workforce.[129] This reality can trigger

123 U.S. Bureau of Labor Statistics, *Profile of the Working Poor*; Antunes, "New Service Proletariat"; Cohen, "Working, but Needing."

124 U.S. Bureau of Labor Statistics, *Profile of the Working Poor*; Antunes, "New Service Proletariat."

125 Bryce Covert, "When Companies Supersize, Paychecks Shrink: Workers Lose Out When Mergers Reduce Competition," *New York Times*, May 13, 2018, www.nytimes.com/; Reich, "Almost 80% of US Workers"; William A. Galston, "How the Vise on U.S. Wages Tightened," *Wall Street Journal*, April 1, 2015, A11.

126 James K. Galbraith, "Why do American CEOs Get Paid So Much?" *The Guardian*, August 20, 2018, www.theguardian.com/; Jeff Stein and Jena McGregor, "Elite CEO Pay Jumps to Average of $19 Million, as Fears Mount Over the Wealthy Pocketing Gains," *Washington Post*, August 16, 2018, www.washingtonpost.com/.

127 Tripp Mickle, "Apple Gives Cook 22% Raise," *Wall Street Journal*, January 9, 2019, B4.

128 Alexia F. Campbell, "CEOs Made 287 Times More Money Last Year Than their Workers Did: Companies Have Finally Started Reporting CEO-Worker Pay Ratios, Now We Know Why They Fought So Hard to Avoid It," *Vox*, June 26, 2019, www.vox.com/; Charlie McGee, "PayPal Chief Tops Software CEOs in Compensation," *Wall Street Journal*, June 18, 2019, B4. The average ratio of CEO-to-employee compensation in the late 1970s was estimated to be 26 times—see Steven Clifford, *The CEO Pay Machine: How It Trashes America and How to Stop It* (New York: Blue Rider, 2017), chapters 5, 6, 8, 9. Many chief executives in the larger oligopolistic technology corporations tend to receive over $100 million in total annual compensation—excluding the customarily high payouts obtained through "golden handshake" and "golden parachute" vestings. During the last decade, the highest-paid 500 U.S. corporate executives (almost all of them in charge of oligopolies, including technology) averaged well over $30 million in annual "realized" compensation (based on actual value rather than "fair value" accounting, stock options, and awards included)—see Stephen Wilmot, "Better Ways to Measure Boss's Pay," *Wall Street Journal*, July 5, 2017, B1.

129 U.S. Bureau of Labor Statistics, *Profile of the Working Poor*; Nicholas Eberstadt, *Men without Work: America's Invisible Crisis* (West Conshohocken: Templeton Press, 2016), chapters 2–5, 8; and his

diverse forms of escapism and addiction—among those who work but cannot cover their needs and those who lose hope of having stable jobs (or any employment). One of the apparent effects has been an epidemic like rise in U.S. opioid medication addiction during the last decade.[130] Opioid addiction rates rose by about 500 percent in barely seven years, while deaths from opioids increased by 343 percent over a 25-year period.[131] Opioid addiction was considered to have reduced workforce participation significantly during the last two decades—accounting for a 20 percent decline among men aged 25–54 and a 25 percent reduction among women.[132] And, along with opioids, other addictive substances—among them heroin, cocaine, and meth-amphetamine—contributed to increase overdose deaths several-fold over a short time.[133]

Related to this panorama was the growing incidence of job stress-related deaths in the workforce and the high stress levels found in workplaces. Work-related issues were estimated to (fully or partially) account for at least 20,000 deaths annually in the U.S. during the last decade, while surveys reported that

"The Idle Army: America's Unworking Men," *Wall Street Journal*, September 2, 2016, A11.

130 See Blue Cross Blue Shield Association, *Addressing America's Opioid Epidemic* (accessed July 29, 2022), and its *America's Opioid Epidemic and Its Effect on the Nation's Commercially-Insured Population*, June 29, 2017, www.bcbs.com/; Quest Diagnostics, *Workforce Drug Testing Positivity Climbed to Highest Rate in 16 Years, New Quest Drug Testing Index Analysis Finds*, August 25, 2020, https://ir.questdiagnostics.com/; its *Drug Positivity in U.S. Workforce Rises to Nearly Highest Level in a Decade, Quest Diagnostics Analysis Finds*, September 15, 2016; and its *Illicit Drug Positivity Rate Increases Sharply in Workplace Testing, Finds Quest Diagnostics Drug Testing Index Analysis*, June 9, 2015, www.questdiagnostics.com/; Anne Steele, "Opioid Addiction Climbs by 500%: Study of Millions of Medical Claims Shows a Surge of Diagnoses in Past Seven Years," *Wall Street Journal*, June 30, 2017, A3; Lauren Weber, "Greater Share of U.S. Workers Testing Positive for Illicit Drugs," *Wall Street Journal*, September 14, 2016, www.wsj.com/. Escapism was also found to be on the rise among the young—see *The Economist, 1843* magazine, "Escape to Another World: As Video Games Get Better and Job Prospects Worse, More Young Men Are Dropping Out of the Job Market to Spend Their Time in An Alternate Reality," April-May 2017, 78–83.

131 Institute for Health Metrics and Evaluation, *County-by-County Study Reveals 600% Increase in Drug-Related Deaths*, www.healthdata.org/ (accessed April 11, 2022); Betsy McKay and Renée Rigdon, "'Deaths of Despair' Take Toll Across U.S.," *Wall Street Journal*, April 11, 2018, A3; Steele, "Opioid Addiction Climbs by 500%." Marketing products that can help control opioid addiction became a promising new market niche for biopharmaceutical oligopolists during the last decade—see Stephanie Armour, "Advisory Recommends Opioid-Reversal Drug," *Wall Street Journal*, April 6, 2018, A3.

132 Alan B. Krueger, "Where Have All the Workers Gone? An Inquiry into the Decline of the U.S. Labor Force Participation Rate," *Brooking Papers on Economic Activity*, September 7, 2017, www.brookings.edu/; Ben Leubsdorf, "Opioids Take a Toll on Worker Participation," *Wall Street Journal*, September 7, 2017, A3; Quest Diagnostics, *Drug Positivity in U.S. Workforce*; and its *Illicit Drug Positivity Rate*.

133 Centers for Disease Control and Prevention, *Drug Overdose Death Data*, www.cdc.gov/ (accessed July 21, 2022); Aimee Cunningham, "Drug Overdose Deaths in America are Rising Exponentially: the Problem is Bigger than Any One Drug, Researchers Say," *Science*, September 20, 2018, www.sciencenews.org/.

as many as 80 percent of workplaces exhibited high stress levels.[134] And, many working people were unable to cover their health care—while employers cut benefits to reduce variable capital outlays. Labor underpayment can thus be added to the (uncompensated) surplus labor effort that underlies surplus value (Δm) in production. Underpayments that do not allow workers to fully regenerate their capacity to work *and* surplus labor—two different but related conditions—are part of this panorama.

Using unpaid "interns"—common among many technology oligopolists during the last decade—was another problem. Interns are, to some extent, comparable to uselabor in social media networks. However, uncompensated interns were part of the conventional labor force—their routines being similar to those of paid labor, and they are subject to dismissal at any time.[135] Many technology startups benefited from using interns—allowing them to reduce variable capital outlays, improve initial stock listings—initial public offerings (IPOs)—and increase their chances of being acquired. Having interns also made it possible to suppress requests for salary raises from the conventional workforce.[136]

Adding to shortfalls in the capacity for work, frequent hiring and compensation practices that discriminated on the basis of age, gender, ethnicity, or race were another problem.[137] Also, collusion among some oligopolists to forgo

134 Jeffrey Pfeffer, *Dying for a Paycheck: Why the American Way of Business is Injurious to People and Companies* (New York: HarperCollins, 2018); Pew Research Center, *The State of American Jobs*, October 2016, www.pewsocialtrends.org/.

135 By the middle of the last decade, internships became so common that they attracted critical attention. See Alex Williams, "For Interns, All Work and No Payoff: Millennials Feel Trapped in a Cycle of Internships with Little Pay and No Job Offers," *New York Times*, February 14, 2014, www.nytimes.com/; Rita Koganzon, "Unpaid Internships are Unregulated, Often Illegal—and Ubiquitous," *National Review*, June 21, 2011, www.nationalreview.com/.

136 See Greg Bensinger, "Startups Scramble to Define 'Employee'," *Wall Street Journal*, July 30, 2015, B1; Rachel Feintzeig and Rachel Silverman, "Haggle over Salary? It's Not Allowed," *Wall Street Journal*, May 27, 2015, B1; Lauren Weber, "Companies Block Staff from Filing Lawsuits," *Wall Street Journal*, April 1, 2015, B1; and her "Some Bosses Reclassify Employees to Cut Costs," July 1, 2015, B1; Stephanie Gleason and Rachel Feintzeig, "At Startups, Pink Slips Come Early and Often," *Wall Street Journal*, December 13, 2013, B1.

137 See Kolakowski, "Racial, Gender Discrimination"; Kari Paul, "Women at Google Miss Out on Thousands of Dollars as a Result of Pay Discrimination, Lawsuit Alleges," *The Guardian*, July 22, 2020, www.theguardian.com/; Magnolia Potter, "The Rise in Age Discrimination in Tech and How to Stop It," *Legal Reader*, August 22, 2019, www.legalreader.com/; Monica Anderson, *Black STEM Employees Perceive a Range of Race-Related Slights and Inequities at Work*, Pew Research Center, January 10, 2018, www.pewresearch.org/; Sam Levin, "Google Accused of 'Extreme' Gender Pay Discrimination by US Labor Department," *The Guardian*, April 7, 2017, www.theguardian.com/; Kim Parker and Cary Funk, *Women are More Concerned than Men about Gender Discrimination in Tech Industry*, Pew Research Center, October 10, 2017, www.pewresearch.org/; Don Clark, "HP, HP Enterprise Hit With Claims of Age Discrimination," *Wall Street Journal*, August 29, 2016, B6; Yoree Koh, "Former Google Employees Allege Bias Against Women," *Wall Street Journal*, September 15, 2017, B4.

hiring from one another—to avoid raising workers' salaries through recruitment or counteroffers.[138] And, the use of "personality" tests, simulations, and related practices in screening applicants—such as "workplace" pre-evaluations, or investigation of past social media behavior—seemed oriented to hire those likely to be submissive when abused.[139]

It should not surprise, therefore, that the largest American technology companies were found to be more likely to undercompensate workers. Salary data analyses in the last decade showed that a large proportion of tech workers (including experienced professionals) were significantly underpaid.[140] And, the termination of conventional pensions—and their replacement by defined contribution [401(k)-type] programs during the past two decades (discussed earlier)—will likely guarantee that many people will not be able to stop working when they reach retirement age (or may never be able to retire).[141]

Labor Intangibles

The reproduction of labor intangibles is a most important aspect of productive transformation. Creativity, knowledge, and experience are vitally important for production and R&D in technology oligopolies. But their social dimension and qualitative character have often led to their neglect. Corporate management's emphasis on the quantitative and on narrow heuristics—along with the longstanding focus on labor's physical performance—contributed much to this situation.[142]

138 Jeff Elder, "Tech Giants Discussed Hiring, Say Documents," *Wall Street Journal*, April 21, 2014, A1, and his "Tech Firms Settle Suit Over Wages," *Wall Street Journal*, April 25, 2014, B1.

139 Eduardo Porter, "Who Discriminates in Hiring? A New Study can Tell," *New York Times*, July 29, 2021, www.nytimes.com/; Greg Bensinger, "Amazon Recruits Face 'Bar Raisers'," *Wall Street Journal*, January 8, 2014, B1.

140 Alison D. Rayome, "61% of Tech Workers Feel Underpaid, Especially at these 20 Companies," *Tech Republic*, July 25, 2018, www.techrepublic.com/; Lauren Weber, "One in Three Tech Workers is Underpaid: Many are Earning at Least 10% Less than They Could Command if They Looked for a New Job Today, Paysa Says," *Wall Street Journal*, January 10, 2017, www.wsj.com/; Paysa, *Top Companies Most Likely to Underpay Their Tech Talent*, February 28, 2017, www.paysa.com/; Covert, "When Companies Supersize." The situation in technology sectors reflects the larger panorama of the American workforce—see Reich, "Almost 80% of US Workers"; U.S. Bureau of Labor Statistics, *Profile of the Working Poor.*

141 See Annie Nova and Carmen Reinicke, "Why the 401(k) Won't Fix the U.S. Retirement Crisis," *CNBC*, February 14, 2021, www.cnbc.com/; Timothy W. Martin, "401(k) Pioneers Lament What They Started: Retirement-saving Vehicles Fall Short of Early Backers' Rosy Expectations," *Wall Street Journal*, January 3, 2017, A1.

142 See Kanigel, *One Best Way*; Eric Hobsbawm, *Labouring Men: Studies in the History of Labour* (London: Weidenfeld and Nicolson, 1964), chapters 3–6, 17. Sumantra Ghoshal's longstanding critical perspective on management's neglect of the qualitative dimension should also be taken into account—see his "Bad Management Theories and Destroying Good Management Practices,"

Intangibles today are estimated to account for a high proportion of the value of technology products and services.[143] Many specialists consider labor intangibles to be the most valuable asset that a technology company can have—an aspect that gained considerable attention during the last decade.[144] Nonetheless, critical analyses of capitalism often ignored them—or simply assumed them to be incidental to labor's physical performance. And when they were considered, they were often associated with managerial performance—rather than with labor.[145]

Reproduction of labor intangibles requires extensive societal mediation. Human–social environment interactions are fundamentally important in this regard. These involve support for creativity, learning, work-based self-development, enhancement of tacit and codified knowledge, and the meaningful accumulation of experience.[146] Social influences outside the corporate domain must therefore be engaged for this mode of reproduction to occur. Learning processes that allow uncodified knowledge to be absorbed, cultural influences and immersions that provide deep insights into social trends or phenomena, peer-to-peer interactions, collectively shared experiences, network-based interactions, freewheeling experimentation, happenstance discoveries, and gaining codified knowledge unavailable within the corporate domain, are some examples of what societal mediation can entail.

Academy of Management Learning and Education 4 (2005), 75–91; Sumantra Ghoshal and Christopher A. Bartlett, *The Individualized Corporation* (New York: HarperBusiness, 1997), chapters 3–5.

143 See *The Economist*, "Immaterial Needs: How to Unleash More Investment in Intangible Assets," May 21, 2022, 74; Ben McClure, *Intangible Assets Provide Real Value to Stocks*, Investopedia, October 19, 2020, www.investopedia.com/; Jason Sandler and Matthew Flug, "Are Intangibles Now the Most Important Asset Class in the Global Economy?" *Brink*, October 17, 2019, www.brinknews.com/; Jonathan Haskel and Stian Westlake, *Capitalism Without Capital: The Rise of the Intangible Economy* (Princeton: Princeton University Press, 2018); *The Economist*, "Insuring Intangible Risks: In Search of a Jelly Mould; The Value of Rich-World Companies Now Lies Mainly in Assets That are Impossible to Touch and Tricky to Insure," August 25, 2018, 61–62; and its "How Intangible Assets are Changing Investment," December 23, 2017, 90; Ahmed Bounfour, *The Management of Intangibles: The Organization's Most Valuable Assets* (Hoboken: Taylor and Francis, 2013); National Research Council, *Intangible Assets: Measuring and Enhancing their Contribution to Corporate Value and Economic Growth* (Washington: National Academies Press, 2009).

144 Growing importance of patenting and IP (brands, logos, copyrights) were major contributors—see John Villasenor, "Why Patents and Copyright Protections are More Important than Ever," *Scientific American*, November 14, 2013, www.scientificamerican.com/; Shira Ovide and John Letzing, "Tech Patents Soar in Value," *Wall Street Journal*, April 10, 2012, B1.

145 This misconception gained favor after the mid-1940s, as oligopolistic consolidation advanced and corporate workplaces became the main source of patent applications—see Luis Suarez-Villa, *Invention and the Rise of Technocapitalism* (Lanham: Rowman and Littlefield, 2000), Chapter 3.

146 Oligopoly capitalism, however, has tended to displace those primary mediations—in the sense provided by István Mészáros in his *Social Structure and Forms of Consciousness*, Vol. 1 (New York: Monthly Review Press, 2010), chapters 3, 8. The result is that second-order mediations take over and result in social alienation—as money, destructive competitism, and consumerism become major objectives.

A very important feature of the reproduction of labor intangibles is that companies typically have limited control, because they involve processes or activities that tend to occur *outside* the corporate domain. Forcing reproduction to be under corporate control can destroy it—or make it largely ineffective. Herein lies an important contrast with the in-house training programs that corporations use to try to improve labor's performance—which are typically under tight control.

Also, labor intangibles are not depleted—nor are they devalued—through usage. The latter tend to enhance their value, by providing new knowledge, experience, or situations that elicit creativity. Thus, the more they are used, the more likely it is that they will improve. And the more they are shared, the better the chance that they will lead others to be more creative, gain knowledge, and make significant contributions.

The reproduction of labor intangibles is qualitative by nature and tends to defy quantification.[147] Attempts to quantify it are often crude and provide limited or no benefit. Also, quantification often yields one-of-a-kind results that are specific to a situation or individual. They therefore tend to be very difficult or impossible to generalize to a larger context. Even when some generalization is possible, the features involved—related to individual creativity, for example—are difficult to transfer between different contexts.

The reproduction of labor intangibles depends on several societal processes that are vitally important for the development of technological capabilities. These processes depend on social relations and on collective or group interests. They are often developed with public resources that have accumulated over long periods of time. They are thus fundamentally different from the accumulative dynamic considered in the previous chapter, in the sense that they are part of the commons—the public or common wealth of a society that no single individual or corporate entity can create, own, or control.

These intangibles-enriching societal processes have a strong qualitative dimension. They are replenished and expanded through the collective contribution of talents, experiences, and knowledge. Public institutions all too often coordinate these processes or at least provide the platforms through which they can occur. Over the years, public funding has made it possible for those institutions to provide such support. And the resources they offer are all too often essential not only for individual and group technological creativity but also for collective advancement.

147 Complex technologies that require substantial societal mediation and qualitative attention are often in this situation. See Suarez-Villa, *Technocapitalism*, 45–54; *The Economist*, *Technology Quarterly*, "Meaning and Machine Intelligence: What Are You Talking About? Machines Still Cannot Conduct Proper Conversations With Humans Because They Do Not Understand the World," January 7, 2017, 9–10; Christopher Mims, "Artificial Intelligence Has a Way to Go," *Wall Street Journal*, December 5, 2016, B1.

Among the societal processes, the acquisition and reproduction of *uncodified* or *tacit knowledge* is particularly important. This process supports most every form of technological creativity. But the kind of knowledge it encompasses is very difficult to transfer to others through written, verbal, or visual communication. This is partly because much of that knowledge will have been acquired through trial and error, specific circumstances, innate talent, or a combination of insights and experiences that are difficult to replicate.

Societal influences that enhance the ability to design (complex equipment, experiments, or software), to understand hidden meanings (in any form of technical specification or language), to detect previously unknown features, symptoms, or behavior, to foresee weaknesses in processes or designs, and to combine elements in new ways are some examples of what uncodified knowledge involves. This form of knowledge has a very direct relationship to invention and innovation. It is fundamental for undertaking basic and applied research and for generating IP.

Patent awards thus depend greatly on uncodified knowledge, given the absolute requirement of novelty. And, such novelty is achieved by coming up with an item, formula, or process that embodies (or embeds) previously unknown possibilities. Novelty cannot exist without such knowledge, inasmuch as any patent application based solely on codified knowledge would likely fail. In some cases, however, combinations of codified knowledge may qualify as novelty, but even there the combination itself would need to be previously unknown.

Uncodified knowledge is thus very important for R&D even when the main objective is product differentiation. The success of the latter all too often depends on being first to come up with an idea, even if the resulting product or service happens to be superfluous. Such cases—socially unnecessary products—manifest the rift between use value and exchange value that characterizes oligopoly capitalism, as noted early in the previous chapter. That they occur frequently in the oligopolistic technology domain can be seen as a symptom of the importance of intangibles and of the difficulty of reproducing them internally.

Another societal process involves the use and reproduction of *codified* or *explicit knowledge*. This form of knowledge can be learned through written, verbal, or visual communication. In some cases, the complexity of the information may require consultation—or prior knowledge of relevant topics—but by and large the knowledge is accessible and can be communicated. Codified knowledge is fundamental for most any professional endeavor, and its learning is legitimized through degrees, certificates, or licenses.

Codified knowledge often also serves as a platform upon which uncodified knowledge will be developed. Patent records and technological histories, for example, provide important insights that can become part of a learning process. Codified knowledge on thermodynamics is fundamental for experimentation that involves any form of energy transfer, while codified knowledge on molecular physics is essential for inventions in nanotechnology. In genetic engineering, codified knowledge involving microbiology is necessary for creating new organisms, much as codified knowledge of software is essential for bioinformatics.

Most everyone who deploys or possesses uncodified knowledge has thus been exposed to related codified knowledge. The two kinds of knowledge tend to be linked, and their accumulation at the societal level can be symbiotic. However, a broader public institutional spectrum—involving primary, secondary, and tertiary education, libraries, communications, and patent data repositories, for example—also supports codified knowledge. The pace and quality of codified knowledge absorption, along with the capacity to use it, is of vital importance for developing labor's technological capabilities.

Societal networks provide a platform where codified and uncodified knowledge can be developed—outside the direct control of corporate power. Possibly the most important networks in this regard are self-organizing and open—focused on certain areas of knowledge. The societal significance of these networks is usually a function of a feature—network extent—discussed previously. Network extent is a multidimensional aspect of all networks, and it consists of three elements—range, accessibility, and composition.[148] These elements—working in unison—are vitally important for networks that diffuse technological knowledge.

Accessibility is vital for networks that serve as a platform for uncodified and codified knowledge, since this feature directly affects their range (or scale), and also their composition. Access and scale, in tandem, affect the quality of a network's social utility—including the new knowledge provided by participants, its significance, the intensity of participation, and their benefit to society.[149] Social utility here is assumed to be synonymous with the definition of socially necessary value—or use value, as noted early in the previous chapter. And, the value of a societal network that supports knowledge accumulation tends to increase with access and scale. Thus, abundance of access and scale—rather than scarcity—is the key to a network's value as an instrument for supporting codified and uncodified knowledge.

Another societal process affecting the reproduction of labor intangibles involves *technological infrastructure*. Research laboratories, advanced educational facilities, public communication systems and facilities, and the community of scientists, engineers, and technologists—broadly defined—contribute to this mode. Technological infrastructure also serves as a platform for societal networks where codified and uncodified knowledge can be accumulated and

148 See Suarez-Villa, *Technocapitalism*, 57–67, 83–84, 162–63.

149 Open-source networks during the first decade of the twenty-first century attracted much hope in this regard. See Joseph M. Reagle, *Good Faith Collaboration: The Culture of Wikipedia* (Cambridge, MA: MIT Press, 2010); Janet Hope, *Biobazaar: The Open Source Revolution and Biotechnology* (Cambridge, MA: Harvard University Press, 2008); Söderberg, *Hacking Capitalism*.

exchanged. A community of scientists, engineers, and technologists can be considered a societal form of technological infrastructure. Such communities are all too often vital for providing guidance on both uncodified and codified knowledge—outside the corporate domain—and they help enrich intangibles by serving as a repository of talent.

Beyond the vast amounts of taxpayer-provided capital required, the recovery of societal investments in infrastructure typically occurs over very long periods of time—returns often being found in qualitative terms. And it is that qualitative dimension regarding benefit that most baffles those who consider the effects of technology only in quantitative terms. Improvements in the level of technological literacy among the population, a more capable pool of scientists, engineers, and technologists, improved institutional capabilities—are some of the qualitative benefits that accrue to society at large.

The indispensable need for societal mediation in the reproduction of intangibles and the fact that such mediation is largely out of the control of the corporate domain pose a dilemma. Oligopolistic corporate power can choose to control the reproduction of intangibles internally—forgoing societal mediation—and thereby possibly end up damaging itself, *or* it can acquiesce to the need for such mediation and end up incurring the risks and uncertainty that accompany it. Among such risks is the failure to appropriate ideas and IP—all the more so if they happen to become part of the public domain, or if another company appropriates them first.

These situations are likely whenever societal mediation is involved, given the knowledge diffusion and interactions that typically accompany it. The histories of invention and innovation are filled with cases of first-mover (or simultaneous first) ideas whose appropriation was preempted because of second-mover takeovers and disputes. And, ideas are at the core of what happens with product development and research.

But, the damage caused by attempting to control—internally—the reproduction of intangibles can be great or possibly worse. Major qualitative aspects involving the all-important objectives of differentiating products or securing IP may fall short of their potential—or fail altogether. And it is usually very difficult for a corporation to reproduce internally the full range of talents, knowledge, creativity, and experience needed to generate the inventions and innovations that it seeks to create.[150]

For labor, attempts to reproduce intangibles internally often translate into greater alienation in the workplace. It should not surprise, therefore, that comprehensive surveys in recent times have shown that the vast majority of workers

150 During the last decade, a widely deployed (and unsuccessful) attempt to remedy this situation involved trying to imitate learn-through-play Montessori school training—see *The Economist*, "Montessori Management: The Backlash Against Running Firms Like Progressive Schools Has Begun," September 7, 2013, 68.

declare themselves to be "alienated, trapped, under-appreciated."[151] The pressure can be such that many individuals have resorted to potentially harmful ways to try to enhance performance—such as transcranial direct current stimulation (tDCS).[152] And, implementing artifices to try to reproduce intangibles internally—such as the use of analytical templates, allowing some autonomous initiative ("intrapreneurship") to selected workers, or emphasizing altruistic considerations that are largely irrelevant to the corporate context—have been largely ineffective.[153]

Capacity Utilization

The impossibility of controlling the reproduction of labor intangibles internally complicates the management of systematized research regimes and product development.[154] This scenario was not as difficult in earlier stages of capitalism, due to the more limited corporate need for intangibles and the emphasis on labor's physical task performance.[155] Also, the intangibles needed were simpler and could be reproduced internally.

Excess Capacity

With the emergence of complex technologies in recent decades, the possibility of fully controlling the reproduction of labor intangibles internally evaporated. This increases uncertainty and risk in the corporate domain, as the absence

151 See TINY Pulse, *The State of Employee Engagement in Tech: 4 Big Bad Trends that are Hitting this Workforce Hard* (2021); its *2015 Employee Engagement Report* and its *2016 Tech Industry Reports (White Paper)*, www.tinypulse.com/ (accessed July 1, 2022); Katie Canales, "Apple is Doing Everything it Can to Keep Employees from Talking About Pay Equity," *Business Insider*, August 31, 2021, www,businessinsider.com/; *The Economist*, "The Other Side of Paradise: Glamorous Tech Startups Can Be Brutal Places for Workers," January 16, 2016, 74.

152 See Wikipedia, *Transcranial Direct-Current Stimulation*, https://en.wikipedia.org/ (accessed July 1, 2022); Mark Harris, "Brain Hackers Beware: Scientist Says tDCS Has No Effect," *IEEE Spectrum*, January 21, 2015, www.spectrum.iee.org/; Jared C. Horvath, Jason D. Forte and Olivia Carter, "Evidence that Transcranial Direct Current Stimulation (tDCS) Generates Little-to-No Reliable Neurophysiologic Effect Beyond MEP Amplitude Modulation in Healthy Human Subjects: A Systematic Review," *Neuropsychologia* 66 (2015), 213–36.

153 Such practices became common in many tech workplaces during the past two decades. See Suarez-Villa, *Technocapitalism*, 128–31. Also, lofty "mission statements" often serve to distract attention from workplace problems—see Rachel Feintzeig, "I Don't Have a Job. I Have a Higher Calling. Some Employees Balk as Many Firms—from Motorcycles to Accounting—Step Up Talk about Changing the World," *Wall Street Journal*, February 25, 2015, B1.

154 A situation addressed in Suarez-Villa, *Corporate Power, Oligopolies*, Chapter "Fundamental Split."

155 See Kanigel, *One Best Way*; Hobsbawm, *Labouring Men*, and his *Age of Capital*; Slichter, *Turnover of Factory Labor*.

of control over intangibles affects most every operational area—especially research, product development, work processes, marketing, pricing, and even enterprise strategy. One result of this scenario is *the oligopolistic practice of sustaining production at levels below full capacity.*[156]

Excess capacity is important for putting new ideas, inventions, and innovations—including product differentiation schemes—into production quickly. It is also important for manipulating product pricing through output adjustments. Excess capacity can help gain flexibility and time when unexpected problems arise. Or, it can help expand output and market reach faster when higher demand materializes.

Rising returns to scale—a characteristic of production in many technology oligopolies—makes it desirable to sustain excess productive capacity. The possibility of reducing unit costs through a rapid increase in output is very attractive—especially for corporations that seek to expand control over a market niche or to capture new ones. Reducing unit costs—the main benefit of larger scale—also makes it easier to set up entry barriers, raise revenue, and acquire other companies.

The cost of maintaining excess capacity can be covered by accumulated and future surpluses—all the more so given that technology oligopolies typically hold vast amounts of idle cash.[157] In contrast with companies engaged in competitive markets, oligopolies are privileged with surpluses through their pricing

156 For general purposes, a 10 percent or greater average of idle production plant capacity—over a continuous period of 12 months or more—may be considered excess capacity. However, sectors can experience significant differences. In social media, for example, a 30 percent or greater average level of idle computer-server capacity may be considered necessary or even desirable, given rapid changes in computing power (needed to adjust to greater demand)—while in computer hardware manufacturing, particularly in assembly production, such a level of idle capacity may be regarded as high. If excess capacity is defined as any excess in the level of capital needed to minimize cost relative to output [used by Robert E. Hall in his *Chronic Excess Capacity in U.S. Industry*, National Bureau of Economic Research Working Paper no. 1973 (Cambridge: NBER, 1986)], then its magnitude is bound to be much higher than if more direct metrics of idle capacity are utilized—such as actual *versus* potential total employment *or* actual *versus* total output possible under a full (24-hour) production run. For debates and historical interpretations on this matter, see Baran and Sweezy, *Monopoly Capital*, 237–48; Josef Steindl, *Maturity and Stagnation in American Capitalism* (Oxford: Blackwell, 1952), chapters II, X; Donald C. Streever, *Capacity Utilization and Business Investment*, University of Illinois Bureau of Economic and Business Research, vol. 57 (Urbana: BEBR, 1960).

157 A matter that attracted attention during the last decade, with regard to tax havens and technology companies. See Ori Wallach, *Mapped: The World's Biggest Private Tax Havens*, Visual Capitalist, July 9, 2021, www.visualcapitalist.com/; Martin Armstrong, *Tax Havens Attracting the Most Foreign Profits*, Statista, July 10, 2020, www.statista.com/; *Berkeley Economic Review*, "Tax Havens: A Paradise for US Tech Giants," November 20, 2019, https://econreview.berkeley.edu/; Jesse Drucker and Simon Bowers, "After a Tax Crackdown, Apple Found a New Shelter for Its Profits: The Tech Giant Has Found a Tax Haven in the Island of Jersey, Leaving Billions of Dollars Untouched by the United States, Leaked Documents Reveal," *New York Times*, November 6, 2017, www.nytimes.com/; Vipal Monga, "New Rules, New Puzzle: Where to Stash Cash?" *Wall Street Journal*, November 4, 2014, B1.

power. And the surpluses can be so vast that it is often difficult to put them to any productive use.

The largest 150 technology corporations—all of them oligopolists in their market segments—often amass several hundred billion dollars annually in cash, even after capital expenditures are accounted for. Their accumulated cash and current profits usually amount to more than 20 percent of their market value.[158] Also, tech corporate profits have increased at a faster rate than the U.S. economy as a whole—a matter that became all too obvious during the last decade.[159] Technology oligopolies were the most profitable companies in the S&P 500 Index during the last decade, and the median corporation in that group often held over 60 percent of its gross operating profit in cash.[160]

Building additional productive capacity can take years, while subcontracting to make up for shortfalls poses problems—having to share (and possibly lose) proprietary technology, quality issues, coordination problems, higher cost, and the possibility that new ideas, processes, or unpatented inventions might be leaked. Sustaining excess capacity can thus seem safer than the alternatives—all the more so given the short-term focus of most executive decision-making and the need for speed when opportunities arise. And, given the fact that reproducing labor intangibles to build additional capacity requires time, is difficult, or is impossible to control, and the results can be uncertain.

Capacity-Price Engineering

Maintaining excess capacity is often accompanied by a strategy that I refer to as *capacity-price engineering*. This strategy involves rapid adjustment of both output and product pricing. *The immediate objective is to sustain pricing by keeping product output below market demand.* To achieve this scenario, prices are kept stable while output is reduced—in the face of stagnant or lower demand. If demand rises, output can be increased so long as pricing can also be made to rise or at least remain stable. Maintaining or increasing the oligopolistic product market surplus (ΔN in the accumulative dynamic) is the desired outcome—a matter that may not be readily apparent if adjustments in capacity or pricing are simultaneously implemented.

158 See Bloomberg, *Investing and Stock Research by Company and Industry*, www.bloomberg.com/ (accessed July 19, 2022); Sebastian Pellejero and Paul J. Davis, "Investors Circle Largest Corporate Cash Hoard Ever," *Wall Street Journal*, December 4, 2020, www.wsj.com/; *The Economist*, "Three Sanity Tests for Whether Tech Firms are Living in a Bubble," February 25, 2017, 58; James Titcomb, "Apple's Cash Reserves Swell to $250bn," *Telegraph*, May 1, 2017, www.telegraph.co.uk/.

159 Justin Lahart, "The Next Problem: Too Much Profit," *Wall Street Journal*, March 28, 2014, C8.

160 Based on data compiled by CSIMarket, https://csimarket.com/ (accessed July 28, 2022); Edward Yardeni and Joe Abbott, *Stock Market Briefing: S&P 500 Sectors & Industries Profit Margins*, Yardeni Research, Inc., August 22, 2017, https://www.yardeni.com/.

With capacity-price engineering, the use of innovations that increase output may be avoided, *if* increases in product demand cannot be anticipated *and* cannot be greater than the projected output levels. This means that older or fairly obsolete technologies may be found in production, even when the oligopolist creates its own cutting-edge technologies and embeds them in its products. Or, it may mean that new and obsolete technologies may coexist within production itself, at different stages or for different purposes. This paradoxical situation highlights oligopolistic technology corporations' dual role as users *and* providers of new technology (noted at the beginning of this chapter). It is a situation unlikely to be found in competitive scenarios, where new technologies in production—and embedding new technologies in products—tend to accompany each other.

Co-respectiveness among oligopolists means that capacity-price engineering can provide some collusive stability. Many technology oligopolists cooperate with one another through supply or outsourcing arrangements. During the last decade, for example, Samsung was found to receive about ten percent of the price consumers pay for every Apple iPhone X—due to its supply of microprocessors and screens.[161] Samsung was also found to use Microsoft's software for its products.[162] Pursuing price competition would not only damage such arrangements but would also likely lower revenues for all.

The effects of capacity-price engineering can be seen in the form of rising prices—even when demand declines, levels off, or remains stagnant. Demand itself can be manipulated, by requiring purchase of accessories or companion items necessary to make a product work. Capacity-price engineering can be effective even when alternative products are readily available for purchase. Rising prices of new smartphones that face constant or weaker demand—with improvements that are minimal over those of a prior model—are one example.[163] Being able to engineer rising prices in such situations can help boost a company's stock market valuation—an important consideration for executives.[164] Rising prices that outstrip increases in demand are another outcome, as the oligopolist adjusts output and pricing simultaneously—a form of manipulation that can be very difficult to detect, especially when a new product is introduced.

161 Timothy W. Martin and Tripp Mickle, "Samsung to Benefit if iPhone X is a Success," *Wall Street Journal*, October 3, 2017, B1.

162 Jay Greene, "Microsoft Gets a Lift in Virtual Reality: New Odyssey Headset from Samsung Uses Windows 10 to Enable Immersive Computing," *Wall Street Journal*, October 4, 2017, B4.

163 A matter that became all too obvious during the last decade. See Dan Gallagher, "New Phone Prices are Going to the Edge," *Wall Street Journal*, August 30, 2017, B1; Tripp Mickle and Timothy W. Martin, "Smartphone Makers Believe You Will Pay $1,000 and Up," *Wall Street Journal*, September 11, 2017, B1.

164 As in the case of Apple during the last decade. Dan Gallagher, "Can the New iPhone Push Apple's Value Above $1 Trillion?" *Wall Street Journal*, September 11, 2017, B10.

For consumers, the effects of capacity-price engineering can be very harmful—beyond the added expense. In the biotechnology and biopharmaceutical sectors, for example, rising prices accompanied by medication shortages—artificially induced, in most cases—were estimated to have added hundreds of millions of dollars annually to healthcare costs during the last decade.[165] Continuous annual shortages over many years were estimated to be in the hundreds—per medication type—affecting tens of millions of patients requiring treatment.[166] The trend in rising prices and constrained output occurred even though in most cases the medications were not affected by a lack of raw materials.[167] And, medication price raises often outstripped increases in demand.

In the agro-biotechnology sector, requiring new seeds to be purchased every year can be considered to be part of a capacity-price engineering strategy. The effects of this strategy were noticeable during the last two decades.[168] Over a 16-year period, corn seed prices were found to have risen by 259 percent, while the average cost of planting an acre of soybeans rose by 325 percent.[169] Oligopolistic influence over regulatory agencies and the judiciary—aspects addressed earlier in this book—have been important supports for capacity-price engineering in this sector.[170] The patent system helped sustain capacity-price engineering, as farmers who mixed seeds or refused to purchase new ones

165 Peter Loftus, "Lack of Cheap Drugs thwarts Treatments: Shortages Add $400 Million to Costs as Doctors Use Pricier and Riskier Alternatives," *Wall Street Journal*, July 3, 2017, B1.

166 See American Society of Health-System Pharmacists, *Information on Drug Product Shortages and Management*, www.ashp.org/drug-shortages/; U.S. Food and Drug Administration, *Drug Shortages*, www.fda.gov/; U.S. Centers for Disease Control and Prevention, *Current Vaccine Shortages and Delays*, www.cdc.gov/; Pharmacy Services, *Drug Shortages*, www.pharmacyservices.utah.edu/ (all accessed July 3, 2019).

167 Peter Loftus, "Scarcity Boosts Drug Cost: Some Prices Triple after Shortages, Recalls," *Wall Street Journal*, January 19, 2019, B1; and his "Lack of Cheap Drugs."

168 See Julie Fidler, *Farmers Reject GM Seeds, Citing High Costs and Few Benefits*, Natural Society, July 30, 2021, https://naturalsociety.com/; Jacob Bunge, "Farmers Reconsider GMO Revolution," *Wall Street Journal*, September 15, 2016, A1; Infinite Unknown, *Monsanto to Charge as Much as 42% More for New Seeds!*, August 18, 2009, https://infiniteunknown.net/; *CBS News*, "Monsanto Strong-Arms Seed Industry," December 14, 2009, www.cbsnews.com/. See also Helena Paul and Ricarda Steinbrecher, *Hungry Corporations: How Transnational Biotech Companies Colonise the Food Chain* (London: Zed, 2003); Daniel Charles, *Lords of the Harvest: Biotech, Big Money, and the Future of Food* (Cambridge, MA: Perseus, 2002).

169 Center for Food Safety and Save Our Seeds, *Seed Giants vs. U.S. Farmers, 2013*, www.centerforfoodsafety.org/. See also Infinite Unknown, *Monsanto to Charge*; *CBS News*, "Monsanto Strong-Arms."

170 Erik Sherman, "Supreme Court Sides with Monsanto on Seed Suit," *CBS News*, May 13, 2013, www.cbsnews.com/; Seed World, *Supreme Court Holds: Patent Exhaustion Does Not Apply to Patented Seeds*, August 21, 2013, https://seedworld.com/; Infinite Unknown, *Monsanto Lobbyists to be Placed in Charge of Food Safety by Obama*, July 29, 2009, https://infiniteunknown.net/.

were sued in court. In a single month, for example, 144 lawsuits were filed against 410 farmers and 56 businesses in at least 27 states.[171]

This panorama was coupled with the inevitable need to use engineered pesticides—seeds and pesticides being manufactured by the same oligopolist.[172] Seed and pesticide prices, rising in tandem, thus accompanied and outstripped increases in demand—as farmers found they could not use one product without the other. In this case, capacity-price engineering was reinforced through changes and requirements in technologies related to the main product—the engineered seeds—despite the pesticides' negative impact on human health.[173]

Capacity-price engineering can stave off a loss of innovation and of control over intangibles, when used in combination with branding. In that scenario, output might be adjusted to meet orders for a brand. The image of a brand associated with wealth or desirable personal qualities can thus help sustain demand—even when its price is very high and the branded product provides little or no improvement over prior versions.[174] Or over similar, lower-priced products marketed by other companies. This seemingly paradoxical situation is known as the "prestige" effect, and it is very desirable for product development and marketing units.

Limiting product output in such cases can lead to higher pricing—and possibly also greater demand—as consumers psychologically accept having to pay more.[175] Also, delaying the introduction of a new, branded product can have a similar effect.[176] Intangibles play a very important role in this panorama, as deep first-hand knowledge of societal trends, consumer psychology, a brand's

171 Rachel Tepper, "Seed Giants Sue U.S. Farmers over Genetically Modified Seed Patents in Shocking Numbers: Report," *Huffpost*, February 13, 2013, www.huffpost.com/; Center for Food Safety and Save Our Seeds, *Seed Giants vs. U.S. Farmers*.

172 See Fidler, *Farmers Reject GM Seeds*; Bunge, "Farmers Reconsider GMO"; Paul and Steinbrecher, *Hungry Corporations*; Charles, *Lords of the Harvest*.

173 Ludwig Burger and Tina Bellon, "Bayer to Pay Up to $10.9 Billion to Settle Bulk of Roundup Weedkiller Cancer Suits," *Reuters*, June 24, 2020, www.reuters.com/.

174 See Yoko Kubota and Tripp Mickle, "Apple to Cut iPhone X Output," *Wall Street Journal*, January 31, 2018, B1; Christopher Mims, "Why There Aren't Enough New iPhones," *Wall Street Journal*, September 18, 2017, B1.

175 A well-known technology journalist, commenting on the availability of Apple's iPhone X during the last decade, wrote: "Shortages of hot new gadgets are so common, it is easy to take them for granted … Are these shortages some kind of Machiavellian marketing play? Calculated risk management?"—Mims, "Why There Aren't Enough," B1. See also Tripp Mickle, "Apple Results Soar on Pricey iPhones: Quarterly Earnings Hit Record Even as Customers Bought Fewer Devices," *Wall Street Journal*, February 2, 2018, B4; Kubota and Mickle, "Apple to Cut."

176 See Tripp Mickle, "Lateness Bedevils Apple CEO Cook," *Wall Street Journal*, January 6, 2018, A1; Kubota and Mickle, "Apple to Cut." An alternative in the case of stagnant or weaker demand is to pressure suppliers to reduce their pricing. See Yoko Kubota, Takashi Mochizuki and Tripp Mickle, "Lower iPhone Demand Bites Apple Suppliers," *Wall Street Journal*, November 20, 2018, A1.

social appeal, and new product placement possibilities are central to prestige-driven marketing.

Also, the brand's image—accompanied by social status considerations or peer pressure—may lead many customers to overlook the fact that the new product provides little or no additional utility.[177] Or, that delivery of the product can require significant waiting time. The branded product may then be sold with all of the most expensive options—at a much higher price—for a shorter delivery time. In such situations, the oligopolist can reduce idle productive capacity—to increase output and fulfill deliveries faster.

Another approach can involve offering a new model—at a very high price—alongside updates of pre-existing models in the same product niche.[178] This can allow the oligopolist to limit the output of the new model, to drive its price higher—while also reducing its own risk if the expected demand does not materialize. And, consumers unwilling to pay the high price of the new model may be enticed to choose updated versions of pre-existing models, despite their minimal improvement.[179]

Apple's marketing of its iPhone X in the last decade—the highest priced smartphone ever—alongside updates of pre-existing models—may be considered an example. Certain features, such as face recognition software to gain access (in the iPhone X), provided a semblance of novelty over the updated models.[180] Limiting opportunities for technology journalists and consumer advocates to test the iPhone X also apparently enhanced Apple's market power over this product, by preventing potential flaws or lack of utility from being exposed to the public.[181] Unveiling updated models of other products simultaneously—such as the Apple Watch Series 3—further enhanced this oligopolist's chances of increasing demand, as potential purchasers were exposed to an array of possibilities—despite the fact that improvements over prior versions were limited.[182]

177 A problem observed during the last decade in some new smartphones. See Josh Zumbrun and Tripp Mickle, "New iPhone Tests Economic Theory," *Wall Street Journal*, September 18, 2017, A2; Tripp Mickle, "Apple Gambles on Allure of Premium Pricing," *Wall Street Journal*, September 13, 2017, A1.

178 See Joanna Stern, "The iPhone 8 is Apple's Middle Child," *Wall Street Journal*, September 14, 2017, B5.

179 Geoffrey Fowler, "iPhone 8: Improvement is Slight for an Upgrade," *Wall Street Journal*, September 20, 2017, B1.

180 See Geoffrey Fowler, "A First Look at Apple's iPhone X: About Face," *Wall Street Journal*, September 13, 2017, B1; Joanna Stern, "iPhoneX Review: How We Tested (and Tricked) FaceID," *Wall Street Journal*, October 31, 2017, www.wsj.com/articles/.

181 See Tripp Mickle, "Apple Limits Lengthy iPhone X Testing for Most Reviewers: 'Unusual' Change in Strategy Means Latest Phone Got Less Testing Than Most of Its Predecessors Before Reviews Could Be Published," *Wall Street Journal*, October 31, 2017, www.wsj.com/articles/.

182 See Joanna Stern, "Apple Watch Series 3: I'll Pass," *Wall Street Journal*, September 21, 2017, B4.

Capacity-price engineering has also been applied by social media, smartphones, on-demand services, online gaming, and entertainment oligopolies to gain control over a very important labor intangibles market—app developers. The latter can be considered equivalent to research workers engaged in TVC-type contracting. By limiting contracts (a form of output) per app developer, restricting the customer data that the latter can appropriate, *and* lowering fees or royalties (equivalent to price control), the oligopolists in charge can achieve much the same effect that consumers experience in product markets. Lawsuits from app developers against some of the largest technology oligopolies during the last decade provided details on such practices.[183]

Typologies

Far from being a monolithic entity, transformation in the oligopolistic technology domain is a fragmented ensemble. The elements and phenomena discussed in this chapter are at the core of this ensemble, and they operate through production, research, assemblage, and extractive regimes that are diverse and multifaceted. The typologies that encompass the reality of the transformative panorama will be addressed in this section.

Extraction and Assemblage

This typology encompasses *mining operations*, *processing*, and *assembly of parts or components*. Commodification tends to be simple—appropriation of commodities and the setting of extractive or assemblage regimes being the main operations. Output may not involve completion of items to be marketed to customers or consumers.

Output in this typology thus often involves a primary or midstream commodity. The latter may undergo further processing or assemblage elsewhere. These may occur under contract and involve multiple sites. Reproduction of skills will likely occur internally. Thus, labor intangibles may be low, requiring limited variable capital. And compensation to reproduce labor's capacity for work may be insufficient.

Mining operations may have dismal working conditions—in some cases comparable to those of forced labor—with long workdays, minimal or no

183 Corrado Rizzi, *Class Action from App Developers Alleges Facebook 'Weaponizes Its Platform to Destroy Competition'*, Class Action, July 10, 2020, www.classaction.org/; Roger Fingas, *Leaked Docs Show Facebook Weaponized User Data Against Competitors, with Little Regard for Privacy*, Apple Insider, April 16, 2019, https://appleinsider.com/; Carole Cadwalladr and Emma Graham-Harrison, "Zuckerberg Set Up Fraudulent Scheme to 'Weaponise' Data, Court Case Alleges: Facebook Exploited Ability to Access Data from Any User's Friend Network, U.S. Case Claims," *The Guardian*, May 25, 2018, www.theguardian.com/.

health care, and low wages.[184] In some cases, armed conflict near mining areas may deepen exploitation—toiling in the mines becoming the only alternative to combat.[185] Conflict minerals mining—a term used by some international organizations—may thus characterize some operations.[186]

Minerals such as cerium, yttrium, indium, beryllium, and coltan can be at the core of extractive operations in this typology. Their limited global availability makes it critical to secure supplies.[187] These minerals are indispensable for batteries, connections, displays, smartphones, and nanotech-enabled microprocessors, among other uses.[188]

A researcher who took an Apple iPhone apart at a laboratory during the last decade, for example, found more than two dozen rare-earth minerals and elements—tracing their extraction to some of the most polluting mining areas on earth, to war zones where child, forced, or slave-like labor occur, and to other areas where the life expectancy of mining workers can be as low as 40 years.[189] Conventional minerals, such as aluminum, zinc, cobalt, or copper—vital for circuitry and controls in most every electronic product—are also mined intensively through subcontracted companies. The latter are all too often oligopolistic in their sector—and divulge little or nothing about their labor practices, thus shielding their technology clientele from responsibility.[190]

184 For extensive treatment of these aspects, see Fuchs, *Digital Labour*, 172–80. See also Henry Sanderson, "LME Probes Cobalt Supplies after Complaints over Child Labour Links," *Financial Times*, November 22, 2017, www.ft.com/.

185 See Billy Batware, *Resource Conflicts: The Role of Multinational Corporations in the Democratic Republic of the Congo*, Academic Council on the United Nations System, http://acuns.org/ (accessed July 18, 2022); Michael W. George, Omayra Bermudez-Lugo and Thomas R. Yager, *Conflict Minerals from the Democratic Republic of the Congo: Gold Supply Chain* (Reston: US Geological Survey, 2015); Peter H. Eichstaedt, *Consuming the Congo: War and Conflict Minerals in the World's Deadliest Place* (Chicago: Lawrence Hill, 2011).

186 See *The Economist*, "Mission Critical: Governments Race to Obtain Minerals Vital to Economic and Military Security," April 3, 2021, 58–60; Batware, *Resource Conflicts*; Michelle Toh, "Apple, Google, Microsoft, Dell and Tesla are Sued Over Alleged Child Labor in Congo," *CNN Business*, December 18, 2019, www.cnn.com/; Scott Patterson and Alexandra Wexler, "Phones, Cars Can't Shed Mining Taint: Supply Chains of Apple, VW and Others Still Link to a Cobalt Mine with Manual Workers," *Wall Street Journal*, September 14, 2018, A1; Emily Chasan, "'Conflict Minerals' Prove Hard to Trace," *Wall Street Journal*, August 4, 2015, B4; John F. Papp, *Conflict Minerals from the Democratic Republic of the Congo: Global Tantalum Processing Plants, A Critical Part of the Tantalum Supply Chain* (Reston: U.S. Geological Survey, 2014).

187 *The Economist*, "The Future of Mining: Rocks and Hard Places," June 26, 2021, 55–56; George, Bermudez-Lugo and Yager, *Conflict Minerals*; Papp, *Conflict Minerals*.

188 See Patterson and Wexler, "Phones, Cars Can't Shed"; Don Clark, "Intel, Micron Claim New Breed of Memory Chips," *Wall Street Journal*, July 29, 2015, B6; Timothy T. Y. Tan's *Rare Earth Nanotechnology* (Singapore: Pan Stanford, 2012).

189 Patterson and Wexler, "Phones, Cars Can't Shed". See also Batware, *Resource Conflicts*; Sanderson, "LME Probes Cobalt Supplies"; Brian Merchant, *The One Device: The Secret History of the iPhone* (New York: Little, Brown, 2017), chapters 8, 9, 12;

190 Approximately 60 percent of cobalt supplies in the world originate in the Democratic Republic of the Congo, where child labor has been found to be common. See Sanderson, "LME Probes

During the last decade, Glencore PLC, one of the world's most powerful mining and minerals corporations, was estimated to mine zinc—vital for producing indium, a zinc byproduct essential for liquid crystal displays—steel, and other metals, at essentially *no* cost to itself.[191] This was due to the very low wages it paid—and the gold byproducts it seized in the minerals it appropriated. In what may be considered an example of capacity-price engineering—this corporation took mines out of production and withheld refined zinc from the global market for extended periods. This practice drove up the price of this vital mineral by over 70 percent in less than two years during the last decade.[192]

When mining companies are contracted by offshore processors, this usually shields technology oligopolies from responsibility for abuses. Arm's-length contracting thus tends to be the preferred relationship. This is convenient, inasmuch as processing or assembly regimes may violate labor safety and environmental rules where they operate. It is not uncommon for offshore processing or assembly contractors to achieve profits of as much as 20 percent of the price paid for each product. For technology oligopolists, profits may amount to as much as 60–70 percent of the price consumers pay (per product)—while the total offshore labor cost incurred may be as little as two percent of that price.[193]

Perhaps then, it should not surprise that some of the largest employers in the world are offshore assembly contractors. Foxconn, for example, employed more than a million workers during the last decade, assembling products for Apple and Microsoft, among many other companies.[194] Being the world's largest offshore contractor helped this company expand across the globe, to diversify its assembly operations and acquire some of its suppliers.[195]

Cobalt Supplies"; *The Economist*, "Battery Minerals: The Whizz of Oz," November 25, 2017, 58–59.

191 Scott Patterson and Timothy Puko, "Glencore Masters the Zinc Market and Revival Ensues," *Wall Street Journal*, March 18, 2017, B1.

192 Patterson and Puko, "Glencore Masters"; *Japan Times*, "Shortage of Rare Minerals Could Upset Global Markets: Study," November 14, 2015, www.japantimes.co.jp/news/; Peter Klimek, Michael Obersteiner and Stefan Thurner, "Systemic Trade Risk of Critical Resources," *Science Advances*, November 2015, http://advances.sciencemag.org/. See also Refinitiv, *Datastream*, www.refinitiv.com/ (accessed July 4, 2022).

193 Christian Fuchs, "Digital Labor and Imperialism," *Monthly Review*, January 2016, 20–22; and his *Culture and Economy in the Age of Social Media* (New York: Routledge, 2015), chapters 4–6; Jack L. Qiu, *Goodbye iSlave: A Manifesto for Digital Abolition* (Urbana: University of Illinois Press, 2016), chapters 2–4.

194 Eva Dou, "How the iPhone Built a City in China: At Sprawling Foxconn Complex, 250,000 Workers Assemble Apple Device," *Wall Street Journal*, July 5, 2017, B1; Jenny Chan, Ngai Pun and Mark Selden, "The Politics of Global Production: Apple, Foxconn and China's New Working Class," *New Technology, Work and Employment* 28 (2013), 100–15.

195 See Takashi Mochizuki, "Foxconn Targets Toshiba Chip Unit," *Wall Street Journal*, April 11, 2017, B3; Eva Dou, "Foxconn Plans to Build China Flat-Panel Factory," *Wall Street Journal*, January 3, 2017, B4; and her "Foxconn Praises China, Prods U.S.," *Wall Street Journal*, March 2, 2017, B2.

Foxconn's labor practices drew global attention when nearly two dozen of its workers attempted suicide at various times during the last decade—some of them successfully—while later another 150 threatened to do so in protest over working conditions.[196] Obtaining the highest task execution efficiency—through production regimes that could require 70-hour work weeks, and in some cases over 90 hours, well above the 48-hour weekly limit stipulated by the International Labor Organization—was a paramount objective.[197] One investigation during the last decade found many workers in its factories enduring 18 consecutive workdays, shifts as long as 16 hours per day, compulsory overtime, many instances of individuals falling asleep while engaged on the production line, and crowded dormitories with as many 12 workers sharing a room.[198] The factories involved also reduced costs by employing minimally educated rural migrants—who had no resources of their own to seek adequate accommodations or fulfill basic needs.

After the economic crisis of 2007–9, some technology oligopolies intensified efforts to pressure governments in low labor cost nations to pursue agendas that would favor their interests. Among the "incentives" requested was low-cost financing of fixed capital outlays and minimal or no taxation. Governments that complied typically had their public treasury (and taxpayers) bear the risk and financing costs. Establishing a production facility to employ labor paying low wages is the outcome when promises are kept. Having a global manufacturing profile is very helpful, as in the case of General Electric and its dealings in India during the last decade.[199]

Over time, a technology oligopolist that has a history of manufacturing in the host nation can erect entry barriers. GE's numerous production facilities in China, for example, provided it with a formidable advantage that few companies could match. Having production facilities around the world then led to an accumulation of influence over time, as politics and surpluses compounded

196 Eva Dou, "Deaths of Foxconn Employees Highlight Pressures Faced by China's Factory Workers: Incidents at iPhone Production Site Reflect Precarious Existences of Migrant Workers," *Wall Street Journal*, August 21, 2016, http://www.wsj.com/; Jenny Chan, "A Suicide Survivor: The Life of a Chinese Worker," *New Technology, Work and Employment* 2 (2013), 84–99; Malcolm Moore, "'Mass Suicide' Protest at Apple Manufacturer Foxconn Factory," *Telegraph*, January 11, 2012, http://www.telegraph.co.uk/. See also Reed Albergotti, "Apple Accused of Worker Violations in Chinese Factories," *Washington Post*, September 9, 2019, www.washingtonpost.com/; Harrison Jacobs, "Inside 'iPhone City,' the Factory Town Where Half of the World's iPhones are Produced," *Business Insider*, May 7, 2018, www.businessinsider.com/.

197 Fuchs, "Digital Labor and Imperialism," 21.

198 Richard Bilton, "Apple 'Failing to Protect Chinese Factory Workers'," *BBC News*, December 18, 2014, http://www.bbc.com/; Brian X. Chen, "BBC Documentary Shows Harsh Conditions for Workers in iPhone Factories," *New York Times*, December 19, 2014, http://bits.blogs.nytimes.com/. See also Albergotti, "Apple Accused of Worker Violations"; Jacobs, "Inside 'iPhone City.'"

199 See Ted Mann and Brian Spegele, "Why GE Builds More Factories Overseas," *Wall Street Journal*, June 30, 2017, A1.

each other.[200] By the end of the last decade, GE had expanded its plants outside the United States by 140 percent over a 35-year period—and the number of nations in which it undertook production had increased by 160 percent.[201] Such experience and scale provided this oligo-conglomerate with much clout to negotiate deals with numerous governments (often with U.S. government assistance).

Integrative Production

Corporate domains in this typology *process or provide finished products and undertake R&D and marketing*. Their products and services are usually branded—often directly to consumers or customers. The range of domains can include dual and compound oligopolies, conglomerates and neo-conglomerates, and niche oligopolists. Many companies can be downstream customers of extractive or assemblage operations. Product development, research, and marketing—functions missing from the previous typology—are distinctive and often have vital importance.

An important challenge confronting corporate domains is *the cleavage between commodification and the reproduction of labor intangibles*. The former must take place within the corporate domain—if the oligopolist is to retain control over labor tasks, processing, and R&D. But the reproduction of labor intangibles tends to depend on external societal mediation.

External social influences thus gain greater weight in this typology. An example during the last decade was the corporate appropriation of ideas and data obtained through open-source networks, customer feedback, user engagement, professional communities, and uselaborers. Indications are that external collaboration, conferences, social interactions, and professional relations now have greater weight than ever in the oligopolistic domain. Thus, many acquisitions in recent times were motivated by the growing importance of intangibles.[202]

Companies that were heavily engaged with socially dependent intangibles often captured important market niches during the last decade. Thus, some networks involved with open-source software became major data cloud service providers.[203] And, across the technology spectrum, increases in market power were often linked to externally sourced intangibles.

200 See Thomas Gryta, Dana Mattioli and David Benoit, "GE Explores Further Spinoffs, Joint Deals," *Wall Street Journal*, April 13, 2018, A1; Mann and Spegele, "Why GE Builds More."

201 Mann and Spegele, "Why GE Builds," A9; Vanessa Fuhrmans, "Companies Disclose Head Count," *Wall Street Journal*, April 12, 2018, B5.

202 Such as Microsoft's acquisition of Xamarin during the last decade—a designer of open-source software tools—see Jay Greene, "A Pivot to Open-Source Software," *Wall Street Journal*, December 17, 2016, A11.

203 See OpenStack, *The Most Widely Deployed Open Source Cloud Software in the World*, www.openstack.org/ (accessed July 16, 2022); Spencer E. Ante and Michael Hickins, "To Build Cloud Services, Some Adopt OpenStack," *Wall Street Journal*, April 16, 2014, B4.

Systematized research regimes—a function missing in the previous typology—are affected by the cleavage between commodification and the reproduction of intangibles. Under stress to support product differentiation and marketing, research regimes often have to confront a dilemma—to pursue research that can lead to inventions (the R in R&D) *or* to differentiate existing products. Short-term considerations—raising revenue, share valuations, and executive compensation, among others—tend to favor the second possibility.[204]

Research deficiencies and excessive emphasis on product differentiation (and revenue) in biopharmaceutical oligopolies were denounced when the Covid-19 pandemic caused devastating human and economic losses—despite warnings over the years about the likely probability.[205] A longstanding lack of timelines for developing vaccine repertories showed a lack of preparation.[206] Problems were then compounded when the very expensive vaccines marketed by the most powerful American biopharmaceutical oligopolists could not stop contagion.

This deficiency—and limited testing before release—led many to believe that the world's population was being submitted to an "experiment," with unknown long-term consequences.[207] Disablement among many survivors

204 See Rafael Corredoira, Brent Goldfarb, Rachelle C. Sampson and Yuan Shi, *The Changing Nature of Firm R&D: Short-Termism and Technological Influence of U.S. Firms*, Harvard Business School, February 19, 2021, www.hbs.edu/; Rachelle C. Sampson and Yuan Shi, "Are U.S. Firms Becoming More Short-Term Oriented? Evidence of Shifting Firm Time Horizons from Implied Discount Rates, 1980–2013," *Strategic Management Journal*, 41 (2020), https://onlinelibrary.wiley.com/. In the last decade, a study of 600 large corporations concluded that 73 percent can be considered "short-termist," based on such practices and strategies as booking sales before customer payments, very limited investment in the company, substantial share buyback activity, aggressive cost reductions to increase profit, and substantial emphasis on fulfilling quarterly profit forecasts—see McKinsey Global Institute, *Measuring the Economic Impact of Short-Termism*, February 2017, https://www.mckinsey.com/.

205 See the warnings in Michael T. Osterholm and Mark Olshaker's *Deadliest Enemy: Our War Against Killer Germs* (New York: Little, Brown Spark, 2017), chapters 1, 7–10, 12–16, 18–20. A biotechnique—labeled mRNA—was rushed into production to create vaccines, despite its unknown effects on certain conditions (such as allergies and vascular coagulation) and possible long-term consequences. The technique was known but apparently was not experimented with due to the high cost of research. Questions remain as to whether a pre-existing research program—a costly and time-consuming endeavor—might have foreclosed contagion, thus saving millions of lives and preventing many millions from suffering lasting disabilities. Among the economic impacts of the pandemic was a simultaneous (and significant) contraction of per capita GDP in nearly 95 percent of the world's national economies—see, for example, Adam Tooze, *Shutdown: How Covid Shook the World's Economy* (New York: Viking, 2021).

206 See Max Nisen, "Deadly Viruses Aren't Pharma's Top Priority. Why Not?" *Bloomberg*, January 23, 2020, www.bloomberg.com/; Stephen Buranyi, "How Profit Makes the Fight for a Coronavirus Vaccine Harder," *The Guardian*, March 4, 2020, www.theguardian.com/.

207 Among them Robert F. Kennedy, Jr., and his immediate best-selling *The Real Anthony Fauci: Bill Gates, Big Pharma, and the Global War on Democracy and Public Health* (New York: Skyhorse, 2021), chapters 1–3.

and adverse vaccine reactions complicated the scenario. Also, the large tax breaks biopharmaceutical oligopolies regularly received for R&D over the years—which usually did not distinguish between basic research and product differentiation—reflected a misuse of vast amounts of public funding. Thus, many taxpayers who funded the tax breaks and other subsidies were prevented from surviving a pandemic that had long been considered likely.

These deficiencies contrasted with longstanding propaganda that touted biopharmaceutical oligopolies' capabilities to deal with most any disease. Further diminishing public confidence is that information on research results is often left unknown to the public and to the research community—due to foreclosure of publication and publicity when trials are unsuccessful, or when research results do not confirm authors' initial expectations. Outcomes and data from only about one in six unsuccessful clinical trials are ever published—an aspect that was repeatedly exposed during the last two decades.[208] This may be attributed to the pressure to show "success"—due to its importance for share valuations, executive compensation, and acquisitions, among other aspects.

Lobbying and applying pressure on regulatory agencies—and providing political contributions—have become a strategic fixture of oligopolistic research regimes. In biopharmaceuticals, for example, during the last decade, money and pervasive lobbying obtained a 12-year window of exclusivity for "biologics"—products based on (or made from) living organisms.[209] This included four years of complete corporate control over data from research and clinical trials *and* eight years of exclusive corporate usage of the product.[210] A major consequence is that a generic equivalent (of a product) cannot be approved by the U.S. Food and Drug Administration (FDA) during that time period—a very advantageous monopolistic lock-in for the corporation in control.

208 *The Economist*, "Clinical Trials: Spilling the Beans; Failure to Publish the Results of All Clinical Trials is Skewing Medical Science," July 25, 2015, 62–63; Bruce M. Psaty and Richard A. Kronmal, "Reporting Mortality Findings in Trials of Rofecoxib for Alzheimer Disease or Cognitive Impairment: A Case Study Based on Documents from Rofecoxib Litigation," *Journal of the American Medical Association* 299 (2008), 1813–17; Peter Lurie and Sidney M. Wofle, "Misleading Data Analyses in Salmeterol (SMART) Study," *Lancet* 366 (2005), 1261–62; James M. Wright, Thomas L. Perry, Kenneth L. Bassett and G. Keith Chambers, "Reporting of 6-Month vs. 12-Month Data in a Clinical Trial of Celecoxib," *Journal of the American Medical Association* 286 (2001), 2398–99; Joseph A. DiMasi, "Success Rates for New Drugs Entering Clinical Testing in the United States," *Clinical Pharmacology and Therapeutics* 58 (1995), 1–14. Distortion of events and results in control groups to enhance a proposed medication's chances of approval—or meet deadlines—has also occurred in some trials—see, for example, Thomas M. Burton, "Doctor Challenges Trial of AstraZeneca Drug," *Wall Street Journal*, February 3, 2014, B1; Daniel Carpenter, Evan James Zucker and Jerry Avorn, "Drug-Review Deadlines and Safety Problems," *New England Journal of Medicine* 358 (2008), 1354–61.

209 See Joel Lexchin, "The Pharmaceutical Industry in Contemporary Capitalism," *Monthly Review*, March 2018, 42; Ameet Sarpatwari, Jerry Avorn and Aaron S. Kesselheim, "Progress and Hurdles for Follow-On Biologics," *New England Journal of Medicine* 372 (2015), http://www.nejm.org/.

210 Lexchin, "Pharmaceutical Industry," 42.

Biologics accounted for almost 40 percent of all medication spending in the United States during the last decade—despite the fact that they made up only about two percent of all prescriptions—with patients paying as much as 20 percent of list prices as co-payments.[211] Substantial, unjustified price increases were part of this dynamic. Thus, for example, a product—Enbrel—launched in the 1990s saw its price rise six-fold by the middle of the last decade—despite having no improvement over its initial version.[212] A result of this panorama is that only ten medications made up almost half of total Medicare-Part B biopharmaceutical spending by the middle of the last decade—eight of them being biologics.[213] Four oligopolistic corporations—Regeneron, Genentech, Amgen, and Johnson and Johnson—marketed the eight biologics.[214]

Research regimes in this typology also benefited greatly from the globalization of U.S. patent rights in recent decades—the biotech and biopharmaceutical sectors providing ample evidence.[215] One result is that the neediest populations in the world have found it very difficult to have access to life-saving medications during a biopharmaceutical's 20-year patent validity—as they are required to pay exorbitant prices that have little or nothing to do with the cost of research or even production. Also, revenue considerations can prevent the production of cheaper medications—if those might replace established, profitable ones (or reduce their sales).[216] Pricing thus tends to be set at whatever level biopharmaceutical oligopolists contrive or wish to charge—not "what the market can bear" (as some financial analysts have long assumed).[217]

Pricing can also be influenced by efforts to expand a conquered market niche, as in Merck's $13,500 monthly pricing of Keytruda—a medication for treating some cancer tumors that generated almost four billion dollars in annual

211 Denny Lanfear, "How Big Pharma Suppresses 'Biosimilars,'" *Wall Street Journal*, June 24, 2019, A17.

212 Lanfear, "How Big Pharma."

213 Sarpatwari, Avorn and Kesselheim, "Progress and Hurdles"; Lexchin, "Pharmaceutical Industry."

214 Sarpatwari, Avorn and Kesselheim, "Progress and Hurdles"; Joseph Walker, "Policy Shift is Win for Drugmakers," *Wall Street Journal*, March 23, 2018, B1; *The Economist*, "Going Large: A Wave of New Medicines Known as Biologics will be Good for Drugmakers, but May Not be so Good for Health Budgets," January 3, 2015, 47–48.

215 See Lexchin, "Pharmaceutical Industry," 42; James Love, "TPP, Designed to Make Medicine More Expensive, Reforms More Difficult," *Medium*, June 8, 2015, https://medium.com/; Kazi Stastna, "Eli Lilly Files $500M NAFTA Suit Against Canada Over Drug Patents: Compensation Sought for Federal Court's Invalidation of Straterra, Zyprexa Patents," *CBC News*, September 13, 2013, http://www.cbc.ca/.

216 Jared S. Hopkins, "Biotech Billionaire is Sued over Deal for Cancer Drug," *Wall Street Journal*, April 4, 2019, B4. See also Robert Pear, "'Shenanigans' to Block Generic Drugs Comes under Scrutiny," *New York Times*, April 15, 2018, www.nytimes.com/; Bruce M. Psaty and Drummond Rennie, "Stopping Medical Research to Save Money: A Broken Pact with Researchers and Patients," *Journal of the American Medical Association* 289 (2003), 2128–31.

217 See William Lazonick and Öner Tulum, "How CEOs are Using Your High Drug Prices to Fill Their Pockets," *New York Times*, February 26, 2019, www.nytimes.com/.

sales during the last decade.[218] Product differentiation and development (the D in R&D) are typically at the core of efforts to find new markets for an existing medication. And, finding new uses for an established niche product all too often leads to higher pricing—rather than the opposite.[219] This is part of the reason *why product differentiation is so often favored over research* in many technology oligopolies. During the last decade, it was noted that, on average, only about one percent of total (after-tax) spending in the biopharmaceuticals sector was actually allocated to research—contradicting the argument that high prices were necessary to support that function.[220]

Other means of favoring product differentiation—to generate more short-term revenue and avoid external mediation on intangibles—may be found in most every oligopolistic technology sector. Engineering obsolescence into products is a fairly common one. It is more feasible when existing products can be rapidly modified and carry a well-known brand—as occurred with Apple's smartphones during the last decade.[221] Locking-in customers through accessories, apps, subscriptions, and services can help this objective—aided by advertising and brand appeal. Depending on a narrow product line for sales can also motivate this strategy. Apple, for example, depended on its iPhone for about two-thirds of sales during the last decade.[222]

Accelerating obsolescence through research regimes' emphasis on product differentiation and short-term revenue was facilitated by changes in microprocessor performance. "Foundries" (fabricators)—such as Intel and Taiwan Semiconductor Manufacturing Company (TSMC)—accelerated their output to take advantage of their clients' product differentiation strategies.[223] Their own emphasis on the short-term and fast results led to flaws that compromised security—exposing users to hacking and intrusions.[224]

218 Peter Loftus, "Merck Bets Big on Cancer Drug," *Wall Street Journal*, April 16, 2018, B3.

219 Loftus, "Merck Bets Big."

220 Lexchin, "Pharmaceutical Industry," 38–39; Daniel M. Hartung, Dennis N. Bourdette, Sharia M. Ahmed and Ruth H. Whitham, "The Cost of Multiple Sclerosis Drugs in the U.S. and the Pharmaceutical Industry: Too Big to Fail?" *Neurology* 84 (2015), www.ncbi.nlm.nih.gov/; Andrew Pollack, "Doctors Denounce Cancer Drug Prices of $100,000 a Year," *New York Times*, April 25, 2013, www.nytimes.com/; Donald W. Light and Joel Lexchin, "Foreign Free Riders and the High Price of U.S. Medicines," *British Medical Journal (BMJ)* 331 (2005), www.bmj.com/.

221 See *The Economist*, "Apple: The Great Successor's Second Act," August 28, 2021, 53–55; Betsy Morris, "What the iPhone Wrought," *Wall Street Journal*, June 24, 2017, B3; *Reuters*, "Apple, Epson Face French Legal Complaints Over Allegedly Shortening Life of Products," December 28, 2017, www.reuters.com/.

222 *The Economist*, "Apple," 53–54; Tripp Mickle, "How iPhone Decade Reshaped Apple," *Wall Street Journal*, June 21, 2017, B1.

223 See *The Economist*, "Silicon Meltdown: Even if Chips are Never Hacked, Their Flaws Have Consequences," January 13, 2018, 57–58; and its "Shifting Silicon: TSMC is Poised to Become the World's Most Advanced Chipmaker," April 7, 2018, 55–56.

224 See Tom Warren, "A Major New Intel Processor Flaw Could Defeat Encryption and DRM Protections," *The Verge*, March 6, 2020, www.theverge.com/; Sam Schechner, Stu Woo and Jay

Research regimes' emphasis on product differentiation—to speed up obsolescence, product replacement, and sales—was felt across the technology spectrum in recent decades. In Microsoft's case, structuring production as an iterative process (as opposed to the "waterflow" or cascade approach) contributed to product flaws.[225] Insufficient testing meant that Microsoft all too often depended on customers to identify problems, making them install "patches" that were often also defective (in other ways).[226] The flaws—and often the prescribed remedies—then exposed them to hacking and diverse security problems. Loading quality control (and its expense) unto customers was a strategic choice—made feasible by Microsoft's oligo-monopolistic control over software.[227]

Pursuing fast product differentiation, obsolescence, and sales led to many other problems in recent times. Among them was defective aircraft design that led to crashes and numerous deaths; addiction-causing medications that resulted in greater demand for the addictive product, and for related treatments; and batteries in smartphones and other gadgets that exploded or caused fires.[228] Accelerating product replacement and imposing monopolies over accessories and supplies was another. Thus, Hewlett-Packard engineered its printers to work only with the ink cartridges it manufactured—much as Monsanto's seeds were to be effective only with its pesticides (discussed earlier).[229] Hewlett-Packard

---

Greene, "Chip Flaws Have Suppliers, Users Seeking Fixes," *Wall Street Journal*, January 6, 2018, B1; Robert MacMillan, "Select Intel Clients Warned Off Patches," *Wall Street Journal*, January 12, 2018, B4; *The Economist*, "Silicon Meltdown."

225 Richard Sharpe, "'Globalization': The Next Tactic in the Fifty-Year Struggle of Labor and Capital in Software Production," in Rick Baldoz, Charles Koeber and Philip Kraft, eds., *The Critical Study of Work: Labor, Technology, and Global Production* (Philadelphia: Temple University Press, 2001), 222.

226 See Rachael King and Danny Yadron, "Microsoft Retires Its XP, but Security Risks Live On," *Wall Street Journal*, April 2, 2014, B1; *Reuters*, "IT Risks, Wariness and Planned Obsolescence," March 12, 2010, www.reuters.com/; Edward Yourdon, *The Dawn of the Guerrilla Programmer* (Philadelphia: Cutter Information, 1994); Sharpe, "Globalization," 222. See also Martin Campbell-Kelly and Daniel D. Garcia-Swartz, *From Mainframes to Smartphones: A History of the International Computer Industry* (Cambridge, MA: Harvard University Press, 2015), chapters 7, 8, 10.

227 King and Yadron, "Microsoft Retires"; Sharpe, "Globalization."

228 See Sinéad Baker, "More than 400 737 Max Pilots are Suing Boeing Over an 'Unprecedented Cover-Up' of Flaws in the Plane's Design," *Business Insider*, June 24, 2019, www.businessinsider.com/; Alana Samuels, "Are Pharmaceutical Companies to Blame for the Opioid Epidemic? Recent Lawsuits Are Asking Courts Whether the Current Crisis is Comparable to the One over Tobacco in the '90s," *The Atlantic*, June 2, 2017, www.theatlantic.com/; Yun-Hee Kim and John D. McKinnon, "Samsung Plans Fixes to Limit Fire Risks," *Wall Street Journal*, September 15, 2016, B1; Steele, "Opioid Addiction Climbs by 500%."

229 Brigette Honaker, *HP Class Action Alleges Printer Ink Defect*, Top Class Actions, April 16, 2020, https://topclassactions.com/; James Salmon, "License to Print Money? HP Faces Backlash after Blocking Customers from Using Cheaper Ink Cartridges in Its Printers," *Daily Mail*, September 19, 2016, www.dailymail.co.uk/. See also Bellon, "Bayer to Pay Up."

also sold ink cartridges designed to deplete quickly—or provide warnings of depletion even when a significant amount of ink was still available.[230]

Labor and production in this typology have undergone important changes during the last two decades. A "flattening" of production regimes occurred—as in-house labor was turned into TVC-type workers, "franchisees," or freelancers.[231] Companies specialized in workforce outsourcing—some of them oligopolistic—contributed to this trend, allowing many technology corporations to access skills without increasing employment.[232] The effect was to make in-house labor processes redundant, often with the help of AI.[233] In-house workers then experienced shorter deadlines, more intrusive monitoring, and performance pressures—even for complex projects that required creativity.[234] Thus, while top executive compensation rose rapidly, for labor the new normal became more difficult workplaces, job insecurity, a lack of employer-paid benefits, and in many cases salaries insufficient to meet needs.[235]

The flattening of production regimes also made it possible to split up production into autonomous units so as to better control labor processes—and implement product differentiation schemes faster. In some cases, these units were likened to "startups" because of their very lean character in terms of costs and budgets, the lack of job security and employer-paid benefits, their

230 Honaker, *HP Class Action*; Salmon, "License to Print."

231 See, for example, Wong, "Revealed: Google's 'Two-Tier'; Weber, "Video Game Makers"; Douglas MacMillan, "YouTube Policies Stir Bitterness: Video Creators, While Condemning Shooting, Complain How they are Treated," *Wall Street Journal*, April 6, 2018, B1.

232 Among the 20 largest global employers by 2017, five were workforce outsourcing oligopolists—compared to only one in 2000—with the value of contracts growing by 300 percent since. See Lauren Weber, "Outsourcing Grabs More of the Workforce," *Wall Street Journal*, December 29, 2017, B3. Research based on data from 70,000 corporations in 134 nations found that, over a 36-year period (1980–2016), outsourcing was associated with declines in labor costs and substantial increases in oligopolistic markups—Jan De Loecker and Jan Eeckhout, *Global Market Power*, NBER Working Paper 24768 (Cambridge: National Bureau of Economic Research, 2018).

233 See David Deming, "AI and Robots are Displacing Science and Tech Workers," *PBS News Hour*, January 22, 2018, www.pbs.org/; Lauren Weber, "Increasingly, Automation Reshapes Workplace Tasks," *Wall Street Journal*, January 18, 2017, B5; *The Economist*, "Manufacturing Technology: The Gemini Makers," July 15, 2017, 58–59; Sam Schechner, "Algorithms Move into Management," *Wall Street Journal*, December 11, 2017, B1.

234 See Barr, "Google Lab Puts a Time Limit"; Eric Schmidt, Jonathan Rosenberg and Alan Eagle, *How Google Works* (New York: Grand Central Publishing, 2017), 12, 22–30, 45–46, 51–53, 237–40. See also *The Economist*, "Big Brotherly Boss: Welcome to the Era of the Hyper-Surveilled Office," May 14, 2022, 62–63; and its "Digital Taylorism"; Haggin, "Wearables."

235 A survey of 356 large American corporations during the last decade found the average CEO-to-employee compensation ratio to be 241:1, with ratios as high as 350:1 in some sectors—see Equilar, *CEO Pay Ratio Survey*, 2018, www.equilar.com/; Tom Foremski, "Equilar Survey: CEO to Worker Pay Level Disparity—$8.4m to $60k: Since 2008 Median CEO Pay Has Been on an Upward Trajectory While Employee Salaries Stagnate," *ZDNet*, February 1, 2018, www.zdnet.com/.

overarching climate of urgency, and the emphasis on task execution.[236] In many cases, product differentiation capabilities were built into the units, to expedite the trajectory to marketing.

A flattening of production regimes in this typology also contributed to blur boundaries between production and product development. In some oligopolies where products are largely intangible—as in software—changes are often made "on the run"—with minimal planning and programming—to speed up differentiation and marketing. Much the same approach has been applied to customized (tangible) tech products in such areas as communication and computing hardware. After all, when in-house labor has been externalized, issues of stress, long hours, and insufficient pay tend to be forgotten by management.

The blurring of boundaries between production and product development made it easier to implement capacity-price engineering schemes, mainly because adjusting productive capacity is easier when much of the workforce is external. Thus, cancellation of (or changes in) pre-established work routines can be executed with minimal or no planning, since reassignments of personnel are largely unnecessary—as such problems are loaded unto an external workforce. A reduction of customization in production in some technology sectors also contributed to the externalization of labor—leading to greater job insecurity.

In software, the flattening of production regimes accompanied reductions in customization in recent decades. This has led to much offshoring of work processes.[237] This panorama of flattened production regimes, externalized labor, decline of in-house customization, and substantial offshoring provide deep contrasts with earlier stages of software's ascendance as a major technology sector.

The first stage of software's emergence (in the 1980s) had involved customization—production being largely *ad hoc*, based on available skills, and having much in common with research. This stage was followed (1990s) by the implementation of production regimes to keep track of schedules, output, and costs.[238] Product development was still based on the model and protocols created in-house, and production consisted largely of adapting them for specific uses.[239] The third stage (starting in the 2000s) involved standardization, along with

236 See Barr, "Google Lab Puts a Time Limit"; Jennifer Alsever, "Startups ... Inside Giant Companies: Innovation Belongs to the Smart and Nimble, Right? That's What GE, IBM, Coke and Others Think. They're Launching 'Startups' Inside Their Walls, Seeking the Elixir of Creativity," *Fortune*, May 1, 2015, 33–36; *The Economist*, "Big Brotherly Boss."

237 See Sharpe, "'Globalization': The Next Tactic," 227.

238 See Philip Kraft, *Programmers and Managers: The Routinization of Computer Programmers in the United States* (New York: Springer-Verlag, 1977), chapters 3, 4, 6.

239 See Michael A. Cusumano and Richard W. Selby, *Microsoft Secrets: How the World's Most Powerful Software Company Creates Technology, Shapes Markets, and Manages People* (New York: Touchstone, 1995), chapters 4, 5.

the flattening of work regimes and the externalization of labor. Globalization became part of this stage as offshore locales—such as Bangalore in India—attracted software production through their low labor cost.[240] Software's intangible character contributed to offshoring, as it eliminated shipping costs and supply chains.

Possibly the extreme example of the flattening of a production regime, if not also the disappearance of boundaries, has been the case of social media oligopolies. From the start, these companies depended on external labor—uncompensated uselaborers, discussed earlier—for production. Expansion of network extent guaranteed that any marginal cost would be more than offset by the advertising and app sales revenue obtained. And they welcomed societal mediation, as it provided ideas and opportunities to mine data, market targeted advertising, and sell access to uselaborer databases.

Their production, moreover, is almost completely automated—through algorithms that mine uselaborer data and target advertisements. They also involve insignificant cost relative to the surpluses obtained. Variable capital outlays are minimal, given the uncompensated nature of uselabor and the very limited conventional labor employed. And, because apps are developed by external contractors, the cost of fixed capital is shifted to them.

The same occurs for uselaborers, as they bear all costs for connectivity, hardware, utilities, time, and effort (and identity theft, should it occur). Thus, in general, capital outlays are very modest for the social media oligopolists—relative to the revenues captured through advertising, apps, and database sales. Research and product development also incur insignificant costs, given the automation of uselaborer data mining—and the fact that societal mediation itself provides the free labor and the raw material.

Inventive Appropriation

Companies that exclusively focus on undertaking research and securing property rights—typically through patents, but in some cases also copyrights and trademarks—characterize this typology. The absence of factory production, assemblage, processing, and raw material extraction differentiates this typology. *A specialized oligo-monopolistic domain therefore revolves around inventive activity and property rights—the product being intangible and largely based on uncodified knowledge.*

A specific IP niche involving a new technology often focuses activities, in the hope that it may serve as a licensing platform. Embedding various licensee business models in the platform can be an important objective. Niche capture, however, usually occurs only after a significant number of patents are

240 See the articles in Anthony P. D'Costa and Eswaran Sridharan, eds., *India in the Global Software Industry: Innovation, Firm Strategies and Development* (New York: Palgrave Macmillan, 2004).

obtained—such that a web of related inventions can become part of the platform. The complexity and time requirements of research can be substantial.

During the last decade, for example, Advanced RISC Machines (ARM)—a microprocessor design oligopolist—estimated that it can take as many as 300 man-years to design a completely new central processing unit.[241] Thus, a high degree of specialization for research regimes is often necessary, given the time commitments, uncodified knowledge, complexity, and the capital requirements.[242] But the range of products that may use the technology can be vast.[243] Legal and regulatory frameworks relevant to IP are thus fundamentally important.

Anchoring those frameworks is the notion of property as an institutionalized artifact. *Any weakening of the legal system involving IP thus poses an existential threat to the oligo-monopolistic domains in this typology*. In some cases, however, the monopoly right conferred by a patent may be lessened if existing products can achieve similar (or satisfactory) results.

To avoid this situation, patent application reviews try to set novelty, usefulness, and non-obvious features as major criteria. Similarity to existing products, treatments, processes, and formulas (or previous patents) may thus cause rejection. The application review process is not foolproof, however—although breaches tend to be uncommon and can be corrected, if discovered. Difficult issues can nonetheless be posed by some fields—such as software—where a design configured for a particular use (such as a type of computer or business process) may gain patent approval, based on its unprecedented application—as opposed to a design that can be applied across a spectrum of uses.[244]

241 *The Economist*, "Armed with A Crystal Ball: Arm Holdings' Chip Designs Already Power the World's Phones," January 5, 2019, 45. ARM—initially Acorn RISC Machine, later renamed Advanced RISC Machines—was founded in 1983, to design RISC-type processors for small computers. See Wikipedia, *Arm*, https://en.wikipedia.org/ (accessed July 29, 2022).

242 As in ARM's case. See Leo Kelion, "What is ARM and why is it worth £24bn?" *BBC News*, July 18, 2016, www.bbc.com/. An eventually unsuccessful attempt to acquire ARM for $40 billion was launched in 2020 by Nvidia—an American company specialized in microprocessor design. See Nvidia, *NVIDIA to Acquire Arm for $40 Billion, Creating World's Premier Computing Company for the Age of AI*, September 13, 2020, https://nvidianews.nvidia.com/. The acquisition was ultimately prohibited by British authorities, on grounds of national interest.

243 See ARM, *IP Products that Transform your Business: 180+ Billion Devices—from Sensors to Smartphones to Servers*, www.arm.com/; Wikipedia, *List of ARM Microarchitectures*, https://en.wikipedia.org/ (both accessed July 7, 2022); *The Economist*, "Armed with Crystal Ball"; Stephen Nellis, "Arm Holdings Unveils Chip Aimed at Self-Driving Car Sensors," *Reuters*, December 18, 2018, www.reuters.com/.

244 See Reed Albergotti, "Apple Sued by App Developer for Alleged Patent Infringement, Antitrust Violation," *Washington Post*, October 5, 2019, www.washingtonpost.com/; Ashby Jones, "Hard Questions on Software: Supreme Court Dives into Muddy Waters over Patents for Computer Applications," *Wall Street Journal*, March 31, 2014, B4; *The Economist*, "Intellectual Property: After Being Blamed for Stymying Innovation in America, Vague and Overly Broad Patents on Software and Business Processes Could Get the Chop," March 8, 2014, 14.

Any questioning of a patent's validity poses a serious threat for the oligo-monopolistic domains in this typology. This is why in the last decade many companies opposed the creation of the Patent Trial and Appeal Board (PTAB)—a review entity under the control of the U.S. Patent and Trademark Office.[245] Among the contrarian arguments was that invalidations would stifle innovation, given the additional uncertainty and risk it would create for research. Many also feared that the creation of this agency could eventually lead to the elimination of patenting—a position advocated by some specialists during the last decade.[246]

By the middle of the decade, it became clear that lawyers and financial speculators could use the PTAB to their advantage, by mounting serial challenges.[247] The latter involve requesting an *Inter Partes* review, to have a patent award re-examined.[248] Patent holders that lose may then have to pay licensing to continue using the patents they previously owned, if they have related products or platforms.

Inter Partes review requests can be coupled with financial speculation. Bets can be made in stock and options markets against the shares of the targeted company *and* its licensees. They would profit when a targeted patent is invalidated, as the owner's share price (and those of licensees) would likely decline. And, when another company (usually the challenger) gains control of the patent, its shares would rise. If a patent exists that can be used in place of the invalidated one, companies may seek licensing from its owner—thus possibly causing the latter's shares to rise. A speculator could thus bet both ways—and profit—when a targeted patent is annulled.

245 See U.S. Patent and Trademark Office, *Patent Trial and Appeal Board*, www.uspto.org/ (accessed July 29, 2022); Joseph Walker, "Patent Rule Would Raise Drug Costs," *Wall Street Journal*, September 1, 2015, B1; Ashby Jones, "New Weapon in Intellectual Property Wars: Panel Can Upend Patent Decisions, but Some Say It Goes Too Far; Like Getting CAT-Scanned, MRI-ed, and X-Rayed," *Wall Street Journal*, March 11, 2014, B4.

246 *The Economist*, "A Question of Utility," August 8, 2015, 50–52; Michele Boldrin and David K. Levine, "The Case Against Patents," *Journal of Economic Perspectives* 27 (2013), 3–22; and the articles in Stephen A. Merrill, Richard C. Levin and Mark B. Myers, eds., *A Patent System for the 21st Century* (Washington: National Academies Press, 2004); Wesley M. Cohen and Stephen A. Merrill, eds., *Patents in the Knowledge-Based Economy* (Washington: National Academies Press, 2003). Difficulties in determining the economic value of patents—an aspect often based on subjective considerations, such as potential royalties and litigation—was part of the debate. See *The Economist*, "Valuing Patents: Billion-Dollar Blueprints," December 4, 2021, 69.

247 Michael T. Renaud, Daniel B. Weinger and Serge Subach, *Better Early than Never: PTAB Confirms Willingness to Deny Institution in Light of Advanced State of Parallel Litigation*, Mintz, www.mintz.com/ (accessed September 7, 2021); Joseph Walker and Rob Copeland, "Kyle Bass Puts Drug Patents in Crosshairs," *Wall Street Journal*, April 8, 2015, B1; Peter J. Pitts, "'Patent Death Squads' vs. Innovation," *Wall Street Journal*, June 11, 2015, A13.

248 See U.S. Patent and Trademark Office, *Inter Partes Review*, www.uspto.gov/ (accessed July 29, 2022); Renaud, Weinger and Subach, *Better Early than Never*.

For the corporate domains in this typology, experimentation is at the core of work processes. Research regimes may therefore be considered pre-systematic, given the frequent need to improvise. A sense of urgency and secrecy tends to permeate these regimes, inasmuch as only first-to-file applicants can be considered for patent awards. Substantial outlays can therefore be wasted if an application's filing time happens to be behind another one involving a similar idea.

Partly because of this uncertainty, companies in this typology try to find ways to lengthen patent validity. A fairly common one involves tweaking an existing (or expired) patent's details in an application—to provide the impression that a new idea is involved.[249] Thus, the ideas behind soon-to-expire (or expired) patents may be reformulated. This approach may also be used in cases when an application is preempted by the first-to-file rule—to provide the impression that an invention is significantly different from that of the early filer.

If a patent has some validity time left, a common strategy involves finding uses that will lead to its licensing or sale. Wants contrivance is not out of the question in this quest, although much of it may be left up to the licensee. However, wants and uses that seem superfluous, or that are catered to by existing patents, can motivate lawyers (and speculators) to file for *Inter Partes* reviews—and bet financially against the company that owns the patent (and its licensees). Thus, a potential check on wants contrivance may unwittingly come from legal specialists as well as speculators.

Product marketing in this typology revolves around recruiting licensees for a patent portfolio. The larger the portfolio, the greater the likely surpluses from the monopoly and licensing rights. Much the same applies to corporate owners of copyrights, especially on branding and digital content. And, the threat of litigation against any company selling a product or service—that can be related to any patent and copyright, contested or not—can be a powerful incentive to purchase a license.

Thus, the best product marketers are often legal specialists who aggressively seek out companies to target—for "invitations" to purchase licenses. "Patent trolling"—the common name for this strategy—often targets small companies with limited resources, which can ill afford the expense of litigation. During the last decade, this became a profitable endeavor for many attorneys and their oligopolistic technology clients. One case, for example, involved sending more than 14,000 letters demanding up to $2,000 per website to small businesses

249 See Sean Hollister, "A Jury Says Intel Owes $2.18 Billion for Infringing a Zombie Chip Company's Patents," *The Verge*, March 2, 2021, www.theverge.com/; Ed Silverman, "How Far can a Drug Firm Go in Protecting its Profits?" *Wall Street Journal*, January 16, 2015, B5; *The Economist*, "Zombie Patents: Drug Companies are Adept at Extending the Lifespan of Patents, at Consumers' Expense," June 21, 2014, 72.

that used a patent-protected type of semiconductor.[250] The court determined that the total amounts owed were $0.10 per website, but the total legal fees incurred were almost $10 million.[251]

Court cases involve much uncertainty about outcomes, given that juries in the United States often lack the expertise to evaluate whether a patent has been infringed. Thus, outcomes may be determined by personality features and body language—as jurors make decisions based on how they are impressed by witnesses and lawyers. It should not surprise, therefore, that about 99 percent of all patent infringement cases are settled out of court—and the settlements, which are usually confidential, may involve large amounts of money. Patent trolling can thus be quite effective—turning the pursuing oligopolist into a rentier of sorts, for the remaining validity of a patent (or until usage stops).

Labor in this typology can be considered an elite, because of the intangible-rich character of work and expertise, and the autonomy to determine work processes on some projects. Experimentation often requires diverse, complex uncodified knowledge, and much collaborative work, particularly in very new fields—for which there is no established educational or professional track. In synthetic biology, genomics, or bio-pharmacology projects, for example, highly specialized research workers from microbiology, medicine, chemistry, bioinformatics, ecology, and epidemiology often collaborate with each other and with legal specialists to file patent applications and design clinical trials. The hardware utilized can involve custom-made laboratory equipment and very fast computers to decode DNA and analyze vast amounts of data, and an understanding of very rare organisms.[252]

In nanotechnology, molecular chemists, materials scientists, toxicologists, industrial engineers, and lawyers often have to collaborate closely to be able to file a patent application—using one-of-a-kind laboratory equipment that requires much expertise. Much the same can be said for other advanced technology fields, such as bio-robotics, laser electronics, and genetic engineering. It would, however, be naïve to think that such talented personnel are fully compensated for the intellectual property they create, or for the future revenue streams that—through licensing or marketing—will accumulate over time. In

250 John Chambers and Myron E. Ullman, "Stopping the Economy-Sapping Patent Trolls," *Wall Street Journal*, February 17, 2015, A9. See also Stefan Lederer, "The Growing Problem of U.S. Patent Trolls, and What Should Happen Next," *Forbes*, July 22, 2021, www.forbes.com/; Roger Parloff, "Taking On the Patent Trolls," *Fortune*, March 17, 2014, 133–40.

251 Chambers and Ullman, "Stopping the Economy-Sapping," A9.

252 Those found at previously inaccessible ocean depths, in particular, have long been targets for DNA decoding and patenting. See Paul Oldham, Stephen Hall and Colin Barnes, *Marine Genetic Resources in Patent Data*, United Nations University, www.un.org/ (accessed April 3, 2022); Marjo Vierros, Curtis A. Suttle, Harriet Harden-Davies and Geoff Burton, *Who Owns the Ocean? Policy Issues Surrounding Marine Genetic Resources*, Association of the Sciences for Limnology and Oceanography, May 2016, htpps://aslopubs.onlinelibrary.wiley.com/; Porter Hoagland, *Patent Activity in the Seabed Mining Industry* (Woods Hole: Woods Hole Oceanographic Institution, 1985).

this sense, labor in this typology can be considered exploited, though not in the same way as that involved in factory production, tech services, or TVC-type arrangements.

The issue of exploitation here is grounded on the surpluses and wealth generated by the inventions created by researchers—who are, after all, labor—and the fact that those surpluses and the results of their work are appropriated by their employer. Patent awards are, paradoxically, granted to individuals, and only afterward can a recipient "assign" a patent to a corporate entity (a standard, legally binding requirement for employment).[253] Thereby, the legal system acknowledges that the research worker whose name appears on the patent award is the author and owner—despite appeals over the years for corporations to be treated as "persons" under patent law.

In sum, the variety of activities that now operate outside conventional notions of production and labor is breathtaking. Internal control is evolving, with intangibles becoming prime assets and commodities, labor facing greater insecurity, workplace rights declining, AI taking over many tasks, and the results of creativity being expropriated more brazenly than ever. Also, the intense drive to come up with ideas and uncodified knowledge—to differentiate products or obtain IP—has split commodification from reproduction. The boundaries and projection of the corporate domain, meanwhile, have become more fluid, as oligopolistic power expands—commanding the public to pay or forgo use or gain usage through free labor.

It should not surprise, then, that the elements and phenomena of transformation involve interactions that are fragmented, complex, and often contradictory. *A common feature binding these elements and phenomena is the exploitation of human toil and talent.* Yet, labor's possibility of partaking in the wealth it creates is diminished.

This sheds light on another important feature of the transformative dynamic—*the exploitation of technology to generate great wealth for a minuscule set of very powerful interests.* Notions of social benefit and utility thus seem to have been discarded—in favor of maximum returns in the shortest possible time—for the minute elite in control. An important and potentially very tragic result of this panorama is that technology is now harnessed to a socioeconomic system that is inherently dysfunctional.

253 See U.S. Patent and Trademark Office, *301 Ownership/Assignability of Patents and Applications [R-07.2015]*, www.uspto.gov/ (accessed April 6, 2022); Quora, "How Do Big Companies Reward their Employees for Patents?" www.quora.com (accessed April 7, 2022); Soonhee Jang, *Inventor Compensation in the U.S.*, American Intellectual Property Law Association, April 2013, www.aipla.org/.

Chapter 5

Dysfunction

The most important dysfunctions of technology oligopoly capitalism are systemic. They result from relations of power that transcend narrow specificity, incidental circumstance, and the vagaries of effect. Yet, paradoxically, the reality of dysfunction is felt through specific scenarios, recurring circumstances, and consequences that persist.

The dysfunctions of technology oligopoly capitalism are diverse, fragmented, and complex. Abuse is their common consequence. Abuse of society, of nature, and of our existence. Abuse that results from exploitive actions and operational modes. And, abuse of technology to make exploitation more lucrative and efficient. Writing a chapter that considers the dysfunctional panorama of technology oligopoly capitalism is therefore a daunting endeavor, but potentially also a rewarding one.

Our journey through the labyrinths of dysfunction will necessarily be broad, with systemic awareness being an important companion. Much evidence will be cited and discussed, and many examples from our time and recent decades will provide perspective. Dysfunction that involves employment, consumption, data appropriation and wants promotion will be given attention first. Consideration of the dysfunctional character of waste and its effects on our existence, nature, and the planet will follow. Dysfunctions involving the commons and their effects on access and the appropriation of resources will be taken up thereafter. Discussions will build upon those of previous chapters to advance an inclusive vision of technology oligopoly capitalism.

Employment

An important dysfunctional mode involves technology oligopoly capitalism's impact on employment. This dysfunction results from a set of factors that are interrelated and difficult to isolate, but which are strongly associated with oligopolistic concentration. Previous chapters have provided much discussion and details on pathologies involving labor. This section will consider aspects of employment and work not addressed previously.

DOI: 10.4324/9781003345893-5

Technocapitalist Control

Intrusive control and deskilling of employment are important dysfunctions of our time. This is underlain by *deepening links between technology, managerial control, and oligopolistic power.* It is a phenomenon that I have referred to as *technocapitalist control*, broadly defined.[1]

Technology and engineering have long been entwined with oligopolistic power—as ways are endlessly devised to obtain efficiency through acceleration of routines, intrusive monitoring, and manipulation of tasks. Such measures are at the core of technocapitalist control. Deskilling of work is an important consequence—an outcome that in our time is accompanied by the introduction of artificial intelligence (AI) and related hardware.

Three aspects are involved in deskilling.[2] The first one is management's manipulation of technical knowledge to control work processes. This asymmetrical relationship between the management and the workers requires subservience and leaves little or no room for negotiation—or autonomy. A second aspect involves the alienation of skills from tasks and processes, as workers become overqualified. The result all too often involves insecure employment, stagnant or lower real compensation, or unemployment.

The third aspect involves the alienation of task execution from conception. Work and employment in this case lose their connection to decisions regarding task design, the organization of what needs to be done, its performance (including measurement), and the final product. These aspects often result in demoralization and disruption of social time—the ensemble of rhythms and routines that underpin how we derive meaning and social gratification from work.[3]

Technocapitalist control also involves highly intrusive monitoring and the near impossibility of negotiating for higher wages.[4] Monitoring involves

1 Luis Suarez-Villa, *Technocapitalism: A Critical Perspective on Technological Innovation and Corporatism* (Philadelphia: Temple University Press, 2009), 8–24, 140–50; and his *Globalization and Technocapitalism: The Political Economy of Corporate Power and Technological Domination* (London: Ashgate, 2012), 97–144.

2 Harry Braverman's pioneering contribution needs to be acknowledged—see his *Labor and Monopoly Capital: The Degradation of Work in the Twentieth Century* (New York: Monthly Review Press, 1974). An updated overview of his analyses is in R. Jamil Jonna and John Bellamy Foster, "Beyond the Degradation of Labor: Braverman and the Structure of the U.S. Working Class," *Monthly Review*, October 2014, 1–23.

3 See Benjamin H. Snyder, *The Disrupted Workplace: Time and the Moral Order of Flexible Capitalism* (New York: Oxford University Press, 2016), chapters 1, 2, 4. See also Henri Lefebvre, *Rhythmanalysis: Space, Time and Everyday Life* (New York: Continuum, 2004), chapters 2, 6; and his *Éléments de Rythmanalyse* (Paris: Syllepse, 1992).

4 A matter that drew attention during the last decade—see Suresh Naidu, Eric Posner and Glen Weyl, "More and More Companies Have Monopoly Power Over Workers' Wages," *Vox*, April 6, 2018, www.vox.com/; Rachel Feintzeig and Rachel Silverman, "Haggle over Salary? It's not allowed," *Wall Street Journal*, May 27, 2015, B1.

intimate surveillance—performed by AI and followed by the second, by specific tasks, physical displacement, and location.[5] Personality characteristics, interpersonal behavior, intimate preferences, contacts—often linked to biometric data—are part of such monitoring.[6]

Monitoring can also involve detailed knowledge of health problems and control over the selection of physicians to treat them—to reduce care costs (if the employer provides such benefit).[7] Database clouds and platforms where that information is stored can be expanded to include details on life preferences, habits, life cycle changes, and relations with management. Such data usually influence evaluations, dismissals, and wages. And, the information might be made available to potential employers and even marketers.[8]

One feature of technocapitalist control is that skills that are scarce often do not garner higher compensation or greater employment security. Also, skills can be diminished through technical adjustments that restructure tasks. No task or activity in existence can now be considered immune to being taken over by AI. And, the number of specialists required to maintain AI tends to be much less than the workers that are displaced.[9]

5 Ivan Manokha, "New Means of Workplace Surveillance: From the Gaze of the Supervisor to the Digitalization of Employees," *Monthly Review*, February 2019, 25–39; Te-Ping Chen, "Three Hours of Work a Day? You're Not Fooling Anyone: Employers are Arming Themselves with New, More Aggressive Technology to Measure How Workers Spend their Time," *Wall Street Journal*, July 20, 2019, B7; Amy Delgado, "Employee Privacy at Stake as Surveillance Technology Evolves," *CBS News*, August 14, 2018, www/cbsnews.com/. Emily Guendelsberger's *On the Clock: What Low-Wage Work Did to Me and How it Drives America Insane* (New York: Little, Brown, 2019), provides insights on the intensity of monitoring that can be expected in precariat-type employment.

6 Sarah Krouse, "The New Ways Your Boss is Spying on You: It's Not Just Your Email—Employers are Mining the Data their Workers Generate to Figure Out What They're Up to, and With Whom; There's Almost Nothing You Can Do About It," *Wall Street Journal*, July 20, 2019, B1; Jeb Su, "Confirmed: Apple Caught in Siri Privacy Scandal, Let Contractors Listen to Private Voice Recordings," *Forbes*, July 30, 2019, www.forbes.com/; Ifeoma Ajunwa, Kate Crawford and Jason Schultz, "Limitless Worker Surveillance," *California Law Review* 105 (2017), 735–76.

7 Melanie Evans, "Employers Seek a Say in Picking Workers' Doctors," *Wall Street Journal*, April 5, 2019, B1.

8 Te-Ping Chen, "Biometrics at Work Trigger Backlash: Some Employees Worry Data from Fingerprint and Facial Scans will End Up with Marketers or Hackers," *Wall Street Journal*, March 28, 2019, B6.

9 Particularly in tech-service occupations. See Mike Colias and Marc Vartabedian, "Robots Tackle Food Delivery," *Wall Street Journal*, March 12, 2019, B1; Christopher M. Matthews, "Technology Spells End of Roughneck Boom: Artificial Intelligence and Automation Replace Oil Industry's Lucrative, Blue-Collar Jobs," *Wall Street Journal*, July 11, 2018, A1; Ben Leubsdorf, "Driverless Cars May Alter 1 in 9 Jobs," *Wall Street Journal*, August 15, 2017, A2; Jon LeSage, "Goldman Sachs: Self-Driving Trucks will Kill 300,000 Jobs per Year," *Business Insider*, November 15, 2017, www.businessinsider.com/.

The rise of precarious employment has thus accompanied greater technocapitalist control.[10] Among the characteristics are low wages that can vary greatly from one week to the next, a lack of pre-determined workdays, hours, and activities, and the absence of defined working spaces and employee rights.[11] The vast majority of tech-service oligopolists already draw most of their employment from this population.

Compensation and Productivity

It should not surprise, then, that during the last decade *workers in large (usually oligopolistic) corporations were found to receive lower compensation and experience greater insecurity*.[12] By the middle of the last decade, as many as 20 million individuals were estimated to be in those categories, with compensation that was 25 percent or less than for in-house workers.[13] And in large software and biopharmaceutical companies, TVC (temporary–vendor–contractor) workers were estimated to be twice as many as in-house employees.[14]

During the last decade, for example, it was estimated that at Google—one of the wealthiest corporations in history—about half of its employees were TVC-type workers.[15] Google's TVC workforce performed some of the more important tasks—such as reviewing legal documents, developing marketing

10 See Robert Reich, "Almost 80% of U.S. Workers Live from Paycheck to Paycheck—Here's Why: America Doesn't Have a Jobs Crisis, it has a 'Good Jobs' Crisis, Where Too Much Employment is Insecure, and Poorly Paid," *The Guardian*, July 29, 2018, www.theguardian.com/; Ricardo Antunes, "The New Service Proletariat," *Monthly Review*, April 2018, 23–29; Guy Standing, *The Precariat: The New Dangerous Class* (London: Bloomsbury, 2016).

11 Antunes, "New Service Proletariat"; Reich, "Almost 80% of U.S. Workers."

12 See Philip Mattera, *Grand Theft Paycheck: The Large Corporations Shortchanging their Workers' Wages* (Washington: Corporate Research Project of Good Jobs First and Jobs with Justice Education Fund, 2018); Lydia DePillis, "Big Companies Used to Pay the Best Wages. Not Any More," *CNN Business*, January 18, 2018, https://money.cnn.com/; Theo Francis, "Bigger Company but Not Big Pay: U.S. Workers Moving from Smaller Firms No Longer Get as Big a Boost in Compensation," *Wall Street Journal*, January 11, 2018, B6; Naidu, Posner and Weyl, "More and More Companies."

13 Lawrence F. Katz and Alan B. Krueger, *The Rise and Nature of Alternative Work Arrangements in the United States, 1995–2015*, March 29, 2016, https://krueger.princeton.edu/.

14 Katz and Krueger, *Rise and Nature*; Lauren Weber, "The End of Employees: U.S. Companies Shift Work Once Considered Core to Contractors, Pruning Costs and Job Security," *Wall Street Journal*, February 3, 2017, A1.

15 *Quora*, "Why do Google Contractors (TVCs) Have Such a Low Chance of Getting Full Time Offers and Such a High Chance of Getting Fired," www.quora.com/ (accessed August 19, 2022); Joshua Brustein, "Apple's 'Black Site' Gives Contract Workers Few Perks and Little Job Security," *Los Angeles Times*, February 12, 2019, www.latimes.com/; Mark Bergen and Josh Eidelson, "Inside Google's Shadow Workforce: About Half of Google's Workers are Contractors Who Don't Receive the Same Benefits as Direct Employees," *Bloomberg*, July 25, 2018, www.bloomberg.com/; Julia C. Wong, "Revealed: Google's 'Two-Tier' Workforce Training Document—Exclusive Internal Document Shows How Google Employees are Trained to Treat Temps, Vendors and Contractors," *The Guardian*, December 12, 2018, www.theguardian.com/.

programs, and managing data software.[16] And, because the TVC workforce was external, it was easier for Google to execute retaliatory actions when grievances were raised.[17]

In other oligopolistic technology corporations, TVC employment during the last decade was estimated to be at least twice as much as that in the conventional, in-house workforce—with compensation that could be 25 percent lower.[18] More than a quarter of all TVC workers were estimated to be receiving public welfare benefits—such as food stamps, partial income support, or health care.[19] Part of the employment cost was thus shifted to taxpayers—a form of corporate welfare that is hardly ever noticed by the public.

This scenario was accompanied by a rapid rise in executive compensation to historically unprecedented levels—leading to a higher concentration of both income and wealth at the top of the economic ladder.[20] A significant, long-term inverse relationship between payrolls and profit accompanied this trend.[21] Thus, employment's share of gross domestic product (GDP) in the American economy continued its five-decade-long decline—a symptom of dysfunctionality in employment that seems set to continue indefinitely.[22] As with other trends, this panorama was accompanied by rising oligopolistic concentration.[23]

Dysfunctionality in employment and compensation is also reflected in the long-term erosion of the middle class. From 61 percent of the population in

16 Bergen and Eidelson, "Inside Google's Shadow"; Wong, "Revealed: Google's."

17 Julia Carrie Wong, "Demoted and Sidelined: Google Walkout Organizers Say Company Retaliated—Staff Who Organized Mass Protests Say in Internal Letter their Roles were Changed after November 2018 Demonstration," *The Guardian*, April 22, 2019, www.theguardian.com/.

18 Ellen Sheng, "Silicon Valley's Dirty Secret: Using a Shadow Workforce of Contract Employees to Drive Profits," *CNBC*, October 22, 2018, www.cnbc.com/; Lauren Weber, "The End of Employees: U.S. Companies Shift Work Once Considered Core to Contractors, Pruning Costs and Job Security," *Wall Street Journal*, February 3, 2017, A1; Bergen and Eidelson, "Inside Google's Shadow Workforce."

19 Katz and Krueger, *Rise and Nature of Alternative Work*; Weber, "End of Employees."

20 Theo Francis, "Big Firms Pay CEOs $1 Million a Month," *Wall Street Journal*, March 18, 2019, B1; Theo Francis and Joann S. Lublin, "CEO Pay Reached New High in 2017," *Wall Street Journal*, March 22, 2018, B1; Robert McMillan, "Big Payday for Apple CEO: In Filing, Cook Says He Received 1.26 million Shares of Apple, Valued at $135 Million," *Wall Street Journal*, August 29, 2016, B6.

21 See Oliver Scott, "10% of the U.S. Richest Hold 69% of the Country's Entire Household Wealth," *Finbold*, April 20, 2021, www.finbold.com/; *The Economist*, "Corporate Realpolitik"; Katz and Krueger, *Rise and Nature*.

22 A major point in Thomas Piketty's *Capital in the Twenty First Century*, A. Goldhammer, trans. [(Cambridge, MA: Harvard University Press, 2014), orig. publ. as *Le Capital au XXI Siècle* (Paris: Seuil, 2013)], chapters 5, 6, 9, 10. Labor's share of corporate income also declined significantly in recent decades—see Paul Kiernan, "Workers Claim a Shrinking Slice of the Pie," *Wall Street Journal*, February 25, 2019, A2; Josh Bivens, *The Decline in Labor's Share of Corporate Income Since 2000 Means $535 Billion Less for Workers*, Economic Policy Institute, September 10, 2015, www.epi.org/.

23 Luis Suarez-Villa, *Corporate Power, Oligopolies, and the Crisis of the State* (Albany: State University of New York Press, 2016), 233–37.

1971, the middle-income segment declined to 51 percent in 2011, and then largely stagnated during the last decade—while the "lower" class (the poor and many working people) increased from 25 percent to almost 30 percent (up to the middle of the last decade).[24] And, inflation-adjusted median weekly income stagnated from the start of the twenty-first century through the end of the last decade.[25] In 1970, inflation-adjusted incomes of about 90 percent of 30-year olds in the United States were higher than those of their parents at the same age. By the middle of the last decade, however, only about 50 percent of those in that age group were in that situation.[26]

These dysfunctions have had a negative impact on productivity. Thus, the long-term stagnation in worker productivity—a trend that started by the end of the twentieth century and continued through the last decade. Levels of about (or below) one percent annual growth became the norm.[27] This trend was accompanied by a long-term—four-decade long—decline in U.S. worker productivity growth vis-à-vis compensation.[28]

It is noteworthy that since the 1970s a massive introduction and use of new technologies occurred that should have substantially improved worker productivity. The declining long-term trend is therefore distressing, inasmuch as *achieving (and sustaining) higher productivity is considered to be the key to greater economic wellbeing*. Stagnant long-term productivity thus all too often leads to declining living standards.

Long-Term Deficit

This dysfunction can be related to a phenomenon that will likely affect employment negatively over the long term. *This is the apparent tendency of new technologies in our time to eliminate more jobs than those they create*. Technologies that may

24 See OECD, *Under Pressure: The Squeezed Middle Class* (Paris: OECD, 2019); Pew Research Center, *The Lost Decade of the American Middle Class: Fewer, Poorer, Gloomier*, August 22, 2012, www.pewsocialtrends.org/. See also Marianne Cooper, *Cut Adrift: Families in Insecure Times* (Berkeley: University of California Press, 2014); Andrew J. Cherlin, *Labor's Love Lost: The Rise and Fall of the Working-Class Family in America* (New York: Russell Sage Foundation, 2014).

25 See *The Economist*, "Social Mobility in America," November 6, 2021, 18–20; Raj Chetty, David Grusky, Maximilian Hell, *et al.*, *The Fading American Dream: Trends in Absolute Income Mobility since 1940*, NBER Working Paper 22910, December 2016, www.nber.org/. For a historical (data-based) overview of changes in the living standard see Robert J. Gordon, *The Rise and Fall of American Growth: The U.S. Standard of Living Since the Civil War* (Princeton: Princeton University Press, 2016), chapters 10–15, 18.

26 Chetty, Grusky, Hell, *et al.*, *Fading American Dream*; *The Economist*, "Social Mobility in America"; and its "Inequality: Fat Tails," January 7, 2017, 21–22.

27 Federal Reserve Bank of St. Louis, Economic Research, *Private Non-Farm Business Sector: Labor Productivity (MPU4910063)*, https://fred.stlouisfed.org/ (accessed March 12, 2022).

28 Economic Policy Institute, *The Productivity-Pay Gap: The Gap between Productivity and a Typical Worker's Compensation has Increased Dramatically Since 1973*, August 2018, www.epi.org/.

gain widespread usage as the twenty-first century advances—such as biocomputing, nano-electroceuticals, molecular robotics, advanced AI, and genetic engineering—may create jobs that will require sophisticated skills that cannot be easily automated—*but* that will employ fewer people. It thus seems unlikely that these new technologies will generate much employment for the middle- or less-skilled population. Or, at least, to the same extent that new technologies in the nineteenth and first half of the twentieth centuries did.

Textile machinery, steam power, steel, railroads, electricity, internal combustion engines, telegraphy, vehicles, telephony, aviation, radio, films, and television all led to the creation of much employment—through vast ecologies of small enterprises, most of them locally based. And, this expansion occurred through the creation of new businesses that all too often remained small—or grew large over a considerable period of time. Also, these businesses created and nurtured jobs that provided skills that could lead to a life-long occupation or a profession. These important features are largely missing from current times.

The contemporary concentration dynamic may thus provide a deep contrast with the employment impact of new technologies in prior times—when oligopolistic power was neither as deep nor as widespread as it is now. Media discussions on this topic during the last decade generated much wishful thinking.[29] Also, the expressed views by and large ignored the oligopolistic panorama that characterizes our time. Thus, the hard reality that new technologies may not generate enough employment to replace the jobs they eliminate is all too easily dismissed or forgotten, despite accumulating evidence.

Short-term fluctuations aside, the long-term trend—1970s onwards—has shown that the decline in manufacturing employment in the United States has been pronounced.[30] And conventional (also referred to as "routine") employment was estimated to have stagnated in recent decades.[31] The long-term

29 See Christopher Mims, "Why Aren't There More U.S. Robots? Automation is the Key to Creating Wealth—and Jobs—Economists, Say, and the U.S. is Falling Behind," *Wall Street Journal*, December 1, 2018, www.wsj.com/; and his "Automation Can Actually Lead to More Job Creation," *Wall Street Journal*, December 12, 2016, B1; Mark P. Mills, "The Cyber Age has Hardly Begun," *Wall Street Journal*, September 18, 2017, A17; Andy Kessler, "The Robots are Coming—Welcome Them," *Wall Street Journal*, August 23, 2016, A11; James B. Hagerty, "Meet the New Robots: They are Nimbler and Work Better with Humans—and they Might Even Help Bring Manufacturing Back to the U.S.," *Wall Street Journal*, June 3, 2015, R1; Martin Neil Baily, "How the U.S. Gets Manufacturing Policy All Wrong: Washington Measures Success by the Number of Jobs—that's a Losing Strategy," *Wall Street Journal*, June 3, 2015, R5. An exception was Greg Ip's "Economic Drag: Few Big Ideas—Dwindling Gains in Science, Technology and Medicine are a Hidden Damper on Economic Growth," *Wall Street Journal*, December 7, 2016, A1.

30 Federal Reserve Bank of St. Louis, Economic Research, *Manufacturing Sector: Employment (PRS30006013)*; its *All Employees: Manufacturing (MANEMP)*; and its *All Employees: Manufacturing/ All Employees: Total Non-Farm Payrolls*, https://fred.stlouisfed.org/ (all accessed July 14, 2022).

31 *The Economist*, "Stay of Execution," June 19, 2021, 72; U.S. Bureau of Labor Statistics, *Civilian labor Force Participation Rate*, www.data.bls.gov/ (accessed July 29, 2022); Maximiliano A. Dvorkin, *Jobs*

employment decline in manufacturing—and the stagnation in conventional employment—occurred as many new technologies were introduced that came into widespread use. Those new technologies did not manage to reverse this dynamic, despite many expectations to the contrary. Also, innovation in long-established industries—such as the replacement of internal combustion engines with electric batteries—failed to overcome this trend.[32]

Accompanying this panorama was the stagnation of long-term total factor productivity—an indicator that encompasses the effects of technological innovation.[33] It peaked in the 1950s, when oligopolistic concentration intensified across the American economy.[34] At that point, the economic impacts of important technologies in various fields—such as steel, electricity, railroads, the internal combustion engine—were leveling off. Since then, the total factor productivity has largely stagnated, with average long-term annual growth rates of about 1 percent.[35] This occurred despite the fact that R&D spending—as a share of GDP—reached historically high levels repeatedly since that time.[36]

Involving Routine Tasks aren't Growing, Federal Reserve Bank of St. Louis, January 4, 2016, www.stlouisfed.org/.

32 See Christoph Rauwald, David Welch and Anurag Kotoky, "Carmakers Shedding 80,000 Jobs as Electric Era Upends Industry," *Bloomberg*, December 3, 2019, www.bloomberg.com/.

33 Although it has been alleged occasionally that official statistics tend to underestimate total factor productivity, this problem has declined over time—and it has been observed that this indicator remains at historically low levels. See Brent R. Moulton, *The Measurement of Output, Prices, and Productivity: What's Changed since the Boskin Commission?* Hutchins Center on Fiscal and Monetary Policy, Brookings Institution, July 2018, www.brookings.edu/; Greg Ip, "The Case Against a Stealth Productivity Boom," *Wall Street Journal*, July 26, 2018, A2; and his "Economic Drag."

34 Federal Reserve Bank of St. Louis, Economic Research, *Total Factor Productivity at Constant National Prices for United States*, https://fred.stlouisfed.org/; Bureau of Labor Statistics, *Multifactor Productivity*, www.bls.gov/ (both accessed July 15, 2022).

35 Stagnation in total factor productivity during the twenty-first century was associated with oligopolistic concentration by Thomas Philippon in his *The Great Reversal: How America Gave Up on Free Markets* (Cambridge, MA: Harvard University Press, 2019), chapters 3–5. Although certain economists argue from time to time that statistics do not measure productivity adequately, better ways to measure productivity have not been devised. Also, new approaches to measurement would introduce discontinuities in the historical data series. See Timothy Aeppel, "U.S. Productivity: Missing or Hiding?" *Wall Street Journal*, July 17, 2015, A1. An explanatory attempt—the "productivity J-curve"—assumed that output is reduced as companies shift resources to intangibles when they adopt new technologies. The result, this approach argues, is lower output that does not correspond with any reduction in employment or capital. Later, as intangibles have an effect, it is assumed that productivity would surge as output increases—the benefit of the new technologies coming into effect. However, the fact that the expected "surge" has *not* materialized in five decades—in the total factor productivity data—is left unexplained. See Erik Brynjolfsson, Daniel Rock and Chad Syverson, *The Productivity J-Curve: How Intangibles Complement General Purpose Technologies*, NBER Working Paper 25148, January 2020, www.nber.org/.

36 OECD, *Gross Domestic Spending on R&D*, https://data.oecd.org/; American Association for the Advancement of Science, *Historical R&D Data*, www.aaas.org/ (both accessed August 15, 2022); Jason Douglas, Jon Sindreu and Georgi Kantchev, "World's Biggest Companies Hog Gains from

Research on automation—assigning probabilistic estimates based on the functional character of occupations—has indicated that during the coming two decades possibly half of American workers may see their jobs automated.[37] The reduction generated by AI alone has been forecast to be 6.2 billion man-hours globally by the early 2020s—much of it in the United States.[38] In occupations that have provided some skill or led to better-compensated employment, the impact would be substantial.[39] In professional driving, for example, it was estimated by Goldman Sachs that the use of autonomous (self-driven) vehicles may lead to 300,000 job losses annually during the 2020s and 2030s.[40]

Some of the most complex or knowledge-intensive occupations—such as software design, scientific research, and navigation—are already being affected by automation.[41] Software programming has been automating rapidly, as specialized AI is now capable of taking ideas and turning them into code without

---

Innovation: Benefits aren't Trickling Down, a Possible Choke on Productivity Growth," *Wall Street Journal*, July 16, 2018, A1; *The Economist*, "Net Gains and Losses: The Internet has Not yet Produced the Hoped-For Productivity Miracle," August 17, 2013, 61. The number of U.S. patent awards *also* filed in Europe and Japan (often taken as an indicator of their importance or potential value) declined by a quarter during the twenty-first century—a matter that Tyler Cowen—in his *The Complacent Class: The Self-Defeating Quest for the American Dream* (New York: St. Martin's, 2017), Chapter 4—attributes to the decline of innovation, and to his assessment that most innovations tend to be incremental rather than transcendental. This evaluation can be associated with the advance of oligopolistic concentration in the American economy, and the emphasis on product development (as opposed to research), discussed earlier in this book.

37 Carl B. Frey and Michael A. Osborne "The Future of Employment: How Susceptible are Jobs to Computerisation?" *Technological Forecasting and Social Change* 114 (2017), 254–80. In subsequent comments, co-author Frey noted that their conclusion is "historical" and that the effect of automation on employment may change over time, possibly generating unspecified positive results—see Carl B. Frey, *Technology Trap: Capital, Labor and Power in the Age of Automation* (Princeton: Princeton University Press, 2019), chapters 12, 13.

38 Gartner, *AI Augmentation Will Create $2.9 Trillion of Business Value in 2021: Decision Support and AI Augmentation to Surpass All Other Types of AI Initiatives*, August 5, 2019, www.gartner.com/; *The Economist*, "The Digital Assembly Line: Technology Firms Vie for Billions in Data-Analytics Contracts," September 7, 2019, 57–58. Additions of "business value" due to AI avoid consideration of reductions in employment. Losses might therefore be greater than expected.

39 See Richard E. Baldwin, *The Globotics Upheaval: Globalization, Robotics, and the Future of Work* (New York: Oxford University Press, 2019), chapters 6, 7; Darrell M. West, *The Future of Work: Robots, AI, and Automation* (Washington: Brookings Institution, 2018), chapters 1, 2, 4; Andrew Keen, *The Internet is Not the Answer* (New York: Atlantic Monthly, 2015), chapters 3, 6–8; Martin Ford, *Rise of the Robots: Technology and the Threat of a Jobless Future* (New York: Basic Books, 2015), chapters 1, 4.

40 Anita Balakrishnan, "Self-Driving Cars could cost America's Professional Drivers Up to 25,000 Jobs a Month, Goldman Sachs Says," *CNBC*, May 22, 2017, www.cnbc.com/; LeSage, "Goldman Sachs: Self-Driving Trucks."

41 See Laura Kusisto, "3-D Printing Reaches Real Estate," *Wall Street Journal*, March 12, 2019, A3; John Bohannon, "A New Breed of Scientist, with Brains of Silicon," *Science*, July 5, 2017, www.sciencemag.org/; Robert Wall and Costas Paris, "Pilotless Sailing is on the Horizon: Freight Carriers Aim to Optimize Use of Vessels, Cut their Fuel and Labor Costs," *Wall Street Journal*, September 1, 2016, B8.

human assistance.[42] A statement by an eminent specialist is indicative of the reality we may be facing: "Almost anything that a typical person can do with less than one second of mental thought, we can either now or in the very near future automate with AI."[43]

Consumer Exploitation

A major systemic dysfunction of technology oligopoly capitalism involves consumption. Oligopolistic price manipulation is at the core of this dysfunction. Only forgoing purchase can provide avoidance—an unrealistic prospect for most consumers. And, switching products is usually unhelpful—price setting all too often involving tacit, follow-the-leader collusion.[44]

Pricing power over markets practically guarantees that consumer exploitation will occur, as this is a most important source of surpluses. Consumer exploitation by technology oligopolies tends to be extensive, and it occurs through various means. New technologies tend to reduce effort and time—making it difficult to avoid purchase. The only options available may be to continue using an older technology—or to do without and incur difficulties. Thus, the consumer's only hope may be that higher pricing can be offset by any reduction in effort and time.

The intrusive character of many technologies promotes exploitation. Most any aspect of life can be a target for sales, surveillance, data mining, and behavioral influence. This can involve inducing purchase of treatments or accessories without which a product may not work well—or at all. Inducing personal habits that tether the consumer to a product—causing addiction that leads to greater consumption—is another way.

At the core of consumer exploitation is that product pricing is rigged, and the bounds—if there are any—are set by the oligopolistic corporations in control. Thus, consumer demand is subordinated to the manipulation of pricing

42 Will Knight, "AI Can Write Code like Humans—Bugs and All," *Wired*, September 20, 2021, www.wired.com/; *The Economist*, "Automating Programming: The Software-Software Engineers; Artificial Intelligence is Transforming the Way Computer Programs are Written," July 10, 2021, 71–72.

43 Andrew Ng (chief scientist at Baidu, also co-founder of education startup Coursera), quoted in Scott Austin, "How AI will Change Everything," *Wall Street Journal*, March 7, 2017, R2. See also Martin Ford, "AI and Automation will Disrupt Our World—but Only Andrew Yang is Warning about it," *The Hill*, November 10, 2019, https://thehill.com/.

44 The importance of oligopolistic pricing was noted by one of the best-known financiers in recent history—Warren Buffett: "the single most important decision in evaluating a business is pricing power ... If you've got the power to raise prices without losing business to a competitor, you've got a very good business." Quoted in Andrew Frye and Dakin Campbell, "Buffett Says Pricing Power More Important than Good Management," *Bloomberg*, February 17, 2011, www.bloomberg.com/. See also *The Economist*, "Pricing Power: Passing the Buck—Businesses' Ability to Pass on Costs is Highly Prized by Investors," November 6, 2021, 57–58.

and the deployment of related strategies—such as capacity-price engineering (considered in the previous chapter), and diverse purchase stimulation schemes. The fact that pricing may be set in tacit ways—without overt collusion—does not make it less harmful. For, oligopolistic pricing involves a zero-sum scenario where only winning or losing can occur—and the consumer is usually the loser.

Pricing Differential

The difference between oligopolistic and competitive product pricing is at the core of consumer exploitation. Recalling accumulation, the *competitive* scenario involves a recurrent dynamic, $M \rightarrow C \rightarrow C' \rightarrow M'$, where new money-capital (M')—a result of each iteration of the productive cycle—is necessary to restart accumulation. A large number of sellers provide a similar product for every market segment, and the price to be paid is left up to the interplay of output supply and consumer demand. Changes in demand thus affect pricing directly, and the competitive price paid by a consumer for any given product may be represented as P'.

In the *oligopolistic* product market scenario, however, the recurrent dynamic, $M \rightarrow C \rightarrow C' \rightarrow M^N$, involves either tacit or overt price collusion. Thus, the price paid by consumers, P^N, is greater than the one paid in the competitive case. The basis of consumer exploitation for any given product's purchase may then be represented as: $P^N - P'$. The oligopolistic surplus (ΔN) obtained depends on that price differential, such that:

$$(P^N - P') = [(M + \Delta m + \Delta N) - (M + \Delta m)] = \Delta N$$

where M and Δm are initial money-capital and surplus value, respectively (as discussed earlier in this book). Estimating these entities is outside the scope of this work, but it should not be more difficult than, say, calibrating the value of such financial instruments as collateralized debt obligations or barrier option contracts.

Add-Ons

Another aspect is that oligopolistic pricing often involves additional cost to consumers (beyond the price differential above). These costs can involve manipulation of product quality or longevity of use. Engineering faster obsolescence in products is an example.[45]

45 See Andrea Soke, *Built to Fail: 7 Examples of Planned Obsolescence*, Durability Matters, January 14, 2021, https://durabilitymatters.com/; John Harris, "Planned Obsolescence: The Outrage of Our Electronic Waste Mountain," *The Guardian*, April 15, 2020, www.theguardian.com/; Kate Jackson,

In a competitive scenario, accelerated obsolescence may be difficult or impossible to implement, as the producer would likely be driven out of business—or would have to cut prices and incur losses. Availability of similar products in any given market segment would provide alternatives and ensure that this tactic is noticed and exposed. A media that serves the public interest would likely draw attention to it. And, the perpetrator might find it difficult to co-opt a regulatory agency.

Designed-in limited effectiveness, or flaws due to insufficient testing, is another cause of damage to consumers—beyond the price differential noted previously.[46] This fairly common practice requires consumers to purchase accessories or treatments, to make a product fulfill its intended purpose. Side effects or addictions can also lead to additional cost.[47]

Setting earlier consumption deadlines than necessary is another damage—a fairly common tactic involving products that deteriorate. Unjustifiably early deadlines often play on consumers' fears about the effectiveness of a product or its side effects—to induce frequent purchase. Designing products to work solely with proprietary accessories or refills—accompanied by high pricing—is another tactic.[48] This lock-in scheme can go unnoticed for a long time—generating substantial revenue for the perpetrator.

Adding compulsory "administrative" fees to services and requiring consumers to pay for subscriptions even when only infrequent purchase is involved are other examples.[49] Some subscription schemes stress access over product ownership, to obtain recurrent revenue.[50] Cloud platforms that provide diverse

---

"Planned Obsolescence Versus the Circular Economy," *Forbes*, August 4, 2020, www.forbes.com/; *Reuters*, "IT Risks, Wariness and Planned Obsolescence," March 12, 2010, www.reuters.com/.

46 See Peter Blumberg, "Zoom Sued for Fraud Over Privacy, Security Flaws," *Bloomberg*, April 8, 2020, www.bloomberg.com/; *The Economist*, "Silicon Meltdown: Even if Chips are Never Hacked, their Flaws have Consequences," January 13, 2018, 57–58; Sam Schechner, Stu Woo and Jay Greene, "Chip Flaws Have Suppliers, Users Seeking Fixes," *Wall Street Journal*, January 6, 2018, B1; Rachael King and Danny Yadron, "Microsoft Retires Its XP, but Security Risks Live On," *Wall Street Journal*, April 2, 2014, B1.

47 National Safety Council, *Prescription Drug Abuse Epidemic; Painkillers Driving Addiction, Overdose*, www.nsc.org (accessed August 10, 2022); Steven Reinberg, "As Opioid Epidemic Rages, Painkiller Prescriptions Don't Drop," *WebMD*, August 1, 2018, www.webmd.com/; Stephanie Armour, "Advisory Recommends Opioid-Reversal Drug," *Wall Street Journal*, April 6, 2018, A3.

48 See Amanda Aronczyk, "Why Printers are the Worst," *NPR*, February 17, 2021, www.npr.org/; Rachel Sandler, "Apple Settles 'Batterygate' Lawsuit for $113 Million," *Forbes*, November 18, 2020, www.forbes.com/; Don Clark, "HP Shifts Course on Printer Update," *Wall Street Journal*, September 29, 2016, B4; James Salmon, "License to Print Money? HP Faces Backlash after Blocking Customers from Using Cheaper Ink Cartridges in Its Printers," *Daily Mail*, September 19, 2016, www.dailymail.co.uk/.

49 Drew Fitzgerald, "Carriers Cash in on Fees," *Wall Street Journal*, June 30, 2018, B1.

50 See Tien Tzuo, *Subscribed: Why the Subscription Model Will Be Your Company's Future—and What To Do About It* (New York: Portfolio, 2018).

services became a convenient vehicle for inducing subscription during the last decade, as in the case of software applications.[51] *The additional cost of these schemes increases consumer exploitation.*

The price differential may then be re-specified as:

$$(P^N + p^\eta) - P'$$

where p^η represents the *add-on* to pricing. This can be included in the overall quantum of the oligopolistic surplus (ΔN). The add-on can be a one-time event or it can accumulate over the life of a product or service. Either way, it will involve an unnecessary expense to the consumer. Diminishment of individual or household budgets is one of the consequences.

Extensive research with large databases has provided evidence of oligopolistic price rises. In biotechnology, for example, an estimate of markups (pricing above marginal cost and inflation)—a plausible measure of oligopolistic pricing differential—found an average increase of over 400 percent (inflation-adjusted) during a 36-year period.[52] Another study based on data from 134 nations (including the United States) and 70,000 companies in numerous sectors (including technology) also found substantial price increases over an extended period.[53] Greater oligopolistic concentration was associated with rising prices in all cases.

Medications that accompany biotech treatments or surgeries experienced substantial increases in recent decades. Pain reduction in such cases is important because of its effect on recovery. Prices for branded, opioid-type biopharmaceuticals in the United States—all of which are produced and distributed by oligopolistic corporations—were found to have increased by 233 percent (inflation-adjusted) over a 24-year period.[54]

Substantial price increases of products that treat addiction—an add-on effect to opioid biopharmaceuticals—provide additional insight. The price of naloxone (Narcan)—a product used to treat opiate overdoses, in use for

51 *The Economist*, "Super Subs: Adobe's Bold Embrace of the Computing Cloud Should Inspire Others," March 22, 2014, 65.

52 Federico J. Diez, Daniel Leigh and Suchanan Tambunlertchai, *Global Market Power and Macroeconomic Implications*, IMF Working Paper WP18137 (Washington: International Monetary Fund, 2018), www.imf.org/. See also *The Economist*, "On the Mark: The IMF Adds to a Chorus of Concern about Falling Levels of Competition," April 6, 2019, 61; William A. Galston, "The Perils of Corporate Concentration," *Wall Street Journal*, June 20, 2018, A15.

53 Jan De Loecker and Jan Eeckhout, *Global Market Power*, NBER Working Paper 24768 (Cambridge: National Bureau of Economic Research, 2018); and their *The Rise of Market Power and the Macroeconomic Implications*, NBER Working Paper 23687 (Cambridge: National Bureau of Economic Research, 2017), www.nber.org/.

54 Based on average pricing per MME (morphine-milligram equivalents)—U.S. Food and Drug Administration, *FDA Analysis of Long-Term Trends in Prescription Opioid Analgesic Products: Quantity, Sales, and Price Trends*, March 2018, www.fda.gov/.

five decades (an off-patent generic)—increased by 552 percent (inflation-adjusted) over a three-year period during the last decade, despite its importance for saving lives.[55] The pressure for higher oligopolistic surpluses—and incentives for medical practitioners to prescribe more—can be linked to these increases.[56]

Across the biotech and biopharmaceutical medication spectra, pricing during the last decade further reflected oligopolistic concentration and its impact on pricing. For the antibiotic doxycycline—necessary for many patients who undergo biotech treatments or surgeries—prices increased by 9,145 percent per bottle over six months.[57] Prices of cycloserine—used against multi-drug-resistant lung infections and tuberculosis—rose by 2,060 percent overnight (for 30 tablets), while prices for two medications used to treat heart disease—Nitropress and Isuprel—increased by 212 and 525 percent (also overnight), respectively.[58] And, prices for 19 brand name dermatologic prescription medications—used to treat diverse but fairly common conditions—were found to have increased by over 500 percent (inflation-adjusted) during a 6-year period.[59] The price of an off-patent, 40-year-old cancer medication increased 15-fold in less than 4 years, placing it out of reach for many patients.[60]

A pack of two treatments was priced at $609 for EpiPen—commonly used for emergency allergy treatments across the age spectrum, but particularly important for schoolchildren—after undergoing 17 price increases (totaling 548 percent, adjusted for inflation) during a nine-year period.[61] Specifying short deadlines for consumption helped increase demand for the oligopolistic owner of this medication. This can be an important way to induce higher sales

55 Eric Berger, "Narcan Price Hikes Troubling as Opioid Epidemic Rages On," *Annals of Emergency Medicine* 70 (2017), A17–A19, www.annemergmed.com/.

56 See Beth Macy, *Dopesick: Dealers, Doctors, and the Drug Company that Addicted America* (New York: Little, Brown, 2018). This work focuses on Purdue Pharmaceuticals, the oligo-monopolistic manufacturer of OxyContin, long a widely used opioid medication.

57 Andrew Pollack, "Drug Goes from $13.50 a Tablet to $750, Overnight," *New York Times*, September 20, 2015, http://nytimes.com/; Peter Loftus, "Drug Prices Soar Without Generics," *Wall Street Journal*, December 26, 2017, B1.

58 Pollack, "Drug Goes"; Loftus, "Drug Prices Soar."

59 Joseph Walker, "Eczema Drug Gets 'Responsible' Price," *Wall Street Journal*, March 29, 2017, B1; Miranda E. Rosenberg and Steven P. Rosenberg, "Changes in Retail Prices of Prescription Dermatologic Drugs from 2009 to 2015," *JAMA Dermatology*, November 25, 2015, http://archderm.jamanetwork.com/; Ron Winslow, "Prices of Skin Drugs Climb, Study Finds," *Wall Street Journal*, November 27, 2015, B1; Peter Loftus, "Monthly Cost for Lilly Drug is $11,430," *Wall Street Journal*, December 12, 2015, B3.

60 Peter Loftus, "Cancer Drug Priced at $850,000," *Wall Street Journal*, January 4, 2018, B2; Andrew Pollack, "Doctors Denounce Cancer Drug Prices of $100,000 a Year," *New York Times*, April 25, 2013, www.nytimes.com/.

61 Jonathan D. Rockoff, "High Cost of EpiPen Stirs Anger," *Wall Street Journal*, August 25, 2016, B1; and his "Drugmaker Stung by EpiPen Backlash," *Wall Street Journal*, August 26, 2016, B1.

or greater demand, especially when the conditions treated are life-threatening or severe complications can occur. Or, when consumers can be made to fear reduced effectiveness if a deadline passes. Reducing output to create shortages in the face of constant demand—a tactic implemented through capacity-price engineering schemes, discussed in the previous chapter—also helps increase pricing.[62]

New treatments and medications marketed at exorbitant prices provide further evidence. A new gene therapy treatment for vision loss was priced at $850,000 (per treatment), while the first gene-inhibiting medication for nerve damage related to heart and digestive diseases was priced at $450,000 annually.[63] And, three medications' initial prices were set at $11,430 monthly, *and* at $32,500 and $37,000 annually—all for treating fairly common conditions.[64] Not having a prior product—to compare with—helps an oligopolist impose a price, based on executives' calculations of desirable surpluses.[65]

Biopharmaceutical and biotech oligopolists often cite the high cost of research to justify high initial prices, but during the last two decades such claims were grossly exaggerated.[66] And, profit margins in some cases were found to be twice the amount declared—and much higher than in most economic sectors—by analysts who examined accounting practices.[67] Also, efforts to produce medications at a lower price—by artisanal "compounders"—faced entry barriers and other serious obstacles from biopharmaceutical oligopolists.[68] Perhaps then it should not surprise that price increases contributed to a 127 percent

62 See Peter Loftus, "Scarcity Boosts Drug Cost: Some Prices Triple after Shortages, Recalls," *Wall Street Journal*, January 19, 2019, B1; Jared S. Hopkins, "Drugmakers Increase Prices in New Year," *Wall Street Journal*, January 2, 2019, A1.

63 Peter Loftus, "Cancer Drug Priced" and his "FDA Approves First 'Gene Silencing' Drug," Wall Street Journal, August 11, 2018, B3.

64 Peter Loftus, "Monthly Cost for Lilly Drug," and his "Cannabis-Based Drug is $32,500," *Wall Street Journal*, August 9, 2018, B3.

65 See William Lazonick and Öner Tulum, "How CEOs are Using Your High Drug Prices to fill their Pockets," *New York Times*, February 26, 2019, www.nytimes.com/.

66 Lazonick and Tulum, "How CEOs are Using"; Donald W. Light and Rebecca Warburton, "Demythologizing the High Costs of Pharmaceutical Research," *BioSocieties* 6 (2011), 34–50; Marcia Angell, *The Truth About the Drug Companies: How They Deceive Us and What to Do About It* (New York: Random House, 2004); Michael Hiltzik, "How Big Pharma Distorts Costs of Developing Drugs," *Los Angeles Times*, April 3, 2011, B1. An unnoticed aspect of research in biopharmaceuticals and biotech is that most results and data on unsuccessful trials are seldom published—and thus remain unknown—raising research costs for other companies through duplication. See *The Economist*, "Clinical Trials: Spilling the Beans; Failure to Publish the Results of All Clinical Trials is Skewing Medical Science," July 25, 2015, 62–63.

67 Aswath Damodaran, *Numbers and Narrative: Value and Price in the Drug Business*, Stern School of Business, New York University, 2019, www.stern.nyu.edu/; *The Economist*, "American Drugmakers are Raising Prices, Again," June 22, 2019, 53.

68 Melanie Evans, "Cheap Custom-Made Drugs Spur Backlash: Compounders Face Tighter Rules, Lawsuits from Traditional Pharmaceutical Makers," *Wall Street Journal*, September 10, 2018, B3.

rise in branded medications' prices between 2008 and 2014—in contrast, the consumer price index rose by only 11 percent during that period.[69]

A seemingly modest annual price increase can be several times the corresponding year's rise in the Consumer Price Index (CPI). This occurred with Johnson and Johnson's average 8.5 percent increase for all its medications—over four times the CPI level—during the middle of the last decade.[70] This and other oligopolists' price increases forced prisons to ration inmate care across the United States and led to cutbacks in health assistance to the poor.[71] And, despite mounting public concern, biopharmaceutical oligopolies continued to raise prices at rates far above the annual CPI during the last decade. As of mid-2018, for example, 3,653 price increases had occurred on 1,043 medications, with a median price rise of 8 percent.[72]

Annual price increases amounting to several times the CPI have thus been common for many years in biopharmaceuticals and biotech—sectors that are now overwhelmingly oligopolistic.[73] Rising medication prices accompanied by output shortages—a result of the capacity-price engineering strategy discussed in the previous chapter—were estimated to have added as much as $400 million in the annual costs of medical care in recent times.[74] Medication price increases thus affect most every area of health care, damaging budgets and contributing to consumer exploitation. It should not surprise then that the cost of medical procedures has contrasted sharply with those of other countries.[75] In the last decade, the United States spent as much as 60 percent more on

69 Joseph Walker, "Drug Prices Jolt Middle Class: Even Insured Patients Struggle to Meet Out-of-Pocket Costs for Powerful New Medications," *Wall Street Journal*, January 2, 2016, A1; *The Economist*, "Drug Pricing in America: Painful Pills," September 26, 2015, 66.

70 Jonathan Rockoff, "J&J Unit: List Prices Rose 8.5% Last Year," *Wall Street Journal*, February 28, 2017, B3.

71 Peter Loftus and Gary Fields, "Costly Drugs for Prisoners Weigh on Public Budgets," *Wall Street Journal*, September 13, 2016, A1; Rockoff, "J&J Unit"; *The Economist*, "Drug Pricing in America."

72 Jonathan D. Rockoff, "Ambien's Price is Rude Awakening: Some Drugmakers Keep Boosting Costs of Products, Despite Mounting Pressures," *Wall Street Journal*, July 16, 2018, B1; and his "Pfizer Again Raises Drug Prices: A Second Round this Year Comes Even as Industry as a Whole is Wary of Public Criticism," *Wall Street Journal*, July 3, 2018, B1; Daniel M. Hartung, Dennis N. Bourdette, Sharia M. Ahmed and Ruth H. Whitham, "The Cost of Multiple Sclerosis Drugs in the U.S. and the Pharmaceutical Industry: Too Big to Fail?" *Neurology* 84 (2015), www.ncbi.nlm .nih.gov/.

73 Kirsten Stewart, *Hospitals Feeling the Pinch of High Drug Prices*, University of Utah Health Sciences, www.uofuhealth.utah.edu (accessed August 28, 2019); U.S. Government Accountability Office, *Drug Shortages: Certain Factors are Strongly Associated with this Persistent Public Health Challenge*, Report to Congressional Committees, GAO-16-595, July 2016, www.gao.gov/.

74 Peter Loftus, "Lack of Cheap Drugs Thwarts Treatments: Shortages Add $400 Million to Costs as Doctors Use Pricier and Riskier Alternatives," *Wall Street Journal*, July 3, 2017, B1.

75 Organization for Economic Cooperation and Development (OECD), *Health Spending*, OECD Data, https://data.oecd.org/ (accessed August 8, 2022); Joseph Walker and Angela Calderon, "Why We Spend So Much on Health Care," *Wall Street Journal*, August 1, 2018, A6; and their "Diagnosing Health Care's Hidden Costs," *Wall Street Journal*, August 1, 2018, A1.

health care (relative to GDP)—with poorer results—than other industrialized nations.[76]

A focus on driving up share prices contributed to this problem—and to consumer exploitation. In one case, a 4,000 percent stock price increase over seven years (during the last decade) was thought to be a prime factor behind medication price rises.[77] Another biopharmaceutical oligopolist provided bonuses to over 100 executives that depended on doubling per-share revenue (or more), over a five-year period.[78] In these and other cases, executive compensation was closely tied to share prices—and to rising medication prices. The five highest-paid executives at oligopolists Regeneron, Mylan, Johnson & Johnson, Pfizer, and Vertex, for example, received over $1.6 billion in compensation—during a four-year period in the last decade.[79] A result of these practices is that consumers were compelled to pay or forgo treatment.[80]

Consumer exploitation by biopharmaceutical and biotech companies also involves hospital oligopolies—their most important corporate allies. Many hospitals have substantial market power due to the services they provide, or because they have a monopoly over locales. In the last decade, prices for in-house services were found to be much higher—by 100 percent or more—than the ones provided by external (often higher-quality) specialists and primary care practitioners.[81] Prices for sigmoidoscopies performed in-house, for example, were found to be as much as $2,597 higher (per patient) than those provided externally, while those for endoscopies were $2,319 higher—in an analysis of insurance for 40 million consumers.[82] Hospital physicians that referred patients to external services experienced pressure to eliminate or curtail them—digitization of patient records facilitates this practice.[83] And, although federal rules

76 See Rabah Kamal and Cynthia Cox, *How Do Health Care Prices and Use in the U.S. Compare to Other Countries?* Peterson-Kaiser System Tracker, May 2018, www.healthsystemtracker.com/; Walker and Calderon, "Why We Spend"; OECD, *Health Spending*.

77 David Benoit and Jacquie McNish, "Architect of Valeant's Turnaround under Fire," *Wall Street Journal*, December 8, 2015, B1; Michael Rapoport and Liz Hoffman, "Valeant's Unconventional Books: The Drugmaker's Accounting Looks Very Different from that of its Peers," *Wall Street Journal*, December 16, 2015, B1.

78 Mark Maremont, "Mylan Tied Pay to Tough Targets," *Wall Street Journal*, September 2, 2016, B1.

79 Mark Maremont, "EpiPen Maker Dispenses Outsize Pay," *Wall Street Journal*, September 14, 2016, A1—based on data from Standard and Poor, Global Market Intelligence, http://markietintelligence.spglobal.com/; and his "Mylan Tied Pay"; Walker and Calderon, "Why We Spend."

80 See Ezekiel Emanuel, "We Can't Afford the Drugs that Could Cure Cancer: Customized Immunotherapies are Ready to Revolutionize Care and Save Lives—If Drug Companies Stop Charging so Much for Them," *Wall Street Journal*, September 22, 2018, C4.

81 Anna Wilde Mathews and Melanie Evans, "Hospitals Push Doctors to Keep Referrals In-House: Hospitals Acquired Primary-Care Practices, and Now They Want those Doctors' Patients for Lucrative Surgeries, MRIs and Tests," *Wall Street Journal*, December 28, 2018, A1.

82 Health Care Cost Institute, *2016 Health Care Cost and Utilization Report*, June 19, 2018, www.healthcostinstitute.org/; Mathews and Evans, "Hospitals Push Doctors," A9.

83 Mathews and Evans, "Hospitals Push Doctors," A9.

attempt to protect physicians from the linking of salaries to external referrals, many employment contracts explicitly require referrals to be made for in-house services.[84]

Across the technology spectrum, the effect of consumer exploitation can be seen in the vast accumulation of idle cash. Several hundred billion dollars—estimated to be as much as one-fifth or more of their stock market value—have been accumulated *annually* by the 150 largest American technology corporations in recent times.[85] A substantial amount has been kept offshore over the years, to evade taxes.[86] Apple alone, for example, was estimated to have as much as $250 billion of accumulated idle capital offshore toward the end of the last decade, while its market capitalization reached $1 trillion at that time—the highest for any company in stock market history.[87]

Apple introduced iPod (30 GB) in the United States in 2006, at a retail price of $299—with the production cost estimated at $144—yielding a gross profit (per iPod) of over half the retail price charged to consumers.[88] And, Apple's first iPhone model—introduced in 2007—yielded a gross profit of almost two-thirds of the retail price charged, a level never seen before in a technology consumer product.[89] This reflected a high level of consumer exploitation, based on the pricing differential discussed earlier. Entering this product niche early allowed Apple to exercise much power over consumers—and to either cripple or acquire companies in related niches.[90] Thus, even though by the middle of

84 Mathews and Evans, "Hospitals Push Doctors," A9.

85 Bloomberg, *Investing and Stock Research by Company and Industry*, www.bloomberg.com/ (accessed July 19, 2022); Justin Lahart, "The Next Problem: Too Much Profit," *Wall Street Journal*, March 28, 2014, C8.

86 Jesse Drucker and Simon Bowers, "After a Tax Crackdown, Apple Found a New Shelter for Its Profits: The Tech Giant Has Found a Tax Haven in the Island of Jersey, Leaving Billions of Dollars Untouched by the United States, Leaked Documents Reveal," *New York Times*, November 6, 2017, www.nytimes .com/. Although some repatriation of idle cash occurred after lower corporate tax rates were implemented in 2018, the amounts held abroad by technology oligopolists continue to be substantial.

87 Adam Shell, "Apple Makes History by Becoming First US Company to Reach $1 Trillion Market Value," *USA Today*, August 2, 2018, www.usatoday.com/; James Titcomb, "Apple's Cash Reserves Swell to $250bn," *Telegraph*, May 1, 2017, www.telegraph.co.uk/; Drucker and Bowers, "After a Tax Crackdown."

88 Greg Linden, Jason Dedrick and Kenneth L. Kraemer, *Innovation and Job Creation in a Global Economy: The Case of Apple's iPod* (Irvine: Personal Computing Industry Center, University of California, 2009), http://pcic.merage.uci.edu/; John Smith, "The GDP Illusion: Value Added versus Value Capture," *Monthly Review*, July 2012, https://monthlyreview.org/.

89 Edward Yardeni and Joe Abbott, *Stock Market Briefing: S&P 500 Sectors & Industries Profit Margins*, Yardeni Research, Inc., August 22, 2017, www.yardeni.com/; Yuqing Xing and Neal Detert, *How the iPhone Widens the United States Trade Deficit with the People's Republic of China*, ADBI Working Paper 257 (Tokyo: Asian Development Bank Institute, 2010), www.adb.org/; Smith, "GDP Illusion."

90 See Brian Merchant's *The One Device: The Secret History of the iPhone* (New York: Little, Brown, 2017), chapters 10–14; Jacquie McNish and Sean Silcoff, "The Inside Story of How the iPhone Crippled BlackBerry," *Wall Street Journal*, May 22, 2015, www.wsj.com/.

the last decade Apple was selling about one-fifth of the world's smartphones, its profit was 92 percent of that product segment's total.[91]

Apple's power over smartphones was compounded by the short life cycle of its models—which often provided limited improvement over prior versions.[92] Much the same applied to some of Apple's other products.[93] A short life cycle is a fairly common strategy to impose higher pricing—based on the status appeal of a product and the oligopolistic power of its producer.[94] Being the leader in higher smartphone pricing during the last decade, Apple broke the $1,000 barrier with its iPhone X—an action followed by other oligopolists across the smartphone segment.[95] For its iPhone XS—introduced barely a year later—Apple then raised prices by 15 percent on average over the iPhone X's.[96]

The main feature of the XS model over its immediate predecessor was a larger screen—a tactic tried previously with the iPhone 6 Plus, which led to increases in sales. The XS model was expected to generate more app sales, mainly because its larger screen could accommodate more icons. Also, Apple's frequent operating system upgrades (usually performed automatically) had caused prior versions of its smartphones to slow down—thus inducing purchase of more expensive models.[97] Limiting testing by journalists and consumer advocates—that prevented in-depth evaluations before introduction—was thought to have helped Apple charge higher prices.[98] And, a very important feature of the iPhone X—face recognition—was subsequently found to be vulnerable to errors or malfeasance—a problem that would most likely have been noticed with sufficient testing.[99]

91 Shira Ovide and Daisuke Wakabayashi, "Apple's Share of Smartphone Industry's Profits Soars to 92%: Apple's Share of Profits is Remarkable Given that It Sells Less than 20% of Smartphones," *Wall Street Journal*, July 12, 2015, www.wsj.com/.

92 Geoffrey Fowler, "iPhone 8: Improvement is Slight for an Upgrade," *Wall Street Journal*, September 20, 2017, B1.

93 See Joanna Stern, "Apple Watch Series 3: I'll Pass," *Wall Street Journal*, September 21, 2017, B4.

94 See Tripp Mickle, "Apple Gambles on Allure of Premium Pricing," *Wall Street Journal*, September 13, 2017, A1; Josh Zumbrun and Tripp Mickle, "New iPhone Tests Economic Theory," *Wall Street Journal*, September 18, 2017, A2.

95 Tripp Mickle and Timothy W. Martin, "Smartphone Makers Believe You Will Pay $1,000 and Up," *Wall Street Journal*, September 11, 2017, B1; Dan Gallagher, "New Phone Prices are Going to the Edge," *Wall Street Journal*, August 30, 2017, B1. Its iPhone X contributed greatly to Apple's record-breaking $1 trillion stock market capitalization in 2018, a matter anticipated by some analysts—see, for example, Dan Gallagher, "Can the New iPhone Push Apple's Value Above $1 Trillion?" *Wall Street Journal*, September 11, 2017, B10.

96 Tripp Mickle, "Apple's Phones Get Bigger, Pricier: Latest Models Cost $949 on Average, 15% More than iPhones Launched a Year Ago," *Wall Street Journal*, September 13, 2018, B1.

97 Mike Murphy, "There's a Reason why iPhones Get Slower after Every iOS Update," *Quartz*, December 20, 2017, https://qz.com/.

98 Tripp Mickle, "Apple Limits Lengthy iPhone X Testing for Most Reviewers: 'Unusual' Change in Strategy Means Latest Phone Got Less Testing Than Most of Its Predecessors Before Reviews Could Be Published," *Wall Street Journal*, October 31, 2017, www.wsj.com/.

99 Joanna Stern, "iPhone X Review: How We Tested (and Tricked) FaceID," *Wall Street Journal*, October 31, 2017, www.wsj.com/articles/; Geoffrey Fowler, "A First Look at Apple's iPhone X: About Face," *Wall Street Journal*, September 13, 2017, B1.

Flaws due to insufficient testing have been found in many technology products over the years, damaging consumers through loss of use or by requiring fixes that involve expense and waste of time or effort, work losses, or payment. *Such flaws can be considered part of the add-on charge* (p^{η}) *to the price differential* discussed before. Batteries—a staple of most every portable consumer electronic product—that catch on fire or explode are one example.[100]

During the last decade one technology oligopolist, for example, was found to have insufficiently tested a new smartphone model. Recalls involved millions of units, causing expense and great inconvenience to consumers.[101] A design flaw that could have been avoided through rigorous testing—an excessively thin electrode separator in its batteries—was the apparent cause. Inadequate testing has also led, over the years, to accidents and fires in expensive technology products, including some that affected public safety.[102]

Another fairly common example of an add-on charge is that of software flaws that allow hacking and malfeasance—resulting in loss of use and work, identity theft, or a need to switch hardware. This is often addressed through "patches," some of which may have problems of their own. During the last decade Microsoft was alleged to depend on consumers to detect flaws—a way to load the expense and time of quality control unto users.[103] A security flaw in Microsoft's Office product, for example, was found to have existed for 17 years before it was detected by users.[104]

Data Exploitation

Oligopolistic power generates important dysfunctions through its appropriation and exploitation of data. The latter are a vital asset for consumer exploitation, pricing,

100 Elizabeth Weise, "Cell Phones Thrown in the Trash are Exploding, Causing 5-Alarm Fires in Garbage Trucks," *USA Today*, May 18, 2018, www.usatoday.com/.

101 Paul Mozur, "Galaxy Note 7 Fires Caused by Battery and Design Flaws, Samsung Says," *New York Times*, January 22, 2017, www.nytimes.com/; Yun-Hee Kim and John D. McKinnon, "Samsung Plans Fixes to Limit Fire Risks," *Wall Street Journal*, September 15, 2016, B1.

102 See *BBC*, "Tesla Autopilot: U.S. Opens Official Investigation into Self-Driving Tech," August 16, 2021, www.bbc.co.uk/; Jonathon Klein, "Parked Teslas Keep Catching on Fire Randomly, and There's No Recall in Sight," *The Drive*, June 18, 2019, www.thedrive.com/; Sean Gallagher, "NTSB Blames Bad Battery Design—and Management—in Boeing 787 Fires: Maker of Lithium-Ion Batteries Didn't Foresee Spreading Short Circuit Danger," *ArsTechnica*, December 2, 2014, https://arstechnica.com/.

103 James Walker, "Security Flaws in Microsoft Software Have Doubled Since 2013," *Digital Journal*, February 19, 2018, www.digitaljournal.com/; Graham Cluley, "Patch Now! Microsoft Fixes over 50 Serious Security Flaws," *WeLiveSecurity*, February 13, 2018, www.welivesecurity.com/; King and Yadron, "Microsoft Retires Its XP."

104 Lee Mathews, "Microsoft Just Fixed a Security Flaw in Office that's 17 Years Old," *Forbes*, November 16, 2017, www.forbes.com/.

and market control. It should not surprise, therefore, that limitations on the use and abuse of personal data are fiercely opposed by technology oligopolies.[105]

Intimate data are at the core of exploitation in consumer markets and in the social media and search sectors. Being made to give up such data can be considered an add-on (p^{η}) charge to the price differential in consumer exploitation. It may also be considered an add-on to the value of uncompensated work that uselaborers are required to give up to search and social media oligopolies.

Personal data can be priced, much as any other commodity—an aspect that the vast majority of consumers and uselaborers do not seem to be aware of. And, since access to such data is routinely sold, estimating its monetary value should not be a difficult matter.[106] Such calibration should not be more complex than, say, estimating the value of derivatives in finance.[107]

The intangibility of data has made its exploitation more difficult to notice. Uselaborers are routinely made to consent to their appropriation and sale—without eliciting any thoughts on their value and importance. Consumers are required to allow their appropriation in order to purchase or receive service and warranties—without attracting concern about their use and misuse. Forced arbitration clauses are embedded in contracts for services and products—to preempt lawsuits on data abuse—without much attention from the public.[108]

Wireless telecom providers were at the forefront of personal data exploitation three decades ago. Timing, location, and contact were the initial targets, but the list eventually expanded to encompass such aspects as movement,

105 Despite restrictions enacted by some states during the last decade, such as California, the appropriation, exploitation, and sale of personal data seem set to continue and increase rapidly—see *The Economist*, "California's Data Sheriffs," December 21, 2019, 94. See also John D. McKinnon and Marc Vartabedian, "Big Tech Wants to Shape Privacy Bill," *Wall Street Journal*, August 7, 2018, A4; Jack Marshall, "Internet Privacy for Sale," *Wall Street Journal*, March 31, 2017, B1.

106 Scandals related to sale of access attracted concern during the last decade—see Cristina Criddle, "Facebook Sued Over Cambridge Analytica Data Scandal," *BBC News*, October 28, 2020, www.bbc.co.uk/; Drew Fitzgerald, "Third Parties Know Exactly Where You Are," *Wall Street Journal*, July 16, 2018, B2; Georgia Wells, "Facebook Details Data Sharing: Company Discloses More Firms than Previously Known Got Special Access," *Wall Street Journal*, July 2, 2018, A1.

107 See Investopedia, *How is the Price of a Derivative Determined?* www.investopedia.com/ (accessed August 17, 2022).

108 Arbitration panels tend to favor corporate interests, a matter that attracted attention from legal experts during the last decade—see Scott Medintz, "Forced Arbitration: A Clause for Concern," *Consumer Reports*, January 30, 2020, www.consumerreports.org/; Elliot Harmon, *Forced Arbitration is a Bad Deal*, Electronic Frontier Foundation, May 3, 2016, www.eff.org/; Joe Valenti, *The Case Against Mandatory Consumer Arbitration Clauses*, Center for American Progress, August 2, 2016, www.americanprogress.org/. See also Katherine V. W. Stone and Alexander J. S. Colvin, *The Arbitration Epidemic: Mandatory Arbitration Deprives Workers and Consumers of their Rights*, Economic Policy Institute, December 7, 2015, www.epi.org/; Jessica Silver-Greenberg and Robert Gebeloff, "Arbitration Everywhere, Stacking the Deck of Justice," *New York Times*, October 31, 2015, www.nytimes.com/; Thomas H. Koenig and Michael L. Rustad, "Fundamentally Unfair: An Empirical Analysis of Social Media Arbitration Clauses," *Case Western Reserve Law Review* 65 (2014), 341–411.

travel, purchases, health, and finance. Consumers provided the latter whenever they signed up and paid for service, and such information was combined with other details to compile intimate profiles.[109] Social media oligopolists then made inroads in this area, mining information on habits and requesting banks to provide data.[110]

Data exploitation can involve not only an individual's information but also that of friends and contacts.[111] The possibilities for corporate use of personal data seem almost boundless. During the last decade, for example, Facebook reportedly used its databases to undertake "opposition research" on prominent individuals who criticized its practices publicly.[112] Obtaining users' financial data to find those more likely to use a service was found to be another project.[113]

For search and social media oligopolies, health is an area with much exploitation potential—as open consultation and targeted advice expand—the proliferation of healthcare apps during the last decade being a symptom.[114] Personal movement also provides many possibilities—involving location, shopping, and most any activity that includes transportation and telecom access.[115] And home connectivity through 5G now affords many new possibilities to mine intimate household habits.

109 See Gal Ringel, "Rethinking Privacy: The Road to Data Ownership," *Forbes*, August 2, 2021, www.forbes.com/; Ryan Knutson, "Verizon Makes It Personal: Wireless Carrier Offers Rewards to Customers but Also Wants to See their Browsing Histories," *Wall Street Journal*, September 6, 2017, B1.

110 Bill Goodwin and Sebastian K. Skelton, "Facebook's Privacy Game—How Zuckerberg Backtracked on Promises to Protect Personal Data," *Computer Weekly*, July 1, 2019, www.computerweekly.com/; Anna Maria Andriotis and Emily Glazer, "Facebook Sought Users' Financial Data for Years," *Wall Street Journal*, September 19, 2018, B1; Emily Glazer, Deepa Seetharaman and Anna Maria Andriotis, "Facebook Asks Banks for Customer Data," *Wall Street Journal*, August 7, 2018, A1.

111 See Carole Cadwalladr and Emma Graham-Harrison, "Zuckerberg Set up Fraudulent Scheme to 'Weaponise' Data, Court Case Alleges: Facebook Exploited Ability to Access Data from Any User's Friend Network, U.S. Case Claims," *The Guardian*, May 25, 2018, www.theguardian.com/.

112 Deepa Seetharaman, "Soros Aide Urges Facebook Review: Philanthropy Chief Seeks Oversight of the Social-Media Firm after Financier Faced Scrutiny," *Wall Street Journal*, November 23, 2018, www.wsj.com/.

113 Seetharaman and Andriotis, "Facebook Asks Banks"; Glazer, "Facebook Sought."

114 Misuse or hacking of health-related apps drew attention during the last decade—see *UpGuard*, "Losing Face: Two More Cases of Third-Party Facebook App Data Exposure," April 3, 2019, www.upguard.com/; John D. McKinnon, "Tech Giants Focus on Health Data," *Wall Street Journal*, August 14, 2018, B2.

115 See Christina Rogers, "What Your Car Knows about You: Automakers Can Now Collect Large Amounts of Data from Internet-Connected Vehicles," *Wall Street Journal*, August 18, 2018, B4.

Clouds

A most important tool to exploit and accumulate databases involves clouds. Data held in clouds are usually proprietary and operations tend to be shrouded in secrecy. The necessary hardware is held in large server "farms" that are guarded and secluded. Their amassment of intimate data has no precedent in history.

Appropriation through clouds is more extensive than any data gathering ever undertaken. A single cloud owned by any of the largest technology or tech-based service oligopolies—such as Facebook, Apple, Alphabet-Google, Microsoft, or Amazon—can contain more personal data than those held by all governments on the planet. And a platform with an array of services can be created for most any activity, enabling its oligopolistic proprietor to use and sell access to the data. Amazon's cloud computing division—Amazon Web Services (AWS)—for example, sells access to its databases to innumerable businesses—and mines client companies' data for its own proprietary services.[116]

Alphabet-Google has long tracked individual searches for certain goods, accumulating details in its clouds—to mine and sell access.[117] Companies that purchase access—or bid for Google's favored placement in searches—find it easier to sell their products. Such proprietary data are also important for finance. During the last decade, for example, consumer purchase data was sold to companies that provide software and data services to banks—the downstream beneficiaries.[118]

Google, provider of nine out of ten web searches during the last decade—whose Android system operates four-fifths of the world's smartphones—expanded into entertainment by acquiring YouTube.[119] Its control over search data provided it with a formidable advantage to market entertainment to uselaborers and target advertisements.[120] The key to exploitation here is thus

116 Dana Mattioli, "Amazon Scooped Up Data from its Own Sellers to Launch Competing Products," *Wall Street Journal*, April 23, 2020, www.wsj.com/.

117 *Deutsche Welle*, "Has Google's Data Collection Gone Too Far? With Google Holding a Chilling Amount of Data on Hundreds of Millions of People around the World, there is an Increasing Sense that It is Neither Moral nor Ethical," July 10, 2019, www.dw.com/.

118 Burt Helm, "Credit Card Companies are Tracking Shoppers Like Never Before: Inside the Next Phase of Surveillance Capitalism," *Fast Company*, December 5, 2020, www.fastcompany.com/; Charles Paikert, "Yodlee is Envestnet's Hottest Act, but Data Security Concerns Mount," *Financial Planning*, May 17, 2018, www.financial-planning.com/; Bradley Hope, "Firm Tracks Cards, Sells Data: Yodlee Provides Online Personal-Finance Tools to Big Banks, Markets Transaction Data to Investors," *Wall Street Journal*, August 7, 2015, A1.

119 Jeff Desjardins, "How Google Retains More than 90 percent of Market Share," *Business Insider*, April 25, 2018, www.businessinsider.com/.

120 See Geoffrey A. Fowler, "How does Google's Monopoly Hurt You? Try these Searches," *Washington Post*, October 19, 2020, www.washingtonpost.com/; *The Economist*, "Antitrust Theatre: Despite a Global Techlash and High Fines in Europe, America's Online Giants Have Not Much to Fear from Regulators," July 21, 2018, 47–48; Desjardins, "How Google Retains."

uselaborers' data—appropriated through searches, entertainment, and advertisement viewings—and the mining of preferences, time, and contact.[121]

And Google's search uselaborers also happen to be consumers. This creates many possibilities to market services. Among these is education. Google's goal of scanning every book in existence—to be the world's library—may allow it to become the world's largest online diploma oligopoly.[122] Since most purchases occur through Android-enabled smartphones—banking, finance, and online commerce may be additional targets. After all, Android software already has access to banking, credit, and purchasing data—a matter that raised concerns during the last decade.[123] Such information can be conflated with other details, such as location, employment, travel, contacts, family, and educational needs to expand Google's reach into new market niches.

Social media oligopolies—such as Facebook—have proprietary clouds *and* sell access to third parties—a practice that attracted attention during the last decade.[124] Selling access and storage flaws can lead to loss or theft of massive amounts of data, as in the case of 600 million users who had their passwords improperly stored by Facebook.[125] This flaw led to loss of detailed data for 50 million individuals at one point during the last decade.[126]

Using its clouds—and the vast intimate data it has appropriated on billions of uselaborers around the world—Facebook expanded into finance by creating a crypto-currency.[127] Its incursion into the monetary realm may lead to control over market niches related to consumer finance. Money, credit, retail banking, and stock market transactions might thus become part of a mega-oligopolistic complex involving uselaborers' contacts, searches, entertainment,

121 Patience Haggin and Kara Dapena, "Search Drives Google's Ad Dominance," *Wall Street Journal*, June 18, 2019, B4; Desjardins, "How Google Retains."

122 Google Books, *Library Partners*, https://books.google.com (accessed August 9, 2022); James Somers, "Torching the Modern-Day Library of Alexandria: Somewhere at Google there is a Data Base Containing 25 million Books and Nobody is Allowed to Read them," *The Atlantic*, April 20, 2017, www.theatlantic.com/.

123 See Desjardins, "How Google Retains"; Reuters, "Google Faces $5 Billion Lawsuit in U.S. for Tracking 'Private' Internet Use: Google 'Cannot Continue to Engage in the Covert and Unauthorized Data Collection from Virtually Every American with a Computer or Phone,' the Complaint Said," *NBC News*, June 2, 2020, www.nbc.news.com/.

124 Dan Patterson, "Facebook Data Privacy Scandal: A Cheat Sheet," *Tech Republic*, July 30, 2020, www.techrepublic.com/; Gabriel J. X. Dance, Michael LaForgia and Nicholas Confessore, "As Facebook Raised Privacy Wall, It Carved an Opening for Tech Giants: Internal Documents Show that the Social Network Gave Microsoft, Amazon, Spotify and Others Far Greater Access to People's Data than It has Disclosed," *New York Times*, December 18, 2018, www.nytimes.com/.

125 Jeff Horwitz and Robert McMillan, "Facebook Stored Users' Passwords Improperly," *Wall Street Journal*, March 22, 2019, A1; Patterson, "Facebook Data Privacy."

126 Horwitz and McMillan, "Facebook Stored"; Patterson, "Facebook Data Privacy."

127 Anna Maria Andriotis, Peter Rudegeair and Liz Hoffman, "Facebook Crypto Coin Gets Backing: Visa, PayPal and Uber to Invest $10 Million Each in Payments System Called Libra," *Wall Street Journal*, June 14, 2019, A1.

shopping, and travel. Possibilities for further data exploitation are vast with new AI-enabled automation. Among them are personal movement and on-demand services—as vehicles are connected to Facebook's data exploitation infrastructure.[128]

Clouds are vital for subscription services, given the vast amount of historical data they amass. Tech-based services can turn subscription data clouds into a formidable tool, to induce sales in specific ways—based on such details as time of day or night, location, home connectivity, companions, news, vehicle use, and prior choices. Netflix, for example, targets consumers with greater precision than television cable channels or rating agencies, because of the specific data it accumulates in its cloud.[129]

Data clouds use AI to predict sales opportunities, target advertising, and expand data exploitation. A very large percentage of consumers, for example, start their online shopping using Amazon—and the vast majority end up buying from its platform.[130] Much of this success has rested on its AI and the data it appropriates through Amazon Web Services (AWS). And, the fact that—unlike Google and Facebook—Amazon is *the* retailer selling the products it advertises.[131] This has allowed Amazon to control *both* sales and advertising, and to charge for each of them to companies that sell through its platform.

Being the retailer also allows Amazon to appropriate and exploit data on purchases. Historical records further enable Amazon to compile preferences and design sales schemes, as individuals advance through the life cycle. Intimate financial details involving credit and purchase frequencies allow it to mine these aspects as well—to provide its own credit option. Amazon's vast data cloud also allowed it to capture other niches during the last decade, such as entertainment and music marketing.[132] Being both retailer and advertiser

128 Expansion of vehicles' computational and communication capabilities during the last decade opened the gate to this possibility—see Ted Greenwald, "Intel Joins Race for 'Servers on Wheels'," *Wall Street Journal*, March 14, 2017, A1; *The Economist*, "Autonomous Vehicles: Who's Self-Driving Your Car?" September 24, 2016, 63–64.

129 A matter that led to much concern during the last decade—see Wikipedia, *Criticism of Netflix*, https://en.wkipedia.org/ (accessed August 19, 2022); Ben Fritz, "Who Decides What You Want? Streaming Services such as Netflix and Spotify Push Music and Movies they Helped Create," *Wall Street Journal*, July 31, 2017, A11. See also Michael D. Smith and Rahul Telang, *Streaming, Sharing, Stealing: Big Data and the Future of Entertainment* (Cambridge, MA: MIT Press, 2016).

130 Randy Wootton, "Marketing in the Age of Amazon," *Forbes*, May 15, 2019, www.forbes.com/; Sarah Hollenbeck, *Amazon Prime Day Survey*, Black Friday, November 15, 2019, https://blackfriday.com/.

131 Wootton, "Marketing in the Age"; Lara O'Reilly and Laura Stevens, "Amazon Emerges as Advertising Giant: Marketers are Conflicted between Desire for the Company's Data and Fear of it as a Competitor," *Wall Street Journal*, November 27, 2018, A1.

132 See Hollenbeck, *Amazon Prime Day*; O'Reilly and Stevens, "Amazon Emerges," A10; Amol Sharma, "Amazon Mines its Data Trove to Bet on TV's Next Hit," *Wall Street Journal*, November 2, 2013, A1.

enables it to operate at a much lower cost than other platforms—employing only one person per every 10 Google workers.[133]

Companies that want to sell through Amazon are induced to purchase ad space for each relevant keyword that a potential customer might search for. This is the only way to ensure that their product will appear at or near the top of the list—as a "sponsored" item.[134] The price charged can be several dollars per any viewer's click—a fee that can provide Amazon with millions of dollars in revenue over a short period of time—for an advertisement attached to a single keyword.[135] Products of companies that decline to purchase are relegated to lower places on the listing and will likely incur lower sales. This form of control over merchants has allowed Amazon to deepen both its consumer and data exploitation capabilities.

The proliferation of "multiple cloud" systems—such as those owned by Amazon's AWS, Google Cloud, and Microsoft's Azure—provides an indication of how data exploitation is being taken to a more intrusive level.[136] Multiple clouds allow more effective exploitation, as connectivity and inter-cloud exchanges make it possible to analyze data intensively. The spread of 5G communication and IoT (Internet-of-Things) technologies is contributing to this reach, as more details of personal life become available. Intimate data exploitation through multiple cloud systems may thus be deepened when smartphones and other gadgets can bypass ground receiving stations—to communicate directly with satellites.[137] This will allow cloud oligopolies to operate anywhere on the planet—appropriating and exploiting data wherever the user happens to be, at any time.[138]

Data exploitation deserves greater concern when it is combined with online commerce and social media. In such cases, uncompensated uselabor must be added to the exploitation of data and consumption. Oligopolies engage in this *exploitive troika* by mining most everything an individual does online—and by selling data and merchandise (directly or through advertising). Data exploitation on identity, contacts, finances, and preferences—along with the

133 O'Reilly and Stevens, "Amazon Emerges"; Sharma, "Amazon Mines."

134 Wootton, "Marketing in the Age"; O'Reilly and Stevens, "Amazon Emerges"; Sharma, "Amazon Mines."

135 Wootton, "Marketing in the Age"; O'Reilly and Stevens, "Amazon Emerges"

136 *The Economist*, "Altocumulus: A New Formation is Rising in the Computing Skies," March 14, 2020, 52. One of the purported benefits of adopting a multiple-cloud strategy is to enhance computing security—see Ion Morozan, *Multi-Clouds Database: A New Model to Provide Security in Cloud Computing*, Vrije Universiteit, www.few.vu.nl/ (accessed May 28, 2022). A multi-cloud strategy could, however, complicate security when hackers exploit software loopholes in inter-cloud exchanges—a necessary feature for making multiple clouds more versatile.

137 See *The Economist*, "A Call from the Heavens: A New Firm Says it has Found a Way to Link Satellites to Ordinary Smartphones," March 7, 2020, 73.

138 *The Economist*, "The Oracle of AI: Flush with Billions, Databricks has Momentum and Big Plans," September 4, 2021, 50–52.

uncompensated time and effort that uselaborers put in—*and* the oligopolistic prices paid are at the core of this regime.[139] The value of the exploitive purchase price differential—and add-ons—is thus conflated with the value of the consumer and uselaborer data appropriated, *and* the value of uselaborers' time, efforts, and ad viewings.

The data are so valuable that even limited mining and sale can generate immense revenue. Self-imposed constraints often have little impact on surpluses. Search engine oligopolists—such as Google—that during the last decade promised not to scan or read email content, for example, reportedly used other information—such as search histories, location, and shopping—to sell to app developers.[140] The latter then mined the data when they purchased access, and paid commissions whenever their apps were sold or used. Thus, intimate data—the most valuable asset an online oligopolist has—can be appropriated and sold in roundabout ways.

Networks

Locking uselaborer-consumers into a large, multipurpose network—made possible by multiple cloud systems—*makes data exploitation more dynamic.* Network lock-in often magnifies the value of appropriated data, *and* the price differentials paid. Add-on charges can then be imposed by making a switch difficult or expensive—*if* there are alternatives. Or, they can be incurred by requiring accessories to be purchased with products and services. Simultaneously, the (uncompensated) value of uselaborers' time and efforts can be boosted as they are induced to stay longer online—by adding games and other services. Thus, a more abundant extent—a composite of range, accessibility, and composition, discussed previously—typically increases the value of a multipurpose network.[141]

This aspect contradicts one of the oldest assumptions of mainstream economics—the relationship between scarcity and pricing at the core of market supply and demand. Thus, abundance of extent—as opposed to its scarcity—is the key to a network's higher value for data exploitation. And, abundant connectivity—a result of greater network extent—typically expands consumer

139 The data repertory is vast, but only some aspects were exposed to the public during the last decade. See Sarah E. Needleman and Parmy Olson, "Google Discloses It Monitors Audio from Digital Assistant," *Wall Street Journal*, July 12, 2019, B1; Douglas MacMillan, Sarah Krouse and Keach Hagey, "Yahoo, Bucking Industry, Scans Emails for Data to Sell: Web Giant Pushes Harder to Analyze Inboxes for Advertisers," *Wall Street Journal*, August 29, 2018, A1.

140 John D. McKinnon and Douglas MacMillan, "Apps can Scan, Share Data from Gmail Accounts," *Wall Street Journal*, September 21, 2018, A4. See also Natalia Drozdiak and Jack Nicas, "Google User-Data Policy Examined," *Wall Street Journal*, January 25, 2017, A1.

141 Key aspects of network structure—complexity, redundancy, and interconnectedness—also affect extent, in both qualitative and quantitative ways. For a discussion of these and related aspects, see Luis Suarez-Villa, *Technocapitalism: A Critical Perspective on Technological Innovation and Corporatism* (Philadelphia: Temple University Press, 2009), 56–85.

lock-in. The combination of greater connectivity with network lock-in then all too often promotes recurrence of purchases. This became obvious in the videogame sector during the last decade, as oligopolists rapidly increased sales while expanding their player-*cum*-uselaborer-consumer population—*and* the data they were made to surrender.[142] Rapidly rising revenue for this sector—to well over $100 billion annually over a short time—reflected the benefit of network lock-in.[143]

Data exploitation through network lock-in also often becomes an important entry barrier. During the last decade, for example, apps became an important tool for network lock-in *and* to keep potential rivals out of the market. Apple's vast network "ecosystem" of apps, most of which only work with its products, is an example.[144] Operating margins of as much as 75 percent—very high even for a powerful technology oligopolist—reflected the importance of this network strategy.[145] And, Apple's network lock-in had the objective of encompassing *all* its services—including cloud computing.[146] The entry barriers structured through its network also allowed Apple to acquire numerous companies, thus extending its consumer and data exploitation regime.[147]

Another network that can generate much data exploitation, lock-in, and entry barriers is a business resource platform. Such platforms can embed specialized, small businesses. Consumer and personal data exploitation can occur indirectly, through the businesses embedded in the platform and its data clouds. Thus, the platform's oligopolistic owner becomes a rentier of sorts, charging for tenancy—and possibly acquiring some of the businesses. The platform itself can be fenced-in through proprietary software that serves multiple operational functions—such as research, testing, communications, scheduling, billing, payroll processing, gaming, or entertainment. For customers and the platform's

142 See Sarah E. Needleman, "Game Developers are Making It Hard for Players to Stop: Availability of Multiple Devices Adds to Allure, Long Hours; 'Gaming Disorder' Draws Concern," *Wall Street Journal*, August 21, 2018, B4; Dan Gallagher, "Microsoft Mines More Out of 'Minecraft'," *Wall Street Journal*, April 12, 2017, B1.

143 PriceWaterhouseCoopers, *U.S. Edition: Global Entertainment & Media Outlook 2018–22: Five-Year Projection of Consumer and Advertiser Spending Data*, www.pwc.com/ (accessed August 2, 2022).

144 Rob Enderle, "Apple and the Dangers of Lock-in," *Techspective*, April 14, 2017, https://techspective.net/; Don Reisinger, "Steve Jobs Wanted to 'Further Lock Customers' into Apple's 'Ecosystem'," *CNet*, April 2, 2014, www.cnet.com/; Merchant, *One Device*; Johnna Montgomerie and Samuel Roscoe, "Owning the Consumer—Getting to the Core of the Apple Business Model," *Accounting Forum* 37 (2013), 290–99.

145 *The Economist*, "Technology Profits: The Secrets of Big Tech," April 30, 2022, 51–52; and its "Big Tech and Antitrust: An UnEpic Victory," September 18, 2021, 57.

146 Enderle, "Apple and the Dangers"; Montgomerie and Roscoe, "Owning the Consumer"; Edwin Yapp, "iCloud: Tale of Apple's Lock-in Strategy," *ZDNet*, June 16, 2011, www.zdnet.com/.

147 Crunchbase, *Apple Acquisitions*, www.crunchbase.com/ (accessed August 5, 2022); Aaron Pressman, "Here's What Apple Could Buy with All its Cash," *Fortune*, January 18, 2018, www.fortune.com/.

embedded tenants, switching to another platform can involve substantial complications and high costs.

In recent decades Microsoft provided an example of this type of network lock-in—based on its software platforms and ancillary services.[148] It acquired many companies, some of them embedded in its platforms (or customers of those already embedded). The platforms and its acquisitions allowed Microsoft to fence-in market niches and reach consumers—to appropriate and exploit their data directly.[149] The platforms and locked-in networks, combined with data and consumer exploitation, increased the company's oligopolistic power substantially. This strategy also allowed Microsoft to evade antitrust action—by claiming that its platforms had helped create small businesses.[150]

Wants Contrivance

The pervasive need of technology oligopoly capitalism to promote wants is a major mode of systemic dysfunction. Wants promotion is both an existential and an operational necessity for technology oligopolies, because of their insatiable appetite for greater surpluses, market power, and executive compensation. The wants contrived—and whatever novel attributes they might have—typically involve an exploitive dimension. That is, to induce customers to purchase products or services sold in the oligopolistic marketplace (even if they are unnecessary). And, wants contrivance is usually conflated with consumer and data exploitation.

The psychological objective of wants contrivance is to make people *learn to want*—or to think that they "need"—a product that happens to be promoted.[151] Advertising is the prime vehicle to induce wants.[152] But the reality is that

148 See Tim Sweeney, "Microsoft Wants to Monopolise Games Development on PC: We Must Fight It," *The Guardian*, March 4, 2016, www.theguardian.com/; Kellogg Brengel, "Microsoft's Strategy to Replace Windows with Office as its Key Monopoly," *ONMSFT*, August 31, 2015, www.onmsft.com/; James Wallace, *Overdrive: Bill Gates and the Race to Control Cyberspace* (New York: Wiley, 1997), chapters 2, 3, 6.

149 Crunchbase, *Microsoft Acquisitions*, www.crunchbase.com/ (accessed August 5, 2022); Mary Jo Foley, "Microsoft Continues Investing in Gaming with Acquisitions, New Xbox Consoles: Microsoft is Stepping Up its Gaming Presence with More Expansions into Gaming Content, Hardware, and, at Some Point, a Game-Streaming Device," *ZDNet*, June 11, 2018, www.zdnet.com/; Sweeney, "Microsoft Wants"; Brengel, "Microsoft's Strategy."

150 Antonio García Martínez, "What Microsoft's Antitrust Case Teaches Us about Silicon Valley," *Wired*, February 11, 2018, www.wired.com/; William H. Page and John E. Lopatka, *The Microsoft Case: Antitrust, High Technology, and Consumer Welfare* (Chicago: University of Chicago Press, 2007).

151 Thorstein Veblen's well-known phrase "invention is the mother of necessity" represents the ethos of much wants contrivance—see his *The Instinct of Workmanship and the State of the Industrial Arts* (New York: Macmillan, 1914), 314.

152 The emergence of advertising as a major economic sector can be traced to the start of pervasive oligopolistic consolidation—as "creating" demand for products became a major corporate priority.

advertising is about giving the advertiser's clients—the oligopolistic technology corporations—what they want (more sales) above giving consumers what they need.[153] And, even when consumers are provided what they need, they are also provided with a lot that they do not need (or want). This applies to both bulk and targeted advertising.

Oligopolistic wants contrivance is directly connected to consumer exploitation—and often also data exploitation. It can be considered an important driver behind the oligopolistic price differential ($P^N - P'$) discussed earlier. And, it all too often drives the add-on charges (p^η) that accompany the price differential and inflate sales.

Wants contrivance can involve products that have limited or false utility. This can occur in a general way, or it can apply to specific situations. This difference is usually not made clear in advertisements, and it may not be provided in technical specifications. Typically, inducing possession of these products plays mostly on acquisitive obsessions that have minimal or no basis on actual need—or utility.[154]

The mélange of possibilities involving wants contrivance can be vast, and marketing programs often choose to cast a wide and far-reaching net. The main sources for wants contrivance are product development units (the D in R&D) that typically work closely with marketing. Their range of activities can be diverse and can include, for example, differentiation of existing products, finding new market niches, extrapolating fashions or societal trends, concocting lock-in schemes, finding ways to promote purchase recurrence, enlisting uselaborers in wants contrivance projects, or tapping loyalty programs. Wants contrivance is thus one of the most flexible and wide-ranging functions that can be found in the oligopolistic technology domain.

Wants contrivance schemes need not involve fraud. Improvements may only be provided with a new product that carries a much higher price than

---

See James Rorty, *Our Master's Voice: Advertising* (New York: Day, 1934), chapters 2, 3, 7, 8; Erik Barnouw, *The Sponsor: Notes on Modern Potentates* (New York: Oxford University Press, 1978), 77–152. For a contemporary perspective on the role of advertising and media in wants promotion, see Tim Wu, *The Attention Merchants: The Epic Scramble to Get inside Our Heads* (New York: Knopf, 2016), parts II-IV.

153 An argument discussed and documented years ago by Robert W. McChesney in his *Digital Disconnect: How Capitalism is Turning the Internet against Democracy* (New York: New Press, 2013), 75–76. See also McChesney's *The Problem of the Media: U.S. Communication Politics in the Twenty-First Century* (New York: Monthly Review Press, 2004), chapters 4, 5. The pervasive character of oligopolistic power, its collusion with the advertising oligopolies, the overarching priority to stimulate consumption—and the role of government in this panorama—were unfortunately missed in early explorations on the importance of the internet. See Jack Goldsmith and Tim Wu, *Who Controls the Internet? Illusions of a Borderless World* (New York: Oxford University Press, 2008), chapters 2, 3, 5.

154 See Crawford B. Macpherson's *Theory of Possessive Individualism: Hobbes to Locke* (Oxford: Clarendon, 1962), Part II, Chapter 3.

a previous model—even though they can be incorporated in the latter. The objective that existing products be abandoned or discarded—to promote sales—drives this strategy. If the existing product has not been fully amortized or has low resale value, the purchaser may incur debt to purchase the new one. Abandonment of the existing product may then generate waste—and negative environmental effects—costs that are seldom included in prices.

Boeing, for example, is considered to have followed this strategy in recent decades.[155] New engines with less negative environmental impact were not placed on existing models that had a long service life left and could accommodate them. Commercial aircraft can have service lives that span several decades, and the new engines could have been accommodated with minor modifications. They were instead sold only with much more expensive new models. Customers were thus induced to purchase the new model—paying tens of millions of dollars (per aircraft) over the cost of a retrofit. And, collusion with engine manufacturers ensured that the new engines would only be installed in the new model.

Given the duopolistic character of large commercial aircraft production—dominated by Boeing and Airbus—such arrangements can be quite advantageous. Producing commercial aircraft that have only one engine supplier—as opposed to the previous customary choice of two or three—can generate greater revenue. And, the sense of novelty of new models can be inflated by, say, advertising greater fuel efficiency that can only occur under ideal conditions—regarding weather, air traffic control, maintenance, passenger and cargo loads, flight software, or airport operations. The complexity of flight software in a new model, which requires additional training, may also be minimized to promote sales—at the cost of greater risk for passengers and customers—as occurred with Boeing's 737 Max 8 aircraft.[156]

Overconsumption

Inducing overconsumption of technology products and services that leads to ill or irreversible effects is a common example of wants contrivance. The initial consumption of a product may not be superfluous, in the sense that it may have utility. But

155 See Jon Ostrower, "At Boeing, Innovation in Small Steps," *Wall Street Journal*, April 3, 2015, B5; Steve Denning, "What Went Wrong at Boeing?" *Forbes*, January 21, 2013, www.forbes.com/; Florence Graves and Sara K. Goo, "Boeing Parts Scandal: Boeing Parts and Rules Bent, Whistle-Blowers Say," *Washington Post*, April 17, 2006, www.washingtonpost.com/; Philip K. Lawrence and David W. Thornton, *Deep Stall: The Turbulent Story of Boeing Commercial Airplanes* (Aldershot: Ashgate, 2005), chapters 3, 5, 8.

156 Martin Peterson, "The Ethical Failures Behind the Boeing Disasters," *Blog of the APA*, April 8, 2019, https://blog.apaonline.org/; Rob Picheta, "Ethiopian Airlines Crash is Second Disaster Involving Boeing 737 Max 8 in Months," *CNN*, March 11, 2019, www.cnn.com/.

greater consumption than necessary—leading to illness, permanent or temporary disability, or death—is the defining feature.

The priority to increase sales and extend the purchase chain is at the root of this problem. Consumer exploitation is entwined with it. The oligopolistic pricing differential thus takes a toll on personal finances through every purchase. And, unnecessary chains of purchases may be considered add-ons to the price differential—compounding exploitation. This is often accompanied by data exploitation—intimate information being mined to advertise and sell more.

Overconsumption of some treatments and medications provides examples. This is often connected to biopharmaceutical and biotech oligopolists' control over knowledge—and its nondisclosure to patients. Conditions for which treatment or medication were not considered necessary in the past—or that were thought to be normal—are one case.[157] Evaluation of new medications and treatments over the years—and of new uses for existing ones—has indicated that many offer no additional benefit and can create problems that offset the benefits they provide.[158] Such knowledge is crucially important for practitioners—who depend on the biopharmaceutical or biotech marketer for guidance. During the last two decades such guidance was found to be accompanied by "incentives" to prescribe more—travel awards to conferences and consulting fee arrangements being examples.[159]

Conflicts of interest in the medical profession—and collusion with biopharmaceutical or biotech providers—have added to this panorama in recent times. Such conflicts were related to overconsumption that led to ill effects, disabilities, or death. In one case, for example, the president of a medical specialty association failed to declare conflicts of interest (as required) in over 50 articles published in some of the most prestigious medical journals—despite the fact that biopharmaceutical and biotech corporations (all of them oligopolistic) had paid $8 million for his research and nearly $114,000 in consulting and

157 Angell, *Truth About the Drug Companies*; H. Gilbert Welch, Lisa Schwartz and Steve Woloshin, *Overdiagnosed: Making People Sick in the Pursuit of Health* (Boston: Beacon, 2012).

158 See the databases in *Prescrire International*, www.english.prescrire.org/ (accessed August 11, 2022); Diane Archer, "Hundreds of New Drugs are Harmful or Ineffective," *Just Care*, August 10, 2017, www.justcare.org/.

159 Charles Ornstein, Mike Tigas and Ryann G. Jones, "Dollars for Doctors—Now there's Proof: Docs Who Get Company Cash tend to Prescribe More Brand-Name Meds; the More Money Doctors Receive from Drug and Medical Device Companies, the More Brand-Name Drugs they tend to Prescribe, A New ProPublica Analysis Shows, Even a Meal Can Make a Difference," *ProPublica*, March 17, 2016, www.propublica.org/; Robert Steinbrook, "Industry Payments to Physicians and Prescribing of Brand-Name Drugs," *JAMA Internal Medicine* 176 (2016), 1123; Jerome P. Kassirer, *On the Take: How Medicine's Complicity with Big Business Can Endanger Your Health* (New York: Oxford University Press, 2006), chapters 1, 3–5.

speaking fees.[160] Beyond such conflicts and the limited information distributed to consumers and physicians, "opinion leaders"—well-known researchers or practitioners who are paid by the manufacturers—have been used to promote greater consumption than necessary, often with ill effects.[161]

Direct publicity to consumers can also induce them to overconsume by pressuring physicians to prescribe more than necessary. In recent times many parents, for example—fearing their children would not excel in school—sought medication for Attention Deficit Hyperactivity Disorder (ADHD) that was considered excessive and harmful. Consumption of medications for this disorder was estimated to be double or even triple the necessary amount during the last decade.[162]

Required testing for new treatments and medications, moreover, is all too often controlled by the biopharmaceutical and biotech oligopolies. Financial considerations often rule over the testing process and can be an important factor in the conduct or termination of trials. Suppressing negative results obtained in trials—by withholding their publication—has long been a problem with testing regimes. This can slow down future research, shortchange treatments, and lead to complications, illnesses, disabilities, and deaths.[163] For perpetrators, the suppression of negative results can keep rivals from saving research resources or time in trials. Also, selective interpretation and publication of trial results

160 Charles Ornstein and Katie Thomas, "What These Medical Journals Don't Reveal: Top Doctors' Ties to Industry," *New York Times*, December 8, 2018, www.nytimes.com/. See also ProPublica, *Dollars for Doctors: How Industry Money Reaches Physicians*, www.propublica.org/ (accessed August 10, 2022); Kasra Ziai, Alessio Pigazzi, Brian R. Smith, Roxana Nouri-Nikbakht, *et al.*, "Association of Compensation from the Surgical and Medical Device Industry to Physicians and Self-Declared Conflict of Interest," *JAMA Surgery* 153 (2018), 997–1002.

161 See For Purpose Law Group, *Conflicts Scandals at Major Medical Centers*, April 11, 2019, https://forpurposelaw.com/; John Mack, "A KOL by Any Other Name: Too Toxic for Everyday Use, or Still the Best Term to Use?" *Pharma Marketing News* 14 (2015), www.pharma-mkting.com/; Sergio Sismondo, *"You're Not Just a Paid Monkey Reading Slides": How Key Opinion Leaders Explain and Justify Their Work*, Working Paper no. 26 (Cambridge: Safra Center for Ethics, Harvard University, 2013).

162 Alan Schwarz, *ADHD Nation: Children, Doctors, Big Pharma, and the Making of an American Epidemic* (New York: Scribner, 2016), chapters 7, 8, 13, 18; Stephen P. Hinshaw and Richard M. Scheffler, "How Attention-Deficit Disorder Went Global," *Wall Street Journal*, March 12, 2014, A19; Pieter Cohen and Nicolas Rasmussen, "A Nation of Kids on Speed," *Wall Street Journal*, June 17, 2013, A17.

163 See Joel Lexchin, "The Pharmaceutical Industry in Contemporary Capitalism," *Monthly Review*, March 2018, 44–45; Martin Enserink, "Withholding Results from Clinical Trials is Unethical, Says WHO," *Science*, April 14, 2015, www.sciencemag.org/; Ben Goldacre, "Trial Sans Error: How Pharma-Funded Research Cherry-Picks Positive Results; Clinical Trial Data is Systematically Withheld from Doctors and Patients, Bringing into Question Many of the Premises of the Pharmaceutical Industry—and the Medicine We Use," *Scientific American*, February 13, 2013, www.scientificamerican.com/.

are not uncommon, due to the power that biotech and biopharmaceutical oligopolies have over most every aspect of testing—and the lack of oversight.[164]

Overconsumption of antibiotics—in biotech treatments, through biopharmaceutical sales, or in agro-tech—is another example. This is a result of the sales drive by biopharmaceutical and biotech oligopolists, insufficient communication of knowledge (or misinformation), faulty regulation, and irresponsible (or unethical) conduct by practitioners. During the last decade, it was estimated that antibiotics used for treating infectious wounds failed to work in about two-thirds of all cases in the United States, and over two million people were estimated to suffer from antibiotic-resistant infections annually during the last decade—leading to a significant number of deaths (directly or through complications).[165]

Overconsumption in this case was estimated by the Centers for Disease Control and Prevention to have occurred in about one in three prescriptions.[166] Deaths from infections with *Clostridium difficile*—a pathogen that can be acquired while taking antibiotics after biotech and biopharmaceutical treatments—rose by 500 percent over a seven-year period, killing tens of thousands annually in the United States.[167] And, the global death toll from antimicrobial-resistant infections—due to antibiotic overconsumption—was estimated to be close to a million annually during the last decade, a figure projected to rise to 10 million by the middle of the twenty-first century.[168]

164 Over the years, insufficient oversight has been attributed to the "partnership" of regulators with biopharmaceutical and biotech corporations—see Lexchin, "Pharmaceutical Industry," 44–46; Joseph Walker, "Doctors Advise FDA and Companies, Too," *Wall Street Journal*, December 9, 2014, A1; Alicia Mundy, *Dispensing with the Truth: The Victims, the Drug Companies, and the Dramatic Story Behind the Battle Over Fen-Phen* (New York: St. Martin's, 2013); Kassirer, *On the Take*; Angell, *Truth About the Drug Companies*; Welch, Schwartz and Woloshin, *Overdiagnosed*.

165 Centers for Disease Control and Prevention, *Antibiotic/Antimicrobial Resistance (AR/AMR)*, September 10, 2018, www.cdc.gov/; Laura Santhanam, "The Problem with Overusing Antibiotics: When They Were Developed Nearly a Century Ago, Antibiotics Were Intended as a Last Resort," *PBS News Hour*, March 29, 2018, www.pbs.org/; Julie Beck, "Antibiotic Resistance is Everyone's Problem: How Can Doctors, Drug Companies, and Governments Prevent a Future Where People Die of Minor Infections?" *The Atlantic*, June 27, 2015, www.theatlantic.com/; *The Economist*, "Antibiotic Resistance: The Drugs Don't Work; Running out of Ammunition in the War on Germs," May 3, 2014, 54.

166 Centers for Disease Control and Prevention, *CDC: 1 in 3 Antibiotic Prescriptions Unnecessary* (accessed August 9, 2022); and its *New CDC Data Show Large Percentage of Antibiotics Misused in Outpatient Settings*, May 3, 2016, www.cdc.gov/.

167 Centers for Disease Control and Prevention, *Clostridioides Difficile Infection* (accessed August 12, 2022); and its *Nearly Half a Million Americans Suffered from Clostridium Difficile Infections in a Single Year*, February 25, 2015, www.cdc.gov/; Robert Roos, "CDC Puts C Difficile Burden at 453,000 Cases, 29,000 Deaths," *CIDRAP News*, February 25, 2015, www.cidrap.umn.edu/.

168 World Health Organization, *Antibiotic Resistance*, February 5, 2018, www.who.int./; Center for Infectious Disease Research and Policy, *WHO Releases its First Report on Global Antibiotic Resistance*, CIDRAP, University of Minnesota, January 29, 2018, www.cidrap.umn.edu/; Francesca Pestinaci, Patrizio Pezzotti and Annalisa Pantosti, "Antimicrobial Resistance: A Global Multifaceted

Indicating the gravity of this trend is that genes of antibiotic-resistant bacteria have been found in remote Arctic locations—8,000 miles away from their natural habitat.[169] Despite this scenario, standard antibiotic dosages increased by 50 percent over a 15-year period around the world—a dynamic that generates greater resistance as microbes evolve.[170] Growing resistance to antibiotics could set back treatment of certain illnesses as much as a century—resulting in extractions and amputations when infections occur, while increasing risk for biotech and biopharmaceutical products or procedures involving transplants, cancer, cardiac interventions, and most every other surgical episode.[171] And, estimates of the cost of treating antibiotic resistance by the middle of the twenty-first century have placed it at four percent of the world's economic product—a prospect that could affect public finances in most nations.[172]

Biotech and biopharmaceutical oligopolists' promotion of overconsumption in this area has gone beyond marketing to humans. Serious effects on the food chain are occurring, which will eventually affect nature *and* humans—a sort of tech-driven biofeedback panorama that will likely have major health impacts as the twenty-first century advances. It has been found that human antibiotic resistance also results from the food chain, due to overconsumption in animals—to increase their weight, accelerate growth, or prevent infection in the crowded conditions in which they are raised.[173] Animal raising has become a largely techno-industrial operation—promoted by biopharmaceutical and biotech oligopolies—with powerful farming companies as clients.

Animals are thus given large amounts of antibiotics through the feed and water they consume—developing antibiotic-resistant bacteria in their organs. Humans who consume the meat of antibiotic-treated animals can be affected. It was estimated during the last decade that farms consumed 80 percent of all

Phenomenon," *Pathogens and Global Health* 109 (2015), 309–18; Sara Reardon, "Antibiotic Resistance Sweeping Developing World: Bacteria are Increasingly Dodging Extermination as Drug Availability Outpaces Regulation," *Nature*, May 6, 2014, www.nature.com/.

169 Clare M. McCann, Beate Christgen, Jenifer A. Roberts, Jian-Qiang Su, *et al.*, "Understanding Drivers of Antibiotic Resistance Genes in High Arctic Soil Ecosystems," *Environment International*, January 2019, www.elsevier.com/; Brianna Abbott, "India Superbug Spread Far, Fast, Researchers Find," *Wall Street Journal*, January 28, 2019, A6.

170 Eili Klein, Ramanan Laxminarayan, Thomas P. Van Boeckel, *et al.*, *Global Increase and Geographic Convergence in Antibiotic Consumption Between 2000 and 2015*, Center for Disease Dynamics, Economics and Policy, April 6, 2018, https://cddep.org/; *The Economist*, "Resistance to Antibiotics," May 3, 2014, 78.

171 Oliver Franklin-Wallis, "The Drugs Don't Work: What Happens After Antibiotics? Antibiotic Resistance is Growing So Fast that Routine Surgery Could Soon Become Impossible," *The Guardian*, March 24, 2019, www.theguardian.com/.

172 International Bank for Reconstruction and Development (World Bank), *Drug-Resistant Infections: A Threat to Our Economic Future*, March 2017, www.worldbank.org/.

173 Maryn McKenna, "How Pharma Hides Data about Farm Antibiotic Use," *Wired*, June 11, 2018, www.wired.com/; and her *Big Chicken: The Incredible Story of How Antibiotics Created Modern Agriculture and Changed the Way the World Eats* (Washington: National Geographic Partners, 2017).

antibiotics sold in the United States—poultry farmers using much more than those who raise livestock or hogs.[174] A chicken's average weight at slaughter (56 days old) was thus found to have increased by 367 percent over a span of almost 50 years, taking (in the last decade) about half the time to achieve it.[175] This is a matter of great importance to the oligopolistic corporations that rule food production technologies, because of the additional revenue it generated. One consequence is that every year almost one-and-a-half million cases of salmonella-related food poisoning—largely from poultry consumption—occur in the United States, resulting in tens of thousands of hospitalizations and hundreds of deaths.[176]

Heavy antibiotic usage, along with genetically engineered hormones, helped accelerate the time needed for cattle to reach slaughter weight from five to just over one year.[177] Livestock raising thus consumes about twice the amount of antibiotics used by humans—a very important market for biopharmaceutical and agro-biotech oligopolists. Effects on humans are already being felt by the most vulnerable. Death rates due to antibiotic resistance are highest among children under six years of age, but vulnerability may soon increase for other age groups.[178] And, the long-term effects on the food chain are largely unknown—raising the likelihood of irreversible damage to not only human health but also the planet's ecology.[179]

Addictions

Wants promotion can also induce addiction through consumption of products or services. Addiction may not be irreversible, in the sense that it might be redressed through individual actions or therapies. Consumer exploitation is embedded in this typology, as each unnecessary purchase damages finances—and is often

174 *The Economist*, "Industrial Farming—Jukes Hazard: How Antibiotics Changed the Way America Eats," September 23, 2017, 28.

175 *The Economist*, "Ruling the Roost: How Chicken Became the Rich World's Most Popular Meat," January 19, 2019, 59–60; Martin J. Zuidhof, B. L. Schneider, Valerie Carney, Doug R. Korver, *et al.*, "Growth, Efficiency and Yield of Commercial Broilers from 1957, 1978 and 2005," *Poultry Science* 93 (2014), 2970–82; *The Economist*, "Industrial Farming."

176 Centers for Disease Control and Prevention, *Reports of Selected Salmonella Outbreak Investigations*, www.cdc.gov/ (accessed August 10, 2022).

177 See Anthony Winson, *The Industrial Diet: The Degradation of Food and the Struggle for Healthy Eating* (New York: New York University Press, 2014); Loren Cordain, S. Boyd Eaton, Anthony Sebastian, Neil Mann, *et al.*, "Origins and Evolution of the Western Diet: Health Implications for the 21st Century," *American Journal of Clinical Nutrition* 81 (2005), 341–54; McKenna, "How Pharma Hides Data."

178 Centers for Disease Control and Prevention, *Antibiotic/Antimicrobial Resistance*; Franklin-Wallis, "Drugs Don't Work."

179 See Rob Wallace, *Big Farms Make Big Flu: Dispatches on Infectious Disease, Agribusiness, and the Nature of Science* (New York: Monthly Review Press, 2016); Winson, *Industrial Diet.*

accompanied by a substantial expenditure of time and effort, along with risk to self and others. Wants contrivance here all too often induces individuals to think that they "need" a product—despite the likelihood that they would be better (or at least as well) off without it.

Intensity of advertising is thought to be an important factor in the rise of addiction-related problems. In recent decades even children have been increasingly drawn to "learn to want" products that end up being addictive.[180] Longer-term (life cycle-long) wants contrivance seems to be a major strategic objective—as vast amounts of intimate data are accumulated and updated.

All too often what starts out as the necessary consumption of a tech service or product—or a simple matter of individual curiosity—turns into recurrent distractions, obsessive use, and impulsive purchases that provide little or no utility, or expose the individual to danger.[181] Such behavior can be seen as part of a continuum between compulsivity and impulsivity, where the former is characterized by false impressions of harm avoidance and the latter by risk-taking behavior based on fantasy.[182] Advice and templates to make tech product consumption addictive were frequently dispensed by management consultants during the last decade.[183]

Software that can detect individual moods was designed to try to induce dependence.[184] Smartphones included such software during the last decade.[185] Telecom oligopolies have strategically used it to promote wants and sales to everyone, anytime, everywhere—an attractive possibility for companies that advertise through smartphones.

180 See *The Economist*, "No Child's Play: Streaming Giants Get More Serious about Children's Shows," January 8, 2022, 54–55; Joel Bakan, *Childhood under Siege: How Big Business Targets Children* (New York: Simon and Schuster, 2011), chapters 3–5; Susan G. Thomas, *Buy, Buy Baby: How Consumer Culture Manipulates Parents and Harms Young Minds* (New York: Houghton Mifflin, 2007), chapters 2, 4, 5.

181 See Wu, *Attention Merchants*; Adam Gazzaley and Larry D. Rosen, *The Distracted Mind: Ancient Brains in a High Tech World* (Cambridge, MA: MIT Press, 2016); Susan Greenfield, *Mind Change: How Digital Technologies are Leaving their Mark on Our Brains* (New York: Random House, 2015).

182 See Zsolt Demetrovics and Marc D. Griffiths, "Behavioral Addictions: Past, Present and Future," *Journal of Behavioral Addictions* 1 (2012), 1–2; Andrea Allen, Audrey King and Eric Hollander, "Obsessive-Compulsive Spectrum Disorders," *Dialogues in Clinical Neuroscience* 5 (2003), 259–71; Thomas, *Buy, Buy Baby*, chapters 4, 5.

183 See *The Economist*, "Getting Hooked: How Digital Firms Create Products that Get Inside People's Heads," January 3, 2015, 53; Nir M. Eyal and Ryan Hoover, *Hooked: How to Build Habit-Forming Products* (London: Portfolio Penguin, 2014), chapters 1, 7, 8; Jill Krasny, "4 Steps to Building Habit-Forming Products," *Inc.*, December 11, 2014, www.inc.com/.

184 *The Economist*, "Your Phone Says 'Cheer Up!' Software that Senses How You are Feeling is Being Pitched to Gadget-Makers," January 3, 2015, 48.

185 A well-known technology journalist, for example, noted receiving 310 notifications through her smartphone in one day that involved picking up the device 210 times—Joanna Stern, "Willpower Eased iPhone Addiction," *Wall Street Journal*, September 12, 2018, B4.

Addictive use of smartphones was estimated to have led to numerous road accidents during the last decade, many of them deadly.[186] More than one-third of individuals surveyed—by one of the largest insurance companies in the United States—admitted to texting while driving a road vehicle, almost one-third reported accessing the internet, and one-quarter declared reading emails.[187] The survey (and related research) led the company to label smartphone usage while driving "an indicator of addiction."[188] Rising insurance rates was an outcome—with negative consequences for individual or household budgets.[189]

Addiction to video gaming has attracted alarm, prompting the World Health Organization to add the category *Gaming Disorder* to its international classification of diseases during the last decade.[190] The American Psychiatric Association, for its part, concluded that "internet gaming disorder" shares similarities with conventional gaming (gambling) disorder—including the term in its *Diagnostic and Statistical Manual of Mental Disorders*.[191] Consumption of videogames was found to be induced in a way that is "designed to hit the pleasure centers of the brain in some of the same ways that gambling can"—by a well-known behavioral research scientist.[192] Gambling casinos long ago understood this aspect—a matter that drove them to create loyalty programs and mine customer databases.[193] And, the likelihood that prolonged video gaming might lead to—or compound—ADHD was raised by prominent researchers who followed 2,500 video gaming teenagers over a two-year period.[194]

186 Cambridge Mobile Telematics, *Distracted Driving Awareness*, www.cmtelematics.com/ (accessed August 12, 2022); Scott Calvert, "Pedestrian Deaths Highest Since 1990s," *Wall Street Journal*, February 28, 2019, A3; Kyle Stock, Lance Lambert and David Ingold, "Smartphones are Killing Americans, But Nobody's Counting: Amid a Historic Spike in U.S. Traffic Fatalities, Federal Data on the Danger of Distracted Driving are Getting Worse," *Bloomberg*, October 17, 2017, www.bloomberg.com/.

187 State Farm Mutual Automobile Insurance Company, *4 Symptoms of Cell Phone Addiction*, www.statefarm.com/ (accessed August 14, 2022); and its *Distracted Driving*, 2016, https://newsroom.statefarm.com/.

188 State Farm Mutual Automobile Insurance Company, *4 Symptoms*.

189 Leslie Scism and Nicole Friedman, "Smartphone Use Lifts Car-Insurance Rates," *Wall Street Journal*, February 21, 2017, A1; Joel J. Kofsky, *The Link Between Smartphones and Insurance Increases*, March 23, 2017, www.prweb.com/.

190 World Health Organization, *Gaming Disorder*, January 2018, www.who.int/; Susan Scutti, "WHO Classifies 'Gaming Disorder' as Mental Health Condition," *CNN*, June 18, 2018, www.cnn.com/.

191 American Psychiatric Association, *Diagnostic and Statistical Manual of Mental Disorders (DSM-5)*, www.psychiatry.org/ (accessed August 20, 2022).

192 Douglas A. Gentile, "The Multiple Dimensions of Video Game Effects," *Child Development Perspectives* 5 (2011), 75–81.

193 Kate O'Keeffe, "Real Prize in Caesars Fight: Data on Players," *Wall Street Journal*, March 20, 2015, B1.

194 Chaelin K. Ra, Junhan Cho, Matthew D. Stone, *et al.*, "Association of Digital Media Use with Subsequent Symptoms of Attention-Deficit/Hyperactivity Disorder among Adolescents," *Journal*

Neuropsychologists and social psychologists are usually contracted to devise ways to keep videogame users engaged and returning. Increasing demand and dependence is a strategic function of product development units (the D in R&D) in technology corporations that sell games. It is not a coincidence that children and youngsters—the main age groups targeted by videogame oligopolists—are the heaviest users.[195]

The hiring of behavioral specialists to promote wants reflects the objective of turning games into a life-long habit. Updating apps or introducing new products—such as virtual and augmented reality—helped promote new demand during the last decade.[196] Storytelling was also found to attract interest in videogames.[197] Streaming then provided a way to increase demand.[198] And the purchase of apps—necessary to allow videogames to work—cemented consumer exploitation.[199]

Gaming platforms thus became a means to induce new wants and to sell any related product. Children and youngsters were turned into consumers *and* uselaborers—generating data, uncompensated online worktime, purchases, and revenue from ad viewings. Then, as their intimate data were appropriated, their efforts, time use, and experiences were mined—to deploy AI algorithms that can track each of them throughout a lifetime.

The arrival of virtual and augmented reality products during the last decade promoted greater consumption of both virtual reality and videogames—despite the rising incidence of identity theft, accidents, and loss of privacy.[200] In the case of identity theft, for example, users who signed up using an Apple iPhone usually gave videogame oligopolists permission to access data associated with a Google account (contacts, calendar, emails, and the like).[201] Risk of injury

of the American Medical Association 320 (2018), 255–63. Their sample included teenagers who used social media and video-streaming sites.

195 *The Economist*, "Addictive Behaviour: Can You Get Hooked on Videogames? Games-Makers Latest Business Models have Bolstered the Case that You Can," January 1, 2022, 46–47; and its "If you Build It: Besides the Tech Titans, Video-Game Firms want a Slice of the Metaverse Pie," November 20, 2021, 64–66; Julie Jargon, "You Spent $1,500 on a Virtual What? Kids are Splurging on Digital Goods such as Outfits for their Videogame Avatars, as 'Money Turns Magical' with Virtual Spending," *Wall Street Journal*, July 17, 2019, A15.

196 *The Economist*, "Addictive Behaviour"; Jack Nicas and Cat Zakrzewski, "Augmented Reality beyond Pokémon: Popularity of the 'Pokémon Go' App is Putting a Spotlight on Other Forms, Uses of the Technology," *Wall Street Journal*, July 14, 2016, B1.

197 See Evelyn M. Rusli, "Oculus VR Seeks to Go Beyond Games: Facebook Unit to Create Lab to Help Studios Create Films Using Virtual Reality Technology," *Wall Street Journal*, January 27, 2015, B4.

198 *The Economist*, "Video Games: The Games are Only Just Beginning," November 7, 2020, 58–59.

199 See Jargon, "You Spent $1,500"; *The Economist*, "Video Games"; Mike Shields and Steven Perlberg, "Ad Agencies Hunt for Pokémon Game Plan," *Wall Street Journal*, July 14, 2016, B4.

200 *The Economist*, "Headset Wars: Seeing and Believing," April 9, 2022, 49–50; and its *The Economist*, "Addictive Behaviour."

201 See *The Economist*, "Video Games"; Nicas and Zakrzewski, "Augmented Reality"; Takashi Mochizuki and Sarah E. Needleman, "Pokémon Game Jolts Nintendo: Augmented Reality App

became a concern, as usage expanded to outdoor settings.[202] And video gaming while driving was estimated to have caused many road accidents—as gaming habits were maintained into adulthood.[203]

Addictive consumption has also affected biotech and biopharmaceuticals—sectors that are entwined and depend on one another to provide effective health care. Reducing pain is particularly important for those undergoing biotech treatments or surgery. Opioid medications have long been used for that purpose, due to their effectiveness. However, over-prescription and excessive usage—promoted by the oligopolistic corporations that produce them—became a major problem.[204]

Addiction rates from opioid medications rose by 500 percent, and deaths increased by almost 350 percent during a quarter-century—while sales more than quadrupled since the start of the twenty-first century.[205] The case of OxyContin—owned by Purdue Pharmaceuticals—sparked much concern, due to its aggressive marketing and payments to physicians.[206] Record-setting rises in mortality rates from certain opioid medications—such as fentanyl—were part of this panorama.[207] Opioid medication addiction is reversible, yet the co-optation of physicians and regulators prevented effective remedial action. Compounding the problem is that after opioid medications lead to addiction,

Fuels Craze, Sends Videogame Maker's Shares Soaring," *Wall Street Journal*, July 12, 2016, B5.

202 See Kate Richards, Kai Wong and Mansoor Khan, "Augmented Reality Game Related Injuries," *New Horizons in Clinical Case Reports* 2 (2017), 27.

203 Mara Faccio and John J. McConnell, *Death by Pokémon GO: The Economic and Human Cost of Using Apps While Driving*, NBER Working Paper 24308, June 4, 2018, https://papers.ssrn.com/. See also State Farm Mutual Automobile Insurance Company, *4 Symptoms*; and its *Distracted Driving*.

204 See Anne Case and Angus Deaton, *Deaths of Despair and the Future of Capitalism* (Princeton: Princeton University Press, 2020), chapters 7–9, 13.

205 Anne Steele, "Opioid Addiction Climbs by 500%: Study of Millions of Medical Claims Shows a Surge of Diagnoses in Past Seven Years," *Wall Street Journal*, June 30, 2017, A3; Blue Cross Blue Shield Association, *America's Opioid Epidemic and Its Effect on the Nation's Commercially-Insured Population*, June 29, 2017, www.bcbs.com/; *The Economist*, "Pharmaceuticals: A World of Pain; Makers and Distributors of Opioid Painkillers are Under Scrutiny," April 8, 2017, 56; Nora D. Volkow, *America's Addiction to Opioids: Heroin and Prescription Drug Abuse*, National Institute on Drug Abuse, May 2014, www.drugabuse.gov/.

206 Patrick R. Keefem, *Empire of Pain: The Secret History of the Sackler Dynasty* (New York: Doubleday, 2021), chapters 17, 25. See also Scott Higham and Sari Horwitz, *American Cartel* (New York: Twelve, 2022), chapters 34–40; Macy, *Dopesick*, chapters 4, 11; Scott Glover and Lisa Girion, "A Closely Guarded List: As Sales Surpass the $27 Billion Mark, OxyContin's Maker Has Privately Identified About 1,800 Doctors Who May Have Recklessly Prescribed the Drug to Addicts and Dealers, Yet it Has Done Little to Alert Authorities," *Los Angeles Times*, August 11, 2013, A1.

207 Centers for Disease Control and Prevention, *U.S. Drug Overdose Deaths*; National Institute on Drug Abuse, *Overdose Death Rates*, August 2018, www.drugabuse.gov/; Christopher Ingraham, "Fentanyl Use Drove Drug Overdose Deaths to a Record High in 2017, CDC Estimates," *Washington Post*, August 15, 2018, www.washingtonpost.com/.

consumers often resort to synthetic, illegal opioids to continue (or supplement) their dependence.[208]

On their part, physicians have all too frequently prescribed powerful, long-acting opioid painkillers for minor injuries, usually under guidance from biopharmaceutical and biotech oligopolists.[209] During the last decade, it was found that many among them engaged physicians for "speaking programs" and provided substantial fees—depending on the amount of prescriptions written.[210] Opioid over-prescription all too often leads to addiction—affecting the population across all age and gender groups, but more severely males between the ages of 25 and 44.[211] This is a prime labor force component, and the rapid growth of addiction and related mortality is a worrisome prospect.[212]

Typologies

Inducing purchase of products that require accessories in order to work is an important typology of wants promotion. The product purchased is practically useless—or may provide limited utility—without the additional purchases. The latter, in turn, compound exploitation as their cost must be added to the oligopolistic price differential. And they can contribute to data exploitation through the data that users are made to provide.

In agro-biotech, Monsanto—the largest provider of genetically engineered seeds—is an example. In recent decades this company sold its glyphosate-based herbicide—Roundup—as an indispensable companion for its seeds.[213] Nine-tenths of all corn and soybean crops in the United States

208 See Matthew P. Prekupec, Peter A. Mansky and Michael H. Baumann, "Misuse of Novel Synthetic Opioids: A Deadly New Trend," *Journal of Addiction Medicine* 11 (2017), 256–65.

209 Travis Rieder, "The Perilous Blessing of Opioids: An Injured Bioethicist Learned Firsthand How Desperately Patients with Severe Pain Need the Relief of Powerful Drugs—and How Little Support They Get to Stop Taking Them," *Wall Street Journal*, June 15, 2019, C3; Anna Lembke, *Drug Dealer, MD: How Doctors Were Duped, Patients Got Hooked, and Why It's So Hard to Stop* (Baltimore: Johns Hopkins University Press, 2016); Jon Kami, "New Painkiller Sparks Abuse Concern," *Wall Street Journal*, May 24, 2014, A3; Glover and Girion, "Closely Guarded List."

210 Joseph Walker, "Doctors' Trial Reveals Tactics to Sell Opioid," *Wall Street Journal*, February 4, 2016, B3. See also Case and Deaton, *Deaths of Despair*; Rieder, "Perilous Blessing."

211 Centers for Disease Control and Prevention, *U.S. Drug Overdose Deaths Continue to Rise; Increase Fueled by Synthetic Opioids*, March 29, 2018, www.cdc.gov/.

212 See Kaiser Family Foundation, *Opioid Overdose Deaths by Age Group*, www.kff.org/ (accessed July 23, 2022); Centers for Disease Control and Prevention, *U.S. Drug Overdose Deaths*.

213 See Marie-Monique Robin, *The World According to Monsanto: Pollution, Corruption, and the Control of the World's Food Supply* (New York: New Press, 2010), and her documentary "The World According to Monsanto" (Ottawa: National Film Board of Canada, 2008); Daniel Charles, *Lords of the Harvest: Biotech, Big Money, and the Future of Food* (Cambridge, MA: Perseus, 2002); Helena Paul and Ricarda Steinbrecher, *Hungry Corporations: How Transnational Biotech Companies Colonise the Food Chain* (London: Zed, 2003).

used it—and it was aggressively marketed for other uses, such as landscaping and gardening.

This strategy allowed Monsanto to obtain the largest surpluses in its sector—leading to its merger with Bayer AG, one of the largest pesticide producers in the world.[214] And, the surpluses also made it possible for Monsanto to acquire numerous companies in related sectors over the years—that allowed it to become involved in the exploitation of large agricultural databases and farming services.[215] Crop damages caused by its powerful pesticide further strengthened its oligo-monopolistic position, by making customers more dependent on its engineered seeds—as ecologies and crops were decimated, making it very difficult to return to natural seeds.[216]

At the same time, farmers were made dependent on more potent versions of its herbicide—to be able to continue farming.[217] The toxicity of Monsanto's herbicide then prompted the World Health Organization to issue a warning during the last decade.[218] And, lawsuits linking its use to cancer led to very substantial monetary awards.[219] Yet, despite mounting evidence, farmers had no choice but to continue using the herbicide, because of a lack of effective alternatives.[220]

Consumer technologies provide many examples of oligopolistic product-*cum*-accessories wants contrivance. Apple's apps—initially intended for its smartphones—are one case. Its App Store has millions for sale—most of which only work with its products—a form of accessory lock-in. Its smartphones would be almost useless without the apps, so they are a compulsory acquisition—an add-on charge (p^{η}) to the oligopolistic price differential.

But the apps, purchased in large quantities by Apple's customers, receive relatively little usage—a symptom of limited utility and of Apple's drive to promote wants and sales. Over three-quarters of Apple's smartphone customers

214 See Brian Fung and Caitlin Dewey, "Justice Department Approves Bayer-Monsanto Merger in Landmark Settlement," *Washington Post*, May 29, 2018, www.washingtonpost.com/.

215 Jason Davidson, "Bayer, Monsanto and Big Data: Who Will Control our Food System in the Era of Digital Agriculture and Mega-Mergers?" *Medium*, March 30, 2018, https://medium.com/; Karl Plume, "Monsanto's Climate Corp to Expand Digital Farming Platform," *Reuters*, August 17, 2016, www.reuters.com/.

216 Jacob Bunge, "Potent Weedkiller Draws Complaints over Crop Damage," *Wall Street Journal*, July 12, 2017, B1.

217 Bunge, "Potent Weedkiller"; Robin, *World According to Monsanto*.

218 World Health Organization, International Agency for Research on Cancer, *IARC Monograph on Glyphosate* (Lyon, France: IARC, 2015), www.iarc.fr/; Center for Food Safety, *Glyphosate and Cancer Risk* (Washington: CFS, 2015), www.centerforfoodsafety.org/.

219 Sara Randazzo and Ruth Bender, "Bayer Loses Weedkiller Verdict," *Wall Street Journal*, March 20, 2019, B1; Sam Levin, "Monsanto Ordered to Pay $289m as Jury Rules Weedkiller Caused Man's Cancer: Court Rules in Favor of DeWayne Johnson, Ill Man Who Was First to Take Roundup Maker to Trial Over Allegations," *The Guardian*, August 10, 2018, www.theguardian.com/.

220 Jacob Bunge, "Farmers Stay with Bayer Herbicide: Roundup's Low Cost and Effectiveness Win Out, for Now, Over Two Cancer Verdicts," *Wall Street Journal*, March 22, 2019, A1.

forgo use of an app within three days after they download it.[221] And, for about one-third of all downloads the user never gets to open an app a third time—while well over three-quarters of each app user's time is spent in only a handful of apps.[222] Less than one-quarter of all Apple's apps are reportedly used in any given month, and most are not used at all.[223]

Low usage may—in addition to limited utility—occur because most apps have to be routinely deleted to free up space, to allow smartphones to work.[224] An accumulation of apps—for those unwilling to delete (and engage in repetitive purchase)—may thus slow down an Apple smartphone to the point that frustration may lead to purchase of a new model.[225] Apps thus play an important (and often unnoticed) part in Apple's product "ecosystem"—beyond their own profitability—when they lead to purchase of new models. In this way, the product-*cum*-accessories wants contrivance chain can be repeated to increase sales (and consumer exploitation).

Apps, software, and personal data are intangible, but they can be as important to an oligopolistic "ecosystem" as blood flow is to human life. Apps are a formidable tool to contrive wants, because of the intimate data they gain access to and accumulate. These, in turn, provide opportunities to advertise, sell, and forecast future preferences—a feature that attracted attention as smartphone use expanded during the last decade.[226] Apple's app-enabled "ecosystem" has also been crucial for fencing-in market niches—by discouraging consumers from surfing the web, to find products offered by other companies.[227]

Apple's smartwatch can be considered another example. An accumulation of (purchased) apps can slow down smartwatches faster than smartphones. As with the latter, this can lead to purchase of new models with greater capacity—thus expanding the purchase chain. Accumulated apps can also end up being deleted at a faster pace than in smartphones, due to the smaller screens. The latter can be a problem for consumers with less-than-perfect vision. Voice command software may not redress it much, given the screens' limitations for video. And, a smartwatch will not keep track of time better than the alternatives—or reduce individual lateness and make its user move faster.[228]

221 Statista, *Mobile App Usage—Statistics and Facts*, www.statista.com/ (accessed July 20, 2022); Christopher Mims, "A Few Ways to Declutter Your Phone," *Wall Street Journal*, February 22, 2016, B1.

222 Statista, *Mobile App Usage*; Mims, "A Few Ways."

223 Statista, *Mobile App Usage*; Mims, "A Few Ways."

224 Mims, "A Few Ways."

225 See Murphy, "There's a Reason why iPhones Get Slower"; Mims, "A Few Ways."

226 See Wakabayashi and Barr, "Apple and Google Race to Predict"; Brian X. Chen and Steve Lohr, "Apple is Becoming a Bigger Target: Regulators, and Hackers, Will Examine Payment Service and Wristwatch," *International New York Times*, September 12, 2014, 17.

227 Christopher Mims, "Apps' Walled Garden Closes Off Wide-Open Web," *Wall Street Journal*, November 17, 2014, B1.

228 Toward the end of a laudatory review, after its introduction, a well-known technology journalist noted: "The Apple Watch has been the most helpful to me as a plain, regular watch, though I've

The smartwatch's very limited battery recharge cycle—about 18 hours when it was introduced—was another drawback.[229] One technology journalist, for example, found that 20 minutes of music listening consumed about one-fifth of its charge.[230] And, most of the smartwatch's functions tended to duplicate what an iPhone provided but in more limited ways—in some cases requiring a smartphone to be nearby to be effective.[231] These drawbacks notwithstanding, Apple seems intent on marketing it as a wearable health diagnostic gadget—to expand its data clouds and sell more apps.[232]

Use of branding to induce wants is a fairly common promotional strategy for technology oligopolies. Brand identification based on psychological factors and social appeal are at the core of this typology. The perception that purchasing a given product is inherently good—because of its brand—motivates the decision to purchase. And the latter can occur even though the product may have little or no utility for the buyer. If there is utility, it may be equal to—or less than—that of a similar product sold for less.

Advertising is a formidable tool to promote brand-based wants. Showing off the brand while using the product—to enhance the consumer's social status or self-esteem—can be an important factor. Branding can contribute to overconsumption, as accessories all too often accompany purchases. It also magnifies consumer exploitation, as the oligopolistic price differential will likely be greater.

Brands are usually trademarked—a type of IP that can be more valuable than some patent portfolios.[233] Fetishizing a brand usually starts with a logotype or symbol that conveys a name, initials, or image to make it recognizable—even to those with limited literacy or vision. The attention expended on logotype creation is—outside the fields of graphic design and advertising—possibly the

---

now perceived that even the highest tech watch won't solve my lifelong problem of being chronically 10 minutes late"—Joanna Stern, "The Hour of the Apple Watch Begins—The Best Reason to Buy It: To Make You Look Good," *Wall Street Journal*, April 9, 2015, D2.

229 *The Economist*, "Wearable Technology: The Wear, Why and How," March 14, 2015, 63–64.

230 Joanna Stern, "The New Apple Watch is a Want, Not a Need," *Wall Street Journal*, September 15, 2016, D4.

231 Christopher Mims, "Why Time Isn't Ripe for Smartwatches," *Wall Street Journal*, April 6, 2015, B1. Much the same drawback was believed to apply to Alphabet-Google's Android Wear smartwatches when they were introduced.

232 Christopher Mims, "In Apple's Third Act, the iPhone Plays a Supporting Role: What Will be the Tech Giant's Next Big Thing? Look for an Expanding Ecosystem of Wearable Computers," *Wall Street Journal*, September 8, 2018, B12; Peter Loftus and Tripp Mickle, "Smartwatch Adds Heart Monitoring and Fall Detection," *Wall Street Journal*, September 13, 2018, B2; Ben Kesling and Tripp Mickle, "Apple to Offer Vets Mobile Health Data," *Wall Street Journal*, November 21, 2018, B1.

233 See Brand Finance, *Valuation Reports*, www.brandfinance.com/ (accessed August 14, 2022); Interbrand, *Best Global Brands 2021*, www.interbrand.com/; *The Economist*, "What are Brands for? Brands are the Most Valuable Assets Companies Possess—But No One Agrees on How Much They are Worth or Why," August 30, 2014, 57–58.

least understood aspect of branding.[234] This is of utmost importance, as all advertising will carry the logotype. The latter will be mentally associated with the qualities a technology oligopolist believes should characterize it—wealth, intelligence, luxury, for example. The effect of frequent repetition on individual cognition is crucially important.[235]

Extensive empirical research during the past five decades showed that less-than-rational decision-making on wants and consumption is quite common. Daniel Kahneman—one of only two behavioral scientists to ever be awarded the Nobel Prize in economics (2002)—found *belief*, as opposed to rationality, to be the most frequent explanation.[236] Decision-making on purchases (and related aspects) was an important part of his meticulous research on preferences. Being well informed about alternatives, the choices to be made—and their consequences—did not change decisions in any significant way.[237] Are decisions based on branding less-than-rational, when they involve technology products that are higher priced but do not provide greater utility than lower-priced alternatives?

Eliciting trust is fundamentally important for branding.[238] Trust is necessary to elicit loyalty and promote sales recurrence. This is especially important when new models provide little or no additional utility beyond existing ones. Appearance and packaging are often crucial for branding—on such aspects as shape, size, color, sound, handling, ergonomics, and even erotic perception.[239] Attention to certain details often indicates the importance of these aspects. During the last decade, for example, Samsung bent the edges of its smartphone screens using flexible organic light-emitting diodes (OLED)—to provide the

234 The work of Paul Rand needs to be taken into account in this regard—Paul Rand, *Paul Rand, A Designer's Art* (New Haven: Yale University Press, 2018); Ellen Shapiro, "Everything is Design, Design is Everything," *Print*, March 3, 2015, www.printmag.com/; Marc Myers, "A Lifelong Allergy to Text," *Wall Street Journal*, March 24, 2015, D5.

235 George Lakoff, *Ten Lectures on Cognitive Linguistics* (Boston: Brill, 2018), "Cognitive Semantics: The Basic Mechanisms of Thought," 18–82.

236 Daniel Kahneman, "Maps of Bounded Rationality: Psychology for Behavioral Economics," *American Economic Review* 93 (2003), 1468, 1470; and the articles in Daniel Kahneman, Paul Slovic and Amos Tversky, eds., *Judgment under Uncertainty: Heuristics and Biases* (New York: Cambridge University Press, 1982).

237 Kahneman, "Maps of Bounded Rationality," 1468, 1470.

238 Consultants' work on trust in branding during the last decade often focused on such aspects as "meaningfulness" and "authenticity"—to target customers. See *Campaign Brief*, "Havas' Meaningful Brands 2017 Report Says Over Half of Content Created by Brands is 'Irrelevant'," March 13, 2017, www.campaignbrief.com/; *The Economist*, "It's the Real Thing: 'Authenticity' is Being Peddled as a Cure for Drooping Brands," November 14, 2015, 69.

239 Wolfgang F. Haug's *Critique of Commodity Aesthetics: Appearance, Sexuality, and Advertising in Capitalist Society* (Cambridge: Polity, 1986) provides an incisive analysis of these aspects. Among the best examples of the importance of appearance and packaging for wants promotion was automotive design in the 1950s and 1960s—see David Gartman, *Auto Opium: A Social History of American Automobile Design* (New York: Routledge, 1994), chapters 4–6.

impression that the gadget "floats" (in the user's hand), despite the fact that contrast and screen size were practically unchanged.[240] This design change drew attention when Apple imitated it for its iPhone.[241]

Branding schemes that target an image of wealth may market a product as part of an established luxury brand. During the last decade Apple, for example, marketed its smartwatch as the Apple Watch Hermès. Hermès's wealthy customers typically paid tens of thousands of dollars for such branded items as handbags, waiting months to receive them—an aspect that undoubtedly drew Apple's attention. Thus, the Apple Watch Hermès was priced approximately 330 percent higher than the price of the non-Hermès version—despite their identical features and capabilities.[242]

Much the same can be done when an image of fitness is targeted. By marketing its smartwatch through a partnership with Nike during the last decade, Apple was able to reach a specialized niche and charge a higher price.[243] Branding can thus involve multiple identities for a product, to charge higher prices and increase sales—despite limited or no additional utility. Through the visibility they provided, these forays allowed Apple to charge higher prices for the smartwatches it sold directly. At that time, for example, the smartwatch Apple sold on its own was priced about 17 percent higher than Samsung's Gear-2, 52 percent higher than LG's G-Watch, and 252 percent higher than that of the comparable Pebble model.[244]

Branding can also facilitate higher pricing for a new model that faces limited demand. The tactic in this case involves first selling the new model only with all the most expensive options for a period of time, and withholding updates for existing models (sold at lower prices than those of the new model). Faster delivery may also be provided for the new model—compared to existing ones—to induce immediate purchase. This scheme can result in the seemingly paradoxical situation of a rising price in the face of limited demand.

In this case, limiting output can lead to a willingness to pay the higher price of the new model, even with unnecessary options—based on branding image and, say, a psychological need to show off the new model early. For consumers unwilling to follow, the updated existing models can become

240 Geoffrey A. Fowler, "An Edgy Bid to Win over Phone Buyers," *Wall Street Journal*, March 30, 2017.

241 Takashi Mochizuki, "Apple Bends in Design of iPhone," *Wall Street Journal*, March 1, 2017, B1.

242 Christina Passariello, "Apple's Foray into Luxury: Inside the Yearlong Collaboration on the Technology and Design of Apple Watch Hermès," *Wall Street Journal*, September 12, 2015, B1.

243 Robert McMillan and Sara Germano, "Apple Watch Shifts Focus to Fitness: Tech Giant Teams Up with Nike to Market New Sports-Themed, Water-Resistant Device," *Wall Street Journal*, September 12, 2016, B4.

244 Daisuke Wakabayashi, "Apple Seeks Identity for Smartwatch: Envisioned as a Health Monitor, it Now Provides Data, Communicates in New Ways and Serves as a Fashion Accessory," *Wall Street Journal*, February 17, 2015, B1.

an alternative—accompanied in some cases by trade-in allowances—to boost overall sales.[245] Apple reportedly followed this tactic with some of its new smartphone models during the last decade—often introduced once a year, followed by updates of existing ones.[246]

This scheme follows the so-called Dutch auction model of sales, targeting consumers willing to pay more to acquire early a branded product, despite the fact that they may have no use for the options they are induced to purchase.[247] Early sales are then followed by targeting those willing to wait for the new model—*minus* the options and higher price. And, subsequently, those who may settle for updated existing models.

Contriving wants through branding can lock in consumers. During the last decade, for example, Apple's iPhone was linked to Apple Land, a vast "ecosystem" of apps and services that can run many aspects of one's life.[248] Chats were then channeled through iMessage, and photos were stored in Apple Photos through iCloud Photo Library—while iTunes made it possible to shop for music, films, and videogames. Television was bundled with other subscription services, such as iCloud data storage and Apple Music, requiring purchase of its proprietary apps. Purchasing the iPhone helped manage a vehicle through CarPlay, after subscribing to Apple Maps. And, operating the iPhone and Apple Watch required purchase of apps from the App Store (as did practically all other services).

Switching out of Apple's branded "ecosystem" therefore became very troublesome, as practically every component would have to be replaced.[249] Also, the consumer might have to subscribe to different providers for the same services—incurring complications. Keeping consumers locked into a brand's "ecosystem" thus depends on ensuring that any advantages provided by switching are more than offset by the disadvantages—a matter helped greatly by brand appeal.

Inducing wants through the appropriation, mining, and selling of personal data is an important promotional typology. A *confiscation of privacy* underlies the mining and sale of intimate information—involving finances, health, contacts, movement, employment, education, family, court records, and most any other aspect of

245 Sarah Krouse, "Trade-In Offers Help to Boost Phone Sales," *Wall Street Journal*, January 9, 2019, B1.

246 Tripp Mickle, Yoko Kubota and Takashi Mochizuki, "Apple Overhauls its iPhone Sales Strategy," *Wall Street Journal*, September 20, 2018, B1; Geoffrey Fowler, "iPhone 8: Improvement is Slight for an Upgrade," *Wall Street Journal*, September 20, 2017, B1; Christopher Mims, "Why an iPhone Priced at $1,400 isn't Crazy," *Wall Street Journal*, July 31, 2017, B1; Daisuke Wakabayashi, "Pricier Gadgets Help Apple Elbow Out Rivals," *Wall Street Journal*, April 28, 2015, A1.

247 See David Easley and Jon Kleinberg, *Networks, Crowds and Markets: Reasoning about a Highly Connected World* (New York: Cambridge University Press, 2010), Chapter 9.

248 Geoffrey A. Fowler, "Why We Keep Buying Each New iPhone," *Wall Street Journal*, September 23, 2015, D1; *The Economist*, "Apple: Frictionless Fruit; Convenience is the Technology Giant's Latest Weapon," June 7, 2014, 70.

249 Fowler, "Why We Keep Buying."

a person's life. Such data, if not directly available, can be obtained from third parties that routinely scour and collate public databases, property records, credit information, and news.

This typology has acquired urgency in recent years, due in part to the (previously discussed) slowdown (or end) of the effects predicted by Moore's Law.[250] Most every technology product in existence depends on microprocessors to increase performance continuously. Sales of new and differentiated models would thus be rendered more difficult, when capacity expansion slows (or ends).[251]

If new ways are found to increase performance, the microprocessors (or their successors) are likely to be more expensive. Due to oligopolistic pricing, the added cost will most likely be passed along to consumers—a matter that may require greater wants contrivance and marketing efforts. More intense targeting—to, say, cultivate branding, recurrent consumption, or even addiction—may then be needed to overcome higher pricing and limited performance.

Pervasive intimate surveillance may thus become the norm.[252] Although policy specialists drew attention to its negative effects during the last decade, its expansion seems unstoppable.[253] Advances in predictive AI allow precision in anticipating moods, behavior, and preferences to induce anyone to want

250 Gordon E. Moore, "Cramming More Components onto Integrated Circuits," *Electronics*, April 19, 1965, 114–17. See also Arnold Thackray, David C. Brock and Rachel Jones, *Moore's Law* (New York: Basic Books, 2015), chapters 6, 9, 10.

251 See David Rotman, "We're Not Prepared for the End of Moore's Law," *MIT Technology Review*, February 24, 2020, www.technologyreview.com/; *The Economist*, "The Semiconductor Industry: Silicon Crumble," February 25, 2017, 53–54; Rachel Courtland, "Transistors Could Stop Shrinking in 2021: A Key Industry Report Forecasts an End to Traditional Scaling of Transistors," *IEEE Spectrum*, July 22, 2016, https://spectrum.ieee.org/; Tom Simonite, "Moore's Law is Dead," *MIT Technology Review*, May 13, 2016, www.technologyreview.com/.

252 See Shoshana Zuboff, *The Age of Surveillance Capitalism: The Fight for a Human Future at the New Frontier of Power* (New York: PublicAffairs, 2019), chapters 2, 3, 6; Elizabeth Dwoskin and Evelyn M. Rusli, "The Technology that Unmasks Your Hidden Emotions: Using Psychology and Facial-Recognition Software to Study People as they Shop, Watch Ads—Breeding Privacy Fears," *Wall Street Journal*, January 29, 2015, B1. See also Franklin Foer and Marc Cashman, *World without Mind: The Existential Threat of Big Tech* (New York: Penguin, 2017), chapters 3–5.

253 See Jathan Sadowski, *Too Smart: How Digital Capitalism is Extracting Data, Controlling Our Lives, and Taking over the World* (Cambridge, MA: MIT Press, 2020), chapters 2–4; Stuart A. Thompson and Charlie Warzel, "Twelve Million Phones, One Dataset, Zero Privacy: An Investigation into the Smartphone Tracking Industry Reveals Surveillance so Omnipresent in our Digital Lives that it seems Impossible to Avoid," *New York Times*, December 19, 2019, www.nytimes.com/; Tom Wheeler, *Time to Fix It: Developing Rules for Internet Capitalism*, Shorenstein Center on Media, Politics and Public Policy, Kennedy School of Government, Harvard University, August 16, 2018, https://shorensteincenter.org/; Deepa Seetharaman, "Report: Big Tech Needs Fixes," *Wall Street Journal*, September 25, 2018, B4; Ken Dilanian, "They're Watching Your Every Move: Internet Giants Like Amazon, Google and Facebook may Well Know More about You than the NSA Does," *Wall Street Journal*, July 10, 2013, A1.

(or try) a product.[254] Also, by collecting detailed information, apps facilitate sophisticated AI deployment.[255] And greater connectivity between gadgets, homes, workplaces, and vehicles is already turning pervasive surveillance for wants contrivance into a reality—despite numerous warnings.[256]

Intimate data can be differentiated by the *exploitability value of the wants* that are induced. The value of smartphone location data, for example, tends to have a very limited time window. Its usage by the oligopolistic appropriator must be immediate if it is to be effective. Wants contrivance in this case must be executed instantaneously and is often based on mining intimate histories of preferences, movement, and purchases. This does not necessarily mean that its exploitability value is low, as other aspects—such as sales quantum and diversity of wants—must also be taken into account.

Wider time windows and a larger target population may enhance exploitability value. Such information can thus attain greater value when combined with similar data from other individuals—as in the case of health technologies. Inducing wants for individuals with certain illnesses may be easier when the target population is in a given geographical area—if personal contact for sale and delivery is required. The exploitability value in this case may depend on the population of individuals with similar ailments—along with the frequency and amount of sales.

A third scenario involves the exploitability value of web-browsing data. This category tends to have temporal flexibility for inducing wants, and may not depend significantly on population size or locational considerations. The value for inducing wants may thus be more a function of the effectiveness of ad targeting—based on mined preferences, prior purchases, and the psychological message conveyed. Instantaneity in this and the previous scenario is thus not as crucial as in the first one.

In general, the exploitability value for inducing wants depends on the amount of data accumulated. The larger the amassment of intimate data, the greater its value. The amount of consumer exploitation executed—discussed

254 Wakabayashi and Barr, "Apple and Google Race to Predict"; Amit Sharma, "How Predictive AI Will Change Shopping," *Harvard Business Review*, November 18, 2016, https://hbr.org/; Steven Perlberg, "Targeted Ads are Coming to Your Television: 'Big Data' Knows Who Likes What—Do You?" *Wall Street Journal*, November 21, 2014, B1.

255 Sam Schechner and Mark Secada, "Apps Sent User Secrets to Facebook," *Wall Street Journal*, February 23, 2019, A1; Jennifer Valentino-DeVries, Natasha Singer, Michael H. Keller and Aaron Krolik, "Your Apps Know Where You Were Last Night, and They are Not Keeping it Secret: Dozens of Companies Use Smartphone Locations to Help Advertisers and even Hedge Funds," *New York Times*, December 10, 2018, www.nytimes.com/; Douglas MacMillan, "App Developers Gain Access to Millions of Gmail Inboxes: Google and Others Enable Scanning of Emails by Data Miners," *Wall Street Journal*, July 3, 2018, A1.

256 See Zuboff, *Age of Surveillance Capitalism*; Foer and Cashman, *World without Mind*; Phil Simon, *The Age of the Platform: How Apple, Amazon, Facebook, and Google Have Redefined Business* (Henderson, NV: Motion, 2013), chapters 5, 6, 9.

previously in this chapter—also needs to be considered. Wants with greater revenue streams—associated with more intensive consumer exploitation—may thus attain higher priority in an inducement agenda. A wider exploitability time window might then be favored, if more effective wants inducement and consumer exploitation can be undertaken.

Health data are among the most valuable for wants promotion—life and health being the most important assets that anyone can have. And individual health can be considered a commodity—an intangible one that can change based on such factors as age, lifestyle, mental condition, employment, accidents, education, and family. Data clouds facilitate tracking and mining such data, to promote wants that target life cycle changes.

The range of health data that can be appropriated through pervasive surveillance is breathtaking. It can include genetic information and treatments, surgeries, illnesses, hospitalizations—in addition to indicators compiled and mined frequently, such as blood content and pressure, medications, organ functions, and addictions. This repertory can attract much surveillance for wants inducement, given the numerous products and accessories linked to health maintenance.

Expansion of some of the largest technology oligopolies into health informatics started during the last decade and is projected to grow. Linkups between healthcare companies and social media or search oligopolies promise to make pervasive surveillance unavoidable.[257] During the last decade, for example, Facebook reportedly started to develop wearable gadgets to track uselaborers' health.[258] Google reportedly gained access—through its Nightingale project—to tens of millions of records that contained vital health information, including names and other identifiable data, without the affected individuals' knowledge.[259] A major healthcare network with facilities in over 20 states had contracted Google to try to improve its information technologies.

Testimony of the power of oligopolies is that the Health Insurance Portability and Accountability Act did not prohibit the sale and mining of personal health information to (and by) third parties.[260] Biotech and biopharmaceutical

257 Ruth Reader, "With a Wearable Reportedly in the Works, Facebook Continues a Quiet Push into Health," *Fast Company*, February 19, 2021, www.fastcompany.com/; Jonathan Shieber, "Facebook Unveils its First Foray into Personal Digital Healthcare Tools," *Tech Crunch*, October 28, 2019, https://techcrunch.com/; Melanie Evans and Laura Stevens, "Amazon Expands Footprint in Health," *Wall Street Journal*, November 28, 2018, A1.

258 Shieber, "Facebook Unveils First Foray"; Reader, "With a Wearable in the Works."

259 Rob Copeland, "Google's 'Project Nightingale' Gathers Personal Health Data on Millions of Americans: Search Giant is Amassing Health Records from Ascension Facilities in 21 States; Patients Not Yet Informed," *Wall Street Journal*, November 11, 2019, www.wsj.com/; Heidi Ledford, "Google Health-Data Scandal Spooks Researchers: Scientists Fear the Controversy over the Nightingale Project will Undermine Trust in Research," *Nature*, November 19, 2019, www.nature.com/.

260 See Wikipedia, *Health Insurance Portability and Accountability Act*, https://en.wikipedia.org/ (accessed August 20, 2022).

companies have profited greatly from the use of such information for wants promotion, since that law's approval. Vast possibilities for pervasive data exploitation were thus created through legislation that had intended to improve healthcare access.

Biopharmaceutical and biotech oligopolies have been the most important beneficiaries, along with clients specialized in treatments. One of the best-known cancer treatment centers in the United States, for example, contracted with an AI startup company—owned and founded by three of its executives—to mine data from 25 million patient tissue slides, along with information on decades of work by its pathologists.[261] The data provided many possibilities to induce wants related to testing, regardless of individual propensity—or the benefit of treatment. Data mining in this area made it possible to sell costly chemotherapy treatments—with Food and Drug Administration (FDA) approval—that extended life for an average of only two months—patients being typically in severe pain and isolated during that time.[262] Advertisements to induce purchase of the treatments nonetheless claimed that they "significantly" increased "the chance of living longer."[263]

Waste

The generation of waste is a major mode of systemic dysfunction. Waste encompasses much more than unnecessary consumption and losses from consumer exploitation. Harm to nature and human wellbeing must also be taken into account.

Waste is closely related to oligopolistic power. Over 70 percent of all greenhouse gas emissions have been attributed to the largest 100 corporations in the world—the majority of them technology oligopolies.[264] Twenty corporations

261 Charles Ornstein and Katie Thomas, "Memorial Sloan Kettering Leaders Violated Conflict-of-Interest Rules, Report Finds," *New York Times*, April 4, 2019; and their "Sloan Kettering's Cozy Deal with Start-Up Ignites a New Uproar," *New York Times*, September 20, 2018, www.nytimes.com/. See also Andrew Dunn, "Memorial Sloan Kettering Scandal Raises Questions for Pharma's Biggest Corporate Boards," *Biopharma Dive*, November 29, 2018, www.biopharmadive.com/; Alyssa Rege, "Memorial Kettering Scandal Prompts Wave of Medical Journal Corrections from Top Facilities," *Becker's Hospital Review*, October 19, 2018, www.beckershospitalreview.com/.

262 Robert Pearl, "Shame, Scandal Plague Healthcare Providers in 2018," *Forbes*, December 10, 2018, www.forbes.com/; Tito Fojo, Sham Mailankody and Andrew Lo, "Unintended Consequences of Expansive Cancer Therapeutics," *JAMA Otolaryngology, Head and Neck Surgery* 140 (2014), 1225–36.

263 Pearl, "Shame, Scandal Plague."

264 Chris Bryant, "The Big Dirty Secret of the World's Biggest Companies," *Bloomberg*, January 28, 2020, www.bloomberg.com/; Carl Folke, Henrik Österblom, Jean-Baptiste Jouffray, *et al.*, "Transnational Corporations and the Challenge of Biosphere Stewardship," *Nature, Ecology and Evolution*, September 2019, www.nature.com/; Matthew Carr and Jeremy Hodges, "Carbon Emissions Hit a Record High," *Bloomberg*, March 25, 2019, www.bloomberg.com/; *The Economist, The World in 2020*, "Corporate Realpolitik," December 2019, 28.

among the 200 with the highest carbon emissions—all of them oligopolistic—account for 70 percent of such emissions.[265]

The discussions in this section will build on the work of two prominent biologists, Richard Levins and Richard Lewontin, who explored the systemic links between natural processes, waste, and capitalism.[266] Their formulation of the *eco-social distress syndrome* set the stage for a broad understanding of the impact of waste on nature and humans. The unprecedented damage to ecosystems, climate, and human health—and to most every form of life—that we now experience can be related to their vision of eco-social dysfunction.

Toxicity and Pollution

Most technology products are very difficult to dispose of, and the toxic chemicals embedded in them can remain in nature and reach the most recondite corners of the planet. Since these chemicals affect animals, plants, air, water, and the food chain, they can cause much damage to nature and health. Thus, the eco-social distress involved is very broad, yet the sources are microscopic and often difficult to detect. Their negative impacts are felt through illnesses and ecological damage that occur after periods of exposure.

Extremely high concentrations of polychlorinated biphenyls (PCBs)—almost 200 times the level of the most polluted sites on the earth's surface—for example, were found in ocean life inhabiting trenches four miles deep during the last decade.[267] Banned in the United States since 1979, these compounds—used in many electronic components, because of their dielectric properties and limited flammability—have nonetheless reached the deepest ocean domains. Banning them in one nation (or several) has therefore not lessened their spread and negative consequences.

PCBs do not break down easily once released into the environment. They accumulate in food crops and above-ground vegetation—and can remain in water, soil, and air. They are thus inevitably ingested by, and stored in, a vast range of mammals, birds, fish, reptiles, insects, and small organisms—part of

265 Bryant, "Big Dirty Secret"; Carr and Hodges, "Carbon Emissions Hit a Record."

266 Richard Levins and Richard Lewontin, *The Dialectical Biologist* (Cambridge, MA: Harvard University Press, 1985), chapters 1, 6, 9; and their *Biology Under the Influence: Dialectical Essays on Ecology, Agriculture, and Health* (New York: Monthly Review Press, 2007), chapters 6, 7, 17, 27, 31.

267 Alan J. Jamieson, Tamas Malkocs, Stuart B. Piertney, Toyonobu Fujii and Zulin Zhang, *Bioaccumulation of Persistent Organic Pollutants in the Deepest Ocean Fauna*, Nature, Ecology and Evolution, 2017, www.nature.com/. See also *The Economist*, "Oceanic Pollution—Entrenched: Nasty Chemicals Abound in What was Thought an Untouched Environment," February 18, 2017, 67; Ellie Kincaid, "Industrial Pollutants Found in the Deepest Corners of the Ocean," *Wall Street Journal*, February 13, 2017, www.wsj.com/.

the food chain of many species, including humans.[268] High levels of PCBs have been associated with the prevalence of diabetes mellitus in adults and with various effects related to prenatal exposure that can disable a child's immune system.[269] PCBs have also been associated with numerous harmful effects that include damage to the liver and to the nervous, endocrine, reproductive, and immune systems, and they have been classified as carcinogenic by the World Health Organization's International Agency for Research on Cancer.[270]

Substantial levels of another class of chemicals—polybrominated diphenyl ethers (PBDEs), used in the United States since the 1970s mainly as flame retardants in a wide range of products, such as electronic components—were also found in high concentrations in very deep ocean waters during the last decade.[271] These chemicals do not experience significant biodegradation, and they can bind strongly to sediments and soil.[272] Researchers found that they can harm air quality significantly, especially in large areas around shredding and recycling facilities.[273]

The food chain has been affected by PBDE pollution, with research on 30 food types of animal origin finding high concentrations in fish and meat products in recent decades.[274] Research on human blood, milk, and tissues found PBDE levels to have increased exponentially by a factor of 100 over a 30-year period—thus doubling every five years on average—with concentrations in the United States as much as 17 times higher than those found in

268 U.S. Environmental Protection Agency, *Polychlorinated Biphenyls (PCBs)*, www.epa.gov/ (accessed August 20, 2022).

269 Agency for Toxic Substances and Disease Registry, *Polychlorinated Biphenyls (PCBs) Toxicity: What are the Adverse Health Effects of PCB Exposure?* www.atsdr.cdc.gov/ (accessed August 21, 2022); Obaid Faroon and Patricia Ruiz, "Polychlorinated Biphenyls: New Evidence from the Last Decade," *Toxicology and Health* 32 (2016), 1825–47.

270 Agency for Toxic Substances and Disease Registry, *Polychlorinated Biphenyls*; International Agency for Research on Cancer, *IARC Monographs on the Evaluation of Carcinogenic Risks to Humans*, https://monographs.iarc.fr/ (accessed August 20, 2022).

271 Jamieson, Malkocs, Piertney, *et al.*, *Bioaccumulation*; Kincaid, "Industrial Pollutants"; *The Economist*, "Oceanic Pollution."

272 Jamieson, Malkocs, Piertney, *et al.*, *Bioaccumulation*; Environmental Protection Agency, *Technical Fact Sheet—Polybrominated Diphenyl Ethers (PBDEs)*, November 2017, www.epa.gov/; Muhammad A. Siddiqi, Ronald H. Laessig and Kurt D. Reed, "Polybrominated Diphenyl Ethers (PBDEs): New Pollutants-Old Diseases," *Clinical Medicine and Research* 1 (2003), 281–90.

273 U.S. Environmental Protection Agency, *Technical Fact Sheet*; Lawrence K. Hearn, Darryl W. Hawker and Jochen F. Mueller, "Dispersal Patterns of Polybrominated Diphenyl Ethers (PBDEs) in the Vicinity of an Automotive Shredding and Metal Recycling Facility," *Atmospheric Pollution Research* 3 (2012), 317–24.

274 Environmental Protection Agency, *Technical Fact Sheet*; Arnold Schechter, Olaf Päpke, Kuang-Chi Tung, Daniele Staskal, *et al.*, "Polybrominated Diphenyl Ethers Contamination of United States Food," *Environmental Science and Technology* 38 (2004), 5306–11; Siddiqi, Laessig and Reed, "Polybrominated Diphenyl."

Europe.[275] PBDEs also have carcinogenic potential and can cause harm to the nervous and endocrine systems—and to specific organs such as the liver, thyroid glands, and the pancreas.[276]

Chemicals used in many technology products to make them water-resistant have accumulated over time. Polyfluoroalkyl (PFAS) substances that include perfluorooctane sulfonate (PFOS), perfluorooctanoic acid (PFOA), GenX, and numerous other chemicals have been manufactured for many decades and were used extensively in the United States.[277] They have also been used in great quantities globally, to the point that there is hardly any nation producing technology hardware where they are not employed. Even though these chemicals are no longer used in the United States, they are found in many imported products.

PFAS substances invade and stay in the natural environment and the human body after products that carry them are discarded. They are routinely ingested by humans and animals through drinking water, many packaged foods, household cleaning products, and the food chain.[278] Among the potential impacts on human and animal health are dysfunctions in immunological, reproductive, and multiple organ systems (thyroid hormones, liver, and kidneys, among others).[279] Unborn babies have also been found to have PFAS substances and—as it is unknown how they can be eradicated—they might remain with an individual throughout a lifetime.

Waste in the form of nanoparticles—resulting from the use and disposal of nanotechnology products—also poses much potential harm to nature and human health. Knowledge about the effects of nanoparticle pollution is limited because of the novel character of the technology, and difficulties in devising testing methods. Nonetheless, early assessments of protein modifications—citrullination, in particular—by nanoparticles indicate that they may harm the immune system of humans and animals.[280] Diseases such as multiple sclerosis and rheumatoid arthritis may be some of the consequences.

275 Environmental Protection Agency, *Technical Fact Sheet*; Ronald A. Hites, "Polybrominated Diphenyl Ethers in the Environment and in People: A Meta-Analysis of Concentrations," *Environmental Science and Technology* 38 (2004), 945–56.

276 National Institutes of Health, *Polybrominated Diphenyl Ethers (PBDEs)*, https://toxtown.nlm.nih.gov/ (accessed August 22, 2022).

277 U.S. Environmental Protection Agency, *Basic Information on PFAS*; and its *Technical Fact Sheet—Perfluorooctane Sulfonate (PFOS), Perfluorooctanoic Acid (PFOA)*, www.epa.gov/ (accessed August 21, 2022); Rob Billott, "The Poisons Found in Everyone, Even Unborn Babies—and Who is Responsible for It: Chemicals called PFAS and PFOS—Known as Forever Chemicals—are in the Blood of Virtually Every Person in the Planet. And they will Only Accumulate," *The Guardian*, December 17, 2020, www.theguardian.com/.

278 Billott, "Poisons Found in Everyone"; U.S. Environmental Protection Agency, *Basic Information on PFAS*.

279 U.S. Environmental Protection Agency, *Basic Information on PFAS*; and its *Technical Fact Sheet (PFOS)*; Billott, "Poisons Found in Everyone."

280 European Union, *Nanotechnologies: What are the Potential Harmful Effects of Nanoparticles?*, https://ec.europa.eu (accessed August 21, 2022); Zannatul Ferdous and Abderrahim Nemmar, "Health Impact of Silver Nanoparticles: A Review of the Biodistribution and Toxicity Following Various

Research on the inhalation and ingestion of nanoparticles has shown that they enter the bloodstream and can cause artery blockages, heart attacks and strokes, liver and kidney damage—while leading to higher risk of brain and neurological disorders such as dementia, Parkinson's, and Alzheimer's diseases.[281] Nanoparticle pollution may spread rapidly, especially if nanoscale circuitry can replace conventional ones in microprocessors—to generate performance increases that might approach those predicted by Moore's Law (discussed earlier). This would affect users of most every type of microprocessor-dependent product.

E-Waste

The problem of "e-waste"—encompassing electronic gadgets that contain hazardous materials such as lead, silver, mercury, and diverse forms of macro and micro-plastics—is an important component of the panorama of waste. This diverse category is increasing rapidly and has been found to pose much harm to nature and to human health.[282] It is a form of eco-social distress that is micro-level, but its negative impacts are also felt at the macro scale of nature and society.

In addition to metals, plastic casings and containers used in diverse technology products are important contributors to e-waste—and they can be found in large quantities in every sea and ocean. A review of deep ocean research involving 5,010 dives over a 30-year period, for example, found that one-third of all plastic debris was macro-plastic, of which 89 percent were single-use.[283]

Routes of Exposure," *International Journal of Molecular Sciences* 21 (2020), 2375, www.mdpi.com/; *Science Daily*, "Nanoparticles in Polluted Air, Smoke and Nanotechnology Products Have Serious Impacts on Health," June 11, 2012, www.sciencedaily.com/; Bashir M. Mohamed, Navin K. Verma, Anthony M. Davies, *et al.*, "Citrullination of Proteins: A Common Post-Translational Modification Pathway Induced by Different Nanoparticles *in Vitro* and *in Vivo*," *Nanomedicine* 7 (2012), www.futuremedicine.com/.

281 See Mićo Tatalović, "'I Wash All my Food Like Crazy': Scientists Voice Concern About Nanoparticles—U.S. Foods are Increasingly Full of Nano-Scale Additives, Even as Researchers Raise Alarm Bells About their Safety," *The Guardian*, May 29, 2019, www.theguardian.com/; Kate Kelland, "Study Finds How Polluting Nanoparticles Get into Blood and Damage Hearts," *Reuters*, April 26, 2017, www.reuters.com/; Mark R. Miller, Jennifer B. Raftis, Jeremy P. Langrish, *et al.*, "Inhaled Nanoparticles Accumulate at Sites of Vascular Disease," *ACS Nano* 11 (2017), 4542–52; Nicholas L, Mills, Mark R. Miller, Andrew J. Lucking, *et al.*, "Combustion-Derived Nanoparticulate Induces the Adverse Vascular Effects of Diesel Exhaust Inhalation," *European Heart Journal* 32 (2011), 2660–71.

282 World Health Organization, *E-Waste and Children's Health*, www.who.int/ (accessed July 21, 2022); Michelle Heacock, Carol B. Kelly, Kwadwo A. Asante, *et al.*, "E-Waste and Harm to Vulnerable Populations: A Growing Global Problem," *Environmental Health Perspectives* 124 (2016), https://niehs.nih.gov/; Kristen Grant, Fiona C. Goldizen, Peter D. Sly, *et al.*, "Health Consequences of Exposure to E-waste: A Systematic Review," *Lancet Global Health* 1 (2013), www.thelancet.com/.

283 Diva Amon, "Deep-Sea Debris in the Western and Central Pacific," *Ocean Exploration*, June 25, 2020, https://oceanexplorer.noaa.gov/; Sanae Chiba, Hideaki Sato, Ruth Fletcher, *et al.*, "Human Footprint in the Abyss: 30-Year Records of Deep-Sea Plastic Debris," *Marine Policy* 96

Increases of 52 and 92 percent in these two categories (respectively)—for ocean areas deeper than 6,000 meters (3.7 miles), located over 1,000 kilometers (621 miles) from mainland coastal zones were registered.[284] By the middle of the twenty-first century, there is likely to be more plastic debris in the ocean than fish—and 99 percent of all seabirds will have ingested plastic, according to a United Nations report.[285] The current, very extensive ocean areas of floating plastic debris—such as the Great Pacific Garbage Patch—may thus be considered an early symptom of a much more serious hazard to come.[286]

Micro-plastics are part of this scenario and can now be found in all the seas and oceans. Because of their extremely small—microscopic or even nanoscale—size, they are very difficult to notice. Specialized, expensive equipment—and repetitive testing—is required to detect them. Micro-plastics have been recently found in human blood—for the first time.[287] As blood circulates through (and connects) most every organ and tissue, the presence of micro-plastics may likely cause diseases throughout the human organism. Much the same applies to animals consumed by humans.

In the United States, it has been estimated that less than one-third of all technology e-waste is recycled, partly because most devices have to be manually disassembled—and their components sorted out at costly, specialized facilities.[288] Most of the e-waste generated is therefore shipped to poorer nations that effectively serve as dumping grounds.[289] A lack of protective equipment for workers who disassemble products and inhale the toxic chemicals—which

(2018), 204–12; Jason Daley, "Even the Deepest Parts of the Ocean Are Polluted with Startling Amounts of Plastic: A Review of Data from 5,010 ROV Dives Reveals an Abundance of Single-Use Plastics Littering the Seas," *Smithsonian*, May 11, 2018, www.smithsonianmag.com/.

284 Chiba, Sato, Fletcher, *et al.*, "Human Footprint"; Amon, "Deep-Sea Debris"; Daley, "Even the Deepest."

285 *UN News*, "Feature: UN's Mission to Keep Plastics out of Oceans and Marine Life," April 27, 2017, https://news.un.org/ (details based on U.N. Environmental Programme data).

286 See American Oceans, *How was the Great Pacific Garbage Patch Created?* www.americaoceans.org/ (accessed July 21, 2022); Jenna R. Jambeck, Roland Geyer, Chris Wilcox, Theodore R. Siegler, *et al.*, "Plastic Waste Inputs from Land into the Ocean," *Science*, February 13, 2015, 768–71; Renee Cho, "Our Oceans: A Plastic Soup," *State of the Planet* (Earth Institute, Columbia University), January 26, 2011, https://blogs.ei.columbia.edu/.

287 Heather A. Leslie, Martin J. M. van Velzen, Sicco H. Brandsma, *et al.*, "Discovery and Quantification of Plastic Particle Pollution in Human Blood," *Environment International* 163 (2022), 1–8; Damian Carrington, "Microplastics Found in Human Blood for First Time," *The Guardian*, March 24, 2022, www.theguardian.com/.

288 Saabira Chaudhuri, "Items Meant to Cut Down on Plastic are Going to Waste," *Wall Street Journal*, January 25, 2019, B5.

289 The World Counts, *A World of Waste*, www.theworldcounts.com/ (accessed July 23, 2022); Syed Faraz Ahmed, "The Global Cost of Electronic Waste: Computers, Phones, and Other Digital Devices Increasingly Are Made to be Thrown Away—Which is Bad for Both Consumers and the Environment; An Object Lesson," *The Atlantic*, September 29, 2016, www.theatlantic .com/.

are also released into the environment—add to public health burdens and environmental damage in those nations.[290]

Exports of such waste constitute a form of subsidy to American technology oligopolies, since the corporations involved do not pay for the harm done to health and nature. The lack of a culture of reuse or repair for most technology products in the United States is part of the problem. Also, the absence of skills and equipment to support reuse and repair—and inadequate recycling—guarantees that this situation will worsen. Pricing of technology products that does not reflect social costs ensures that most products will be discarded after relatively short usage.

Agro-Tech

Harmful consequences involving use of agro-tech products are part of the waste panorama. This is a form of eco-social distress that is broad and far-reaching. It affects the food chain and health—not only of humans but also of most species. Its effects on human health can lead to death or permanent disability, and its destruction of entire ecologies is now part of our reality.

Although questions remain unanswered about the long-term consequences of genetically engineered seeds, evidence is accumulating about the harmful effects of the pesticides that accompany them. Highly toxic herbicides are an essential companion of genetically engineered seeds—to protect them (and the crops they generate) from weeds. But their toxicity has increased considerably over time, as weeds evolve and neutralize their effects—leading to yet more toxic herbicides that in turn generate more resistant weeds.

Crops generated by engineered seeds—among them corn, soybeans, and alfalfa—use large quantities of herbicides to eliminate weeds, mainly because these evolve and reappear.[291] Their toxic chemicals are now used intensively in farming, due to the spread of engineered seeds. American companies led in this technology sector—driven since its early days by agro-biotech oligopolists such as Monsanto (now part of Bayer), Dow, and DuPont.

290 The World Counts, *World of Waste*; Charlotte Edmond, *This is What the World's Waste does to People in Poorer Countries*, World Economic Forum, May 16, 2019, www.weforum.org/; Mari Shibata, "Inside the World's Biggest E-Waste Dump: 215,000 Tonnes of Second Hand Consumer Electronics, Mainly from Western Europe and the U.S., Come Through Ghana a Year," *Motherboard*, June 11, 2015, https://motherboard; *National Public Radio*, "After Dump, What Happens to Electronic Waste?" December 21, 2010, www.npr.org/.

291 Pesticide Action Network, *Big Ag's Dirty Little Secret: Herbicide-Resistant GE Seeds Have Driven Dramatic Increases in Pesticide Applications Since They Hit the Market in the 1990s—and That's No Accident*, www.panna.org/ (accessed August 14, 2022); Jacob Bunge, "Farmers Reconsider GMO Revolution," *Wall Street Journal*, September 15, 2016, A1; Beth Hoffman, "GMO Crops Mean More Herbicide, Not Less," *Forbes*, July 2, 2013, www.forbes.com/.

Glyphosate—the main chemical in Monsanto's branded Roundup herbicide—has been used about four times more than the second most heavily used chemical—atrazine.[292] Glyphosate residue has thus been found in food, water, and air—in the United States and in most nations where engineered seeds are planted.[293] Intense promotion of Roundup as a want—despite its toxicity—led to it becoming a staple of landscaping and gardening, especially around homes, buildings, and parks.

The promotion of Roundup belied the fact that one of its inert ingredients—polyethoxylated tallowamine (POEA)—was found during the last two decades to be capable of killing human cells, especially in umbilical cords and in placental and embryonic tissues.[294] This ingredient was found to be more toxic than glyphosate itself, even at concentrations much more diluted than those used in farms and lawns.[295] This toxicity in a commonly used farming and landscaping product is very likely to have long-term effects on health and nature.

During the last decade the World Health Organization's International Agency for Research on Cancer listed glyphosate as a "probable carcinogen"—based on findings from various nations around the world.[296] And the first lawsuit brought against Monsanto for its Roundup herbicide—by a groundskeeper who contracted cancer after years of using the product—resulted in an award of $289 million.[297] Despite mounting evidence—such as findings of significant

292 Pesticide Action Network, *Big Ag's Dirty*; Charles M. Benbrook, "Trends in Glyphosate Herbicide Use in the United States and Globally," *Environmental Sciences Europe* 28 (2016), www.ncbi.nlm.nhi.gov/.

293 Benbrook, "Trends in Glyphosate"; Adam Wernick, "An FDA Scientist Finds Traces of Weed Killer in Many Common Foods," *PRI*, June 2, 2018, www.pri.org/; Vincenzo Torretta, Ioannis A. Katsoyiannis, Paolo Viotti and Elena C. Rada, "Critical Review of the Effects of Glyphosate Exposure to the Environment and Humans through the Food Supply Chain," *Sustainability* 10 (2018), www.mdpi.com/.

294 Giles-Eric Sérralini, Emilie Clair, Robin Mesnage, *et al.*, "Republished Study: Long-Term Toxicity of a Roundup Herbicide and a Roundup-Tolerant Genetically Modified Maize," *Environmental Science Europe* 26 (2014), www.ncbi.nlm.nih.gov/; Crystal Gammon, "Weed-Whacking Herbicide Proves Deadly to Human Cells: Used in Gardens, Farms, and Parks Around the World, the Weed Killer Roundup Contains an Ingredient that can Suffocate Human Cells in a Laboratory, Researchers Say," *Scientific American*, June 23, 2009, www.sceintificamerican.com/.

295 Sérralini, Clair, Mesnage, *et al.*, "Republished Study: Long-Term Toxicity"; Gammon, "Weed-Whacking Herbicide."

296 World Health Organization, International Agency for Research on Cancer, *IARC Monograph on Glyphosate* (Lyon, France: IARC, 2015), www.iarc.fr/; Center for Food Safety, *Glyphosate and Cancer Risk* (Washington: CFS, 2015), www.centerforfoodsafety.org/; Daniel Cressey, "Widely Used Herbicide Linked to Cancer: The World Health Organization's Research Arm Declares Glyphosate a Problem Carcinogen. What's the Evidence?" *Scientific American*, March 25, 2015, www.scientificamerican.com/.

297 Sam Levin, "Monsanto Ordered to Pay $289m as Jury Rules Weedkiller Caused Man's Cancer: Court Rules in Favor of DeWayne Johnson, Ill Man Who Was First to Take Roundup Maker to Trial Over Allegations," *The Guardian*, August 10, 2018, www.theguardian.com/.

residue in many food staples, including those in children's diets—regulatory authorities in the United States did not ban glyphosate or any other pesticide containing POEA.[298] Many nations where glyphosate, POEA, and other toxic pesticides—and genetically engineered seeds—are used usually look to U.S. authorities for guidance, before issuing bans.

One result of this panorama is that in recent decades large areas of U.S. farmland developed "super weeds" that are resistant to pesticides and herbicides.[299] Increasing toxicity has affected natural ecologies, soils, and vegetation—especially those that sustained non-engineered seeds. Significant residues have thus been found in many organisms located far away from areas where herbicides and pesticides are used. And hormones or metabolisms of diverse species—such as frogs, bees, trout, sheep, and rodents—were found to have been disrupted in studies undertaken during the last decade.[300]

The accumulation of these disruptions can lead to the extinction of species or to disease. The testing criteria to detect these problems, however, seem to have been tailored to suit the interests of the agro-biotech corporations that produce seeds and herbicides.[301] And, those of the also-oligopolistic agribusiness companies that control farming and food distribution.

298 Carey Gillam, "Weedkiller Found in Granola and Crackers, Internal FDA Emails Show: The FDA Has Been Testing Food Samples for Traces of Glyphosate for Two Years, But the Agency Has Not Yet Released Any Official Results," *The Guardian*, April 30, 2018, www.theguardian.com/; Mihir Zavery, "Report Finds Traces of a Controversial Herbicide in Cheerios and Quaker Oats," *New York Times*, August 15, 2018, www.nytimes.com/; *Sustainable Pulse*, "US FDA and Cornell University Show Glyphosate Residues in Corn, Soybeans and Pet Food," October 4, 2018, https://sustainablepulse.com/.

299 H. Claire Brown, "Attack of the Superweeds: Herbicides are Losing the War— and Agriculture Might Never be the Same Again," *New York Times*, August 18, 2021, www.nytimes.com/; Ian Berry, "Pesticides Make a Comeback: Many Corn Farmers Go Back to Using Chemicals as Mother Nature Outwits Genetically Modified Seeds," *Wall Street Journal*, May 22, 2013, B1. See also Carey Gillam, *Whitewash: The Story of a Weed Killer, Cancer, and the Corruption of Science* (Washington: Island Press, 2017), chapters 3–6, 10.

300 Kelly Smalling, *Pesticides Found in Amphibians from Remote Areas in California*, U.S. Geological Survey, Environmental Health Program, www.usgs.gov/ (accessed July 21, 2022); Carsten A. Brühl, Thomas Schmidt, Silvia Pieper and Annika Alscher, "Terrestrial Pesticide Exposure of Amphibians: An Underestimated Cause of Global Decline?" *Scientific Reports* 3 (2013), www.nature.com/; Damian Carrington, "Common Pesticides 'Can Kill Frogs Within an Hour': New Research Suggests the Chemicals are Playing a Significant and Previously Unknown Role in the Global Decline of Amphibians," *The Guardian*, January 24, 2013, www.theguardian.com/; Brad Balukjian, "Pesticides Found in Frogs Far from Crops: Researchers are Concerned that the Chemicals Made their Way to Distant Sites," *Los Angeles Times*, July 29, 2013, AA3.

301 See Marie-Monique Robin, *The World According to Monsanto: Pollution, Corruption, and the Control of the World's Food Supply* (New York: New Press, 2010); and her documentary "The World According to Monsanto" (Ottawa: National Film Board of Canada, 2008); Gillam, *Whitewash*; J. Somerville Park, *Seeds of Reprisal: Monsanto vs. Michael Park* (Jupiter, FL: Provident House, 2014); Dominic Clover, *Monsanto and Smallholder Farmers: A Case Study on Corporate Accountability*, IDS Working Paper (Brighton: Institute for Development Studies, University of Sussex, 2007).

Microbiome Disruption

One of the most difficult impacts of the previously considered forms of waste involves the disruption of the microbiome. Advances in genomics, microbiology, and bioinformatics in recent decades have revealed the importance of the microbiome—the population of micro-organisms that inhabit the human body.[302] Disruptions of the microbiome that affect the *microbiota*—the organisms in the microbiome that regulate the immune system and physiological functions—can be very harmful.

This is a micro-level mode of eco-social distress that has macrosocial ramifications. Toxic chemicals and nanoparticles can affect the microbiota of humans and mammals severely, particularly in the gastrointestinal and respiratory tracts—where the immune system plays a vital role and many metabolic functions are performed.[303] The gut's microbiota are the most complex component of the human microbiome, encompassing about 40 trillion micro-organisms—with interactions that are largely symbiotic.[304] Over nine million unique genes that influence development and hereditary traits can be found in this ecosystem.[305] Gut microbiota are a vulnerable component of the microbiome, because of their sensitivity to disruption from sustained, harmful changes in the food chain and the natural environment.[306]

302 See Chan School of Public Health, Harvard University, *The Nutrition Source*, www.hsph.harvard.edu/ (accessed August 12, 2022); Michael Friedman, "Metabolic Rift and the Human Microbiome," *Monthly Review*, July 2018, 70–104; Courtney J. Robinson, Brendan J. M. Bohannan and Vincent B. Young, "From Structure to Function: The Ecology of Host-Associated Microbial Communities," *Microbiology and Molecular Biology Reviews* 74 (2010), 453–76; Peter J. Turnbaugh, "The Human Microbiome Project: Exploring the Microbial Part of Ourselves in a Changing World," *Nature*, October 18, 2007, 804–10.

303 Humans and many other mammals have been found to possess similar gut microbiota, based on dietary intake—an aspect that can affect health if deficiencies are passed along. See Zhenjiang Xu and Rob Knight, "Dietary Effects on Human Gut Microbiome Diversity," *British Journal of Nutrition* 113 (2015), S1–S5; Ruth E. Ley, Micah Hamady, Catherine Lozupone, *et al.*, "Evolution of Mammals and their Gut Microbiomes," *Science*, June 20, 2008, 1647–51.

304 Chan School of Public Health, Harvard University, *Nutrition Source*; Ed Yong, *I Contain Multitudes: The Microbes within Us and a Grander View of Life* (New York: HarperCollins, 2016); Eva Boon, Conor J. Meehan, Chris Whidden, *et al.*, "Interactions in the Microbiome: Communities of Organisms and Communities of Genes," *FEMS Microbiology Reviews* 38 (2014), 90–118; Sascha Krause, Xavier Le Roux, Pascal A. Niklaus, *et al.*, "Trait-Based Approaches for Understanding Microbial Biodiversity and Ecosystem Functioning," *Frontiers in Microbiology*, May 27, 2014, www.frontiersin.org/.

305 Chan School of Public Health, Harvard University, *Nutrition Source*; Xing Yang, Lu Xie, Yixue Li and Chaochun Wei, "More than 9,000,000 Unique Genes in Human Gut Bacterial Community: Estimating Gene Numbers Inside a Human Body," *PLoS One* 4 (2009), www.ncbi.nlm.nih.gov/.

306 Yong Fan and Oluf Pedersen, "Gut Microbiota in Human Metabolic Health and Disease," *Nature Reviews, Microbiology* 19 (2021), 55–71; Andreas J. Bäumler and Vanessa Sperandio, "Interactions between the Microbiota and Pathogenic Bacteria in the Gut," *Nature*, July 6, 2016, 85–93; Felix Sommer and Fredrik Bäckhed, "The Gut Microbiota—Masters of Host Development and Physiology," *Nature Reviews Microbiology* 11 (2013), 227–38; Stephen M. Collins, Michael G.

During the last decade, it was found that the most serious disruptions involve reduction of microbial diversity.[307] Microbial reductions can be related to certain health conditions—such as Parkinson's disease.[308] Diversity reductions—involving bacteria such as *Lactobacillus reuteri*—for example, are thought to be associated with autism.[309] The full range of effects on human health is still unknown, but these are likely to be substantial.[310]

Because the microbiome's ecosystem develops in phases, disruptions of the early ones can generate harmful effects later.[311] The most important early phases involve fetal development and infancy, due to their influence on the immune system and organ development.[312] Exposure to toxic chemicals and nanoparticles during these phases can have negative impacts that may persist and affect genes.

Surette and Premysl Bercik, "The Interplay between the Intestinal Microbiota and the Brain," *Nature Reviews Microbiology* 10 (2012), 735–42.

307 Erica D. Sonnenburg, Samuel A. Smits, Mikhail Tikhonov, *et al.*, "Diet-Induced Extinctions in the Gut Microbiota Compound over Generations," *Nature*, January 14, 2016, 212–15; Fan and Pedersen, "Gut Microbiota"; Kenya Honda and Dan R. Littman, "The Microbiota in Adaptive Immune Homeostasis and Disease," *Nature*, July 7, 2016, 75–84; Christoph A. Thaiss, Niv Zmora, Maayan Levy and Eran Elinav, "The Microbiome and Innate Immunity," *Nature*, July 7, 2016, 65–74.

308 Zhenzhen Yan, Fan Yang, Jingwei Cao, *et al.*, "Alterations of Gut Microbiota and Metabolome with Parkinson's Disease," *Microbial Pathogenesis* 160 (2021), www.sciencedirect.com/; Nicola Segata, "Gut Microbiome: Westernization and the Disappearance of Intestinal Diversity," *Current Biology* 25 (2015), R611–13; Thaiss, Zmora, Levy and Elinav, "Microbiome and Innate Immunity."

309 Martina Sgritta, Sean W. Dooling, Shelly A. Buffington, Eric N. Momin, *et al.*, "Mechanisms Underlying Microbial-Mediated Changes in Social Behavior in Mouse Models of Autism Spectrum Disorder," *Neuron* 101 (2019), 246–59; *The Economist*, "Autism—Gut Feelings: Experiments on Intestinal Bacteria May Point the Way to a Treatment of Autism," December 8, 2018, 76–77; Michael C. Toh and Emma Allen-Vercoe, "The Human Gut Microbiota with Reference to Autism Spectrum Disorder: Considering the Whole as More than a Sum of its Parts," *Microbial Ecology in Health and Disease* 26 (2015), www.ncbi.nlm.nih.gov/.

310 See Rodney R. Dietert and Janice M. Dietert, "The Microbiome and Sustainable Healthcare," *Healthcare* 3 (2015), 100–29; Martin J. Blaser and Stanley Falkow, "What Are the Consequences of the Disappearing Human Microbiota?" *Nature Reviews Microbiology* 7 (2009), 887–94.

311 Fan and Pedersen, "Gut Microbiota"; Juan M. Rodriguez, Kiera Murphy, Catherine Stanton, *et al.*, "The Composition of the Gut Microbiota throughout Life, with an Emphasis on Early Life," *Microbial Ecology in Health and Disease* 26 (2015), www.ncbi.nlm.nih.gov/; Trisha Gura, "Nature's First Functional Food," *Science*, August 15, 2014, 747–49; Boon, Meehan, Whidden, *et al.*, "Interactions in the Microbiome."

312 Juliana Durack and Susan V. Lynch, "The Gut Microbiome: Relationships with Disease and Opportunities for Therapy," *Journal of Experimental Medicine* 216 (2019), 20–40; Thomas Gensollen, Shankar S. Iyer, Dennis L. Kasper and Richard S. Blumberg, "How Colonization by Microbiota in Early Life Shapes the Immune System," *Science*, April 29, 2016, 539–44; Samuli Rautava, Raakel Luoto, Seppo Salminen and Erika Isolauri, "Microbial Contact during Pregnancy, Intestinal Colonization and Human Disease," *Nature Reviews Gastroenterology and Hepatology* 9 (2012), 565–76.

Microbiome disruption can occur through antibiotic overconsumption—a problem that accompanies many biotech and biopharmaceutical treatments.[313] In the agro domain, antibiotic over-usage in animals, especially poultry and livestock, can contribute to disruption—with effects on human health and the food chain. This is one of the results of the industrialization of animal raising, noted previously. Broad-spectrum antibiotics—the most commonly used—can generate serious microbiome disruptions.[314]

Pathogens that overcome antibiotic treatments—the so-called superbugs—can eliminate entire microbiota ecosystems. This is a problem that affects an increasing number of people around the world. Genes that provide antibiotic resistance can be passed along horizontally to other organisms in the microbiome, compounding negative effects.[315] Children are among the most affected, as reductions of microbiome diversity can severely damage their immune system and numerous metabolic functions.[316]

Promoting antibiotic overconsumption and that of other products—such as opioid medications—also contribute to microbiome disruption. Medications that neutralize the immune system to achieve quick results often reduce microbial diversity. This can eventually weaken immune response in a lasting way.[317] Excessive promotion of wants and consumption by biotech and biopharmaceutical oligopolies has contributed greatly to these problems.

Eco-Planetary

A larger dimension of waste—the planetary—must also be taken into account. *This involves technology oligopoly capitalism's contribution to the destruction of nature*

313 Megan Cully, "Antibiotics Alter the Gut Microbiome and Host Health," *Nature Portfolio*, June 17, 2019, www.nature.com/; Martin J. Blaser, "Antibiotic Use and Its Consequences for the Normal Microbiome," *Science*, April 29, 2016, 544–45; Les Dethlefsen and David A. Relman, "Incomplete Recovery and Individualized Responses of the Human Distal Gut Microbiota to Repeated Antibiotic Perturbation," *Proceedings of the National Academy of Sciences* 108 Supplement 1 (2011), 4554–61.

314 Ian Angus, "Superbugs in the Anthropocene: A Profit-Driven Plague," *Monthly Review*, June 2019, 1–28; Katherine Y. King, Kamilla Josefsdottir and Megan T. Baldridge, "Antibiotics Impair Murine Hematopoiesis by Depleting Intestinal Microbiota," *Open Forum Infectious Diseases* 3 Supplement 1 (2016), 2230; Blaser, "Antibiotic Use and Its Consequences."

315 Cully, "Antibiotics Alter"; Blaser, "Antibiotic Use and Its Consequences"; Amy Langdon, Nathan Crook and Gautam Dantas, "The Effects of Antibiotics on the Microbiome throughout Development and Alternative Approaches for Therapeutic Modulation," *Genome Medicine* 8 (2016), 39.

316 Cully, "Antibiotics Alter"; Blaser, "Antibiotic Use and Its Consequences"; Pajau Vangay, Tonya Ward, Jeffrey S. Gerber and Dan Knights, "Antibiotics, Pediatric Dysbiosis, and Disease," *Cell Host and Microbe* 17 (2015), 553–64; Katri Korpela, Anne Salonen, Lauri J. Virta, Riina A. Kekkonen, *et al.*, "Intestinal Microbiome is Related to Lifetime Antibiotic Use in Finnish Pre-School Children," *Nature Communications*, January 26, 2016, www.nature.com/.

317 Cully, "Antibiotics Alter"; Blaser, "Antibiotic Use and Its Consequences"; Robert A. Britton and Vincent B. Young, "Interaction between the Intestinal Microbiota and Host in Clostridium Difficile Colonization Resistance," *Trends in Microbiology* 20 (2012), 313–19.

through greenhouse gases. Eco-social distress thus manifests itself not only through the dysfunctions generated by toxicity, e-waste, contamination, and microbiome disruption. It also involves a dysfunctional panorama that encompasses the planet's natural ecosystems and all of humanity.

One metric that can help us understand this phenomenon involves carbon concentration. A 450 ppm concentration of carbon in the atmosphere—associated with a two-degree (centigrade) increase in the planet's average temperature—promises to become an immediate reality.[318] This could lead to a compounding of feedback effects—that may raise our planet's average temperature by as much as four to five degrees during the twenty-first century. Indications are that the trajectory toward this unfortunate reality is accelerating—as shown, for example, by the findings that ocean temperatures have risen 40 percent faster (on average) than estimated by a United Nations report barely five years earlier.[319] Even if the (unlikely) possibility is accepted that nature might (in some as yet unknown way) partially repair itself, the long-term impact is likely to be very harmful.

Ecologically, waste also involves energy losses—in the form of gases, chemicals, nanoparticles, plastics, and non-recyclable products.[320] And, rising energy losses from production and extractive activities—involving the typologies discussed in the previous chapter—have contributed to altering energy flows in the ecosphere. Disruption of such flows has been linked to negative health effects that are likely to become more pervasive.[321]

Among the macro-level impacts are rising levels of greenhouse gases and average temperatures—triggering harmful changes in the chemistry of the

318 See Rebecca Lindsey, "Climate Change: Atmospheric Carbon Dioxide," *Climate*, August 14, 2020, www.climate.gov/; John Bellamy Foster, "Making War on the Planet: Geoengineering and Capitalism's Creative Destruction of the Earth," *Monthly Review*, September 2018, 1–2; Nicola Jones, "How the World Passed a Carbon Threshold and Why It Matters," *Yale Environment 360*, January 26, 2017, Yale School of Forestry and Environmental Studies, https://e360.yale.edu/; Jerry H. Bentley, "Environmental Crises in World History," *Procedia – Social and Behavioral Sciences* 77 (2013), 108–15.

319 U.S. Environmental Protection Agency, *Climate Change Indicators: Sea Surface Temperature*, www.epa.gov/ (accessed August 14, 2022); LuAnn Dahlman and Rebecca Lindsey, "Climate Change: Ocean Heat Content," *Climate*, August 17, 2020, www.climate.gov/; Lijing Cheng, John Abraham, Zeke Hausfather and Kevin E. Trenberth, "How Fast are the Oceans Warming?," *Science*, January 11, 2019, 128–29; Kendra Pierre-Louis, "Ocean Warming is Accelerating Faster than Thought, New Research Finds," *New York Times*, January 10, 2019, www.nytimes.com/.

320 The dissipation of energy by all forms of life—a core aspect of biology—may also be applied to economic processes. See Erald Kolasi, "Energy, Economic Growth, and Ecological Crisis," in V. Upadhyay and Paramjit Singh, eds., *Global Political Economy: A Critique of Contemporary Capitalism* (London: Routledge, 2022), 376–404; Erald Kolasi, "The Physics of Capitalism," *Monthly Review*, May 2018, 29–43; Peter Atkins, *Four Laws That Drive the Universe* (New York: Oxford University Press, 2007).

321 David Herring and Rebecca Lindsey, "How will Global Warming Harm Human Health and Well-Being?" *Climate*, October 29, 2020, www.climate.gov/; World Health Organization, *Climate Change and Health*, February 1, 2018, www.who.int/; Alan H. Lockwood, *Heat Advisory: Protecting Health on a Warming Planet* (Cambridge, MA: MIT Press, 2016).

oceans and ecosystems. This includes the extinction of numerous animal and plant species—along with more serious natural disasters. Other impacts will likely involve lower quality of air, water, and soils, damage to the food chain, and disruption of the microbial ecosystems of humans and animals.

This scenario adds to the unsustainable character of the *status quo*, beyond the problems addressed previously. The catastrophic effects of waste at the macro level also reflect the impossibility of treating it as an "externality"—as mainstream economics has long assumed. Waste is at the core of the economic system we have—an aspect that the media, politicians, and the public usually overlook.[322]

Techno-Fixes

The contribution of waste to greenhouse gases thus poses a potentially catastrophic long-term threat to life on our planet. And it is difficult to think that this threat can be contained through purely technological solutions. Nonetheless, a frantic search for technological fixes is underway, to try to manipulate the ecosphere and the climate.

The solutions proposed so far seem infeasible. Their scale, the monetary cost, their time parameters, and the negative effects on nature that they will likely generate pose very difficult obstacles.[323] Also, most of the technologies that would be needed are either unknown or untried.

A very important aspect is that all of the proposed techno-fixes would allow the existing oligopolistic relations of power to be sustained, deepened, or extended. The most favored proposal would involve burning biomass to capture the resulting carbon dioxide and generate electricity—or storing it and postponing its release to the atmosphere for years or decades.[324] This proposal depends on an extensive

322 See John Bellamy Foster and Brett Clark, *Capitalism and the Ecological Rift: The Robbery of Nature* (New York: Monthly Review Press, 2020), chapters 1, 9, 10; John Bellamy Foster, Brett Clark and Richard York, *The Ecological Rift: Capitalism's War on the Earth* (New York: Monthly Review Press, 2010); Douglas F. Dowd, *The Waste of Nations: Dysfunction in the World Economy* (Boulder, CO: Westview, 1989).

323 See Kurt Cobb, "Geoengineering the Climate: The Zombie Idea that Just Won't Die," *Resource Insights*, April 4, 2021, www.resilience.org/; Carolyn Gramling, "In a Climate Crisis, is Geoengineering Worth the Risks?" *Science News*, October 6, 2019, www.sciencenews.org/; Michael Friedman, "Why Geoengineering is Not a Remedy for the Climate Crisis: An Ecological Point of View," *Monthly Review*, May 2018, https://mronline.org/; ETC Group, Biofuels Watch and Heinrich Böll Stiftung, *The Big Bad Fix: The Case Against Climate Geoengineering*, November 2017, www.biofuelwatch.org.uk/; James Hansen, Makiko Sato, Pushker Kharecha, *et al.*, "Young People's Burden: Requirements of Negative CO_2 Emissions," *Earth System Dynamics* 8 (2017), 577–616; Clive Hamilton, *Earthmasters: The Dawn of the Age of Climate Engineering* (New Haven: Yale University Press, 2013); Alan Robock, "20 Reasons Why Geoengineering May Be a Bad Idea," *Bulletin of the Atomic Scientists*, May 1, 2008, https://thebulletin.org/.

324 Drax, *BECCS and Negative Emissions*, www.drax.com (accessed July 23, 2022); Clair Gough, Samira Garcia-Freites, Christophe Jones, *et al.*, "Challenges to the Use of BECCS as a Keystone

planting of crops that can generate the necessary biomass, the availability of suitable soils and of extremely large land areas, a massive supply of water to sustain the crops, and a vast network of very expensive storage infrastructure.

To obtain biomass that could help reduce planetary carbon emissions in any significant way, a vast area of land would be needed—equivalent to about half of all the world's currently farmed land.[325] The amount of water needed annually would be roughly equivalent to the total presently used for agriculture on our planet, *and* the cost of the storage infrastructure could be as much as one-half of one quadrillion dollars (deflated, 2017) over the course of the twenty-first century.[326] Monocrop cultivation would most likely be involved—despite its lower carbon sequestration, compared to diverse cultivation and the associated ecosystems—because of the need to plant and harvest on an industrial scale.[327]

And the crops would most likely involve genetically engineered seeds, accompanied by very toxic pesticides. This would provide a bountiful bonanza of surpluses and market power to agro-biotech oligopolists. The (previously considered) negative effects of agro-tech chemicals and pesticides would thus be magnified many times over their current level.

If fully implemented, it is assumed that this approach—already endorsed by the United Nations' Intergovernmental Panel on Climate Change (IPCC) and incorporated in its climate simulation models—would lead to a reduction of planetary carbon dioxide emissions over time.[328] Nations would thus be able to exceed their annual emission quotas over the short and medium term—on the assumption that at some future time the excess would be redressed *or* be more than offset through expanded carbon capture and storage. The greatest beneficiaries of this approach would be global oligopolistic corporations—typically the most important single sources of carbon dioxide emissions. These corporations would have the most resources to engage in carbon trading schemes, evade quotas and restrictions, and co-opt national governments to seek exemptions.

As noted in the previous chapter—in the discussion on capacity-price engineering—old and new production technologies all too often coexist in

Technology in Pursuit of 1.5°C," *Global Sustainability*, June 13, 2018, www.cambridge.org/; Julia Rosen, "Vast Bioenergy Plantations Could Stave Off Climate Change—and Radically Reshape the Planet," *Science*, February 15, 2018, www.sciencemag.org/; Abby Rabinowitz and Amanda Simpson, "The Dirty Secret of the World's Plan to Avert Climate Disaster," *Wired*, December 10, 2017, www.wired.com/; Leo Hickman, "Timeline: How BECCS Became Climate Change's 'Saviour' Technology," *Carbon Brief*, April 13, 2016, www.carbonbrief.org/.

325 Rosen, "Vast Bioenergy Plantations."

326 Hansen, Sato, Kharecha, *et al.*, "Young People's Burden"; Rosen, "Vast Bioenergy Plantations."

327 Friedman, "Why Geoengineering is Not"; Foster, "Making War on the Planet," 5.

328 See Foster, "Making War on the Planet," 4; Rabinowitz and Simpson, "The Dirty Secret"; United Nations Intergovernmental Panel on Climate Change, *Global Warming of 1.5°C*, 2018, https://report.ipcc.ch/.

oligopolistic corporations. Keeping obsolescent or less efficient production technologies in operation—despite their higher carbon emissions—is part of the effort to maintain significant levels of idle productive capacity, in order to manipulate output and pricing. And, unlike companies in competitive market scenarios, oligopolistic corporations usually have the resources to sustain both idle capacity and higher production costs. Their influence over government also makes it less likely that they will be required to upgrade their technologies to reduce emissions. Thus, it cannot be expected that the vast resources of these corporations might be used to invest in new, emission-reducing technologies—when (or if) they become available.

Regrettably, all of the other approaches for reducing planetary carbon emissions seem less feasible than the IPCC-endorsed one. They would involve either carbon capture and sequestration (CCS) *or* the limitation of solar radiation (LSR). One of two proposals in the former category would capture carbon dioxide by burning the exhaust of coal-fired power plants, to store it indefinitely. It has been estimated, however, that this approach would reduce planetary carbon dioxide emissions by only about 20 percent of the twenty-first century's projected total.[329] Decades would be required to build the carbon storage infrastructure, at a cost that would likely be about twice the current monetary worth of all existing petrochemical facilities on the planet.[330] Also, storage facilities would have to be built continuously and indefinitely, to try to achieve lower carbon levels—in a race against time.

The second CCS proposal would carry the captured power plant emissions to deep ocean areas, through a vast network of pipes.[331] These networks would not only be very difficult and extremely costly to build and maintain but are also likely to raise ocean temperatures. The latter would pose a serious risk to deep ocean species and marine life in general.

Fertilizing the oceans with iron—to try to absorb more carbon from the ecosphere—has also been proposed and can be related in part to the CCS typology. Iron fertilization, however, would likely make the oceans either highly populated with phytoplankton—with very harmful effects on zooplankton and many marine species—*or* it could render many ocean areas lifeless.[332]

329 Foster, "Making War on the Planet," 5–6; Hamilton, *Earthmasters*, 47–50.

330 Andy Skuce, "'We'd Have to Finish One New Facility Every Working Day for the Next 70 Years'—Why Carbon Capture is No Panacea," *Bulletin of the Atomic Scientists*, October 4, 2016, https://thebulletin.org/; Vaclav Smil, "Global Energy: The Latest Infatuations," *American Scientist*, May 2011, www.americanscientist.org/.

331 Oliver Morton, *The Planet Remade: How Geoengineering Could Change the World* (Princeton: Princeton University Press, 2016), 137–38; Cesare Marchetti, *How to Solve the CO_2 Problem Without Tears* (Laxenburg, Austria: International Institute for Applied Systems Analysis, 1991); and his *On Geoengineering and the CO-2 Problem* (Laxenburg, Austria: International Institute for Applied Systems Analysis, 1976).

332 Foster, "Making War on the Planet," 4; Hamilton, *Earthmasters*, 27–35; Wynne Parry, "Could Fertilizing the Oceans Reduce Global Warming?" *Live Science*, July 18, 2012, www.livescience

Difficulties in simulating (and analyzing) the impact of marine carbon dioxide removal also make it very difficult to assess whether one or the other outcome might prevail.[333] The lack of concrete data about the effects of this proposal thus raises questions about its feasibility—and its potential compliance with international laws.[334]

The main feature of two proposals in the LSR category would involve manipulating the atmosphere. One approach would modify clouds over the oceans, increasing their mass through vast, sustained releases of microscopic seawater particles—using a very large fleet of remote-controlled ships.[335] It is assumed that the sun would cause water in the particles to evaporate, reflecting solar radiation away from the earth—thus reducing carbon absorption and emissions. The effects on marine life, however, seem likely to be harmful as the oceans' sulfur content would rise—triggering disruptions of the food chain and exterminating numerous species.[336] Also, the sulfur in the atmosphere could lead to acid rain over large areas of the planet.

A second approach in the LSR category would involve massive injections of aerosol in the stratosphere, using large fleets of aircraft built for that purpose.[337] The sulfates released would be expected to limit solar radiation, thus lowering carbon levels in the ecosphere. A major problem with this approach—besides the very high cost—would be its potential depletion of the ozone layer *and* its disturbance of the planet's hydrology—both of which would have harmful consequences for all forms of life.[338] And, among the unanswered questions is

.com/; Hugh Powell, "Fertilizing the Ocean with Iron: Should We Add Iron to the Sea to Help Reduce Greenhouse Gases in the Air?" *Oceanus*, November 13, 2007, www.whoi.edu/.

333 See Lennart T. Bach and Philip W. Boyd, "Seeking Natural Analogs to Fast-Forward the Assessment of Marine CO_2 Removal," *Proceedings of the National Academy of Sciences* 118 (2021), www.pnas.org/.

334 See Hamilton, *Earthmasters*; Parry, "Could Fertilizing the Oceans"; Powell, "Fertilizing the Ocean"; Randall S. Abate and Andrew B. Greenlee, "Sowing Seeds Uncertain: Ocean Iron Fertilization, Climate Change, and the International Environmental Law Framework," *Pace Environmental Law Review* 27 (2010), 555–98.

335 Foster, "Making War on the Planet," 3; Andy Jones, Jim Haywood and Olivier Boucher, "A Comparison of the Climate Impacts of Geoengineering by Stratospheric SO_2 Injection and by Brightening of Marine Stratocumulus Cloud," *Atmospheric Science Letters*, September 17, 2010, https://rmets.onlinelibrary.wiley.com/; Alan Robock, Luke Oman and Georgiy L. Stenchikov, "Regional Climate Responses to Geoengineering with Tropical and Arctic SO_2 Injections," *Journal of Geophysical Research* 113 (2008), https://agupubs.onlinelibrary.wiley.com/; Robock, "20 Reasons."

336 See Michael E. Mann and Tom Toles, *The Madhouse Effect: How Climate Change Denial is Threatening Our Planet, Destroying Our Politics, and Driving Us Crazy* (New York: Columbia University Press, 2016), Chapter 7; Robock, "20 Reasons."

337 See John Bellamy Foster, "Late Soviet Ecology and the Planetary Crisis," *Monthly Review*, June 2015, 7–10; Mikhail I. Budyko, *Climate and Life* (New York: Academic Press, 1974).

338 Foster, "Making War on the Planet," 3, and his "Late Soviet Ecology."

how stratospheric aerosol injections would affect weather in areas that are vital for agriculture.[339]

A less well-known approach—outside the scope of the previous categories—would use nuclear reactors to replace all existing fossil fuel power generation. The main argument offered is that anti-nuclear policies have been influenced by longstanding "phobias" about radiation. Thus, it is proposed that "hundreds of reactors" should be built annually around the world to try to reduce carbon emissions.[340] The possibility of accidents is minimized by this approach, and problems associated with uranium mining—and the genotoxic, mutagenic, and carcinogenic effects of this mineral—are ignored, along with its long-established harmful impact on human reproduction and development.[341]

Because of their unintended—and harmful—side effects, their extremely high cost, or their limited effectiveness in reducing carbon emissions, all of these proposals seem impossible to implement. And, beyond the specifics of what they propose, the fact remains that they do not address the source of the problem—the socioeconomic system we have, and its dysfunctions. Nonetheless, *the fact that they have been considered at all reflects the urgency of the effects posed by greenhouse gases.*

Efficiency Mirage

Adding to the urgency of this panorama is the flawed assumption that technological efficiency will reduce carbon emissions in any significant way. Technological fetishism (discussed in the previous chapter) may be at play here, along with the notion that new technologies always have positive effects. The adoption of more efficient technologies, unfortunately, may not change the trajectory toward higher levels of greenhouse gases.

Two factors are at work in this panorama. One is that there are absolute, long-term limitations to improvements in technological efficiency. The end of the effects predicted by Moore's Law (discussed previously) is an example. This is a matter that almost no one took into account as electronics—and

339 See Weiyi Sun, Bin Wang, Deliang Chen, *et al.*, "Global Monsoon Response to Tropical and Arctic Stratospheric Aerosol Injection," *Climate Dynamics* 55 (2020), 2107–21.

340 Joshua S. Goldstein and Staffan A. Qvist, *A Bright Future: How Some Countries Have Solved Climate Change and the Rest Can Follow* (New York: PublicAffairs, 2019); and their "Only Nuclear Energy Can Save the Planet: Do the Math on Replacing Fossil Fuels; To Move Fast Enough, the World Needs to Build Lots of Reactors," *Wall Street Journal*, January 12, 2019, C4.

341 See Jose L. Domingo, "Reproductive and Developmental Toxicity of Natural and Depleted Uranium: A Review," *Reproductive Toxicology* 15 (2001), 603–09; Darryl P. Arfsten, Kenneth R. Still and Glenn D. Ritchie, "A Review of the Effects of Uranium and Depleted Uranium Exposure on Reproduction and Fetal Development," *Toxicology and Industrial Health* 17 (2001), 180–91; World Health Organization, *Health Effects of Depleted Uranium: Report by the Secretariat*, 54th World Health Assembly, A54/19 Add.1, April 26, 2001, www.who.int/.

information and communication technologies—developed into major economic sectors. Another example is the effort to make supersonic commercial aviation economically and environmentally viable. This barrier has limited mass air travel to subsonic speeds for over six decades, making it impossible to reduce flight times.

Carnot's principle regarding thermodynamic engines and the conversion of heat into work (in the form of motion, energy, or refrigeration) provides another example.[342] Following rules of physics, this principle has long been able to explain why even frictionless engines—the dream of every mechanical inventor—cannot convert anywhere close to 100 percent of their heat inputs into work. And, the hope that innovation can overcome such barriers seems misplaced—taking into account the priorities of technology oligopolies.

Innovations that reduce oligopolistic power are unlikely to be pursued. And, the capacity of the public purse to provide incentives seems limited, given the breadth and depth of the problems likely to be faced in coming decades. The trajectory of oligopoly capitalism is, after all, filled with instances of obsolescent technologies being kept in use, when more efficient ones are available. This seemingly paradoxical situation can be explained by capacity-price engineering—a strategy discussed previously. It may also be explained, in part, by offshoring—as low labor costs and high productivity in certain locales offset the benefit of deploying newer techniques.

The second factor involves the effect known as the Jevons paradox. William Stanley Jevons brought it to public attention (in the mid-nineteenth century) when he noticed that more efficient use of coal in a broad range of industries led to its greater consumption.[343] Also known as the "rebound effect," this empirically derived insight showed that the adoption of more efficient technologies all too often leads to more emissions and waste.[344] *Input reductions due to greater efficiency thus tend to be more than offset by greater consumption*—as products become more affordable *or* new uses are found.

This outcome seems all the more likely in the case of technology oligopolies, given their emphasis on wants contrivance and marketing. As consumption increases so will emissions and waste, especially over the long term—even though they might be reduced immediately after adoption. Reductions per user or per unit of product may thus likely occur, but *aggregate emissions and waste would nonetheless rise over the life of the new technology or even soon after it is adopted.*

342 Nicolas. L. S. Carnot, *Reflections on the Motive Power of Heat* (New York: Wiley, 1897; trans. and edited by R.H. Thurston), Part IV. See Peter Atkins, *The Laws of Thermodynamics: A Very Short Introduction* (New York: Oxford University Press, 2010), chapters 3–5; and his *Four Laws that Drive the Universe* (New York: Oxford University Press, 2007).

343 William S. Jevons, *The Coal Question: An Enquiry Concerning the Progress of the Nation, and the Probable Exhaustion of Our Coal Mines* (London: Macmillan, 1865), chapters X, XI.

344 See Kolasi, "Physics of Capitalism," 38–39.

Also, the totality of the generation of waste and emissions must be taken into account. For example, greater usage of electric vehicles will show a substantial reduction in per-vehicle emissions, but additional electric power will have to be generated to keep batteries charged.[345] And the toxic minerals built into the batteries must be considered. Mining those minerals is itself a source of harmful emissions and ecological depredation—all the more so when open pit or strip-type operations are involved. The disposal of the electric vehicle then aggravates the situation, because of the vast amount of plastics, electronic circuitry, gadgets, and the battery's toxic chemicals and metals—many of which cannot be recycled.[346] The global, total positive effect of electric car usage might therefore be limited over the long term—and may make little difference in the overall panorama of greenhouse gas emissions.

The effect noted by Jevons—and oligopolistic concentration—may thus explain the fact that carbon emissions have continued to rise rapidly. And this has occurred despite the fact that a great number of more efficient technologies have been adopted during the past seven decades. Even if the effect noted by Jevons does not occur in some cases, the question remains as to whether additional technological efficiency can be enough to reduce emissions significantly—in an aggregate way, over the long term.

So far, the data indicate that more efficient technologies—far from reducing or even containing planetary carbon emissions—have had the opposite effect, in substantial ways.[347] It may therefore be that only radical alternatives to oligopoly capitalism's dependence on overconsumption and wasteful resource

345 See Alex Brown, "Electric Cars will Challenge State Power Grids," *Pew Trusts Stateline*, January 9, 2020, www.pewtrusts.org/; F. Todd Davidson, Dave Tuttle, Joshua D. Rhodes and Kazunori Nagasawa, *How Much Electricity will it Take to Power Electric Cars of the Future?* Inverse, December 6, 2018, www.inverse.com/; Chris Sinclair, *Just How Environmentally Friendly are Electric Cars?* Stanford University Management Science and Engineering, July 21, 2017, https://mse238blog.stanford.edu/; Will Oremus, "How Green is a Tesla, Really? As Green as a Golf Cart? A Prius? An SUV?" *Slate*, September 9, 2013, https://slate.com.

346 Perry Gottesfeld, "Electric Cars have a Dirty Little Recycling Problem—Batteries,' *National Observer*, January 22, 2021, www.nationalobserver.com/; Tilak Doshi, "The Dirty Secrets of 'Clean' Electric Vehicles," *Forbes*, August 2, 2020, www.forbes.com/.

347 See NASA, *Global Climate Change, Facts: Carbon Dioxide*, https://climate.nasa.gov/ (accessed July 24, 2022); U.S. Energy Information Administration, *Greenhouse Gases and the Climate: Greenhouse Gas Emissions and Atmospheric Concentrations have increased over the Past 150 Years*, www.eia.gov/ (accessed August 14, 2022). See also Eric Rignot, Jérémie Mouginot, Bernd Scheuchl, *et al.*, "Four Decades of Antarctic Ice Sheet Mass Balance from 1979–2017," *Proceedings of the National Academy of Sciences*, January 14, 2019, www.pnas.org/; Cheng, Abraham, Hausfather and Trenberth, "How Fast are the Oceans Warming?"; Pierre-Louis, "Ocean Warming is Accelerating"; Tom DiChristopher, "Planet-Warming Carbon Emissions are Rising in Wealthy Nations for the First Time in Five Years," *CNBC*, December 4, 2018, www.cnbc.com/; William J. Ripple, Christopher Wolf, Thomas M. Newsome, *et al.*, "World Scientists' Warning to Humanity: A Second Notice," *BioScience* 67 (2017), 1026–28.

usage can provide solutions. Painful and difficult as those could turn out to be, they may be the only hope for survival on our planet.

The Commons

Systemic dysfunction also involves the oligopolistic takeover of resources that belong to all. Reducing their sustainability, causing the public to forgo their use, or rationing access are at the core of this dysfunction. Exclusion, alienation, and damage are the main vehicles. Necessities are the usual target. Greater surpluses and market power are the motives.

Lauderdale Paradox

The takeover of the commons by oligopolistic power can be related to an important classical contribution. Long before oligopolies existed, the contradiction between the interests of society *and* those of private entities attracted concern—as early industrial capitalism began to affect social life in myriad ways. Patterns of social alienation and exclusion that had accompanied the emergence of mercantile capitalism two centuries earlier deepened and were extended to new areas.

In the early nineteenth century, James Maitland (8th Earl of Lauderdale) posited that *an inverse relationship exists between public wealth—essentially the commons—and the accumulation of private riches.*[348] His contribution stood the test of time. It remains valid today despite the different social and economic circumstances we experience.

Maitland's formulation—known as the Lauderdale Paradox—noted that a rise in private riches (oligopolistic surpluses, in our time) is all too often accompanied by a decline in public wealth—society's common endowment of resources. Thus, the conclusion that the former occurs at the expense of the latter becomes inescapable—a relationship that has been verified numerous times during the past two centuries. In the context of technology oligopoly capitalism, we see it as a minuscule elite—and the corporations they control—amass greater wealth while society's dysfunctions deepen.

Given that the value of the commons is realized through public usage—the cornerstone of social use value—any reduction of such utility must be assumed to harm the public interest. At the core of movements to improve society, therefore, is the attempt to balance access and the management of our common endowment of resources—the public's wealth—with the accumulation of private riches. Oligopolistic power has triggered the most severe imbalances

348 James Maitland, *An Inquiry into the Nature and Origin of Public Wealth, and into the Means and Causes of its Increase, by the Earl of Lauderdale* (Edinburgh: Constable, 1804), chapters II, V

between these two opposed interests during the past seven decades—with technology oligopolies at the forefront.

New technologies have all too often cemented these imbalances. Their exploitation has created great wealth for a few, limited benefits for the many, and destroyed nature in ways that may spell catastrophe for all. In the context of oligopoly capitalism, technology is thus neither neutral nor does it necessarily provide a way out of the labyrinth of dysfunction that we now experience.

Access and Benefit

The commons encompasses tangible and intangible resources and involves social rights related to access and benefit. This categorization partially consolidates the typologies provided by Elinor Ostrom in her work.[349] Diminishment of the right to access will comprise withdrawal and exclusion. Damaging the right to benefit will involve preemption of collective sharing. This modification is deemed necessary because of the character of technology and the realities imposed by oligopolistic power.

Oligopolistic control brings up a major contradiction insofar as these rights are concerned. *Oligopolistic corporate power tends to deny free access and collective benefit as it makes management of the commons subservient to its priorities.* Pricing power and the prospect of greater surpluses thus take precedence over access and the public's right to benefit from a collective resource. The damage can be intangible, as it can involve a qualitative loss that is difficult or impossible to quantify. Or it can be tangible, when it forces the public to forgo use that entails material loss.

With social media networks—a component of the social communication commons—the privatization of contact means that those unwilling to allow their data to be expropriated are excluded. And if they comply, they are made to surrender the right to decide how their information is used. Uselaborers are also excluded from partaking in the oligopolistic surpluses obtained from the sale of their data. And they are alienated from the value of the effort, time, and experiences they provide. Even if some benefit is obtained from satisfying the need for contact, the exploitive character of the relationship denies the purpose of a common resource.

A patent monopoly over the product of invention—part of the technological knowledge commons—denies usage to all except the corporate owner. And, charging for usage—if the owner grants licenses—curtails access to those

349 Elinor Ostrom, *Governing the Commons: The Evolution of Institutions for Collective Action* (New York: Cambridge University Press, 1990), chapters 1, 4; Edella Schlager and Elinor Ostrom, "Property-Rights Regimes and Natural Resources: A Conceptual Analysis," *Land Economics* 68 (1990), 249-62. See also Antoine Dolcerocca and Benjamin Coriat, "Commons and the Public Domain: A Review Article and a Tentative Research Agenda," *Review of Radical Political Economics* 48 (2016), 127–39.

unable to pay. Exclusion here involves a privatization of knowledge that is all too often collective in origin and development—much of which is financed by the public through investment in education.

Alienation of the technological knowledge commons starts when individual inventors—who are essentially highly skilled labor—are made to reassign patent awards to their corporate employer.[350] This is usually a legally binding requirement for employment. And the patent system is itself a tool for alienation and exclusion—as the knowledge it circumscribes is usually built up over generations, through additions and combinations. Innovation thus often results from stages going back centuries and depends on knowledge spanning societies, diverse expertise, and multiple phases of social development.[351]

The benefits of innovation, however, accrue primarily to corporations. Exclusion is institutionalized—patents being part of the apparatus of property rights that sustain oligopolistic power. Much the same can be said about copyrighting and the intellectual commons—a domain entwined with technological knowledge. In this area, however, alienation can occur immediately after completion of any work—if access is priced or usage by society is barred. In parallel with patents, there is thus another level of alienation involving copyrights.[352] This form of alienation is all too often unavoidable if intellectual work is to be disseminated—and it can encompass technological knowledge not specified in a patent.

The oligopolistic pricing mechanism that accompanies exclusion is typically justified on the basis of a presumed need for efficiency. Curtailment of access is the usual result, for those who cannot pay or have to ration usage. Making access scarce is thus the key to increase pricing, manipulate output through capacity-price engineering, exploit the public, and obtain oligopolistic

350 See IBM, *IBM Earns Record 9,100 Patents in 2018, Tops U.S. Patent List*, January 18, 2019, https://newsroom.ibm.com/. See also Innovent Law, *Employees and Patents*, https://kgulick.com/ (accessed August 15, 2022); FindLaw, *Law Regarding the Rights to Inventions Made by Employees*, February 16, 2018, www.findlaw.com/.

351 The collective, accumulative social character of invention and innovation is typically disregarded, or ignored altogether, by those who subscribe to the romantic vision of the beleaguered individual inventor as the sole originator of new technology—a mindset long ago countered by S. Colum Gilfillan in his *The Sociology of Invention* (Chicago: Follett, 1935). See also Clarence E. Ayres, *The Theory of Economic Progress* (Chapel Hill: University of North Carolina Press, 1944); William M. Dugger and James T. Peach, *Economic Abundance: An Introduction* (Armonk, NY: Sharpe, 2009); William M. Dugger, "Technology and Property: Knowledge and the Commons," *Review of Radical Political Economics* 48 (2016), 111–26.

352 Copyrighting generally occurs by default—and can only be neutralized through deliberate action by authors. Initially—in the nineteenth century—the copyright monopoly right lasted 14 years, but extensions over time increased it to 70 years after the death of an author. See Dolcerocca and Coriat, "Commons and the Public Domain," 132; Pamela Samuelson, "Mapping the Digital Domain: Threats and Opportunities," *Law and Contemporary Problems* 66 (2003), 147–71; David Lange, "Recognizing the Public Domain," *Law and Contemporary Problems* 44 (1981), 147–78.

surpluses. Efficiency of access, therefore, does not seem to be the real motive or objective.[353]

The true motive is grounded in the fact that making a resource scarce—especially when it is part of the commons—results in higher pricing and larger surpluses. This applies to tangible resources, as their materiality diminishes with usage or consumption. The oligopolist in control can therefore benefit from diminished stock—more so if the resource is non-renewable or cannot be easily replaced.

A contradiction occurs, however, in the case of intangible resources that are part of the commons. With intangibles, usage or consumption does *not* result in their diminishment. Access by any user or consumer does not reduce others' possibility of using the resource—nor does it lead to their having to pay more to access it. Much the opposite often happens—especially with technological knowledge—as greater usage leads to new ideas, better applications, and potentially more benefit.

Herein lies an argument against allowing the technological knowledge commons to be appropriated by oligopolies. Exclusion—through a patent's monopoly right—can be considered detrimental to the public. Its main purpose is to obtain surpluses for the oligopolistic owner of the patent. And, the longstanding argument that such monopoly constitutes an incentive to invent seems lost in our day and age, as the work of inventors is typically appropriated by employers.

The notion that patent monopoly rights foster invention and innovation is also contradicted by history. In the mid-1950s, telecommunications monopolist AT&T was made to agree—through an antitrust "consent decree"—to license all of its patents (then owned by Bell Laboratories) for free to any company.[354] This action led to the emergence of numerous companies that went on to create important inventions and innovations—such as Fairchild Semiconductors, Comsat, Texas Instruments, and Motorola.[355] AT&T continued with its monopoly over telecom, albeit in a more restricted way (with regulatory oversight). Loosening up a monopoly—over patents and a market segment—thus led to more invention and innovation.

353 The fallacy of scarcity as a tool for imposing efficiency, its justification in mainstream economics, its undemocratic nature, and its use as a means of social control has long been a source of interest for some scholars—see Costas Panayotakis, *Remaking Scarcity: From Capitalist Inefficiency to Economic Democracy* (London: Pluto, 2011); Dugger and Peach, *Economic Abundance*; Dugger, "Technology and Property."

354 See Martin Watzinger, Thomas A. Fackler, Markus Nagler and Monika Schnitzer, "How Antitrust Enforcement Can Spur Innovation: Bell Labs and the 1956 Consent Decree," *American Economic Journal* 12 (2020), 328–59.

355 See Wikipedia, *Fairchild Semiconductor*; its *COMSAT*; its *Texas Instruments*; and its *Motorola*, https://en.wikipedia.org/ (all accessed August 8, 2022).

In the 1970s, IBM—through a 13-year-long antitrust prosecution—was made to allow software to be designed by other companies.[356] This action, although ultimately unsuccessful (in terms of its original objective), set the stage for Microsoft to emerge.[357] In the late 1990s an antitrust case against Microsoft itself led to its agreement to allow browsers other than its own Internet Explorer to use Windows.[358] This action—although also unsuccessful in terms of its original objective—made it possible for Google and others to emerge.[359] The fact that the new companies went on to become oligopolists in their market segments should not obscure the fact that the innovations they created—in their early years—would not have been possible without antitrust action. Regretfully, however, many resources of the technological knowledge commons were appropriated as these companies accumulated power.

Appropriation

New opportunities for appropriating the knowledge commons are usually of great interest to technology oligopolies. *Any unexploited collective resource can thus become a target—all the more so if the knowledge involved has the potential to generate surpluses.* Life—our planet's most precious common feature—is one such resource.

Exploring deep ocean areas to find unknown species, organisms, or plants, decoding their genetic information, and obtaining patents on modified codes have attracted great interest in recent decades. The companies involved thus essentially mine nature to appropriate life. This applies even when patenting is circumscribed to modifications of the codes. One oligopolistic biochemical corporation, for example, was found to own almost half of all existing patents on marine genes—a vast and valuable data trove that can be used in numerous fields—biomedicine, ocean farming, biopharmaceuticals, for example.[360]

356 See Franklin M. Fisher, John J. McGowan and Joen E. Greenwood, *Folded, Spindled and Mutilated: Economic Analysis and U.S. v. IBM* (Cambridge, MA: MIT Press, 1983), chapters 1, 4, 6, 8.

357 See Britannica, *Microsoft Corporation*, www.britannica.com/ (accessed July 28, 2022).

358 See *New York Times*, "United States v. Microsoft," May 19, 1998, www.nytimes.com/; U.S. Department of Justice, *U.S. v. Microsoft: Court's Findings of Fact*, www.justice.gov/ (accessed July 28, 2022).

359 See Jonathan Taplin, *Move Fast and Break Things: How Facebook, Google and Amazon Cornered Culture and Undermined Democracy* (New York: Little, Brown, 2017), chapters 6–9; and his "Can the Tech Giants be Stopped?" *Wall Street Journal*, July 15, 2017, C1; Britannica, *Microsoft Corporation*.

360 Ryan P. Smith, "Nearly Half the Patents on Marine Genes Belong to Just One Company: Who Owns Biodiversity? No One and Everyone—Or Maybe, a German Chemical Company," *Smithsonian*, June 13, 2018, www.smithsonianmag.com/; Heather Murphy, "What 13,000 Patents Involving the DNA of Sea Life Tell Us about the Future," *New York Times*, September 17, 2018, www.nytimes.com/. See also University of British Columbia, "Patenting Marine Genetic Resources: Who Owns Biodiversity?" *Science Daily*, June 6, 2018, www.sciencedaily.com/.

Decoded DNA databases for many species have increased exponentially since the early twenty-first century. There were, for example, nearly 10 million gene sequences compiled in the Barcode of Life database by the start of the current decade.[361] Genome assemblies for nearly 20,000 species of mammals (humans excluded), birds, fish, insects, plants, and fungi had been placed in the NCBI BioProject database at that time.[362] The genetic makeup of vast geo-zones—such as coastal areas—is also being analyzed, mapped, and compiled through metagenomics studies that target environmental DNA (eDNA).[363] All the various life forms of entire geographical areas of the planet may thus be genetically inventoried—and likely made available or sold for exploitation.

Oligopolistic appropriation of the life commons in these cases may face relatively few limitations. The complexity of the knowledge involved can preclude much scrutiny from regulators or the public—partly because the knowledge commons taken over requires combining expertise from diverse fields. Thus, no scientific discipline can provide the necessary knowledge on its own, and no degree program can generate all the talent needed, at least initially. The techniques a company deploys may only be known to itself—solely used in-house—and the necessary hardware may be unique. The early stages can thus confer immense advantage to the corporations that take over any part of the technological knowledge commons related to life.

Corporations that can build on the takeover of the life commons—such as those that control genetic editing through applications of CRISPR (Clustered Regularly Interspaced Short Palindromic Repeats) techniques—stand to gain much wealth and power.[364] Most any area of biotechnology, medicine, biopharmaceuticals, farming, animal raising, food chains, and any ecosystem on the planet may thus be affected by the oligopolistic takeover of life that targets genetic decoding. And, any organism that has been—or can be—genetically deciphered is likely to be re-engineered, whenever doing so can generate surpluses and power.

361 Bold Systems, *Barcode of Life Data System*, www.barcodinglife.org/ (accessed August 21, 2022); *The Economist, Technology Quarterly*, "DNA Analysis: Cracking the Code," June 19, 2021, 5–7.

362 NCBI, *BioProject*, www.ncbi.nlm.nih.gov/ (accessed August 6, 2022); NCBI, "Database Resources of the National Center for Biotechnology Information," *Nucleic Acids Research* 44 (2016), D7–19.

363 Universiteit Leiden, *Metagenomics for Community Ecology; A Next Generation of eDNA Monitoring Tool for Biomass Studies in Freshwater Environments*, www.universiteitleiden.nl/ (accessed July 26, 2022); Dominique A. Cowart, Katherine R. Murphy and C.-H. Christina Cheng, "Metagenomic Sequencing of Environmental DNA Reveals Marine Faunal Assemblages from the West Antarctic Peninsula," *Marine Genomics* 27 (2018), 148–60.

364 See Henry Greely, *CRISPR People: The Science and Ethics of Editing Humans* (Cambridge. MA: MIT Press, 2021), chapters 3, 5, 13–15; Katrina Megget, "Money from Genes: CRISPR Goes Commercial; The New DNA-Changing Tech Has Attracted Millions of Dollars from AstraZeneca, DuPont and Other Big Companies," *Scientific American*, January 22, 2016, www.scientificamerican.com/.

New oligopolistic markets—based on genetic trait modification—are already being developed. This will deepen the privatization of the life commons. Wants promotion here involves making everyone aware that certain illnesses that can affect an individual (or that have affected family) might be avoided. This likely large consumer market would involve the engineering of body cells—with changes that cannot be passed on.[365]

The potentially more lucrative (and transcendental) germline cell editing of traits would, however, involve changes that can be passed down to offspring.[366] It is not currently available to humans, but its immense oligopolistic profit potential ensures that it may become reality. A major objective will likely be to make offspring more capable at performing certain endeavors—science, finance, music, warfare, for example—or to reduce susceptibility to certain illnesses.[367] Might we see a new sort of eugenics develop through this market, as the life commons is further privatized and commodified?

Oligopolistic technology platforms that can support human genetic engineering as a consumer market have already been set up. One company specialized in providing hardware for gene testing, for example, controls 90 percent of its market in the United States.[368] This corporation seems set to control the "software" of diagnostic testing—as it owns the company that first developed predictive screening for illnesses, based on blood sampling.[369] Such platforms can therefore support body cell genetic engineering—and possibly germline engineering as well, eventually. The next stage of oligopolistic privatization of the life commons in this area may thus acquire momentum soon.

A focus on genetic design could preempt consideration of social and environmental factors that induce skill or disease. Farming and natural ecologies stand to be affected, as genetic modification ends up targeting most every non-human life form—whenever doing so can generate greater oligopolistic power

365 See Greely, *CRISPR People*, chapters 3, 4.

366 Greely, *CRISPR People*, chapters 2, 11–14. Regulatory approval will be required. For discussions on the first known modification of human germline cells (by Dr. He Jiankui) see Greely, *CRISPR People*, chapters 6–9; Walter Isaacson, *The Code Breaker: Jennifer Doudna, Gene Editing, and the Future of the Human Race* (New York: Simon and Schuster, 2021), Chapter 37.

367 See Greely, *CRISPR People*, chapters 11–14; Rob Stein, "New U.S. Experiments Aim to Create Gene-Edited Human Embryos," *NPR*, February 1, 2019, www.npr.org/; Peter Loftus, "FDA Approves First 'Gene Silencing' Drug," *Wall Street Journal*, August 11, 2018, B3; Amy Dockser Marcus, "In U.S. First, Scientists Edit Out Gene Defect," *Wall Street Journal*, August 3, 2017, A1; Stuart A. Newman, "The Divisive Gene," *Monthly Review*, November 2017, 38–44.

368 *The Economist*, "Illumina and the Holy Grail: The 'Google of Genomics' Meets the Techbashers of Antitrust," September 11, 2021, 66; Immy Mobley, *How did Illumina Dominate the Sequencing Market?* Front Line Genomics, August 6, 2021, https://frontlinegenomics.com/; Ben Remaly, *Illumina Illegally Monopolised DNA Sequencing Market, Rival Says*, GCR, January 12, 2021, https://globalcompetitionreview.com/.

369 Conor Hale, *Grail Launches Long Awaited Galleri Blood Test, its Groundbreaking Multi-Cancer Screening Diagnostic*, Fierce Biotech, June 7, 2021, www.fiercebiotech.com/; *The Economist*, "Illumina and the Holy Grail."

and surpluses.[370] Branding, based on the status appeal of certain products, procedures, or results, the upscale market power of the oligopolists in control, and the social class that patronizes them may be part of that panorama.

A most troubling aspect of the dysfunctions considered in this chapter is that they either spring from, or are deeply associated with, the most powerful organizations in history. *The corporations that potentially hold the key to human advancement, and to the survival of life on the planet, are thus major contributors to the most serious social, economic, and ecological pathologies of our time.* Technology oligopoly capitalism has become a core component and cause of the most serious problems we face, in a way that would have been difficult to imagine a few decades ago.

And, it seems to be becoming clearer that new technologies may not avert a worse future for humanity or for nature and the planet. On the contrary, new technologies have in many ways become part of that worse future and its potentially catastrophic outcomes. The key to technology's role in that unfortunate panorama lies with the powerful corporate interests that control it. Deep-seated, multifaceted conflicts between the social good—what is important for humanity and for life on the planet—*and* corporate objectives are thus taking us down a perilous road.

As we advance down that road our common journey may become more difficult, and the dysfunctions more intractable. Thus, the fact that a corporation may come up with one or another—or many—path-breaking technologies does *not* necessarily translate into a sustainable future or greater wellbeing for humanity and nature. Large surpluses might be obtained and accumulated through such technologies, but that does not mean that they will change our trajectory toward a worse future.

370 See Stein, "New U.S. Experiments"; Newman, "Divisive Gene"; Dennis Berman, "Data Science Will Transform Farming: Hugh Grant of Monsanto and James C. Collins Jr. of DuPont on the Impact of New Gene-Editing Technologies and Big Data," *Wall Street Journal*, October 16, 2017, R7; Megget, "Money from Genes."

Chapter 6

Domination

Our understanding of technology oligopoly capitalism must take into account the panorama of domination. It is impossible to think that technology oligopolies could have become as influential as they are without an apparatus of control that reaches far and wide, across nations and continents. This apparatus is—as with all previously considered topics—systemic in character, complex, and multifaceted.

The apparatus of domination has a planetary projection that is impossible to escape. It is totalistic in its reach, sparing no society or economy that can provide greater surpluses and power. The means and phenomena that sustain this projection will be considered in this chapter, taking into account the realities they have imposed. Discussions will encompass geopolitics, commodity chains, arbitrage, control hierarchies, the martial domain, and those who are made to pay for the vast apparatus of domination. Numerous examples and references on recent events will anchor discussions.

Commodity Chains

Oligopolistic technology corporations control more resources than most nations on earth. *Their control is sustained by the articulation of commodity flows and the relations of power they embed.* These flows have much strategic importance, due to their relationship with geopolitics and its planetary projection.

Geopolitical domination depends greatly on commodity input and product chains.[1] Their significance is rooted in the fact that they articulate almost three-

1 The terms "value chain" and "supply chain" may be considered synonymous with commodity chain. The latter has been adopted for this chapter because of the fundamental importance of commodities for technology oligopolies. Production of commodities by means of commodities is, after all, as much a core feature of capitalism as it is of technology. Although interest in supply flows can be traced to trade in ancient times, historians have granted much attention to their management in warfare—see, for example, Earl J. Hess, *Civil War Logistics: A Study of Military Transportation* (Baton Rouge: Louisiana State University Press, 2017), chapters 1, 3–5.

DOI: 10.4324/9781003345893-6

quarters of all trade flows on earth.[2] And four-fifths of those flows are under the control of oligopolistic corporations.[3] Technology oligopolies are the most important among the latter—due to their global reach, their wealth, and their impact on our existence.

Today, commodity chains involving technology trade are the most complex in history. Constellations of offshore contractors are involved in their operation and maintenance. Their complexity is such that most contractors reportedly ignore the networks and identities of upstream and downstream participants.[4] Studies of shipping flows and their disruption, during the last decade and in recent years, provided much evidence on this aspect—a matter of grave geopolitical concern.[5]

The worldwide networks that commodity chains help articulate have two fundamental objectives—to reduce cost *and* to appropriate value.[6] Both are closely related to the quantum of surpluses that a technology oligopolist can obtain, and they influence how other important aspects of oligopolistic power—such as labor, investment, and political influence—are managed. At the same time, they condition the geopolitical relations of power on technology production, especially on how nations and locales are viewed in the larger scheme of planetary control.

Arm's length contracting is characteristic of technology commodity chains.[7] It provides a convenient way for technology oligopolists to evade regulations

2 Organization for Economic Cooperation and Development, *OECD Factbook Statistics*, www.oecd-library.org/ (accessed June 22, 2022). See also Global Input-Output Database, *World Input-Output Tables, Release 2016*, www.woid.org/; International Labor Organization, *The Impact of Global Supply Chains on Employment and Production Systems* (Geneva: ILO, 2018); Wen Chen, Pieter Woltjer, Marcel P. Timmer and Reitze Gouma, *WIOD Socio-Economic Accounts (SEA) 2016: Sources and Methods* (Groningen: WIOD, 2018). Input-output studies—whose origins can be traced to Francois Quesnay and his Tableau Economique (1758)—were important for raising awareness about material links and flows.

3 See International Labor Organization, *Impact of Global Supply Chains*; Organization for Economic Cooperation and Development, *OECD Factbook Statistics*.

4 After the Fukushima earthquake, for example, it reportedly took a Japan-based semiconductor manufacturer over 12 months and about 100 of its executives to find out the identities and relationships of all participants in the commodity chains it was linked to—*The Economist*, "Special Report, Global Supply Chains, Bumpy New World," July 13, 2019, 4.

5 See Gina Roos, "Resilinc: Supply Chain Disruptions Nearly Doubled in 2017," *EPS News*, February 1, 2018, https://epsnews.com/; *Material Handling and Logistics*, "Supply Chain Disruptions at Highest Rate in 3 Years," November 27, 2018, www.mhlnews.com/. See also Steven A. Altman, Pankaj Ghemawat and Phillip Bastian, *DHL Global Connectedness Index 2018* (Bonn: Deutsche Post DHL, 2019).

6 Recent work on global commodity flows provides important insights on these objectives. See Intan Suwandi, *Value Chains: The New Economic Imperialism* (New York: Monthly Review Press, 2019), chapters 1–3; William Milberg and Deborah Winkler, *Outsourcing Economics: Global Value Chains in Capitalist Development* (New York: Cambridge University Press, 2013), chapters 4, 5; John Smith, *Imperialism in the Twenty-First Century: Globalization, Super-Exploitation, and Capitalism's Final Crisis* (New York: Monthly Review Press, 2016), chapters 2–4, 7–9.

7 See United Nations Conference on Trade and Development, *World Investment Report 2019*, Chapter 1, "Global Investment Trends and Prospects" (Geneva: UNCTAD, 2019), 1–32; International Labor

wherever processing occurs. Companies that have no equity ties to the entities that contract them are therefore in charge of hiring labor and managing operations. Raw material extraction is also typically managed by companies other than the ones that will place their brand on a product. Arm's length contracting arrangements thus insulate American technology oligopolists from compliance expenses and direct contact with labor.

Multiple sourcing has introduced greater complexity in technology commodity chains in recent decades, as processing became more fragmented and dispersed. Thus, a microprocessor placed in a smartphone may be manufactured in one nation—receiving its raw materials or parts from elsewhere—while the screen is manufactured in another country and the casing in yet another one. Other parts will have been manufactured in several nations, while final assembly may occur elsewhere. And the intellectual property for the parts and the product may be owned by a corporation based in a different nation from those where all stages of the chain occur. Chains linked to marketing may further complicate this panorama, if the technology embedded in a product is differentiated to increase sales.

These complexities are part of a global system of control that is largely invisible to the public, but which has coherence and purpose. In this regard, Immanuel Wallerstein's work on commodity chains and systemic global power deserves to be recognized.[8] The "world-economy" model that Wallerstein postulated is relevant to our reality—given the interrelated character of geopolitical power and technological domination. And his formulation of a dualistic global division of labor also needs to be considered, as—technology-wise—the have-nots today depend on (and are in many ways dominated by) the haves.[9] Both the world-economy model and the dualistic division of labor require powerful corporate structures to articulate commodity flows. And, as we shall see later, they also require a far-flung military apparatus to enforce control.

Technology commodity chains have played an important function in this panorama, as they provided the means for the haves to gain advantages that

Organization, *Impact of Global Supply Chains*; Intan Suwandi, R. Jamil Jonna and John Bellamy Foster, "Global Commodity Chains and the New Imperialism," *Monthly Review*, March 2019, 1–2; World Bank, *Special Focus 2, Arm's Length Trade: A Source of Post-Crisis Trade Weakness*, Global Economic Prospects, June 2017, 61–69.

8 Immanuel Wallerstein, *World-Systems Analysis: An Introduction* (Durham: Duke University Press, 2004), chapters 2, 3. See also his *Geopolitics and Geoculture: Essays on the Changing World System* (New York: Cambridge University Press, 1991), chapters 8, 9.

9 See Wallerstein, *World-Systems Analysis*, chapters 3, 5; and his "Protection Networks and Commodity Chains in the Capitalist World-Economy," in Jennifer Bair, ed., *Frontiers of Commodity Chain Research* (Stanford: Stanford University Press, 2009), 83–90. See also the articles in Immanuel Wallerstein, ed., *The World is Out of Joint: World-Historical Interpretations of Continuing Polarizations* (New York: Routledge, 2016).

cemented domination—and that today seem insurmountable to the have-nots.[10] Seizing the advantages provided by lower cost and value capture, discussed earlier in this book, allowed the United States—and its technology oligopolies—to set the terms for the rest of the planet. Thus, most every important aspect related to distribution, production, and labor is under the influence of the largest technology corporations.

Arbitrage

The exploitation of arbitrage is a fundamental component of technological domination and its geopolitical dimension. Two kinds of arbitrage are found in the global domination panorama. One involves labor cost, the other focuses on value appropriation. Both occur through offshore processing and depend on commodity chain flows. Labor and value appropriation are inextricably linked in the context of technology oligopoly capitalism, as value cannot exist without labor.

Labor Arbitrage

For oligopolistic technology corporations, labor arbitrage involves taking advantage of labor cost differentials across nations, such that processing can occur at the lowest possible cost.[11] Such differentials are largely due to the limited mobility of labor—because of migratory restrictions imposed by advanced nations—compared to the high mobility of capital.[12] Securing lower labor costs has therefore often involved pitting officials in one nation or locale against another, to obtain the most favorable terms.[13] Labor arbitrage is thus grounded in the existence of a

10 See Wallerstein, "Protection Networks"; Gary Gereffi, John Humphrey and Timothy Sturgeon, "The Governance of Global Value Chains," *Review of International Political Economy* 12 (2005), 78–104; Jennifer Bair, "Global Capitalism and Commodity Chains," *Competition and Change* 9 (2005), 153–80.

11 Stephen Roach is credited with initial use of the term labor arbitrage—see his *The World Economy at the Crossroads: Outsourcing, Protectionism, and the Global Labor Arbitrage* (New York: Morgan Stanley Special Economic Study, 2003); and his "More Jobs, Worse Work," *New York Times*, July 22, 2004, www.nytimes.com/.

12 An important component of the asymmetrical relations of power involving trade and migration—a topic of longstanding interest among critical political economists. See Arghiri Emmanuel, *Unequal Exchange: A Study of the Imperialism of Trade* (New York: Monthly Review Press, 1972), orig. published as *L'échange inégal* (Paris: Maspero, 1969); Suwandi, Jonna and Foster, "Global Commodity Chains," 5.

13 A strategy that consultants have long espoused. See, for example, James Peoples and Roger Sugden, "Divide and Rule by Transnational Corporations," in Christos N. Pitelis and Roger Sugden, eds., *The Nature of the Transnational Firm* (New York: Routledge, 2000), 177–95; Boston Consulting Group, *International Business*, www.bcg.com/ (accessed June 12, 2022).

vast global "reserve army" of labor—a very large population of workers with a disposition to work for very low wages.[14]

The global labor arbitrage accounts for much commodity chain-related employment, driven by offshoring from the United States and other advanced nations.[15] About one-fifth of global employment is estimated to be commodity chain-linked, with related low-wage jobs increasing by over half since the mid-1990s.[16] But labor participation in offshore commodity chains—although contributing immensely to oligopolistic surpluses—has not had a correspondingly upward effect on labor compensation. Thus, long-term differences in wage levels have tended to increase—between nations where processing occurs *and* the United States and other advanced nations.[17]

Rising wage differentials are therefore behind widening income gaps between rich and poor nations—a trend that seems set to continue in the future and that is fundamentally important for labor and value arbitrage. This increase is related to the rise in offshore outsourcing by large corporations—most of all in technology sectors—and the relations of power that highly favor oligopolistic power and capital.[18] For technology oligopolists labor costs have thus tended to decline in less developed nations—in relative terms—even as worker productivity keeps rising, a phenomenon that underlies a higher rate of offshore labor exploitation.

This is due to the fact that more labor power is obtained for each unit of product, while real wage levels either remain stagnant or increase less rapidly than productivity. For oligopolistic technology corporations that contract offshore this is a formidable advantage, due to the vast populations of underemployed or unemployed workers—compared to a much smaller labor force in the United States.[19] These deeply contrasting labor force numbers help sustain the global labor arbitrage—a major factor in the panorama of domination.

14 See Intan Suwandi, "Labor-Value Commodity Chains: The Hidden Abode of Global Production," *Monthly Review*, July 2019, www.monthlyreview.com/; John Bellamy Foster, Robert W. McChesney and R. Jamil Jonna, "The Global Reserve Army of Labor and the New Imperialism," *Monthly Review*, November 2011, www.monthlyreview.org/.

15 See Suwandi, "Labor-Value Commodity Chains," 9; Benjamin Selwyn, "Beyond Firm-Centrism: Re-Integrating Labour and Capitalism into Global Commodity-Chain Analysis," *Journal of Economic Geography* 12 (2012), 205–226.

16 International Labor Organization, *Impact of Global Supply Chains*; World Bank, *Arm's Length Trade*.

17 International Labor Organization, *Impact of Global Supply Chains*; and its *Global Wage Report* (various years), www.ilo.org/ (both accessed June 14, 2022); U.S. Bureau of Labor Statistics, *Technical Notes: International Comparisons of Hourly Compensation Costs in Manufacturing*, www.bls.gov/ (accessed June 17, 2022); World Bank, *Arm's Length Trade*. See also *The Economist*, "The Headwinds Return," September 13, 2014, www.economist.com/; Jason Hickel, *The Divide* (London: Heinemann, 2017), chapters 1, 2.

18 See International Labor Organization, *Global Wage Report* (various years); Suwandi, *Value Chains*.

19 See Lowell Bryan, "Globalization's Critical Imbalances," *McKinsey Quarterly*, June 2010, www.mckinsey.com/.

For technology oligopolists the labor cost advantage can be very substantial as, for example, profit can amount to as much as 70 percent of the price paid by customers for a product, while the total cost of offshore labor can be as little as two percent of that price.[20] If the same product happened to be entirely manufactured in the United States, profit might likely be four to six times less and the labor cost at least ten times greater.[21] And such profitability tends to be greater the more a product is processed offshore. The global labor arbitrage thus allows technology oligopolies to obtain more labor power for much less money-capital than they could hope to attain in the United States.

The cost advantage is such that even advanced forms of automation may not overcome it. At the core of this matter is the fact that unit labor cost differences between the United States and lower-cost labor nations tend to be greater than the respective differences in productivity.[22] Thus, even if higher productivity in the United States is taken into account, this does not offset the cost advantage of producing or assembling technology products in those nations.[23]

This applies to many parts, components, and raw materials used in military technology, including advanced weaponry—a matter that is typically not disclosed to offshore factories and mining operations where extraction, processing, or assembly occur. Many parts needed for techno-military products are not manufactured in the United States—a matter that makes offshore commodity chains indispensable.[24] Prohibitions on national security grounds can be voided if a part or component has dual commercial and military use, or if eventual usage can be kept secret from offshore subcontractors. And in the case

20 See International Labor Organization, *Global Wage Report* (various years); Christian Fuchs, "Digital Labor and Imperialism," *Monthly Review*, January 2016, 20–22; and his *Culture and Economy in the Age of Social Media* (New York: Routledge, 2015), chapters 4–5; John Smith, "The GDP Illusion: Value Added versus Value Capture," *Monthly Review*, July-August 2012, 86–102. See also Jenny Chan, Ngai Pun and Mark Selden, "The Politics of Global Production: Apple, Foxconn and China's New Working Class," *New Technology, Work and Employment*, 28 (2013), 100–15.

21 By the end of the last decade a well-known Goldman Sachs analyst estimated labor compensation for a "typical" firm in the United States to be about 13 percent of sales—quoted in *The Economist*, "Earnings Reprieve," July 20, 2019, 53.

22 Based on unit labor costs—ratio of (current) real total labor compensation per hour *to* (current) gross output per hour. This avoids calibration problems related to relative wage and productivity data—see International Labor Organization, *World Employment and Social Outlook: The Changing Nature of Jobs—Trends* (various years), www.ilo.org/; Suwandi, Jonna and Foster, "Global Commodity Chains," 13–14, 19–21.

23 Differences in average hourly labor compensation in manufacturing—measured as unit labor costs—between the United States and major offshore manufacturing nations have remained fairly constant since the mid-1990s, at approximately 10 times higher. See U.S. Bureau of Labor Statistics, *Technical Notes*; International Labor Organization, *Global Wage Report* (various years), www.ilo.org/; Suwandi, Jonna and Foster, "Global Commodity Chains," 13.

24 See Dario Leone, "The F-35: Made in China? We explain," *National Interest*, August 4, 2019, https://nationalinterest.org/; Michael Peck, "The U.S. Military's Greatest Weakness? China 'Builds' a Huge Chunk of It," *National Interest*, May 26, 2018, https://nationalinterest.org/.

of certain weapons, the final assembly of the product may occur in the United States—whenever secrecy is considered important. Techno-military contractors thus tend to benefit from much the same low labor cost advantage that commercial technology producers do.

Minerals mining is at the genesis of technology commodity chains and of labor and value arbitrage. Rare-earth minerals—such as tantalum, yttrium, indium, or beryllium—are fundamental for commercial and military technologies, especially those that enable communication, computation, data storage, navigation, and targeting. Many products thus embed dozens of rare-earth minerals in their manufactured parts or components. And some of the mining sites where these minerals are extracted or refined are known to use forced or slave-like labor and child workers—with life expectancies as low as 40 years.[25]

Conventional minerals—such as copper, iron, silver, gold, and zinc—are also fundamentally important for commercial and military technology hardware—and labor conditions and wages are often the worst that can be found on earth. Such minerals vitally involve commodity chain flows and both labor and value arbitrage. Trading oligopolies that sell these minerals have been found to take advantage of the extremely low wages and miserable working conditions at the mining sites. Thus, for example, during the last decade a global minerals trade oligopolist—one of the wealthiest companies in its sector—was found to essentially obtain its conventional minerals for free, due to very low wages and the fact that it appropriated (and sold) all gold extracted—a byproduct of some of the minerals it bought, such as zinc.[26] The value of the gold it appropriated and traded with thus completely offsets what it paid for the other minerals. And the most important customers of those mineral-trading oligopolies are the largest American technology companies and techno-military contractors.

Techno-military oligopolists are thus major beneficiaries of the global labor arbitrage, as the commodity chains that supply them not only engage low-cost labor offshore—and appropriate much value—but are also protected by the U.S. military and intelligence apparatus. Dual-use oligopolistic contractors are possibly the greatest beneficiaries of this panorama, as parts, components and raw materials obtained offshore can be directed to commercial *or* military use

25 See *CBS News*, "CBS News Finds Children Mining Cobalt for Batteries in the Congo," March 5, 2018, www,cbsnews.com/; Scott Patterson and Alexandra Wexler, "Phones, Cars Can't Shed Mining Taint: Supply Chains of Apple, VW and Others Still Link to a Cobalt Mine with Manual Workers," *Wall Street Journal*, September 14, 2018, A1; Henry Sanderson, "LME Probes Cobalt Supplies after Complaints over Child Labour Links," *Financial Times*, November 22, 2017, www.ft.com/; Brian Merchant, *The One Device: The Secret History of the iPhone* (New York: Little, Brown, 2017), chapters 8, 9.

26 See Scott Patterson and Timothy Puko, "Glencore Masters the Zinc Market and Revival Ensues," *Wall Street Journal*, March 18, 2017, B1; Peter Klimek, Michael Obersteiner and Stefan Thurner, "Systemic Trade Risk of Critical Resources," *Science Advances*, November 2015, www.advances.sciencemag.org/.

depending on market demand and the Pentagon's budget. These synergies apply not only to hardware and raw materials but also to intangibles, such as software and even research.

Boeing, one of the two most important U.S. military contractors—and also the nation's most important commercial exporter—has long offshored much of its software design, testing, and development.[27] Its offshore software subcontractors usually work around the clock and have mostly temporary employees—comparable in status to *precariat* workers in the United States.[28] Individuals performing similar work at home would be paid at least ten times more and, in addition, would likely receive certain benefits, such as health insurance and paid vacations. In 2010 Boeing opened a major center with one of its subcontractors in India—engaged in "stress analyses, design and software engineering"—for its commercial aircraft and presumably also for certain (undisclosed) military models.[29] At home, many of Boeing's software engineers were laid off, along with flight testing personnel—who must use flight software intensively and provide feedback.[30]

27 See Peter Robison, "Boeing's 737 Max Software Outsourced to $9-an-Hour Engineers," *Bloomberg*, June 28, 2019, www.bloomberg.com/; and his *Flying Blind: The 737 Tragedy and the Fall of Boeing* (New York: Doubleday, 2021), chapters 6–9; Kyle Peterson, "Outsourcing at Boeing: How the Aerospace Giant Looks Abroad for Key Suppliers in Dreamliner," *Huffpost*, January 20, 2011, www.huffpost.com/.

28 Flaws with some of Boeing's in-flight software for its best-selling commercial aircraft model—that resulted in two accidents and 346 fatalities—have been associated with its software offshoring. Although Boeing denied that it relied on offshore subcontractors for its MCAS (Maneuvering Characteristics Augmentation System) software, resumes posted by offshore workers on social media long before the accidents indicated this had occurred. Boeing's offshore subcontractors in this case were HCL for flight display and Cyient for flight test software (both based in India). One HCL software employee, for example, noted in one post at the time work was being performed: "Provided quick workaround to resolve production issue which resulted in not delaying flight test of 737-Max (delay in each flight test will cost very big amount for Boeing)"—Robison, "Boeing's 737 Max Software." See also Dominic Rushe, "Boeing's 'Culture of Concealment' Led to Fatal 737 Max Crashes, Report Finds: Preliminary Findings Conclude Boeing 'Jeopardized the Safety of the Flying Public' in Its Attempt to Get Max Approved by Regulators," *The Guardian*, March 6, 2020, www.theguardian.com/; U.S. House of Representatives, Transportation Committee, *Nearly One Year After Launching its Boeing 737 Max Investigation, House Transportation Committee Issues Preliminary Investigative Findings*, March 6, 2020, https://transportation.house.gov/. Boeing and U.S. air safety regulators had refused to cooperate with Dutch officials on a fatal crash remarkably similar to that of the 737 Max disasters, involving in-flight software in another model (737 NG) a decade earlier—see Chris Hamby and Claire Moses, "Boeing Refuses to Cooperate with New Inquiry into Deadly Crash," *New York Times*, February 6, 2020, www.nytimes.com/; Alan Levin, "Latest 737 Max Fault that Alarmed Test Pilots Rooted in Software," *Bloomberg*, July 26, 2019, www.bloomberg.com/.

29 Robison, "Boeing's 737 Max Software"; Anita Sharpe and Peter Robison, "Pilots Flagged Software Problems on Boeing Jets Beside Max," *Bloomberg*, June 27, 2019, www.bloomberg.com/. Offshoring software work to India was considered important in winning a $22 billion order for commercial aircraft—the largest ever for Boeing in that nation.

30 *Plane and Pilot*, "Boeing Fires Flight Training Pilots and Outsources the Work," September 22, 2020, www.planeandpilotmag.com/; Robison, "Boeing's 737 Max Software."

For hardware, Boeing began taking advantage of the global labor arbitrage substantially at the start of the twenty-first century, when it decided to transfer responsibility for quality control and technical details to subcontractors.[31] The latter were given technical specifications and were expected to design parts and components on their own.[32] Partly because of this strategy, Boeing has reportedly been outsourcing to offshore subcontractors over one-third of all its parts and components.[33] Its vast and diverse combination of commercial and military products—such as satellites, missiles, combat jets, bombers, passenger and military transport aircraft—means that this scenario will likely expand.

Other dual-use oligopolistic military technology contractors also started to take substantial advantage of the global labor arbitrage at about the same time as Boeing. Companies whose operations had been mainly confined to the United States during the Cold War began to engage in offshoring in the 1990s—as U.S. geopolitical power became largely hegemonic, with control over commodity chains most anywhere, everywhere. Rockwell Collins, a military technology contractor with dual-use products—among them aircraft cockpit displays and avionics systems—started to offshore significant amounts of work at the start of the century.[34] Its military business is quite substantial as it supplies a very large proportion of all the avionics and communication systems used in combat and transport aircraft. By the start of the last decade, one of its offshore subcontractors had more than 400 people working on the design, verification, and development of almost all of its products.[35]

Well before its $30 billion acquisition by United Technologies during the last decade—at the time the most important one in aerospace history—Rockwell Collins had increased its offshore subcontracting to increase surpluses, thus making itself more attractive as a merger target.[36] Its business as a military contractor improved substantially at the time of the merger—a matter influenced by offshore operations—especially on labor. In 2018, the Pentagon then awarded Rockwell Collins a $288 million contract for radios to update

31 See Peterson, "Outsourcing at Boeing."

32 Sharpe and Robison, "Pilots Flagged Software"; Rushe, "Boeing's 'Culture of Concealment'."

33 Peterson, "Outsourcing at Boeing"; Nick Vyas, "Four Compass Points for Global Supply Chain Management … Revisited," *Supply Chain Management Review*, September 5, 2018, www.scmr.com/.

34 Rockwell Collins, *Rockwell Collins in India: Rockwell Collins India Design Center Engineering Capabilities*, www.rockwellcollins.com/ (accessed June 12, 2022); Andrew McIntosh, "Rockwell Collins Plans Job Cuts in Everett as it moves work to the Philippines," *Puget Sound Business Journal*, July 19, 2017, www.bizjournals.com/; HCL, *HCL Technologies' and Rockwell Collins' Strategic Aerospace Engineering Agreement Reaches Ten Year Milestone: Companies Look to Expand Relationship*, May 6, 2010, www.hcltech.com/.

35 McIntosh, "Rockwell Collins plans."

36 See *CNBC*, "United Technologies to Buy Rockwell Collins for $30 Billion, Combine Aerospace Operations," September 4, 2017, www.cnbc.com/.

most every aircraft in service with the Navy, Air Force, and Marines.[37] The updates involved hardware produced through far-ranging commodity chains that also supplied other military technology contractors.

Value Arbitrage

Appropriating value at each stage of a commodity chain network is vitally important for technological domination. The appropriation of value is thus closely linked to the global labor arbitrage—and to commodity chain flows—to the point that it is impossible to disassociate them from each other. And, as both arbitrage modes—and the related chains—contribute to reducing costs, the quantum of value appropriated through offshore processing will rise.[38]

Every stage of a commodity chain thus adds exchange value to a technology product. Value appropriation starts when a raw material is mined and increases as the various phases of transformation occur. All the more so if the entire product is fabricated offshore, as the value-to-cost differential is bound to be greater than if processing occurred onshore. Exchange value thus rises as processing advances, even though it will only be realized when the product is sold.[39]

The gains obtained through value arbitrage—and the financial capital saved—may allow oligopolists to acquire other companies, set up stronger entry barriers, capture new market niches, lobby politicians and government officials, or engage in financial speculation. Offshore value arbitrage may thus provide a formidable advantage to technology oligopolists. The vast amounts of cash held by such companies offshore can be considered part of that advantage. It should not surprise then that the total hoarded by only 12 technology oligopolists—Boeing, Microsoft, IBM, Alphabet-Google, Apple, Intel, Oracle, Cisco, Qualcomm, Meta-Facebook, Amazon, and General Electric—was estimated to be well over one trillion dollars by the end of the last decade.[40]

37 See *Defense World*, "Rockwell Collins Wins $288 Million Contract for AN/ARC-210 Aircraft Radios," August 21, 2018, www.defenseworld.net/.

38 As oligopoly capitalism has distorted notions of value (an aspect noted earlier in this book), it is important to understand the evolution of its meaning. Significant insights on this matter can be found in Ronald L. Meek, *Studies in the Labour Theory of Value* (London: Lawrence and Wishart, 1979), 230–35; Rudolf Schlesinger, *Marx: His Time and Ours* (London: Routledge and Kegan Paul, 1950), chapter VI; Paul A. Baran and Paul M. Sweezy, *Monopoly Capital: An Essay on the American Economic and Social Order* (New York: Monthly Review, 1966), 52–78.

39 A matter that will—misleadingly—cause the entire market value of a product to be credited to the economy where sale occurs. John Smith refers to this distortion as "value capture"—an important point to be taken into account in the context of value arbitrage and commodity chains—see his "The GDP Illusion: Value Added versus Value Capture," *Monthly Review*, July-August 2012, 86–102; and his *Imperialism in the Twenty-First Century* (New York: Monthly Review Press, 2016), chapters 3, 8. See also Mariana Mazzucato, *The Value of Everything* (New York: PublicAffairs, 2018), chapter 7.

40 *The Economist*, "Technology Profits: The Secrets of Big Tech," April 30, 2022, 51–53; Kriti Gupta, "Big Tech, Flush with Cash, Sticks to Sidelines of Bond Market," *Bloomberg*, February 12, 2019,

It is possible that for all American technology oligopolies the total amount of cash kept offshore may be over four trillion dollars—a sum that is more than the gross domestic product of most nations around the world.[41] The cash holdings are of such magnitude that most technology oligopolists seem unable to put them to use in productive ways. Share buybacks—a speculative tactic to drive up share valuations artificially (discussed previously in this book)—is a fairly common use for offshore excess cash when it is repatriated.[42]

For offshore workers, gains from their toil may be minimal—compared to the vast amount of wealth obtained through value arbitrage. An immense transfer of wealth thus occurs, from offshore labor *to* the technology oligopolists in control of arbitrage and commodity chains and—in a lesser way—to the subcontracted companies.[43] The latter are also often oligopolistic.

One such company is Foxconn, the largest manufacturing contractor in the world.[44] Among the many technology products it assembles is Apple's smartphone. Foxconn's profit on each smartphone has been estimated to be about one-fifth of Apple's unit profit (per smartphone)—while the daily wage it pays to workers amounts to about two percent of the price charged by Apple to consumers.[45] Foxconn also assembles products for other technology oligopolists—among them Microsoft—obtaining similar profit margins on their products.

The importance of value arbitrage for technology oligopolies can be seen when the U.S. government imposes import tariffs on certain products. Such tariffs often target a nation that is non-compliant with U.S. geopolitical interests. The publicly announced intent may be to induce a relocation of stages in the offshore commodity chain to the United States—to try to generate employment at home or reduce a trade deficit. However, the real or immediate objective—until compliance with geopolitical dictates occurs—will be to

www.bloomberg.com/. See also Bloomberg, *Global Technology Tracker*, www.bloomberg.com/ (accessed September 14, 2021); Centre for Applied Research, Norwegian School of Economics, *Financial Flows and Tax Havens*, December 2015, www.gfintegrity.org/.

41 *The Economist*, "Technology Profits"; Bloomberg, *Global Technology Tracker*.

42 See Nico Grant and Ian King, "Big Tech's Big Tax Ruse: Industry Splurges on Buybacks," *Bloomberg*, April 14, 2019, www.bloomberg.com/; Todd Haselton, "Apple's Cash Hoard Now at $225.4 Billion," *CNBC*, April 30, 2019, https://cnbc.com/.

43 A form of exploitation that has long drawn attention in the critical politico-economic literature—see Emmanuel, *Unequal Exchange*; Martin Hart-Landsberg, *Capitalist Globalization: Consequences, Resistance, and Alternatives* (New York: Monthly Review Press, 2013), 14–70; Samir Amin, *Unequal Development: An Essay on the Social Formations of Peripheral Capitalism* (New York: Monthly Review Press, 1976).

44 See Wikipedia, *Foxconn*, https://en.wikipedia.org/ (accessed June 12, 2022).

45 Fuchs, "Digital Labor and Imperialism," 20–21; Reed Albergotti, "Apple Accused of Worker Violations in Chinese Factories," *Washington Post*, September 9, 2019, www.washingtopost.com/; Jamie Condliffe, "Foxconn is Under Scrutiny for Worker Conditions. It's Not the First Time," *New York Times*, June 11, 2018, www.nytimes.com/; Gethin Chamberlain, "Apple Factories Accused of Exploiting Chinese Workers," *The Guardian*, April 30, 2011, www.theguardian.com/.

pit the targeted nation against others using value and labor arbitrage. The difference here is that the U.S. government will be undertaking arbitrage, not a technology oligopolist.

This scenario became all too real when the U.S. government started a trade war with China during the last decade, imposing substantial tariffs on a vast range of technology products.[46] But, rather than processing being relocated to the United States, the effect was to drive some of it—and the corresponding stages in their commodity chains—to several other low-cost nations.[47] American consumers were negatively affected, as the tariffs were estimated to cost them $1.4 billion per month by the end of the last decade—largely because of oligopolistic pricing power at each stage of every supply chain.[48] And, some production was shifted elsewhere from China to evade the tariffs—but not to the United States. The losers in this scenario were thus American consumers and Chinese workers—the winners (in a very limited way) were the few nations that received some relocated processing.

Another way in which the importance of value arbitrage is revealed involves the imposition of sanctions by the U.S. government on offshore financial transactions against nations and their companies.[49] The objective is to damage value appropriation and accumulation by blocking transactions and, implicitly, benefit nations that comply with U.S. geopolitical interests. This is an extraterritorial form of economic aggression—"weaponized" value arbitrage, in a way—that can target non-compliant nations. Underlying the sanctions is all too often the (unstated) objective of seizing certain natural resources vital for technology commodity chains and weaponry, such as rare-earth and conventional minerals. Strategic location on or near commodity chain flows may also play a part.

U.S. banks, foreign banks with operations in the United States—and any use of the U.S. dollar by parties involved in value arbitrage for any stage of commodity chains—are thus severely penalized if they engage in a transaction with the targeted nation or its companies. The Society for Worldwide Interbank Financial Telecommunication (SWIFT), the global organization that

46 See John W. Schoen and Jacob Pramuk, "Trump Reignites the China Trade War—Here's How We Got Here," *CNBC*, March 2, 2019, www.cnbc.com/; Dorcas Wong and Alexander C. Koty, "The US-China Trade War: A Timeline," *China Briefing*, September 11, 2019, www.china-briefing.com/.

47 *The Economist*, "Supply-Chain Reaction," December 21, 2019, 99; ITC Tradeweb, *Monthly Activity Report*, 2019 (various months), www.tradeweb.com/; Panjiva Research, *U.S. Ocean Freight Trade*, 2019 (various months), https://panjiva.com/; Sankalp Phartiyal and Sudarshan Varadhan, "Foxconn to Begin Assembling Top-End Apple iPhones in India in 2019—Source," *Reuters*, December 27, 2018, www.uk.reuters.com/.

48 Mary Amiti, Stephen J. Redding and David Weinstein, *The Impact of the 2018 Trade War on U.S. Prices and Welfare*, NBER Working Paper 25672, March 2019, www.nber.org/.

49 See Henry Farrell and Abraham L. Newman, "Weaponized Interdependence: How Global Economic Networks Shape State Coercion," *International Security* 44 (2019), 42–79.

tracks all financial flows—under U.S. influence since its inception—is a formidable surveillance tool for these measures, as its data clouds can reveal every banking transaction that occurs in the world.[50] The U.S. Treasury's Center for Financial Intelligence (FINCEN) is another vital tool in this regard, as it adds detail or correlates information with SWIFT data—and with information provided by such intelligence organizations as the CIA (Central Intelligence Agency) and the NSA (National Security Agency).[51] The U.S. dollar's global supremacy—and its widespread use in value arbitrage transactions—has also made such measures feasible.

The most intensively targeted nations for punishment through value arbitrage during the last seven decades have been North Korea, Cuba, Iran, Venezuela, and lately Russia. U.S. sanctions against North Korea date to 1950 and the Korean War—a matter that arguably led its government to develop nuclear weapons and long-range missiles as a sort of insurance against military aggression.[52] North Korea's strategic location relative to some of the most important commodity chain flows in East Asia—and to South Korea's advanced technology research and production complexes—may also be considered significant factors.

In the other cases, aggression through value arbitrage can be related to strategic location relative to important commodity chain flows, or important mineral resources for technology. In Cuba's case—a nation with minimal mineral resources but a very strategic location related to commodity chain flows—over six decades of sanctions through value arbitrage and limited warfare transcended the end of the first Cold War.[53] Iran's valuable natural resources—many of them important for advanced technologies—and its strategic location near some of the most important commodity chain flows in the planet, partially underlie its targeting.[54] Venezuela, with the world's largest proven oil reserves

50 SWIFT is based in Belgium—a NATO member nation closely bound with the U.S. military and intelligence establishment. See SWIFT, *SWIFT History*, www.swift.com/ (accessed June 19, 2022); *The Economist*, "The Pros and Cons of a SWIFT Response," November 20, 2014, www.economist.com/; Susan V. Scott and Markos Zachariadis, *The Society for Worldwide Interbank Financial Telecommunication (SWIFT)* (London: Routledge, 2014), chapters 2–3.

51 Wikipedia, *Financial Crimes Enforcement Network*, https://en.wikipedia.org/; FINCEN, *Financial Crimes Enforcement Network*, www.fincen.gov/ (both accessed June 20, 2022).

52 See Wikipedia, *Sanctions against North Korea*, https://en.wikipedia.org/ (accessed June 14, 2022); Semoon Chang, "The Saga of U.S. Economic Sanctions against North Korea," *Journal of East Asian Affairs* 20 (2006), www.jstor.org/.

53 At the beginning of the last decade estimates placed economic damages at one trillion dollars, but additional actions by the U.S. government during the last decade may have increased them significantly. See Wikipedia, *United States Embargo against Cuba*, https://en.wikipedia.org/ (accessed May 14, 2022); United Nations, Meetings Coverage, *As General Assembly Demands End to Cuba Blockade, for Twenty-Third Consecutive Year, Country's Foreign Minister Cites Losses Exceeding $1 Trillion*, October 28, 2014, www.un.org/; Portia Siegelbaum, "Cuba: U.S. Embargo Causes $1 Trillion in Losses," *CBS News*, September 14, 2011, www.cbsnews.com/.

54 See *Global Defense Analysis*, "Iran's FM: $1 Trillion Economy Damage due to US Sanctions," February 24, 2021, www.globaldefenseanalysis.com/; Wikipedia, *United States Sanctions against Iran*, https://en.wikipedia.org/ (accessed June 14, 2022).

and vast deposits of varied minerals—many of them indispensable for advanced technologies—along with its strategic location close to very important commodity chain routes can be considered decisive factors.[55]

It may be argued that value arbitrage promotes oligopolistic consolidation. For technology oligopolies, the larger scale that consolidation provides strengthens negotiating power with commodity chain subcontractors—all the more so when arm's-length relationships are the norm. Such added power can, in turn, further reduce costs and lead to additional value appropriation.

For the U.S. military and intelligence apparatus, a foreign constraint to oligopolistic consolidation will likely be regarded as a threat—to be met with additional increases in military and intelligence budgets. Such increases are fundamentally important for the advancement of careers—and for techno-military contractors they represent additional surpluses. *The interests of the oligopolistic and the martial domains thus become synergistically linked through value arbitrage.* One set of actors must therefore keep feeding the other if the dynamics of arbitrage, geopolitical domination, and oligopolistic power are to be sustained.

During the last decade the merger of UTC (United Technologies)—supplier of Pratt and Whitney jet turbines for both commercial and military use, among other products—and Raytheon (a producer of missiles, and specialist in high-temperature materials technology), illustrated how consolidation can enhance arbitrage.[56] Raytheon had previously acquired Rockwell Collins—another military technology contractor—for $30 billion by the end of the last decade.[57] The merged UTC–Raytheon company became the second largest aerospace military technology contractor—after Boeing—thereby acquiring a much larger scale and gaining greater clout to impose its terms on offshore contractors—for its commercial and military operations. And although doubts were expressed about the merger, it nonetheless fit in quite well with the logic favoring consolidation among military technology contractors.[58]

55 Sanctions have involved embargoes, confiscation of Venezuelan state property and companies in the United States, hybrid warfare, and interception at sea (including confiscation) of Venezuelan commercial shipments, among other actions—see Amy Goodman (interviewer), *Economist Jeffrey Sachs: U.S. Sanctions have Devastated Venezuela and Killed Over 40,000 Since 2017*, Democracy Now!, May 1, 2019, www.democracynow.org/; Marc Weisbrot and Jeffrey Sachs, *Economic Sanctions as Collective Punishment: The Case of Venezuela*, Center for Economic and Policy Research, April 2019, https://cepr.net/; Sanctions Wiki, *Venezuela*, httsp://sanctionswiki.org/ (accessed June 14, 2022).

56 See *The Economist*, "Fighting the Next War: Military and Industrial Forces are Behind America's Biggest Defense Merger," June 15, 2019, 58; Marcus Weisgerber, "Pentagon Sees 'No Major Concerns' with Raytheon-United Technologies Merger: The Defense Department's Top Weapons Buyer, Ellen Lord, Gives Stamp of Approval to What Would be the Second-Largest Defense and Aerospace Company Ever," *Defense One*, August 26, 2019, www.defenseone.com/.

57 *The Economist*, "Fighting the Next War."

58 See Jon Sindreu, "Sharing Tech Won't Vindicate UTC-Raytheon Megamerger: An Analysis of Both Companies' Patent Portfolios Confirms that They Have little in Common," *Wall Street Journal*, August 7, 2019, www.wsj.com/; Weisgerber, "Pentagon Sees"; *The Economist*, "Fighting the Next War."

The merger also allowed UTC to spin off two of its commercial units as oligopolistic subsidiaries, to better control its value arbitrage and associated activities.[59] The two subsidiaries—one focused on fabricating elevators (Otis) and the other temperature control systems (Carrier)—attracted more capital from Wall Street. The spun off subsidiaries were then able to engage in diverse forms of financial speculation—targeting certain niches, such as real estate. More important, the two subsidiaries obtained a stronger position to improve their arbitrage through offshore supply chains—by subcontracting more work abroad independently.

The acquisition of Sikorsky by Lockheed Martin during the last decade provides another example of consolidation, the importance of arbitrage, and the supportive attitude of the military establishment.[60] Lockheed Martin—one of the two largest military technology contractors in the world—expanded its aerospace repertory to include helicopters, along with their related weaponry and services. This was the most expensive purchase of a military contractor in two decades. Many of the parts and components utilized by the two companies were manufactured offshore. Shortly after, Lockheed Martin even asked the Pentagon to pay it $212 million in restructuring costs—thus expecting taxpayers to further subsidize its acquisition.[61] The purchase of Sikorsky also allowed Lockheed Martin to shift away from being an integrator of communications and weapons to becoming an owner of military technology platforms—strengthening its power to lobby politicians, Pentagon officials, and offshore contractors.

The asymmetrical relations of power that result from arbitrage and oligopolistic consolidation mean that offshore subcontractors at any stage in a commodity chain may have practically no choice but to accept demands. The larger scale of the consolidated corporation practically guarantees a more powerful unidirectional, arm's-length relationship. The importance of arbitrage along the commodity chain may thus increase for the oligopolist in control, while net benefits to offshore subcontractors—and workers—may be very limited. For techno-military contractors that engage in consolidation this is an almost ideal situation to be in, as increased domination over offshore contracting translates into lower costs and greater surpluses.

Control Hierarchies

Technological domination involves control hierarchies that are global in scope and scale. The ways and means of control tend to be fragmented and opaque, but they

59 See *The Economist*, "Fighting the Next War"; Thom Forbes, "United Technologies will Spin off Otis and Carrier over Two Years," *MediaPost*, November 27, 2018, www.mediapost.com/.

60 Andrew Clevenger, "Lockheed Completes Sikorsky Acquisition," *Defense News*, November 6, 2015, www.defensenews.com/; Doug Cameron, "Deal for Sikorsky Raises Lockheed Bet on Military," *Wall Street Journal*, July 21, 2015, A1.

61 Anthony Carpaccio, "Lockheed Wants Pentagon to Help Pay its Costs to Absorb Sikorsky," *Bloomberg*, January 24, 2018, www.bloomberg.com/.

are closely related to geopolitical influence, commodity chain flows, and arbitrage. Without these hierarchies, oligopolistic power—and the martial domain to which it is symbiotically connected—would become largely ineffective. The multifaceted global predominance of American technology oligopolies depends on how these modes of control are managed and enforced.

Hierarchic domination has been subject to misinterpretation in recent decades. The rapid expansion of technology-related commodity chains since the early 1990s—linked to the spread of multiple sourcing, the rising diversity of flows, and the increasing number of processing sites—led to network configurations that seemingly dissolved or inverted hierarchical power, but in fact retained and deepened concentration.[62] The misinterpretation seems, to a large extent, to have been due to neglect of network structures and their complexities.

In particular, the spread of hub-and-spoke (or circuit) network structures in commodity chains—vital to sustaining multiple sourcing and flexible production—and the large number of new processing sites contributed to the mirage of an inversion of control. These network structures reduced the reach (distance-wise) of many commodity chains, contributing to the aforementioned interpretation. The dispersion that characterizes circuit networks also promoted the perception that a dilution of hierarchic corporate power had occurred. But commodity chain flows actually retained and expanded their complexity—despite appearances to the contrary—as noted by analysts who researched this aspect empirically.[63] Thus, the complexity of commodity chain networks—and their hierarchic control by a relatively small number of very large corporations—was *not* reduced by globalization or by the emergence of new production sites.

Continental processing hubs, an outcome of circuit network structures, became necessary to manage multiple sourcing, appropriate value, and more intensively exploit the global labor arbitrage—adding to the impression that control over commodity chains was shifting out of the United States and other advanced nations.[64] Such hubs were—and have remained—under the control

62 See Thomas L. Friedman, *The World is Flat: A Brief History of the Twenty-First Century* (New York: Farrar, Straus and Giroux, 2006); and Richard Baldwin's *The Great Convergence: Information Technology and the New Globalization* (Cambridge, MA: Harvard University Press, 2016), Part III.

63 See Mark Millar, "Deconstructing Global Supply Chains: Despite a Shift toward Regionalization, the Era of Complex Supply Ecosystems is Far from Over," *Inbound Logistics* 39 (2019), www.inboundlogistics.com/; and his *Global Supply Chain Ecosystems: Strategies for Competitive Advantage in a Complex, Connected World* (London: Kogan Page, 2015), chapter 8.

64 The impression of a shift in control saw a decentralization from the "triad" at the core—the United States as global hegemon supported by Western Europe and Japan. This impression rested on the assumption that globalization had advanced to a point that national sovereignty and the concept of nation had become irrelevant—for *all* nations, including the United States. Thus, it was argued that any notion of imperialism was no longer valid, as imperial hegemony and its concentration of decision-making power had decentralized (or become dispersed) around the planet. The notion of a

of U.S. oligopolistic power—especially for technology corporations and for techno-military contractors. And, despite the attention granted to China as a rising industrial power, it has been estimated that about 85 percent of this nation's technology exports are largely links and stages in the commodity chains of global oligopolistic corporations based in—and controlled by—the United States and several other advanced nations.[65]

Despite appearances to the contrary, control over the largest global technology corporations remains highly concentrated. Ninety-six percent of the 200 largest corporations in the world—among them the most powerful American technology oligopolies—have their headquarters in only eight nations, with the United States in the lead by far.[66] All of the nations involved are close allies of, or depend on, the United States—economically and militarily. Membership in those corporations' boards of directors is almost all (98 percent) composed of citizens of their home-base nation. And, all of their chief executives are citizens of each of those countries.

The United States—and to a lesser extent seven other advanced nations, all of them geopolitically subordinated—thus largely control global commodity chains. Such control involves the most important decisions that govern their existence. *This hierarchic concentration is fundamental for deciding strategies and imposing priorities regarding the most advanced technologies—including those that enable enforcement of geopolitical domination.* This aspect has largely remained unchanged over the past six decades, despite globalization. Hierarchic power thus remained nation-based—and continued to be

---

decentralization of hegemonic power—and the assumption of irrelevance of the nation-state—was challenged early on by several authors, among them Atilio A. Borón in his *Empire and Imperialism: A Critical Reading of Michael Hardt and Antonio Negri* (London: Zed, 2005); Samir Amin in his *The Law of Worldwide Value* (New York: Monthly Review Press, 2010) and his *Capitalism in the Age of Globalization: The Management of Contemporary Society* (London: Zed, 2014); Leo Panitch and Sam Gindin in their *The Making of Global Capitalism: The Political Economy of American Empire* (London: Verso, 2012); Utsa Patnaik and Prabhat Patnaik in their *A Theory of Imperialism* (New York: Columbia University Press, 2017); and by Ernesto Screpanti in his *Global Imperialism and the Great Crisis: The Uncertain Future of Capitalism* (New York: Monthly Review Press, 2014). The impression of a dissolution of global hegemonic control—and of imperialism—was most prominently explicated by Michael Hardt and Antonio Negri in their *Empire* (Cambridge, MA: Harvard University Press, 2000) and their *Multitude: War and Democracy in the Age of Empire* (New York: Penguin, 2004). A nuanced view of hegemonic dissolution was also taken up by David Harvey in his *The New Imperialism* (New York: Oxford University Press, 2003), chapters 4–5.

65 See Hart-Landsberg, *Capitalist Globalization*, 45; Suwandi, Jonna and Foster, "Global Commodity Chains," 8.

66 See Suwandi, Jonna and Foster, "Global Commodity Chains," 13–18; Boron, *Empire and Imperialism*, 46; Fortune, *Fortune 500*, https://fortune.com/ (accessed February 24, 2022); Data.gov, *Fortune 500 Corporate Headquarters*, December 2, 2019, https://catalog.data.gov/; Wikipedia, *List of S&P 500 Companies*, and its *List of Largest Companies by Revenue*, https://en.wikipedia.org/ (both accessed February 24, 2022); Renee Lightner and Theo Francis, "Inside America's Board Rooms," *Wall Street Journal*, January 19, 2016, www.wsj.com/.

controlled from the United States—contradicting the notion that it had become "multinational" in terms of control or priorities.

It is important to recognize that the United States' hierarchic influence over commodity chains and arbitrage—a very important feature of its global technological domination—developed over a long period of time. Such control is an outcome of several global hierarchic projections that involve both oligopolistic commercial power and the martial domain. These global projections of U.S. hierarchic power did not emerge simultaneously, however. Their occurrence was a result of influences and prior events that will be considered in this discussion.

Biotechnology

Control over biological technologies is at the forefront of oligopolistic domination. The engineering of life, and any modification thereof, are major concerns. Life itself is thus turned into a commodity through this projection—arbitrage and commodity flows providing materials, supporting processing, and making it possible for marketing and research to occur.

Hierarchic control is reflected by the fact that the vast majority of biotechnology patents are held by American oligopolistic corporations.[67] The highest *per capita* proportion of bio-scientists in the world helps sustain this control scenario.[68] These aspects ensure that domination over biological technologies will deepen, as a vast range of genomic products are marketed. And, biological technologies are likely to have stronger ties with warfare.

Commodity chains support this hierarchic projection in three ways. One typology involves supply of raw materials, some of which may be plants or live specimens, or extracts thereof. Among the specimens, viruses are particularly important—as they are diverse and vital for both disease control and bio-warfare. The second typology involves the provision of processed substances and equipment. Laboratory and processing hardware are, after all, subject to cost considerations involving commodity chain flows, and to both labor and value arbitrage. Then, there is the supply of finished products, to be used in such diverse activities as medical treatments, farming, animal raising, environmental remediation, and bio-warfare.

Offshore contracting occurs through any of the commodity chain typologies, with relatively greater emphasis on the first two. A vast diversity of

67 See OECD, *Patents by Technology*, and its *Key Biotechnology Indicators*, https://stats.oecd.org/ (both accessed June 7, 2022); World Intellectual Property Organization, *Statistical Country Profiles*, www.wipo.int/ (accessed June 28, 2022); Statista, *Content Marketing Trend Study 2019, Distribution of Global Life Science PCT Applications in 2012, by Region*, www.statista.com/.

68 See OECD, *Employment Database*, and its *Main Science and Technology Indicators*, https://stats.oecd.org/ (both accessed June 27, 2022); Statista, *Market Size and Growth of the Global Life Sciences Industry in 2016, by Sector*, www.statista.com/.

materials and products is characteristic of these chains, and they support not only biotechnology but also biopharmaceuticals and biomedicine. American oligopolistic corporations overwhelmingly control—hierarchically—the commodity chains and most processing steps. This is partly due to the fact that U.S. companies were pioneers in biotechnology and in most of the techniques that have emerged in related sectors.

CRISPR (Clustered Regularly Interspaced Short Palindromic Repeats) technologies are possibly the most important and are likely to have much impact on life as the twenty-first century advances. These technologies (addressed earlier in this book) allow genetic code editing in any living organism, including humans.[69] A vast global market for genetic engineering is thus emerging—controlled largely from the United States.[70]

Treatments for genetically derived diseases, organ replacements, and (eventually) the passing of engineered traits to offspring will be some of the products.[71] Humans, animals of all species, viruses, and plants are targets for genetic modification—for medical, economic, or aesthetic reasons, and also for warfare. And the commodity chains that sustain CRISPR materials, equipment, and processing stages possibly have some of the highest monetary value—per unit of weight—across the technology spectrum.

DARPA (Defense Advanced Research Projects Agency)—a very important component of the military apparatus—is the organization through which oligopolistic technology contractors usually link up with the bio-military dimension.[72] Numerous projects articulate the needs of the military in ways that can engage corporations.[73] Although the U.S. government officially gave up

69 See Wikipedia, *CRISPR*, https://en.wikipedia.org/ (accessed May 26, 2022); Congressional Research Service, *Advanced Gene Editing: CRISPR-Cas9*, December 7, 2018, https://crsreports.congress.org/; Rodolphe Barrangou and Jennifer A. Doudna, "Applications of CRISPR Technologies in Research and Beyond," *Nature Biotechnology* 34 (2016), 933–41; *The Economist*, "Genome Editing: The Age of the Red Pen," August 22, 2015, 19–22.

70 AEI, *Thinking about the CRISPR Revolution and Economic Growth*, November 2, 2020, www.aei.org/; Peter Loftus, "FDA Approves First 'Gene Silencing' Drug," *Wall Street Journal*, August 11, 2018, B3; Lydia R. Pflanzer, "A Revolutionary Gene-Editing Technology is On Track to be a $10 Billion Market by 2024," *Business Insider*, November 2, 2017, www.businessinsider.com/; Amy D. Marcus, "In U.S. First, Scientists Edit Out Gene Defect," *Wall Street Journal*, August 3, 2017, A1; McKinsey and Company, *Realizing the Potential of CRISPR*, January 24, 2017, www.mckinsey.com/; *The Economist*, "Genome Editing."

71 See Clara Rodríguez Fernández, *10 Unusual Applications of CRISPR Gene Editing*, Labiotech, March 30, 2020, www.labiotech.eu/; Victor Tangermann, *A CRISPR Future: Five Ways Gene Editing will Transform Our World*, Futurism, January 30, 2018, https://futurism.com/.

72 DARPA, *Creating Breakthrough Technologies and Capabilities for National Security*, www.darpa.mil/ (accessed June 17, 2022); DARPA, *Bolstering the Front Line of Biological Warfare Response*, February 12, 2013, www.darpa.mil/. See also RAND Corporation, *Biological Weapons and Warfare*, www.rand.org/ (accessed October 17, 2021).

73 See Moderna, *mRNA Strategic Collaborators: Government Organizations*, www.modernatx.com/ (accessed October 17, 2021); Lindy Kyzer, *Pfizer Awarded DARPA Biodefense Contract—DoD*

its biological weapons program in 1973, its research (labeled "biodefense") reportedly continued—and many projects have been considered to tacitly involve bioweapon creation and development.[74]

The intense attention and vast resources devoted to bioweapon-related research may indicate the importance of this projection for the martial domain. Hundreds of the Pentagon's biological or bioweapon research labs are reportedly located in the United States and around the world—with highly secretive research programs that have raised safety concerns.[75] Allegations and evidence have surfaced occasionally about the United States' use of biological agents, to test on the public or against nations that defy U.S. geopolitical interests.[76] And in the few cases where there is any public information, the targeted nations can be linked to commodity chains and geopolitics in various ways—as sources of raw materials, as stage platforms, or because of their strategic location.[77]

Daily Contracts, Clearance Jobs, December 4, 2013, https://news.clearancejobs.com/. See also Jade Tungui, "Inside the U.S. Government's Top-Secret Bioweapons Lab," *Business Insider*, April 11, 2021, www.businessinsider.com/; *SWFI Institutional Investor, DARPA Displays Human Implant Microchip that can Detect Viruses*, April 12, 2021, www.swfinstitute.org/; Harm Venhuizen, "8 Weird DARPA Projects that Make Science Fiction Seem like Real Life," *Military Times*, September 4, 2020, www.militarytimes.com/; DARPA, *Bolstering Front Line Biological Warfare*.

74 See Wikipedia, *United States Biological Weapons Program*, https://en.wikipedia.org/ (accessed September 25, 2021); CRISPR Society, *The Military as a Disease Vector and Covid-19*, October 15, 2021, https://thecrisprsociety.com/; Sharon Lerner and Maia Hibbett, "Leaked Grant Proposal Details High-Risk Corona Virus Research," *The Intercept*, September 23, 2021, https://theintercept.com/; Dilyana Gaytandzhieva, "New Data Leak from the Pentagon Biolaboratory in Georgia," *Arms Watch*, September 6, 2020, https://armswatch.com/; Sherwood Ross, "U.S. Biowarfare Programs have 13,000 Death Scientists Hard at Work," *State of the Nation*, December 19, 2020, https://stateofthenation.co/; Candice Choi and Seth Borenstein, "Scientists: U.S. Military Program can be Seen as Bioweapon," *AP*, October 4, 2018, www.apnews.com/; Arms Control Association, *Chemical and Biological Weapons Status at a Glance*, June 2018, www.armscontrol.org/; Arthur Neslen, "US Military Agency Invests $100M in Genetic Extinction Technologies," *The Guardian*, December 4, 2017, www.theguardian.com/. The military and intelligence apparatus justifies its involvement with bioweapons and biowarfare as a "response" capability, mainly to counter bioterrorism—see, for example, DARPA, *Bolstering Front Line Biological Warfare*.

75 See Emily Baumgaertner, "Biosafety Reforms Still Lagging at Military Labs," *New York Times*, September 20, 2018, www.nytimes.com/; Alison Young and Nick Penzenstadler, "Inside America's Secretive Biolabs," *USA Today*, May 28, 2015, www.usatoday.com/.

76 See Michelle Bentley, *USA's History of Testing Bioweapons on the Public—Were Ticks Used Too?* Lyme Disease, July 22, 2019, www.lymedisease.org/; Baumgaertner, "Biosafety Reforms Still Lagging"; Kevin Loria, "Over and Over Again, the Military has Conducted Dangerous Biowarfare Experiments on Americans," *Business Insider*, September 25, 2016, www.businessinsider.com/.

77 See *Veterans Today*, "Russia Accuses U.S. of Bio-Warfare in Shocking Report," April 10, 2021, www.veteranstoday.com/; Wikipedia, *Allegations of Biological Warfare in the Korean War*, https://en.wikipedia.org/ (accessed October 17, 2021); Jimmy Falls, *JFK Files Reveal Biological Warfare Plans against Cuba*, Who What Why, May 9, 2018, https://whowhatwhy.org/; Shane Harris and Matthew M. Ald, "Exclusive: CIA Files Prove America Helped Saddam as He Gassed Iran," *Foreign Policy*, August 26, 2013, https://foreignpolicy.com/; Hank P. Albarelli Jr. and Zoe Martell, *Dengue Fever Outbreak Leads Back to CIA and Army Experiments*, Voltairenet, July 17, 2010, www

Military contracting can involve diverse, mostly oligo-monopolistic, corporate research laboratories. Poisoning nature to damage a targeted nation's ecosystems, ruin its agriculture or fauna, impoverish its population, and cause penuries that will lead to governance changes can conceivably become an expected research result. Most of the corporate research laboratories contracted for these endeavors depend greatly on commodity chains for their inputs, some of which can only be found in remote locales or in deep ocean areas around the world.[78] And their research results may be one-of-a-kind—created for a single use or purpose.

The potential (or eventual) application of CRISPR gene editing technologies to U.S. military personnel reflects the importance of the bio-dimension for the martial domain.[79] Improving combat performance would seem to be an important objective. Although the avowed intent might be to protect soldiers, it seems obvious that genetically equipping individuals to be more capable in combat—to more effectively eliminate enemies—would be a purpose.[80]

Among other possible CRISPR uses are modifications of viruses to turn them into bioweapons. There are 264 known virus species on earth, and about 800,000 that infect animals which could be passed to humans.[81] Genetically engineering viruses using CRISPR techniques—for use as bioweapons—could, for example, generate accelerated mutation to evade vaccines and antiviral medications.[82] The genetic code of the virus itself might be engineered

.voltairenet.org/; Geoff Simons, *The Scourging of Iraq: Sanctions, Law, and Natural Justice* (New York: St. Martin's, 1996).

78 See Wikipedia, *Deep Sea Mining*, https://en.wikipeida.org/ (accessed June 19, 2022); Alan Weedon, "Warfare's Next Frontier Might be the Ocean Floor," *ABC News*, October 18, 2019, www.abc.net.au/; Olive Heffernan, "Seabed Mining is Coming—Bringing Mineral Reaches and Fears of Epic Extinctions," *Nature*, July 24, 2019, www.nature.com/; Maja V. Folkersen, Christopher M. Fleming and Syezlin Hasan, "The Economic Value of the Deep Sea: A Systematic Review and Meta-Analysis," *Marine Policy* 94 (2018), 71–80.

79 See DARPA and Renee Wegrzyn, *Safe Genes*, www.darpa.mil/ (accessed September 26, 2021); DARPA and Todd Lopez, *DARPA Director Talks Promise of Life Sciences Research*, September 24, 2019, www.darpa.mil/.

80 See Nicholas Cropper, *CRISPR is Making Bioweapons More Accessible,* American Security Project, April 29, 2020, www.americansecurityproject.org/; Russ Read, "Military Wants to Use Gene Editing to Protect Troops Against Chemical and Biological Weapons," *Washington Examiner*, September 23, 2019, www.washingtonexaminer.com/; Joe Pappalardo, "Short-Term Superhuman: If We Create Augmented Soldiers, Can We Turn Them Back?" *Popular Mechanics*, September 25, 2018, www.popularmechanics.com/.

81 *The Economist, Technology Quarterly*, "Forecasting: All in the Blood," March 27, 2021, 11–12. See also Centers for Disease Control and Prevention, *Diseases that can Spread between Animals and People*, www.cdc.gov/ (accessed October 17, 2021); Anne Harding, Nicoletta Lanese, "The Deadliest Viruses in History," *Live Science*, March 4, 2020, www.livescience.com/; *The Economist*, "Genome Editing."

82 See Rafael Sanjuán and Pilar Domingo-Calap, "Mechanisms of Viral Mutation," *Cellular and Molecular Life Sciences* 73 (2016), 4433–48; Barrangou and Doudna, "Applications of CRISPR Technologies"; Wikipedia, *CRISPR*.

(using CRISPR techniques) to hide its modification or make it appear as if it originated in nature. These possibilities seem to be under constant consideration and experimentation, and they reflect the high priority placed on sustaining domination over this projection—even when the cost to humanity through say, accidents or leaks, might be substantial.

Speedy contagion could be another objective of a bioweapon virus engineered using CRISPR techniques, by targeting its spread through such unavoidable human functions as breathing or touching. Among the collateral effects—beyond deaths—could be disabilities (temporary or permanent), economic damage, fear, social alienation, loss of trust in government, or the incapacitation (if not death) of vulnerable populations that tend to occupy leadership positions (such as mature adults and the elderly).[83] The diffusion dynamic can be a problem, however, as release of the virus could end up having a "boomerang" effect on the perpetrator—due to mass travel or customary human contact. Such an effect might be acceptable to the martial domain, however—if it is assumed or anticipated that the virus would inflict greater damage on the targeted nation. Perhaps it is not difficult to see why a prominent scientist considers CRISPR to be potentially more dangerous than nuclear weapons.[84]

Other life forms are also being experimented with by the martial domain. The range is reportedly very broad, and it includes insects, plants, bats, and miscellaneous animals.[85] Reports from the last decade indicated that new life forms were also being engineered, to perform specialized duties—such as surveillance, assassinations, espionage, and combat penetration.[86] Among these were seaborne organisms that could detect submarines, bird-like creatures to enter and bomb areas (such as caves and tunnels) that drones would have a difficult

83 See Linda Geddes, "Long Covid has More than 200 Symptoms, Study Finds," *The Guardian*, July 15, 2021, www.theguardian.com/; *The Economist*, "Post-Covid Syndrome: The Sting in the Tail, Researchers are closing in on Long Covid. The Results are Alarming," May 1, 2021, 65–67; Frances Williams, "Long Covid: Who is at Risk?" *The Conversation*, January 4, 2021, https://theconversation.com/.

84 Eric Werner, *The Coming CRISPR Wars: Or Why Genome Editing can be More Dangerous than Nuclear Weapons*, 2019 (Preprint), www.ericwerner.com/. Dr. Werner is Research Scientist, Oxford Advanced Research Foundation.

85 See Lilyana Gaytandzhieva, *Project G-2101: Pentagon Biolab Discovered MERS and SARS-like Coronaviruses in Bats*, May 2, 2020, www.dilyana.bg, and her "New Data Leak"; Christina Lin, "Why US Outsourced Bat Virus Research to Wuhan," *Asia Times*, April 22, 2020, https://asiatimes.com/; Max-Planck-Gessellschaft, "A Step towards Biological Warfare with Insects?" *Science Daily*, October 9, 2018, www.sciencedaily.com/; Brandon Specktor, "The Pentagon Wants to Make an Army of Virus-Spreading Insects—Scientists are Concerned," *Live Science*, October 5, 2018, www.livescience.com/; Choi and Borenstein, "Scientists: U.S. Military Program."

86 See Specktor, "Pentagon Wants"; Patrick Tucker, "The U.S. Military is Genetically Engineering New Life Forms to Detect Enemy Subs," *Defense One*, December 1, 2018, www.defenseone.com/; Antonio Regalado, "U.S. Military Wants to Know What Synthetic-Biology Weapons Could Look Like: Re-Created Viruses, Toxic Bacteria Top New Ranking of Risks," *MIT Technology Review*, June 19, 2018, www.technologyreview.com/.

time accessing, and microscopic gadgets that could be introduced into any organism to damage organ functions or cause death. Coupled with advances in such fields as nanotechnology and bio-mimetics, the potential to create new organisms for warfare and espionage seems vast.[87] The fact that these and other possibilities are being experimented with reflects the importance placed on this hierarchic control mode.

Intellectual Property

Control over intellectual property is vitally important for domination over new technologies. Arbitrage and commodity flows are interrelated with IP—as restrictions influence fabrication, marketing, and distribution of inputs and products around the world. And restrictions often cover raw material processing and extraction, depending on the technologies deployed. IP is itself a commodity, after all—created through labor, sold through licensing or purchase, and involved in market exchange through the products and services in which it is embedded.

This hierarchic projection gained much relevance during the last seven decades, as IP became a major asset class in corporate portfolios. It is now an important consideration for mergers and acquisitions, as its ownership can influence which technologies will be deployed. In recent times it also became a target for financial speculation—bets being placed on the future value of patents and trademarks. And, commercially embedded IP can be used by the martial domain.[88]

U.S. hierarchic control over IP strengthened globally after the dissolution of the Soviet Union and market reforms in China. These nations had treated invention and technology as collective goods until the early 1990s, based on their philosophical and political rejection of capitalist property regimes. As they began to install IP regimes similar to those of the United States—and to engage more in international trade—they therefore became subject to American control. The imposition of rules—through the World Trade Organization and other mechanisms—propelled changes in China and Russia and cemented American control over IP regulation worldwide.[89]

87 See *EurAsian Times*, "US Army's New Research Frontier—Squirrel-Inspired Land-Based Drones that are Agile, Intelligent, and Great Spies," October 4, 2021, https://eurasiantimes.com/; Kenneth Payne, *I, Warbot: The Dawn of Artificially Intelligent Conflict* (New York: Oxford University Press, 2021); Abishur Prakash, *The Age of Killer Robots*, 2020, chapters 3, 6, https://abishurprakash.com/; *The Economist*, "New Materials: Joint Approach, 3-D Printing is about to Borrow an Ingenious Idea from Biology," October 10, 2020, 72–73; Michael Peck, "Army Seeks Shape-Changing Biomimetic Aircraft," *Defense Systems*, July 25, 2017, https://defensesystems.com/.

88 Navigation software, for example—see EESA Navipedia, *Military Navigation*, www.gssc.esa.int/ (accessed June 10, 2022).

89 See World Trade Organization, *Intellectual Property: TRIPS-Trade Related Aspect of Intellectual Property Rights*; its *Overview: The TRIPS Agreement*; and its *TRIPS: Issues, Technology Transfer*, www.wto

Hierarchic control over IP occurs for all of the most advanced technologies. For state-of-the-art semiconductors, for example, the corporations—all of them oligopolistic—designing and manufacturing them use IP protocols set by the United States.[90] These companies are either in the United States or in subordinate nations and territories—NATO (North Atlantic Treaty Organization) members of Western Europe, South Korea, Japan, or Taiwan. In the vast majority of cases, the inventions they use were initially patented in the United States.

The most advanced semiconductors can be used in both commercial and military hardware. U.S.-based Intel, for example, produces most of the microprocessors that enable data centers to operate—vital tools for the military and intelligence apparatus, and for any commercial activity that depends on data clouds. Commodity chains that supply Intel must observe U.S. IP protocols—directly or through companies in subordinate nations, all of which must observe restrictions on potential military use.[91] Intel—along with U.S.-based AMD (Advanced Micro Devices)—produces the x86 microprocessor for commercial supercomputers, *and* for the military ones implanted in such weapons as hypersonic missiles, nuclear submarines, and stealth drones.[92]

Intel is also one of three oligopolists that serve as "foundries" to process silicon incorporated in microprocessors.[93] Two other oligopolists that serve

.org/ (all accessed June 16, 2022). See also Semiconductor Industry Association, *Semiconductors and the World Trade Organization*, November 2020, www.semiconductors.org/.

90 See *The Economist*, "Chipmaking: Neutral but not Idle, The Technological Brain Trust at the Heart of the $550bn Global Chipmaking Business," September 25, 2021, 51–52; Semiconductor Industry Association, *Semiconductors and the World Trade Organization*. Symptomatic of hierarchic control is that, despite many efforts and much funding in recent decades, *none* of the most advanced microprocessors are manufactured in Europe—*The Economist*, "Chipmaking: Fabs with Benefits," February 12, 2022, 56 (based on manufacturing capacity data from Kearney).

91 *The Economist*, "Global Technology: Pinch Points—The First of Two Articles about Supply Chains Maps their Vulnerabilities," June 8, 2019, 58–59; Information Network, *Global Semiconductor Equipment: Markets, Market Shares and Market Forecasts*, August 2019, www.theinformationnet.com/. The Wassenaar Arrangement (1996) established U.S-led hierarchic control over exports of semiconductors (and other technologies) that might have military use—setting the stage for extensive surveillance of commodity chains. See Wikipedia, *Wassenaar Arrangement*, https://en.wikipedia.org/ (accessed June 19, 2022); *The Economist*, "A Global Contest over Semiconductors," January 29, 2022, 47–48.

92 See Kontron, *Military Design Trends: Applications Migrating to Intel x86 Architecture*, Whitepaper, www.kontron.com/ (accessed June 14, 2022). Among its diverse uses, the x86 microprocessor has been considered for implants in soldiers, to monitor vital aspects of their health and (possibly) their performance—see Matthew Loffhagen, "U.S. Military Testing Mind-Control Chips on Soldiers' Brains to Alter their Moods," *Outer Places*, November 29, 2017, www.outerplaces.com/; Robert Johnson, "The U.S. Wants to 'Microchip' Troops," *Business Insider*, May 6, 2012, www.businessinsider.com/.

93 Intel, *Intel Annual Reports and Anniversary Publications*, various years, www.intel.com/ (accessed August 10, 2021); *The Economist*, "Poker Chips: Intel Should be Wary of Becoming an American National Champion," April 3, 2021, 55, and its "Global Technology," 59.

as foundries—Samsung and TSMC (Taiwan Semiconductor Manufacturing Company)—are heavily dependent on the United States.[94] Qualcomm, based in the United States, fabricates about half of the world's baseboard microprocessors—the kind that enable most every mode of wireless communication to function—while Broadcom and Nvidia (both U.S.-based) design or fabricate advanced microprocessors and related software.[95] ARM Limited (based in Britain, previously known as Advanced RISC Machine) is very important for microprocessors that enable smartphones to operate, and its software is considered essential for the so-called Internet-of-Things—the stage of interconnectivity that artificial intelligence (AI) and 5G systems enable.[96] Protocols set by the United States govern all IP obtained or commercialized by these companies, regardless of where they operate.

All these corporations are linked to a highly specialized oligo-monopolist—also subject to U.S.-set protocols—that enables them to equip their factories: ASML, based in the Netherlands (a NATO member).[97] Its hardware is essential to fabricate components needed by the most advanced microprocessors. IMEC (Interuniversity Microelectronics Centre)—based in (NATO member) Belgium—undertakes research for all advanced microprocessor designers and manufacturers—and for ASML—helping ensure that IP rules are observed.[98] Japan-based Nikon and Canon—the only other manufacturers of lithographic hardware outside China—also operate in accordance with U.S.-set IP protocols.[99] All of these companies are very important participants in the global commodity chains that, in one way or another, involve IP rules.

ASML's production of EUVL (Extreme Ultraviolet Lithography) hardware can illustrate the importance of U.S. hierarchic domination over IP. This company supplies American oligopolistic semiconductor manufacturers—such as Intel, Qualcomm, and AMD—and those based in nations that closely depend

94 *The Economist*, "Taiwan Semiconductor Manufacturing Company: Living on the Edge, The World's Biggest Chipmaker is Learning How to Thrive Amid the Sino-American Tech War," May 1, 2021, 52–53, and its "Global Technology," 59; Taiwan Semiconductor Manufacturing Company, *TSMC Annual Report 2021*, www.tsmc.com/; *The Economist*, "Samsung Electronics: The Third Star," October 23, 2021, 59–62.

95 See Wikipedia, *Qualcomm*, its *Broadcom, Inc.*, and its *Nvidia*, https://en.wikipedia.org/ (all accessed October 19, 2021); *The Economist*, "Global Technology (1)," 58.

96 See ARM, *Delivering Next-Generation AI Experiences for the 5G World: CPU, GPU and ML Processors Upscale Performance for 5G and AI*, www.arm.com/ (accessed June 10, 2022); *The Economist*, "Global Technology," 58; Wikipedia, *ARM Architecture*, http://en.wikipedia.org/ (accessed June 20, 2022).

97 See ASML, *Changing the World, One Nanometer at a Time: ASML Gives the World's Leading Chipmakers the Power to Mass Produce Patterns on Silicon*, www.asml.com/ (accessed May 10, 2022); *The Economist*, "ASML, Industrial Light and Magic: A Low-Key Dutch Company has Monopolised a Critical Link in the Global Technology Supply Chain," February 29, 2020, 49–50; *The Economist*, "Global Technology," 59; and its "Chipmaking."

98 See *The Economist*, "Chipmaking."

99 *The Economist*, "ASML, Industrial Light and Magic"; and its "Global Technology."

on the United States.[100] ASML had over 5,000 suppliers by the end of the last decade, which provided most every component it uses—an example of a vast and complex commodity chain.

Much of ASML's research funding reportedly comes from the United States (from Intel, in particular).[101] The United States thus pressured the Dutch government to refuse an export license (which would include IP) when a Chinese company sought to be ASML's customer. The Dutch government complied—despite the great financial advantage of ASML being able to sell to China, the vast size of its market, and the immense future profit potential.[102] And, taking into account that—due to this rejection—a Chinese producer might in the future achieve EUVL capabilities similar to, or more advanced than, ASML's—thus preempting its entry into China, and possibly even curtailing its global oligo-monopolistic power.

China—despite all concerns generated about its potential rise as a U.S. technology rival—has reportedly only one large company (SMIC, Semiconductor Manufacturing International Corporation) that could be considered a potential future fabricator of the most advanced microprocessors.[103] Nonetheless, the importance of sustaining U.S. domination became obvious in another case, when an attempt was made to sell advanced semiconductor technology to China—a matter that would benefit an American technology company greatly. This occurred when AMD engaged a Chinese company in a partnership, to keep itself from going into bankruptcy and possible liquidation.[104] At the time AMD pursued the partnership its stock had sunk to a record low price of $3 per share, its need for cash was desperate, and its indebtedness was very high and growing rapidly.[105] However, its sharing advanced microprocessor technology with its Chinese partner was deemed a national security breach by

100 *The Economist*, "ASML, Industrial Light and Magic," 50.

101 *The Economist*, "ASML, Industrial Light and Magic," 50; ASML, *Changing the World*.

102 *The Economist*, "ASML, Industrial Light and Magic," 50; Ramish Zafar, "ASML NXE:3400B Might be the Scanner Blocked by the U.S. in Chinese Sale," *WCCF Tech*, January 6, 2020, https://wccftech.com/.

103 See Edward White, "China's Ability to Make Computer Chips Still 'Years Behind' Industry Leaders," *Financial Times*, January 21, 2019, www.ft.com/; Josh Horwitz, "China Chip Industry Insiders Voice Caution on Catch-Up Efforts," *Reuters*, June 13, 2019, www.reuters.com/; *The Economist*, "Global Technology," 59. See also Seamus Grimes and Debin Du, "China's Emerging Role in the Global Semiconductor Value Chain," *Telecommunications Policy*, April 2020, www.sciencedirect.com/.

104 See Wikipedia, *AMD-Chinese Joint Venture*, http://en.wikipedia.org/ (accessed May 11, 2022); Kate O'Keeffe and Brian Spegele, "Chip Maker Shared 'Keys to Kingdom': AMD Helped China Get World-Class Product, Sparking Battle over U.S. National Security," *Wall Street Journal*, June 28, 2019, A1; Alex Fang, "U.S. Expands China Blacklist to Supercomputers and AMD Partners: Two Sides Battle over Next-Gen Machines Vital to Nuclear, Space and Biotech," *Nikkei Asian Review*, June 22, 2019, www.asia.nikkei.com/.

105 O'Keeffe and Spegele, "Chip Maker Shared," A11.

U.S. officials—despite the fact that AMD had pre-announced it, the agency designated to review it was properly consulted, and government agencies did not stop it.[106]

Much complaining occurs among U.S. ruling circles and the martial elites, about China's requirement for foreign companies to engage in a partnership—and share IP (through licensing)—with a Chinese company if they wish to manufacture in China.[107] In such arrangements the foreign company may hold no more than a 49 percent stake. Because of these requirements, China has been repeatedly accused of "stealing" technology from American companies that undertake operations in China, and of forcing them to hand over their knowledge. Such arguments, however, ignore the fact that in the U.S. inventors typically see their patents and knowledge routinely expropriated, as they are required by their employers to reassign them—as a condition for employment (a matter addressed earlier in this book). Even when employee-inventors are allowed to share some of the benefits, these tend to be only a small fraction of the value created.

U.S. ruling circles and martial elites also seem to ignore the historical baggage of U.S. pilfering of foreign technology—to gain strategic advantages, for military and commercial purposes. As early as 1912, for example, the U.S. Supreme Court's decision on the *Crozier v. Krupp* case extended eminent domain powers to IP—by allowing the U.S. Navy to expropriate a German gun carriage design it had copied and replicated, without any permission.[108] That year, the U.S. Navy also reportedly stole plans for a secret British long-range torpedo—a matter that would have longstanding favorable consequences for the United States.[109] This action was judicially "protected" under eminent domain—despite the fact that this legal principle was never intended to cover such purposes. And the United States expropriated German companies' and

106 O'Keeffe and Spegele, "Chip Maker Shared," A11; U.S. Department of the Treasury, *The Committee on Foreign Investment in the United States (CFIUS)*, home.treasury.gov/ (accessed June 11, 2022). AMD initially argued that the agreement was not under CFIUS's purview, and the Committee had agreed with AMD's position. See also Saif M. Khan, *U.S. Semiconductor Exports to China: Current Policies and Trends*, Center for Security and Emerging Technologies, Georgetown University, October 2020, https://cset.georgetown.edu/; Elaine Chan and Daniel Ren, "China's Long March for the Soul of the Nation's Digital Future Faces an Ever-Shifting End-Point: Chinese Semiconductor Companies are Up Against a Formidable Intel-Microsoft Alliance that has Ring-Fenced an Eco-System and Peripheral Sub-Sectors of Hardware Producers, Chip Designers, Software and App Developers," *South China Morning Post*, May 26, 2018, www.scmp.com/.

107 Kun Jiang, Wolfgang Keller, Larry D. Qiu and William Ridley, "China's Joint Venture Policy and the International Transfer of Technology," *VoxChina*, February 6, 2019, http://voxchina.org/. See also Seamus Grimes and Debin Du, "China's Emerging Role in the Global Semiconductor Value Chain," *Telecommunications Policy*, April 2020, www.sciencedirect.com/

108 U.S. Library of Congress, *U.S. Reports: Crozier vs. Krupp, 224 U.S. 290 (1912)*, www.loc.gov/ (accessed May 1, 2022).

109 See Katherine C. Epstein, *Torpedo: Inventing the Military-Industrial Complex in the United States and Great Britain* (Cambridge, MA: Harvard University Press, 2014), chapters 1, 3, 6.

citizens' patents held in the United States during the First and Second World Wars, providing significant advantages to American corporations that took them over.[110]

Cybernetics

Hierarchic control over cybernetic technologies and cyberspace is a fundamental component of oligopolistic technology domination. This control mode is closely related to commodity chains and arbitrage, as most of its products depend on materials obtained or processed offshore. And it is related to hierarchic control over IP—as protocols govern patents issued for computation, software, microprocessors, and related technologies.

This projection can be traced to the late 1960s and the founding of ARPANET (Advanced Research Projects Agency Network) by the Pentagon, which led to the creation of the internet.[111] Initially intended to allow communication between military bases in case of nuclear war, it became a most important commercial technology. And it would eventually lead to the creation of the world wide web in the mid-1990s.[112]

Sustaining global control over cyberspace made it essential for technology oligopolies to forge strong links with the martial domain. These can be indirect, allowing corporations that are wholly commercial to provide support through products they sell on the market. Or they can be direct, as in the case of contracted-for tools that have specific military uses and that may have secrecy conditions attached. But there are other ways. One, for example, involves setting up "advisory boards" composed of corporate CEOs—a way for the military to seek advice on strategic aspects of cyberspace. During the last decade, this approach reportedly allowed the Pentagon to gain knowledge and implement multiple new strategies.[113]

Another way can involve using cyber-tech startups for secretive military missions, without a contract or official disclosure—a matter reported on during

110 Julian A. Gross, "World War I: 100 Years Later—The U.S. Confiscated Half a Billion Dollars in Private Property during WWI," *Smithsonian*, July 28, 2014, www.smithsonianmag.com/; John Nugent, "The Great Patents Heist," *Wintersonnenwende* (orig. publ. in *Barnes Review*, March 1999, 27–33), www.wintersonnenwende.com/ (accessed November 3, 2021).

111 See Britannica, *ARPANET: United States Defense Program*, www.britannica.com/ (accessed May 19, 2022); Giovanni Navarria, "How the Internet was Born," *The Conversation*, October 29 and November 2, 2016 (four-part series), www.theconverstation.com/.

112 See World Wide Web Foundation, *History of the Web*, https://webfoundation.org/ (accessed June 18, 2022); *The Economist*, "Histories of the Web: Paradise Lost—Two Dotcom Memoirs Point to a Pressing Question: Whose Internet is it, Anyway?" February 22, 2020, 80.

113 See Doug Cameron, "Pentagon Begins New Tech Détente: Military Chiefs will Seek Help from Tech Bosses, Conduct a Defense Systems 'Hackathon'," *Wall Street Journal*, March 3, 2016, B7.

the last decade.[114] Very important was the creation of venture capital funds to invest in companies that can be connected to the military or intelligence apparatus. The CIA created such a fund during the past two decades, for example—based in Silicon Valley—to observe and evaluate startups, formulate projects, and provide capital.[115] Yet another way has involved the outright acquisition of advanced technologies by Silicon Valley–based military outfits, as in the case of companies that can design cyberweapons.[116]

The National Security Agency (NSA)—founded in 1952 to collect and decrypt foreign communications—would become instrumental for the cybernetic control mode.[117] Decryption and data collection activities provided entry to the cybernetic dimension and to all related surveillance possibilities.[118] The NSA has been essential for implementing cyberspace actions related to commodity chains and arbitrage and for imposing geopolitical dictates. Other

114 See Christopher Kirchhoff, "Silicon Valley Must Go to War," *International New York Times*, May 4, 2018, 10.

115 In-Q-Tel, *1999–2019, Strategic Investor, Technology Accelerator, Trusted Partner*, www.iqt.org/ (accessed May 23, 2022); Damian Paletta, "The CIA's Venture Capital Firm, Like its Sponsor, Operates in the Shadows: In-Q-Tel Provides Only Limited Information About its Investments, and Some of its Trustees Have Ties to Funded Companies," *Wall Street Journal*, August 30, 2016, www.wsj.com/; Dion Nissenbaum, "Top Venture Funds Back Spycraft Software Startups," *Wall Street Journal*, July 23, 2013, B2; Rick E. Yanuzzi, "In-Q-Tel: A New Partnership Between the CIA and the Private Sector," *Defense Intelligence Journal* 9 (2000), 25–38. Among the Silicon Valley startups that reportedly gained considerable support was Palantir—a data analytics company created by the founder of PayPal—whose first (and for a time its only) client was the CIA, according to Randall Stross (see Margaret P. O'Mara, Book Review, *The Code*, *Wall Street Journal*, July 16, 2019, A13). See also *The Economist*, "Palantir Technologies: A Prickly Patriot, A Secretive Software-Maker Says Hello to the Stockmarket—and Waves Goodbye to Silicon Valley," August 29, 2020, 52.

116 The Defense Innovation Unit (DIU)—based in Mountain Valley, California—founded in 2015—for example, had such objectives. See Defense Innovation Unit, *Accelerating Commercial Technology for National Security*, www.diu.mil/ (accessed June 18, 2022); Billy Mitchell, "'No Longer an Experiment'—DIUx Becomes DIU, Permanent Pentagon Unit," *FedScoop*, August 9, 2018, www.fedscoop.com/; Gordon Lubold, "Pentagon Pledges Support for Flexible Electronics," *Wall Street Journal*, August 31, 2015, B4. Silicon Valley itself had significant military links from the beginning. Starting in 1949 the Pentagon saw electronics as important and became the Valley's first venture capitalist—see Margaret P. O'Mara, *The Code: Silicon Valley and the Remaking of America* (New York: Penguin, 2019), 24–25.

117 See Wikipedia, *National Security Agency*, https://en.wikipedia.org/ (accessed May 21, 2022); National Security Agency, Office of the Inspector General, *History of the NSA OIG*, https://oig.nsa.gov/ (accessed June 18, 2022). See also James Bamford, *Spy Factory: The National Security Agency and 9/11* (Alexandria, VA: PBS, 2009), and his *The Shadow Factory: The Ultra-Secret NSA from 9/11 to the Eavesdropping on America* (New York: Anchor, 2009).

118 See James Bamford, *Body of Secrets: Anatomy of the Ultra-Secret National Security Agency, from the Cold War to the Dawn of a New Century* (New York: Doubleday, 2007); and his "Infiltration, Sabotage, Mayhem: For Years, Four-Star General Keith Alexander has been Building a Secret Army Capable of Launching Devastating Cyberattacks—Now It's Ready to Unleash Hell," *Wired*, July 2013, 90–99.

agencies, such as the highly secretive Special Collection Service (SCS, code named F6)—founded by the CIA and NSA in the late 1970s, to conduct covert surveillance for U.S. embassies—were important for detecting shifts in geopolitical alliances that can affect technology companies, their commodity chains, and arbitrage.[119] The SCS—part of a larger surveillance program known as STATEROOM—would also become vital for targeting and destabilizing governments that defy geopolitical interests.[120]

Another agency involved in cybernetic and cyberspace hierarchic control is the Central Security Service (CSS).[121] Founded in 1972, the CSS has been involved with signals intelligence, cryptology, and surveillance to provide tactical support to the various combat branches of the U.S. military apparatus.[122] Coordination with the CIA or any unit of the NSA is part of its mission. Intercepting foreign military communications—including wireless transmissions—and tapping undersea cables have reportedly been among its operations. This is very important for monitoring worldwide communications involving advanced technologies, commodity chain issues, and arbitrage.

CSS's mission can be considered offensive, as it is vital for preparing the conditions for—and during—military campaigns. Its signals intelligence capabilities are important for destabilization efforts against targeted governments. And they are used to conduct surveillance of all military capabilities—including the most mundane details involving communications, habits, and movements.[123] The CSS is important for imposing geopolitical dictates on any non-compliant government, and it can help re-establish commodity chain flows.

In the 1990s, the NSA and the CIA sought ways to apply supercomputing technology to undertake surveillance on a massive scale. Cracking or violating any and all forms of encryption would turn into a major objective.[124] A core undertaking was the creation of the Massive Digital Data Systems (MDDS) research program in 1993, to recruit university specialists—Stanford,

119 See Wikipedia, *Special Collection Service*, and its *Stateroom (Surveillance Program)*, https://en.wikipeida.org/ (both accessed May 18, 2022); Matthew M. Aid, "The CIA's New Black Bag is Digital," *Foreign Policy*, July 17, 2013, https://foreignpolicy.com/; Bamford, "Infiltration, Sabotage, Mayhem."

120 See Wikipedia, *Stateroom (Surveillance Program)*, https://en.wikepedia.org/ (accessed June 18, 2022).

121 See Wikipedia, *Central Security Service*, https://en.wikipedia.org/ (accessed May 21, 2022); Bamford, "Infiltration, Sabotage, Mayhem."

122 National Security Agency, *Central Security Service (CSS)*, www.nsa.gov/ (accessed June 18, 2022).

123 See Wikipedia, *Central Security Service*; Bamford, *Shadow Factory*, 175–206, 234–70.

124 See Trevor Aaronson, "A Declassified Court Ruling Shows How FBI Abused NSA Mass Surveillance Data," *The Intercept*, October 10, 2019, www.theintercept.com/; Michael Winter, "NSA Uses Supercomputers to Crack Web Encryption, Files Show," *USA Today*, September 5, 2013, www.usatoday.com/.

MIT, Harvard, and Cal Tech at the forefront—through the National Science Foundation (NSF).[125]

Over a dozen grants involving millions of dollars were initially provided by the NSF to the recruited analysts and universities.[126] Among the objectives were mining and data analyses on communications involving individuals and entire populations—vital for implementing pervasive surveillance. Such efforts would also (eventually) become important for monitoring global commodity chains, as their management became digitized. Managerial communications could, much like those involving populations or individuals, be analyzed to anticipate disruptions.

Among the group of enlisted analysts by the MDDS program were the two future founders of Google (at the time both at Stanford), who reported regularly to two key individuals in charge of the MDDS operation.[127] One such individual was reportedly from MITRE, a military technology contractor for the NSA, CIA, the combat branches, and their research units—while the second individual was from the CIA's research department.[128] The MDDS program created the Query Flocks System for mining vast amounts of data—and one of its results was the search engine that would become Google.[129] The NSA and the CIA—along with other components of the military and intelligence apparatus—thus had a fundamental role in the creation of a most important technology oligopolist. This is a fact that was reportedly concealed in official documents and related materials.[130]

The growing importance of the cybernetic and cyberspace projection led to the creation of new agencies. Possibly the most prominent was the U.S. Cyber Command (USCYBERCOM)—founded in 2010 to oversee the militarization of cyberspace. With very generous funding, the initial recruitment of over 14,000 cyber specialists (along with combat troops), and close cooperation with

125 See Hal Curran, Robert Kluttz, Claudia Pierce, Rick Steinheiser and Bhavani Thuraisingham, *Intelligence Community Initiative in Massive Digital Data Systems*, front page posted as a pdf document in www.personal.utdallas.edu/ (accessed May 18, 2021). See also Jeff Nesbit, "Google's True Origin Partly Lies in CIA and NSA Research Grants for Mass Surveillance," *Quartz*, December 8, 2017, https://qz.com/; National Science Foundation, *On the Origins of Google*, August 17, 2004, www.nsf.gov/.

126 See National Science Foundation, *Origins of Google*; and its *A Brief History of the NSF and the Internet*, August 13, 2003, www.nsf.gov/.

127 See Tyler Durden, "How the CIA Made Google," *Zero Hedge*, August 28, 2017, www.zerohedge.com/; Nesbit, "Google's True Origin."

128 See Kit Klarenberg, "Suppressed History: How the CIA and NSA Helped Create Google to Spy on Citizens," *Sputnik News*, September 27, 2018, https://sputniknews.com/. Klarenberg reportedly worked at MITRE and was a colleague of individuals in charge. See also Durden, "How CIA Made Google"; Nesbit, "Google's True Origin."

129 Klarenberg, "Suppressed History."

130 Klarenberg, "Suppressed History"; National Science Foundation, *On the Origins*; Nesbit, "Google's True Origin."

the NSA and the CIA, this agency was targeted to become a major asset for global control.[131] Also in 2010, the Joint Functional Command for Network Warfare (JFCC-NW)—created in 2005 as part of the U.S. Strategic Command, which controls the nuclear arsenal—was merged with the Cyber Command.[132] The capacity to execute major cyberwarfare operations that could, for example, disable completely a targeted nation's cyberinfrastructure—and include ransomware attacks—was thus established.[133]

This merger allowed the Cyber Command to reach into the nuclear arsenal, to combine cyberwarfare with nuclear war. The combination of the two modes of warfare might have led some strategists to imagine that the United States could get away with a nuclear first strike without sustaining much (or any) damage—if the targeted nation would be sufficiently disabled through a massive cyberattack.[134] The main objective of the Cyber Command has thus been offensive cyberwarfare.[135] Routine attacks against other nations' cyberinfrastructure—both military and civilian—reportedly became its main activity.[136] This was considered necessary to find vulnerabilities in each nation's cyberinfrastructure that could be exploited for further action—including blackmail to induce compliance with geopolitical interests. Offensive cyberwarfare capabilities would also allow the Cyber Command to retaliate if any targeted nation decided to counterattack.

The Cyber Command and the NSA are assisted by specialized intelligence agencies—such as the National Geospatial-Intelligence Agency—that focus on cybernetic geo-imagery and mapping everywhere.[137] The fusion of the cyber-

131 See Wikipedia, *United States Cyber Command*, https://en.wikipedia.org/ (accessed May 21, 2022); Bamford, "Infiltration, Sabotage, Mayhem."

132 See Wikipedia, *Joint Functional Component Command–Network Warfare*, https://en.wikipedia.org/ (accessed June 20, 2022); *The Economist*, "The Future of Armed Conflict: Warfare's Worldwide Web, America's Armed Forces are Designing a New Approach to Command and Control," January 9, 2021, 67–69; Bamford, "Infiltration, Sabotage, Mayhem."

133 *The Economist*, "Over There in the Shadows: A Spate of Ransomware Hacks Highlights the Challenges Governments Face as they Try to Defend Themselves—and Attack Others—Online," June 19, 2021, 22–24. See also Wikipedia, *Joint Functional Component Command*; *The Economist*, "Future of Armed Conflict." Paralyzing and damaging a targeted nation's conventional infrastructure (utilities, road, air) may also be achieved, along with cyberinfrastructure attacks.

134 See Greg Mitchell, "U.S. Must End Nuclear 'First-Strike' Policy," *Newsweek*, August 24, 2020, www.newsweek.com/; Jim W. Dean, "US Confirms First Strike Policy with Nukes," *Veterans Today*, March 29, 2019, www.veteranstoday.com/; Diana Johnstone, "Doomsday Postponed?" in Paul H. Johnstone, ed., *From MAD to Madness: Inside Pentagon Nuclear War Planning* (Atlanta: Clarity, 2017), 275–77.

135 Mitchell, "U.S. Must End Nuclear 'First-Strike'"; Dean, "U.S. Confirms First Strike Policy"; Wikipedia, *Joint Functional*, and its *Cyber Command*; Bamford, "Infiltration, Sabotage, Mayhem."

136 *The Economist*, "Over There in the Shadows," 23; and its "Future of Armed Conflict."

137 Wikipedia, *National Geospatial-Intelligence Agency*, https://en.wikipedia.org/ (accessed May 21, 2022); James Bamford, "The Multibillion-Dollar U.S. Spy Agency You Haven't Heard Of," *Foreign Policy*, March 201, 2017, https://foreignpolicy.com/.

netic and geospatial dimensions is a most important strategic tool for military and intelligence planning and for espionage.[138] The work of this agency is thus vital for mounting armed aggression against any targeted government, as it can map all of its territory in great detail and provide guidance for all operations.

Special operations that seek precision—combining different modes of aggression and combat—depend greatly on the data provided by this agency. Identifying topography, port facilities, vessels, airports, storage areas, and supply points, for example, would be part of the commodity chain-related data it can provide.[139] Its data clouds can thus help sustain or recover commodity chains—by tracking all geographical features vital for their operation—as a targeted government's military capabilities are destroyed.

Through the Cyber Command, the U.S. military and intelligence apparatus has placed cyberwarfare at the same level as missile, aerial, and outer space warfare. And the establishment of the Cyber Command made it possible for frontline troops to request cyberwarfare support, in much the same way as they ask for artillery fire or aerial bombing. The result was that the martial domain began to treat cyberspace as a major weapon against targeted nations—with higher priority than conventional armed action. Prime targets for Cyber Command attacks would thus be governments that defy geopolitical dictates, are sources of raw materials, or have strategic locations near major commodity flows.[140] And, because combat or bombing are not involved, it was likely assumed that destruction will be more acceptable to politicians.[141]

The cyber-military and intelligence apparatus spends vast amounts on software, hardware, and personnel—a matter that seems to escape public awareness. Software and social network designs that facilitate manipulation of social behavior—such that a targeted government can be blamed for the privations that result from cyberattacks on infrastructure—can be part of this scenario. Among the many oligopolistic technology contractors that supplied software and hardware to execute such operations during the last decade were reportedly General Dynamics, Boeing, Google, Raytheon, SAIC, and Booz-Allen-Hamilton.[142] Google's Project Maven, developed in partnership with the Pentagon during the last decade—to create AI platforms for interpreting data

138 *The Economist*, "Espionage: Ears in the Sky, By Listening for Radio and Radar Signals, a New Generation of Satellites can Track Human Activity, Both Licit and Illicit," March 20, 2021, 71–72; Bamford, "Multibillion-Dollar U.S. Spy Agency."

139 See *The Economist*, "Espionage: Ears in the Sky," and its "Over There in the Shadows."

140 See Alexander Klimburg, *The Darkening Web: The War for Cyberspace* (New York: Penguin, 2018), chapters 14–17; Bamford, "Infiltration, Sabotage, Mayhem."

141 See *The Economist*, "Future of Armed Conflict"; Lucas Kello, *The Virtual Weapon and International Order* (New Haven: Yale University Press, 2017). Richard A. Clarke and Robert K. Knake's *Cyber War: The Next Threat to National Security and What to do About It* (New York: HarperCollins, 2012) provides insights on cyberwarfare planning.

142 See Bamford, "Infiltration, Sabotage, Mayhem"; Ralph Nader, "Corporatizing National Security," *Counterpunch*, June 21, 2013, www.counterpunch.org/.

provided by UAVs (unmanned aerial vehicles or drones)—is one example.[143] Booz-Allen-Hamilton alone reportedly had as many as nine cyberwarfare-focused facilities by the end of the last decade, all shrouded in secrecy.[144]

These and hundreds of other oligopolistic technology contractors are part of a vast "ecosystem" of corporations that design, test, or deploy cyberwarfare tools. Some contractors are engaged in devising methods and tools for cyber-penetration of any system, such that "network situational awareness" can be achieved.[145] This cyberespionage mode can provide locations, digital addresses, software in use, operating system, and other details of any device connected to the internet in the world—such that a targeted computer system can be penetrated.[146] Concocting hacking tools and malware is important for this corporate ecosystem—a matter revealed when Wikileaks disclosed details on approximately 500 CIA projects during the last decade—almost all engaging oligopolistic technology contractors.[147]

Once penetration occurs, cyber-kinetic attacks can incapacitate a targeted government's cyberinfrastructure—and the conventional one involving utilities, movement, and logistics. The first known infrastructure cyberattack was the so-called Stuxnet operation against Iran—reportedly undertaken by the CIA and Israeli intelligence.[148] The malware implanted reportedly required thousands of hours of work by highly experienced specialists.[149] The Stuxnet case provided an example of the kind of cyberwarfare that can be undertaken

143 U.S. Department of Defense and Cheryl Pellerin, *Project Maven to Deploy Computer Algorithms to War Zone by Year's End*, July 21, 2017, www.defense.gov/. After Google's involvement with this project became known, many of its employees requested that the company cancel the contract—see Adam Frisk, "What is Project Maven? The Pentagon AI Project Google Employees Want Out of," *Global News*, April 5, 2018, htpps://globalnews.ca/.

144 Edward J. Snowden, *Permanent Record* (New York: Metropolitan, 2019), Part 2. See also Bamford, "Infiltration, Sabotage, Mayhem"; Nader, "Corporatizing"; Wikipedia, *Booz Allen Hamilton*, https://en.wikipedia.org/ (accessed May 21, 2022).

145 See Snowden, *Permanent Record*, Part 3; Tim Shorrock, "A New Spy Scandal Exposes the Corruption of Privatized Intelligence," *The Nation*, October 14, 2016, www.tehnation.com/; Jeff Larson, "Revealed: The NSA's Secret Campaign to Crack, Undermine Internet Security," *ProPublica*, September 5, 2013, www.propublica.org/; Ian Black, "NSA Spying Scandal: What We Have Learned, Key Players and Programmes in the National Security Agency's Secret Operation Mining Phone and Internet Data," *The Guardian*, June 10, 2013, www.theguardian.com/. See also CBS News, *NSA Surveillance Exposed*, www.cbsnews.com/ (accessed June 20, 2022).

146 See Bamford, *Spy Factory*, and his "Infiltration, Sabotage, Mayhem"; Klimburg, *Darkening Web*.

147 Allan Cullison, "Wikileaks Reveals CIA Hacking Projects, from Weeping Angel to Hammer Drill: Documents Exposed Agency Projects that Allegedly Infect CDs, Hack Samsung Smart TVs and More," *Wall Street Journal*, March 9, 2017, www.wsj.com/; Wikileaks, *Vault 7: CIA Hacking Tools Revealed*, March 7, 2017, htpps://wikileaks.org/ciav7p1/.

148 See Kim Zetter, *Countdown to Zero Day: Stuxnet and the Launch of the World's First Digital Weapon* (New York: Crown, 2014).

149 David Kushner, The Real Story of Stuxnet: How Kaspersky Lab Tracked-Down the Malware that Stymied Iran's Nuclear Fuel Enrichment Program," *IEEE Spectrum*, February 26, 2013, https://spectrum.ieee.org/; Langner, *The Stuxnet Story*, July 23, 2020, www.langner.com/.

against any nation's industrial base, the commodity chains that supply industry, and power grids.[150]

The NSA—largely in charge of enforcing U.S. global cybernetic domination, in collusion with technology oligopolies—collaborates closely with Britain's Government Communications Headquarters (GCHQ).[151] This agency is reportedly at the core of the so-called Five Eyes Anglophonic intelligence combine.[152] This alliance has added "partners" over the years, mostly for cyberespionage—engaging nations dependent on U.S. military and economic power.[153] And it has long been reported that this alliance, under NSA influence, has tapped bulk cables carrying practically all global internet and telephone communications—oceanic or overland.[154] Such data can be correlated with U.S. domestic information obtained from telecommunications, search engines, and social media oligopolists.[155]

Bulk cable tapping can be much more comprehensive and thorough than tapping servers, and the data obtained can involve any aspect that concerns U.S. geopolitical domination—related to commodity chains, arbitrage, any government, company, or individual. Decryption of such data can be contracted to companies that may be located abroad, to evade exposure or

150 Cyber-attacks against power grids are important because of their ramifications and the extensive damage they can cause—to commodity chain flows and to industrial activity. See, for example, David E. Anger and Nicole Perlroth, "U.S. Escalates Online Attacks on Russia's Power Grid," *New York Times*, June 15, 2019, www.nytimes.com/.

151 See Richard J. Aldrich, *GCHQ* (London: Collines, 2019); *Electrospaces*, "INCENSER, or How NSA and GCHQ are Tapping Internet Cables," November 29, 2014, https://electrospaces.blogspot.com/.

152 See Wikipedia, *Five Eyes*, https://en.wikipedia.org/ (accessed May 7, 2022); Paul Farrell, "History of 5-Eyes—Explainer: Partnership Forged in Wartime to Monitor Enemy Radio Transmissions Now Scoops up Data about Ordinary Citizens," *The Guardian*, December 2, 2013, www.theguardian.com/. Creating obstacles to oversight and accountability have allegedly long been problems for this alliance—see, for example, Scarlet Kim, Diana Lee, Asaf Lubin and Paulina Perlin, "Newly Disclosed Documents on the Five Eyes Alliance and What They Tell Us about Intelligence-Sharing Agreements," *Lawfare*, April 23, 2018, www.lawfareblog.com/.

153 See Bram Jansen, *Five, Nine, Fourteen Eyes—Intelligence Alliances Explained*, VPN Alert, August 20, 2021, https://vpnalert.com/; Philip Dorling, "Singapore, South Korea Revealed as Five Eyes Spying Partners," *Sydney Morning Herald*, November 25, 2013, www.smh.com.au/.

154 See Caleb Larson, *Intelligence Coup: How One U.S. Nuclear Submarine Tapped Russian Undersea Cables*, The National Interest, May 30, 2020, https://nationalinterest.org/; Snowden, *Permanent Record*, Part 3; Laura Mallonee, "Photos of the Submarine Internet Cables the NSA Probably Tapped," *Wired*, September 20, 2016, www.wired.com/; Glenn Greenwald, *No Place to Hide: Edward Snowden, the NSA, and the U.S. Surveillance State* (London: Hamilton, 2014); Electrospaces, *NSA's Largest Cable-Tapping Program: DANCINGOASIS*, May 24, 2014, https://electrospaces.blogspot.com/; Joe Wolverton, "NSA Taps Directly into Undersea Fiber-Optic Data Cables," *New American*, July 24, 2013, www.thenewamerican.com/.

155 See Ryan Gallagher and Henrik Moltke, "The Wiretap Rooms: The NSA's Hidden Spy Hubs in Eight U.S. Cities," *The Intercept*, June 25, 2018, https:theintercept.com/; Steven Levy, "NSA vs. the Internet," *Wired*, February 2014, www.wired.com/.

oversight.[156] NSA—and Five Eyes alliance—espionage based on bulk cable tapping is said to be the most extensive in history, and it can include data on new technologies and on confidential corporate matters that can benefit military technology oligopolists. Over the years, the NSA has been seen as an economic espionage agency, extending its capabilities to look into confidential details on foreign companies—justifying such intrusion on grounds of U.S. national security.[157]

Disclosures of foreign confidential corporate data can occur through the drafting of a contract—and the contractors selected can turn out to be the U.S. companies that would be most negatively affected.[158] Passing such information along might be justified on national security grounds, or if the American technology company that receives it has a history of contracts with the NSA or the Pentagon.[159] Individuals connected with surveillance operations against foreign corporations during the last decade were reportedly found to use such data to speculate in stock markets.[160]

The immense scope of U.S. global economic and military cybernetic espionage—the most extensive undertaken in history—points to the persistence of hierarchic control and its importance for technological and geopolitical domination. The growing profile of cybernetic military and intelligence capabilities is reflected by the existence of numerous secret programs over the years, to gather detailed economic, military, technological, corporate, political, and individual data around the world. During the last decade PRISM, for example, collected immense amounts of data on communications by entities and individuals, and it reportedly involved NSA cooperation with over 100 corporations

156 See Kaelan Deese, "CIA Used Encryption Company to Spy on other Countries for Decades," *The Hill*, February 11, 2020, https://thehill.com/.

157 See Electrospaces, *The NSA Tried to Spy on Danish and Other European Targets via Cable Tapping in Denmark*, July 6, 2021, www.electrospaces.net/; Sebastian Moss, *Danish Whistleblower Details NSA Collaboration, Submarine Cable Spying, Surveillance Data Center: The NSA Worked with the Danish Intelligence Agency to Spy on Denmark*, Data Center Dynamics, November 18, 2020, www.datacenterdynamics.com/; Bill Blunden, "How the NSA is a Servant of Corporate Power: Top-Secret Intercepts Prove that Economic Spying by the U.S. is Pervasive and Wielded to Benefit Powerful Corporate Interests," *Alternet*, July 22, 2015, www.alternet.org/; Bill Blunden and Violet Cheung, *Behold a Pale Farce: Cyberwar, Threat Inflation, and the Malware Industrial Complex* (Walterville, OR: Trine Day, 2014), chapters 3–7, 10; Olga Khazan, "The Creepy, Long-Standing Practice of Undersea Cable Tapping: The Newest NSA Leaks Reveal that Governments are Probing 'the Internet's Backbone'. How does that Work?" *The Atlantic*, July 16, 2013, www.theatlantic.com/.

158 Blunden, "How the NSA is a Servant"; Blunden and Cheung, *Behold a Pale Farce.*

159 Shorrock, "New Spy Scandal Exposes"; Deese, "CIA Used Encryption Company"; Blunden, "How the NSA is a Servant"; Blunden and Cheung, *Behold a Pale Farce.*

160 See Price, "New Surveillance Normal," 49; Arindrajit Dube, Ethan Kaplan and Suresh Naidu, "Coups, Corporations, and Classified Information," *Quarterly Journal of Economics* 126 (2011), 1375–409.

to use or mine the data they gathered.[161] Microsoft, Google, Facebook, Apple, Yahoo, and YouTube (in various years)—and various telecommunications oligopolists—were found to be among the cooperating entities.[162]

And, despite restrictions on such espionage within the United States, indications are that hundreds of millions of records were occasionally obtained by the NSA over the years—for metadata analyses and for individually targeted surveillance.[163] The NSA had actually started its own program of warrantless domestic wiretapping in 2001—on telephone calls—with the assistance of two communication oligopolists, AT&T and Verizon.[164] Indications are that, over the years, the NSA's domestic data collection provided a platform for other U.S. federal agencies to undertake their own warrantless surveillance. Using NSA data, the FBI reportedly engaged in frequent mining to conduct domestic "backdoor searches" on millions of individual citizens and legal residents, despite the supposed safeguards.[165] The misuse of the Foreign Intelligence Surveillance Act (FISA) law and courts, and the alleged bending of the FBI from a law enforcement agency to undertake domestic espionage and intel-

161 See Wikipedia, *PRISM (Surveillance Program)*, http://en.wikipedia.org/ (accessed August 19, 2021); Lavanya Rathnam, "PRISM, Snowden and Government Surveillance: 6 Things you Need to Know," *Cloudwards*, April 19, 2017, www.cloudwards.net/; David Greene and Katitza Rodriguez, *NSA Mass Surveillance Programs: Unnecessary and Disproportionate*, Electronic Frontier Foundation, May 29, 2014, www.eff.org/.

162 See Barton Gellman and Laura Poitras, "U.S. Intelligence Mining Data from Nine U.S. Internet Companies in Broad Secret Program," *Washington Post*, June 6, 2013, www.washingtonpost.com/; Glenn Greenwald and Ewen MacAskill, "NSA Taps in to Internet Giants' Systems to Mine User Data, Secret Files Reveal—Top-Secret Prism Program Claims Direct Access to Servers of Firms Including Google, Apple and Facebook—Companies Deny Any Knowledge of Program in Operation Since 2007," *The Guardian*, June 6, 2013, www.theguardian.com/.

163 See Christine Fisher, "NSA Improperly Collected Even More Call Records than We Thought—Months After it Admitted Error and Deleted 600 million Records, the NSA Violated Federal Laws Once Again," *Engadget*, June 26, 2019, www.engadget.com/; Dustin Volz, "NSA Improperly Collected Data Again," *Wall Street Journal*, June 27, 2019, A4. Adding to this aspect is that "the NSA chooses what it discloses, and any relevant documents can only be reviewed in a dedicated room and not removed"—as reported by *The Economist*, "Collecting Private Information: Uses and Abuses," April 4, 2015, 80. See also Bruce Schneier, *Data and Goliath: The Hidden Battles to Collect Your Data and Control Your World* (New York: Norton, 2015), chapters 2, 3, 5–7.

164 See Robert W. McChesney, *Digital Disconnect: How Capitalism is Turning the Internet against Democracy* (New York: New Press, 2013), 165; Glenn Greenwald, *With Liberty and Justice for Some: How the Law is Used to Destroy Equality and Protect the Powerful* (New York: Metropolitan, 2011), 75–76.

165 In 2017, 3.1 million such searches were undertaken by the FBI—compared with approximately 7,500 domestic individual data mining searches by the CIA and the NSA in the same year—see Trevor Aaronson, *A Declassified Court Ruling Shows How the FBI Abused NSA Mass Surveillance Data*, The Intercept, October 10, 2019, www.theintercept.com/. And the U.S. government is said to routinely obtain—without any judicial warrant—daily access to data on tens of millions of individual cellphone locations and personal details, based on app-generated marketing information—see *Wall Street Journal*, "How the U.S. Government Obtains and Uses Cellphone Location Data," February 7, 2020, www.wsj.com/.

ligence on citizens, has—in parallel with NSA operations—been blamed for the tech-enabled abuse of privacy and constitutional rights.[166] These domestic tech-driven intrusions and violations can be considered extensions of what has long been done abroad, to cement geopolitical domination.

Another surveillance program is MUSCULAR—an extensive, longstanding, and very secretive global operation by the NSA and the GCHQ—one of the various programs generally known by the code name WINDSTOP, which reportedly collected billions of sensitive data records over short periods of time during the last decade.[167] MUSCULAR broke into the main communication cables that connect Google, Yahoo, and other internet-based corporations, mining most every form of economic, personal, and other data held in servers.[168] The program XKeyscore reportedly enabled the NSA to spy on most everything any user can do on the internet—including browsing histories, social media, and emails—and its analysts allegedly were not required to obtain prior authorization to access or mine such data.[169] Vast data clouds with intimate details can be assembled through the software and hardware technologies associated with this program—data that can be used to secure concessions from individuals, groups, and organizations linked to technology and geopolitical power.

ECHELON—a longstanding joint NSA-GCHQ program that has often involved other intelligence agencies in the Five Eyes alliance—was started in the 1960s to spy on the Soviet Union's military and diplomatic communications, but became engaged in economic and technological espionage over the years.[170] Benefits to the U.S. military and intelligence apparatus—and its technology contractors—were allegedly much more than those gained by all other

166 In this regard, a retired FBI Special Agent and former legal attaché stated: "The use of FISA to target a U.S. citizen is the most egregious abuse. … FISA was never intended as a tool to pursue Americans. … It was not intended to be used in criminal prosecutions. … To seek a warrant under the Foreign Intelligence Surveillance Act, with its lower standard of probable cause, when one would ultimately pursue a prosecution was considered an abuse of FISA. It is still an abuse."—Thomas J. Baker, "What Went Wrong at the FBI," *Wall Street Journal*, March 20, 2018, A19.

167 See Wikipedia, *MUSCULAR (Surveillance Program)*, http://en.wikipedia.org/ (accessed June 18, 2022); Barton Gellman and Matt DeLong, "One Month, Hundreds of Millions of Records Collected," *Washington Post*, October 30, 2013, www.washingtonpost.com/; Barton Gellman and Ashkan Soltani, "NSA Infiltrates Links to Yahoo, Google Data Centers Worldwide, Snowden Documents Say," *Washington Post*, October 30, 2013, www.washingtonpost.com/.

168 Gellman and DeLong, "One Month, Hundreds of Millions"; Gellman and Soltani, "NSA Infiltrates Links."

169 See Wikipedia, *XKeyscore*, https://en.wikipedia.org/ (accessed May 20, 2022); Glenn Greenwald, "XKeyscore: NSA Tool Collects 'Nearly Everything a User Does on the Internet," *The Guardian*, July 31, 2013, www.theguardian.com/.

170 See Wikipedia, *ECHELON*, https://en.wikipedia.org/ (accessed May 22, 2022); Dan Froomkin, "After 27 Years, Reporter who Exposed ECHELON finds Vindication in Snowden Archive," *The Intercept*, August 3, 2015, www.theintercept.com/; Lucas Matney, "Uncovering ECHELON: The Top Secret NSA/GCHQ Program that has been Watching You your Entire Life," *Tech*

Five Eyes participants combined. Among data obtained through ECHELON were those that provided advantages to American corporations in international bidding or negotiation—such as the ones involving Boeing and Airbus for Pentagon military contracts, and the U.S.–Canada–Mexico trade agreements.[171] ECHELON's espionage operations possibly involved the most diverse set of communication technologies ever, starting with landline telephone and cable and shortwave radio communications, moving on to wired global banking transactions—including those handled through SWIFT—along with the internet, the web, and all forms of wireless communications, transcending boundaries and sovereignty.[172]

The cyberspace projection of the United States—militarily and commercially—has reportedly grown more intrusive than ever during the past three decades, and it seems reasonable to note that the intensity of espionage and the amount of data collected is possibly much more than those collected by all other nations in history combined. Control over global commodity chains is fundamentally important for this facet of geopolitical domination and for the global power of American technology oligopolies. *The commercial cybernetic domain therefore depends as much on global economic power—through technology oligopolies, their arbitrage, and commodity chains—as it does on the martial domain.*[173]

Data clouds are today a very important vehicle for U.S. hierarchic control over global cyberspace. They are intimately related to commodity chains, inasmuch as the management of inputs and products and the global scope of transactions depend on them. Amazon, Microsoft, IBM, and other large technology oligopolists were at the core of such control during the last decade.[174] Their clouds provide an immense amount of personal and corporate data that is vital for *both* the commercial and the martial domains.

The importance of this relationship may be exemplified by the censoring of Wikileaks revelations on NSA domestic espionage in 2010—by Amazon

Crunch, August 3, 2015, www.techcrunch.com/; Aldrich, *GCHQ*; Patrick R. Keefe, *Chatter: Dispatches from the Secret World of Global Eavesdropping* (New York: Random House, 2005).

171 See Project Freedom, Human Rights Watch, *ECHELON Part Two, The NSA's Global Spying Network*, www.bibliotecapleyades.net/ (accessed June 19, 2022); Laurent Bloch, *L'Internet: Vecteur de Puissance des États Unis?* (Paris: DiploWeb, 2017); European Parliament, *Report on the Existence of a Global System for the Interception of Private and Commercial Communications (ECHELON Interception System)*, July 2001, https://cryptome.org/.

172 See Project Freedom, *ECHELON*; Matney, "Uncovering ECHELON"; Bloch, *L'Internet*; SWIFT, *SWIFT History*; Scott and Zachariadis, *The Society for Worldwide*, chapters 4–5.

173 See Gellman and Poitras, "U.S. Intelligence Mining Data"; Yasha Levine, "American Internet Companies are Privatized Instruments of U.S. Geopolitical Power, and They're not even Hiding It," *The Grayzone*, April 7, 2019, www.thegrayzone.com/; Greenwald, *No Place to Hide*.

174 See Asher Schechter, "Google is as Close to a Natural Monopoly as the Bell System was in 1956," *Pro-Market*, May 9, 2017, https://promarket.org/; Jonathan Taplin, *Move Fast and Break Things: How Facebook, Amazon, and Google Cornered Culture and Undermined Democracy* (London: Macmillan, 2017).

(denial of access to servers), Apple (cancellation of apps)—and the severance of financial services after Amazon's and Apple's actions by PayPal, Visa, MasterCard, and Bank of America.[175] All *without* any apparent order from the U.S. government to implement such censorship, and despite the fact that the revelations (and documentation provided) were legitimate. The oligopolists involved reportedly sought to safeguard their interests—as either current or future contractors for the U.S. government—above the right of the public to know.[176]

The new JWCC (Joint Warfighting Cloud Capability) and JEDI (Joint Enterprise Defense Infrastructure) programs—proposed massive data cloud projects between the Pentagon and selected cyberspace oligopolies—may well indicate the close future connections between oligopolistic power and the military and intelligence apparatus.[177] These projects promise to eventually become the largest ever cloud data mining operation by the martial domain with a commercial company. The solicitation process for the JEDI winner-take-all contract initially drew complaints of favoritism and unethical lobbying from several cloud-based oligopolists (including Amazon) that hoped to receive the contract.[178]

U.S. hierarchic global control over a most important aspect of cyberspace—artificial intelligence—is set to be closely linked to the cloud platforms and the martial domain. As with the JEDI program and most every project involving cyberspace, technology oligopolists seem set to be the prime enablers and developers. AI will be crucially important for control over warfare, based on processing vast amounts of data independently from human supervision.[179] As AI is being utilized to manage many aspects of commodity chains, its interface with the martial domain seems assured. AI-based global control strategies are thus likely to span both military and commercial operations—sustenance and expansion of commodity chains being an important strategic priority.

Cybernetic-intensive managerial and organizational consultants may also be considered an important component of this control hierarchy. Several

175 McChesney, *Digital Disconnect*, 164–65.

176 McChesney, *Digital Disconnect*, 164–65. See also Greenwald, *No Place to Hide*; Taplin, *Move Fast and Break Things*.

177 See *The Economist*, "Can Tech Reshape the Pentagon? Silicon Valley Gets Back Together with the Military-Industrial Complex," August 13, 2022, 57–58; Jared Serbu, "Microsoft Wins Controversial DoD JEDI Cloud Contract," *Federal News Network*, October 25, 2019, https://federalnewsnetwork.com/; Lauren C. Williams, "DOD Releases $10 Billion JEDI Cloud Contract," *Defense Systems*, July 26, 2018, https://defensesystems.com/.

178 John D. McKinnon, "Amazon Meetings Draw Scrutiny to Pentagon Project," *Wall Street Journal*, July 8, 2019, B1.

179 See *The Economist*, "Battle Algorithm: Artificial Intelligence is Transforming Every Aspect of Warfare," September 7, 2019, 71–73; Michael Horowitz, Kara Frederick, Elsa B. Kania, Ashley J. Llorens, *et al.*, *American Leadership in the Age of Artificial Intelligence*, Center for a New American Security, June 14, 2019, www.cnas.org/.

global American oligopolists in this area—such as Accenture, McKinsey, and Deloitte—get to know the most sensitive details of their clients, which include advanced technology companies around the world. Very sensitive details on commodity chains and their management is part of such knowledge. Accenture—previously part of Andersen Consulting—alone has over half a million employees, many of them reportedly low-cost labor based in India and the Philippines.[180] Its annual revenue has reached as much as $45 billion in recent times, and it has spent one billion dollars or more annually acquiring dozens of other companies—to apparently fence-in market niches and erect entry barriers.[181]

This company's oligopolistic power over most any area of organizational cybernetics—AI, clouds, cyber-security, mobile communications, and data analytics, among others—has allowed it to amass the most detailed information on the technologies they use, their company strategies, their future plans, and their key personnel. Its client companies include a vast number of non-U.S.-based corporations in most every field imaginable—along with Google, Facebook, and others.[182] The intimate knowledge Accenture gains on its clients might be transferred to others, especially those at home. Its global power—and the vast amount of sensitive information it gains on client technology companies around the world—provides the United States with much potential leverage on other nations and their companies—as intelligence and military contractors are reportedly among Accenture's clients.[183]

Operating systems provide another example of cybernetic hierarchic domination, as practically all wireless or smartphone communications in the world (except China's to some extent), and the vast majority of smartphones, portable and desktop computing, depend on systems owned by American technology oligopolies.[184] Apple's Android operating system, for example, commanded almost 90 percent of sales market share in the world's mobile phone market (smartphones included) during the last decade.[185] Even Open Source software programs do not escape global hierarchic control, as licensing to entities in nations targeted as a "foreign adversary" can be banned.[186]

180 See Wikipedia, *Accenture*, https://en.wikipedia.org/ (accessed June 6, 2022); *The Economist*, "The Rise and Rise of Accenture: How a Consultant has Ballooned into a White-Collar Leviathan," March 14, 2020, 53.

181 *The Economist*, "Rise and Rise."

182 *The Economist*, "Rise and Rise"; Wikipedia, *Accenture*.

183 Wikipedia, *Accenture*; *The Economist*, "Rise and Rise."

184 A matter that seemed to make it easier for U.S. intelligence agencies to hack such devices—see Shane Harris and Paul Sonne, "WikiLeaks Dumps CIA Spy Trove," *Wall Street Journal*, March 8, 2017, A1; Paul Sonne, "IPhones, TVs could be Vulnerable," *Wall Street Journal*, March 8, 2017, A4.

185 Statista, *Global Mobile OS Market Share in Sales to End Users from 1st Quarter 2009 to 2nd Quarter 2020*, www.statista.com/ (accessed June 21, 2022).

186 See Homeland Security Digital Library, *Executive Order 13873: Securing the Information and Communications Technology and Services Supply Chain*, May 15, 2015, www.hsdl.org/.

The importance of sustaining hierarchic global domination over cyberspace seemed obvious in the case of the U.S. ban on Huawei—the world's second most important producer of smartphones—and the pressure applied on subordinate governments to impose similar prohibitions. And this occurred despite predictions that the bans would harm 5G technology development—not only in the nations that gave in but also in the United States itself.[187] This occurred despite the fact that six important American technology corporations received a significant portion of their annual revenue from sales to Huawei.[188] Broadcom—a global semiconductor supplier based in the United States—estimated it would lose at least two billion dollars annually in revenue due to the ban.[189] Apple was also likely to experience substantial revenue losses, as its Android operating system—along with millions of proprietary apps sold through its App Store monthly—was in almost all Huawei smartphones sold outside China.[190]

More than any other aspect, the United States ban targeted Huawei's global commodity chains, with the intent of severely disrupting or destroying them—to cause the company to experience substantial losses and to possibly collapse.[191] The raw geopolitical game of domination seemed to be very much at the core, and the key factor was the perception among U.S. military and intelligence elites that China is a rising technology rival and will not bend to American geopolitical power.[192] Killing off a technology company in a nation perceived to be an up-and-coming rival—through bans and sanctions—thus became an

187 See Vijay Vaitheeswaran, "Splinternet of Things: The Transformative Potential of 5G will be Diminished by America's Blacklisting of Huawei," *The Economist, World in 2020*, December 2019, 117–18.

188 Dan Strumpf and Asa Fitch, "Huawei Ban Yanks Supply Chain," *Wall Street Journal*, June 29, 2019, B3 (based on data from Bernstein Research).

189 Asa Fitch, "Broadcom to take $2 Billion Hit from Huawei Ban: Company Cuts Outlook, Misses Second-Quarter Revenue Targets," *Wall Street Journal*, June 13, 2019, www.wsj.com/.

190 Jesus Diaz, "Trump's Huawei Ban could end Android as we know it and Damage Apple (Update)," *Tom's Guide*, May 21, 2019, www.tomsguide.com/; Jay McGregor, "How the Huawei Ban Affects Android," *Forbes*, May 22, 2019, www.forbes.com/.

191 See Kenneth Rapoza, "Without U.S. Tech Ban, Huawei Phones Would Rival Samsung and Apple Nearly Everywhere," *Forbes*, June 20, 2019, www.forbes.com/.

192 China's refusal to acquiesce to U.S. geopolitical interests is often assumed to be connected to its espionage capabilities, especially through cybernetics. For historical overviews of the complex U.S.–China espionage relationship and its links to technology—as seen from the U.S. and Western perspectives—see Roger Faligot, *Chinese Spies: From Chairman Mao to Xi Jinping* (London: Hurst, 2019), chapters 11, 12; Peter Mattis and Matthew Brazil, *Chinese Communist Espionage: An Intelligence Primer* (Annapolis, MD: Naval Institute Press, 2019), chapters 4, 6, 7. Among the few accounts of U.S. cyberespionage against China is the CIA and NSA's extensive 11-year hacking (known as APT-C-39) of a wide range of sectors, including technology, aviation, oil, gas, and various government agencies—see Pierluigi Paganini, "Chinese Security Firm Qihoo 360 Revealed that the U.S. CIA has Hacked Chinese Organizations in Various Sectors for the Last 11 Years," *Security Affairs*, March 4, 2020, https://securityaffairs.co/.

obvious part of the global strategy to sustain domination.[193] A reportedly new Cold War to sustain U.S. global technological supremacy may be taken as evidence of the importance attached to this priority. And, lost in the arguments for the bans was the fact that the U.S. intelligence apparatus long spied on Huawei through the NSA and kept the data it obtained secret—thus, in a way, undertaking much the same actions that it alleged Huawei might be capable of doing.[194]

Financial

Control over financial transaction technologies is a vital support of domination. The emergence of this projection can be traced to the end of the 1940s. Unlike all other industrialized nations, the United States emerged from the Second World War with its entire technological infrastructure—and industrial base—undamaged and expanded.[195] This formidable advantage enabled finance to invest in transaction technologies and look abroad. The main beneficiaries were the largest corporations, the dollar, Wall Street, and the martial domain.

Much demand for technologies that could provide greater speed and security accompanied a rising volume of global transactions. The creation of SWIFT (noted earlier) cemented control over finance and transaction technologies—making it possible to monitor finance. Wider usage of SWIFT then helped track financial transactions globally.[196] Although nominally not under U.S. control, SWIFT would become a formidable tool for undertaking surveillance and imposing embargoes—against governments and companies that might disrupt commodity chains, arbitrage, or defy geopolitical interests. And it also allowed record-keeping on an unprecedented scale, providing greater speed and security.

193 See Sean Lyngaas, "No 'Smoking Gun' Evidence Coming on Huawei, NSA Official Says," *Cyberscoop*, March 7, 2019, www.cyberscoop.com/; Zak Doffman, "Huawei Claims U.S. Onslaught is Because their 5G Technology Prevents Widespread NSA Spying," *Forbes*, February 28, 2019, www.forbes.com/.

194 See David E. Sanger and Nicole Perlroth, "NSA Breached Chinese Servers seen as Security Threat," *New York Times*, March 22, 2014, www.nytimes.com/; *RT*, "U.S. Used FISA Warrant to Spy on Huawei and Keep Evidence Secret," April 4, 2019, www.rt.com/.

195 Industrial production increased by 90 percent while real aggregate output rose by 65 percent during 1941–1944, allowing the United States to account for almost two-thirds of the world's manufacturing output by 1945—see Richard B. DuBoff, *Accumulation and Power: Economic History of the United States* (New York: Routledge, 2016), 90–94.

196 SWIFT reportedly handled $140 trillion, and amounts totaling 150 percent of global GDP during 2020, connecting 11,000 banks in over 200 nations—see *The Economist*, "The Geopolitics of Money: Be Swift, Be Bold," October 23, 2021, 17. See also SWIFT, *SWIFT History*; Stansfield Smith, "World Police: Washington Seeks to Imprison Foreign Businesspeople for Violating Illegal U.S. Sanctions," *The Grayzone*, April 27, 2021, https://thegrayzone.com/; Karen Yeung, "How the US Uses the Dollar Payments System to Impose Sanctions on a Global Scale," *South China Morning Post*, August 25, 2020, www.scmp.com/.

Another element of financial control and the use of transactions technology was the creation of CHIPS (Clearing House Interbank Payments System). This is a U.S.-based network that by the end of the last decade was processing about $1.6 trillion in daily transactions.[197] Owned by the financial institutions that use it—most of all the largest U.S. banks and financial corporations—it compiles transaction data between participating entities worldwide. Foreign banks with a regulated U.S. presence can participate, thus enlarging CHIPS' scope, helping promote the dollar's global supremacy, and—in combination with SWIFT—allowing the U.S. government to monitor any targeted government or company. Denial of access to CHIPS can lead to isolation from the global financial system—inflicting much damage on targeted governments and companies and on national economies. Bans can also damage foreign banks with any business of their own in the United States, any banks or companies that use U.S.-based back-end accounting systems—for any transaction, even if not denominated in dollars—any use of email services with servers in the United States, and any transaction that involves a U.S. citizen or resident to process, facilitate, or approve it.[198]

Yet another control mode over finance and the use of transactions technology is Continuous Linked Settlement (CLS).[199] By the end of the last decade, this entity settled about four-fifths of all global foreign exchange turnover—involving the U.S. dollar and 17 other currencies—through more than 24,000 client firms, 66 settlement members, and 79 shareholders. CLS is vital for reducing settlement risk, as it prevents the possibility that an organization may go without payment from a counterparty using the currencies it supports—most of all the U.S. dollar. Nations excluded from using CLS would suffer higher currency transaction costs and much difficulty financing trade—likely leading to deepening export deficits, insurmountable import obstacles, larger trade imbalances, debt defaults, and substantial reductions in national income. In combination with CHIPS and SWIFT, CLS thus contributes greatly to U.S. domination over global finance. This troika of financial control is unprecedented—no nation or empire in history was able to wield such deep and far-reaching power over the rest of the world.

Related to these organizations is the tech-enabled consumer payments duopoly that dominates credit transactions. Neither could have attained the power they have over credit payments without advanced transaction technologies. Visa and MasterCard operate in over 200 nations and territories, coordinating a complex system of financial intermediaries between merchants and consumers.

197 See Federal Reserve Bank of New York, *CHIPS*, www.newyorkfed.org/; Wikipedia, *Clearing House Interbank Payments System*, https://en.wikipedia.org/ (both accessed January 28, 2022).

198 See Federal Reserve Bank of New York, *CHIPS*; *The Economist*, "American Financial Hegemony," January 18, 2020, 64.

199 See Wikipedia, *CLS Group*, https://en.wikipedia.org/ (accessed March 20, 2021); CLS, *CLS FX Trading Activity January 2020*, www.cls-group.com/.

Being barred from their transaction networks can devastate a nation's financial infrastructure—cash or cash-transfer payments becoming the only alternatives. By the end of the last decade Visa alone connected over 60 million merchants to more than 3.5 billion of its branded cards—almost one for every two inhabitants in the world.[200] Through its vast tech-enabled system it coordinated almost $10 trillion in transactions annually—nearly 10 percent of the world's gross domestic product (GDP), with an operating profit rate of about 65 percent—one of the three highest in the world for any listed company.

The creation of FINCEN in 1990 to conduct global surveillance on transactions of any type—including any use of the U.S. dollar—further deepened hierarchic control over finance and the use of transaction technologies.[201] Run by the U.S. Treasury Department—with close ties to the CIA, NSA, and other intelligence organizations—this agency acquired unprecedented power. Technology oligopolies reportedly provide advice and much support for its transaction surveillance hardware and software. FINCEN technically gained the capacity to classify as "illicit" financial activities considered to be adverse to any aspect of U.S. geopolitical power—including those related to global arbitrage and commodity chains. Such classification automatically subjects any targeted individuals, entities, or governments to U.S. criminal and economic sanctions—leading to account freezes, confiscation, imprisonment, or bans on operation and entry.[202]

In this regard, FINCEN became a most important, tech-enabled tool for U.S. domination over finance and transactions—and over most any type of economic activity around the world. Governments and entities targeted for destabilization—because of their non-compliance with geopolitical dictates, including any reorientation of commodity chains that diminish U.S. economic and military power—could thus find themselves classified as money launderers, traffickers, terrorism facilitators, or violators of U.S. laws. The vast, historically unprecedented *extraterritorial* projection of U.S. financial laws—achieved through FINCEN, complemented by control over CHIPS and SWIFT—further deepened U.S. domination over finance and the use of transaction technologies.

Closely related to FINCEN is the Office of Foreign Assets Control (OFAC)—also managed by the U.S. Treasury Department.[203] Its prime func-

200 See *The Economist*, "Processing Power: Visa is the Global Digital Network that Everyone Underestimated," March 21, 2020, 59; Stephen Connolly, "Veni, Vidi, Visa: Profits from Payment Processing—Visa, the Payment Network Giant, is a Highly Profitable Operator Dominating the Global Market," *MoneyWeek*, May 22, 2019, https://moneyweek.com/.

201 See Wikipedia, *Financial Crimes Enforcement Network*, https://en.wikipedia.org/; FINCEN, *Financial Crimes Enforcement Network*, www.fincen.gov/ (both accessed June 16, 2022).

202 See Smith, "World Police."

203 See Wikipedia, *Office of Foreign Assets Control*, https://en.wikipedia.org/ (accessed June 20, 2022); Samuel Rubenfeld, "OFAC Rises as Sanctions Become a Major Policy Tool," *Wall Street Journal*,

tion is enforcement and usage of advanced transaction technologies to gather intelligence. OFAC used the Patriot Act and the post-9/11 situation to codify extraordinary, extraterritorial powers into U.S. financial laws.[204] It has thus been vital for the expansion of sanctions and coercive measures—estimated to have reached nearly 15,000 during the past four decades, the largest number ever imposed by any nation in history.[205]

Intelligence "targeters"—supported by the most advanced transaction surveillance technologies—are considered to be OFAC's most important employees.[206] It is thought to be one of the most secretive government agencies, and it has the power to target any government, entity, and individual considered to be adverse to U.S. interests. The entities or individuals targeted may operate completely outside—and have no ties whatsoever to—the U.S. Actions have reportedly driven numerous banks and businesses around the world to fail—in most cases for transactions that were legal in their home nations.[207] Or, for actions and transactions about which OFAC allegedly had no conclusive proof.[208]

Confiscations, embargoes, bans, extraditions, and financial account freezes are at the core of OFAC's tech-enabled repertory. Any government, entity, or individual targeted is likely to be classified as a criminal violator of U.S. laws—even when the alleged offense did not involve any U.S. citizens, residents, or entities, did not occur within the territory of the United States, use of dollars, and did not break any laws.[209] Also, any individuals extradited to the United States Will be made to stand trial and likely serve prison time. Practically all transactions with nations and companies targeted for "weaponized" value arbi-

February 5, 2014, www.wsj.com/.

204 Juan C. Zarate's *Treasury's War: The Unleashing of a New Era of Financial Warfare* (New York: PublicAffairs, 2013), parts I, II—provides insights on the legal arguments deployed. See also *The Economist*, "American Financial Hegemony"; *China Daily*, "U.S. Economic Hegemony against World Reality," May 5, 2016, www.chinadaily.com.cn/.

205 *The Economist*, "Economic Sanctions: Handle with Care," April 24, 2021, 59–63; Gibson Dunn, *2020 Year-End Sanctions and Export Controls Update*, February 5, 2021, www.gibsondunn.com/; Scott Sumner, "How the US Bullies the World into its Sanctions Regime," *FEE*, May 30, 2018, https://fee.org/. Nicholas Mulder's *The Economic Weapon: The Rise of Sanctions as a Tool of Modern War* (New Haven: Yale University Press, 2022) provides historical perspective on the use of sanctions from the First to the Second World Wars.

206 See *The Economist*, "Economic Sanctions"; Zarate, *Treasury's War*, chapters 3, 4, 9, 10, 16.

207 *The Economist*, "Economic Sanctions"; Sumner, "How the U.S. Bullies." See also Victor Gao, "Failure to Follow Due Process in the Meng Wanzhou Case Weakens Canada's Rule of Law," *CGTN*, November 1, 2020, https://news.cgtn.com/; Julia Horowitz, "Huawei CFO Meng Wanzhou Arrested in Canada, Faces Extradition to United States," *CNN Business*, December 6, 2018, www.cnn.com/.

208 See Smith, "World Police"; *The Economist*, "American Financial Hegemony"; Yeung, "How the US Uses"; Horowitz, "Huawei CFO."

209 See Sumner, "How the U.S. Bullies"; Yeung, "How the US Uses"; *The Economist*, "American Financial Hegemony"; Gao, "Failure to Follow"; Horowitz, "Huawei CFO."

trage (discussed earlier) are monitored and can be pursued. Much the same can apply to commodity chain disruptions that might affect U.S. interests negatively, including those of American technology oligopolies.

Socio-political

Control over technologies that influence socio-political culture is an important support for oligopolistic domination. The means used in this projection are hybrid and diffuse, but they have three elements in common—technology, oligopolistic power, and the martial domain. *The engineering of public perception is their shared objective.*

Achieving control over socio-political culture can involve several functions. All of them are supported by communication technologies, advanced software, and data clouds. First, political "content designers" and "influencers" create slogans, memes, videos, and symbols—that are diffused through social media.[210] These are often accompanied by messaging that tries to amplify content—and reach as many people as possible. The creation of templates by content designers—to avoid errors and contradictions—may be part of this function. These tasks can be supported by constellations of apps that facilitate connectivity with supportive online sites.

These activities help sustain a second vital function—generating awareness in a targeted population. Certain communication and social media technologies—messaging algorithms, data clouds, apps, smartphones—are vital for this function. Larger network extent (a concept discussed previously in this book) is very important, as it will likely result in greater diffusion. Expanded network extent can also make diffusion more dynamic, such that more people can be reached in a shorter period of time. Such diffusion efficiency can help amplify awareness and promote action.[211]

Outreach in this function can involve an extrapolation of some of the same general socio-psychological appeals used by technology oligopolies in their advertising campaigns. The symbolism deployed might also draw insights from marketing involving brand fetishism (discussed earlier in this book). Enhancing self-esteem and social gratification may be important tactical features, especially when there are many among a targeted population who have experienced disadvantage.

A third function then involves facilitating appropriation of the ideas put out, and of the symbols, memes, and slogans—by anyone—such that they will appear to be spontaneous and collectively created. The mainstream,

210 See Whitney Phillips and Ryan M. Milner, *You Are Here: A Field Guide for Navigating Polarized Speech, Conspiracy Theories, and Our Polluted Media Landscape* (Cambridge: MIT Press, 2021), chapters 1–3, 6; *The Economist*, "The Globalisation of Politics," June 12, 2021, 53–54.

211 Use of specialized "influencer" consultants and platforms may be sought. See *The Economist*, "Globalisation of Politics," 54; HypeAuditor, *Industry Standard Analytical Platform for Transparent and Fraud-Free Influencer Marketing*, https://hypeauditor.com/ (accessed October 22, 2021).

corporate-controlled media can help greatly in this regard, by providing legitimacy to what the political content designers created. Thus, news media sites with substantial global circulation may end up replaying or building upon the messages put out.[212] The three most visited global English-language online news platforms during the last decade—those of the BBC, CNN, and *New York Times*—can be important in this regard.[213] Mainstream media articles can provide legitimacy, partly because they may add details—such as interviews, reports on incidents, and official declarations. Blogs, videos, and messaging sites may then diffuse supportive comments on the articles and reports. All content can be biased (subtly or not) against a targeted government, and no contrarian views or facts may be provided.

Awareness—and the collective appropriation of ideas—can be tacitly assisted by social media oligopolies through *uselabor*-driven campaigns that involve much the same methods as advertising and wants contrivance. Uselabor (discussed in previous chapters) thus—in addition to being uncompensated labor—becomes an instrument for socio-political manipulation. Technology products usually convey a sense of novelty, effectiveness, or higher social status—features that are vehicles for communication and awareness—and that facilitate mass appropriation of ideas and symbols. Tech products often target demographic groups—young adults, especially—whose views on politics and social action are malleable. This can make it easier to overcome collective reticence in nations that have not been compliant with geopolitical interests.

Establishing an ancillary unit to make contact with official agencies and provide propaganda can serve the dual purpose of marketing and influencing socio-political attitudes. The announced objective of Google's Jigsaw unit—launched during the last decade—for example, was to "explore threats to open societies."[214] This mission statement seemed consonant with the oft-stated U.S. State Department goal of promoting "open" societies—taken by many people around the world to mean acquiescence to U.S. geopolitical interests.[215] The fact that Jigsaw's founding executive was formerly one of the most influential State Department officials—regarded as the main advocate of the Department's "21st Century Statecraft" policy platform—seemed to confirm such suspicions.[216] The close association—possibly the clearest one articulated in recent

212 See Edward S. Herman and Noam Chomsky, *Manufacturing Consent: The Political Economy of the Mass Media* (New York: Pantheon, 2002), chapters 1, 3–5; *The Economist*, "Globalisation of Politics," 54.

213 *The Economist*, "Globalisation of Politics," 54.

214 Google, *Jigsaw*, www.jigsaw.google.com/ (accessed April 26, 2022).

215 See U.S. Department of State, *21st Century Statecraft*, www.state.gov/ (accessed June 9, 2022).

216 See Paul B. Carr, "Google Launches 'Jigsaw', Headed by Former State Department Official, to 'Tackle Geopolitical Challenges'," *Pando*, February 17, 2016, www.pando.com/; David Dayen, "The Android Administration: Google's Remarkably Close Relationship with the Obama White House, in Two Charts," *The Intercept*, April 22, 2016, www.theintercept.com/; Mario

times—led some observers to note a definite symbiosis between American technology companies and geopolitics.[217]

Google put "statecraft" in action when—working closely with the State Department—it offered to provide internet connectivity to Cuba during the last decade.[218] The U.S. government (and all American companies) had—since the inception of the internet—completely denied access to this service through its marine, landline, and satellite networks—forcing Cuba to recur to costly, insufficient satellite connections provided from other nations.[219] Later, Google would facilitate connections through broadband and WiFi and provide other services.[220] These connectivity services are fundamental for setting up an awareness "stage"—that can lead to a massive appropriation of the ideas put out—such that the social and political reality can be influenced. Once these services and the stage are in place, socio-political agendas can be deployed—using messaging services, social media, blogs, and text or video created by content designers and strategic influencers.

Seemingly unrelated services can then be enlisted to further support statecraft staging operations. One of Google's most strategic—and geopolitically connected—services, for example, involves mapping.[221] Related data clouds contain much vital information that intelligence agencies and the military can use. The mapping service typically compiles and analyzes vast amounts of data on elements of commodity chains—ports, processing sites, mines, roads, rail, air cargo facilities, warehousing, control centers, power generation, and com-

---

Trujillo, "Report Finds Hundreds of Meetings between White House and Google," *The Hill*, April 22, 2016, www.thehill.com/. See also Christina Larson, "State Department Innovator Goes to Google: Jared Cohen, a High-Profile Advocate of the State Department's Forays into '21st Century Statecraft' is Leaving Foggy Bottom for New York," *Foreign Policy*, September 7, 2010, www.foreignpolicy.com/. Not long after Jigsaw's foundation, reports surfaced about a difficult internal environment—see, for example, Lorenzo Franceschi-Bicchierai, "Google's Jigsaw was Supposed to Save the Internet: Behind the Scenes, It Became a Toxic Mess," *Motherboard-Vice*, July 2, 2019, www.vice.com/.

217 See Julian Assange, *Google is Not What It Seems*, www.wikileaks.org/ (accessed September 9, 2021), and his *When Google Met Wikileaks* (New York: OR Books, 2014).

218 Brody Mullins and Carol E. Lee, "Google's Cuba Connection: Obama Administration Shared Company's Interest in Bringing Internet Connectivity to Island," *Wall Street Journal*, March 24, 2016, A1.

219 Cuba's first internet connection via submarine cable occurred during the last decade, through a specially built fiber optic connection from Venezuela—financed by that nation. See U.S. Department of State, *Cuba Internet Task Force: Final Report*, June 16, 2019, www.state.gov/; Tamara Pearson, "Venezuela Helps Cuba Overcome US-Imposed Internet Restrictions," *Venezuela Analysis*, November 4, 2010, https://venezuelanalysis.com/.

220 See Paresh Dave and Sarah Marsh, "Google to Announce Deal with Cuba on Improving Connectivity: Source," *Reuters*, March 26, 2019, www.reuters.com/; Laurel Wamsley, "Google Spins Up its First Servers in Cuba," *NPR*, April 27, 2017, www.npr.org/.

221 Satellite imagery has helped Google by making it possible to map most every nation on earth, including the most restrictive ones (without site inspections). See North Korean Economy Watch, *North Korea Uncovered—(Google Earth)*, www.nkeconwatch.com/ (accessed June 9, 2022).

munication nodes, among others—that can be used for statecraft staging. Such data can be vitally important for identifying locations that can be used for demonstrations, violent confrontation, sabotage, or targeted military attacks and false-flag operations.

Another geopolitically sensitive Google service (offered at no charge) involves archiving national libraries—repositories of any nation's most important documents—to place all content in its clouds. Such information can support statecraft staging by providing ideas, slogans, or phrases that can be used in propaganda created by content designers. Possibly the most clever statecraft staging programs are based on specific data related to a nation's or a people's history, past struggles, tragic events, and most any memorable detail. This information can also help foundations, think tanks, non-governmental organizations (NGOs), and U.S. intelligence agencies formulate socio-political action programs with greater accuracy—attuned to the culture and history of a targeted nation.

Some technology corporations may be less willing to disclose their links to the State Department, intelligence agencies, or the Pentagon. Nonetheless, it is known that most technology oligopolies have ties to such agencies as contractors, consultants, or commercial providers. Also, their organizations tend to be owned by the most powerful segment of American society. The majority of Twitter's and Netflix's shares, for example, were found to be owned by some of the wealthiest individuals and Wall Street firms. And, a majority of members in their boards of directors were found to be closely associated with large oligopolistic corporations—technology and tech-service companies included.[222] During the last decade numerous former high-level U.S. government officials were reported to be members of such boards, and of financial firms that own their stock.[223]

222 See Twitter, Investor Relations, *Board of Directors*, www.investor.twitterinc.com/ (accessed June 8, 2022); Netflix, Netflix Investors, *Officers and Directors*, www.netflixinvestor.com/ (accessed May 18, 2022); *Wall Street Journal*, "Netflix Inc.: NFLX (U.S.: Nasdaq)," September 8, 2019, www.wsj.com/; Kurt Wagner, "Who Owns Twitter? A Look at the Players who could Make or Break a Deal," *Vox*, August 11, 2016, www.vox.com/; Edward Cox, "Twitter Sale: Top 5 Stakeholders with Decision Making Influence," *Heavy*, October 4, 2016, www.heavy.com/.

223 See Emily Birnbaum, "12 Former Security Officials who Warned against Antitrust Crackdown have Tech Ties," *Politico*, September 22, 2021, www.politico.com/; Menqi Sun and Ian Talley, "Former Treasury Officials Positioned to Shape Fintech from Private Sector," *Wall Street Journal*, June 8, 2020, www.wsj.com/; National Center for Public Policy Research, *Netflix Appoints Obama Crony Susan Rice to its Board of Directors*, March 29, 2018, www.nationalcenter.org/; Timothy M. LaPira and Herschel F. Thomas, *Revolving Door Lobbying: Public Service, Private Influence, and the Unequal Representation of Interests* (Lawrence: University Press of Kansas, 2017), chapters 1, 4, 7, 9; Rupert Neate, "Washington Revolving Door Speeds Up as Obama Officials Head for Lobbying Jobs," *The Guardian*, March 7, 2015, www.theguardian.com/; Glenn H. Reynolds, "Tax the Revolving Door: Column," *USA Today*, January 29, 2013, www.usatoday.com/; Bruce E. Levine, "The Myth of U.S. Democracy and the Reality of U.S. Corporatocracy," *Huffpost*, My 25, 2011, www.huffpost.com/.

Diverse forms of manipulation are embedded in the socio-political hierarchic projection—using cyberspace and its interphase with election campaigns, balloting, and data compilation. Subtlety and subterfuge can be important for this mode of "soft" tech-enabled intervention. Cyberattacks may also be employed—as catalysts for demonstrations, election losses, revolts, and coups. A major objective for exercising control through socio-political technologies is, after all, "regime change" in a targeted nation—such that governance compliant with U.S. geopolitical interests can be installed.

Regime change can also involve *systemic change*—politically, economically, and militarily. Regime change, however, can be easier to accomplish. Systemic change may then follow, if conditions allow it, to impose a new mode of governance—to deconstruct or eliminate institutions and to reconfigure the state. Both are bound to be more cost-effective than conventional warfare, as loss of U.S. military lives and hardware will be avoided—along with the expense of reconstructing infrastructure. Losses of innocent lives can be minimized or ignored by the press—much as social media spin campaigns do in the commercial arena, when products are not as effective as they were advertised to be. Thus, the amoral character of this hierarchic projection may end up being largely ignored—raw power and a lack of accountability ensuring that negative results will end up disregarded.

In recent decades tech-enabled, richly funded think tanks and foundations became important for formulating socio-political control strategies—to try to achieve regime or systemic change—by influencing the media, the public, and politicians.[224] Tacit censorship of contrarian ideas in social media and related entertainment activities can be part of the agenda—a matter that can be helped by engaging with certain technology oligopolists.[225] Placing "their people" in key government positions through which they can influence the public was considered to be another.[226] Yet another component has involved influencing universities on teaching programs and faculty hiring—to promote dissemination of agendas and influence students.[227] Philanthropy to support research

224 Among such organizations the Council on Foreign Relations has long attracted attention—see Lawrence H. Shoup, *Wall Street's Think Tank: The Council of Foreign Relations and the Empire of Neoliberal Geopolitics, 1976–2019* (New York: Monthly Review Press, 2019); Lawrence H. Shoup and William Minter, *Imperial Brain Trust: The Council of Foreign Relations and U.S. Foreign Policy* (New York: Monthly Review Press, 2004).

225 See Kirsten Grind and John D. McKinnon, "Facebook, Twitter turn to Right-Leaning Groups to Help Referee Political Speech," *Wall Street Journal*, January 8, 2019, www.wsj.com/; Nat Ives, "Twitter Hires Ad Executive to Engage with User Groups," *Wall Street Journal*, November 2, 2018, www.wsj.com/.

226 See Jonathan Mahler, "A Conservative Think Tank Stocks the Trump Government: By Placing its People Throughout the Administration—the Heritage Foundation Has Succeeded in Furthering its Right-Wing Agenda," *New York Times*, June 20, 2018, www.nytimes.com/.

227 *The Economist*, "Free Speech: Money Talks," October 16, 2021, 24.

projects that can be related to regime change—such as those involving tech-enabled behavior modification—can be part of this panorama.[228]

Technological capabilities and support have been at the core of all such efforts, often enlisting help from technology oligopolies or their executives. Billionaires (including some tech company founders or former executives) have been sources of funding.[229] Very powerful people and their funded entities—and often their corporations, indirectly—may thus be found behind these activities. Most of the influential individuals contribute greatly to favored politicians and super-political action committees (super-PACs) (an aspect considered earlier in this book). And the richly funded entities they support usually employ—as consultants or staff—specialists with deep knowledge of a targeted government and nation, the themes to attract attention to, and the communication technologies that can be deployed.[230]

Regime (and systemic) change efforts can work in concert with government agencies that serve as quasi-intelligence organizations on occasion. During the last decade the U.S. Agency for International Development (AID), for example, reportedly created a Twitter-like program to induce Cuba's population to use it as a social media network—with the local telephone system as a platform, without permission.[231] This program was implemented to complement official U.S. shortwave radio and television transmissions targeting that nation.[232] It

228 See Wikipedia, *Electronic Harassment*, https://en.wikipedia.org/; Biblioteca Pleyades, *Psychotronic Weapons: Brain Manipulation from a Distance*, www.bibliotecapleyades.net/ (both accessed May 8, 2022). Connections with the martial domain and its research apparatus might also occur—see, for example, Jim Marrs, *Psi Spies: The True Story of America's Psychic Warfare Program* (Franklin Lakes, NJ: New Page Books, 2007), chapters 1, 5–7, 9; Harold E. Puthoff, "CIA-Initiated Remote Viewing at Stanford Research Institute," *Journal of Scientific Exploration* 10 (1996), 63–76.

229 See Ben Norton, "Billionaire-Backed Human Rights Watch Lobbies for Lethal U.S. Sanctions on Leftist Governments as Covid Crisis Rages: Regime-Change Hungry HRW Proudly Taking Credit for Crushing New U.S. Sanctions on Nicaragua while Pushing to Escalate Washington's Economic War on Venezuela." *The Grayzone*, April 8, 2020, https://thegrayzone.com/; Jane Mayer, *Dark Money: The Hidden History of the Billionaires behind the Rise of the Radical Right* (New York: Anchor, 2017), chapters 1–3, 6, 9. See also Daniel Bessner, "The George Soros Philosophy—and its Fatal Flaw," *The Guardian*, July 6, 2018, www.theguardian.com/; Open Society Foundations, *George Soros, Founder/Chair*, www.opensocietyfoundations.org/ (accessed June 7, 2022); Dave Levinthal, *The Koch Brothers' Foundation Network Explained: In All, Six Separate Private Foundations are Tied to One or Both Koch Brothers*, Center for Public Integrity, November 3, 2015, www.publicintegrity.org/.

230 See Wikispooks, *Foundation for Defense of Democracies*, https://wikispooks.com/; Foundation for the Defense of Democracies, *Military and Political Power*, www.fdd.org/ (both accessed June 2, 2022); Daniel McCarthy, "The Foundation for the Defense of Democracies goes on Offense," *The American Conservative*, November 17, 2003, www.amconmag.com/.

231 See Alberto Arce, "US Secretly Built 'Cuban Twitter' to Stir Unrest," *AP*, April 3, 2014, www.apnews.com/.

232 See Wikipedia, *Radio y Televisión Martí*, https://en.wikipedia.org/ (accessed May 7, 2022); Jerry Iannelli, "A Brief History of Miami's CIA Ties and Propaganda Efforts," *Miami New Times*, August 26, 2018, www.miaminewtimes.com/.

concealed the fact that the U.S. government was involved, that users' personal data were being compiled and mined, that such data would be used to rank personal political tendencies, and that it would likely be used in future destabilization programs.[233]

The apparent objective was to (eventually) induce users to organize antigovernment demonstrations and violent actions. The user base—which reportedly had over 40,000 subscribers at the time it was exposed—initially provided items about sports, weather, news, and assorted trivia. AID's alleged plan was to gradually introduce political content, such that an action program could be organized.[234] Cuba—a nation of barely 11 million people—has long been defiant of U.S. geopolitical interests and has been subjected for over six decades to innumerable acts of sabotage, terrorism, military incursions, assassination attempts, bans, sanctions, and a very aggressive economic embargo. It has longstanding ties to Latin American nations that defy U.S. geopolitical control and that have vast mineral resources vital for commodity chains and technology oligopolies.[235] And it is strategically located at the confluence of major commodity chain shipping routes.

The ecology of organizations that assist with destabilization can also include "front companies" that pose as businesses but in fact provide cover for intelligence and socio-political influence operations.[236] The companies tend to have much technological expertise—to provide support—and they can in turn receive assistance and hardware from technology oligopolists. The front

233 Arce, "US Secretly Built"; José de Córdoba and David Luhnow, "U.S. Set up Twitter-Like Program to Reach Cubans," *Wall Street Journal*, April 4, 2014, A14;

234 The destabilization objective of this program became obvious after it was exposed, and the U.S. government and AID refused to reveal—to a congressional committee and to the public—those who had designed and implemented it. See Steven Nelson, "Another USAID Cuba Spy Program Exposed: Senator says Scheme Tarnishes Relief Agency," *U.S. News and World Report*, August 4, 2014, www.usnews.com/.

235 Cuba's ties to Venezuela have been an important aspect. Venezuela has substantial deposits of rare-earth minerals vital for most every technology product, the largest proven oil reserves in the world, among the world's largest gold deposits, and a vast array of other mineral resources. It also has an important strategic location for commodity shipping routes, excellent ports, and extensive coastal areas along the Caribbean and the Atlantic Ocean, some islands, and substantial land areas on the Amazon—possibly the richest and largest unexplored area of the world for minerals. See Wikipedia, *List of Countries by Proven Oil Reserves*, https://en.wikipedia.org/ (accessed May 3, 2022); Investopedia, *10 Countries with the Most Natural Resources*, June 25, 2019, www.investopedia.com/; *Latin American Herald Tribune*, "Venezuela Confirms Coltan Deposits, $100 Billion in Gold Reserves," February 4, 2019, www.laht.com/.

236 The known (or supposedly known) list and variety of CIA front companies is breath-taking. See, for example, Jar2, *CIA Front Companies*, http://jar2.com/ (accessed September 2, 2021); Jeff Stein, "The Biggest Little CIA Shop You've Never Heard of," *Newsweek*, November 14, 2013, www.newsweek.com/; Walt Hickey, "25 Cutting Edge Firms Founded by the CIA," *Business Insider*, August 11, 2012, www.businessinsider.com/; James Corbett, "CIA Front Companies: How Much of the Economy is owned by 'The Company'?" *FourWinds10*, November 4, 2011, http://fourwinds10.com/.

companies can even be technology companies—in the sense that they may have some business of their own, to help conceal operations and obtain some revenue. Front organizations can also serve as political content designers and diffusers involving any or all of the functions discussed previously.[237] Venture capital funds set up by an intelligence agency—such as the CIA—might assist, seeking to gain access to natural resources or markets after a targeted government is deposed.[238]

Data clouds are very important to organizations involved in socio-political manipulation. Consultants specialized in diffusion—often data analytics firms that mine social media information compiled in clouds—can craft strategies. In this way, social media networks can be turned into a platform for destabilization, even when the companies that own them are unaware.[239] Spreading false information is another tactic that often goes unnoticed and can be very difficult (if not impossible) to correct.[240]

Political content designers, data analytics companies, and intelligence contractors can be assisted by apps that track individual location, contacts, and preferences. App developers routinely gain access to such data to improve their software and can sell access—along with the social media network oligopolists to which they are linked. During the last decade, the latter were found to have used such data to track location, analyze contacts, and mine preferences.[241]

237 See Wayne Madsen, *The Mayor Purveyor of 'Fake News' is the CIA-Corporate Complex*, Strategic Culture Foundation, November 28, 2016, www.strategic-culture.org/; Stein, "Biggest Little CIA Shop."

238 See In-Q-Tel, *1999–2019, Strategic Investor*; Yanuzzi, "In-Q-Tel"; Paletta, "The CIA's Venture Capital Firm."

239 See Casey Newton, "Why these Facebook Research Scandals are Different: How the Company Found Itself in the Biggest Crisis since Cambridge Analytica," *The Verge*, September 23, 2021, www.theverge.com/; Carole Cadwalladr, "Fresh Cambridge Analytica Leak 'Shows Global Manipulation is Out of Control': Company's Work in 68 Countries Laid Bare with Release of More than 100,000 Documents," *The Guardian*, January 4, 2020, www.theguardian.com/; Julia C. Wong, "The Cambridge Analytica Scandal Changed the World—But it didn't Change Facebook," *The Guardian*, March 18, 2019, www.theguardian.com/; Deepa Seetharaman and Kirsten Grind, "Lax Data Policies Haunt Facebook: Approach to Policing those with Access to User Information Led to Company's Crisis," *Wall Street Journal*, March 21, 2018, A1.

240 Peter Dizikes, "Study: On Twitter, False News Travels Faster than News Stories. Research Project Finds Humans, not Bots, are Primarily Responsible for Spread of Misleading Information," *MIT News*, March 8, 2018, https://news.mit.edu/; Robinson Meyer, "The Grim Conclusions of the Largest-Ever Study of Fake News: Falsehoods Almost Always Beat Out the Truth on Twitter, Penetrating Further, Faster and Deeper into the Social Network than Accurate Information," *The Atlantic*, March 8, 2018, www.theatlantic.com/. See also Olivia Solon and Sam Levin, "How Google's Search Algorithm Spreads False Information with a Rightwing Bias," *The Guardian*, December 16, 2016, www.theguardian.com/.

241 See Carole Cadwalladr and Emma Graham-Harrison, "Facebook Accused of Conducting Mass Surveillance through its Apps: Company gathered Data from Texts and Photos of Users and their Friends, Court Case Claims," *The Guardian*, May 25, 2018, www.theguardian.com/.

Tracking location is very important for planning demonstrations—a matter facilitated by smartphone apps.[242]

Tracking data and social media can be important for destabilization programs in which a political candidate is to be discredited. For the companies involved concealing their participation is a standard—and expected—practice. That may not be too difficult to engineer, given the nature of social media platforms. This was the case with one of the best-known international data analytics companies, whose top executive reportedly claimed that his organization "put information into the bloodstream of the internet, and then, and then watch it grow, give it a little push every now and again."[243] Entrapment can also be part of the manipulation repertory, as the same company's executive reportedly claimed it could "send women to seduce a politician and set up hidden cameras."[244]

Censorship or blocking of social media communications can accompany socio-political manipulation. During the last decade, for example, tens of thousands of accounts of Iranians, Russians, Chinese, Venezuelans, and Cubans who expressed opinions contrarian to those of the U.S. government were reportedly blocked or deleted.[245] And, in an example of what could be considered collusion of a social media oligopolist with the U.S. government, Twitter suspended accounts of Cuba's journalists when they prepared to report on shortages caused by U.S. sanctions.[246]

Among other examples of censorship, Google reportedly deleted 210 YouTube accounts, Twitter deleted over 200,000 personal accounts, and

242 See Charlie Savage, "Intelligence Analysts Use Smartphone Location Data without Warrants, Memo Says," *New York Times*, January 22, 2021, www.nytimes.com/; *NBC News*, "Location Data Companies Tracking and Selling Smartphone Users' Information, Report Reveals," December 19, 2019, www.nbcnews.com/. During the last decade, some software tools—such as Apple's "Differential Privacy"—made it possible to collect vast amounts of individual data without specifically identifying anyone. See Ian Bogost, "Apple's Empty Grandstanding about Privacy: The Company Enables the Surveillance that Supposedly Offends its Values," *The Atlantic*, January 31, 2019, www.theatlantic.com/; Andy Greenberg, "Apple's 'Differential Privacy' is About Collecting your Data—But not Your Data," *Wired*, June 13, 2016, www.wired.com/.

243 Quoted in Rebecca Ballhaus, "Firm Pitches Entrapment Tactics on Video," *Wall Street Journal*, March 20, 2018, A6. See also Wikipedia, *Cambridge Analytica*, and its *Facebook-Cambridge Analytica Data Scandal*, https://en.wikipedia.org/ (both accessed June 9, 2022).

244 Quoted in Ballhaus, "Firm Pitches Entrapment."

245 See Anya Parampil, "U.S. Government Censorship? Social Media Giants Disappear Accounts of Iranian, Venezuelan Academics, Journalists," *The Grayzone*, January 30, 2020; https://thegrayzone.com/; *France24*, "Twitter Blocks Accounts of Iranian State Media Outlets," July 20, 2019, www.france24.com/; Ben Norton, "Twitter Relying on US/European Government-Funded Regime-Change Groups to Crack Down on Foreign States," *The Grayzone*, August 24, 2019, https://thegrayzone.com/; *Reuters*, "Iran Says Twitter Shut Legitimate Accounts, but not Anti-Government Ones," September 16, 2018, www.reuters.com/.

246 *TeleSur*, "Twitter Suspends Accounts of Cuba's Largest Media Outlets," September 12, 2019, www.telesurenglish.net/.

Facebook removed 7 pages, 3 groups, and 5 private accounts during the initial weeks of the Hong Kong 2019 protests.[247] And this occurred reportedly without provision of any proof about what they alleged the account holders were attempting to do. Simultaneously, they reportedly retained accounts favorable to the protests.[248]

To apparently facilitate the Hong Kong protests, Apple reportedly provided an app—purchased through its App Store—that allowed protesters to track police movements, plan attacks on officers, and block roads and metro stations.[249] Among other planned actions were repeated blockages of a major global airport terminal, and closure of the entire airport—with thousands of flight cancellations over a short period of time—that inflicted severe damage on the tourism and financial services-dependent economy.[250] Also, the use of incendiary devices and bombs, inflicting extensive damage on shops and public buildings, beating up individuals thought to be unsympathetic, and attacking government representatives who tried to serve as negotiators.[251] And a university campus with one of the largest enrollments in Asia had to be closed for several months—causing the loss of an entire semester to all students—due to severe destruction and fires.[252]

For its part, mainstream U.S. news media largely alleged that the demonstrations were about "democracy," when the real sources of unrest were reportedly rising inequality and a lack of housing affordability—due to the immense power wielded by local land development oligopolists and the low wages paid relative to the cost of living.[253] Hong Kong billionaires' wealth—as a share of its GDP—is the highest in the world, and almost two-thirds has been obtained

247 Darryl Coote, "Facebook, Twitter Remove Chinese Accounts Attacking Hong Kong Protests," *UPI*, August 19, 2019, www.upi.com/; Boris Djuric, "Twitter Closed Accounts of Chinese Opponents of the Hong Kong Demonstration," *Newswire*, August 21, 2019, https://newswire .net/.

248 Djuric, "Twitter Closed"; Coote, "Facebook, Twitter."

249 Verna Yu, "'Protecting Rioters': China Warns Apple over App that Tracks Hong Kong Police—State Media Says 'Poisonous' App Made Apple an Accomplice in the Hong Kong Protests," *The Guardian*, October 9, 2019, www.theguardian.com/.

250 Helen Regan, Ben Westcott, James Griffiths and Jessie Yeung, "Hong Kong Grounds All Flights as Protest Paralyzes Airport," *CNN*, August 19, 2019, https://edition.cnn.com/.

251 See Dan Cohen, "Behind a Made-for-TV Hong Kong Protest Narrative, Washington is Backing Nativism and Mob Violence," *The Grayzone*, August 17, 2019, https://thegrayzone.com/.

252 See Ken Moritsugu and Kelvin K. Chan, "Hong Kong Polytechnic University Campus Burns as Protesters, Police Clash," *Global News*, November 18, 2019, https://globalnews.ca/.

253 *The Economist*, "Hong Kong's Tycoons: Check Your Privilege," May 22, 2021, 54–55; Alexandra Stevenson and Jin Wu, "Tiny Apartments and Punishing Work Hours: The Economic Roots of Hong Kong's Protests," *New York Times*, July 22, 2019, www.nytimes.com/; *The Economist*, "Hong Kong: Property and Protest—The Link between the Unrest and the Unbearable Expense of Housing," August 24, 2019, 31–32; Michelle Wong, "Why the Wealth Gap? Hong Kong's Disparity between Rich and Poor is Greatest in 45 Years, so what can be Done?" *South China Morning Post*, September 27, 2018, www.scmp.com/; Elson Tong, "Hong Kong Household

through real estate speculation—leading to some of the highest rents in the world per square meter and the highest property prices.[254] Although frustrations with democratic representation undoubtedly existed, it became clear that the underlying causes of the protests were economic—due to serious injustices related to housing, rents, and affordability.

Links to certain American foundations and think tanks—and government representatives—were reportedly uncovered, indicating that the Hong Kong demonstrations and violence were apparently not spontaneous, as the mainstream U.S. media had reported.[255] Even the U.S. Congress chose to encourage the protests—with both the Republican and Democratic parties passing resolutions that would have been considered gross interference in U.S. domestic affairs had any nation adopted them.[256] And the demonstrations occurred during the trade war initiated by the U.S. government against China, a few months after a ban on Huawei's technology, and after multiple bans on technology transfer—leading many to suspect it was an orchestrated operation aimed at destabilizing both Hong Kong and China.[257]

A symptom of the overarching priority attached to domination was that the bans on technology transfer occurred despite the fact that American oligopolies have benefited greatly from their China operations over the years. Almost half of all American corporations surveyed by the end of the last decade reported that their businesses in China were significantly more profitable than elsewhere—with consistent annual increases during the decade.[258] Important among these was Apple, whose sales in that nation provided as much as one-fifth of total annual revenue over the years.[259] General Motors, long an American industrial icon that pioneered many vehicle technologies, was

---

Income Inequality Rises to Record High, Census Shows," *Hong Kong Free Press*, June 9, 2017, www.hongkongfp.com/.

254 See *The Economist*, "Hong Kong: Property and Protest"; its "Our Crony-Capitalism Index: Planet Plutocrat," March 15, 2014, 57–58; and the figure "The Crony-Capitalist Index," 58 (based on data from Forbes, IMF, World Economic Forum).

255 See Steven Lee Myers, "In Hong Kong Protests China Angrily Connects Dots Back to U.S.," *New York Times*, September 5, 2019, www.nytimes.com/; Ajit Singh, "Hong Kong's Opposition Unites with Washington Hardliners to 'Preserve the US's Own Political and Economic Interests,'" *The Grayzone*, November 22, 2019, https://thegrayzone.com/; Mnar Muhawesh, "The NED Strikes Again: How Neocon Money is Funding Hong Kong Protests," *MintPress News*, November 9, 2019, https://mintpressnews.cn/; Cohen, "Behind a Made-for-TV."

256 See Daniel Flatley and Justin Sink, "Congress Passes Bill Supporting Hong Kong Protests," *Bloomberg*, November 20, 2019, www.bloomberg.com/.

257 See Singh, "Hong Kong's Opposition"; Muhawesh, "NED Strikes Again."

258 *The Economist*, "American Firms in China: Still Worth It—Despite Political Complications, America Inc. is still Doing Surprisingly Well in China," January 4, 2020, 45–46.

259 *The Economist*, "Apple: The Great Successor's Second Act," August 28, 2021, 54. Apple also contracted during the last decade to have its new Mac Pro desktop computer manufactured in China—see Tripp Mickle and Yoko Kubota, "Apple Picks China for Production of New Mac Pro," *Wall Street Journal*, June 29, 2019, A1.

practically saved from liquidation—and from having to accept larger federal bailouts (2008–2009)—by the magnitude of its revenues in China.[260] General Electric, over the years a pioneer of innumerable technologies—with over 100 factories in China—would have likely been liquidated during the last decade, were it not for the revenues it obtained in that nation.[261] Yet, the importance attached to technological and geopolitical domination overshadowed these realities.

Enforcement

The enforcement of domination inevitably links technology oligopolistic power, commodity chains, arbitrage, hierarchic controls, and geopolitics with the martial domain. The binding agent for enforcement is raw military power—based on the most advanced warfare and surveillance technologies that contractors can provide. Domination thus ultimately depends on a platform of diverse military capabilities that can be deployed anywhere. And the platform's expense seems to have no bounds.[262] No nation in history was ever able to amass the range and depth of military power that the United States currently possesses.[263] And no nation that defies its supremacy can consider itself safe from the reach of that power.[264]

260 See Bill Vlasic, "G.M., Once a Powerhouse, Pleads for Bailout," *New York Times*, November 11, 2008, www.nytimes.com/; Chris Isidore "GM: Almost Out of Cash, No. 1 Automaker Posts Huge Loss—Says it has Made Case to Washington for Rescue," *CNN Money*, November 26, 2008, https://money.cnn.com/.

261 See Thomas Gryta and Ted Mann, "GE Powered the American Century—Then It Burned Out," *Wall Street Journal*, December 14, 2018, www.wsj.com/.

262 Early concerns about the rising expense and power of the military apparatus and its contractors were voiced by none other than President (and former General) Dwight Eisenhower, days before the end of his term—see Yale Law School, Avalon Law Project, *Military-Industrial Complex Speech, Dwight D. Eisenhower, 1961*, https://avalon.yale.law.edu/ (accessed June 5, 2022). U.S. National Security Council, *NSC 68: United States Objectives and Programs for National Security*, April 14, 1950 (www.mtholyoke.edu/), Part IX—is thought to have set the basis for the creation of the "military-industrial complex" that President Eisenhower denounced.

263 The drive for global power can be traced to the 1890s, when advances in fuels and metallurgical technologies required greater and more diverse supplies of raw materials. Brooks Adams's *The New Empire* (New York: Macmillan, 1902) and Charles Conant's "The Economic Basis of 'Imperialism'," *North American Review* 167 (1898), 326–40, were influential at the time. Two sentences from Conant's article (p. 326) are noteworthy: "Almost as if by magic, the importance of naval power as the advance agent of commercial supremacy has flashed upon the mind of the country. The irresistible tendency to expansion, which leads the growing tree to burst every barrier, which drove the Goths, the Vandals, and finally our Saxon ancestors in successive and irresistible waves over the decadent provinces of Rome, seems again in operation, demanding new outlets of American capital and new opportunities for American enterprise."

264 The notion of gaining—and enforcing—global supremacy found support in the views of Halford Mackinder on British imperial power. Ludwig von Mises's arguments on the need for supremacy based on liberal principles were also influential. See Halford J. Mackinder, *Britain and the British Seas* (London: Heinemann, 1902), chapters XVIII–XX, and his *Democratic Ideals and Reality: A Study in the Politics of Reconstruction* (New York: Holt, 1919), chapters III–V; Ludwig von Mises, *Liberalismus* (Stuttgart: Fischer, 1927), parts I, III. In the 1940s, Nicholas Spykman's *America's*

Enforcement Platform

The enforcement platform can involve a vast repertory of weapons and scenarios—such as deep ocean robots, engineered pathogens, nanotech devices, cyberattack software, and outer space. The latter—a most important warfare "frontier"—depends greatly on earthbound commodity chain inputs, arbitrage, and tech control hierarchies. Rare minerals, requiring complex and expensive refining processes, shipping, and surveillance, are essential for this scenario. The United States has been estimated to spend about three times as much as the rest of the world on military space projects—reflecting the high priority given to area. And this level of spending occurred before the creation of the Space Force at the end of the last decade—a matter likely to increase future allocations considerably.[265]

Control over space rests on three vital functions—surveillance, navigation, and warfare. All are related to earthbound enforcement of geopolitical interests and to commodity chain and arbitrage controls. For surveillance, the U.S. Space Surveillance Network has about two dozen known centers around the world.[266] These bases are important for gathering intelligence, guiding missiles and spacecraft, and monitoring commodity flows. Navigation and surveillance have many routine military and civilian uses—boundaries between them becoming blurred. The Pentagon's Defense Advanced Research Projects Agency (DARPA) Blackjack program reflects the ongoing fusion, given its declared intention to place military equipment—such as sensors and targeting tools—in commercial satellites.[267] This would render commercial space operations inseparable from the military ones.

Strategy in World Politics: The United States and the Balance of Power (New York: Harcourt, Brace, 1942), and his *The Geography of Peace* (New York: Harcourt, Brace, 1944) were influential in charting a postwar agenda. Spykman's emphasis on maritime power was largely complementary to Mackinder's focus on territorial domination. Implicitly, both approaches had control over commodity chains and arbitrage at their core. An important articulation in favor of global hegemony at the end of the Cold War was posited by Zbigniew Brzezinski—see his *The Grand Chessboard: American Primacy and its Geostrategic Objectives* (New York: Basic Books, 1997), 3–4, 10–11, 30–38. His earlier formulations were also influential among foreign policy and military elites—see Charles Krauthammer, "Universal Dominion: Toward a Unipolar World," *The National Interest* 18 (1989), 46–49; Thomas P. M. Barnett, *The Pentagon's New Map: War and Peace in the Twenty-First Century* (New York: Putnam, 2004).

265 See Theresa Hitchens, "Space Force: What is it Good for?" *Breaking Defense*, July 15, 2019, www.breakingdefense.com/. A phrase prominently posted at the Pentagon's Combined Space Operations Center reflects the overarching objective: "this is where space superiority begins"—*The Economist*, "Using the Force," July 20, 2019, 18.

266 *The Economist*, "Using the Force," 19.

267 Defense Advanced Research Projects Agency and Paul Thomas, *Blackjack*, www.darpa.mil/ (accessed June 17, 2022); John Keller, "Two Companies Join Project to Design SWaP-C-Optimized Communications and Surveillance Satellites," *Military and Aerospace Electronics*, January 9, 2019, www.militaryaerospace.com/.

The third function enables war in outer space *and* on earth—dimensions that are intertwined and depend on commodity chains and arbitrage for resources.[268] Among the earliest space warfare missions may be the destruction of other nations' satellites and space vehicles, whenever enforcement of domination is made to justify it.[269] The possibility that few lives might be lost seems to ensure that this warfare mode will occur—nations that own the targeted craft also likely finding themselves under threat from economic sanctions and destabilization programs (discussed previously). Space warfare is set to be handled by the National Space Defense Center—created during the last decade.[270] Oligopolistic contractors—such as Boeing, Rockwell Collins, United Technologies, and Lockheed Martin, among others—are heavily involved and can be expected to benefit immensely.

Among third-function technologies are hypersonic missiles and nuclear weapons that can be launched from space *or* earth. Improved precision and evasion of interception have cemented the assumption that a nuclear first strike can avoid retaliation.[271] Advances in nuclear weapons, on their part, have increased explosive power substantially—along with radiation output.[272] These developments have led some Pentagon elites to believe that a nuclear war can be "won."[273] Disabling a targeted nation's cybernetic, communication, and nuclear military infrastructures simultaneously—as a first-strike attack is launched—would be essential.[274] The rationale and its execution—unrealistic

268 The importance of commodity chain flows and arbitrage for Space Force missiles and satellites was stressed by shortages of ammonium perchlorate during the last decade. See Andy Pasztor, "Rocket Fuel Sparks Debate: Proposed Use of a Propellant Made Overseas Leads to U.S. Security Concerns," *Wall Street Journal*, December 30, 2017, B2.

269 *The Economist*, "Using the Force," 18.

270 See Air Force Space Command, *National Space Defense Center Transitions to 24/7 Operations*, January 26, 2018. www.afspc.af.mil/; Oriana Pawlyk, "U.S. Air Force Preparing for War in Space," *Military.com*, April 4, 2017, www.military.com/.

271 See Mitchell, "U.S. Must End Nuclear 'First-Strike'"; Dean, "U.S. Confirms First Strike Policy."

272 The current cost of nuclear weapon programs is difficult to ascertain. In 1996, shortly after the end of the Cold War—when nuclear weapon spending had presumably declined—the cost of such programs was estimated to be over $5 trillion, an amount that exceeded that of all other peacetime weapon programs (in real dollars)—see Stephen I. Schwartz, *Atomic Audit: The Costs and Consequences of U.S. Nuclear Weapons since 1940* (Washington: Brookings Institution Press, 1998), chapters 8, 10, Appendix A.

273 Mitchell, "U.S. Must End Nuclear 'First-Strike'." Number of warheads may be an important support for the first-strike mindset. The U.S. reportedly had stockpiled 3,750 nuclear warheads, with an additional 2,000 available (but awaiting dismantlement) as of mid-2021—Chandelis Duster and Nicole Gaouette, "Biden Administration Reveals Number of Nuclear Weapons in U.S. Stockpile," *CNN*, October 5, 2021, www.cnn.com/; Kelsey Reichmann, "Here's How Many Nuclear Warheads Exist, and Which Countries Own Them," *Defense News*, June 16, 2019, www.defensenews.com/.

274 The possibility that a conflagration may occur by accident—without the possibility of disabling a targeted nation's infrastructure—needs to be considered. The Pentagon has long been regarded as negligent in its handling of nuclear weaponry—see Wikipedia, *List of Military Nuclear Accidents*,

as they might be—should not be underestimated, as they eliminate the notion of "mutually assured destruction" that prevented nuclear war during the past seven decades.[275]

The all too realistic scenario that the earth's atmosphere would be covered with soot and ash—leading to the extinction of species that depend on plant life or sunlight—was apparently disregarded by the first-strike mindset. As higher explosive power (and radiation) is necessary for a first strike, this must also be taken into account. Nuclear weapons depend greatly on uranium refinement technology. This vital but highly toxic mineral is closely connected to far-flung commodity chains that require strategic surveillance from space and earth. Negative health impacts of uranium use—and its placement in munitions to increase kinetic power—have raised many concerns in recent decades.[276] And, uranium processing and mining sites have been found to have dismal work and safety conditions—involving illnesses and forced labor.[277]

Unmanned Aerial Vehicles (UAVs) and their warfare and surveillance capabilities are also enabled by the third function. In line to replace combat and surveillance aircraft, this technology depends extensively on satellite communications, mapping, AI software, and data clouds. Their future widespread usage rests on their capacity to increase kill ratios and the avoidance of American military casualties.[278] Combat pilots are most expensive to train, and replacement costs are substantial. In contrast, UAVs require ground-station (or satellite) AI software for guidance and a programmer. These features have helped

https://en.wikipedia.org/ (accessed June 30, 2022); Jaya Tiwari and Cleve J. Gray, *U.S. Nuclear Weapons Accidents*, Center for Defense Information, November 13, 2011, www.cdi.org/.

275 See Johnstone, *From MAD to Madness*; Edward Kaplan, *To Kill Nations: American Strategy in the Air-Atomic Age and the Rise of Mutually Assured Destruction* (Ithaca: Cornell University Press, 2015), chapters 5, 7, 8.

276 Especially in war zones—see Wikipedia, *Depleted Uranium*, and its *International Coalition to Ban Uranium Weapons*, https://en.wikipedia.org/ (accessed June 8, 2022); Mike Ludwig, "Iraqi Kids Test Positive for Depleted Uranium Remnants near Former U.S. Air Base," *Truthout*, September 19, 2019, https://truthout.org/; Andrew Womack, "The Latest Nuclear War: Does the Use of Depleted Uranium Armaments and Armors Constitute a War Crime?" *Vermont Law Review* 41 (2016), 407.

277 John Vidal, "Uranium Workers Dying After Time at Namibia Mine, Report Warns: Miners Who Dug Ore to Supply the Military Found to be Dying of Cancers and Other Illnesses at Rio Tinto's Rössing Mine," *The Guardian*, April 15, 2014, www.theguardian.com/; David Rose, "'Safe' Uranium that Left a Town Contaminated: They Were Told Depleted Uranium Was Not Hazardous; Now, 23 Years after a U.S. Arms Plant Closed, Workers and Residents Have Cancer—and Experts Say their Suffering Shows the Use of Such Weapons May Be a War Crime," *The Guardian*, November 18, 2007, www.theguardian.com/.

278 The spread of U.S. military drone bases around the world indicates the growing importance of this technology. See Wikiwand, *List of United States Drone Bases*, www.wikiwand.com/ (accessed June 9, 2022); Nick Turse, "Secret U.S. Military Documents Reveal a Constellation of American Military Bases Across Africa: Newly Disclosed Numbers Contradict More than a Decade's Worth of Dissembling by U.S. Africa Command," *The Nation*, April 27, 2017, www.thenation.com/.

UAV contractors greatly, including those that provide accessories—such as targeting and navigation software, missiles, and satellites. These contractors are among the wealthiest and most powerful military technology oligopolists—among them Boeing, Lockheed Martin, and Northrop Grumman.[279]

Multimodality

Tech-intensive, earthbound warfare modes—designed for "anywhere, anytime" action—are also enabled by the third function. They depend on satellite communications, real-time terrain surveillance, mapping, data clouds—and tactical missile support from space to destroy land and sea targets. These modes require speed, are often hybrid—reaching across multiple technical domains—and can be deployed in conjunction with destabilization programs.[280] *Their multimodal technological capabilities are part of a "fast and lean" form of warfare that can be used to control commodity chain or arbitrage scenarios, neutralize disruptions, and otherwise impose geopolitical dictates.*

Mercenary warfare companies can be contracted as enforcement agents, and they tend to (conveniently) operate outside the rules of war.[281] Much the same applies to intelligence outsourcing, a multimodal segment that often uses advanced surveillance technologies—such as UAVs, satellite imagery, and data clouds—with minimal accountability.[282] Deployment thus becomes a contractual business matter—operating above issues of sovereignty, local laws,

279 *Market Watch*, "Military Surveillance Drones Market 2021: Top Manufacturers, Industry Demands, Top Key Players, Industry Analysis, Forecast by 2025," October 25, 2021, www.marketwatch.com/.

280 The term "hybrid warfare" was initially used to refer to combat that uses diverse weaponry and tactics—see Frank G. Hoffman, *Conflict in the 21st Century: The Rise of Hybrid Wars* (Arlington, VA: Potomac Institute for Policy Studies, 2007)—but can now encompass "soft" tactics (sabotage, disinformation, assassinations). See also Theresa Hitchens, *DARPA's Mosaic Warfare—Multi Domain Ops, But Faster*, Breaking Defense, September 10, 2019, https://breakingdefense.com/.

281 The privatization of warfare through mercenary armies has raised concerns. See Sean McFate, *The Modern Mercenary: Private Armies and what they Mean for World Order* (New York: Oxford University Press, 2017); P.W. Singer, *Corporate Warriors: The Rise of the Privatized Military Industry* (Ithaca: Cornell University Press, 2008), Part I. An early example was Blackwater—created in 1997 as a security company, it was later contracted by the CIA and the Pentagon. It became known for its violence in Iraq after 2003 and was later to change its name to Xe (2009) and to Academi (2011)—see Jeremy Scahill, *Blackwater: The Rise of the World's Most Powerful Mercenary Army* (New York: MJF, 2012).

282 See Kit Klarenberg, "Bellingcat Funded by U.S. and U.K. Intelligence Contractors that Aided Extremists in Syria," *The Grayzone*, October 9, 2021, https://thegrayzone.com/; Tim Shorrock, "5 Corporations Now Dominate Our Privatized Intelligence Industry: This Unaccountable Oligarchy of Spies Controls the Information that Guides Our Military and Civilian Leaders," *The Nation*, September 8, 2016, www.thenation.com/; and his *Spies for Hire: The Secret World of Intelligence Outsourcing* (New York: Simon and Schuster, 2009).

moral principles, or human rights.[283] The U.S. government's rejection of the International Court of Justice is undoubtedly important in this regard.[284] Possibly among the most important reasons for this refusal may be the U.S. government's past deployment of chemicals as weapons, the use of fraud and deception to start highly destructive wars, the incidence of massacres and war crimes, and the numerous innocent casualties that have resulted over the years.[285]

The "customer" (the Pentagon) thus places itself as both judge and jury, on such matters as whether the kill ratios achieved—by any contractor or by its own forces—justify the quantum of innocent civilian casualties.[286] Such

283 The notion that a nation (the United States in this case) and its military apparatus should be motivated by base self-interest first and foremost—a precept applied in rational choice theory to individual consumers—seems to be at the core of this practice. International law can thus become largely irrelevant when imposing geopolitical dictates—see Jens D. Ohlin, *The Assault on International Law* (New York: Oxford University Press, 2015), chapters 2–4.

284 See Sean D. Murphy, *The United States and the International Court of Justice: Coping with Antinomies*, Law School, George Washington University, 2008, https://scholarship.law.gwu.edu/; International Court of Justice, *The Court: History*, www.icj-cij.org/ (accessed June 5, 2022).

285 Use of the Agent Orange defoliant as a war chemical in Vietnam is one example. See Wikipedia, *Agent Orange*, https://en.wikipedia.org/ (accessed June 8, 2022); Jennifer Newton, "Four Decades after Agent Orange—Heartbreaking Pictures show Babies in Vietnam are Being Born with Horrific Defects," *Daily Mail*, April 25, 2014, www.dailymail.co.uk/; Gary G. Kohls, *War Crimes: Agent Orange, Monsanto, Dow Chemical and Other Legacies of the Vietnam War*, Global Research, Centre for Research on Globalization, November 13, 2015, www.globalresearch.ca/. Thousands of American veterans who served in or near the zones targeted for Agent Orange spraying died of diverse cancers and maladies over the years—see U.S. Department of Veteran Affairs, *Public Health: Veterans; Diseases Associated with Agent Orange*, www.publichealth.va.gov/ (accessed June 9, 2022). Fraudulent information used as justification to start wars has long been documented—see, for example, Julian Borger, "There were no Weapons of Mass Destruction in Iraq: 1,625 U.N. and U.S. Inspectors Spent Two Years Searching 1,700 Sites at a Cost of more than $1Bn. Yesterday they Delivered their Verdict," *The Guardian*, October 7, 2004, www.theguardian.com/; Don D. Guttenplan, "When Presidents Lie to Make a War: Fifty Years on we Know the Trigger for War with Vietnam was a Fiction," *The Guardian*, August 2, 2014, www.theguardian.com/; UPI, *The Pentagon Papers*, 1971, www.upi.com/. See also Kendrick Oliver, *The My Lai Massacre in American History and Memory* (Manchester: Manchester University Press, 2006); Deborah Nelson, *The War behind Me: Vietnam Veterans Confront the Truth about U.S. War Crimes* (New York: Basic Books, 2008); Wikipedia, *Operation Rolling Thunder*, https://en.wikipedia.org/ (accessed March 14, 2022).

286 Rising tolls of civilian casualties in U.S. military interventions have attracted attention during the past three decades. See John Tirman, *The Deaths of Others: The Fate of Civilians in America's Wars* (New York: Oxford University Press, 2015), chapters 1, 2, 9–11; James A. Lucas, *U.S. has Killed more than 20 Million People in 37 'Victim' Nations since World War II*, Global Research, Centre for Global Research, June 30, 2019, www.globalresearch.ca/; *The Economist*, "Bombs Astray: How Many Civilians Does America Kill in Air Strikes? The Pentagon Doesn't Know," April 6, 2019, 21–22. See also MIT Center for International Studies, *Iraq: The Human Cost*, https://web.mit.edu/ (accessed June 10, 2022); Gilbert Burnham, Shannon Doocy, Elizabeth Dzeng, Riyadh Lafta, *et al.*, *The Human Cost of the War in Iraq: A Mortality Study, 2002–2006*, Bloomberg School of Public Health, Johns Hopkins University, www.stat.columbia.edu/ (accessed March 17, 2022); Wikipedia, *Civilian Casualties in the War in Afghanistan (2001-present)*, https://en.wikipedia.org/ (accessed April 17, 2022).

ratios, a performance measure partially derived from marketing, are an important indicator for mercenary warfare contractors.[287] Stocks of companies that engage in these and related forms of warfare are traded in Wall Street, much as those of any other company—some having been created as Silicon Valley "startups," with capital from private sources, hedge funds, or government entities.[288]

The spectrum of enforcement possibilities that multimodal warfare encompasses can be vast. Actions can be labeled "special operations" and, although often executed by mercenary contractors, can also involve conventional military units. The latter often include units of subordinate nations—especially those enlisted in NATO—to spread responsibility and costs.[289] This is convenient, inasmuch as it is more difficult to blame several nations than one—for violations of sovereignty and human rights, war crimes, displacement of populations, or destruction of infrastructure. And many such operations can be labeled "anti-terrorist" to justify them.[290] By the end of the last decade the Pentagon or its mercenary contractors had reportedly intervened through "special ops" in 85 nations over a three-year period.[291]

287 See U.S. Army, *Force Ratio Calculator*, https://rdl.train.army.mil/; SF, *Inventory to Sales Ratio*, https://studyfinance.com/ (both accessed June 9, 2022).

288 See *The Economist*, "The Midas of Mordor: Peter Thiel is Reinventing America's Military-Industrial Complex," September 25, 2021, 58; Peter Lattman, "Cerberus to Buy Defense Contractor DynCorp: Private-Equity Firm Pursues Broader Government-Related Business with $1 Billion Deal, as LBOs Make a Comeback," *Wall Street Journal*, April 13, 2010, B3.

289 See MIT Center for International Studies, *Iraq*; United Nations Assistance Mission in Afghanistan, *Midyear Update on the Protection of Civilians in Armed Conflict*, July 30, 2019, https://unama.unmissions.org/; Horace Campbell, *Global NATO and the Catastrophic Failure in Libya* (New York: Monthly Review Press, 2013). As a subsidiary of the Pentagon, NATO has contributed to enrich American techno-military contractors greatly over the years—see NATO, *Defence Expenditure of NATO Countries (2011–19)*, March 14, 2019, www.nato.int/; Gökan Ergöçün, "NATO Countries to Spend Over $1T for Defense in 2019," *AA*, June 25, 2019, www.aa.com.tr/.

290 See Brett Wilkins, "'Counter-Terrorism'? Two Decades after 9/11, New Interactive Map Details Footprint of US War Machine in 85 Countries," *Common Dreams*, February 25, 2021, www.commondreams.com/; Gian Gentile, *Wrong Turn: America's Deadly Embrace of Counterinsurgency* (New York: New Press, 2013). High cost and rising human tolls have attracted much concern about counter-terrorism operations over the years—see Brown University, Cost of War Project, *Costs of the 20-Year War on Terror: $8 Trillion and 900,000 Deaths*, www.brown.edu/ (accessed June 5, 2022).

291 George Petras, Karina Zaiets and Veronica Bravo, "Exclusive: US Antiterrorism Operations Touched 85 Countries in the Last 3 Years," *USA Today*, February 25, 2021, www.usatoday.com/; Nick Turse, "Special Operations Forces Continue to Expand Around the World—Without Congressional Oversight: Even Congress Doesn't Know the Extent of American Military Reach," *The Nation*, July 17, 2018, www.thenation.com/. A vast worldwide network of U.S. military bases is part of this panorama—the largest ever deployed by any nation—almost all at locations relevant for surveillance of commodity flows. See Wikipedia, *File: US Military Bases in the World*, https://en.wikipedia.org/ (accessed June 9, 2022); David Vine, *Base Nation* (New York: Metropolitan Books, 2015).

The rising frequency and reach of "special ops," the numerous mercenary outfits, the vast array of warfare technologies, the many innocent casualties, and the Pentagon's wealthy contractors have led some specialists in recent decades to note that the United States is engaged in a state of *permanent war*.[292] Warfare that seems to have no bounds—in its expense, brutality, or its negative effects on humanity and nature. Warfare that greatly enriches a circumscribed group of oligopolistic corporations, whose executives are at the very top of the American income and wealth pyramid.[293] Warfare and techno-military corporations that are essentially sustained by American taxpayers, at immense cost to themselves—a matter that is usually ignored by the public and the media.

Taxpaying

Enforcement and techno-military contracting are supported by taxation rather than markets. This important aspect of domination must always be kept in mind. Spending and contracting are therefore sustained by taxpayers. And the latter—forcibly and under threat of punishment—have no choice but to contribute.

Taxes are thus the source of contractors' vast surpluses and wealth. Allocations of taxpayer funds cannot be considered money-capital, as they are *not* derived from market pricing in the capital accumulation dynamic (discussed earlier in this book). And, unlike in the market domain—where possibilities exist for customers to forgo, postpone, or switch purchases—taxpayers do not have such options.

Another aspect is that oligopolistic surpluses obtained through the military apparatus—dependent as they are on taxes—are *contractual* in character and practice. Contractual money collection in the martial domain does *not* involve market exchange. Thus, there is *no* real exchange value to speak of, and neither is there any use value *or* social value. These value modes can only be obtained in market settings, through voluntary purchase (even under oligopolistic conditions).

The term *value* will thus be excised when referring to military contracting and warfare. Only through market exchange—and the use of capital, productive labor, and investment—can value be generated. Notions of value cannot

292 See Rosa Brooks' *How Everything Became War and the Military Became Everything: Tales from the Pentagon* (New York: Simon and Schuster, 2016), chapters 4, 8, 9, 13, 15; Andrew J. Bacevich, *Washington Rules: America's Path to Permanent War* (New York: Metropolitan, 2010), chapters 1, 2, 5, 6; Eric Hobsbawm, *On Empire: America, War, and Global Supremacy* (New York: Pantheon, 2008), chapters II, IV; James Bamford, *A Pretext for War: 9/11, Iraq, and the Abuse of America's Intelligence Agencies* (New York: Anchor, 2005).

293 See Stephen Semler, *The Top 5 Military Contractors Ate $2 Trillion during the Afghanistan War*, Speaking Security, August 23, 2021, https://stephensemler.substack.com/; Sarah Almukhtar and Rod Norland, "What did the U.S. Get for $2 Trillion in Afghanistan?" *New York Times*, December 9, 2019, www.nytimes.com/.

be attached to warfare, as this endeavor typically involves much destruction of value and great waste (even when its deployment might have some moral or legal justification). After all, loss of life—the most precious endowment we have—is part of the destruction of value that warfare perpetrates.

Contractual Money

Tax-funded, contractual money collection cannot be considered analogous to capital accumulation. Only capital that is reproduced through market exchange, investment, and the expenditure of labor power can involve accumulation. The root of such accumulation involves market settings where voluntary purchase is the norm, even when pricing and the terms of exchange are under oligopolistic control. In the discussions of this section, therefore, the term accumulation will not be used to refer to the collection of money through taxpayer-supported contracting.[294]

Contractual amounts tend to be artificial, moreover. Their magnitude is subject to politics, influence, lobbying, bureaucratic dictates—and the system of "legalized corruption" that so characterizes American governance (discussed earlier in this book). Excessive budgets, faulty accounting, waste, delays, and deficient performance are all too common in military contracting. Such practices reflect a lack of accountability that is difficult or impossible to perpetrate in markets—even in oligopolistic ones. It should not surprise, therefore, that the question of whether a major objective of the martial domain is to benefit contractors, at taxpayers' expense, is repeatedly asked.[295]

Bidding processes involving military contracting cannot be considered analogous to markets, moreover—as allocated funds are usually spent regardless of the number of bidders or the amounts involved. Not doing so all too often translates into lesser funding allocations in subsequent years. Cost overruns are common, and delivery deadlines are often violated and extended. Also, cancellation of projects tends to be rare—and contract amounts are often increased after award.

Bidding, furthermore, usually comprises a handful of companies, or in some cases one. The process thus typically involves an oligopolistic scenario, a duopoly, or even a monopoly. Also, the interplay of market supply and demand is absent in the contractual accumulation dynamic. Awarding taxpayer-funded contracts cannot be considered equivalent to market demand—or to the myriad

294 Also for these reasons, consideration of taxpayer-funded, contractual money collection was excluded from the chapter "Accumulation."

295 See Gareth Porter, *America's Permanent War Complex: Eisenhower's Worst Nightmare has Come True, as Defense Mega-Contractors Climb into the Cockpit to Ensure We Stay Overextended*, Global Research, Centre for Global Research, November 18, 2018, www.globalresearch.ca/; David Vine, *The United States of War* (Oakland: University of California Press, 2020), chapters 14–17, and his *Island of Shame* (Princeton: Princeton University Press, 2009), chapters 2, 7.

individual and collective decisions the latter encompasses. And contracting cannot be considered analogous to market supply—not even in a monopolistic sense—as taxpayers are forcibly locked into contributing regardless of whether the purpose of contracts is fulfilled. Contractors, moreover, are not typically accountable to the ultimate "customers"—taxpayers.

And taxpayers have no choice but to pay. They must forcibly accept the contracts—and the weaponry turned out—even when those fall short of expectations. They must also unavoidably accept the actions that will be executed with the weaponry they pay for—no matter how destructive and wasteful they may be. And, unlike in markets—even oligopolistic ones—taxpayers cannot return weaponry to request refunds or compensation. Arbitration and lawsuits—important in market processes—are also impossible for taxpayers to undertake.

The contractual money collection dynamic comprises several entities that deserve to be considered. Inputs, suppliers, processing, and outcomes are part of this dynamic. These are systemic features of techno-military contracting and the enforcement apparatus.

The oligopolistic contractual money collection dynamic can be represented as:

$$T \rightarrow W \rightarrow W' \rightarrow T^Z \text{ where } T^Z = T + \Delta z + \Delta Z$$

with T as initial contractual—taxpayer-provided—money to initiate design or fabrication of weaponry, W as inputs (workers included), and W' the completed weaponry. T^Z represents new contractual—also taxpayer-provided—money disbursed upon completion of W'. The oligopolistic contractual surplus—represented by ΔZ—is obtained through bidding, addressed previously. The quantum of these surpluses can, in whole or in part, be a function of contractors' influence on politicians and officials—inflated budgets and overruns being the norm.

The contractual money surplus created by human toil is represented as Δz—an amount to which contractors' workers have a rightful claim. Worker exploitation occurs in the contractual collection scenario, as those who invent and fabricate typically do not share in the full monetary benefit of their toil. Such exploitation can be acute—due to secrecy restrictions, intrusive monitoring, accident frequency, oppressive workplace conditions, absent union bargaining, round-the-clock routines, exposure to toxic substances and explosives, and the influence of contractors with Pentagon officials and politicians.[296]

296 See Guy Burdick, *GAO Finds History of Safety Violations Among Defense Contractors*, EHS Daily Advisor, July 9, 2019, https://ehsdailyadvisor.blr.com/; Wikia, *List of Accidents and Incidents involving Military Aircraft (2000-Present)*, (also available for prior decades), https://military.wikia.org/ (accessed June 6, 2022).

And, monopolistic control over the worker population tends to be the norm whenever the skills required are unique or scarce.[297]

In the contractual money collection dynamic, all or part of T^Z need not be used to restart the collection cycle, as each cycle may be a discrete event. This may hold even when separate stages of design or fabrication occur—assuming that each one is contracted for and funded separately. However, techno-military oligopolists with continuous or overlapping contracts may use all or part of T^Z to restart a cycle. It is possible for such contractors to build a long-lasting relationship with the martial domain—or to be entirely dedicated to contracting. The latter can be considered advantageous, to avoid the vagaries of markets—as in the case of commercial aircraft production.[298]

Much waste and misplaced priorities—a matter repeatedly pointed out by specialists during the last decade and before—may result from such long-lasting relationships. A prominent analyst, for example, noted that a drone—costing taxpayers almost $30 million (each) to build, which flies for almost $4,000 per hour and fires a missile that costs about $70,000—has often been used to kill someone (in, say, the Middle East or Central Asia) who earns less than one dollar per day.[299] And, the drone (and its missile) can end up killing more than two dozen innocent civilians for every targeted individual.[300] Yet, typically, such taxpayer-funded spending and tragedies occur with little or no public discussion—and the loss of innocent lives is simply written off as unintended collateral damage.[301]

The cost per taxpayer for sustaining military contracting and the martial domain is difficult to estimate.[302] During the last decade, general tabulations indicated that almost 25 percent of every annual tax dollar paid went to military spending (veterans' benefits excluded).[303] This level of spending shortchanges outlays for such vital needs as education, health care, infrastructure, and

297 As occurs with testing personnel—see Christian Gelzer, *Remembering Test Pilots who Lost their Lives*, NASA Science, January 25, 2018, https://solarsystem.nasa.gov/.

298 See Airliners, *Why did Lockheed Abandon Commercial Production?* www.airliners.net/; Wikipedia, *Lockheed Martin*, https://en.wikipedia.org/ (both accessed June 6, 2022).

299 Andrew Bacevich, as quoted in Carl Kline, "Can We All Find a Better, Richer Life?" *Brookings Register*, March 7, 2020, https://brookingsregister.com/.

300 *The Economist*, "Bombs Astray."

301 See Bacevich, *Washington Rules*; Kline, "Can We All Find."

302 Possibly the more accurate estimates are those that refer to specific wars—see Anthony Cordesman, *U.S. Military Spending: The Cost of Wars*, July 10, 2017, Center for Strategic and International Studies, www.csis.org/; Joseph E. Stiglitz and Linda J. Bilmes, *The Three Trillion Dollar War: The True Cost of the Iraq Conflict* (New York: Norton, 2008). U.S. military spending has long been, by far, the highest of any nation in the world, according to international estimates—see Stockholm International Peace Research Institute, *65 Years of Military Spending: Trends in SIPRI's New Data*, www.sipri.org/ (accessed June 8, 2022).

303 See Third Way, *National Security*, various years, https://thirdway.org/ (accessed March 4, 2022); Laura Saunders, "Three Questions for April 15," *Wall Street Journal*, April 12, 2014, B9, and her "Tracking Your Federal Tax Dollars," *Wall Street Journal*, November 6, 2010, B9.

safeguarding nature. Allocation of tax revenue for contracting in any given period is, after all, part of a zero-sum scenario. And this applies even when the government borrows to try to increase outlays, as debt incurred must eventually be covered by taxpayers.

Taxpayer Exploitation

Consideration of contractual money collection raises the question of taxpayer exploitation. As in the case of consumer exploitation (discussed in an earlier chapter) this mode of exploitation occurs through the absence of competition. However, as there are no markets to speak of, the oligopolistic exploitive medium involves bidding and contracting itself. A fusion of interests between contractors and officials practically ensures that substantial oligopolistic contractual surpluses (ΔZ) will result from most every contract. These surpluses are at the core of taxpayer exploitation—beyond any questions on the need for weaponry or the magnitude of the military apparatus.

Obtaining ΔZ involves, conceptually, the difference between the amount represented by T^Z (amount of taxpayer funds disbursed upon completion of weaponry) *and* the amount of taxpayer-provided funding that would be paid—if competitive bidding and contracting could occur. This assumes that a competitive scenario would involve:

$$T \rightarrow W \rightarrow W' \rightarrow T' \text{ where } T' = T + \Delta z$$

with T' representing new taxpayer-provided funds disbursed upon completion of weaponry (W')—all other variables as before. Thus, the amount of taxpayer exploitation can be represented as $(T^Z - T')$. As in the case of consumer exploitation, the oligopolistic surplus obtained through contracting (ΔZ) is a function of this difference. For all military contracting, the aggregate taxpayer exploitive quantum may then be represented as $\sum (T^Z - T')$.

The inflation of contract amounts magnifies the exploitive quantum. Cost overruns, budget extensions, delays, unnecessary accessories, poor performance, and the like can add substantial amounts to initial budgets. Such inflation can be considered an add-on charge (t^{ω}) to the differential $(T^Z - T')$ that the public seldom hears about. Add-on charges thus increase the taxpayer exploitive quantum significantly.[304] Because many weapon programs use little-known technologies—requiring much testing and changes—the add-on charges can build up substantially over time.

304 Cost of veteran support is an important (and necessary) add-on charge. See Linda Bilmes, *Current and Future Projected Costs of Caring for Veterans of the Iraq and Afghanistan Wars*, Watson Institute, Brown University, https://watson.brown.edu/ (accessed March 10, 2022); Alan Zarembo, "Wars' Future Cost is Vast: Veterans' Care and Other Expenses from Afghanistan and Iraq could bring Total to $6 Trillion, Study Finds," *Los Angeles Times*, March 29, 2013, AA2.

Analyses during the last decade showed that accountability for the vast amount of tax revenue obtained by the martial domain and its contractors is possibly the worst of any area of government.[305] The Department of Defense is, according to specialists, the only federal agency that is unable to pass a professionally conducted audit.[306] Military bases around the world absorb much taxpayer-funded spending, yet controls are reportedly very flawed.[307] The Commission on Wartime Contracting—established by the U.S. Congress—for example, estimated that as much as $60 billion in contracting fraud involving military bases in or near Afghanistan and Iraq occurred during 2002–2010.[308] One estimate of contracting outlays for military bases abroad during 2001–2013 came up with $385 billion, but the total spent was thought to be possibly closer to one-half trillion dollars or more—with about one-third paid to only ten contractors, all of them oligopolists in their fields.[309]

Assembling any kind of partially complete information on the actual contract, operational, and base expenses can reportedly require months or even years, and the result can be misleading if not downright inaccurate.[310] Pentagon accounting has often been considered farcical, where even one billion dollars can be regarded as a "rounding error," according to an experienced

305 See Jay Syrmopoulos, "Audit: Pentagon cannot Account for $6.5 Trillion Dollars in Taxpayers' Money—Adding to the Appearance of Impropriety is the Fact that Thousands of Documents that Should be on File have Been Removed and Disappeared without any Reasonable Explanation," *MPN News*, August 8, 2016, www.mintpressnews.com/; Jeffrey Smith, "Pentagon's Accounting Shambles May Cost an Additional $1 Billion," *Center for Public Integrity*, March 23, 2012, http://publicintegrity.org/; Brooks, *How Everything Became War*, Chapter 13.

306 Vine, *United States of War*, chapters 14–15; and his "'We're Profiteers': How Military Contractors Reap Billions from U.S. Military Bases Overseas," *Monthly Review*, July 2014, 84.

307 Vine defines a base as "any structure, facility, or place regularly used for military purposes of any kind"—see his "'We're Profiteers'," 100 (Note 13). The early emphasis on a worldwide network of bases—1,400 in 31 nations by the end of the 1950s—reflected the importance of geopolitical control—see Baran and Sweezy, *Monopoly Capital*, 183–85, 190–202. See also Donald A. Carter, *Forging the Shield* (Washington: Center for Military History, U.S. Army, 2015), chapters 8–10; Chalmers Johnson, *Blowback: The Costs and Consequences of American Empire* (New York: Holt, 2000), chapters 1, 9, 10.

308 Vine, "'We're Profiteers'," 84, 89, 94; and his *Base Nation*, Part IV. See also Project on Government Oversight, *Federal Contractor Misconduct Database (FCMD)*, www.contractormisconduct.org/ (accessed March 13, 2022), and its *POGO Updates Misconduct Records and Rankings for Top 100 Government Contractors*, April 26, 2010, https://pogoblog.typepad.com/.

309 Vine, "'We're Profiteers," 83–84, 89; and his *Base Nation*, Chapter 13. See also Linda Bilmes, "Who Profited from the Iraq War?" *EPS Quarterly* 24 (2012), www.epsusa.org/.

310 Vine, "'We're Profiteers," 83–85; Chalmers Johnson, *Sorrows of Empire: Militarism, Secrecy, and the End of the Republic* (New York: Holt, 2004), Chapter 6. Among the most daunting tasks is estimating the immense monetary cost of wars to taxpayers—see, for example, Neta C. Crawford, *United States Budgetary Costs of the Post-9/11 Wars through FY2019: $5.9 Trillion Spent and Obligated*, Costs of War Project, Watson Institute, Brown University, November 2018, www.watson.brown.edu/.

researcher.[311] During the last decade, it was considered that estimates of actual total spending might be twice the officially reported amounts, if a comprehensive list of military outlays could be compiled.[312]

These details can convey why many specialists consider the military use of taxpayer funds to be a most important example of non-representative governance. Many thousands of individuals—who are neither elected nor accountable to taxpayers—make decisions and spend the largest sums for weapons and warfare in history. Oligopolistic military technology contractors are at the core of this vast apparatus that underpins domination—not only over taxpayers but also over much of the world. Their existence, their influence, and the vast wealth they obtain make it possible to impose this reality. Perhaps it should not surprise that some scholars have concluded that the checks and balances mandated by the U.S. Constitution were collapsed long ago in the case of military spending.[313]

Although nominally, bidding for contracts might seem to involve some competition—duopolistic, or even monopolistic, scenarios tend to be characteristic. For the construction of Ford-class aircraft carriers during the last decade, for example, only one company reportedly submitted a bid. Costs soon increased by almost one-quarter over initial estimates—the first carrier entering service almost two years behind schedule and billions of dollars over budget.[314] For the construction of nuclear submarines, destroyers, and support vessels—also during the last decade—two companies reportedly submitted bids.[315] This scenario is fairly common for most weapons, and the number of bidding companies is all too often less than a handful, with contract details shrouded in secrecy.[316]

Military technology contracting is thus quite advantageous to the corporations involved. Even when bidding involves more than a duopoly, "cost-plus"

311 Vine, "'We're Profiteers," 89. See also the articles in Catherine Lutz, *The Bases of Empire: The Global Struggle against U.S. Military Posts* (New York: New York University Press, 2009).

312 Robert W. McChesney, "The Labyrinth of U.S. Military Spending," 112–15, in his *Blowing the Roof Off the Twenty-First Century: Media, Politics, and the Struggle for Post-Capitalist Democracy* (New York: Monthly Review Press, 2014).

313 See Andrew Cockburn, *The Spoils of War: Power, Profit and the American War Machine* (New York: Verso, 2021), parts I, II, IV; Michael J. Glennon, *National Security and Double Government* (New York: Oxford University Press, 2015), chapters 2–4; Bacevich, *Washington Rules*; Vine, *United States of War*.

314 Christopher P. Cavas, "Modly: Carrier Ford Continues Progress," *Defense and Aerospace Report*, March 9, 2020, https://defaeroreport.com/. The sole bidder for this project was Huntington Ingalls—see Wikipedia, *Huntington Ingalls Industries*, https://en.wikipeida.org/ (accessed June 1, 2022).

315 Doug Cameron, "Ship Maker for Navy to Bolster Investment," *Wall Street Journal*, February 20, 2015, B1; Andrea Shalal-Esa, "Huntington Ingalls, General Dynamics Win U.S. Navy Orders," *Reuters*, June 3, 2013, www.reuters.com/.

316 See Craig Hooper, "Secrecy is Distorting the 4-Way Race for America's Next Frigate," *Forbes*, November 11, 2019, www.forbes.com/.

arrangements can essentially guarantee a large surplus regardless of the eventual cost. Once a project is underway, it is unlikely to be abandoned as the waste involved can attract negative reactions—and cancellation can jeopardize future allocations. Also, career advancement of military officials can be negatively affected by cancellations. Thus, officials and politicians may choose "fixes"—that require yet more taxpayer funding—to induce hope that problems might be resolved in the end. Unjustified minimization of the problems may also allow projects to drag on for years, consuming vast amounts of funding.

Military contractor chief executives are among the highest paid in the United States—their compensation estimated to be significantly higher than that of the highest paid bank chief executives.[317] Their compensation reportedly places military contractor executives among the highest paid individuals within the one percent top range of both income and wealth—an elite of the elite, in a sector that has the lowest public accountability of all taxpayer-funded activities.[318] Military contractor outlays for lobbying of politicians and officials are also reportedly higher—by as much as three times in some cases—than the lobbying budgets of the largest banks in the United States.[319]

Military technology contractors, moreover, are prime candidates for bailouts during economic crises or when they become insolvent—at further taxpayer expense. And the larger they become, the more likely it is that they will be rescued. Thus, there is a built-in incentive for contractors to acquire or merge with other companies. Becoming too-big-to-fail can be a great asset for contractors. And the military apparatus tacitly encourages consolidation, as it is more convenient to obtain weaponry from a single contractor than from two or several—even though this can damage taxpayers' interests.[320]

Once a contract is awarded, the interest of the military technology contractor is to increase costs as much as possible. The thought that officials may seriously try to prevent this seems misplaced. Military officials know that higher

317 See Sarah Anderson and Brian Wakamo, *Soaring CEO Pay at Pentagon Contractors*, Inequality, September 22, 2021, https://inequality.org/; Mandy Smithberger, *Brass Parachutes: The Problem of the Pentagon Revolving Door*, Project on Government Accountability, November 5, 2018, www.pogo.org/; Robert Greenwald, "Meet the 0.01 Percent: War Profiteers," *Huffpost*, December 6, 2017, www.huffpost.com/; David C. Johnston, "The U.S. Government is Paying through the Nose for Private Contractors," *Newsweek*, December 12, 2012, http://newsweek.com/.

318 Greenwald, "Meet the 0.01 Percent."

319 Greenwald, "Meet the 0.01 Percent." See also Smithberger, *Brass Parachutes*; Johnston, "U.S. Government is Paying."

320 See Weisgerber, "Pentagon Sees 'No Major Concerns' Raytheon-United Technologies Merger"; Sindreu, "Sharing Tech Won't Vindicate UTC-Raytheon Megamerger"; *The Economist*, "Fighting the Next War." Another aspect is that military technology oligopolists that have commercial operations can benefit greatly from the latter, because of the synergies involved. During the last decade, it was found that U.S. military grants to foreign governments were often accompanied by commercial sales—especially in such sectors as aerospace. See Loren Thompson, "Why Defense has a Secure Future in Boeing's Business Mix," *Forbes*, October 1, 2014, www.forbes.com/.

costs typically justify larger budget requests and allocations in subsequent years. Pentagon spending is allegedly guided by the "use it or lose it" principle, and cost overruns can therefore serve as justification to request more funding subsequently.[321]

Cost inflation has been considered endemic for military technology contracting, and there are various ways to achieve it. One example is to customize solutions for a given need when commercially available products can perform as well. Unnecessary customization may thus be considered an important driver of inflated costs and budgets.[322] Forgoing purchase of lower-cost, commercially available technologies is a form of cost-inflation-by-default that is all too common in military contracting.

Permanent warfare can add to this scenario, by serving as another justification to purchase new technology and replace equipment continuously—at any cost. Thus, it is counterproductive for officials to induce contractors to exercise much cost control, when doing so is against the interests of both parties. Vast arsenals willfully left behind, as in Afghanistan and Iraq, also help increase contract purchases (and costs).[323] Military strategy can help as well, as rapid dominance (or "shock-and-awe") combat scenarios tend to waste much weaponry, due to excessive use and partly because locales often have to be re-taken later.[324] And lax cost control is not as much of a liability as in other areas of government, given the high level of secrecy that characterizes projects. Also, revolving door arrangements whereby contractors' executives take up high-level positions in the military apparatus—or the inverse—help perpetuate this scenario.[325]

321 See John W. Whitehead, "Pity the Nation: War Spending is Bankrupting America," *CounterPunch*, March 15, 2019, www.counterpunch.org/.

322 See Zuri Davis, "The Air Force Spent Over $300,000 on 391 Special Coffee Mugs: As it Turns Out the 3-D Printed Solution Costs 50 Cents," *Reason*, October 24, 2018, https://reason.com/; Aaron Gregg, "The Air Force's $10,000 Toilet Cover," *Washington Post*, July 14, 2018, www.washingtonpost.com/; Airon A. Mothershed, "The $435 Hammer and the $600 toilet Seat Scandals: Does Media Coverage of Procurement Lead to Procurement Reform?" *Public Contract Law Journal* 41 (2012), 855–80.

323 See Elie Kaufman, "U.S. Left Behind $7 Billion of Military Equipment in Afghanistan After 2021 Withdrawal, Pentagon Report Says," *CNN*, April 28, 2022, www.cnn.com/; Adam Andrzejewski, "Staggering Costs—U.S. Military Equipment Left Behind in Afghanistan," *Forbes*, August 23, 2021, www.forbes.com/; Dan Froomkin, "U.S. to Hand Over Iraq Bases, Equipment Worth Billions," *Huffpost*, September 26, 2011, www.huffpost.com/.

324 See Wikipedia, *Shock and Awe*, https://en.wikipedia.org/ (accessed June 19, 2022); Harlan K. Ullman and James P. Wade, *Shock and Awe: Achieving Rapid Dominance* (Washington: National Defense University, 1996), chapters 2, 3.

325 See Open Secrets, *Revolving Door: Mark Esper Employment Summary*, www.opensecrets.org/ (accessed June 5, 2022); Sam Bright, "Government Departments Breaking Guidance on Board Members' Conflict of Interest," *Byline Times*, April 19, 2021, https://bylinetimes.com/; Jason Paladino, *The Chairman of the Revolving Door*, Project on Government Oversight, March 6, 2020, www.pogo.org/; Peter Castagno, "New Defense Secretary Poised for Confirmation Despite Vast

Weaponry, such as aircraft, vessels, and missiles, involve some of the most complex technologies in existence. In addition, arguments for secrecy—and an official classification to that effect—are an impenetrable barrier to public awareness. Cost inflation through secrecy may thus be considered a tacit objective of much techno-military contracting. This is one of the reasons the Pentagon has been estimated to account for more than half of all discretionary federal spending, every fiscal year, in recent times.[326]

Another way is to engineer unnecessary complexity or to design a weapon—such as a jet fighter—with a vast array of (also unneeded) accessories that may require it to be in maintenance for as much as 85 percent of its service life.[327] Contracts for such maintenance are typically awarded to the company that designed and fabricated the weapon—given its intimate knowledge of the technology. This ensures a long future stream of service contracts that can be renewed sequentially and provide revenue and surpluses for as long as three or four decades, if not longer. Cumulative revenues obtained through maintenance can thus be 50 times or more the amount of the initial design and fabrication contract.

Unnecessary delays are another way to inflate costs and enlarge allocations. This can be compounded when the military request additional features or change specifications, or when there are basic flaws in a weapon's design.[328] The F-35 jet fighter—with an estimated cost of almost two trillion dollars to design and fabricate—was over five years behind schedule and had to be grounded frequently due to poor performance and short maintenance intervals.[329] And it was considered by some analysts to be the most expensive military project in history. Contracting for this aircraft followed that of the extremely costly and

Conflicts of Interest," *Citizen Truth*, July 29, 2019, https://citizentruth.org/; Jared Keller, "Meet Your Brand New Secretary of the Army," *Task and Purpose*, November 16, 2017, https://taskandpurpose.com/.

326 See Cockburn, *Spoils of War*, chapters 4, 5, 15–17; Neta C. Crawford, *Pentagon Fuel Use, Climate Change, and the Cost of War*, Costs of War Project. Watson Institute, Brown University, June 12, 2019, www.watson.brown.edu/.

327 See *New York Times*, "The Fighter Jet that is Too Pricey to Fail: The F-35 is a Boondoggle. Yet We're Stuck with It," March 12, 2021, www.nytimes.com/; Eric Tegler, "WTF-35: How the Joint Strike Fighter Got to be Such a Mess—The Story of the F-35 Fighter, and What Went Wrong to put the Joint Strike Fighter So Far over Budget and Behind Schedule," *Popular Mechanics*, July 27, 2018, www.popularmechanics.com/; Sebastien Roblin, "Is the F-35 Program Really Worth the $1,500,000,000,000 Price Tag?" *The National Interest*, April 21, 2018, https://nationalinterest.org/.

328 See Ryan Pickrell, "Here are 5 of the Worst Weapons Projects the U.S. Military Has in the Works," *Business Insider*, May 31, 2019, www.businessinsider.com.au/; Roblin, "F-35 Program"; Tiefer, "10 Most Blatantly Wasteful Defense."

329 See Tegler, "WTF-35"; Roblin, "F-35 Program"; Dan Grazier, *F-35 Cutting Corners to 'Complete' Development: Officials Altering Paperwork instead of Pursuing Actual Fixes*, Project on Government Oversight, August 29, 2018, www.pogo.org/; Doug Cameron, "U.S. Air Force Deems Delayed F-35 Fighter is Ready for Combat," *Wall Street Journal*, August 2, 2016, B2.

deficient F-22 Raptor jet fighter program—an immense cost to taxpayers over the years.[330]

Yet another way to achieve cost inflation and unnecessary spending by military technology contractors is to design and manufacture non-reusable weaponry. Loading such weapons with the most expensive—and often unnecessary (or little used)—features is part of this mode of cost inflation. A related practice is to make one-time-use weapons—such as missiles—as expensive as possible. Usage rates of such weaponry can be very high, partly because they can increase kill ratios. Thus, it should not surprise that more than 40,000 precision-guided missiles—each costing as much as $120,000—were reportedly used up in a single campaign against Islamic State (in Iraq and parts of Syria), during the last decade.[331] That campaign served to justify a warfare program in which U.S. military aircraft expended almost 18 times more weapons than in Afghanistan over a similar period of time.[332]

At this point it seems appropriate to characterize domination as a phenomenon that entwines technology oligopolistic power with a vast geopolitical and military apparatus. This occurs in myriad, fragmented ways that are difficult to detect and expose. *The result is a state of waste, mismanagement, and permanent warfare that is meant to increase taxpayer-funded allocations for oligopolistic technology contractors.* Imposition of geopolitical dictates around the world—made possible by the most advanced technologies—sustains this unjust panorama.

For the public, official narratives on national security are meant to obliterate any questioning of this reality. Such narratives also tend to eliminate any awareness of taxpayer exploitation and of the need for funding to address vital needs at home. The greatest beneficiaries of this state of affairs are oligopolistic technology contractors, rather than national security or the American people. *This reality of technology-enabled warfare and waste does not therefore seem to be about national security, but about domination and exploitation.*

Domination therefore involves a grievous panorama of dysfunction. Its institutionalization in the apparatus of governance—usually undertaken out of public sight—can render it more harmful than the dysfunctions that result from commercial corporate practices. Never in history has a nation amassed so much military technology, with such vast destructive capabilities and so little accountability. Domination and exploitation on a planetary scale seem to be the core objectives, with technology oligopolies in command.

330 See Robert Farley, "Forget the F-35 and the F-22: These Two Fighter Jets Almost Replaced Them," *The National Interest*, January 10, 2020, https://nationalinterest.org/; David Axe, "Buyer's Remorse: How Much has the F-22 Really Cost?" *Wired*, December 14, 2011, www.wired.com/.

331 Paul Sonne, "For Missile Makers, U.S. Demand Surges," *Wall Street Journal*, January 7, 2017, B4. Among the "missile-makers" cited in this case were Boeing and Lockheed-Martin. See also Airwars, *News and Investigations* (selected articles), https://airwars.org/; Wikipedia, *List of Active Missiles in the United States Military*, https://en.wikipedia.org/ (both accessed June 10, 2022).

332 Sonne, "For Missile Makers."

Chapter 7

Techno-oligarchy

Technology oligopoly capitalism is at an existential impasse. Its social dysfunctions are unsustainable, its economic rationality is inhuman, and its effects on nature will likely be catastrophic. Technology's longstanding promise to improve human and natural wellbeing thus seems spent under oligopoly capitalism. Most alarming, technology has been turned into a formidable tool for oppression—to alienate and exploit the majority so that a few can benefit.

To perpetuate its power, a techno-oligarchic elite has imposed an apparatus of societal control—a supra-structure of sorts—that affects most everything we do. A supra-structure that is invisible yet commands more power than most established institutions. A supra-structure that seems designed to impose control over most every aspect of our existence. *A supra-structure that alienates in order to dominate.*

Alienation that can now be found in most everything we do. From cradle to grave, intimate details of our lives are monitored and conditioned as never before. How we think, what we know or believe, what we consume, our contacts, the way we work, our preferences, our health, our employers, how and where we travel, our finances, whom we elect, our daily habits, how we communicate and are censored—are now tracked to an extent that would have been difficult to imagine not long ago.

What we receive in exchange—convenience, efficiency, contact—seem meager in comparison with what we are made to give up. For, in the technology treadmill, oligopolistic power always looks for ways to more cleverly alienate and exploit. Always giving up as little as possible in return for all it takes.

Inducing consumption of what we do not need. Locking us in to appropriate our identities and sell our data. Turning our contact time, searches, and effort into uncompensated toil. Engineering life to turn it into a commodity. Destroying nature by generating ever more waste and pollution. Seizing our taxes to concoct the most destructive weapons. Placing us at risk as it turns the planet into a stage for permanent war. Buying up politicians to bend our governance. Imposing submission to block questioning of its ways. Occluding justice so that a minuscule elite can increase its power and wealth all the time, anytime—at our expense.

DOI: 10.4324/9781003345893-7

Yet, for all its power, the supra-structure that sustains technology oligopoly capitalism is not part of the state. Rather, it seems to operate as an *alter* state. But it does not want to be perceived as such—even as it vacates functions of the state to impose its power.

The supra-structure that sustains the techno-oligarchy is thus a sort of shadow state. A shadow state that has taken over many of the roles of the state. A shadow state that has the power and means to alienate as no state has ever been able to. Quietly—by conditioning our behaviors and routines, by manipulating how we toil, create, and communicate, by tracking us incessantly, by inducing habits that are difficult or impossible to vacate.

The power elite that commands the supra-structure—the techno-oligarchy—seems fragmented and amorphous. It does not look like a social class, much less a government. Many of its actions seem to have divergent aims. Its pronouncements can be devoid of meaning. A lack of perspective and social awareness seems all too common. Flights of fancy or hedonism can involve much waste and malfeasance. Hidden, self-serving agendas pervade its philanthropy. Many of its decisions seem confused and unrealistic. But a close look can show that the ensemble is purposeful. And effective.

The effectiveness of the supra-structure can be found in the alienation it induces. For, the power and perpetuation of the techno-oligarchy depend on its capacity to alienate. To alienate us from our human condition as it conquers our habits and behavior. To alienate us from nature as it destroys more of it every day. To alienate us from learning as it turns education into menial tasking. To alienate us from our governance as it turns politics into legalized corruption. To alienate us from the world as it turns geopolitics into permanent warfare. To alienate us from our social condition by making society more dysfunctional. To alienate us from the product of our toil as we are made to give up what we create.

Our alienation is thus systemic. It is induced by the system we must perforce live in, regardless of our intent or disposition. It is technologically induced in the sense that advanced technologies are deployed to condition our submission. Our alienation is therefore *not* really about us, individually or personally. Our alienation is social and—as such—can be found in all the dysfunctions and pathologies considered in this work.

Take, for example, our alienation from nature. The damage inflicted by technology oligopoly capitalism on nature cannot be treated as an "externality"—as the techno-oligarchic elite and its apologists have long sought to do. Damage to nature is internal to the system of oligopoly capitalism. Technology oligopolies are active perpetrators. Waste—a result of wants contrivance and the hyper-consumption it induces—is a major vehicle. Permanent warfare—fueled by our compulsory, exploitive taxation—is another contributor. Engineering agriculture through seeds and pesticides that destroy food chains is yet another. The destruction of nature may thus be considered an alienation of life—in any form, not only the humankind.

From planetary processes involving the atmosphere, to the food chain of all species, to the microbiome and microbiota that sustain organisms, to all ocean life, to all flora and soils, to freshwater resources and the seas—the alienation of nature that the techno-oligarchy and its supra-structure induce can be considered an expropriation of life. Alienation conflated with expropriation that leads to destruction. Technology oligopoly capitalism is the great facilitator of this destruction. The minuscule techno-oligarchic elite is the greatest beneficiary.

Life in all forms—including us, humanity—is the damned. And no advances in genetic engineering, no clever techniques that attempt to modify or mold life, seem likely to stave off catastrophe. Discussion of this matter in an earlier chapter addressed the challenges we face. The breadth of the panorama of alienation we experience is daunting. It is an alienation that belongs to no one—because it belongs to everyone.

Invention and innovation provide another example. Their contribution to expanding efficiency frontiers—saving time, effort, and cost—has long been regarded as *the* solution to many of the problems we face. But the techno-oligarchy seems to have turned these important endeavors into sales accessories. Means to sell more and to contrive wants—to trigger yet more sales. Engineering greater sales thus seems to have become the prime function of invention and innovation. Their involvement in research that is not geared to sell seems out of place in the corporate domain. Might it surprise—as noted in an earlier chapter—that the incidence of important innovations was found to have declined substantially during the last five decades?

Our alienation from invention and innovation also involves talent. Most everyone is now required to "reassign" patent awards to employers. Even when creation or research occur outside the workplace and worktime. And, if any benefits are shared, the inventor might receive only a small fraction of the total appropriated (over the life of the patent and beyond). May it seem reasonable to note that alienation of invention and innovation is shortchanging technological development?

Alienation also involves the martial domain. Military technology is developed by contractors—typically among the most powerful corporations in the oligopolistic spectrum. Mostly controlled by an elite *within* the techno-oligarchic elite—a minuscule group at the very top of the wealth and income pyramids. The one percent of the one percent. Not many in charge of the largest Wall Street banks tend to be found among that select elite.

Warfare technology alienates life by destroying it. And in many ways, the techno-oligarchy is in charge of warfare today. They are not only its enablers—they are also its promoters, its profiteers, and in many cases its mercenary executors. The techno-oligarchy then further alienates us—from life and the rest of humanity—by turning geopolitics into a vehicle for permanent conflict. Warfare meant to consume—or waste—ever more weaponry. Driven by profit, supported by our taxes—with minimal or no accountability.

The techno-oligarchy thus also alienates us as taxpayers. From the taxes we must compulsorily pay, under penalty of punishment. Taxes that are the main—in many cases the only—source of their vast wealth and privilege. Politicians and military officials seem very eager partners in this form of alienation, as they allocate ever larger amounts of our tax money—benefiting from promotions, donations, and schemes over which we have no say. Might it surprise that a billion dollars is often considered a "rounding error" in military spending? Or, that many military technologies can cost several thousand times more than their similar commercial counterparts?

Our alienation as taxpayers also involves the many tax breaks and loopholes that immensely benefit the techno-oligarchy. Innumerable breaks and loopholes now populate the tax code—more than at any time in history. Not only for technology oligopolies but also for the elite that controls them. And this does not take into account the vast amounts of untaxed wealth that technology companies hold offshore. Wealth and profit that do not show up in declarations at home. Might it seem reasonable to assume that—if tribute were to be paid on such wealth—the taxes we are made to pay would be much lower?

Alienation, then, can be found everywhere. It is anywhere and everywhere because there is nowhere to hide. Alienation is entwined with the techno-oligarchy and its command over oligopoly capitalism. The topics addressed in this work have, in one way or another, provided insights on the root causes of our alienation. The amassment of power, how capital is accumulated, the structuring of production, how myriad dysfunctions and pathologies are induced, the destruction of nature, the use of geopolitics and the martial domain to dominate, how we are conditioned to submit. All of these topics and phenomena have alienation at their core.

The techno-oligarchy and its control supra-structure may be characterized as *totalistic*. Their power is inescapable—impossible to avoid, compliance guaranteed by the absence of a systemic alternative. But unlike totalitarian systems of the past, what the supra-structure lacks in the way of a centralized, despotic authority is more than made up by its apparatus of alienation. An apparatus capable of reproducing itself but which—to do so—needs to deploy the power of an *alter* state. A non-state that has the power of a state. A non-state that has concocted its own *alter* legality. A non-legality that is, in effect, law but is not codified as such.

The panorama of alienation and control imposed by the techno-oligarchy thus involves a major contradiction. The conventional state is *not* well suited to impose the overarching control the techno-oligarchy needs to perpetuate itself. The stipulations and precedent of the conventional state—conflictive in many ways and historically specific—make it difficult for the oligarchic elite to streamline its domination. The latter, after all, depends on the alienation of individuals and social classes from the levers of power. This, however, is contrarian to what the conventional state nominally seeks to achieve.

Also—despite technology oligopoly capitalism's worldwide reach—the techno-oligarchy has found it impossible to concoct a global state of its own. A global state tailored to its needs, to rule over all conventional states. Totalistic in character and domination. The United States, for its part, has proved incapable of replicating its state apparatus on a global scale, because of its internal contradictions and historical specificities. Partly for this reason, a state of permanent warfare now seems to be the norm. Permanent warfare that is as technological as it is harmful. Permanent warfare that is highly profitable for those contracted to provide it. The symbiosis of technology oligopoly capitalism, the techno-oligarchy, and the martial domain has thus bore fruit. And it is a very wasteful and dangerous *modus operandi*—one that may end up destroying our planet.

At this point it seems appropriate to note that the existential crisis of technology oligopoly capitalism faces two trajectories. Both, it may be argued, require radical change. One would involve the complete dismantlement of the techno-oligarchic supra-structure—and of oligopolistic power itself—no less. This path would necessarily involve a radical metamorphosis. One that must engage humanity in constructing a better, sustainable future.

The other trajectory would most likely be violent, with unknown but probably very tragic outcomes. Some of its profile seems to be gaining visibility. And it is a trajectory we may not be able to alter. Deterioration of nature seems to be beyond the help of the most sophisticated technologies of our time, as discussed earlier. Deterioration of our social condition and of our capacity to coexist may lead to conflagrations the likes of which our planet, its nature, and human society have never witnessed. War is, after all, technological. And the technologies of war today are the most destructive ever.

Reform of the status quo, for its part, seems incapable of avoiding the approaching catastrophe that nature and humanity face. Or, of resolving the pathologies generated by pervasive alienation and the panorama of abuse it engenders. Reformist approaches, in any case, would most likely be co-opted by the techno-oligarchy for its own ends. Much as it has co-opted our governance and so many other aspects of our existence.

It seems reasonable to argue that a dismantlement of the supra-structure will require eliminating the alienation that it fosters—and upon which it depends. Doing away with alienation in every sphere of our existence—regarding work, consumption, capital accumulation, innovation, taxation, the commons, nature, and governance, for example—must be undertaken systemically and in unison. This seems essential, as the techno-oligarchy's imposed order is one of mutually reinforcing dysfunctions and pathologies. Dismantlement cannot therefore occur in isolated ways, as doing so will most certainly be countered and defeated—forcefully, possibly ruthlessly.

Dismantlement of the techno-oligarchy and its supra-structure will also require radical change in another aspect—the relations of power that perpetuate the commodification of human existence and of nature. Those relationships must be re-purposed to be of—and for—humanity and nature. This will require an end to commodity value as the sole determinant of economic worth. It will also require a collective determination of needs—as opposed to unfettered wants contrivance and consumer exploitation. Socially necessary value—as a guide and measure of economic value—should thus displace commodity value.

Innovation and work will necessarily have to be placed under the control of labor—if the alienation of those who toil and create is to be dismantled. This will entail an end to exploitation—and the placement of use value, generated through production and research, to benefit those who work. Democratization of workplaces will necessarily require not only the latter but also the self-organization of labor to make important decisions regarding work, innovation, and production. This is in opposition to the current regime of oligopolistic power. Thus, the infinitive expansion of surpluses—the primordial objective of oligopolistic power—must be replaced by a redefinition of the relations of production, such that those who work and consume can benefit on the basis of what is socially necessary.

And what is socially necessary must by all means work in concert with the metabolic reality of nature. This is essential if life on earth is to be sustained—given the damage that has already been done, the demographic realities we face, and the fact that nature's resources are finite. Nature must therefore also be disengaged from commodity value, if life on earth is to be safeguarded. Social necessity *and* necessary value will thus have to be engaged—and balanced—with the metabolism of nature. This is a most difficult but necessary undertaking, if we are to have any hope of averting catastrophe.

Technology is indispensable for the dismantlement of the techno-oligarchic supra-structure. It must be constructively engaged at all levels, and this must occur outside the dictates of commodity value and oligopolistic power. Technology at all levels must therefore be engaged organically with society's needs and with nature—if the dismantlement of the supra-structure is to lead to constructive solutions. This is not an option; it is an urgent and unavoidable necessity for survival.

Index